THE UNITED
STATES SINCE
1945

THE UNITED STATES SINCE 1945

Historical Interpretations

Doug Rossinow and Rebecca Lowen, editors

PEARSON
Prentice
Hall

Upper Saddle River, New Jersey 07458

Library of Congress Cataloging in Publication Data

The United States since 1945: historical interpretations/[edited by] Doug Rossinow, Rebecca Lowen.

   p. cm.
   Includes bibliographical references.
   ISBN 0-13-1840339
   1. United States—History—1945– 2. United States—History—1945—Historiography.
   3. United States—History—1945—Sources. I. Rossinow, Douglas C. (Douglas Charles)
   II. Lowen, Rebecca S.
   E742. U56 2007
   973.91—dc22   2006005407

Editorial Director: *Charlyce Jones Owen*
Editorial Assistant: *Maureen Diana*
Senior Marketing Manager: *Emily Cleary*
Marketing Assistant: *Jennifer Lang*
Production Liaison: *Marianne Peters-Riordan*
Manufacturing Buyer: *Ben Smith*
Art Director: *Jayne Conte*
Cover Design: *Kiwi Design*
Cover Illustration/Photo: *Photodisc Red/Getty Images, Inc.*
Director, Image Resource Center: *Melinda Reo*
Manager, Cover Visual Research & Permissions: *Karen Sanatar*
Composition/Full-Service Project Management: *Jodi Dowling/Techbooks*
Printer/Binder: *R.R. Donnelley & Sons*

Credits and acknowledgments borrowed from other sources and reproduced, with permission, in this textbook appear on appropriate page within text.

Pearson Education LTD. London
Pearson Education Singapore, Pte. Ltd
Pearson Education, Canada, Ltd
Pearson Education–Japan
Pearson Education Australia PTY, Limited

Pearson Education North Asia Ltd
Pearson Educación de Mexico, S.A. de C.V.
Pearson Education Malaysia, Pte. Ltd
Pearson Education, Upper Saddle River, New Jersey

10 9 8 7 6 5 4 3 2 1
ISBN 0-13-184033-9

Contents

Acknowledgments

Many people helped bring this project to completion. We wish to thank all the authors who kindly permitted us to reprint their work. Special thanks are due Bart Bernstein, Jagdish Bhagwati, Dinesh D'Souza, Barbara Ehrenreich, Sara Evans, Thomas Frank, Chalmers Johnson, and Allen Matusow, all of whom made things easier than they might otherwise have been. Thanks also to Nina Johns at *Foreign Affairs,* Jill Jones at ICM, Mimi Ross of Houghton Mifflin, Matthew Kull at Temple University Press, and Sami Aknine of *Global Agenda* for their helpfulness. Our book is better for having been scrutinized, in whole or in part, by Brian Balogh, Michael Bernstein, Bob Buzzanco, Mark T. Gilderhus, Roy Rosenzweig, Karen Manners Smith, Robert K. Tomes, the anonymous readers for Prentice Hall, and the students in History 336 at Metropolitan State University in spring 2003 and fall 2004. All offered useful insights; we take responsibility for any of the book's remaining shortcomings. We are also grateful to Randy Getchell, for his impressive literature survey; Carl Frie of Metropolitan State, for reliable staff support; Emily and Norman Rosenberg, for their early endorsement of the project; and Shona Dockter, John Haas, and Sadie Dockter Haas, for generous and well-timed assistance. Our editors, Charlyce Jones Owen and Charles Cavaliere, expertly guided us from this book's inception to its completion. We thank them and others at Prentice Hall, including Marianne Peters Riordan and Jana Stambaugh, and Jodi Dowling of Techbooks. Finally, we thank Siri for providing good company and entertaining distractions; Addie for her patience as well as her insistence, at times, that the book could wait; and Bram for opening a new chapter in our lives.

About the Authors

Doug Rossinow is the author of *The Politics of Authenticity: Liberalism, Christianity, and the New Left in America* (New York: Columbia University Press, 1998) and numerous articles. He teaches history at Metropolitan State University in St. Paul, MN. His areas of interest include progressive politics in twentieth-century America, religion and politics in U.S. history, the social movements of the 1960s, and America in the 1980s. He serves on the advisory board of H-1960s, an electronic listserve devoted to the history of the 1960s. He received his Ph.D. in history from The Johns Hopkins University.

Rebecca Lowen is the author of *Creating the Cold War University: The Transformation of Stanford* (Berkeley: University of California Press, 1997) and numerous articles. She teaches history and women's studies at Metropolitan State University in St. Paul, MN. Her areas of interest include twentieth-century U.S. political and institutional history, and the history of science, medicine, and public health. She has served on the editorial advisory board of *Isis*, the journal of the History of Science Society. She received her Ph.D. in history from Stanford University.

Note to Students

History is about interpreting the past; it is a "spin" on the historical facts. As the scholar E. H. Carr noted, history has been called a "hard core of facts" surrounded by a "pulp of disputable interpretation." Without interpretation—"the pulpy part of the fruit"—there is no meaning, only disconnected facts. Even if an historian is not explicit about his or her viewpoint, an interpretation is always lurking somewhere in what he or she writes. Through interpretation, historians say what they believe the past *means*. They attempt to explain why and how things happened as they did and why particular elements in the past are important.

To Carr, interpretation was the key to writing history. But according to his metaphor, the "fruit" cannot exist without the core—the facts. Any subject can become the source of argument and dispute. As one of our students speculated regarding one historical controversy—the atomic bombings of Japan—an Internet search would produce lots of different opinions about this event. But historical interpretation is more than opinion. It must be informed by a knowledge of the facts—procured from sources such as government documents, personal letters, diaries, and oral histories, to name a few—and an understanding of how they fit together to create a coherent story of the past.

This factually based story or interpretation is always subject to challenge. In almost all cases, sooner or later, an interpretation is questioned, found inadequate, refined, or sometimes completely overthrown by a new, more convincing explanation. At times, as in the case with the history of the origins of the cold war, one interpretation dominates and may go unchallenged for many years. In other cases, such as the scholarship on the end of the cold war, different and sharply conflicting interpretations emerge at the same time. And in some instances, such as the history of the civil rights movement, historians are not in sharp conflict over their interpretation of events; they share an overarching interpretation but focus on telling different pieces of a larger story. The collection of different interpretations produced over time—historiography—may best be understood as a long-running discussion among historians about the meaning of past events.

This volume offers an historiographic approach to the history of the United States since 1945, seeking to familiarize you with the major historical interpretations regarding particular events and developments since the end of the Second World War. The individual chapters include two or three readings—excerpts from essays or books. Each reading presents an interpretation of the topic under consideration. At times, the interpretations in a given chapter conflict with one another, forming something that resembles an argument over how to view the facts. But some topics in post-1945 U.S. history, as already noted, have not spurred the formation of sharply opposed or conflicting interpretations, and we have not artificially imposed such a conflict on the chapters dealing with those topics. In those instances, the different readings are complementary rather than contradictory.

Each chapter begins with an introduction, in which we offer basic factual information about the topic under consideration and summarize the historiography on that particular subject. We analyze the major schools of interpretation to highlight salient points of dispute or difference. We then summarize the main points of the readings and indicate the ways in which the readings are similar or different. Finally, we offer a brief, annotated bibliography designed to help you locate additional material if you wish to read further on the subject, along with a list of Web sites that contain historical documents on the topic should you wish to examine primary sources.

Any book with as broad a subject as post-1945 U.S. history must be selective in what it covers. Although we provide chapters on the topics that most historians would consider significant, we have also had to make choices. To some extent, the historiography itself has made the choices for us. For example, there is an ample and growing literature on domestic life in the 1950s, a topic we include here. But the economic developments of that era have attracted less attention from historians in recent years and so, although we regard this as an important subject, we do not cover it in this volume. In the later part of this book, which covers more recent history, most topics are too new to have a well-developed historiography; in some cases, there is no significant published work by historians. In these sections, we have chosen topics that we believe to be important and that we expect to become topics of concern to historians in the future. This volume has also been shaped by our interest in representing the various approaches to the study of history. Thus there are chapters that focus on foreign policy and diplomatic history, as well as chapters that present the work of social historians, cultural historians, and political historians.

We have divided the book into three roughly chronological parts. The first section, "The Cold War System Abroad and at Home" covers the years from 1945 to 1960, during which the United States began to play a dominant role globally and when white middle-class American citizens began to enjoy a general level of material comfort previously unknown. It begins with a chapter on the atomic bombings of Japan, an event commonly understood as ending the Second World War but one that also ushered in the nuclear age and positioned the United States for a time as the technologically dominant world power. Chapter 2 addresses the origins of the cold war, the ideological and geopolitical conflict that developed between the United States and the USSR and whose potential to become "hot"—and possibly to "go nuclear"—loomed over most of the second half of the twentieth century. Chapter 3 deals with the political and cultural repercussions of the cold war on the home front—the events from the mid-1940s to the early 1960s commonly known as the Red Scare. If the first fifteen years after World War II were a period of anxiety and repression at home, they are also commonly remembered with nostalgia, as a time when family life was celebrated, when stay-at-home mothers, suburban homes (with televisions), and backyard barbeques were, if not the norm, then the standard to which people aspired. Chapter 4 explores domestic life in the period known as the Fifties, looking particularly at the roles of women and how they did, and did not, fit the stereotype of the decade promulgated in popular television shows from *Father Knows Best* to *Happy Days*.

The second section of the book, "The System Under Stress" covers the years 1960 to 1975. These years may best be seen as a period of dramatic challenge to the structures of power and the values that they represented. Most of these challenges came from "below"—from citizens who organized to demand changes in American society. The first such challenge, and the one that paved the way for subsequent ones, was the black freedom struggle, often referred to as the civil rights movement. This is the subject of Chapter 5. The next chapter focuses on the "new left," the term for the young radicals of this era. Many in the new left were inspired by or participated in the civil rights movement; in seeking to reform American society, they significantly influenced American culture and politics. Chapter 7 explores the reawakening of feminism in America in the 1960s and 1970s and its relationship to both the civil rights movement and the labor movement. Whereas Chapters 5, 6, and 7 focus on demands for change "from below"—from people and groups within society who felt in some way disenfranchised—the next three chapters cover the same span of years but look at the actions of the "top," specifically the initiatives, programs, and foreign policy of the U.S. government. Chapter 8 focuses on one component—the War on Poverty—of President Lyndon Johnson's Great Society, the effort in the tradition of Franklin Roosevelt's New Deal to use the powers of the federal government to eliminate suffering. Chapter 9 addresses American foreign policy in the 1960s, looking specifically at U.S. involvement in the Vietnam War, a conflict that had profound effects on American society, culture, and politics. Chapter 10, which concludes this section, looks at the culminating event in this period of "stress" to the "system"—the resignation of President Richard M. Nixon in response to his certain impeachment by the U.S. Congress.

The final section of the book covers the years from 1975 to the present and is titled "A New Domestic and World Order." Many historians view the political, cultural, and economic developments in these years as a response to, or backlash against, the cultural permissiveness and political liberalism of the Sixties. Some, particularly in the realm of foreign policy, disagree as to whether these post-1975 years are more reflective of change from, or continuity with, the previous decades. Chapter 11 explores the rise of the political right—typically referred to as the conservative movement—to a position of power in American life; this development played a role in the presidential election of both Jimmy Carter in 1976 and Ronald Reagan four years later. Chapter 12 examines "Reaganomics"—the challenge from the political right to the economic ideas and policies identified with the American welfare state—looking at the policies and their socioeconomic impact in both the Reagan and the Clinton years. If, in the 1980s and 1990s, there were significant political, cultural, and economic challenges to the status quo, so there was also an apparent dramatic change in the foreign policy status quo—the end of the cold war in the late 1980s. Chapter 13 presents readings that analyze this unexpected event, seek to apportion credit, and assess the longer term foreign policy significance of the way in which the cold war ended. Chapter 14 addresses the social realities of "globalization," presenting views both praising and criticizing the economic integration of the world that has been a major trend in global affairs since the end of the cold war. The last chapter of the book addresses the issue of America's relations with the world since the cold war, looking specifically at the traumatic events of September 11, 2001, and their significance. Implicitly, these readings ask whether 9/11 represents the beginning of a new era for the United States or whether this act of terrorism and the U.S. response to it is continuous with American policy since 1945. In studying each of the topics in this volume, you may wish to consider, similarly, just how much has changed since 1945, or whether continuity with the past is more striking.

You can learn many of the facts about post-1945 U.S. history from the readings in these chapters. We encourage you, however, to focus on each author's presentation of the facts, on the way the author interprets them, and on the broader argument that each author makes. As you read, consider yourself to be in a conversation of sorts with each author. Although you obviously cannot ask questions directly of the author, you can interrogate what the author has written and seek answers to your questions through a careful reading of the text. It may be helpful to keep in mind the following questions as you read each excerpt:

- What events and developments does the author emphasize? Does he or she see some as more important than others?
- What is the author's attitude toward these developments and the historical actors to whom he or she refers? Is the author impressed? Scornful? Neutral? Disappointed?
- Does the author explain how or why things happened as they did? If so, what does he or she say? Does he or she emphasize ideas? The actions of particular individuals? Large economic and social forces?
- How does the author build his or her argument? Is it convincing to you? Why or why not?

These are just some of the questions you may wish to consider in reading the selections in this book. Asking questions such as these will help you uncover the interpretive framework employed by each author and, we hope, to develop your own interpretation of the events under discussion.

THE UNITED
STATES SINCE
1945

The Cold War System Abroad and at Home

CHAPTER 1

The Atomic Bombings

INTRODUCTION

In early August 1945, the United States dropped two atomic bombs on Japan, instantly killing approximately 115,000 inhabitants of the cities of Hiroshima and Nagasaki and injuring over 100,000. Shortly afterwards, Japan surrendered, ending a fierce and costly war that had begun with the Japanese attack on Pearl Harbor on December 7, 1941. In announcing to the American people the use of the atomic bomb, President Harry S Truman declared, "It is an awful responsibility which has come to us. We thank God that it has come to *us* instead of to our enemies." At the time, the American public would have had no doubt that by "enemies," Truman was referring to the Germans and the Japanese. But historians have since debated whether the bomb was necessary to end the war with Japan and, if not, whether it was in fact used to intimidate the Soviet Union, which by 1945 was beginning to seem to many U.S. officials more like a potential postwar foe than a wartime ally.

The American public overwhelmingly hailed the use of the bomb against Japan, accepting the official explanation put forward by Truman and echoed over the years by others: that the atomic bombing of Japan had been a regrettable necessity to speed the end of the war in the Pacific and thereby avert the need to invade Japan, a military campaign that might have cost the lives of hundreds of thousands, and by some assertions, millions. The effort to develop and build the bomb—the Manhattan Project—was celebrated as an unprecedented collaboration between science and government, and, at a cost of $2 billion, also one of the most expensive scientific and technological feats in history. Hiroshima and Nagasaki were described as war production centers and, by implication, legitimate military targets.

There were no significant challenges to this official explanation in the ensuing two decades. A few commentators did argue that Japan, by the summer of 1945, was so weakened that neither the atomic bombs nor an invasion was necessary to bring the war to a close. And some Americans concluded that the use of the atomic bombings had been immoral, especially in light of information about the devastation and suffering that had been wrought on Japanese civilians, not just by the bomb's blast, but in subsequent years, from its radioactive aftereffects. But it was not until 1965 that a scholar, in the course of studying the Truman administration's postwar policy planning with respect to Europe, posed a serious challenge to the traditional explanation. Gar Alperovitz, a political economist, concluded that Truman had engaged in "atomic diplomacy," using the fact of America's nuclear monopoly in the summer of 1945 to make Stalin more tractable to U.S. plans for postwar Europe. Contrary to the assertions of Truman and others, Alperovitz suggested that the bomb had in fact not been used primarily to speed the end of the Pacific War, and that there had been other options available but not pursued by America's leaders, including Soviet entry into the war against Japan. He speculated that Truman had dropped the bomb to impress the Soviets with America's nuclear power.

This revisionist view of the bomb gained adherents among scholars during the 1960s and 1970s as the political and cultural climate during and after the Vietnam War shifted and Americans became increasingly willing to doubt the wisdom as well as the truthfulness of their leaders, particularly in their descriptions of dealings with an Asian nation. Extensive archival research bolstered the revisionist view and led to a more fully elaborated understanding of the bomb's use. Attention was drawn to documents showing that official estimates of the number of American lives that might be lost in an invasion ranged from 25,000 to 46,000, nowhere near the figures put forward by the official or traditional view. Documents also revealed that Nagasaki and Hiroshima had been selected as targets not because they were the locations of military installations but because they afforded opportunities to impress the Japanese with the bomb's power. Truman's diary as well as new information about Truman's Secretary of War James Byrnes provided additional support for the claim that Truman had indeed been brandishing the bomb in negotiations with the Soviets. Questions about the morality of the bomb's use were renewed, with many historians seeing the bomb not as the closing act of World War II but as the opening act of the cold war and of a dangerous, expensive, and potentially lethal nuclear arms race. Some also wondered whether the bomb, had it been ready in time, would have been used against Nazi Germany, or whether racism toward the Japanese—evidenced by the internment of Japanese Americans during the war, among other things—was an important factor in Truman's decision.

By the end of the century, experts in the history of the atomic bombings overwhelmingly embraced as least some aspects of the revisionist view, the most significant being the contention that the Pacific War could have been ended without an invasion *or* the atomic bombings. The American public, however, remained generally unaware of this virtual scholarly consensus, drawing its understanding of the decision to use the bomb from admiring biographies of Truman or from popularized military histories that imply that the bomb was justified "payback" for Japan's treachery.

The first essay in this chapter, by Gar Alperovitz, presents an updated and expanded version of his classic revisionist interpretation. It emphasizes the centrality of the looming conflict with the Soviet Union over the fate of Eastern Europe, as well as the desire of the United States to keep the Red Army out of the Japanese conflict, in Truman's decision to drop the bomb. Alperovitz sees Truman as heavily influenced by the hard-line anticommunists among his advisors; by implication, he suggests that had Roosevelt remained president, the atomic bombs might not have been used.

The second essay, by historian Barton J. Bernstein, combines elements of the revisionist and traditional views. Drawing on the same documents used by Alperovitz (in fact, Bernstein is credited with drawing attention to the lower estimated mortality figures), Bernstein accepts the contention that there were alternatives to both the bomb and an invasion, and acknowledges that Truman did brandish the bomb in the expectation of impressing the Soviets. He also emphasizes that the targets of the bombs were chosen with the understanding that civilians would be killed. However, Bernstein departs from Alperovitz in concluding that Truman's primary purpose in dropping the bombs was as Truman had stated—to end the war and save American lives. In supporting his contention, Bernstein draws particular attention to the moral climate of World War II. This was a war during which the traditional proscription against the killing of civilians had been abandoned; the United States itself had engaged in terror bombings of both German and Japanese civilians. In the context of a brutal, total war, the atomic bomb did not raise new questions of morality, contends Bernstein. Truman, according to Bernstein, inherited assumptions about the bomb that had been present at the outset and likely shared by Roosevelt—that the bomb was a legitimate weapon of war.

GAR ALPEROVITZ

Why the United States Dropped the Bomb

Ask the average person why the United States exploded the atomic bomb over Hiroshima and Nagasaki . . . and the answer will almost always be straightforward: "To save thousands of lives by making an invasion unnecessary at the end of World War II." ABC's Ted Koppel expressed such a view in a special "Nightline" broadcast a few years ago: "What happened over Japan . . . was a human tragedy. . . . But what was planned to take place in the war between Japan and the United States would almost certainly have been an even greater tragedy."

The only problem with this morally comforting explanation is that it is now known to be false. . . .

Scholarly judgment has shifted with the discovery of a wide range of previously unavailable documents, diaries, and private journals. . . .

The bare chronology of events in 1945 itself raises questions about U.S. motives for dropping the bomb. Germany surrendered on May 8, and the Allied powers knew that Japan's situation was deteriorating rapidly. At the Yalta conference of Allied leaders in February, Stalin had agreed to declare war on Japan three months after the defeat of Germany—roughly August 8. The United States originally sought Soviet support for an invasion of Japan, but by late summer the shock of a Russian declaration of war seemed likely to end the war without a U.S. offensive. . . .

President Truman's oft-quoted estimate that a U.S. invasion might have cost a million American lives is the basis for much of the conventional wisdom about why the bomb was dropped. Unfortunately, that figure has no basis in military planning records. Stanford historian Barton Bernstein has shown that the Joint War Plans Committee—a high-level advisory group to the U.S. Joint Chiefs of Staff—concluded that about 40,000 Americans would die if an assault were launched on both the island of Kyushu and, thereafter, the main Japanese home island.

But as early as mid-June 1945 . . . it appeared that the smaller Kyushu landing alone might "well prove to be the decisive operation which will terminate the war," according to the committee. U.S. Army Chief of Staff General George C. Marshall informed President Truman that casualties

From "Why the United States Dropped the Bomb," by Gar Alperovitz, from *Technology Review,* Vol. 93 (Aug.–Sept. 1990). Reprinted by permission of Alumni Association, Massachusetts Institute of Technology.

for the Kyushu operation were not expected to exceed 31,000 during the first and costliest month of the operation—a figure that included dead, wounded, and missing. Extrapolating from contemporary combat statistics would yield an estimate of less than 7,500 dead.

However, these deaths would occur only if such a landing were actually attempted, and by mid-summer 1945 that possibility had become "remote," in the judgment of a newly discovered intelligence study. Massive documentation now shows that Japan's military, economic, and political condition deteriorated dramatically from the spring of 1945 on. Even as early as April 1945, General Douglas MacArthur, commander of U.S. troops in the Pacific, reported that "the Japanese fleet has been reduced to practical impotency. The Japanese Air Force has been reduced to a line of action which involves uncoordinated, suicidal attacks against our forces. . . . Its attrition is heavy and its power for sustained action is diminishing rapidly."

As the situation in Japan worsened, Japanese "peace feelers" began to erupt throughout Europe. On May 12, 1945, Office of Strategic Services Director William Donovan reported to President Truman that Shunichi Kase, Japan's minister to Switzerland, wished "to help arrange for a cessation of hostilities." He believed "one of the few provisions the Japanese would insist upon would be the retention of the Emperor."

Truman received a similar report concerning Masutaro Inoue, Japan's counselor in Portugal, who, according to an Office of Strategic Services informant, "declared that actual peace terms were unimportant so long as the term 'unconditional surrender' was not employed. The Japanese, he asserted, are convinced that within a few weeks all of their wood and paper houses will be destroyed."

Though such feelers were not yet official, in mid-June Admiral William D. Leahy—who both chaired the Joint Chiefs of Staff and served as the president's chief of staff—concluded that "a surrender of Japan can be arranged with terms that can be accepted by Japan and that will make fully satisfactory provision for America's defense against future trans-Pacific aggression."

Even more important evidence of Japan's desire to end hostilities reached the White House through intercepted diplomatic cables. U.S. intelligence experts had broken Japanese codes early in the war. During the late summer, these experts learned that the emperor of Japan was secretly attempting to arrange a surrender through Russia. The emperor wished to send a personal representative, Prince Konoye, to Moscow: "The mission . . . was to ask the Soviet Government to take part in mediation to end the present war and to transmit the complete Japanese case in this respect. . . . Prince Konoe [*sic*] was especially charged by His Majesty, the Emperor, to convey to the Soviet Government that it was exclusively the desire of His Majesty to avoid more bloodshed."

. . . The emperor's personal initiative, however, was "real evidence," as Secretary of the Navy James Forrestal put it, of a determination to end the fighting. The intercepted cables also indicated that the only significant condition appeared to be an assurance that the emperor could retain his title.

Truman later acknowledged that he had generally been informed of these messages, but his personal, handwritten journal—kept secret and, so we are told, then misfiled until 1979—is particularly revealing. In it he goes so far as to characterize one crucial Japanese intercept as the "telegram from [the] Jap Emperor asking for peace."

As these cables made clear, and as several top officials advised the president, one option that appeared likely to end the war was simply to let Japan know that "unconditional surrender" did not require removing the emperor. Indeed, since the Japanese people considered the emperor a deity, U.S. and British intelligence experts argued that without such assurances, Japan would be forced to fight to save face until the very end. U.S. military leaders also believed that only if the emperor were allowed to keep his throne would anyone have enough authority to order Japanese soldiers to put down their arms.

It is important to understand that a variety of documents, including the diaries of Secretary of War Henry L. Stimson and the papers of Acting Secretary of State Joseph C. Grew, show that President Truman had no fundamental objection to offering assurances to the emperor: he made this quite clear to both men at different points during the summer. And, of course, Truman ultimately did allow the emperor to remain: Japan has an emperor to this day.

The president chose to wait, however, until after using the atomic bomb before providing the assurances Japan sought. One common interpretation is that he feared domestic political opponents would criticize him for being "soft" on the Japanese. He may have hoped the bomb would make even small changes in the surrender terms unnecessary. But by July 1945 the choice was clearly no longer the simple one of mounting an invasion or relying on the devastating power of the new weapon.

. . . Repeated U.S. intelligence studies judged as early as mid-April 1945 that "the entry of the U.S.S.R. into the war would . . . convince most Japanese at once of the inevitability of complete defeat." In mid-June 1945, General Marshall advised President Truman directly that the impact of the expected Soviet declaration of war "on the already hopeless Japanese" might well "lever" them into capitulation immediately or shortly thereafter "if" the United States landed in Japan. A month later—with still more information in hand—Britain's General Sir Hastings Ismay summarized joint American-British intelligence conclusions for Prime Minister Churchill, saying: "[W]hen Russia came into the war against Japan, the Japanese would probably wish to get out on almost any terms short of the dethronement of the Emperor."

Truman's private journal, along with his letters, also illuminates his recognition, well before the atomic bomb was used, that the Soviet declaration of war—on its own—seemed all but certain to end the fighting. After Stalin confirmed that Russia would declare war against Japan in early August, Truman privately noted: "Fini Japs when that comes about." And writing to his wife, the president observed that with the Soviet declaration, "We'll end the war a year sooner now, and think of the kids who won't be killed!" (Military planners advised that if an invasion were undertaken, the war's likely maximum duration would be about a year.) So important did the Russian declaration seem before the first atomic test that Truman told several people it was his main reason for traveling to Potsdam, Germany, to meet with Stalin in July.

Since the U.S. bombings of Japan and the Soviet declaration of war occurred within days of each other, and since Japan formally surrendered only after Truman acknowledged the role of the emperor, historians continue to debate precisely how much weight to accord each factor in ending the conflict. But a top-secret 1946 War Department intelligence study discovered only last year bluntly concludes that the atomic bomb had little to do with Japan's decision to surrender. Rather, it states that the Soviet Union's entry was unquestionably the decisive factor that ended World War II. Like the official Strategic Bombing Survey, the study also concludes that a large-scale U.S. invasion would likely never have taken place: it is "almost a certainty that the Japanese would have capitulated upon the entry of Russia into the war."

Despite the accumulating evidence that Japan was all but defeated, plans to ready the bomb continued throughout the spring of 1945. However, as Japan's situation worsened during May, June, and July, the specific role the bomb was to play appears to have shifted. Initially some U.S. leaders felt the weapon should be employed in the course of an invasion against strictly military targets. Even as late as May 29, General Marshall thought "these weapons might first be used against straight military objectives such as a large naval installation and then if no complete result was derived from the effect of that, . . . we ought to designate a number of large manufacturing areas from which people would be warned to leave—telling the Japanese that we intend to destroy such centers."

By early June, however, Japan's condition had so deteriorated that a psychological shock—not an attack to destroy "straight military objectives"—seemed likely to produce surrender. But the Interim Committee, a high-level group formed to decide how to handle the new technology and chaired by Secretary of War Henry L. Stimson, rejected the option of giving an explicit warning to civilians. According to the committee's records, *The Secretary expressed the conclusion, on which there was general agreement, that . . . we should seek to make a profound psychological impression on as many of the inhabitants as possible. At the suggestion of Dr. Conant* [the president of Harvard] *the Secretary agreed that the most desirable target would be a vital war plant employing a large number of workers and closely surrounded by workers houses.*" [Emphasis in original.] . . .

Various scientists, upset that the bombing would proceed even though Germany had been defeated and Japan had been reduced to dire straits, attempted to head it off. New research has also given us a clearer picture of the many ways their efforts were blocked. Peter Wyden, for instance, describes . . . how J. Robert Oppenheimer deftly sidetracked Chicago scientists opposed to using the atomic weapon. General Leslie Groves, the military leader of the Manhattan Project, and other top officials also simply delayed a petition to the president registering scientists' opposition until it was too late. . . .

Historians are divided in attempting to explain why, in the face of the evidence we now have, U.S. leaders chose to use the atomic bomb. But a number of experts agree that a once-controversial factor—the U.S. hope of strengthening the West's hand against the Soviet Union—played a significant role.

The clearest evidence points to a strong U.S. desire to end the war before the Russians attacked Japan. Truman and his advisors knew that the Red Army would engage the Japanese in Manchuria and North China, a move that would put them in a position to dominate the area after the war. Although there was plenty of time to test Japan's reaction to the Soviet declaration of war, once U.S. and British officials knew the atomic bomb actually worked they desperately wanted to end the fighting before the Red Army crossed into Manchurian and Chinese territory.

For example, the private journal of Walter Brown, personal assistant to Secretary of State James F. Byrnes, notes that Byrnes was "hoping for time, believing that after [the] atomic bomb Japan will surrender and Russia will not get in so much on the kill, thereby being in a position to press claims against China." Prime Minister Churchill also observed on July 23, 1945, "It is quite clear that the United States do not at the present time desire Russian participation in the war against Japan." And the diary of Navy Secretary James V. Forrestal records that Secretary of State Byrnes was now "most anxious to get the Japanese affair over with before the Russians got in." . . .

Modern documentary discoveries also indicate that U.S. officials expected the bomb to provide a second political advantage. From April 1945 on, they calculated that the weapon would enormously bolster negotiations with the Soviets over the fate of postwar Europe as well as Asia. The Red Army had moved into Eastern Europe while defeating Germany, and the Allies were struggling over the control and composition of the government in each country. Churchill, Stalin, and Truman had agreed to meet in Potsdam, Germany, to discuss these and other European matters.

The general assumption that the weapon would strengthen the overall U.S. and British diplomatic position can be traced to the early Roosevelt years. When Roosevelt died, the new president initially received a full briefing on the atomic bomb mainly because of its likely impact on diplomacy, not its role vis-à-vis Japan. In late April, for example, in the midst of an explosive fight with Stalin over the composition of the postwar Polish government, Secretary of War Stimson urged discussion of the bomb because (as he told Truman) it had "such a bearing on our present foreign relations and . . . such an important effect upon all my thinking in this field."

Stimson's diaries show that although he regarded the atomic bomb as the "master card" of diplomacy toward Russia, he believed sparring with the Soviet Union in the early spring, before the weapon was demonstrated, would be counterproductive. After a mid-May meeting on Far Eastern issues, for instance, Stimson observed that "the questions cut very deep and . . . [were] powerfully connected with our success with S-1 [the atomic bomb]." Two days later he noted that "it may be necessary to have it out with Russia on her relations to Manchuria and Port Arthur and various other parts of North China, and also the relations of China to us. Over any such tangled weave of problems the [atomic bomb] secret would be dominant and yet we will not know until after that time, probably . . . whether this is a weapon in our hands or not. We think it will be shortly afterwards, but it seems a terrible thing to gamble with such big stakes in diplomacy without having your master card in your hand."

Stimson therefore urged delaying diplomatic fights with Russia, as he indicated in another mid-May diary entry after a conversation with Assistant Secretary of War John J. McCloy: "[T]he time now and the method now to deal with Russia was to keep our mouths shut and let our actions speak for words. The Russians will understand them better than anything else. It is a case where we have got to regain the lead and perhaps do it in a pretty rough and realistic way. [T]his [is] a place where we really held all the cards. I called it a royal straight flush and we mustn't be a fool about the way we play it. They can't get along without our help and industries and we have coming into action a weapon which will be unique.

"Now the thing is not to get into unnecessary quarrels by talking too much and not to indicate any weakness by talking too much; let our actions speak for themselves."

Stimson's files and other documents show that President Truman had come to similar conclusions. Quite specifically—and against the advice of Churchill (who wanted an early meeting with Stalin before American troops were withdrawn from Europe)—the president postponed his only diplomatic encounter with the Soviet leader because he first wanted to know for certain that the still untested atomic bomb actually worked. "If it explodes, as I think it will," he told a close associate, "I'll certainly have a hammer on those boys." After a May 1945 meeting with Truman, Ambassador Joseph E. Davies' diaries record that "to my surprise, he said he did not want it [the heads-of-government meeting] until July. The reason which I could assign was that he had his budget on his hands. . . . 'But,' he said, 'I have another reason . . . which I have not told anybody.' He told me of the atomic bomb. The final test had been set for June, but now had been postponed until July. I was startled, shocked and amazed." (After Truman told Stimson of his overall strategy toward the Potsdam meeting, the secretary of war agreed: "We shall probably hold more cards in our hands later than now.")

Strong evidence now shows that Secretary of State James F. Byrnes, an influential former Supreme Court Justice, played a central role in determining Truman's view of the bomb's utility. Byrnes had been one of Truman's mentors when the young unknown from Missouri first came to the Senate. By choosing Byrnes as his personal representative on the Interim Committee, Truman arranged to secure primary counsel on both foreign policy and the atomic bomb from a single trusted advisor. (If Truman had been interested in a strictly military appraisal of the bomb, of course, he would have relied primarily on the War Department for advice.)

There is not much doubt about Byrnes' consistently hardline viewpoint. In one of their very first meetings, Byrnes told Truman that "in his belief the atomic bomb might well put us in a position to dictate our own terms at the end of the war." At the end of May, Byrnes met at White House request with atomic scientist Leo Szilard. Szilard found that "Mr. Byrnes did not argue that it was necessary to use the bomb against the cities of Japan in order to win the war. . . . Mr. Byrnes's . . . view [was] that our possessing and demonstrating the bomb would make Russia more manageable in Europe. . . . Russian troops had moved into Hungary and Rumania; Byrnes thought . . . that Russia might be more manageable if impressed by American military might."

In May of 1945, Byrnes also intervened forcefully to oppose General Marshall and others on the Interim Committee who suggested that the Russians be told of the bomb's existence before it was used. Marshall further urged that Russian scientists be invited to witness the test—a proposal also rejected. In general, Byrnes, representing the president, took a very tough line against any attempt to seek international control of the new weapon. He was intensely interested in how long the U.S. nuclear monopoly would last, pressing scientists on the question in meetings of the committee's scientific panel on May 31. Byrnes also repeatedly stressed the need to accelerate research to stay ahead.

After discussions at Potsdam, Ambassador Davies recorded in his diary that "Byrnes' attitude that the atomic bomb assured ultimate success in negotiations disturbed me. . . . I told him the threat wouldn't work, and might do irreparable harm." Assistant Secretary of War John J. McCloy, too, met with Byrnes a few weeks after Hiroshima and reported to Stimson that Byrnes, about to depart for a meeting with Soviet Foreign Minister Vyacheslav Molotov, "was quite radically opposed" to any effort to reach an understanding with the Russians to control nuclear weapons. Stimson himself talked with Byrnes on September 4, 1945, and noted that "Jim Byrnes had not yet gone abroad and I had a very good talk with him afterwards sitting in the White House hall. . . . I took up the question which I had been working at with McCloy up in St. Huberts, namely how to handle Russia with the big bomb. I found that Byrnes was very much against any attempt to cooperate with Russia. His mind is full of his problems with the coming meeting of foreign ministers and he looks to having the presence of the bomb in his pocket, so to speak, as a great weapon to get through the thing."

The timing of Truman's summer strategy to delay negotiations with Stalin worked exquisitely: the first successful atomic test occurred on July 16, 1945. Truman sat down for discussions with the Soviet premier the very next day, July 17. Secretary of War Stimson's diary includes this entry after he received a full report of the test results: "[Churchill] told me that he had noticed at the meeting of the Big Three yesterday that Truman was evidently much fortified by something that had happened and that he stood up to the Russians in a most emphatic and decisive manner, telling them as to certain demands that they absolutely could not have and that the United States was entirely against them. He said 'Now I know what happened to Truman yesterday. I couldn't understand it. When he got to the meeting after having read this report he was a changed man. He told the Russians just where they got on and off and generally bossed the whole meeting.'"

A July 22, 1945, entry in the diary of Field Marshall Alan Brooke, chief of the British imperial general staff, further describes Churchill's reaction—and provides more indirect evidence of the atomic bomb's impact on American attitudes: "[The Prime Minister] . . . had absorbed all the minor American exaggerations and, as a result, was completely carried away. . . . We now had something in our hands which would redress the balance with the Russians. The secret of this explosive and the power to use it would completely alter the diplomatic equilibrium which was adrift since the defeat of Germany. Now we had a new value which redressed our position (pushing out his chin and scowling); now we could say, 'If you insist on doing this or that, well . . .' And then where are the Russians!"

A number of historians now agree that long-term diplomatic interests—beyond a specific desire to end the war before the Red Army crossed the Manchurian border—influenced Truman, Stimson, and Byrnes, consciously or unconsciously, when they chose the bomb over other readily available ways to stop the fighting. Experts differ, of course, in the precise weight to accord this motive in the thinking of each U.S. leader, and some continue to hold that solely military factors were involved, or that the weapon's use was "inevitable" because of the technological, bureaucratic, and military momentum built up during the war. Other historians argue that because huge sums were spent developing the new weapon, political leaders found it impossible not to use it. Still others believe a roughly even mix of political-diplomatic considerations and military concerns were at work, and some writers look to bureaucratic infighting to explain the outcome. But the late Herbert Feis, a friend of Stimson's, an advisor to three secretaries of war, and a historian with impeccable connections, judged a quarter-century ago that "impressing" the Soviets almost certainly played a role in the decision to use the atomic bomb. . . .

In fact, some historians now believe that the atomic bomb probably even prolonged the war and cost American lives rather than saved them, since Acting Secretary of State Joseph Grew advised the president as early as May 1945 that changing the surrender terms might well halt the fighting—and since the president apparently delayed until the bomb was ready. "Many more American soldiers and Japanese of all types," Tufts University historian Martin Sherwin writes, "might have had the opportunity to grow old if Truman had accepted Grew's advice." Secretary of War Stimson, too, came subsequently to believe "that history might find the United States, by its delay in stating its position [on surrender terms], had prolonged the war."

In a post-victory visit to Moscow, General Dwight Eisenhower observed that "before the atom bomb was used, I would have said, yes, I was sure we could keep the peace with Russia. Now I don't know. . . . People are frightened and disturbed all over. Everyone feels insecure again." At the September 1945 London Conference of Foreign Ministers, Byrnes—relying upon the atomic bomb—did, in fact, attempt to make Russia "more manageable" in such Eastern European nations as Bulgaria and Rumania. John Foster Dulles, who was present, believed the tensions that became the Cold War started at this time.

In Washington, Secretary Stimson—now profoundly troubled by Byrnes' attitude and the developing momentum of U.S. policy—undertook what is undoubtedly one of the most remarkable, if unsuccessful, reversals in American history. Acknowledging that "I was wrong" to think the U.S. should "hang onto the bomb as long as possible," Stimson came to believe this would be "by far the more dangerous course."

In a direct approach to the president, Stimson urged an immediate initiative to establish cooperative international control of the new weapon. He emphasized that the Russians were unlikely to respond if the approach were made in a public arena like the United Nations, or if it were made "after a succession of express or implied threats or near threats." The alternative, Stimson warned, would likely be "a secret armament race of a rather desperate character." He stressed: "If the atomic bomb were merely another though more devastating military weapon to be assimilated into our pattern of international relations, it would be one thing. . . . But I think the bomb instead constitutes merely a first step in a new control by man over the forces of nature too revolutionary and dangerous to fit into the old concepts. . . . "

"To put the matter concisely, I consider the problem of our satisfactory relations with Russia as not merely connected with but as virtually dominated by the problem of the atomic bomb."

. . . [T]he full record of what happened in the summer of 1945 is still not available. We especially lack knowledge of many private discussions between Secretary Byrnes and President Truman during April, May, and June 1945, when Byrnes served as the president's personal representative on the Interim Committee. We know almost nothing about the critical planning sessions the two men held during the eight-day Atlantic crossing before the Potsdam conference and the bombing itself. Beyond this, many official documents—ranging from selected Japanese "intercepts" to specific Manhattan Project files—are still classified, and some private journals have not been made public.

We shall undoubtedly learn the full truth one day. As the Cold War winds down, there is renewed interest in the Hiroshima story—and in the profound questions Secretary Stimson and others came to understand were posed by the first use of nuclear weapons, and by the U.S. contribution to the tensions that were to dominate international relations for more than four decades.

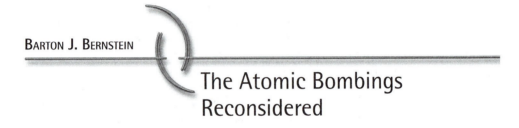

BARTON J. BERNSTEIN

The Atomic Bombings Reconsidered

Before Hiroshima and Nagasaki, the use of the A-bomb did not raise profound moral issues for policymakers. The weapon was conceived in a race with Germany, and it undoubtedly would have been used against Germany had the bomb been ready much sooner. During the war, the target shifted to Japan. And during World War II's brutal course, civilians in cities had already become targets. The grim Axis bombing record is well known. Masses of noncombatants were also intentionally killed in the later stages of the American air war against Germany; that tactic was developed further in 1945 with the firebombing of Japanese cities. Such mass bombing constituted a transformation of morality, repudiating President Franklin D. Roosevelt's prewar pleas that the warring nations avoid bombing cities to spare civilian lives. Thus, by 1945, American leaders were not seeking to avoid the use of the A-bomb on Japan. . . .

In 1941, urged by émigré and American scientists, President Roosevelt initiated the atomic bomb project—soon code-named the Manhattan Project—amid what was believed to be a desperate race with Hitler's Germany for the bomb. At the beginning, Roosevelt and his chief aides assumed that the A-bomb was a legitimate weapon that would be used first against Nazi Germany. They also decided that the bomb project should be kept secret from the Soviet Union, even after the Soviets became a wartime ally, because the bomb might well give the United States future leverage against the Soviets.

By mid-1944, the landscape of the war had changed. Roosevelt and his top advisers knew that the likely target would now be Japan, for the war with Germany would undoubtedly end well before the A-bomb was expected to be ready, around the spring of 1945. In a secret September 1944 memorandum at Hyde Park, Roosevelt and British Prime Minister Winston Churchill ratified the shift from Germany to Japan. Their phrasing suggested that, for the moment anyway, they might have had some slight doubts about actually using the bomb, for they agreed that "it might *perhaps,* after mature consideration, be used against the Japanese" (my emphasis).

Four days later, mulling over matters aloud with a visiting British diplomat and chief U.S. science adviser Vannevar Bush, Roosevelt briefly wondered whether the A-bomb should be dropped on Japan or whether it should be demonstrated in America, presumably with Japanese observers, and then used as a threat. His speculative notion seemed so unimportant and so contrary to the project's long-standing operating assumptions that Bush actually forgot about it when he prepared a memo of the meeting. He only recalled the president's remarks a day later and then added a brief paragraph to another memorandum.

Put in context alongside the dominant assumption that the bomb would be used against the enemy, the significance of F.D.R.'s occasional doubts is precisely that they were so occasional—expressed twice in almost four years. All of F.D.R.'s advisers who knew about the bomb always unquestioningly assumed that it would be used. Indeed, their memoranda frequently spoke of "after it is used" or "when it is used," and never "*if* it is used." By about mid-1944, most had comfortably concluded that the target would be Japan.

The bomb's assumed legitimacy as a war weapon was ratified bureaucratically in September 1944 when General Leslie Groves, the director of the Manhattan Project, had the air force create a special group—the 509th Composite Group with 1,750 men—to begin practicing to drop atomic bombs. So dominant was the assumption that the bomb would be used against Japan that only one high-ranking Washington official, Undersecretary of War Robert Patterson, even questioned this notion after V-E Day. He wondered whether the defeat of Germany on May 8, 1945, might alter the plans for dropping the bomb on Japan. It would not.

The Manhattan Project, costing nearly $2 billion, had been kept secret from most cabinet members and nearly all of Congress. Secretary of War Henry L. Stimson, a trusted Republican, and General George C. Marshall, the equally respected army chief of staff, disclosed the project to only a few congressional leaders. They smuggled the necessary appropriations into the War Department budget without the knowledge—much less the scrutiny—of most congressmen, including most members of the key appropriations committees. A conception of the national interest agreed upon by a few men from the executive and legislative branches had revised the normal appropriations process.

In March 1944, when a Democratic senator heading a special investigating committee wanted to pry into this expensive project, Stimson peevishly described him in his diary as "a nuisance and pretty untrustworthy . . . He talks smoothly but acts meanly." That man was Senator Harry S Truman. Marshall persuaded him not to investigate the project, and thus Truman did not learn any more than that it involved a new weapon until he was suddenly thrust into the presidency on April 12, 1945.

In early 1945, James F. Byrnes, then F.D.R.'s "assistant president" for domestic affairs and a savvy Democratic politician, began to suspect that the Manhattan Project was a boondoggle. "If [it] proves a failure," he warned Roosevelt, "it will be subjected to relentless investigation and criticism." Byrnes' doubts were soon overcome by Stimson and Marshall. A secret War Department report, with some hyperbole, summarized the situation: "If the project succeeds, there won't be any investigation. If it doesn't, they won't investigate anything else."

Had Roosevelt lived, such lurking political pressures might have powerfully confirmed his intention to use the weapon on the enemy—an assumption he had already made. How else could he have justified spending roughly $2 billion, diverting scarce materials from other war enterprises that might have been even more useful, and bypassing Congress? In a nation still unprepared to trust scientists, the Manhattan Project could have seemed a gigantic waste if its value were not dramatically demonstrated by the use of the atomic bomb.

Truman, inheriting the project and trusting both Marshall and Stimson, would be even more vulnerable to such political pressures. And, like F.D.R., the new president easily assumed that the bomb should and would be used. Truman never questioned that assumption. Bureaucratic developments set in motion before he entered the White House reinforced his belief. And his aides, many inherited from the Roosevelt administration, shared the same faith.

Groves, eager to retain control of the atomic project, received Marshall's permission in early spring 1945 to select targets for the new weapon. Groves and his associates had long recognized that they were considering a weapon of a new magnitude, possibly equivalent to the "normal bombs carried by [at least] 2,500 bombers." And they had come to assume that the A-bomb would be "detonated well above ground, relying primarily on blast effect to do material damage, [so that even with] minimum probable efficiency, there will be the maximum number of structures (dwellings and factories) damaged beyond repair."

On April 27, the Target Committee, composed of Groves, army air force men like General Lauris Norstad, and scientists including the great mathematician John Von Neumann, met for the first time to discuss how and where in Japan to drop the bomb. . . .

By early 1945, World War II—especially in the Pacific—had become virtually total war. The firebombing of Dresden had helped set a precedent for the U.S. air force, supported by the American people, to intentionally kill mass numbers of Japanese citizens. The earlier moral insistence on noncombatant immunity crumbled during the savage war. In Tokyo, during March 9–10, a U.S. air attack killed about 80,000 Japanese civilians. American B-29s dropped napalm on the city's heavily populated areas to produce uncontrollable firestorms. It may even have been easier to conduct this new warfare outside Europe and against Japan because its people seemed like "yellow subhumans" to many rank-and-file American citizens and many of their leaders.

In this new moral context, with mass killings of an enemy's civilians even seeming desirable, the committee agreed to choose "large urban areas of not less than three miles in diameter existing in the larger populated areas" as A-bomb targets. The April 27 discussion focused on four cities: Hiroshima, which, as "the largest untouched target not on the 21st Bomber Command priority list," warranted serious consideration; Yawata, known for its steel industry; Yokohama; and Tokyo, "a possibility [though] now practically all bombed and burned out and . . . practically rubble with only the palace grounds left standing." They decided that other areas warranted more consideration: Tokyo Bay, Kawasaki, Yokohoma, Nagoya, Osaka, Kobe, Kyoto, Hiroshima, Kure, Yawata, Kokura, Shimonoseki, Yamaguchi, Kumamoto, Fukuoka, Nagasaki, and Sasebo.

The choice of targets would depend partly on how the bomb would do its deadly work—the balance of blast, heat, and radiation. At their second set of meetings, during May 11–12, physicist J. Robert Oppenheimer, director of the Los Alamos laboratory, stressed that the bomb material itself was lethal enough for perhaps a billion deadly doses and that the weapon would give off lethal radioactivity. The bomb, set to explode in the air, would deposit "a large fraction of either the initial active material or the radioactive products in the immediate vicinity of the target; but the radiation . . . will, of course, have an effect on exposed personnel in the target area." It was unclear, he acknowledged, what would happen to most of the radioactive material: it could stay for hours as a cloud above the place of detonation or, if the bomb exploded during rain or in high humidity and thus caused rain, "most of the active material will be brought down in the vicinity of the target area." Oppenheimer's report left unclear whether a substantial proportion or only a small fraction of the population might die from radiation. So far as the skimpy records reveal, no member of the Target Committee chose to dwell on this matter. They probably assumed that the bomb blast would claim most of its victims before the radiation could do its deadly work. . . .

The Target Committee selected their four top targets: Kyoto, Hiroshima, Yokohama, and Kokura Arsenal, with the implication that Niigata, a city farther away from the air force 509th group's Tinian base, might be held in reserve as a fifth. Kyoto, the ancient former capital and shrine city, with a population of about a million, was the most attractive target to the committee. "From the psychological point of view," the committee minutes note, "there is the advantage that Kyoto is an intellectual center for Japan and [thus] the people there are more apt to appreciate the significance of such a weapon." The implication was that those in Kyoto who survived the A-bombing and saw the horror would be believed elsewhere in Japan.

Of central importance, the group stressed that the bomb should be used as a terror weapon—to produce "the greatest psychological effect against Japan" and to make the world, and the U.S.S.R. in particular, aware that America possessed this new power. The death and destruction would not only intimidate the surviving Japanese into pushing for surrender, but, as a bonus, cow other nations, notably the Soviet Union. In short, America could speed the ending of the war and by the same act help shape the postwar world.

By the committee's third meeting, two weeks later, on May 28, they had pinned down matters. They chose as their targets (in order) Kyoto, Hiroshima, and Niigata, and decided to aim for the center of each city. They agreed that aiming for industrial areas would be a mistake because such targets were small, spread on the cities' fringes, and quite dispersed. They also knew that bombing was imprecise enough that the bomb might easily miss its mark by a fifth of a mile, and they wanted to be sure that the weapon would show its power and not be wasted.

The committee understood that the three target cities would be removed from the air force's regular target list, reserving them for the A-bomb. But, the members were informed, "with the current and prospective rate of . . . bombings, it is expected to complete strategic bombing of Japan by 1 Jan 46 so availability of future [A-bomb] targets will be a problem." In short, Japan was being bombed out.

On May 28, 1945, physicist Arthur H. Compton, a Nobel laureate and member of a special scientific panel advising the high-level Interim Committee newly appointed to recommend policy about the bomb, raised profound moral and political questions about how the atomic bomb would be used. "It introduces the question of mass slaughter, really for the first time in history," he wrote. "It carries with it the question of possible radioactive poison over the area bombed. Essentially, the question of the use . . . of the new weapon carries much more serious implications than the introduction of poison gas."

Compton's concern received some independent support from General Marshall, who told Secretary Stimson on May 29 that the A-bomb should first be used not against civilians but against military installations—perhaps a naval base—and then possibly against large manufacturing areas after the civilians had received ample warnings to flee. Marshall feared "the opprobrium which might follow from an ill considered employment of such force." A graduate of Virginia Military Institute and a trained soldier, Marshall struggled to retain the older code of not *intentionally* killing civilians. The concerns of Compton the scientist and Marshall the general, their values so rooted in an earlier conception of war that sought to spare noncombatants, soon gave way to the sense of exigency, the desire to use the bomb on people, and the unwillingness or inability of anyone near the top in Washington to plead forcefully for maintaining this older morality.

On May 31, 1945, the Interim Committee, composed of Stimson, Bush, Harvard President James Conant, physicist and educator Karl T. Compton, Secretary of State designate James F. Byrnes, and a few other notables, discussed the A-bomb. Opening this meeting, Stimson, the aged secretary of war who had agonized over the recent shift toward mass bombing of civilians, described the atomic bomb as representing "a new relationship of man to the universe. This discovery might be compared to the discoveries of the Copernican theory and the laws of gravity, but far more important than these in its effects on the lives of men."

Meeting, as they were, some six weeks before the first nuclear test at Alamogordo, they were still unsure of the power of this new weapon. Oppenheimer told the group that it would have an explosive force of between 2,000 and 20,000 tons of TNT. Its visual effect would be tremendous. "It would be accompanied by a brilliant luminescence which would rise to a height of 10,000 to 20,000 feet," Oppenheimer reported. "The neutron effect [radiation] would be dangerous to life for a radius of at least two-thirds of a mile." He estimated that 20,000 Japanese would be killed.

According to the committee minutes, the group discussed "various types of targets and the effects to be produced." Stimson "expressed the conclusion, on which there was general agreement, that we could not give the Japanese any warning; that we could not concentrate on a civilian area; but that we should seek to make a profound psychological impression on as many of the inhabitants as possible. At the suggestion of Dr. Conant, the secretary agreed that the most desirable target would be a vital war plant employing a large number of workers and closely surrounded by workers' houses."

Directed by Stimson, the committee was actually endorsing terror bombing—but somewhat uneasily. They would not focus exclusively on a military target (the older morality), as Marshall had recently proposed, nor fully on civilians (the emerging morality). They managed to achieve their purpose—terror bombing—without bluntly acknowledging it to themselves. All knew that families—women, children, and, even in the daytime, during the bomb attack, some workers—dwelled in "workers' houses."

At the committee's morning or afternoon session, or at lunch, or possibly at all three times—different members later presented differing recollections—the notion of a noncombat demonstration of the A-bomb came up. The issue of how to use the bomb was not even on Stimson's agenda, nor was it part of the formal mandate of the Interim Committee, but he may have showed passing interest in the subject of a noncombat demonstration. They soon rejected it. It was deemed too risky for various reasons: the bomb might not work, the Japanese air force might interfere with the bomber, the A-bomb might not adequately impress the Japanese militarists, or the bomb might incinerate any Allied POWS whom the Japanese might place in the area. . . .

Two weeks after the Interim Committee meeting, on June 16, after émigré physicists James Franck and Leo Szilard and some colleagues from the Manhattan Project's Chicago laboratory raised moral and political questions about the surprise use of the bomb on Japan, a special four-member scientific advisory committee disposed of the matter of a noncombat demonstration. The group was composed of physicists Arthur Compton, J. Robert Oppenheimer, Enrico Fermi, and Ernest O. Lawrence. By one report, Lawrence was the last of the four to give up hope for a noncombat demonstration. Oppenheimer, who spoke on the issue in 1954 and was not then controverted by the other three men, recalled that the subject of a noncombat demonstration was not the most important matter dealt with during the group's busy weekend meeting and thus did not receive much attention. On June 16, the four scientists concluded: "We can propose no technical demonstration likely to bring an end to the war; we see no acceptable alternative to direct military use."

At that time, as some members of the scientific panel later grudgingly acknowledged, they knew little about the situation in Japan, the power of the militarists there, the timid efforts by the peace forces there to move toward a settlement, the date of the likely American invasion of Kyushu, and the power of the still untested A-bomb. "We didn't know beans about the military situation," Oppenheimer later remarked pungently.

But even different counsel by the scientific advisers probably could not have reversed the course of events. The bomb had been devised to be used, the project cost about $2 billion, and Truman and Byrnes, the president's key political aide, had no desire to avoid its use. Nor did Stimson. They even had additional reasons for wanting to use it: the bomb might *also* intimidate the Soviets and render them tractable in the postwar period. . . .

During 1945, Stimson found himself presiding, with agony, over an air force that killed hundreds of thousands of Japanese civilians. Usually, he preferred not to face these ugly facts, but sought refuge in the notion that the air force was actually engaged in precision bombing and that somehow this precision bombing was going awry. Caught between an older morality that opposed the intentional killing of noncombatants and a newer one that stressed virtually total war, Stimson could neither fully face the facts nor fully escape them. He was not a hypocrite but a man trapped in ambivalence.

Stimson discussed the problem with Truman on June 6. Stimson stressed that he was worried about the air force's mass bombing, but that it was hard to restrict it. In his diary, Stimson recorded: "I told him I was anxious about this feature of the war for two reasons: first, because I did not want to have the United States get the reputation of outdoing Hitler in atrocities; and second, I was a little fearful that before we could get ready the air force might have Japan so thoroughly bombed out that the new weapon would not have a fair background to show its strength." According to Stimson, Truman "laughed and said he understood."

Unable to reestablish the old morality and wanting the benefits for America of the new, Stimson proved decisive—even obdurate—on a comparatively small matter: removing Kyoto from Groves' target list of cities. It was not that Stimson was trying to save Kyoto's citizens; rather, he was seeking to save its relics, lest the Japanese become embittered and later side with the Soviets. As Stimson explained in his diary entry of July 24: "The bitterness which would be caused by such a wanton act might make it impossible during the long post-war period to reconcile the Japanese to us in that area rather than to the Russians. It might thus . . . be the means of preventing what our policy demanded, namely, a sympathetic Japan to the United States in case there should be any aggression by Russia in Manchuria."

Truman, backing Stimson on this matter, insisted privately that the A-bombs would be used only on military targets. Apparently the president wished not to recognize the inevitable—that a weapon of such great power would necessarily kill many civilians. At Potsdam on July 25, Truman received glowing reports of the vast destruction achieved by the Alamogordo blast and lavishly recorded the details in his diary: a crater of 1,200 feet in diameter, a steel tower destroyed a half mile away, men knocked over six miles away. "We have discovered," he wrote in his diary, "the most terrible bomb in the history of the world. It may be the fire destruction prophesied." But when he approved the final list of A-bomb targets, with Nagasaki and Kokura substituted for Kyoto, he could write in his diary, "I have told Sec. of War . . . Stimson to use it so that military objectives and soldiers and sailors are the target and not women and children. Even if the

Japs are savages, ruthless, merciless, and fanatic . . . [t]he target will be a purely military one." Truman may have been engaging in self-deception to make the mass deaths of civilians acceptable.

Neither Hiroshima nor Nagasaki was a "purely military" target, but the official press releases, cast well before the atomic bombings, glided over this matter. Hiroshima, for example, was described simply as "an important Japanese army base." The press releases were drafted by men who knew that those cities had been chosen partly to dramatize the killing of noncombatants.

On August 10, the day after the Nagasaki bombing, when Truman realized the magnitude of the mass killing and the Japanese offered a conditional surrender requiring continuation of the emperor, the president told his cabinet that he did not want to kill any more women and children. Rejecting demands to drop more atomic bombs on Japan, he hoped not to use them again. After two atomic bombings, the horror of mass death had forcefully hit the president, and he was willing to return partway to the older morality—civilians might be protected from A-bombs. But he continued to sanction the heavy conventional bombing of Japan's cities, with the deadly toll that napalm, incendiaries, and other bombs produced. Between August 10 and August 14—the war's last day, on which about 1,000 American planes bombed Japanese cities, some delivering their deadly cargo after Japan announced its surrender—the United States probably killed more than 15,000 Japanese.

Before August 10, Truman and his associates had not sought to avoid the use of the atomic bomb. As a result, they had easily dismissed the possibility of a noncombat demonstration. Indeed, the post-Hiroshima pleas of Japan's military leaders for a final glorious battle suggest that such a demonstration probably would not have produced a speedy surrender. And American leaders also did not pursue other alternatives: modifying their unconditional surrender demand by guaranteeing the maintenance of the emperor, awaiting the Soviet entry into the war, or simply pursuing heavy conventional bombing of the cities amid the strangling naval blockade.

Truman and Byrnes did not believe that a modification of the unconditional surrender formula would produce a speedy surrender. They thought that guaranteeing to maintain the emperor would prompt an angry backlash from Americans who regarded Hirohito as a war criminal, and feared that this concession might embolden the Japanese militarists to expect more concessions and thus prolong the war. . . .

Similarly, most American leaders did not believe that the Soviet entry into the Pacific war would make a decisive difference and greatly speed Japan's surrender. Generally, they believed that the U.S.S.R.'s entry would help end the war—ideally, before the massive invasion of Kyushu. They anticipated Moscow's intervention in mid-August, but the Soviets moved up their schedule to August 8, probably because of the Hiroshima bombing, and the Soviet entry did play an important role in producing Japan's surrender on August 14. Soviet entry without the A-bomb *might* have produced Japan's surrender before November.

The American aim was to avoid, if possible, the November 1 invasion, which would involve about 767,000 troops, at a possible cost of 31,000 casualties in the first 30 days and a total estimated American death toll of about 25,000. And American leaders certainly wanted to avoid the second part of the invasion plan, an assault on the Tokyo plain, scheduled for around March 1, 1946, with an estimated 15,000–21,000 more Americans dead. In the spring and summer of 1945, no American leader believed—as some later falsely claimed—that they planned to use the A-bomb to save half a million Americans. But, given the patriotic calculus of the time, there was no hesitation about using A-bombs to kill many Japanese in order to save the 25,000–46,000 Americans who might otherwise have died in the invasions. Put bluntly, Japanese life—including civilian life—was cheap, and some American leaders, like many rank-and-file citizens, may well have savored the prospect of punishing the Japanese with the A-bomb. . . .

No one in official Washington expected that one or two atomic bombs would end the war quickly. They expected to use at least a third, and probably more. And until the day after Nagasaki, there had never been in their thinking a choice between atomic bombs and conventional bombs, but a selection of both—using mass bombing to compel surrender. Atomic bombs and conventional bombs were viewed as supplements to, not substitutes for, one another. Heavy conventional bombing of Japan's cities would probably have killed hundreds of thousands in the next few months, and might have produced the desired surrender before November 1.

Taken together, some of these alternatives—promising to retain the Japanese monarchy, awaiting the Soviets' entry, and even more conventional bombing—very probably could have ended the war before the dreaded invasion. Still, the evidence—to borrow a phrase from F.D.R.—is somewhat "iffy," and no one who looks at the intransigence of the Japanese militarists should have full confidence in those other strategies. But we may well regret that these alternatives were not pursued and that there was not an effort to avoid the use of the first A-bomb—and certainly the second. . . .

Administration leaders did not seek to avoid the use of the A-bomb. They even believed that its military use might produce a powerful bonus: the intimidation of the Soviets, rendering them, as Byrnes said, "more manageable," especially in Eastern Europe. Although that was not the dominant purpose for using the weapon, it certainly was a strong confirming one. . . .

Americans also came slowly to recognize the barbarity of World War II, especially the mass killings by bombing civilians. It was that redefinition of morality that made Hiroshima and Nagasaki possible and ushered in the atomic age in a frightening way.

That redefinition of morality was a product of World War II, which included such barbarities as Germany's systematic murder of six million Jews and Japan's rape of Nanking. While the worst atrocities were perpetrated by the Axis, all the major nation-states sliced away at the moral code—often to the applause of their leaders and citizens alike. By 1945 there were few moral restraints left in what had become virtually a total war. Even F.D.R.'s prewar concern for sparing enemy civilians had fallen by the wayside. In that new moral climate, any nation that had the A-bomb would probably have used it against enemy peoples. British leaders as well as Joseph Stalin endorsed the act. Germany's and Japan's leaders surely would have used it against cities. America was not morally unique—just technologically exceptional. Only it had the bomb, and so only it used it.

To understand this historical context does not require that American citizens or others should approve of it. But it does require that they recognize that pre- and post-Hiroshima dissent was rare in 1945. Indeed, few then asked why the United States used the atomic bomb on Japan. But had the bomb not been used, many more, including numerous outraged American citizens, would have bitterly asked that question of the Truman administration.

Further Reading

One of the earliest published versions of the traditional view is "The Decision to Use the Atomic Bomb" (*Harper's*, vol. 194/1161 [February 1947], 97–107), by Henry L. Stimson, secretary of war to President Roosevelt—an essay that purported to provide a faithful recounting of the decisions leading up to the use of the atomic bombs. The most recent book-length treatment of the subject from a traditional perspective is Robert Maddox's *Weapons for Victory: The Hiroshima Decision Fifty Years Later* (Columbia: University of Missouri Press, 1995). Maddox's work is notably lacking in the nuance of earlier traditional interpretations such as Herbert Feis, *The Atom Bomb and the End of World War II* (Princeton, NJ: Princeton University Press, 1966). A reprint of Stimson's article and an excerpt from Feis's book, along with other essays and primary documents, can be found in *The Atomic Bomb: The Critical Issues* (Boston: Little, Brown, 1976), edited by Barton J. Bernstein.

Research in the past decade revealed that Stimson's article was in fact not primarily written by Stimson but was a carefully orchestrated effort to quiet doubts about Truman's decision; thus, it is no longer viewed as a faithful effort to present Stimson's perspective on the decision. This new understanding of myth-making, along with a full presentation of his revisionist perspective, may be found in Gar Alperovitz, *The Decision to Use the Atomic Bomb and the Architecture of an American Myth* (New York: Knopf, 1995). A significantly less-detailed revisionist account, but the first full-length treatment to stress the racist dimensions of the decision to drop atomic bombs on Japan, is Ron Takaki's *Hiroshima: Why America Dropped the Atomic Bomb* (Boston: Little, Brown, 1995). A recent and compendious collection of primary and secondary sources that emphasizes the revisionist viewpoint is *Hiroshima's Shadow* (Stony Creek, CT: Pamphleteers Press, 1998), edited by Kai Bird and Lawrence Lifschulz. P. M. S. Blackett, *Fear, War and the Bomb: Military and Political Consequences of Atomic Energy* (New York: Whittlesey House, 1949) is an early critical work.

Book-length studies that, like Bernstein's essay in this volume, embrace some aspects of the revisionist interpretation but do not reject fully the traditional understanding of the use of the bomb include *A World Destroyed: Hiroshima and the Origins of the Arms Race* (New York: Knopf, 1975), by Martin Sherwin, and *Prompt and Utter Destruction: Truman and the Use of the Atom Bombs Against Japan* (Lincoln: University of Nebraska Press, 1997), by J. Samuel Walker, historian of the U.S. Nuclear Regulatory Commission. Journalist Murray Sayle's "Did the Bomb End the War?" (*The New Yorker*, 31 July 1995, 40–64) presents a forceful argument supporting Bernstein's contention that, in the context of total war, the atomic bombs appeared to be legitimate combat weapons. He also argues that the bombs themselves did not lead to Japan's surrender, but that it was Stalin's declaration of war on August 8, 1945, that spurred Japan finally to give up. Emphasizing that Japan did, in fact, surrender in response to the bombings is Sadao Asada, "The Shock of the Atomic Bomb and Japan's Decision to Surrender—A Reconsideration," *Pacific Historical Review* (vol. 67/4 [November 1998], 447–512).

A growing literature focuses not on executive decision making but on the scientists involved in the Manhattan Project and their relationship to the federal government. The most recent, complete, one-volume treatment of the subject that is at once detailed and accessible is Richard Rhodes's award-winning *The Making of the Atomic Bomb* (New York: Simon & Schuster, 1987). Also see David Holloway, *Stalin and the Bomb: The Soviet Union and Atomic Energy, 1939–1956* (New Haven, CT: Yale University Press, 1994). Studies of the cultural effects of the atomic bomb in the United States include Allan Winkler, *Life Under a Cloud: American Anxiety about the Atom* (New York: Oxford University Press, 1993) and Paul Boyer, *By the Bomb's Early Light* (New York: Pantheon Books, 1985). Elaine Tyler May's *Homeward Bound: American Families in the Cold War Era* (New York: Basic Books, 1988) focuses on gender issues. A good general history of the antinuclear movement that arose in response to the use of the bomb is Lawrence S. Wittner's *One World or None: A History of the World Nuclear Disarmament Movement Through 1953* (Stanford, CA: Stanford University Press, 1993).

Primary Sources

The primary sources documenting the decision to drop two atomic bombs on Japan, as well as the development of nuclear weapons and their effect on Nagasaki and Hiroshima, are voluminous. For a selection of the most relevant primary documents (including excerpts from President Truman's diary, petitions from scientists opposing use of the bomb without a prior warning or demonstration, minutes of the Target Committee, and eyewitness accounts of the Trinity test), see "Atomic Bomb: Decision: Documents in the Decision to use Atomic Bombs on the Cities of Hiroshima and Nagasaki" at www.dannen.com/decision/index.html. See also www.dannen.com/moreinfo.html for links to other online documents (including those at the Truman library), to secondary sources, and to video on the related topics of nuclear testing and the Manhattan Project. Another good site with numerous primary documents is www.nuclearfiles.org/menu/key-issues/nuclear-weapons/history/pre-cold-war/hiroshima-nagasaki/index.htm. For an extensive set of links to both primary and secondary sources, go to www.mtholyoke.edu/acad/intrel/hiroshim/htm. Many primary documents are located at the Harry Truman Presidential Library and are available on the Internet at www.trumanlibrary.org.whistlestop/study_collections/bomb/large/index.php. Documents produced by the Manhattan Project, including discussions of the bomb's likely effect, as well as studies of its impact after the bombing, may be found at www.yale.edu/lawweb/avalon.abomb/mpmenu.htm. For oral histories of the Hibakusha—those who witnessed and survived the bombing of Hiroshima, see www.inicom.com/hibakusha. For information about the bombing of Nagasaki that was collected by the Scientific Data Center for the Atomic Bomb Disaster in Nagasaki, go to www.sdc.med.nagasaki-u.ac.jp/n50/index.html. A number of scholarly exchanges concerning Alperovitz's interpretation can be found at www.doug-long.com/debate.htm.

CHAPTER 2

The Origins of the Cold War

INTRODUCTION

For almost half a century, the United States and the Soviet Union were locked in a costly ideological and geopolitical struggle known as the cold war. Never taking the form of direct military engagement, the conflict was instead marked on each side by belligerent rhetoric, a massive buildup of weapons of mass destruction, and proxy wars in third world countries such as Vietnam and Afghanistan. The dismantling of the Soviet Union over a decade ago, which left the United States as the sole superpower and victor, renewed scholarly interest in long-standing questions about the origins of the cold war. How and why did the World War II alliance between the United States and the Soviet Union dissolve? Was the clash between capitalist and communist superpowers inevitable once their common enemy, Nazi Germany, had been defeated? Or was the cold war the tragic result of a series of misunderstandings? And if it was not inevitable, as the latter question suggests, was one nation or leader more culpable than the other for starting the conflict?

As the relationship between the United States and the USSR deteriorated after World War II, President Harry Truman and his advisors blamed the developing cold war entirely on the Soviets. So did the American historians of the orthodox school who wrote about the conflict. They charged that the USSR was an expansionist power seeking to spread socialist revolution and, ultimately, to dominate the world. Even before World War II had ended, they pointed out, Stalin had begun making territorial demands, insisting, for example, that the United States accept his annexation of the Baltic States and part of Poland. He also imposed a puppet regime in Romania and helped the Communists come to power in Poland, both actions reflecting Stalin's desire for compliant governments along the Soviet Union's western and southern borders. Whether observers attributed these acts to Marxist–Leninist fervor or to Russia's determination to protect its borders, borne of traditional fears of foreign invaders, Soviet behavior was said to violate a key principle articulated by U.S. President Franklin Roosevelt and British Prime Minister Winston Churchill in 1941 in the Atlantic Charter: the right of all peoples to determine their own fates and their own forms of government. Germany's disregard of this basic right had triggered World War II; according to the orthodox view, Stalin had behaved no differently from Hitler, and his actions had made a cold war inescapable.

In contrast to the Soviet Union, the United States was seen, from the orthodox perspective, as forbearing, its actions even bordering initially on appeasement. For example, Roosevelt had accepted the expansion of Soviet borders. And at the Allied Conference at Yalta in 1945, he had essentially acquiesced to Communist domination of postwar Poland. But as Soviet aggression continued, American policymakers realized that Stalin—whom they had come to see as deeply paranoid and perhaps unbalanced—was beyond the reach of reason and that conciliation could not stop the juggernaut of Soviet expansionism. Rejecting the idea of trying to roll back Soviet gains, they wisely adopted the policy of containment, which committed the United States to preventing communism from spreading to new countries, including those in Western Europe and the third world.

This explanation of Soviet and American behavior and intentions was the dominant one in the early years of the cold war, a dominance illustrated by the fact that only one official in the Truman administration—Commerce Secretary Henry A. Wallace—objected to this characterization of the Soviets, and he was dismissed as a result. The historians' challenge to the orthodox view began in 1959 with the publication of *The Tragedy of American Diplomacy,* a widely influential work by William Appleman Williams, which placed the cold war in the longer history of U.S. power relations and American imperialism. Williams regarded the cold war as but the latest phase in a long-standing antagonism between capitalism and its opponents, which had been marked, among other things, by U.S.-armed intervention to oppose the 1917 Communist revolution in Russia. America, in other words, had always been hostile to the Soviet Union. In this respect, Williams shared with the traditionalists a sense of inevitability about the cold war, although he focused on the actions of U.S. policymakers rather than on the behavior of Stalin.

In Williams's view and that of other revisionist scholars who published in his wake, the United States had done much to provoke Soviet enmity while still allied with the USSR. For example, Roosevelt and Churchill had, despite promises to the contrary to Stalin, delayed the opening of a second front in Europe for two years, leaving the Soviet Union to assume the brunt of the ferocious battle with the Nazis. Additionally, Roosevelt had shared the secret of the atomic bomb with Churchill, but not with Stalin; at the end of the war, President Truman had worn the bomb "on his hip" during negotiations with the Soviets in an effort, many revisionist historians believe, to intimidate them (see Chapter 1).

Revisionists also raised the issue of the relative power of the United States and the USSR at the onset of the cold war. With 27 million dead, 25 million homeless, and 31,000 factories and 100,000 collective farms in ruins, the Soviet Union was devastated. In contrast, the United States, which lost 400,000 lives, nonetheless emerged from the war an economic and military powerhouse, indisputably the strongest nation on the globe. Given this gross disparity in strength, revisionists asked whether the Soviet Union had really posed a significant threat to the United States or Western Europe at the end of the war.

In their view, the United States had been far from the benign presence, forced into responding to Stalin's aggression, that the orthodox school asserted. America itself had an expansionist, aggressively anticommunist agenda: to secure markets in postwar Europe for American goods and to ensure that the rebuilding of European political and economic structures was compatible with U.S. economic interests. Moreover, the United States enjoyed predominance in its own "sphere of influence"—Latin America—where the United States honored the principle of self-determination only in the breach. Simply put, American policymakers had a double standard; they were criticizing the USSR for things that the United States was itself doing.

The revisionist interpretation heavily influenced subsequent scholarship on the cold war and spawned new revisionist lines of inquiry. A number of scholars expanded their focus to include the third world, recognizing that the cold war only became hot in such countries as Korea and Vietnam. Applying "world-systems theory" to the conflict, some have suggested that the cold war was really one aspect of a larger struggle of "core" nations for dominance, or hegemony, over the resources and markets of the rest of the world: the "periphery" and "semiperiphery." Even scholars in the orthodox camp took note of the revisionists, and there were hints in the 1980s that a "postrevisionist synthesis" was emerging. However, the American victory in the cold war gave new life to the orthodox interpretation. Hopes that access to previously unavailable Soviet archives would settle interpretive disputes have not been borne out; both revisionist and orthodox scholars have found evidence in newly released documents to support their own interpretations.

The three excerpts that follow represent recent versions of orthodox and revisionist scholarship. The first, from a 1997 book by the foremost historian of the orthodox school, John Lewis Gaddis, begins by briefly acknowledging the revisionist point that the United States sought to reshape the Western European economy to benefit American capitalism. Gaddis emphasizes, however, that the chief American postwar aim was to establish a collective security organization—the United Nations—to prevent another major conflict. He then quickly returns to the traditional emphasis on Stalin as a malevolent, essentially irrational dictator who instigated the cold war by refusing to accept the notion of collective security and instead making a bid for new territory. It was not so much Stalin's interest in controlling neighboring states in Eastern Europe that offended American policymakers, according to Gaddis (who notes, as have revisionists, the loose way in which U.S. leaders have always interpreted the concept of self-determination), but the way in which Stalin went about things: unilaterally and brutally. The attention to Stalin's methods implies an argument that Gaddis made in a previous work: that the response of American presidents to foreign policy situations is shaped by the views of the public that elects them. Thus, unlike the dictator Stalin, who could act without reference to the desires of Soviet citizens, President Truman had to attend to the concerns of voters of Polish ancestry who were appalled by Stalin's treatment of Poland.

Seeing Stalin as the driving force toward the cold war, Gaddis also dismisses the argument of some historians that President Roosevelt, had he not died in office and been succeeded by the inexperienced Truman (whose advisors, such as diplomat George Kennan, tended to be hard-line anticommunists), could have prevented the breakdown of the U.S.–USSR alliance. Roosevelt, the argument goes, was the one leader whom Stalin trusted and who knew how to negotiate with him. In Gaddis's view, Stalin trusted no one, not even Roosevelt. Although the selection by Gaddis begins by stressing that the cold war was not inevitable, it concludes otherwise: with Stalin in the picture, no other outcome in the relationship between the United States and the USSR was possible. Gaddis's essay hinges on his analysis of Stalin's personality and his argument by extension: a man who behaved so distrustfully and cruelly towards his own people could not be expected to behave otherwise in matters of foreign policy. Gaddis offers scant evidence of Stalin's actual dealings with Western leaders or of his responses to the policies and actions of the United States and is allies.

The second selection is a factually-rich excerpt from Carolyn Eisenberg's prize-winning book, *Drawing the Line.* A revisionist scholar, Eisenberg, like Gaddis, states a commitment to revisiting the beginnings of the cold war with an open mind and without the sense of inevitability that has marked so many studies of the conflict. Her work focuses on the decision to divide Germany, a decision, according to Eisenberg, that marked the point of no return in the deterioration of U.S.–USSR relations. Although agreeing readily that Stalin was a dictator who often acted brutally, she disagrees with Gaddis that he was impervious to reason and resistant to any compromises. She concludes instead that it was U.S. policymakers, not the Soviets, who were adamantly opposed to negotiations and committed to acting unilaterally. The Americans were the ones who pushed for the division of Germany, contrary to wartime agreements that a unified Germany would be supervised jointly by the United States, the USSR, and the other Allies. Eisenberg reminds us that the seminal crisis of the early cold war—the 1948 Soviet blockade of Berlin—was actually a last-ditch effort by the USSR to *prevent* the division of Germany, and not the aggressive act to create division, as it was portrayed to the American public.

Although mentioned only briefly here, it is Eisenberg's belief that the death of President Roosevelt did decisively affect the unfolding of events. Roosevelt had appreciated Stalin's concern that Germany not be permitted to become a significant power that might again threaten Russian security, as it had in two world wars, as well as Russia's dire need for reparations from Germany to help rebuild the USSR's shattered infrastructure. President Truman's advisors, on the other hand, were determined to resurrect Germany as an industrial powerhouse that would foster the economic recovery of the rest of war-ravaged Western Europe, even if it meant forgoing denazification of the country, backing away from a previous commitment to provide Russia with reparations, and ultimately, violating wartime agreements by dividing Germany in two. The source of this determination, in Eisenberg's view, was policymakers' concern that working with the Soviets might slow Europe's recovery and, in so doing, provide opportunities for popular left-wing political parties to offer their own economic solutions that were not amenable to American economic interests.

Eisenberg clearly finds regrettable the rigidity of U.S. policymakers, and she laments the results of their actions, among them the abandonment of the citizens of East Germany to life under a Soviet-style dictatorship. Here, she implicitly challenges the argument made by the orthodox school that U.S. policymakers were driven chiefly by concerns over Stalin's brutality toward those in the East. She also questions the orthodox claim that the actions of U.S. leaders were in some measure shaped by the electorate's view of Soviet actions, noting that most policy regarding Germany was made without significant input from elected officials, and that the public, far from influencing decisions, was deliberately misinformed about the course of events.

The third selection is by Bruce Cumings, the foremost American historian of the Korean War. Although Cumings only refers briefly to Roosevelt, he shares the view of Gaddis that Truman carried forward his predecessor's policies rather than departing from them. But like Eisenberg, Cumings emphasizes geopolitical and economic concerns as underlying America's approach to the Soviet Union and the ensuing cold war. He departs from both Gaddis and Eisenberg by arguing that the focus of cold war scholarship on Europe is misplaced. In his view, the real stakes in the cold war were in the third world, particularly Asia, where, after all, two crucial "hot" wars were fought.

Cumings sees the United States as having dual motivations. One aim, as most scholars have said, was to contain communism; the second, equally significant goal was to gain control over the resources and potential markets of third world nations and to integrate them into one system, for the benefit of the United States and its allies, West Germany and Japan. These twin aims—of containment and hegemony—came together in the war in Korea, an area of no direct strategic significance to the United States but one of central importance to Japan and thus to America's hegemonic project. If the cold war was not a foregone conclusion before 1950, the Korean War marked the point of no return. Proponents of American globalism had already pushed successfully for the enunciation of the Truman Doctrine, in which the president stated America's readiness to intervene in any nation in the world to prevent a socialist government from coming to power. They now used North Korea's incursion into South Korea to win congressional approval of a proposal—known as NSC 68 and conceived well before the Korean War—to vastly expand America's military arsenal. This marked the beginning of the so-called "national security state" (sometimes referred to as the "military-industrial complex"): a well-funded and far-reaching intelligence and military apparatus, closely linked to universities and large industries engaged in research on, and the production of, military technologies.

The course of the Korean War proved significant for containment proponents as well. While U.S.-led United Nations forces swiftly pushed the North Koreans back to the 38th parallel, U.S. General Douglas MacArthur, with Truman's approval, led the army deep into North Korea to the Yalu River in an apparent challenge to the governments of both North Korea and China, which had recently become a communist nation. China responded by entering the war, driving UN forces out of North Korea and leading the U.S. military and policymakers to accept the policy of containment; efforts at rolling back communism would be limited to covert activities, as in Iran in 1953, and later, in the Bay of Pigs in Cuba.

JOHN LEWIS GADDIS

Rethinking Cold War History

When a power vacuum separates great powers, as one did the United States and the Soviet Union at the end of World War II, they are unlikely to fill it without bumping up against and bruising each other's interests. This would have happened if the two postwar hegemons had been constitutional democracies: historians of the wartime Anglo-American relationship have long since exposed the bumping and bruising that did take place, even among these closest of allies. Victory would require more difficult adjustments for Russians and Americans because so many legacies of distrust now divided them: the distinction between authoritarian and democratic traditions; the challenge communism and capitalism posed to one another; Soviet memories of allied intervention in Russia after World War I; more recent American memories of Stalin's purges and his opportunistic pact with Hitler. It was too much to expect a few years of wartime cooperation to sweep all of this away.

At the same time, though, these legacies need not have produced almost half a century of Soviet–American confrontation. The leaders of great nations are never entirely bound by the past: new situations continually arise, and they are free to reject old methods in attempting to deal with them. Alliance in a common cause was as new a situation as one can imagine in the Russian–American relationship. Much would depend, therefore, upon the extent to which Roosevelt and Stalin could—in effect—*liberate* their nations' futures from a difficult past.

The American President and his key advisers were determined to secure the United States against whatever dangers might confront it after victory, but they lacked a clear sense of what those might be or where they might arise. Their thinking about postwar security was, as a consequence, more general than specific. They certainly saw a vital interest in preventing any hostile

From *We Now Know: Rethinking Cold War History* (1997), by John Lewis Gaddis. By permission of Oxford University Press.

power from again attempting to dominate the European continent. They were not prepared to see military capabilities reduced to anything like the inadequate levels of the interwar era, nor would they resist opportunities to reshape the international economy in ways that would benefit American capitalism. They resolved to resist any return to isolationism, and they optimistically embraced the "second chance" the war had provided to build a global security organization in which the United States would play the leading role.

But these priorities reflected no unilateral conception of vital interests. A quarter century earlier, Wilson had linked American war aims to reform of the international system as a whole; and although his ideas had not then taken hold, the coming of a second world war revived a widespread and even guilt-ridden interest in them as a means of avoiding a third such conflict. Roosevelt persuaded a skeptical Churchill to endorse Wilson's thinking in August, 1941, when they jointly proclaimed, in the Atlantic Charter, three postwar objectives: self-determination—the idea here was that people who could choose their own forms of government would not want to overthrow them, hence they would achieve, to use a Rooseveltian term, freedom from fear; open markets—the assumption was that an unrestricted flow of commodities and capital would ensure economic prosperity, hence freedom from want; and collective security—the conviction that nations had to act together rather than separately if they were ever to achieve safety. . . .

The United States would seek power in the postwar world, not shy away from it as it had done after World War I. It would do so in the belief that only it had the strength to build a peace based on Wilsonian principles of self-determination, open markets, and collective security. It would administer that peace neither for its exclusive advantage nor in such a way as to provide equal benefits to all: many as yet ill-defined possibilities lay in between these extremes. Nor would Roosevelt assume, as Wilson had, public and Congressional approval; rather, the administration would make careful efforts to ensure domestic support for the postwar settlement at every step of the way. There would be another attempt at a Wilsonian peace, but this time by the un-Wilsonian method of offering each of the great powers as well as the American people a vested interest in making it work. It was within this framework of pragmatism mixed with principle that Roosevelt hoped to deal with Stalin.

The Soviet leader, too, sought security after World War II: his country lost at least 27 million of its citizens in that conflict; he could hardly have done otherwise. But no tradition of *common* or *collective* security shaped postwar priorities as viewed from Moscow, for the very good reason that it was no longer permitted there to distinguish between state interests, party interests, and those of Stalin himself. National security had come to mean personal security, and the Kremlin boss saw so many threats to it that he had already resorted to murder on a mass scale in order to remove all conceivable challengers to his regime. It would be hard to imagine a more *unilateral* approach to security than the internal practices Stalin had set in motion during the 1930s. Cooperation with external allies was obviously to his advantage when the Germans were within sight of his capital, but whether that cooperation would extend beyond Hitler's defeat was another matter. It would depend upon the ability of an aging and authoritarian ruler to shift his own thinking about security to a multilateral basis, and to restructure the government he had made into a reflection of himself.

It is sometimes said of Stalin that he had long since given up the Lenin–Trotsky goal of world revolution in favor of "socialism in one country," a doctrine that seemed to imply peaceful coexistence with states of differing social systems. But that is a misunderstanding of Stalin's position. What he really did in the late 1920s was to drop Lenin's prediction that revolutions would arise spontaneously in other advanced industrial countries; instead he came to see the Soviet Union itself as the center from which socialism would spread and eventually defeat capitalism. The effect was to switch the principal instrument for advancing revolution from Marx's idea of a historically determined class struggle to a process of territorial acquisition Stalin could control. "The idea of propagating world Communist revolution was an ideological screen to hide our desire for world domination," one of his secret agents recalled decades later. "This war is not as in the past," Stalin himself explained to the Yugoslav communist Milovan Djilas in 1945: "whoever occupies a territory also imposes his own social system. . . . It cannot be otherwise."

Stalin was fully prepared to use unconventional means to promote Soviet interests beyond the territories he ruled. . . . And he by no means excluded the possibility of an eventual war with capitalism involving the Soviet Union itself. "Stalin looked at it this way," his foreign minister, Viacheslav Molotov recalled: "World War I has wrested one country from capitalist slavery; World War II has created a socialist system; and the third will finish off imperialism forever."

It would be easy to make too much of Stalin's words, for reality always separates what people say from what they are able to do. What is striking about Stalin, though, is how small that separation was. To a degree we are only now coming to realize, Stalin *literally* imposed his rhetoric upon the country he ran: this was a dictator whose subordinates scrutinized his every comment, indeed his every gesture, and attempted to implement policies—even the most implausible scientific doctrines—on the basis of them. Not even Hitler ran so autocratic a system. The result was a kind of self-similarity across scale, in which the tyrant at the top spawned smaller tyrants at each level throughout the party and state bureaucracy: their activities extended down to the level of scrutinizing stamp collections for evidence that their owners might value the images of foreign potentates more than those of Lenin and Stalin. It was typical of the Kremlin boss, the most consummate of narcissists, that he thought very far ahead indeed about security. But it was always and only his own security that he was thinking about.

Here, then, was the difficulty. The Western democracies sought a form of security that would reject violence or the threat of it: security was to be a *collective* good, not a benefit denied to some in order to provide it to others. Stalin saw things very differently: security came only by intimidating or eliminating potential challengers. World politics was an extension of Soviet politics, which was in turn an extension of Stalin's preferred personal environment: a zero-sum game, in which achieving security for one meant depriving everyone else of it. The contrast, or so it would seem, made conflict unavoidable.

But is this not putting things too starkly? The United States and its democratic allies found ways to cooperate with the Soviet Union, after all, in fighting Germany and Japan. Could they not have managed their postwar relationship similarly, so that the safety Stalin demanded could have been made to correspond with the security the West required? Could there not have been a division of Europe into spheres of influence which, while they would hardly have pleased everybody, might have prevented an ensuing four and a half decades of superpower rivalry?

. . . Even if Stalin's long-range thinking about security did clash with that of his Anglo-American allies, common military purposes provided the strongest possible inducements to smooth over such differences. It is worth asking why this *practice* of wartime cooperation did not become a *habit* that would extend into the postwar era.

The principal reason, it now appears, was Stalin's insistence on equating security with territory. Western diplomats had been surprised, upon arriving in Moscow soon after the German attack in the summer of 1941, to find the Soviet leader already demanding a postwar settlement that would retain what his pact with Hitler had yielded: the Baltic states, together with portions of Finland, Poland, and Romania. Stalin showed no sense of shame or even embarrassment about this, no awareness that the *methods* by which he had obtained these concessions could conceivably render them illegitimate in the eyes of anyone else. When it came to territorial aspirations, he made no distinction between adversaries and allies: what one had provided the other was expected to endorse.

Stalin coupled his claims with repeated requests for a second front, quite without regard to the fact that his own policies had left the British to fight Germany alone for a year, so that they were hardly in a position to comply. He reiterated his military and territorial demands after the Americans entered the war in December, despite the fact that they were desperately trying to hang on in the Pacific against a Japanese adversary against whom the Soviet Union—admittedly for good strategic reasons—had elected not to fight. This linkage of postwar requirements with wartime assistance was, as the Russians used to like to say, "no accident." A second front in Europe in 1942 would have been "a completely impossible operation for them," Molotov later acknowledged. "But our demand was politically necessary, and we had to press them for everything."

On the surface, this strategy succeeded. After strong initial objections, Roosevelt and Churchill did eventually acknowledge the Soviet Union's right to the expanded borders it claimed; they also made it clear that they would not oppose the installation of "friendly" governments in adjoining states. This meant accepting a Soviet sphere of influence from the Baltic to the Adriatic, a concession not easily reconciled with the Atlantic Charter. But the authors of that document saw no feasible way to avoid that outcome: military necessity required continued Soviet cooperation against the Germans. Nor were they themselves prepared to relinquish spheres of influence in Western Europe and the Mediterranean, the Middle East, Latin America, and East Asia. Self-determination was a sufficiently malleable concept that each of the Big Three could have endorsed, without sleepless nights, what the Soviet government had said about the Atlantic Charter: "practical application of these principles will necessarily adapt itself to the circumstances, needs, and historic peculiarities of particular countries."

That, though, was precisely the problem. For unlike Stalin, Roosevelt and Churchill would have to defend their decisions before domestic constituencies. The *manner* in which Soviet influence expanded was therefore, for them, of no small significance. Stalin showed little understanding of this. Having no experience himself with democratic procedures, he dismissed requests that he respect democratic proprieties. "[S]ome propaganda work should be done," he advised Roosevelt at the Tehran conference after the president had hinted that the American public would welcome a plebiscite in the Baltic States. "It is all nonsense!" Stalin complained to Molotov. "[Roosevelt] is their military leader and commander in chief. Who would dare object to him?" When at Yalta F.D.R. stressed the need for the first Polish election to be as pure as "Caesar's wife," Stalin responded with a joke: "They said that about her, but in fact she had her sins." Molotov warned his boss, on that occasion, that the Americans' insistence on free elections elsewhere in Eastern Europe was "going too far." "Don't worry," he recalls Stalin as replying, "work it out. We can deal with it in our own way later. The point is the correlation of forces."

The Soviet leader was, in one sense, right. Military strength would determine what happened in that part of the world, not the enunciation of lofty principles. But unilateral methods carried long-term costs Stalin did not foresee: the most significant of these was to ruin whatever prospects existed for a Soviet sphere of influence the East Europeans themselves might have accepted. This possibility was not as far-fetched as it would later seem. The Czechoslovak president, Eduard Beneš, spoke openly of a "Czech solution" that would exchange internal autonomy for Soviet control over foreign and military policy. W. Averell Harriman, one of Roosevelt's closest advisers and his ambassador to the Soviet Union after 1943, was keenly interested in such an arrangement and hoped to persuade the Poles of its merits. F.D.R. and Churchill—concerned with finding a way to respect both Soviet security interests and democratic procedures in Eastern Europe—would almost certainly have gone along.

Nor was the idea out of the question from Stalin's point of view. He would, after all, approve such a compromise as the basis for a permanent settlement with Finland. He would initially allow free elections in Hungary, Czechoslovakia, and the Soviet occupation zone in Germany. He may even have *anticipated an enthusiastic response* as he took over Eastern Europe. "He was, I think, surprised and hurt," Harriman recalled, "when the Red Army was not welcomed in all the neighboring countries as an army of liberation." "We still had our hopes," Khrushchev remembered, that "after the catastrophe of World War II, Europe too might become Soviet. Everyone would take the path from capitalism to socialism." It could be that there was another form of romanticism at work here, quite apart from Stalin's affinity for fellow authoritarians: that he was unrealistic enough to expect ideological solidarity and gratitude for liberation to override old fears of Russian expansionism as well as remaining manifestations of nationalism among the Soviet Union's neighbors, perhaps as easily as he himself had overridden the latter—or so it then appeared—within the multinational empire that was the Soviet Union itself.

If the Red Army could have been welcomed in Poland and the rest of the countries it liberated with the same enthusiasm American, British, and Free French forces encountered when they landed in Italy and France in 1943 and 1944, then some kind of Czech–Finnish compromise might have been feasible. Whatever Stalin's expectations, though, this did not happen. That non-event, in turn, removed any possibility of a division of Europe all members of the Grand Alliance could have endorsed. It ensured that an American sphere of influence would arise there largely by consent, but that its Soviet counterpart could sustain itself only by coercion. The resulting asymmetry would account, more than anything else, for the origins, escalation, and ultimate outcome of the Cold War. . . .

Social psychologists make a useful distinction between what they call "dispositional" and "situational" behavior in interpreting the actions of individuals. Dispositional behavior reflects deeply rooted personal characteristics which remain much the same regardless of the circumstances in which people find themselves. One responds inflexibly—and therefore predictably—to whatever happens. Situational behavior, conversely, shifts with circumstances; personal traits are less important in determining what one does. Historians need to be careful in applying this insight, though, because psychologists know how tempting it can be to excuse one's own actions by invoking situations, while attributing what others do to their dispositions. It would be all too easy, in dealing with so controversial a matter as responsibility for the Cold War, to confuse considered judgment with that most satisfying of sensations: the confirmation of one's own prejudices.

By the end of 1945 most American and British leaders had come around—some reluctantly, others eagerly—to a dispositional explanation of Stalin's behavior. Further efforts to negotiate or compromise with him were likely to fail, or so it seemed, because success would require that he cease to be what he was. One could only resolve henceforth to hold the line, remain true to one's own principles, and wait for the passage of time to bring a better world. Such at least was the view of a new George Kennan, whose top secret "long telegram" from Moscow of 22 February 1946, would shape American policy over the next half century more profoundly than his distant relative's denunciations of tsarist authoritarianism had influenced it during the preceding one. Nor was "containment" just an American strategy: Frank Roberts, the British *chargé d'affaires* in the Soviet capital, was dispatching similar arguments to London even as former prime minister

Winston Churchill, speaking at Fulton, Missouri, was introducing the term "iron curtain" to the world. It was left to Kennan, though, to make the dispositional case most explicitly in a lesser-known telegram sent from Moscow on 20 March: "Nothing short of complete disarmament, delivery of our air and naval forces to Russia and resigning of powers of government to American Communists" would come close to alleviating Stalin's distrust, and even then the old dictator would probably "smell a trap and would continue to harbor the most baleful misgivings."

If Kennan was right, we need look no further in seeking the causes of the Cold War: Stalin was primarily responsible. But how can we be sure that this perspective and the policies that resulted from it did not reflect the all too human tendency to attribute behavior one dislikes to the *nature* of those who indulge in it, and to neglect the *circumstances*—including one's own behavior—that might have brought it about? Is there a test historians can apply to avoid this trap?

One might be to check for evidence of consistency or inconsistency, within a particular relationship, in each side's view of the other. Attitudes that show little change over the years, especially when circumstances have changed, suggest deep roots and hence dispositional behavior. Trees may bend slightly before the wind, but they stay in place, for better or for worse, until they die. Viewpoints that evolve with circumstances, however, reflect situational behavior. Vines, after all, can creep, climb, adhere, entwine, and if necessary retreat, all in response to the environment that surrounds them. Roosevelt's vine-like personality is universally acknowledged, and needs no further elaboration here: there could hardly have been a *less* dispositional leader than the always adaptable, ever-elusive F.D.R. But what about Stalin? Was he capable of abandoning, in world politics, the paranoia that defined his domestic politics? Could he respond to conciliatory gestures, or was containment the only realistic course?

Stalin's behavior toward fellow-authoritarians did twist and turn. He gave Hitler the benefit of the doubt at several points, but viewed him as an archenemy at others. His attitudes toward Josef Broz Tito in Yugoslavia and Mao Zedong in China would evolve over the years, albeit in opposite directions. But Stalin's thinking about democratic capitalists remained rooted to the spot: he always suspected their motives. "Remember, we are waging a struggle (negotiation with enemies is also struggle) . . . with the whole capitalist world," he admonished Molotov as early as 1929. He dismissed Roosevelt's and Churchill's warnings of an impending German attack in 1941 as provocations designed to hasten that event. He authorized penetration, by his spies, of the Anglo-American atomic bomb project as early as June 1942, long before his allies made the formal but by then futile decision to withhold such information from him. He placed repeated obstacles in the path of direct military cooperation with the Americans and the British during the war. He not only arranged to have Roosevelt's and Churchill's living quarters at the Tehran Conference bugged; he also had Beria's son, a precocious linguist, translate the tapes daily and report to him on what was said. "Churchill is the kind who, if you don't watch him, will slip a kopeck out of your pocket," Stalin famously warned on the eve of the landings in Normandy in June 1944, surely the high-point of allied cooperation against the Axis. "Roosevelt is not like that. He dips in his hand only for bigger coins."

A compliment? Perhaps, in Stalin's grudging way, but hardly an expression of trust. The Soviet leader is on record as having expressed compassion—once, at Yalta—for the president's physical infirmity: "Why did nature have to punish him so? Is he any worse than other people?" But the very novelty of the remark impressed Gromyko, who heard it: his boss "rarely bestowed his sympathy on anybody from another social system." Only a few weeks later the same Stalin astounded and infuriated the dying Roosevelt by charging that secret Anglo-American negotiations for the surrender of Hitler's forces in Italy were really a plot to keep the Red Army out of

Germany. Many years later a Soviet interviewer would suggest to Molotov that "to be paralyzed and yet to become president of the United States, and for three terms, what a rascal you had to be!" "Well said," the old Bolshevik heartily agreed. . . .

If Stalin's wartime attitude toward Roosevelt was half as distrustful as Molotov's in retirement, then a significant pattern emerges: neither American nor British sources reveal anything approaching such deep and abiding suspicion on the Anglo-American side. Churchill subsequently credited himself, to be sure, with having warned of Soviet postwar intentions; but the archives have long since revealed a more complex pattern in which his hopes alternated with his fears well into 1945. In the case of Roosevelt, it is difficult to find *any* expressions of distrust toward Stalin, public or private, until shortly before his death. If he had doubts—surely he had some—he kept them so carefully hidden that historians have had to strain to find traces of them. Kennan first put forward his dispositional explanation of Stalin's actions in the summer of 1944. But in contrast to Molotov, he found no sympathy at the top, nor would he for some time to come.

From this perspective, then, one has to wonder whether the Cold War really began in 1945. For it was Stalin's disposition to wage cold wars: he had done so in one form or another throughout his life, against members of his own family, against his closest advisers and their families, against old revolutionary comrades, against foreign communists, even against returning Red Army war veterans who, for whatever reason, had contacts of any kind with the West in the course of defeating Nazi Germany. "A man who had subjected all activities in his own country to his views and to his personality, Stalin could not behave differently outside," [Yugoslav Communist] Djilas recalled. "He became himself the slave of the despotism, the bureaucracy, the narrowness, and the servility that he imposed on his country." Khrushchev put it more bluntly: "No one inside the Soviet Union or out had Stalin's trust."

Roosevelt's death in April 1945, then, is not likely to have altered the long-term course of Soviet–American relations: if Stalin had never trusted him, why should he have trusted that "noisy shopkeeper" Harry S. Truman, or the harder-line advisers the new president came to rely upon? . . .

If doubts remained about Stalin's disposition, he thoroughly dispelled them in his first major postwar address, made on the eve of his own "election" to the Supreme Soviet in February 1946. The speech was not, as some Americans regarded it, a "declaration of World War III." It was, though, like Molotov's reminiscences, a revealing window into Stalin's mind. World War II, the Kremlin leader explained, had resulted *solely* from the internal contradictions of capitalism, and *only* the entry of the Soviet Union had transformed that conflict into a war of liberation. Perhaps it might be possible to avoid future wars if raw materials and markets could be "periodically redistributed among the various countries in accordance with their economic importance, by agreement and peaceful settlement." But, he added, "that is impossible to do under present capitalist conditions of the development of world economy." What all of this meant, Stalin's most perceptive biographer has argued, was nothing less than that "the postwar period would have to be transformed, in idea if not in actual fact, into *a new prewar period.*"

"There has been a return in Russia to the outmoded concept of security in terms of territory—the more you've got the safer you are." The speaker was former Soviet foreign minister and ambassador to the United States Maxim Litvinov, who had personally negotiated the establishment of Soviet–American diplomatic relations with Franklin D. Roosevelt. The occasion was an interview, given in Moscow to CBS correspondent Richard C. Hottelet a few months after Stalin's speech. The cause, Litvinov explained, was "the ideological conception prevailing here that conflict between Communist and capitalist worlds is inevitable." What would happen, Hottelet wanted to know, if the West should suddenly grant all of the Soviet Union's territorial demands? "It would lead to the West's being faced, after a more or less short time, with the next series of demands." . . .

Would there have been a Cold War without Stalin? Perhaps. Nobody in history is indispensable.

But Stalin had certain characteristics that set him off from all others in authority at the time the Cold War began. He alone pursued personal security by depriving everyone else of it: no Western leader relied on terror to the extent that he did. He alone had transformed his country into an extension of himself: no Western leader could have succeeded at such a feat, and none attempted it. He alone saw war and revolution as acceptable means with which to pursue ultimate ends: no Western leader associated violence with progress to the extent that he did.

Did Stalin therefore seek a Cold War? The question is a little like asking: "does a fish seek water?" Suspicion, distrust, and an abiding cynicism were not only his preferred but his necessary environment; he could not function apart from it.

CAROLYN EISENBERG

The American Decision to Divide Germany

He was in the lead jeep when they first spotted the Russians, stretched along the east bank of the Elbe River. His commanding officer saw the sun glinting off the soldiers' medals and remembered hearing that the Red Army wore their decorations in combat. Certain now that these were Soviet troops and not Germans, the elated Americans shot up two green flares and shouted their greetings into the stiff wind that was blowing across the water. It was 11:30 in the morning, April 25, 1945. . . .

The man standing in the first jeep was Private Joseph Polowsky of Chicago, a rifleman with G Company, 273rd Infantry, Third Platoon, Sixty-ninth Division, First Army. Polowsky had been awarded a Bronze Star in the Battle of the Bulge and was part of a unit that had fought its way across Germany. One day earlier the men had reached Trebsen, a town twenty miles west of the Elbe. There, G Company had been ordered to dispatch a patrol in the direction of the river to obtain more precise information about the location of the Red Army. The soldiers were under instructions not to attempt an actual linkup, lest there be accidental casualties.

But the emotions of the moment had proved overwhelming. In the final stage of the most devastating war in human history, the prospect of actually meeting the Russian troops and helping

From *Drawing the Line: The American Decision to Divide Germany,* 1944–1949, by Carolyn Eisenberg. Copyright © 1998 by Cambridge University Press. Reprinted with the permission of Cambridge University Press.

sever the German army was irresistible. On the morning of the 25th the group's leader, Lieutenant Alfred "Buck" Kotzebue, chose to ignore headquarters' restriction and to push ahead to the Elbe. Later the same day, two other patrol leaders from the Sixty-ninth Division would also ignore their instructions, as their troops surged forward in search of the Red Army.

Kotzebue's men were the first to make contact. Joe Polowsky had been placed in front so he could talk to the Russians. Because nobody in the unit knew their language, the lieutenant was counting on Polowsky's German to permit communication.

As they pulled up to the Elbe the Americans were perplexed about how to get across. The closest bridge had been obliterated in an earlier battle and the river, which was swollen by the spring rain, was flowing swiftly. Suddenly Kotzebue spotted some small boats chained to the shore. Unable to unfasten them by hand, he balanced a grenade on the knot of chains, pulled the pin, and took cover. The explosion released one of the sailboats, and six of the men eagerly climbed in. Using makeshift oars, they paddled through the heavy currents and reached the eastern bank.

An appalling spectacle met their eyes as they tried to disembark. Extending along both sides of the ruined bridge were hundreds of corpses of German civilians. These old men, women, and children had been fleeing the Red Army in horse-drawn carts. The previous night the Russians had seen the light of their encampment, and mistaking the people for German soldiers had bombarded the location with their artillery. Now the bodies were "piled up like cordwood" along the water.

In order to greet the Soviet soldiers, the Americans "literally waded knee-deep through the bodies of the German refugees." Private Polowsky later recalled being overcome by the scene, unable to remove his gaze from the body of a young girl who was lying on the ground, clutching her doll with one hand and her fallen mother with the other.

Despite the surrounding horror, there was a feeling of exhilaration as the Americans recognized that their rendezvous spelled the defeat of the Third Reich. Visibly moved, Kotzebue turned to his translator proposing that we "make a resolution with these Russians here," that "this would be an important day in the lives of the two countries." Polowsky recollected that the suggestion was "very informal, but it was a solemn moment. There were tears in the eyes of most of us. . . . We embraced. We swore never to forget."

The Russians quickly produced some bottles of vodka along with German wine and beer. In a tumultuous outpouring of excitement, hope, and grief, the six soldiers from G Company joined the men from the Red Army in repeated toasts and pledges. Standing beside the bodies of the slain civilians, they promised that they would remember the destruction and forever honor the memory of the Elbe. With impassioned words flowing from many lips, Private Polowsky found his work unexpectedly arduous and affecting.

Company G had encountered the Russians in the town of Strehla, sixteen miles south of Torgau. Because there were no reporters present, this first linkup received little publicity. Four and one half hours later a second American patrol, headed by Lieutenant Robertson, found the Red Army at Torgau. Hundreds of reporters were nearby, and it was this meeting that was immediately immortalized in the Allied press by photographs of the first handshake.

The euphoria at Strehla was replicated at Torgau. Bill Robertson later remembered that

> We three Americans were standing with the Russians on the river bank laughing, shouting, pounding each other on the back, shaking hands with everyone. Frank, George and I were shouting in English, our hosts in Russian. Neither understood the other's words, but the commonality of feeling was unmistakable. We were all soldiers, comrades in arms. We had vanquished a common enemy. The war was over, peace was near. All of us would live for another hour, another day.

Andy Rooney, reporter for the army's *Stars and Stripes,* described "a mad scene of jubilation on the east and west banks of the Elbe at Torgau as infantrymen of Lieutenant Courtney H. Hodges, First U.S. Army, swapped K rations for a vodka with soldiers of Marshal Kornian's Ukrainian army, congratulating each other, despite the language barrier on the link-up." Later the men from the Sixty-ninth Division sat in warm sunshine on the banks of the Elbe, with the enemy guns finally silent, passing around bottles with their new Russian friends and watching the soldiers of the Red Army dance and sing. Reflecting on this panorama, Rooney wrote, "You get the feeling of exuberance, a great new world opening up." . . .

At the time of Joe Polowsky's death [1983], there were few who treasured the symbolism of the Elbe. That sudden explosion of fraternal feeling as the Allied armies joined in Germany had been virtually buried in historic memory. Yet in April 1945, the import of the occasion had been evident not only to the soldiers who were there, but to millions of people around the world.

In a period darkened by vast atrocities and unimaginable suffering, the linking of American and Soviet troops was a source of inspiration, signifying the potential for human cooperation across barriers of language, nationality, and social systems. Amidst the ruins of the European Continent the urgency of international friendship, trust, and mutual accommodation required little explanation. And as battered veterans wept and danced and told their stories, the preciousness of peace was never more apparent.

Under the influence of the Cold War, historical studies of the Grand Alliance have generally emphasized the sources of future discord. The Western powers and the Soviet Union had been hostile to each other before the Second World War. The partnership had been dictated by absolute necessity. The Soviet Union was fighting for its life and needed all the help it could get. The United States and Britain saw the Red Army as the last hope for stopping Hitler. Despite a surface collaboration, each of the principals continued to nourish private resentments, ideologies, and plans. Even at the height of their cooperation, Roosevelt, Stalin, and Churchill had quarreled over many issues.

All of these elements seem more important in hindsight than they did at the time. When the war ended, the compelling fact was that the United States, the United Kingdom, and the Soviet Union had worked together successfully to defeat Germany. Faced with a common peril, they had submerged differences of experience and ideology. Whatever the discomforts of the Alliance, bonds of sympathy and appreciation had been forged among the participants, and the publics of all three nations had come to value the connection.

Like the dramatic imagery of the Elbe encounter, these hopeful developments were nearly erased from historical consciousness. But in disregarding this part of the past, the meaning of subsequent events is also lost. What is forgotten is how unwelcome and unexpected the U.S.–Soviet rupture really was. From our present standpoint we are apt to see the Cold War as an automatic by-product of the divergent patterns of society and governance, an inevitable resumption of hostilities once the specter of fascism had been exorcised. During the Second World War, however, there were many wise people on both sides of the Atlantic who were convinced that such divergences could be managed peacefully. This assessment flowed directly from the knowledge, born of the Grand Alliance, that heterogeneous societies—even Marxist and capitalist ones—could compromise when survival required it.

By recalling these original perceptions, we can penetrate the cloud of inevitability that hangs so heavily over the Cold War, and observe that the East–West conflict was the product of human decisions. In 1945 other aspirations had existed and other outcomes had seemed possible. To understand why the Great Powers failed to establish a durable peace, it is necessary to focus on the choices that were made, the reasons for their adoption, and the identity of the choosers. Though this is no longer the fashion, the search for Cold War origins must entail the exploration of responsibility. . . .

Though the division of Germany was one of the most crucial decisions of the postwar period, it has received little serious study in the United States. This omission is especially curious because the division of Germany was not only the most dramatic embodiment of the collapse of Great Power cooperation; it was also a fundamental cause of global polarization. So long as the Allies were controlling Germany in a unified way, there was hope of reconciling other European quarrels. Leaders on both sides recognized that a pacific, neutral German nation could be a model for the rest of the Continent, as well as a bridge between eastern and western Europe. Furthermore, Germany was the place where both the United States and the Soviet Union had their greatest stakes. If they could satisfy important interests in this arena, less weighty controversies might be defused.

Once Germany was cut in two, these prospects disappeared. With U.S.–Soviet aspirations embodied in rival German sovereignties, the European split proved irreversible. Superimposed on the preexisting tensions was a powerful new anxiety on the part of Americans and Russians: that Germany would be reunified on principles favorable to the other. In muted form, this had been a concern since the inception of the occupation. But it became far more serious once the major powers were actively strengthening two rump states. From this apprehension sprang two military alliances and the fortification of the blocs with the most lethal weapons ever deployed.

. . . U.S. policy makers had intended to cooperate with the Soviets in the supervision of a unified Germany. However, their ability to reach agreements at Yalta and at Potsdam was conditioned by the lingering influence of New Deal liberals over American foreign policy. The combined efforts of Henry Morgenthau Jr., Harry Dexter White, Harry Hopkins, and President Roosevelt himself had tilted U.S. directives toward a program of deindustrialization and draconian reform. This seemed to meet Stalin's economic and security requirements, and to provide him with an incentive to curb the German Communists.

With Roosevelt's death and the conclusion of the Second World War, however, the liberal New Dealers disappeared from the highest counsels. Administration conservatives such as Henry Stimson, John McCloy, and William Clayton, who were looking toward the establishment of a new multilateral trading order, consolidated their control over German policy. Though they favored collaboration with the Soviets and the maintenance of unity, they were also determined to rebuild postwar Germany so that it could be integrated with the capitalist economies of Europe.

Not surprisingly, the ascendance of this group led to increasingly bitter conflict with the Soviet Union. . . .

Underlying the American approach to the German negotiations was the self-serving conviction that legitimate Soviet needs could be met within the framework of a free market economy. Though genuinely desirous of an accommodation with the Russians, policy makers saw no reason to modify fundamental goals. What they were unable to envision was a process of mutual concessions in which both sides would accept substantial restrictions on their national objectives.

This stance was partly conditioned by an awareness of Soviet vulnerability. Weakened internationally by the massive wartime damage and its nonpossession of the atomic bomb, the Soviet Union also held the poorer hand inside Germany. Because the eastern zone had less land, fewer people, and reduced industrial resources as compared to the western portion of the country, they seemed less likely to succeed in their area of occupation. That gave hope that the Russians would eventually surrender control on western terms, and that the partition of the country would not prove permanent.

But even if this did not happen, the Americans thought it safer to forfeit the shredded alliance with the Soviet Union than to risk the failure of their plans for Western Europe. . . .

Ahead were forty years of Cold War, which ended abruptly on November 9, 1989, when euphoric Germans from east and west breached the wall in Berlin. Their reunion, oddly reminiscent of an earlier rendezvous when the two joyous Allied armies joined at the Elbe, terminated an exceptionally dangerous and tragic period of international relations.

To an American audience, the denouement in Germany held an obvious meaning: The Russians had split the country, and they had lost. For a generation, the Berlin Wall had been the prime symbol of the Cold War era. It exemplified the Soviet habit of foisting communism on unwilling people and imprisoning them forever. Although erected in 1961, twelve years after the establishment of two separate German states, it was the tangible proof of the Soviet Union's culpability.

Despite their manifold violations of human freedom, the Soviets were not the architects of the German settlement. It was the Americans and their British partners who had opted for partition with the associated congealment of the continental division. In contrast to their British confederates, U.S. policy makers had made their decision slowly and reluctantly, but it was America's wealth and power that assured its realization.

Though long forgotten, the Americans and British had initiated all the formal steps toward separation. . . . In each instance, there was some equivalent move in the eastern zone. Yet the pattern of U.S.–British action and Soviet response was a consistent one.

As in a divorce where the party filing papers is not necessarily the one who caused the rupture, formal situations are not always illuminating. Indeed at the time they adopted these measures, the Americans and British maintained that the Soviets had created the schism through their unofficial obstruction of German unity. Such claims nurtured the impression of both their publics that Germany was divided because the Soviet Union had closed off the east.

From the beginning of its occupation in April 1945, the Soviet authorities had imposed a repressive regime, which significantly curtailed German liberties. However, at the point when the Americans and British began their formal moves toward partition, the eastern zone was still a relatively open place—certainly in comparison to what it subsequently became. Not surprisingly, the greatest latitude existed in the quadripartite city of Berlin where, under the protection of the Allied Kommandatura, people and goods were circulating freely and political parties were competing fiercely for public support. Because Berlin was inside the Soviet zone, this ferment and diversity spilled over to the surrounding areas, limiting the Russians' ability to control the sentiments and activities of the populace.

While the relationship among the four zones was less fluid than the situation in Berlin, there was controlled trade and travel with an associated transmission of books, newspapers, and ideas. Political conditions inside the eastern zone tightened appreciably after March 1946, when the Soviets forced the merger between the Communist and Social Democratic parties. . . . Even then, two bourgeois parties—the Christian Democrats (CDU) and the Liberal Democrats (LDP)—were allowed to operate independently with their own press and regular public meetings. Though frequently harassed, these anticommunist groups participated actively in provincial elections and polled a strong vote during the fall of that year.

The same mixed pattern obtained in the economic sphere, where the Soviets pursued an inconsistent, opportunistic policy. In late 1945 they had pushed through a radical land reform measure, which divided all estates over one hundred hectares, but the resulting parcels were widely distributed into the private hands of landless settlers and poor farmers. In the industrial field, they had authorized the Länder to sequester "ownerless property" as well as the property of the German government, the Nazi organizations, and the "leading members and influential followers" of the Nazi Party. Yet they were slow to transfer ownership to the state. During the summer of 1946 the eastern provinces held referenda on the disposition of the sequestered facilities, thus paving the way for substantial socialization. However, some portion of these confiscated enterprises were returned or resold to private individuals. In conjunction with those properties that had not qualified for sequestration, this meant that much of the eastern industry was still under private ownership.

Between 1947 and 1949 Soviet policy accelerated in a dictatorial direction. By the end of the period, their alleged commitment to political and social pluralism had given way to one-party control and state direction of economic life. However, in distinguishing cause-and-effect, the chronology remains pertinent. In the summer of 1947, when the Americans and British reached a clear decision to divide Germany, the presence of these trends had not yet obliterated the alternative voices, political organizations, and social institutions in the east.

Furthermore, while the American and British officials deplored the internal trends in the Soviet zone, this was never their primary focus. . . . When they referred to Soviet intransigence and obstructionism, they had chiefly in mind the Soviet Union's conditions for amalgamating the zones.

To a remarkable extent, these Soviet conditions remained unchanged from the time of Yalta and were devoid of Marxist content. Especially noteworthy was the Soviet negotiating position at the Moscow Council of Foreign Ministers in March–April 1947. . . .

As presented by Foreign Minister Molotov, the Russian package was designed to meet pragmatic security and material requirements. In speeches grown stale with repetition, Molotov stressed the necessity for reparations and reaffirmed the figure of 10 billion dollars, which he insisted should come from current production rather than capital equipment. He also recycled demands for four-power control of the Ruhr and a vigorous policy of "democratization"—by which he denoted land reform, denazification, decartelization, the rapid reconstruction of trade unions and other social initiatives. In the biggest change of Soviet policy, he accepted the concept of a freely elected German provisional government, which he expected to be centralized along the lines of the Weimar constitution.

. . . Off the record, the Russians intimated to their Western colleagues that many of their planks could be modified if reparations demands were satisfied.

Whatever the merits of the Soviet program, it did not differ appreciably from that previously advanced by liberals in the Roosevelt administration, whose ideas had been partly embodied in the Yalta reparations clauses, the German provisions of Potsdam, and the Joint Chiefs of Staff Directive 1067. Such convergence was admittedly of slight comfort to the less reform-minded members of the Truman team who viewed these documents skeptically. Their displeasure notwithstanding, the Soviet Union was still exhibiting a surface willingness to accept the norms of parliamentary democracy and to open a wider door for capitalism in the eastern zone.

During the Moscow meetings, U.S. officials recognized that the Russians were desirous of German unification, even though some versions would not be acceptable. The Soviets would not, for example, forfeit reparations removal from their zone in order to reintegrate the country. However, the Soviets' appetite for a bargain was apparent for a reason that was scarcely mysterious. As prescribed by Yalta, the western zones of Germany included the majority of the land, people, and resources of the country. The Ruhr alone contained sufficient coal, steel, and chemicals to make West Germany an economic and political power in its own right. Should the country be split, not only would the Soviet Union lose access to the wealthiest portion; it ran the risk that West Germany could, in association with the Western nations, become a grave military threat. . . .

As they implemented the division of the country, the Americans and British were not simply ratifying an already existing situation. The conditions of the eastern zone remained unsettled and the Soviet bargaining position showed numerous signs of flexibility. In the gathering momentum for a separate West German state, there was continuing evidence that unification could be achieved.

Why did U.S. officials prefer schism? At the end of the Second World War, American policy had been different. The prevailing view then, even among administration conservatives, was that Germany should be kept together and supervised by the Great Powers. During 1946–47, as this attitude was reevaluated, one pervasive element was the mounting fear of Soviet aggression. Washington policy makers were strongly affected by the reports from George Kennan and others, who perceived a Soviet plan to take over Western Europe. As applied to Germany, that analysis presumed the Soviet Union would use any centralized machinery to subvert democratic institutions in the western zones. Thus even if unification was attainable, it would be too dangerous.

Significantly, the leaders of U.S. Military Government in Germany did not share Kennan's assessment. In hundreds of cables and oral reports, they highlighted the weakness of the Communist Party in western Germany. . . . These observers also believed the Russians were economically desperate, and would forfeit political advantages in order to garner reparations.

If Washington officials listened more to Kennan than their representatives in Germany, this was because his gloomy prognostications fit their policy preferences. The core of realism in their position was the appreciation of a genuine clash of interests between even the minimum Soviet program for reparations and security, and their own aspiration for West European recovery and integration. Though it had initially seemed possible to reconcile the two agendas, difficulties in procuring coal, steel, and chemicals from the Ruhr, and restoring the German market for West European goods had reduced that prospect. As the western zones stagnated, each Russian demand—for reparations deliveries, for quadripartite controls in the Ruhr, for a breakup of the large German combines, for denazification of management, for a politicized labor movement— became harder to tolerate. Ultimately, it became an intellectual fine point whether these Russian claims reflected sincere anxieties about German militarism or nefarious schemes for taking over the country. To U.S. officials what mattered was the Soviet interference with their plans for German rehabilitation.

After mid-1947 there was even less room for argument as Soviet rhetoric and behavior became significantly more provocative. Within Europe, the formation of the Comintern was accompanied by a summons to Western communist parties to engage in disruption and sabotage, and by mounting repression in Hungary, Rumania, and Poland. Inside Germany itself, the western Communist Party (KPD) was mobilizing working-class resistance to the Marshall Plan, while the Soviet military authorities were accelerating the trend to one-party rule in the east. Taken in aggregate, these developments seemed to confirm the analysis of those American officials who viewed the Soviets as unscrupulous partners, whose only genuine goal was world revolution. When these transgressions were capped by a Russian decision to blockade Berlin, the brief against the Soviet Union hardened into doctrine.

Yet even in this latter phase, there was a willful narrowness in American thinking. If Soviet behavior was getting worse, it was also true that they were being locked out of western Germany and denied the benefits of their World War II victory. The likelihood that these situations were connected, that Soviet belligerence was partly the result of feeling cheated and threatened, were topics that could not be probed. Only on the political fringes would a dissident like Henry Wallace wonder if a German compromise could still reverse the most dangerous developments in Western and Eastern Europe. Within mainstream circles, such an inquiry was anathema.

. . . For all their alarms about Russian aggression, U.S. policy makers saw the Soviets as weak both economically and militarily. This judgment allowed them to make careless calculations, to disregard the Soviet interests with a sense of impunity, and to sacrifice potentially favorable bargains with the expectation of a complete collapse down the road.

The road was very long, and there is reason to wonder if ordinary citizens would have chosen it. In retrospect, it is shocking to consider how inaccurately the U.S. government communicated its German policy to constituents. For the first two years after the war, little was said about the effort to rebuild the country. As far as most Americans knew, the main goal was to punish Nazis and reform the society.

After mid-1947, the focus shifted to the containment of Soviet aggression. With the inception of the Berlin blockade, President Truman articulated a simple story that featured the Russians, trampling the wartime agreements in their ruthless grab for the former German capital. The president did not explain that the United States had abandoned Yalta and Potsdam, that it was pushing the formation of a West German state against the misgivings of many Europeans, and that the Soviets had launched the blockade to prevent partition.

In offering this distorted account, Truman was partly responding to the pressures of confrontation and the need for a short, intelligible description that would rally public support. Yet since his experience at Potsdam, the president had never involved himself in the German problem, and it is doubtful that he understood its complexities. . . . [H]e did not seem aware that his subordinates were propelling separation, nor did he apprehend the gravity of the Soviet response.

The importance of German policy, notwithstanding, momentous decisions were made without the significant participation of any elected officials. Even Senator Vandenberg, the most informed of Washington legislators, was startled when Secretary Acheson came before the foreign Relations Committee in 1949 and outlined the State Department's approach. Until that point, neither Vandenberg nor his colleagues on the committee had realized how determined the State Department was to create a separate West German state, regardless of Soviet terms.

This abdication of political leadership framed the public's obliviousness to the issues. Without accountable officials, able and willing to outline the existing options, there was little opportunity for democratic debate. Instead, policy was established by the national security bureaucracies, with their strong penchant for secrecy. Lacking pertinent information, citizens were relegated to the sidelines. . . .

There are some grounds for claiming that the public interest was well served, even in the absence of informed consent. U.S. policy makers aimed to protect the nation's security by salvaging free market economies in Western Europe. For this purpose the exclusion of the Russians from the western portion of Germany seemed increasingly attractive. Once the severance had occurred, West Germany played the projected role, reviving quickly and providing goods and markets to its neighbors. . . .

One price of these accomplishments was that East Germany was abandoned to the Russians, along with the rest of Eastern Europe. Ironically, it was George Kennan—the earliest and most vigorous proponent of "containment"—who became most disturbed by this consequence. For years, he had lamented the Soviet infringements of eastern rights and called upon his government to disassociate itself. But at the point of partition, Kennan apprehended how much more repressive the regimes could become and discarded his own counsel.

Another charge for the division of Germany was the militarizing of Europe. As illustrated by the Berlin blockade, the splitting of the country meant that the United States and the Soviet Union would become mortal enemies, whose urgent interests could engender armed conflict. U.S. policy makers reckoned that their monopoly of nuclear weapons and ability to join with Western Europe in a buildup of conventional forces would deter Soviet advances.

However, the very reliance on military power made the international environment more menacing. Not only did it insure that the Soviets would cling to every scrap of territory they had gained; it guaranteed a costly arms race and endowed even remote places on the globe with a strategic significance they might not otherwise have held. Later many would wonder why young Americans were dying in Korea and South Vietnam, but the logic of a military rivalry lent reason to these encounters.

Among the small circle of Americans who set policy for Germany there was little attempt to weigh alternatives. What finally gave shape to their deliberations was a conception of national security that took the expansion of West European free trade as an absolute requirement for the United States. Though this reflected the aspirations of the large internationally oriented corporations and banks, it was less clearly in line with the predilections of the public, for whom issues of East European freedom and the maintenance of peace held greater salience.

From the perspective of the mid-1990s, with Soviet communism so severely discredited, there is a temptation to again lay at their feet the blame for every international transgression. This disposition has been quite naturally strengthened by the opening of archives, which offer new manifestations of Eastern bloc despotism.

Though the atmosphere is unpropitious, there is still good reason for historical fairness. The oppressive internal policies of the Soviet Union that were gradually imposed upon the population of East Germany were not the source of the postwar schism. In the aftermath of victory, what produced that unwanted result was an ambitious American agenda, which was juxtaposed on a European continent that was more impoverished, strife-ridden, and unruly than anyone in Washington had envisioned. In conjunction with America's preponderance of military and economic power, this yielded high-risk policies, whose most painful consequences were mainly borne by others.

Had American officials been more flexible and sought a compromise solution in occupied Germany, it is possible that the Soviets would have blocked or overturned it. But this is something we cannot know since the United States selected a different course. In the wreckage of the Cold War, America has yet to acknowledge responsibility for the structures that it built.

BRUCE CUMINGS

The Wicked Witch of the West is Dead. Long Live the Wicked Witch of the East

What was the Cold War? Ostensibly it was a global struggle between communism and democracy, with frightening military formations arrayed along the central front in Europe. Three "Berlins" seemed to typify the conflict and to place the appropriate emphasis on Europe: the airlift in 1948 at the Cold War's reported beginning, the crisis in 1961 that summed up its

From "The Wicked Witch of the West Is Dead. Long Live the Wicked Witch of the East," by Bruce Cumings, from *The End of the Cold War: Its Meaning and Implications,* edited by Michael J. Hogan. Copyright © 1992 by Cambridge University Press. Reprinted with the permission of Cambridge University Press.

bipolar and intractable nature, and the dismantling of the wall in 1989 that presumably ended it. Hardly any lives were lost along the central axis of division in Europe, which encourages historians like John Lewis Gaddis to speak of a "long peace" in our time. Gaddis argues for the success of George Kennan's containment doctrine, conceived as a long twilight struggle to hold the existing lines of the postwar settlement, until the Soviet Union saw the error of its ways and reformed itself. When Gorbachev proceeded to dismantle the Soviet empire, Kennan's wisdom seemed triumphant. Only a myopic Eurocentrism could yield such conclusions.

In fact, Europe fought a "shadow conflict," obscuring the real history of the past four decades. Kennan's strategy had a curiosity in an unspoken premise: The doctrine was meant both to contain the enemy, the Soviet Union, *and* the allies—mainly West Germany and Japan. Kennan was one of the architects of a strategy in which West Germany and Japan were shorn of their previous military and political clout during the period of American occupation, but their industrial economies were encouraged to revive, and they were posted as engines of growth in the world economy. Meanwhile, the United States kept both countries on defense dependencies and shaped the flow of essential resources to each, thus to accumulate a diffuse leverage over all of their policies and to retain an outer limit veto on their global orientation.

The major wars of the "long peace" were part of this American hegemonic project, which was articulated and developed coterminous with the Truman Doctrine to bolster regional positions of strength. In Korea, the United States picked up the glove of the Japanese empire and sought to keep South Korea and Taiwan within Japan's historic economic area, thus to aid its reviving industry. In Vietnam, we picked up the French glove, but again for reasons connected to the needs of the French and Japanese economies. Lesser interventions, like those in Greece in 1947 and Iran in 1953, were similarly connected to the revival of the industrial economies and the American desire to police the lines of resource flow to the industrial states.

The real reason for the long European peace between the superpowers was that the Soviet Union shared the American perspective to a much greater degree than is generally recognized. Stalin's doctrine, which became the life-long doctrine of Foreign Minister Andrei Gromyko, was to contain not just the United States but also any hint of *revanche* in Germany and Japan; to contain an Eastern Europe that had been fertile ground for conflict before both world wars . . . and also a restive Third World with clients who might draw Soviet might and prestige into unwanted peripheral clashes with the United States. When push came to shove the Soviet Union pulled its forces out of northern Iran in 1946, cut off the Greek guerrillas, distanced itself from direct involvement in the wars in Korea and Vietnam, and withdrew from the brink over Cuba in 1962. Meanwhile it laid siege against West Germany and Japan.

Thus, when the United States found itself in the best of all possible worlds in 1990, having won the Cold War but still retaining immense leverage over Germany and Japan, it was not by accident, because the Cold War consisted of two systems: the containment project, providing security against both the enemy and the ally; and the hegemonic project, providing for American leverage over the necessary resources of our industrial rivals. Both the hegemonic project and the allied-containment system survive today.

The shadow conflict of the Cold War period shaded our vision, obscuring the hegemonic project and highlighting threats that could never stand the glare of realpolitik analysis: above all the obsession with China beginning in 1949, which for a generation made the People's Republic seem far more important than it really was. . . . More importantly, Russia is now seen for what many "revisionists" always argued it to be, a regional power of the second rank (except in regard to inherently unusable nuclear weapons), inflated out of all proportion by the hot air of Cold War ideology. Finally, the United States can now be seen to be what it always has been since the 1940s—the only hegemon, the Great Britain of our time.

That the Cold War ended essentially through the unilateral acts of the Soviet Union also helps to explain why the American projects of global hegemony and allied containment continue: Nothing really changed in American policy. It was as if two horses were racing around a track, one broke its leg, and the other kept on running anyway. But our treatment of U.S. global policy is not sufficient to explain why Reagan and Bush kept on racing. The rise of the Cold War system had a domestic corollary as well in the emergence of mechanisms that served the twin projects of containment and hegemony: a military-industrial complex and a national security state. Although the twin projects were conceived in 1947, the system necessary to service them took several years to develop.

A diverse American coalition of left and right, located in small business, labor, and farming constituencies and known colloquially as "isolationists," resisted the Roosevelt–Truman march toward world power, and up until 1950 had been unwilling to countenance the major defense expenditures deemed necessary to service the new global commitments. It was the Korean War that "came along and saved us," as Secretary of State Dean Acheson later remarked, a necessary crisis that galvanized Congress and the public. Only with the Korean War did the mechanisms and bureaucracies of hegemonic maintenance proliferate in the federal government and the defense industries (the CIA, for example, was still little more than a rump operation in early 1950). . . .

Perhaps nothing would have surprised George Frost Kennan more in 1947 than if someone had told him that the major wars that the United States would fight in pursuit of "containment" would be in Korea and Vietnam, two countries that never held more than his momentary attention, and then only as he figured out how they might make themselves useful to someone else (usually Japan). Nor could Kennan have imagined that when the Cold War finally ended and the Soviet Union returned to its Russian roots, the Cold War would persist intractably in Korea. Yet distant, remote Korea provides an optic that highlights almost all of the important history of the Cold War.

Korea was there before the beginning of the Cold War and it is still there after the end. The full panoply of conflict that we associate with the Cold War appeared in Korea in the last months of 1945. . . . Korea is a museum of that awful conflict, the only place in the world where Cold War confrontation remains predominant. What does this have to teach us about the Cold War?

It teaches us that the Cold War was only indirectly about U.S.–Soviet strategic conflict. No realpolitik worthy of the name, no military doctrine before, during, or after the Korean War could sustain the argument that possession of Korea (or half of it) made a significant difference militarily or strategically in the balance of power. That Soviet power occupied northern Korea in 1945 simply intensified a different conflict, that between Japanese and American power and indigenous popular forces seeking to orient Korea's future independently. This struggle began in the waning period of Soviet–American cooperation in 1945 and would have happened had Korea been on the other side of the globe: let's say, in Central America.

In other words, the Cold War was also about confrontation between the First and Third worlds, and this is where its major violence came: four million deaths in Korea, nearly an equal number in Vietnam. It was a conflict between core and periphery, especially in that contingent, intermediate zone that Immanuel Wallerstein terms the semi-periphery. And here we find the logic of American policy in Korea; all sorts of historical conundrums can be unpacked when we understand that Korea's primary significance for the United States was not its proximity to the Soviet Union, but its proximity to Japan.

When traditional American noninvolvement in Korea was reversed during World War II, it was Japanophiles in the State Department who did the about face, linking postwar Korean security to that of Japan and the Pacific. When Secretary of State George Marshall, at the onset of "the fifteen weeks" in 1947, gave post facto blessing to the American Occupation's eighteen-month-old effort to contain revolution and establish a separate southern government, he did so to "connect [Korea] up" with Japan. When his successor Dean Acheson spoke publicly in 1950 about a "defense perimeter" in Asia, he was thinking privately about a "great crescent" delineating a 1940s "Pacific Rim" political economy, linking Tokyo with the East Asian rim and ultimately with the oil of the Middle East. Acheson's decision six months later to take American forces into the Korean War had to do internationally with holding the lines of this developing political economy and domestically with finding a crisis that would win congressional approval of NSC 68 and thus commit the American people to maintaining an enormous, far-flung, and historically unprecedented hegemony.

What Acheson and Truman found in Korea was quite different from their expectation. The Koreans fought tenaciously and ultimately pulled a rabbit called China out of their hat. By December 1950, U.S. policy was in ruins, and a crisis beyond imagination was at hand that destabilized and ultimately destroyed the Truman administration (according to Acheson). Paradoxically, this dark moment stabilized the Cold War system financially and strategically. By December 1950, authorized defense spending had nearly quadrupled from its $13 billion level in June 1950. More generally, Korea was a crisis enabling the second major wave of state-building in this American century: The New Deal was the first, and the national security state was the second, with security bureaucracies growing exponentially from the early 1950s onward.

Furthermore, an unstable compromise on containment from 1947 to 1950, lacking bipartisanship on Asia and on how to respond to the dynamism of communism, was brought together into a temporary consensus via the march to the Yalu; when this exploded in everyone's face, centrists like Acheson and Dulles retreated to de facto containment thereafter, even though Dulles continued to give voice to rollback rhetoric in the 1950s. In this sense, the Chinese limited the war for an America that could not. China understood that the wars in Korea and Vietnam were proxy wars for the United States, that the Chinese revolution was the real issue. Therefore, China established definitive limits on American expansionism in these two former tributary states, and in so doing taught a lesson that lasted down to the worldwide end of the Cold War: Communist territory was off limits, except to covert forays.

Fear of China then decisively affected the course of the Vietnam War by deterring an American invasion of North Vietnam and causing successive administrations to define "success" as a permanently divided Vietnam. Within the American state and polity, the failed rollback attempt in Korea and the crisis it caused also explain the stalemate between conservatives and liberals over the Bay of Pigs in 1961 and over Nicaragua throughout the 1980s. From this standpoint the Korean War was far more important to the construction of postwar American foreign policy than the Vietnam War. Only the latter, however, stuck itself irrevocably in the American heart.

The enemy in Korea did not seek or want any of this. The North Koreans and the Chinese sought to drive a stake into the heart of Acheson's "great crescent" political economy, to declare their territories off limits to American hegemony and Japanese economic influence. Today it appears that they merely succeeded in delaying for two decades the dynamism of the regional Northeast Asian economy, which had its origin in colonial development in the 1930s. Neither North Korea nor China could contain the automaticity of a dynamic regional capitalist economy once it got going again in the mid-1960s. In the 1990s, capitalism laps at their doors, and increasingly integrates the most advanced parts of the Chinese economy.

North Korea, however, remains outside this realm, and dangerously so. The only question Americans have ever wanted to ask about the Korean War was "who started it?"—a snapshot in time that buries the war's origins and embodies its own ideological answer. So also Americans today view Korea through one "snapshot" that seeks to silence and bury the history that explains why the Cold War lives on in Korea: satellite photos showing some sort of nuclear facility at Yongbyôn. American policy points at that issue and at North Korea as another "renegade state" like Iraq; the media uncritically repeats the line, or goes beyond it (*Chicago Tribune* editors have twice called for a military attack on Yongbyôn); hardly anyone points out that we are still technically at war with North Korea, that the real reason that the Bush administration points the finger at P'yôngyang's unusable (and as yet nonexistent) nuclear weapon is to keep Japan from going nuclear, to keep American troops in Korea and Japan to retain leverage on both, and to continue the postwar settlement regardless of the ostensible end of the Cold War.

Further Reading

The literature on the origins of the cold war is enormous, and some of it is highly specialized. For a general overview of the conflict from a traditional perspective, a good starting point is a book-length, early treatment by John Lewis Gaddis, *The United States and the Origins of the Cold War, 1941–1972* (New York: Columbia University Press, 1972). His article proposing a "postrevisionist" approach ("The Emerging Post-Revisionist Synthesis on the Origins of the Cold War") may be found in *Diplomatic History* (vol. 7 [Summer 1983], 171–90). An earlier stab at postrevisionism that, in the end, really restates the orthodox position is "Origins of the Cold War," by presidential advisor and prominent cold warrior Arthur M. Schlesinger, Jr., published in *Foreign Affairs* (vol. 46/1 [October 1967], 22–52). For a pointed rebuttal to "postrevisionism," see Bruce Cumings, "'Revising Postrevisionism,' or, The Poverty of Theory in Diplomatic History" in *Diplomatic History* (vol. 17/4 [Fall 1993], 539–70). Other readings from the orthodox perspective include Randall B. Woods and Howard Jones, *Dawning of the Cold War: The United States' Quest for Order* (Athens: University of Georgia Press, 1991).

For a highly readable overview of the cold war from a revisionist perspective, see Thomas G. Paterson, *On Every Front: The Making and Unmaking of the Cold War* (New York: Norton, 1992), which sees the cold war as emerging from the destabilization of the old international system wrought by World War II but also emphasizes the roles of particular world leaders, notably Truman, in creating the conflict. Also engaging is Melvyn Leffler, *The Specter of Communism: The United States and the Origins of the Cold War, 1917–1953* (New York: Hill and Wang, 1994), a concise version of his magisterial *A Preponderance of Power: National Security, the Truman Administration, and the Cold War* (Stanford, CA: Stanford University Press, 1992). Leffler argues persuasively that the Soviet Union posed no immediate threat to the United States after World War II, but unlike most revisionists, he does believe that U.S. leaders for the most part acted prudently and correctly, given their fears that the USSR could in some way in the future challenge American interests. Arnold A. Offner, *Another Such Victory: President Truman and the Cold War, 1945–1953* (Stanford, CA: Stanford University Press, 2002) is a detailed work highly critical of Truman. Thomas J. McCormick, *America's Half-Century: United States Foreign Policy in the Cold War and After* (Baltimore: The Johns Hopkins University Press, 1995) emphasizes geopolitical concerns and economic interests as the basis for the cold war. For a classic revisionist account that stresses economic motives—specifically, the concerns of American corporations to secure international markets to prevent another Depression—see Gabriel Kolko and Joyce Kolko, *The Limits of Power: The World and the United States Foreign Policy, 1945–1954* (New York: Harper & Row, 1972). Another revisionist classic that is periodically updated is Walter LaFeber, *America, Russia and the Cold War, 1945–2002* (rev. ed. [New York: McGraw-Hill, 1994]).

For a good account of the cold war from Stalin's perspective that makes use of recently available archival materials, see Vladislav Zubok and Constantine Pleshakov, *Inside the Kremlin's Cold War: From Stalin to Khrushchev* (Cambridge, MA: Harvard University Press, 1996), which is compatible with some of the revisionist interpretations of the cold war. For the orthodox view, see Adam Ulam, *Expansion and Coexistence: Soviet Foreign Policy, 1917–1973* (New York: Praeger, 1974) and Vojtech Mastny, *The Cold War and Soviet Insecurity: The Stalin Years* (New York: Oxford University Press, 1996).

The literature on the cold war that focuses on individual countries or on regions outside of Western Europe is growing; some basic works include Bruce R. Kuniholm, *The Origins of the Cold War in the Near East: Great Power Conflict and Diplomacy in Iran, Turkey, and Greece* (Princeton, NJ: Princeton University Press, 1980); Geir Lundestad, *America, Scandinavia and the Cold War: Expansion and Its Limitations in U.S. Foreign Policy, 1945–1949* (New York: Columbia University Press, 1980); Irwin M. Wall, *The United States and the Making of Postwar France: 1945–1954* (Cambridge: Cambridge University Press, 1991); Michael M. Boll, *Cold War in the Balkans: American Foreign Policy and the Emergence of Communist Bulgaria, 1943–1947* (Lexington: University Press of Kentucky, 1984); Akira Iriye, *The Cold War in Asia: A Historical Introduction* (Upper Saddle River, NJ: Prentice Hall, 1974); Nancy Bernkopf Tucker, *Taiwan, Hong Kong, and the United States, 1945–1992: Uncertain Friendships* (New York: Twayne, 1994); and Robert J. McMahon, *Colonialism and the Cold War: The United States and the Struggle for Indonesian Independence: 1945–1949* (Ithaca, NY: Cornell University Press, 1981).

For a quick introduction to a variety of perspectives on the cold war, see the collection of essays, *The Origins of the Cold War* (Boston: Houghton Mifflin, 1999), edited by Robert McMahon and Thomas G. Paterson.

Primary Sources

The Web site www.mtholyoke.edu/acad/intrel/coldwar.htm offers a vast collection of documents (as well as links to other Web sites with documents) related to the cold war. These include excerpts from George Kennan's 1947 "Long Telegram" (www.mtholyoke.edu/acad/intrel/longtel.html) and Kennan's famous "Mr. X" article, "The Sources of Soviet Conduct" (www.mtholyoke.edu/acad/intrel/coldwar/x.htm). The text of NSC-68 may also be found here (www.mtholyoke.edu/acad/intrel/nsc-68/nsc68-1.htm). The text of the Yalta agreement is available at www.yale.edu/lawweb/avalon/wwii/yalta.htm. For the text of the July 23, 1946, letter from Henry A. Wallace to President Harry Truman, in which Wallace lays out the case against containment, go to historymatters.gmu.edu/d/6906. For the text of Winston Churchill's Iron Curtain speech, go to www.fordham.edu/halsall/mod/churchill-iron.html. For Stalin's response, go to www.fordham.edu/halsall/mod/1946stalin.html. The text of the Truman Doctrine is available at www.fordham.edu/halsall/mod/1947TRUMAN.html. Go to www.trumanlibrary.org/whistlestop/study_collections/marshall/large/index.php (particularly the letters to and from

Charles P. Kindleberger of the State Department), for documents with discussions of U.S. plans for postwar Germany and their deviation from the commitments made at Yalta and Potsdam. For documents concerning the onset of the Korean War from the perspective of the Truman administration, see the copy of the June 25, 1950, memo, "Points Requiring Presidential Decision," prepared by the Departments of State and Defense and summarized for the president by Dean Acheson at www.trumanlibrary.org/whistlestop/study_collections/korea/large/week1/elsy_5_1.htm and other documents at www.trumanlibrary.org/whistlestop/study_collections/korea/large/koreaweek1docs.htm.

The Red Scare

INTRODUCTION

In the ten years after 1945, as the U.S. government escalated its conflict with the forces of communism abroad, powerful forces in American society also went on the attack against alleged left-wing traitors and subversives at home. The resulting atmosphere of fear and punishment became known as the "Red Scare." The federal government, state governments, and private groups sought to ferret out hidden Communists and anyone else they suspected of "Red" sympathies. Many Red-hunters defined subversive sympathies very broadly, drawing large numbers of Americans under a cloud of suspicion because of their past or current political associations, or simply because they dissented from the intense conservatism that prevailed during this era. The best known Red-hunter of all was U.S. Senator Joseph R. McCarthy, Republican of Wisconsin; his notoriety was so great that the term "McCarthyism" became synonymous with the Red Scare.

McCarthy made two claims: that there were secret Communists in the U.S. government who worked for the Soviet Union, and that the treason of these saboteurs explained the foreign-policy setbacks that America experienced in 1949 and 1950. In these years, the Soviets detonated an atomic bomb, ending the U.S. monopoly on this weapon; the Communists won the Chinese civil war over their rivals, the Nationalists; and Communist North Korea invaded South Korea, drawing the United States into a land war in Asia only five years after the end of World War II. To many Americans it seemed incredible that Russian and Asian Communists could mount these challenges to U.S. power on their own. They were thus receptive to the frightening assertion made by McCarthy in 1950 in Wheeling, West Virginia, in a speech often viewed as the opening salvo in the Red Scare. He intoned, "This must be the product of a great conspiracy."

McCarthy himself was controversial from the start. Critics revealed him as a serial fabricator early on and used terms such as "guilt by association" and "witch-hunt" to suggest the kind of unfair, destructive, and dangerous tactics he used. A Senate committee, led by Millard Tydings, a Democrat from Maryland, called McCarthy's charges a hoax in 1950, and the Senate censured him in 1954, after he accused the Army of coddling Communists in its ranks. Discredited and in poor health, McCarthy died in 1957. Yet in his heyday he gained much attention for his wild charges, deftly using reporters who knew he was a charlatan but wanted good copy; the charges, not the questions about their basis in fact, got the headlines. Most important, his smear tactics caught on with many other Red-hunters and long outlasted McCarthy's career.

In the 1950s, virtually all mainstream political and intellectual figures in the United States were staunchly anticommunist, and this complicated the desire many of them felt to distance themselves from McCarthy's unsavory tactics. Republican party leaders, despite their privately expressed disdain for McCarthy, embraced his Red-hunting crusade as a means of gaining political power; one consistent claim by McCarthy and his fellow Red-hunters was that Democrats were lax when it came to Communist subversion. Although Democrats feared that McCarthyism held the potential to raise the fortunes of Republicans, a great many liberals were deeply anticommunist themselves and believed that Communist sabotage either was or had been real and dangerous. For example, they supported the sensational charges made in the late 1940s by Whittaker Chambers, a *Time* magazine editor and a former Communist, that Alger Hiss, a former State Department diplomat, had been, while in government service, Chambers's partner in spying for the Soviet Union. The liberal anticommunists, many of them former Communists or leftists themselves, saw American Communism as the extension of a hostile foreign government, not as a legitimate political movement, and they often expressed doubts that Communists deserved the protection of the freedoms outlined in the U.S. Constitution. But they saw McCarthy as a liar and a demagogue who targeted innocents along with the guilty. They wanted to discredit him, but they feared that an anti-McCarthy backlash could blind Americans to the dangerous and immoral nature of communism. Therefore liberal anticommunists worked hard during the 1950s both to denounce McCarthy and to justify "responsible" Red-hunting.

Historians and sociologists in the 1950s sought to understand the substantial popular enthusiasm for McCarthy, a man they thought was an obvious fraud. They advanced the idea that "status anxiety" propelled support for McCarthy. This interpretation, which was most closely associated among historians with Richard Hofstadter, postulated that American society, unlike those of Europe, was egalitarian, with a fluid class structure. As a result, Americans had a relatively weak sense of status or position, causing them anxiety about where they "fit in." Furthermore, particular segments of American society—those undergoing rapid movement either down or up the social scale—experienced particularly acute levels of status anxiety. According to Hofstadter, these people were likely recruits for hyper-nationalist movements like McCarthyism, which let them loudly proclaim their "Americanness" by disputing the patriotism of others. McCarthy's followers felt that they were the "real" Americans, betrayed by the governmental and social elite—"the bright young men who are born with silver spoons in their mouths" who had "been selling this Nation out," in McCarthy's words. The status-anxiety scholars, influenced by psychoanalytic and sociological research on the nature of prejudice, saw similarities among McCarthyism, the American "Populist" movement of the late nineteenth century, and fascism, viewing them all as dangerous "mass movements" that built up the status of their own members by attacking other groups of purported lesser virtue. McCarthy and his supporters seemed fueled by resentments against people other than Communists: intellectuals or "eggheads," "eastern elites," Jews, and liberals. This proved, in the view of the status-anxiety scholars, how irrational and dangerous McCarthyism was. This interpretation of the Red Scare dominated academic discussion for many years, despite the fact that its advocates summoned little factual data in support of it.

In the late 1960s, a new generation of historians developed a revisionist interpretation of the Red Scare, and largely discredited the status-anxiety theory. The revisionists emphasized partisan politics as the essential background to the Red Scare, and argued that neither the resentments of provincials against cosmopolitan elites nor a sincere fear of Communist subversion had lain at the heart of McCarthyism. Since the 1930s, Republicans and conservatives had claimed that domestic Communists were a dangerous presence within Franklin D. Roosevelt's Democratic administration. This charge was sharpened into specific allegations, like those against Hiss, during Harry S Truman's presidency, amid the sharp partisan conflict of the late 1940s, when control of Congress passed from Democrats to Republicans and back again. The revisionists focused on these early postwar years as the crucial period of the Red Scare and saw McCarthyism as a tactic employed by the Republican Party when out of power to discredit the Democrats. Moreover, under the revived intellectual influence of the political left in the 1960s, these scholars also concluded that Democrats such as Truman bore a great deal of responsibility for the Red Scare. Frightened by Republican charges of being "soft" on communism, Democrats and liberals joined the Red-hunting crusade, differing with McCarthyites only over how broadly to draw the circle of suspicion and how the government should police the citizenry's political beliefs and activities. Finally, the revisionist historians of the Red Scare tended to view the left in general and even American Communists in particular more kindly than had either the liberal anticommunists or the status-anxiety scholars. The revisionists embraced an "anti-anticommunist" perspective. Many of them saw American Communism as a legitimate political movement that pursued needed reforms and combated racism and fascism. They did not view the Red Scare primarily as a crusade to ferret out traitors nor as a neurotic attack on objects of status resentment. Rather, they saw it as a calculated and wholesale attempt to repress the political left and advance the fortunes of the right, an attempt that largely succeeded during the 1950s and that the revisionists lamented.

In the 1990s, some historians attacked revisionist anti-anticommunism as, at best, naïve. These new anticommunist scholars used recently disclosed Soviet records, and U.S. government intercepts of World War II communications, to bolster their case. However, little of this recent anticommunist literature actually deals directly with the postwar Red Scare; it focuses on the earlier history of American Communism. The idea that there really had been Soviet spies in America, and that at least some elements in the Red Scare therefore were justified, was not new. It had been a mainstream view since McCarthy's day, and recent writings along these lines differ little, in their essential outlook, from the anticommunist writings of the 1950s.

The first reading in this chapter, a 1954 article by the literary critic Leslie Fiedler, expresses the liberal anticommunist view of McCarthyism, and also incorporates elements of the status-anxiety interpretation. This article was published in *Encounter,* a sophisticated journal of opinion published in Great Britain starting in 1953 by the Congress for Cultural Freedom (CCF), an organization of anticommunist intellectuals. *Encounter* was secretly funded by the U.S. Central Intelligence Agency (CIA) as a means of putting a worldly face, both liberal and anticommunist, on U.S. culture abroad. Britain, like most other Western countries, did not experience a Red Scare during the 1950s, even though a large Communist movement had existed there, and U.S. elites saw a need to explain American politics in a way that would reassure Europeans about the soundness of American leadership.

Fiedler, no doubt sincerely, depicted McCarthyism as a dangerous reaction against a real and malignant Communist presence. Fiedler saw McCarthyism as irrational, because it was a reaction to, in Fiedler's view, a past rather than a present danger. Communism had been important in the United States during the 1930s and 1940s, but was politically dead by the 1950s. In the excerpt reprinted here, he mentions the "popular front" and "fellow traveling," references to the open alliance between Communists and liberals that was forged in the 1930s. Fiedler bemoans this former alliance as a deal with the devil, one that was forged by liberal intellectuals. He portrays the Red Scare as the expression of resentment by "plain people" and their representatives, like McCarthy, against these procommunist intellectuals. Many McCarthyite targets tended to fit the role of the intellectual with an air of superiority. Examples include Hiss; the China scholar Owen Lattimore, whom McCarthy, despite having no proof, charged with spying for the Soviet Union; J. Robert Oppenheimer, the former head of the U.S. wartime atomic bomb project whose opposition to the development of the hydrogen bomb resulted in his reliability being questioned and the loss of his security clearance; and Julian Wadleigh, a State Department employee who admitted to having spied for the Soviets. Essentially, Fiedler views the struggle over McCarthyism as an early version of what observers in the 1990s would call a "culture war" between affected cosmopolitan liberals and right-wing Americans who styled themselves as the salt of the earth. He finds McCarthy dangerous, but understandable in light of the moral obtuseness of liberals concerning communism, and he shows little sympathy for the Red Scare's victims, some of whom he views as guilty of either crimes or bad politics.

The second of the three selections reproduced in this chapter, an excerpt from *No Ivory Tower*, Ellen Schrecker's 1986 study of McCarthyism in U.S. universities, effectively summarizes the revisionist case against liberals for joining in the Red Scare. Schrecker examines the practice of blacklisting, which denied employment in the private sector to those accused of insufficient fealty to the anticommunist orthodoxy. This practice prevailed in the movie and television industries, in labor unions, and in universities—places that might be thought of as strongholds of liberalism and freedom of thought. Schrecker explains how those who thought the Red Scare was dangerous and irrational nonetheless went along with it, and even helped to extend it to new areas. She views this as a betrayal of freedom by political liberals, and she places events in the universities in the context of the Truman administration's aggressive moves to advance the Red Scare, starting in the late 1940s. In Schrecker's anti-anticommunist telling of the story, American communism occupies a place of distinctly secondary importance. In her most recent work, Schrecker embraces many of the research findings of the recent anticommunist literature, but finds these not very consequential for her concerns. She maintains that the Red Scare was a cynical enterprise, one not at all justified by the work of Communists in an earlier time, one that terrified people with no connection to government work or national security, and one that did horrendous damage to American universities and intellectual life, as well as to politics and society.

The third and most recent selection, by K. A. Cuordileone, brings the newer perspectives of cultural history and gender studies to an analysis of the anticommunist crusade. Careful observers (including Fiedler) long have noted how suggestions of effeminacy, extending to what we today recognize as gross homophobic innuendo, marked the debates over communism and McCarthyism in the 1950s. Cuordileone catalogues these charges and countercharges, arguing that they tell us a good deal about the anxieties over masculine and feminine identity that many have associated with the Fifties. In a sense, this analysis returns to the framework of anxiety, even of neurosis, that shaped the status-anxiety scholarship on McCarthyism. Although Cuordileone assumes, rather than proves, that the rhetoric of masculinity and femininity reflected real and deep cultural disturbances, her discussion demonstrates that no area of American life, no matter how private and personal, was insulated from the turmoil and fear that the Red Scare generated.

LESLIE A. FIEDLER

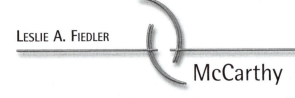

McCarthy

From the moment he rose before the Women's Republican Club of Wheeling, West Virginia, to announce that he had the names of 205 Communists in the State Department, McCarthy's history has been in the public domain. What most people know of his earlier career in the Senate: his opposition to sugar rationing and public housing; his leading, though unofficial, role in saving from their death-sentences German storm troopers convicted of shooting down 250 American and Belgian prisoners at Malmédy in 1944—all this has been reinterpreted in the light of the unbroken series of charges and counter-charges that have followed the Wheeling Lincoln's Day Address.

McCarthy on the one side; the State Department, the Democratic Party, the internationalist Republicans on the other; a threatened America between—this is . . . a melodrama played over and over with an almost mindless persistence and lack of variation, in the newspapers, over the radio, on television. But who is the hero, who the villain? Sitting in the same playhouse, two audiences see two quite different plays acted simultaneously by the same cast.

From the very first, the tone was set, half-comic, half-terrifying: the attack without warning, wild, self-contradictory, almost random; and never well documented or well prepared really, merely better prepared *for:* the press conference that announces another press conference at which the hyperbolic accusation is launched in a conspiratorial setting, as McCarthy raps a pencil against the mouthpiece of his telephone, turns on the water in the sink—he is surrounded by enemy dictaphones, he gives us to understand, spied on and harried. No matter how often the performance is repeated, the air of improvisation is never lost, the sense of one who rides the tiger, driven endlessly to defend and justify the indefensible first statement by an indefensible second, the indefensible second by a shameless diversion: "a list of 205 known to the Secretary of State as being members of the Communist Party . . . still working and shaping policy. . . ." "I do not believe I mentioned the figure 205. I believe I said 'over 200. . . .'." "I told him three times. I read the speech to him. I told him there were 57 Communists in the State Department. . . ."

We hesitate between laughter and exasperation until we realise that some are neither annoyed nor amused, that our buffoon and villain is someone else's hero, and certainly his own. . . .

Many people have deplored what they consider the excessive attention paid to McCarthy by the American press. But McCarthy apparently docs more to sell newspapers than newspapers do to sell McCarthy. In an annual poll of political reporters in Washington, McCarthy has more than once been voted the worst of the forty-eight Senators by those who do most to spread his name and fame. Between McCarthy and the press in general, there is a state of chronic feud . . . and yet he has, so far as publicity goes, the best press in the country. The very reporters who, as men, despise him, as reporters recognise in him the newsman's blessing: the story that writes itself. His statements do not have to be touched up or toned down to make good journalistic fare; McCarthy must have babbled in headlines as precociously as certain poets are said to have

From "McCarthy," by Leslie A. Fiedler, from *Encounter,* No. 11 (Aug. 1954). Reprinted with permission.

lisped in numbers. His press releases have to begin with that swollen, emotion-ridden air, that immunity to documentation, of the journalistic statement at its lowest level; and his heroic legend has been dreamed by the kind of mind to which the tabloid press habitually condescends.

But McCarthy is not his only press agent; he has also the Communist Party and some liberals, who by a simple act of inversion turn his own hyperpatriotic image into one of *their* stereotypes; and this in turn is adapted by vague anti-capitalists all over the world, who borrow whatever "facts" are useful to deprecate America. These people assume (and would like to believe) that because McCarthy bellows against Communist infiltration, this is sufficient proof that the whole idea is absurd. Like McCarthy, though for different political reasons, they are uninterested in an assessment of the truth, and prefer to keep the whole business in the realm of political mythology.

The Tydings Committee's investigation of McCarthy's original charges is a case in point. A mere glance at the documents makes clear how shifty and unreliable a witness McCarthy was, uneasily dodging from number to number, completely contemptuous of dates, and unwilling, despite boasts to the contrary, to strip himself of Senatorial immunity and take the legal consequences of his statements. But any approximately objective study of the relevant documents reveals that the investigation itself was partisan and inefficient, a mere token glance at the questions raised, and that its official report misrepresents what the Committee did, or rather failed to do. From its title page on, the Tydings report is dubious, for it claims to be a report of a whole Committee to which it was never submitted, as indeed it was not even submitted before release to the minority (Republican) members of the subcommittee actually involved. Moreover, the findings of the Tydings Committee have been falsified in discussion ever since, as they are, for instance, in a recent (and generally useful) issue of the *Progressive* devoted wholly to McCarthy, where Senator Lodge is quoted as having said that the investigations found no Communists in the State Department, but his qualification, that most of the case-material was insufficiently followed up to prove anything either way, is misleadingly omitted.

The case of Owen Lattimore and the Institute of Pacific Relations, in their relation to State Department policy, is another instance. This case, which was the first major pitched battle between McCarthy and the liberals, was a liberal disaster. Not that McCarthy was proved right—he wasn't. But the liberals were proved wrong, and have been on the defensive ever since. McCarthy did almost succeed in obscuring the facts of the Lattimore case in his attempts to re-make a waspish, party-line professor, with considerable influence among State Department policy-makers, into a "top espionage agent." But those who sprang so quickly to Lattimore's defence on the simple grounds that, being accused by McCarthy, he *must* be blameless (this might be called the theory of "innocence by association") had to writhe with him as he tried, before the McCarran Committee, to explain in what sense he thought the Moscow Trials a higher form of justice, or why, after he had authoritatively informed the American ambassador in Moscow that Outer Mongolia was a state completely independent of Russia, he applied for a travel visa to that country at the Russian Foreign Office.

To write off the whole desire to learn of the role of Communist influence in shaping American policy in China as a bugaboo scared up by the "China Lobby" is as facile and wrong as interpreting that policy as the fabrication of disloyal or suborned officials. The notion of the Chinese Communists as "agrarian reformers" was merely a particular development of a general liberal willingness to see the better side of Communism even where it did not exist. To label that impulse harmless is to the advantage only of the Communists; to indict it as utterly treacherous is only to McCarthy's advantage; but to see it in all its ambiguity is to the advantage of those whose first allegiance is to the truth.

We must, I am convinced, see this ambiguity or become its victims. I do not mean, of course, that we must moderate our fight against McCarthyism in an excess of scrupulosity; merely that we must understand what it is that we are fighting, so we do not waste our energy in stalking the enemy where he is not. It is better, I am sure, to fight windmills than not to fight; but where there are real monsters it is a pity to waste one's blows on windmills. Even the rallying cry which seems superficially most sound, the contention that McCarthyism has by its methods created an atmosphere of suspicion, a stifling pressure of conformity, is only one piece of a double truth.

It can be asserted with almost equal justice that there is nothing easier in America at the present moment than speaking ill of McCarthy. In academic circles, for instance, particularly in the East, it is generally the pro-McCarthy position which occasions resentment and even ostracism; while in the country's major newspapers, and on the chief radio networks, the majority opinion, quite openly expressed, is unfavourable to the Senator from Wisconsin. For intellectual respectability (and one can understand "intellectual" in its broadest possible scope), it is *de rigueur* that one consider McCarthyism a major threat to liberty. I doubt that there has ever been gathered together a broader or more articulate united front than the one which opposes the behaviour of the present Chairman of the Permanent Sub-Committee on Investigations. Aside from the Communists and their more intimate friends (actually well aware that it is to their best interests that McCarthy continue to spread confusion), this front includes socialists and libertarians, Old Guard and New Deal Democrats, leading spokesmen for Jewish, Protestant, and liberal Catholic groups, and a strong representation of Republicans, including apparently the President and Vice-President of the United States.

It need hardly be said that such a group has little trouble in making itself heard; the daily press and the radio is open to its statements; its books are prominently and favourably reviewed; whereas the partisans of McCarthy find a certain resistance not easy to overcome. McCarthy is notoriously well covered by day-to-day reporting, to be sure, but I do not find in the Book Review Index, for instance, a single notice of his book, *The Fight Against Communism;* and a recent book favourable to McCarthy (*McCarthy and His Enemies* by W. F. Buckley and L. Brent Bozell) has received universally hostile comment. It is instructive, in this regard, to look through the additional material included in the Appendix to the *Congressional Record,* in which the opponents of McCarthy are able to quote from the leading newspapers of his own state, and from journals ranging from the Social Democratic *New Leader* to the Jesuit *America* and the Republican *Time,* while he and his friends can supplement the Hearst and McCormick press only with excerpts from the scarcely literate editorials of back-country weeklies.

And yet the statement made in article after article by the attackers of McCarthy, a statement repeated by commentators and re-echoed by commentators on the commentators, is that McCarthyism threatens, if it does not actually bludgeon into silence, all free criticism. From one end of the country to another rings the cry, "I am cowed! I am afraid to speak out!" and the even louder response, "Look, he is cowed! He is afraid to speak out!" In my own town, where it proved almost impossible to turn up a pro-McCarthy speaker for a recent forum, and where no library contains a copy of McCarthy's book, though Lattimore's version of his story is available, I have been told over and over that there is "something" now in the air which makes one swallow unsaid what once might have been spoken without a second thought.

One is tempted to laugh at first, to find only comedy in this constant frightened twittering back and forth among people who are in almost universal agreement. And yet—and yet, it was only with difficulty that I refrained from adding a parenthesis to the last sentence of the preceding paragraph, reading: "needless to say, our librarians are far from being Communists." The "needless to say" would have been a sop; there was some nagging fear in my mind that a careless reference, under the circumstances, might get the unimpeachable guardians of our books into trouble. I am convinced that the intellectual community has been an accomplice in creating this situation of fear; but it has been an accomplice after the fact. There *have* been some reprisals against the holders of ideas unpopular with McCarthy: a handful of nervous regents have dropped instructors in a few universities and colleges; in the public school system, there has been an occasional firing; sponsors on the radio have been particularly jittery; and in certain government agencies there has been a real terror, as McCarthyism has combined with the standard vagaries of bureaucratic administration and the usual rumour-mongering of bureaucratic underlings.

I would suggest that the loud fears of the intellectuals, in so far as they are more than a tic of anxiety, are based on the suspicion that McCarthy represents not merely himself, his own ambition and chicanery, but a substantial popular hostility, immune to argument and logical proof, to much of what the intellectual community stands for. Certainly, it was disconcerting to discover not many months back that the majority of the American people were favourably disposed towards McCarthy, despite the fact that the larger part of their semiofficial spokesmen were bitterly opposed to him. In a certain sense, McCarthyism not only flourishes in, but *is*, this hostility between the community and its intelligence.

The forces which McCarthy really represents (I mean his mass support, not the Texas millionaires of whom so much is made; anyone who persists in politics in America, whether he be right or left or centre, can get himself a millionaire or two) find their expression in the resolutely anti-intellectual small-town weeklies and in the professionally reactionary press, which continue to say in his name precisely what they have been saying now for thirty-five years. To realise this is to understand that McCarthyism, generally speaking, is an extension of the ambiguous American impulse towards "direct democracy," with its distrust of authority, institutions, and expert knowledge; and that more precisely, it is the form which populist theory takes when forced to define itself against such a competing "European" radicalism as Communism. McCarthy is a new voice for these forces; though scarcely a different one. The astonishing thing about McCarthy is his closeness to a standard kind of mid-western political figure, usually harmless and often comical. What defies analysis is the aura of fear which surrounds him and which cannot be justified in terms of what he is as a person. . . .

There has always been a greater or lesser split in the United States between the Ordinary Voter and the Man Seriously Interested in Politics; and this difference was exaggerated and specially defined in the years between the triumph of the Russian Revolution and the Great Depression. Unlike Western Europe, where a gradually Marxist-influenced working-class and intelligentsia have found a way of neutralising old tensions in finding common attitudes towards the Soviet Union, in America the influence of Marxism, however remote, has served only to separate the intellectuals decisively from the mass of people.

The intellectuals, including brighter college students, newspaper reporters, lawyers, and professional people, as well as artists and political theorists, had—during the 1930's—as a typical initiation into the intellectual community (the case of Robert Oppenheimer, recently much bruited, is a classic instance) a brief bout of fellow-travelling, or, at least, the experience of collaboration and friendly intercourse with Communists and fellow-travellers. Communists and liberals seemed once to be bound together, not only by a passionate revulsion from war and the inequities of capitalism, but more positively, too, by certain tastes in books and in the arts, by shared manners and vocabulary—and especially by the sense of moral engagement that used to be called "social consciousness." From this feeling of fellowship, the great Popular Front organisations of the 1930's were forged; in the teeth, as it were, of the ordinary voter, who—immune to all this—identified not only the Communists but their most distant friends with free love, looting, and general iniquity; and who were condescended to majestically by the enlightened, thus storing up a special resentment for the hour of disillusion.

From the time of the Sacco and Vanzetti Case—that is to say, from 1927—until 1946, it seemed that America had chosen sides in a bloodless civil war. To the liberal-intellectual, "We" consisted of the supporters of trade-unionism, social security, and the rights of Negroes, Jews, and other minorities, including socialists and even Communists ("rude but on our side"); while "They" were constituted of Red-baiters, readers of the Hearst press, supporters of Franco, and, *ad libitum,* members of the Catholic hierarchy, William Green and the AFL, Southern Senators, football players, American Legionnaires, etc. The questioning by McCarthy of Reed Harris, Deputy Administrator of the International Information Administration, illustrates the difficulties such a conventional categorising can occasion years later. Despite his record of loyal and excellent service in government, Harris was quizzed at length over a book he had written when just out of college, called *King Football;* and the McCarthy Committee thought it worth while to quote, as a presumable example of "disloyalty," Harris' identification of someone as "a sadistic butcher who is now probably the commander of some American Legion Post." The complicated innocence of such a remark made in the 1930's is almost impossible to explain to an American veteran who is very proud of his membership in the Legion.

I do not want to seem to exaggerate the Communist influence on American life; in a political sense, the movement was a failure in the United States, for it never appealed to any large number of the workers and poorer farmers to whom it presumably spoke most directly. Indeed, it never won even the total allegiance, much less the actual adherence, of the intellectuals. But it *did* manage to establish itself in the intellectual community as an acceptable variant of the liberal-humanistic tradition—and even more, made its recognition as such a variant the very test of political decency. This confusion not only enabled such Party members as Hiss to regard their activities as the expression of a higher loyalty to "Humanity," but even made it possible for others like Julian Wadleigh, too "liberal" to join the Party, to commit espionage for the Soviet Union. And it has bequeathed to us the bewildering concept of an undefinable "left," which obscures for us the actualities of the political situation.

Indeed, the childish division of the world into good and evil was never really politics in a practical sense, but the translation of social and economic problems into ethical melodrama. Yet, for a while, when the free world and Russia were allies against the Nazis, even history itself seemed to connive in the illusion. The war against Hitlerism added to "our side" (i.e. the liberals' side) the glow of war-time solidarity and even the patriotic slogans hitherto usurped by the "other side." But even without a Hitler, the desire to make virtue depend, not so much on what one did as on what one was, would have triumphed; and the temptation to simplify international conflict into the confrontation of sheer wrong and simple right could not have been resisted.

The liberal-internationalists found justification for their self-righteousness in the knowledge that they were immune to platitudes and conventional rhetoric; that they were more intelligent, read better books, liked superior music and pictures, could use the vocabularies of advanced thought. Certainly, intelligence in itself is an advantage, and the majority of the intelligent were on the liberal side: but intelligence is not synonymous with virtue nor is it a specific against either political error or malice. The intelligent do not make the same mistakes as others, or at least they do not make them for the same reasons; but even when they are buttressed with goodwill, they do err. And they were wrong, drastically wrong, about the most important political fact of our time.

It is true that McCarthy himself has revealed no dangerous hidden Communists; has proved little beyond the foolishness and uncertainty of many who have appeared before his Committee. But insofar as he is the personification of a long-inarticulate movement, of the sullen self-consciousness of a sizeable minority (at least), he *begins* with a victory that he cannot fritter away, no matter how many errors he makes or how many downright lies he tells.

The emergence of McCarthy . . . in Wisconsin is a clue to what he represents. He inherits the bitterest and most provincial aspects of a Populism to which smooth talking has always meant the Big City; and the Big City, the Enemy. Traditionally, that Enemy has been identified with "Wall Street," but from the middle twenties on there has been a tendency to give an equal status to "internationalism" and "international Communism." It was not until 1950, however, that McCarthy discovered a symbolic butt in "the State Department Communist," "the Park Avenue Pinko," capable of welding together the fractured Populist image of the Enemy. In light of this, it is just as important that McCarthy's initial attack was directed against the State Department under Acheson (and against Harvard behind him) as that it was directed against the Communists. Acheson is the projection of all the hostilities of the mid-Western mind at bay: his waxed moustache, his cultivated accent, his personal loyalty to a traitor who also belonged to the Harvard Club; one is never quite sure that he was not invented by a pro-McCarthy cartoonist.

With something like genius, McCarthy added the connotation of wealth and effete culture to treachery, topping it all off with the suggestion of homosexuality. His constant sneering references to "State Department perverts" are not explained by his official view that such unfortunates are subject to blackmail, but represent his sure sense of the only other unforgivable sin besides being a Communist. The definition of the Enemy is complete; opposite in all respects to the Ideal American, who is simple, straightforward, ungrammatical, loyal, and one hundred percent male. Such an Enemy need not be proven guilty; he is guilty by definition.

But the Enemy for McCarthy is not only a dandy, a "queer," an intellectual, and a Communist; he is, or was at least in the beginning, a Democrat or Democrat's friend. The struggle between the liberal intellectual and the old-line "red-baiter" has been absurdly confused with the contest for votes between the Democratic and Republican Parties. This seems, in part, clearly accidental. McCarthy himself was for a while a Democrat (and Mr. Roy Cohn still proudly declares himself one); and, at the start, his charges were taken up largely as ammunition to be used against the Ins, who happened to be Democrats, by the Outs, who happened to be Republicans. It was possible at first to believe that there was no anti-Communist conviction at all behind McCarthy's campaign against the State Department, merely a desire to slander his opponents and advance the fortunes of his own party; but one senses in him the happy coincidence of conviction and strategy.

Does the Republican Party have any right to claim the mantle of anti-Communism as its own? Certainly, there have been leading "red-baiters" in both parties, and dupes of the Communists in both, too. Yet it is true that the Democratic Party had become in the early days of the New Deal, not liberal perhaps, but certainly liberal-coloured; finding a place in its ranks, somewhere between the big city bosses and the Southern reactionaries, for fellow-travelling professors, left-wing C.I.O. trade-unionists, and especially for a new kind of practical politician who had learned to adapt the vocabulary and attitudes of the true liberal to his own constant opportunism. Roosevelt himself was a representative of this heterogeneous group, and his own approach to the Soviet Union was deeply conditioned by the stereotypes and conventional allegiances of the liberal, at a point when the liberals were most victimised by illusions about the Soviet Union.

The Roosevelt Administration pushed safeguards for labour and provisions for social security to the verge of what Republican conservatives like to call "The Welfare State"; and though these latter can, of course, not undo such measures, they can deplore them—or condemn the "philosophy" behind them: which is to say, they can call liberal-coloured improvisation a philosophy, and name it "creeping socialism." The spokesmen for this ideological opposition to the New Deal were tempted to use the exposure of real or alleged Communists in the Roosevelt bureaucracy as objective proof of a kinship of ideas between left-wing Democrats and Bolsheviks. And they found in the jittery and uninformed reactions of men like Truman more fuel than they had hoped for. Fearful that granting any truth to the Republican charges might lose them votes, the Democrats arrayed themselves in strict party lines, and put themselves in the absurd position of denying Chambers' allegations about Hiss as a "red herring." The way was open for McCarthy to make the whole New Deal seem nothing but a cover-up for Communist infiltration and espionage. It would, of course, be absurd to accuse the Democrats of any real desire to assist Communists; but they did often choose to deny what they knew to be true, in the interests of vote-getting.

It was a strange and embarrassing opportunity for the Republicans, who found themselves on the popular side of an issue for the first time since 1932. Anti-Communism in America has always been strongest among farmers, industrial workers (where there is a strong Catholic influence), and the lowest level of the middle class. The votes which clinched McCarthy's first Senatorial victory came not only from the wealthier Catholic farmers of Wisconsin, but from the working-class districts of Kenosha, Racine, and Milwaukee, ordinarily considered safe for the Democrats. And once McCarthy had brought into the open a problem which opposed to "the People," not the "Economic Royalists," but the "Intellectuals," a new kind of Republican was needed to assume leadership. This Senator Taft appears to have seen; and perhaps he knew all along that though he was called "Mr. Republican," he could not himself have made the populist appeal; certainly, in this light his otherwise inexplicable support of McCarthy, his willingness to tout him in speeches dedicated to "political morality," makes a kind of sense.

If there is a blackness in McCarthy, it is not the reactionary blackness of the oil interests or of the Catholic hierarchy, but of something in the American people which distrusts equally "red tape" and "reds," which grows impatient with law and order, with understanding and polite talk, when it feels it has been betrayed. The fight against McCarthyism must be carried on, but those who wage it must be aware that they are faced with a situation in which a widespread moral indignation against Communists and their sympathisers has far outstripped the community's legal procedures for dealing with them.

ELLEN SCHRECKER

McCarthyism and the Universities

By February 3, 1960, Joseph R. McCarthy had been dead for nearly three years, and the movement that had received his name was presumably over. But not for Chandler Davis. On that day, Davis, a former instructor of mathematics from the University of Michigan, ended a six-year struggle against McCarthyism, said good-bye to his family, and surrendered to a fed-eral marshal in Grand Rapids to begin serving a six-month prison term. Davis's crime had occurred on May 10, 1954, when he refused to tell the House Un-American Activities Committee (HUAC) whether or not he had ever been a Communist. Davis challenged the com-mittee, insisting that its questions about his politics infringed upon his freedom of speech and, as he put it, overstepped "the bounds placed on Congress by the First Amendment." He knew that he would probably lose his job and be convicted for contempt of Congress, but he hoped that the Supreme Court would eventually exonerate him. Instead, on June 8, 1959, the Court in effect ruled against him in the similar case of Lloyd Barenblatt, another former college teacher who had also defied HUAC on First Amendment grounds. The 5 to 4 decision affirmed that the committee did not violate its witnesses' constitutional rights by asking them about their rela-tionship with the Communist Party (CP). That ruling sent both Barenblatt and Davis, whose case was determined by Barenblatt's, to Danbury Federal Penitentiary.

These two academics went to prison because, as Justice John Marshall Harlan stated for the majority in the *Barenblatt* decision, the Supreme Court "has consistently refused to view the Communist Party as an ordinary political party" and has let the government behave in ways that "in a different context would certainly have raised constitutional issues of the gravest character." Thus, even as late as 1959, almost five years after the Senate censured Joseph McCarthy, the Supreme Court could still cite the Cold War as an excuse for depriving American Communists and suspected Communists, like Davis and Barenblatt, of their constitutional rights. In this, of course, the Court was only echoing the anti-Communist consensus that swept the country in the late 1940s and 1950s, a consensus that viewed the American Communist Party as one of the gravest threats to its security the United States had ever faced.

In retrospect, it now appears that this assessment was wrong. Whatever perils the Cold War might have brought on the international level, the danger that a few thousand American Communists, acting on secret instructions from Moscow, were about to take over the United States was not one of them. And yet, so pervasive was the image of the Party as a lethal foreign conspiracy and so useful was that image as a way to cope with the uncertainties of the new atomic age that few American leaders could or would accept a more realistic assessment. The onset of the Cold War had shocked and confused them. . . . The Communist coup in Czechoslovakia in the spring of 1948 touched off a frightening war scare, intensified a few months later by the Berlin blockade. Then, the following year came the news that the Soviets had detonated an atomic bomb. A few months later, China "fell" to the Communists.

To give the American Communist Party any credit for these revolutionary changes was ridiculous. Even during its supposed heyday in the 1930s the CP had been neither numerous nor popular. Yet the logic of politics demanded that the Truman administration, which had committed itself to combatting the spread of Communism abroad, confront it at home as well. The Republican party, its own anti-Communist credentials never in doubt, was ready to pounce on any indication of laxity. Accordingly, both Democrats and Republicans threw themselves into the domestic Cold War against the American CP. Local Communists suddenly became potential Soviet agents, who, if they were not about to take over the government, could nonethe-less subvert it in more subtle ways or, at least, send vital secrets back to Moscow. Each politician had his own assessment of the extent of this conspiracy and his own formula for fighting it. But almost everybody agreed that the danger was immense. If nothing else, the nation's security demanded that there be no reds in the government.

Truman was already under considerable pressure from the Republican-controlled 80th Congress when, on March 22, 1947, he issued Executive Order 9835 establishing a new loyalty-security program for federal employees. Since the security measures already in place had largely eliminated most Communists and other dissidents from sensitive positions, the new program was superfluous, except as a political gesture. Its real function was to protect the Democratic administration from the Republican party. It failed. It did, however, succeed in establishing anti-Communism as the nation's official ideology, and, several years before Senator Joseph McCarthy entered the scene, it laid the foundations for the movement we now call McCarthyism. Until then anti-Communism had been a haphazard crusade, the province of right-wing ideologues and embittered former reds. The CP was unpopular, of course, but opposition to it had not yet become central to the nation's politics. When in 1947 Truman promulgated Executive Order 9835 and created a loyalty-security system, he legitimized, as only a President could, the project of eradicating Communism from American life.

No other event, no political trial or congressional hearing, was to shape the internal Cold War as decisively as the Truman administration's loyalty-security program. It authorized the economic sanctions that were crucial to the success of McCarthyism. Communists and suspected Communists could now be fired from their jobs. Other institutions followed and they, too, began to examine their employees' politics. Within a few years, this process had spread far beyond the Potomac; political tests were being used to screen individuals for almost everything from jobs and passports to insurance policies and fishing licenses. In addition, because the federal government's loyalty-security program borrowed so many of its procedures and ideas from traditional right-wing anti-Communism, it was administered in a disturbingly reactionary manner. Other employers copied this aspect of the program as well.

Executive Order 9835 not only barred Communists, fascists, and other totalitarians from the federal payroll, it also excluded anybody guilty of "sympathetic association" with such undesirables or their organizations. Every federal employee had to be checked out, usually by the FBI or a similar investigatory organization. People with "derogatory information" in their files then had to clear themselves. Despite the existence of some individual safeguards, abuses flourished. "Sympathetic association" was hardly a precise tool for separating the pinks from the reds. Nor was the list of potentially subversive organizations that the Executive Order authorized the Attorney General to compile any more meticulous. It included the Communist Party, of course, but it also cited many already defunct left-wing groups in which both Communists and non-Communists had been active in the 1930s and 1940s. In addition, because the FBI, which handled most of the investigative work, insisted that it would not be effective if it had to reveal the identity of its informers, anonymous accusations could cost people their jobs. The program had its critics; Truman himself deplored its injustices. But, once in place, its flaws were not corrected. And in fact, as political pressures increased, first the Truman and then the Eisenhower administration were to revise the loyalty program to make it easier to discharge undesirable employees.

As the 1948 election approached, the Truman administration took other steps to prove its devotion to the anti-Communist cause. The third-party campaign of former Vice President Henry Wallace, who had broken with the administration over its hard-line policy toward the Soviet Union, gave the Democrats a perfect opportunity to distance themselves from the left.

Since the Communist Party supported Wallace, it was easy for Truman and his allies to accuse Wallace of being its tool. Such attacks not only diverted attention from Truman's own alleged softness on Communism, but, by so thoroughly identifying Wallace's rather mild critique of the Cold War with the hated CP, they also eliminated all effective domestic opposition to American foreign policy. This was probably not what the liberals who led the assault on Wallace intended. They did not think that they were McCarthyites, but because their red-baiting narrowed American politics by excommunicating its left, they inadvertently fostered the furor to come.

Perhaps the most obvious indication of the Truman administration's conversion to a tough anti-Communist position was its decision in the summer of 1948 to prosecute the top leaders of the American Communist Party under the Smith Act, an infrequently used 1940 statute that made it illegal to "teach and advocate the overthrow and destruction of the Government of the United States by force and violence." Putting the Party's top brass on trial served several functions. It crippled the CP, first by forcing it to divert its energies to self-defense, and then by jailing its leaders. Even more important, the Smith Act trial gave the government a way to publicize the menace of Communism. The prosecution put the Party's ideology on trial and sought to show that Communist theory, as contained in the writings of Marx, Engels, Lenin, and Stalin, committed the CP to force and violence. Instead of arguing that the Truman administration had no right to prosecute them because the Smith Act violated their First Amendment right of free speech, Party General Secretary Eugene Dennis and the other Communist leaders accepted the battle on the government's terms and tried to refute the prosecution quote for quote. They lost; the ex-Communists and undercover agents who were the government's main witnesses had little trouble convincing the jury that Dennis and his colleagues were violent revolutionaries. A few years later, the Supreme Court upheld that verdict by a 5 to 2 margin, thus giving the Constitution's blessing to the government's purge of American Communists.

By the summer of 1951, when the Supreme Court rendered its decision in the *Dennis* case, the McCarthyist furor was at its height. It had grown slowly since the late forties, the product of an interaction between the insecurities of the Cold War and the Republican party's essentially partisan attempt to exploit those insecurities. The international crises of the late forties had been deeply unsettling. By the time the Soviet Union got its bomb and the United States "lost" China, it seemed as if Communism was unstoppable. Of course, China had never been an American possession, nor was the secret of nuclear fission an American monopoly. But from the perspective of an edgy public, worried about America's apparently slipping primacy in a dangerous world, each of these crises seemed increasingly more frightening and more difficult to understand. The Communist invasion of South Korea in June 1950 confirmed everyone's worst fears.

The Republican right offered an explanation. America had been betrayed by a worldwide Communist conspiracy. Stalin's agents had penetrated the Democratic administration and subverted the nation's foreign policy; Soviet sympathizers elsewhere had filched the secret of the bomb. Since there *had* been Russian spies, the slight core of truth in this scenario made it all the more attractive to the GOP. This was especially the case after Truman's surprise victory in the 1948 presidential election revealed that the Democrats were relatively invulnerable with regard to traditional domestic issues. Accordingly, the Republican party, looking for a way to recoup its electoral fortunes, began to attack the Truman administration as "soft" on Communism. By claiming that the Democrats had condoned Soviet subversion, the conservatives in the GOP could mount an assault on the New Deal, which they could not do on social or economic grounds. Moreover, since Truman had already enlisted the government in the anti-Communist crusade, he was in a poor position to rebuff the Republicans' claim that they were simply trying to help him clean house.

Most of this housecleaning took place at congressional hearings. Legislative investigations gave the conservatives a perfect arena for their campaign against the New Deal and its supposed sympathy for Communist subversion. To begin with, as congressmen constitutionally immune from lawsuits, they could make accusations without having to worry about being sued for libel. In addition, since legislative investigations were not judicial proceedings, these politicians could use witnesses whose testimony did not have to stand up in court. Best of all, committee hearings created headlines. American politics had never offered a more dramatic spectacle than the confrontation between the investigators and their witnesses, especially when those witnesses pulled microfilms out of pumpkins and talked of false names, clandestine meetings, secret passwords, and the arcane workings of a shadowy underworld peopled by Soviet agents and urbane upper-class spies. Once the rise of Richard Nixon showed how a smart politician could parlay his berth on an investigating committee into the Vice Presidency, congressmen clamored for such positions. In 1952, 185 of the 221 Republicans in Congress applied for seats on the House Un-American Activities Committee, an unpopular assignment only a few years before. . . .

In charging that the Truman administration was harboring some 57—later 205, 81, 10, or 116—Communist agents within the State Department, the junior senator from Wisconsin was only doing, albeit more flamboyantly, what many other reactionary politicians had done before. Even his charges were old-hat; they had been circulating for years within the network of professional anti-Communists who proffered their expertise to individuals and institutions eager to eliminate subversives. McCarthy's first round of attacks, like those on the eminent Johns Hopkins University China expert Owen Lattimore, were related to the GOP's contention that the Truman administration had betrayed China to Mao Zedong. As a result, McCarthy received the tacit support of the more respectable leaders of the Republican party, who welcomed the damage that their disreputable colleague was inflicting on the incumbent Democrats. The outbreak of the Korean war in June, 1950, gave McCarthy's charges added saliency; the electoral defeat of some of his main critics in the fall only increased his clout. Within a few years, McCarthy's erratic campaign against the Army ended his political career. Because he was so uniquely pathological, it is easy to forget how much McCarthy resembled the other right-wing politicians who also used the issue of Communism as a way to further their own fortunes and those of their party. After all, what made McCarthy a McCarthyite was not his bluster but his anti-Communist mission, one which, in one way or another, almost every American political leader claimed to support.

McCarthy never found any subversives. Most of the men and women he denounced were perfectly loyal, though politically unpopular, American citizens. So, too, were most of the witnesses who appeared before the other anti-Communist investigators of the period. These people were not, however, selected at random. Almost all of them had once been in or near the Communist Party. Except for a handful of people like Owen Lattimore, there were few "innocent liberals." This was crucial. McCarthyism succeeded because the people it targeted were already political outcasts. They were Communists or ex-Communists. And, by the late forties and early fifties, the Truman administration, the Supreme Court, and most private citizens believed or claimed to believe that Communism was so alien to the American way of life that its adherents did not deserve to be protected by the Constitution. Many decent people deplored the excesses of McCarthyism; they just did not think that punishing Communists was excessive. Those who did, though they fought valiantly for the rights of individuals, did so in vain.

Moreover, once the political establishment legitimated the denial of civil rights to members of the Communist Party, it was relatively easy for the more reactionary practitioners of anti-Communism to extend that denial to yet other types of political undesirables by claiming that those people also served the Party's cause.

McCarthyism was amazingly effective. It produced one of the most severe episodes of political repression the United States ever experienced. It was a peculiarly American style of repression—nonviolent and consensual. Only two people were killed; only a few hundred went to jail. Its mildness may well have contributed to its efficacy. So, too, did its structure. Here, it helps to view McCarthyism as a process rather than a movement. It took place in two stages. First, the objectionable groups and individuals were identified—during a committee hearing, for example, or an FBI investigation; then, they were punished, usually by being fired. The bifurcated nature of this process diffused responsibility and made it easier for each participant to dissociate his or her action from the larger whole. Rarely did any single institution handle both stages of McCarthyism. In most cases, it was a government agency which identified the culprits and a private employer which fired them.

We know the most about the first stage of McCarthyism, for it received the most attention at the time. Yet the second stage is just as important. For without the almost automatic imposition of sanctions on the people who had been identified as politically undesirable, the whole anti-Communist crusade would have crumbled. In a sense, it was this second stage that legitimated the first. Had HUAC's targets been able to survive their encounters with the committee without losing their jobs, the committee would have lost its mandate. This did not happen. On the contrary, private employers often rushed to impose sanctions on these men and women, sometimes without waiting for the official machinery to run its course. The fate of the Hollywood Ten is illustrative here. When these radical screen-writers and directors refused to cooperate with HUAC in October, 1947, it was not clear which side had won, the witnesses or the committee. The movie studios' decision to fire the Ten before either the judiciary or public opinion had delivered a verdict may well have influenced that outcome as significantly as the Supreme Court's later refusal to review their conviction for contempt. Other employers followed the studios' example. By the time the investigative furor that characterized the first stage of McCarthyism abated in the late fifties, thousands of people had lost their jobs. And thousands more, whether realistically or not, feared similar reprisals and curtailed their political activities.

Every segment of society was involved. From General Motors, General Electric, and CBS to the *New York Times,* the New York City Board of Education, and the United Auto Workers, there were few, very few, public or private employers who did not fire the men and women who had been identified during a first-stage investigation. The academic community went along as well and dismissed those of its members McCarthy, HUAC, and the FBI had nominated for such treatment. There were quite a good number of these people, for the nation's faculties housed hundreds of men and women whom official and unofficial red-hunters were to single out as undesirable. Exact figures are hard to come by, but it may well be that almost 20 percent of the witnesses called before congressional and state investigating committees were college teachers or graduate students. Most of those academic witnesses who did not clear themselves with the committees lost their jobs.

Chandler Davis, the young mathematician who went to prison for defying HUAC, was no exception. A few months after he appeared before the committee, the University of Michigan fired him. He was not, however, dismissed without a hearing. Although Davis lacked tenure, the Michigan administration was sufficiently concerned about academic freedom to draw up formal charges against him and convene a faculty committee to hear his case. Actually, Michigan's authorities were so punctilious that Davis received three separate hearings before he was finally dismissed. His experiences were not unique. Unfriendly witnesses at other schools had similar trials. While these elaborate proceedings did not, in the end, protect many people, they did produce thousands of pages of testimony. An ironic legacy, these records contain what well may be the most comprehensive, cogently argued, and carefully thought-out defense of McCarthyism available. They also show how the academy, an institution ostensibly dedicated to intellectual freedom, collaborated in curtailing that freedom.

At no point did the college teachers, administrators, and trustees who cooperated with McCarthyism by evicting unfriendly witnesses and other suspected Communists from their faculties admit that they were repressing dissent. On the contrary, in their public statements and in the documentary record that they produced, they often claimed that they were standing up to McCarthyism and defending free speech and academic freedom. It is important, therefore, to go beyond the rhetoric of the period and examine what these people were doing rather than what they were saying. They said that they were opposing Senator McCarthy and the more rabid red-baiters of the period. Yet, when given an opportunity to transform that opposition into something more concrete than words, almost all of these essentially liberal academics faltered. Either they participated in and condoned the dismissals or else, when they opposed them, did so in such a limited fashion that they must have known they would not succeed.

It is important to identify the players here. Since there are only a handful of instances in which an academic institution itself instigated these dismissals, it is clear that the nation's colleges and universities would not have purged their left-wing faculty members during the McCarthy era without pressure from outside. It is also clear that not every group within the academic community had equal responsibility for those purges. . . . Administrators and faculty members. . .were the men and women who had made a full-time, life-time commitment to the academy. Though they lacked the formal authority of the trustees they nonetheless exercised considerable power and could have, had they wanted to, prevented much of what happened. That they did not is the most interesting aspect of the academy's response to McCarthyism. . . .

The extraordinary facility with which the academic establishment accommodated itself to the demands of the state may well be the most significant aspect of the academy's response to McCarthyism. It was the government, not some fringe group of right-wing fanatics, which initiated the movement to eliminate Communism from American life. It administered the first stage of McCarthyism, acting through the agency of investigating committees and the FBI to identify political undesirables on campus. It let the universities handle the second stage and get rid of the targeted individuals. . . .

The academy did not fight McCarthyism. It contributed to it. The dismissals, the blacklists, and above all the almost universal acceptance of the legitimacy of what the congressional committees and other official investigators were doing conferred respectability upon the most repressive elements of the anti-Communist crusade. In its collaboration with McCarthyism, the academic community behaved just like every other major institution in American life. Such a discovery is demoralizing, for the nation's colleges and universities have traditionally encouraged higher expectations. Here, if anywhere, there should have been a rational assessment of the nature of American Communism and a refusal to overreact to the demands for its eradication. Here, if anywhere, dissent should have found a sanctuary. Yet it did not. Instead, for almost a decade until the civil rights movement and the Vietnam war inspired a new wave of activism, there was no real challenge to political orthodoxy on the nation's campuses. The academy's enforcement of McCarthyism had silenced an entire generation of radical intellectuals and snuffed out all meaningful opposition to the official version of the Cold War. When, by the late fifties, the hearings and dismissals tapered off, it was not because they encountered resistance but because they were no longer necessary. All was quiet on the academic front.

K. A. CUORDILEONE

Cold War Political Culture and the Crisis in American Masculinity

If the male homosexual became a sexual bogeyman by the early 1950s, it is perhaps no coincidence that he also became a threat to national security. . . . [F]ear of homosexuality surfaced in the political arena in an unprecedented fashion. When Undersecretary of State John Puerifoy revealed in 1950 that most of the ninety-one employees recently dismissed from the State Department were homosexuals, politicians expressed alarm at what had long been rumored about the diplomatic corps but never so publicly confirmed. Conservatives quickly turned the issue to their advantage. GOP party chairman Guy Gabrielson circulated a letter to thousands of party members saying that "sexual perverts . . . have infiltrated our government" and were "perhaps as dangerous as the actual Communists." He spoke of the new "homosexual angle" in Washington and advised Republicans to express their outrage, especially since "decency" prevented the media from discussing the matter too openly. The Republican floor leader in the Senate, Kenneth Wherry, called for a full inquiry into the presence of homosexuals in government.

The result was to unleash . . . the image of the "homosexual menace." That image rested on the notion that homosexuals were by definition morally bankrupt and, as such, politically suspect. As Wherry explained to the *New York Post's* Max Lerner in 1950, "you can't hardly separate homosexuals from subversives. Mind you, I don't say every homosexual is a subversive, and I don't say every subversive is a homosexual. But a man of low morality is a menace in the government, whatever he is, and they are all tied up together." The senator also claimed that Joseph Stalin had obtained Adolf Hitler's "world list" of homosexuals who could be enlisted for the purposes of subversion. Thus Wherry's call for measures to secure "seaports and major cities against sabotage through [a] conspiracy of subversives and moral perverts in government establishments."

The outcome of the Senate investigation was the report *Employment of Homosexuals and Other Sex Perverts in Government.* The report's operative assumption was that "those who engage in overt acts of perversion lack the emotional stability of normal persons." Because their "moral

From " 'Politics in an Age of Anxiety': Cold War Political Culture and the Crisis in American Masculinity, 1949–1960," by K. A. Cuordileone, from the *Journal of American History,* Vol. 82 (Sept. 2000). Copyright © Organization of American Historians. Reprinted with permission.

fiber" had allegedly been weakened by sexual indulgence and because they were compromised by a socially unacceptable affliction that left them vulnerable to extortion, the report deemed homosexuals blackmail-prone and thus national security risks. Echoing Kinsey's observation that the outward appearance of homosexuals did not always correspond to the stereotype of the effete male, the report called for more rigorous efforts to detect and remove homosexuals in government.

McCarthy, for one, understood all too well the utility of the homosexuality issue, hence his "Communist and queer" epithets. When questions arose about his list of Communists who had allegedly infiltrated the State Department, McCarthy, lacking evidence, fell back on a guilt-by-association strategy and stressed to his Senate colleagues that a few cases involved homosexuality and revealed the "unusual mental aberrations of certain individuals in the department," citing "one of our top intelligence men" who believed that practically every Communist is "twisted mentally or physically in some way." McCarthy continued thereafter to employ the image of the homosexual menace to bolster his charge of twenty years of treason.

Other conservatives used the homosexuality issue to put Democrats on the run. Thomas Dewey blamed the Truman administration for tolerating sex offenders in government. The excitable *New York Daily News* considered homosexual subversion the "primary issue" of the 1950 congressional race: "The foreign policy of the U.S., even before World War II, was dominated by an all-powerful, super-secret, inner circle of highly educated, socially highly placed sexual misfits in the State Department, all easy to blackmail, all susceptible to blandishments by homosexuals in foreign nations." When Rev. Billy Graham praised the patriots who were "exposing the pinks, the lavenders, and the reds who have sought refuge beneath the wings of the American Eagle," liberals, homosexuals, and Communists had been linked by virtue of their common moral weaknesses. To the far right, the pink-lavender-red trinity was inseparable from its affluent breeding grounds: the eastern establishment, the Ivy League, and the State Department.

For some observers, such associations may have been suggested by the sexual subtext of the Alger Hiss case. In many ways, the personal drama of its two principal actors was paradigmatic for the era unfolding. Hiss, a Harvard Law School graduate, New Deal liberal, and former official in Franklin D. Roosevelt's State Department, was accused in 1948 by the former Communist party operative Whittaker Chambers of passing classified State Department documents to the Soviet Union in the 1930s. By now both a devout Catholic and an anticommunist, Chambers privately confessed to the Federal Bureau of Investigation (FBI) that he had been gay in the 1930s, claiming to have "conquered" his homosexual "affliction" at the same time he presumably conquered his Communist "affliction." That the defense would raise the issue of Chambers's homosexuality in court (which in any case became widely known) to discredit him was doubtful, since the FBI had learned that Hiss's stepson had been discharged from the navy for an alleged homosexual offense. The FBI's "hints" about its discovery of this information apparently prevented Priscilla Hiss's son from testifying altogether. Defense lawyers begged Hiss to let his stepson take the witness stand to refute Chambers's testimony about crucial facts at issue in the case. Hiss, however, fearing the consequences for his wife's son, nixed the only defense strategy that might have helped him win an acquittal.

While some observers speculated about a previous infatuation with Hiss on Chambers's part or even a past sexual relationship between Chambers and Hiss or Hiss's stepson—something that might explain disparities in the two sides' account of the nature of their past friendship—what is significant here is not the truth of such speculations, but the ideological fallout of the case's subtext. Chambers's self-proclaimed sexual affliction fed the imagination that linked political subversion and "sexual perversion"; his mysterious friendship with Hiss in the 1930s implicated the latter in Chambers's murky past. And although the sexual overtones of the case did not result in explicit accusations that Hiss was homosexual, he did become the prototypical weak-willed, effete, treasonous eastern establishment liberal, whose softness left him prone to transgressions of a political, moral, and perhaps even of a sexual nature. . . .

The connections between liberals, subversives, and homosexuals (and the State Department, Hiss's terrain) were slyly alluded to by McCarthy in his 1952 manifesto, *McCarthyism: The Fight for America.* Citing the Senate report on "homosexuals and other sex perverts" in that election year broadside, McCarthy pointed out that "in addition to the security question, . . . individuals who are morally weak and perverted and who are representing the State Department . . . certainly detract from the prestige of this nation." He proceeded to attack Acheson (who had vowed not to turn his back on his friend Hiss), stressing that it was Acheson who had sent Hiss to Yalta and thus conjuring up a conspiratorial connection between pinks, reds, and lavenders.

The image of the effete "striped-pants diplomat" of the State Department was not McCarthy's invention, however; by the early 1950s the diplomatic corps had become an object of derision and ridicule in some political circles. The tendency to link homosexuality with the State Department went back to the early 1940s; the notion of aristocratic "sexual misfits" under-mining United States foreign policy was clearly a reference to Sumner Welles, FDR's undersec-retary of state, who resigned amid allegations of homosexuality. Yet insinuations about the diplomatic corps could be heard from all partisan quarters, even before the Puerifoy speech. . . . The conservative authors of *Washington Confidential,* a 1951 best-selling tell-all exposé of the "dirtiest community in America" that targeted the capital's dissolute "parlor pinks," joked that "until the recent purges of the State Department, there was a gag around Washington you had to speak with a British accent, wear a homburg hat, or have a queer quirk if you wanted to get by the guards at the door."

Others took the State Department's reputation more seriously. In 1953 John Foster Dulles instructed Charles Bohlen, the newly appointed ambassador to the Soviet Union, to travel to his post on the same plane with his wife. Such a scenario would presumably quell any doubts that Bohlen was less than a "normal" family man. The Harvard educated Bohlen, who had been close to the Roosevelt and Truman administrations and present at Yalta, had been the subject of a security-clearance investigation into his private life and sexual preferences, which were insin-uated to be for men.

The first gay advocacy organization in the United States, the Mattachine Society, worried some observers. Founded in 1951 by several ex–Communist party members, the society came under the scrutiny of the *Los Angeles Mirror* in 1953. Reporting Mattachine leaders' Communist party ties, the *Mirror* warned readers that homosexuals were known national security risks and that, if united, they could potentially "swing tremendous political power." The FBI must have concurred: it infiltrated the Mattachine Society in the 1950s and kept the organization under constant surveillance. Whatever J. Edgar Hoover's own sexual orientation (in response to FBI harassment, Mattachine leaders made their own arguably ironic point by putting the director on the society's regular mailing list), Hoover used the same "logic" that linked moral, sexual, and political subversion as did other anticommunists. His pledges to root out "sex deviates" from the FBI, his surveillance and smear campaigns against sexually suspect political enemies, and his profile of the "maladjusted" Communist in his book *Masters of Deceit*—all suggest that for Hoover the enemy was sexual as well as ideological. And like other anticommunists, he depicted the typical Communist as "neurotic" and "twisted" and cited, among other reasons why people joined the party, "sexual pleasure."

Though Hoover did not elaborate on the nature of that sexual pleasure, other critics pondered the psychosexual basis of the Communist party's erotic lure. The scholar John Kosa noted the party's appeal to the lonely, neurotic person who gains "an almost sexual satisfaction from his relationship with the Communist movement." Always attuned to the red psyche, Schlesinger stressed more pointedly the "psychology of clandestinity" that Communists found enticing, comparing their ability to identify each other on casual meeting to the way homosexuals allegedly identify each other: "by the use of certain phrases, the names of certain friends, by certain enthusiasms and certain silences. It is reminiscent of . . . the famous scene in Proust where the Baron de Charlus and the tailor Jupien suddenly recognize their common corruption."

Whether it was Marcel Proust who provided the operative model for the high-brow crowd or the Hiss-Chambers drama that fed the imagination of less erudite observers, the threat of Communism became entangled with the threat of an unrestrained sexuality and, by extension, homosexuality. Surely sexually loaded rhetoric and lavender-baiting served personal, partisan, or nationalistic interests for those who sought to stigmatize political enemies and shore up their own manly, heterosexual credentials. This was the view of David Riesman and Nathan Glazer, who in 1955 attributed right-wing attacks on "sissified" liberals to an exploitation of the growing fear of homosexuality in America. The homosexual, the authors observed, had become "a much more feared enemy than the Negro." What Michael Rogin has more recently called "political demonology" has a long, complex history in American political culture; sexual fears and fantasies have often underlain the demonization of those perceived as a threat to American order and civility.

As a political weapon, sexually charged rhetoric clearly relied upon real anxieties about both Communism and sexuality. Just what was the nature of those anxieties and how might they be linked? While similar in their rhetorical expression (for example, the imagery of penetration), are fears of Communism and fears of an unrestrained sexuality *parallel* fears that derive from separate sources and intersect only at the point of heightened national security concerns?

To some observers, sexual containment was necessary for the containment of Communism. Indeed, an Indiana Catholic archdiocesean newspaper attacked Kinsey's studies (which showed that Americans were hardly chaste) because they "pave the way for people to *believe in* Communism and to *act like* Communists." Yet here, as elsewhere, a deeper connection was being made between sexuality, Communism, and liberalism, suggesting anxieties that were not just parallel but deeply intertwined in their origins. To Billy Graham, the word "tolerant" was synonymous with "liberal" and "broad-minded." Liberal permissiveness and moral relativism, it seemed, invited the subversion and perversion of all that was normal and sacred: freedom, God, private property, the family, and *sex polarity*. Communism, insofar as it was the final, hideous denouement of liberal-progressive inclusivity and naïveté overturned all "natural" hierarchies and relations—free man and the state, God and man, the individual and the collective, and at a most basic level, man and woman. Popular depictions of hard, mannish Soviet women and slavish, emasculated Soviet men provided one negative referent against which the United States could be defined, its moral superiority imagined, its order and civility restored. . . .

When viewed from the vantage point of sexuality, anticommunism was more than a defense against Communism (or liberalism); in its broadest cultural manifestations and most feverish imaginings, it was a defense against America itself—its self-indulgence, its godlessness, its laxity and apathy, its lack of boundaries, its creeping sexual modernism—which is why it could be so readily wedded to family values and sexual containment. Norman Mailer may have overstated his case in 1960 when he said that "the excessive hysteria of the Red wave was no preparation to face an enemy, but rather a terror of the national self: free-loving, lust-looting, atheistic, implacable." But it is hard to escape the conclusion that underlying the excesses and absurdities of anticommunist rhetoric—of which the image of the communist-as-homosexual was only the most lurid—was an anxiety about unsettling trends at home as well as abroad, not least among them sexual modernism. That creeping sexual modernism—whether it was evidenced by the decline of masculinity, the rising tide of working women or assertive wives, Alfred Kinsey's portrait of the collective sexual sins of the nation, or the rise of gay and lesbian communities in the postwar United States—was projected onto an enemy whose quasi-Victorian culture and rigid material theology made it an altogether unworthy repository of American anxieties and frustrations.

To say that the specter of sexual chaos underlay certain fears of and fantasies about Communism is not to say that sexual modernism caused anticommunism; rather it was a source of an anxiety that gave the emergent opposition to Communism an ideological unity and a moral intensity and purpose that could be immediately and viscerally felt. It helped to lay the basis for what Bell called "the equation of Communism with sin," thereby elevating the Communist issue from the level of a serious national security matter to the level of a *moral* issue worthy of extraordinary fervor. And the more that resistance to the red menace became entangled with homegrown fears and frustrations, the more it became a useful medium for the expression of so many extra-Communist concerns. Whatever else anticommunism most certainly was, once unleashed in the culture it served to redefine America against the tide of social change, operating in some cases as an ideological buffer against discomforting postwar trends or perceived social ills. Racial integration, secularism, materialism, apathy, commercialism, conformity, youth rebellion, Jewish upward mobility, internationalism, and welfare statism were among the trends that were not infrequently imagined as subversive to American order and thus discouraged under the aegis of anticommunism. Sexual modernism was uniquely disquieting inasmuch as it could be so readily personalized; fears of being less than a real man, less than a real woman, less than heterosexual, less than *normal* could strike deep emotional chords in a way that fears of materialism or secularism or perhaps even the bomb could not.

If the reputation for softness became something like the political kiss of death, the ultimate casualty of the anxieties of the era may have been Adlai Stevenson. Stevenson had all of the attributes that the right wing suspected: an Ivy League pedigree, style, intellect, a penchant for verbosity, and a prior association with Hiss. (He had vouched for Hiss's character in the first trial.) Anticommunism was at its high point in 1952, and the fallout from the Hiss and Rosenberg cases, the "loss of China," and the first Soviet explosion of an atomic bomb—all of which occurred under a fifth successive Democratic administration—surely meant that any Democrat would have been at a considerable disadvantage. Yet at a time when Sen. Everett Dirksen could promise that, if elected, Republicans would drive all "lavender lads" out of the State Department, Stevenson was unusually vulnerable to a campaign to impugn his manhood.

Perhaps in no other United States presidential election was hard/soft imagery more conspicuous. The *New York Daily News* called Stevenson "Adelaide" and claimed he "trilled" his speeches in a "fruity voice." His proponents were "Harvard lace-cuff liberals," "lace-panty diplomats" who, in the face of McCarthy's charges, wailed in "perfumed anguish" and sometimes "giggled" about anticommunism. McCarthy, who saw a kindred spirit in the Republican vice presidential candidate, Richard M. Nixon, predicted that a Nixon victory would be "a body blow to the Communist conspiracy" and threatened to expose the "pinks, pansies and punks" on the Stevenson campaign staff. And while Dwight D. Eisenhower took the high road with his tough-minded "Korea, corruption and Communism" platform, his running mate used the strategy that had served him so well in the past, implying that his opponent was a hopelessly soft Communist dupe. Nixon called Stevenson "Adlai the appeaser," a "Ph.D. from Dean Acheson's cowardly college of Communist containment."

Even when Stevenson was not explicitly charged with effeminary, the contrast between Eisenhower's paternal, military persona and reputation as an *ordinary* American and Stevenson's sophistication, style, and "teacup words" left the latter at an oft-noted disadvantage. Stevenson's speech at the Democratic convention no doubt projected weakness more than the humility and integrity he wanted to project. "I accept your nomination," he said, adding "I should have preferred to hear these words uttered by a stronger, a wiser, a better man than myself." And while Stevenson had served the military only as a civilian, working as an assistant to the secretary of the navy during World War II, Ike had led the D day invasion of Europe, and in the political climate of the time the general's admission that he had never registered to vote may not have been much of a political liability.

Yet the reputation for effeminacy that Stevenson acquired was not the inevitable result of his persona; it also rested upon a determined effort to call his sexuality into question. Indeed, the 1952 presidential campaign may have been a high-water mark in the history of dirty politics in America. Eisenhower maintained his dignity, as Senators Nixon, McCarthy, and William Jenner handled the innuendoes and smears against Stevenson. The source of what one journalist called the "ugly whispering campaign" about Stevenson was Hoover's FBI, which had supposedly obtained information that Stevenson had been arrested in Maryland and Illinois for homosexual acts and that a cover-up had ensued. According to Hoover's biographer Curt Gentry, the FBI "channeled this and any other derogatory information to Nixon, McCarthy, and members of the press. Although most newspaper editors had the story, none used it. But it was widely circulated, as anyone who worked in the campaign could attest." Receiving reports claiming that "Stevenson and Bradley University President David Owen were the two best known homosexuals" in the state and that Stevenson was known in gay circles as "Adeline," Hoover entered the governor's name in one of his special files marked "Stevenson, Adlai Ewing—Governor of Illinois—Sex Deviate."

The national political unconscious is impossible to measure. Stevenson's defeats cannot be blamed on right-wing aspersions; liberalism was clearly on the decline, given not just what ultra-conservatives were calling "twenty years of treason" but what cooler heads were calling a "time for a change" after five successive Democratic administrations. Stevenson was also hurt by his divorce and rumors that he was a womanizer. But if the press did not report his alleged arrests because no police record could be documented, Stevenson's enemies, if only by insinuation, stigmatized him by calling him "Adelaide" and ridiculing his "fruity voice," among other suspicious feminine attributes. And while such innuendoes may not have cost him the election, they did earn him a reputation as the consummate effete liberal "egghead." Lacking a record in military combat, sports, or anything else that might have shored up his manly credentials, Stevenson was "only a gentleman with an Ivy League background," as Richard Hofstadter noted, "and there was nothing in his career to spare him from the reverberations this history set up in the darker corners of the American mind." (Stevenson was still dogged by innuendo in 1956: Walter Winchell told his Mutual Radio Show audience that "a vote for Adlai Stevenson is a vote for Christine Jorgensen," the first well-known recipient of a sex-change operation.) . . .

For liberals . . . the lesson of McCarthyism (and of the invective heaped on Stevenson) was to fight fire with fire. When the liberal *New York Post* ran a series of articles on McCarthy in

1951 entitled "Smear, Inc.: The One-Man Mob of Joe McCarthy," the writers pointed out that "the man who flamboyantly crusades against homosexuals as though they menace the nation employed one on his office staff for many months." Occasionally, liberals vented their hatred of McCarthy with a heftier dose of the senator's own medicine, as did the famous liberal journalist Drew Pearson, who not only charged in his column that a convicted homosexual had been on McCarthy's staff but also kept a file of affidavits from men who claimed to have had sex with McCarthy. Pearson preferred to circulate the affidavits within insider circles rather than put them into print, but others were not so cautious. Pearson's dubious testimonies found their way into the *Las Vegas Sun,* which in the midst of the 1952 election identified McCarthy: "Joe McCarthy is a bachelor of 43 years. He seldom dates girls and if he does he laughingly describes it as window dressing. It is common talk among homosexuals in Milwaukee . . . that Senator Joe McCarthy has often engaged in homosexual activities." Troubled by the "homo stories," McCarthy consulted the Anti-Defamation League about suing the *Sun* but in the end decided against a criminal libel suit. When insinuations about his private life surfaced in a Syracuse paper, however, McCarthy sued the paper and won.

Though such efforts to malign McCarthy may not have damaged him much politically, they speak to a climate in which charges of homosexuality were made with such ease that no politician—not even Tail Gunner Joe—was spared. But the taint of homosexuality did hover over McCarthy's downfall in 1954. Suspicions about the sexual orientation of McCarthy staff members Roy Cohn and David Schine among observers of the Army-McCarthy hearings raised, as Joseph Alsop put it in his column, "certain suggestions as to the nature of the McCarthy-Cohn-Schine relationship." Those suspicions—real, inflated, or fabricated—surfaced dramatically when Sen. Ralph Flanders delivered to the Senate a devastating, innuendo-laden attack on McCarthy. Likening him to both Adolf Hitler and Dennis the Menace, Flanders spoke of the "mysterious personal relationship" between Cohn and Schine. "It is natural that Cohn should wish to retain the services of an able collaborator, but he seems to have an almost passionate anxiety to retain him. Why?" Flanders then raised the question of McCarthy. "Does the assistant have some hold on him, too? Can it be that our Dennis . . . has at last gotten into trouble himself? Does the committee plan to investigate the real issues at stake?" Given prevailing Senate protocol, Flanders had broached the subject of homosexuality as delicately as he could. The dialogue about "pixies" and "fairies" that arose during the Army-McCarthy hearings was a fitting token of the sexual undertones of the entire spectacle, the undoing of McCarthy, and the waning of the peak red scare years. . . .

Masculinity was clearly a rhetorical terrain on which political images were forged and partisan battles were fought, but how decisively the masculinity crisis shaped the political history of the era is a question whose answer is necessarily speculative. There *was* a world beyond the feverish imaginings of some cold warriors; standing tough in the face of Stalinism was not simply or uniformly a political posture born out of sexual anxiety or political opportunism but a moral and political commitment to many anticommunists for whom the lessons of Munich and the Moscow trials were deeply and inescapably real. No less real (and inescapable) is the inherently gendered nature of language itself, which inevitably colors political rhetoric along masculine/feminine lines.

But in the heady atmosphere of Cold War political culture, the hard/soft dichotomy gradually took on a life of its own, existing quite apart from tangible political and strategic considerations and operating in a symbolic milieu in which it often seemed as if the very manhood of the nation, and by extension that of its male citizenry, was at stake. The hard/soft opposition certainly limited the possibility of more meaningful political discourse and led to much gratuitous posturing; it may have influenced the outcome of national elections (Kennedy won by a slim margin). Yet perhaps a more important historical by-product of the hard/soft dynamic was that it led Democrats to overcompensate for previous deficiencies. . . . The Kennedy administration's much-commented-upon cult of toughness did not arise in a vacuum, but amid a political culture that turned muscularity into a prerequisite for Democrats, style into a commodity, and failure to act boldly and decisively into another Munich, another failure of nerve, another *male character defect*. And to the extent that Lyndon B. Johnson inherited the cult of toughness, he, like Kennedy, was beholden to a rhetoric that had reinvented the liberal's relationship to the "exercise of power" and demanded action. Certainly a constellation of powerful political forces and geopolitical interests converged to shape state policy making in these years. But inasmuch as individual self-image and institutional reputation—and an arguably new and unequaled self-consciousness about leadership style—played a role in that policy-making process, the cult of toughness and virility should not be underestimated. In foreclosing the possibility of more searching, effective, open dialogue and decision making within the White House and the national security bureaucracy, the premium placed on courage and hardness may have rendered the Bay of Pigs invasion of Cuba and the flexing of liberal muscle in Vietnam a seeming masculine imperative.

Further Reading

The most complete treatment of this topic is Ellen W. Schrecker's bulky *Many Are the Crimes: McCarthyism in America* (Boston: Little, Brown, 1998). Although it softens the edges of earlier revisionist interpretations, it remains a staunchly anti-anticommunist work. Stephen J. Whitfield, *The Culture of the Cold War* (Baltimore: The Johns Hopkins University Press, 1991) presents a highly readable, liberal anticommunist view of the Red Scare's impact on American popular and intellectual culture. Paul Buhle and Dave Wagner's *Hide in Plain Sight: The Hollywood Blacklistees in Film and Television, 1950–2002* (New York: Palgrave Macmillan, 2003) and Lary May, *The Big Tomorrow: Hollywood and the Politics of the American Way* (Chicago: University of Chicago Press, 2000) offer alternative views. *The CIO's Left-Led Unions* (New Brunswick, NJ: Rutgers University Press, 1992), edited by Steve Rosswurm, offers up-to-date scholarship on the politics of anticommunism within the U.S. labor movement, an important topic; its authors write in sympathy with the purge victims. For those interested in Joseph McCarthy specifically, David M. Oshinsky, *A Conspiracy So Immense: The World of Joe McCarthy* (New York: The Free Press, 1985), a detailed work if not always a probing one, is the place to start. Some would say that J. Edgar Hoover, not McCarthy, was the most important single figure in the Red Scare. Kenneth O'Reilly, *Hoover and the Un-Americans: The FBI, HUAC, and the Red Menace* (Philadelphia: Temple University Press, 1983) reveals Hoover's role.

The essays in *The New American Right* (New York: Criterion Books, 1955; revised as *The Radical Right* [Garden City, NY: Doubleday, 1963]), edited by Daniel Bell, offer the interpretation of McCarthyism as a destabilizing mass movement based in status anxiety, an interpretation that Fiedler partly embraces in his essay. Frances Stonor Saunders, *The Cultural Cold War: The CIA in the World of Arts and Letters* (New York: The New Press, 2000) details the story of *Encounter* and similar efforts. Michael Paul Rogin, *The Intellectuals and McCarthy: The Radical Specter* (Cambridge, MA: MIT Press, 1967), a work of rhetorical power and impressive research, was the earliest work to refute the status-anxiety interpretation. The revisionist work that followed demonstrates the centrality of traditional, anti-New-Deal conservatism to "McCarthyism," while also blaming the Truman administration for the Red Scare, as discussed previously. Much of that important scholarship can be sampled in the essays collected in *The Specter: Original Essays on the Cold War and the Origins of McCarthyism* (New York: Franklin Watts, 1974), edited by Robert Griffith and Athan Theoharis, the authors of the most significant such work.

Allen Weinstein, *Perjury: The Hiss-Chambers Case* (rev. ed. [New York: Random House, 1997]) and Ronald Radosh and Joyce Milton, *The Rosenberg File: A Search for the Truth* (rev. ed. [New Haven, CT: Yale University Press, 1997]) bring in "guilty" verdicts in the famous cases of Hiss and of the alleged "atom spies," Julius and Ethel Rosenberg. Declassified Soviet documents are summarized in *Venona: Decoding Soviet Espionage in America* (New Haven, CT: Yale University Press, 1999), by John Earl Haynes and Harvey Klehr. Haynes surveys the recent literature from an anticommunist perspective in "The Cold War Debate Continues: A Traditionalist View of Historical Writing on Domestic Communism and Anti-Communism," *Journal of Cold War Studies* (vol. 2, no. 1 [Winter 2000], 76–115). Rebuttals from the anti-anticommunist camp have come largely in the form of reviews and opinion pieces. Pointed rejoinders include Michael E. Parrish and Joseph W. Esherick, "Looking for Spies in All the Wrong Places," *Reviews in American History* (vol. 25, no. 1 [March 1997], 174–85), and Ellen Schrecker and Maurice Isserman, "The Right's Cold War Revision," *Nation* (vol. 271, no. 4 [24 July 2000], 22–24).

Primary Sources

The text of the McCarran Act (which made membership in the Communist Party illegal) may be found at www.historycentral.com/documents/McCarran.html#. Transcripts of the executive sessions of the Senate Permanent Subcommittee on Investigations of the Committee on Government Operations (the McCarthy Hearings) for 1953–54 have recently been made public and may be found at www.gpo.gov/congress/senate/senate12cp107.html. (Scroll down to S. Prt. 107–84 and click on the links.) Audio of a small portion of the Army/McCarthy hearings from April–June 1954 is available on line at www.c-span.org/special/mccarthy.asp (click on Tues. Aug. 22—Thurs. Aug. 24). A number of documents related to McCarthy, including correspondence between McCarthy and President Eisenhower, correspondence by Eisenhower which mentions McCarthy, and diary entries related to McCarthy by Eisenhower's press secretary, may be found at www.eisenhower.archives.gov/dl/McCarthy/Mccarthydocuments.html. Documents related to two of the notable "spy" cases of the era—that of the Rosenbergs and that of Alger Hiss—are available on the Web. Regarding the Rosenbergs, visit www.law.umkc.edu/faculty/projects/ftrials/rosenb/ROSENB.HTM for lengthy trial transcript excerpts, defense and prosecution summary statements, the sentencing statement of the trial judge, appellate court decisions and excerpts from the Rosenbergs' prison letters. For information on the Hiss case, including excerpts from the minutes of the Hiss grand jury, as well as FBI notes on statements made by Whittaker Chambers and copies of the Venona documents purporting to relate to Hiss, go to homepages.nyu.edu/~th15/home.html, a page created with a grant from the Alger Hiss Research and Public Project of the Nation Institute. The texts of the principal documents and letters of the Personnel Security Board of the U.S. Atomic Energy Commission in the matter of J. R. Oppenheimer (which stripped the "father of the atomic bomb" of his security clearance in 1953 on the grounds that he presented a security risk to the United States), may be found at www.yale.edu/lawweb/avalon/abomb/oppmenu.htm. A brief excerpt of the trial transcript of *Dennis v. U.S.* may be found at www.english.upenn.edu/~afilreis/50s/dennis-opening.html. Go to www.authentichistory.com/images/1950s/red_channels/redchannels.html to view pages from the "blacklist." For an excellent discussion of the impact of the Red Scare on one state—Washington—along with approximately fifty primary documents from that state's equivalent of the House Un-American Activities Committee, and the decision of the University of Washington to fire three tenured professors for their left-wing political views, visit www.washington.edu/uwired/outreach/cspn/curcan/main.html#concordance.

CHAPTER 4

Affluence, Domesticity, and the Fifties

INTRODUCTION

For many Americans, "The Fifties" connotes an era of affluence, consumer abundance, suburban living, stay-at-home mothers and, of course, the baby boom. Reruns of classic 1950s television programs such as *Father Knows Best* and *Leave It to Beaver,* as well as the 1970s-era "sitcom," *Happy Days,* which was set in the Fifties, have reinforced these images of an era when life was easy, when even the thorniest of problems—should the Beav be punished for ditching a sweater that he didn't like?—could be solved through family discussion or by Dad.

This image of the 1950s came under attack before the decade was even over. To one commentator, the Fifties were years of "flabbiness and self-satisfaction and gross materialism." To another, it was "the dullest and dreariest" decade in American history, marked by political quietude and mind-numbing conformity. As discussed in the previous chapter on the Red Scare, it was also a period of unusually intense repression against those on the political left, as well as homosexuals and others seen as deviating from the "norm." For William H. Whyte, the Fifties were notable as the age of the "organization man," the corporate factotum who had traded individual initiative and creativity for financial security. For Betty Friedan, writing in 1963, it was a decade in which women had been forced into domestic roles that were stultifying and left them feeling empty. The Beat poets and later, the counterculture of the 1960s, scorned what they saw the Fifties as representing: mindless consumerism, sexual repression, social conformity, and prohibitions on free expression.

But beginning in the mid-1970s, the Fifties came back into fashion as movies like *American Graffiti* resurrected the music and replayed the hijinx of the period, and as Americans facing double-digit inflation and the family stresses of two working parents looked back with longing to a decade when families, it was remembered, lived well on one salary. (*American Graffiti* was in fact set in 1962, evidence that the term "the Fifties" is used loosely, by filmmakers as well as historians and cultural commentators. The term is often used to encompass the period, roughly, from the end of World War II in 1945 to the beginning of the 1960s.)

Fifties nostalgia reached its peak during the politically conservative decade of the 1980s, as "family values" advocates and other commentators argued that America had taken a wrong turn in the Sixties—not in the Fifties, as some earlier critics had suggested. Pointing to rising rates of divorce, single motherhood, and out-of-wedlock births, they looked to the 1950s as a time of family togetherness and harmony, of prosperity, national unity, and shared moral values. Scholarly work with titles such as *The Proud Decades* and *American High* shared this positive view of the 1950s, focusing on the prosperity, peace, and technological innovations of the period. Other studies have taken a much dimmer view of the decade, with titles such as *The Dark Ages* and *The Way We Never Were,* which argued just that—that the Fifties were, in fact, never as they were depicted in sitcoms and that the reality of that decade had become clouded by nostalgia and wishful thinking. These works reminded readers that the 1950s, although a period of prosperity for many Americans—for example, home ownership jumped to over 60 percent during the decade—was also a time of great inequality. Poverty was extensive, racism and segregation continued (although they started to come under attack during this period), and sexism was prevalent. Numerous studies have shown that teenage rebellion and teenage mothers were much discussed as serious problems during the Fifties, that many women found the role of stay-at-home mom unsatisfying and even oppressive, and that beneath the appearance of security and comfort, a strong undercurrent of anxiety marked much of the popular culture of the 1950s.

Whether generally positive or negative about the decade, most historians have agreed that the 1950s were somehow anomalous and distinct from the eras that came before and after, representing a break from and reversal of longer term trends begun earlier in the century, such as the rise in the average age at marriage and in the rate of divorce, a declining birth rate, the increasing participation of women in the paid labor force, an increase in sexual freedom for women, and in terms of the political culture, a stubborn progressive spirit that challenged the prevailing inequities of the day. The astounding growth of the American middle class was another notable characteristic of the Fifties that separated the decade from previous ones. As cultural historian Lary May put it in the introduction to *Recasting America,* a collection of essays on the culture and politics of the Fifties, America after 1945 underwent "a paradigm shift of major proportions." How can this dramatic departure from the past be explained? May's volume focused on the cold war to explain the distinctive features of the 1950s. The first excerpt, from an essay by historian Elaine Tyler May which summarizes the argument of her widely read and cited study of the 1950s, *Homeward Bound,* is an example of this perspective.

May focuses on the 1950s' family and argues that the end of World War II and the beginning of economic prosperity simply cannot account for the unusually strong cultural emphasis on marriage and family life, for the phenomenon of the baby boom, or for the promotion of clearly defined gender roles for men—the breadwinners—and for women—full-time mothers and erotic companions to their husbands. These distinctive cultural and social characteristics of the Fifties, in May's view, are attributable to the cold war. Just as American foreign policy focused on containing communism, so the domestic ideology of the period emphasized the containment of women, economically and sexually, within the home and family. Experts urged Americans to see early marriage and childrearing as normative and other choices as deviant. Americans, according to May, largely followed this advice, viewing the family as a haven from the insecurity of life in the nuclear age. In the ideology of the day, the family—especially mothers—would not only provide comfort in difficult times but would also act as a bulwark in the cold war, instilling and propagating the values and even the survival skills necessary for America to triumph over the Soviet Union. Although the dominant images of the 1950s in American popular culture today are of happy couples and contented children, May asserts in *Homeward Bound* that many women—and men—found conforming to the dominant social norms stressful and unsatisfying and that they had married, produced children, and in the case of women, foregone work outside the home in response to social pressure rather than from deep personal desire. Although a central problem with May's work is that it offers little in the way of evidence that Americans' turn toward the home and away from the public world was in fact driven by cold war anxieties, her work gained considerable attention for attempting to tie together the social, cultural, and foreign policy aspects of the Fifties.

The second excerpt is from an essay by eminent historian Alan Brinkley, which appeared in an edited collection entitled *Cold War Culture* and which, like several other essays in that volume, suggests that other factors in addition to the cold war played a pivotal role in defining the distinctive features of the 1950s. Focusing on the postwar economic boom, the phenomenal growth of the middle class, the trend toward suburban living, the bureaucratization of white-collar work, and the ideology of consensus, Brinkley concludes that none of these developments hinged on the cold war and that, in fact, all would have occurred in the absence of the postwar conflict between the United States and the USSR. Brinkley's essay effectively calls into question the assumptions about cause and effect underlying May's influential work. He does not, however, address one central query of May's work—how to explain the baby boom, which ran counter to long-term trends of decreasing family size. Nor does Brinkley directly address the role of women in the 1950s.

The last selection is by Margaret Rose, from a highly regarded volume on women in the 1950s, *Not June Cleaver*. As the title suggests, the volume contests the notion that women in the 1950s were all stay-at-home mothers who deferred to their husbands, found fulfillment in child-rearing, and wore high heels and pearls while vacuuming. Nor were they the victims of an ideology of domesticity. As with many essays in *Not June Cleaver*, the article by Rose acknowledges that the dominant cultural role for women in the 1950s was motherhood. But Rose shows how the Mexican American women in her study used this domestic ideology to achieve their own aims—in this instance, to advocate for improved conditions for their communities. Rose's essay makes several other important points about the 1950s. First, the ideology of domestic containment described so well in May's article clearly did not reflect the lives of many Mexican American households, many of which lacked the financial resources that permitted the lifestyles prescribed by the cultural norms of the Fifties. This raises the broader point that the supposedly ubiquitous June Cleaver role model in fact represented only a particular segment of American women—those in the (white) upper-middle class. Second, the stories of women such as Dolores Huerta and Hope Mendoza presented by Rose make clear that many women were not "contained" within the home in the 1950s, but were, in fact, active politically and determined to bring change to their communities. As Rose writes, "far from being a stagnant period for Mexican-heritage women, the late 1940s and 1950s were years of involvement and commitment." This calls into question the truism that the 1950s were a politically quiescent decade. Finally, Rose's article implicitly challenges the idea put forward by May and others that the Fifties were an aberration, divorced from the trends of the past and from the developments of the future. Instead, the activities and thinking of the women (and men) in Rose's article suggest that the 1950s were in many respects not distinct or notably different from the previous or subsequent eras. The struggles for economic justice and improved social and political conditions for their communities depicted in Rose's essay began before the 1950s and continued well after that decade came to an end. Thus Rose's work implies, as does the work of other essayists in *Not June Cleaver*, that the Fifties might be best viewed not as an anomaly, good or bad, but as a bridge between the years preceding World War II and the era of the Sixties.

ELAINE TYLER MAY

Politics and the Family in Postwar America

In 1959, Vice-President Richard M. Nixon traveled to the Soviet Union to engage in what would become one of the most noted verbal sparring matches of the century. In a lengthy and often heated debate with Soviet premier Nikita Khrushchev at the opening of the American National Exhibition in Moscow, Nixon extolled the virtues of the American way of life, as his opponent promoted the Communist system. What is remarkable about this exchange is its focus. The two leaders did not discuss missiles, bombs, or even modes of government. Rather, they argued over the relative merits of American and Soviet washing machines, televisions, and electric ranges. According to the American vice-president, the essence of the good life provided by democracy was contained within the walls of the suburban home.

For Nixon, American superiority rested on a utopian ideal of the home, complete with modern appliances and distinct gender roles. He proclaimed that the "model home," with a male breadwinner and a full-time female homemaker, and adorned with a wide array of consumer goods, represented the essence of American freedom. Nixon insisted that American superiority in the cold war rested not on weapons but on the secure, abundant family life available in modern suburban homes, "within the price range of the average U.S. worker." Houses became almost sacred structures, adorned and worshiped by their inhabitants. Here women would achieve their glory, and men would display their success. Consumerism was not an end in itself, but rather the means for achieving a classless ideal of individuality, leisure, and upward mobility.

With such sentiments about gender and politics widely shared, Nixon's remarks in Moscow struck a responsive chord among Americans at the time. He returned from Moscow a national hero. The visit was hailed as a major political triumph; popular journals extolled his diplomatic skills in this face-to-face confrontation with the Russian leader. Many observers credit this trip with establishing Nixon's political future. Clearly, Americans did not find the kitchen debate trivial. The appliance-laden ranch-style home epitomized the expansive, secure life-style postwar Americans wanted. Within the protective walls of the modern home, worrisome developments like sexual liberalism, women's emancipation, and affluence would lead not to decadence but to wholesome family life. Sex would enhance marriage; emancipated women would professionalize homemaking; affluence would put an end to material deprivation. Suburbia would serve as a bulwark against communism and class conflict, for, according to the widely shared belief articulated by Nixon, it offered a piece of the American dream for everyone. Although Nixon vastly exaggerated the availability of the suburban home, one cannot deny the fact that he described a particular type of domestic life that had become a reality for many Americans, and a viable aspiration for many more.

What gave rise to the widespread endorsement of this familial consensus in the cold war era? The depression and war laid the foundations for a commitment to a stable home life, but they also opened the way for what might have become a radical restructuring of the family. The yearning for family stability gained momentum and reached fruition after the war; but the potential for restructuring did not. Instead, that potential withered, as a powerful ideology of domesticity became imprinted on the fabric of everyday life. Traditional gender roles revived just when they might have died a natural death, and became, ironically, a central feature of the "modern" middle-class home.

Since the 1960s, much attention has focused on the plight of women in the fifties. But at the time, critical observers of middle-class life considered homemakers to be emancipated and men to be oppressed. Much of the most insightful writing examined the dehumanizing situation that forced middle-class men, at least in their public roles, to be "other-directed" "organization men," caught in a mass, impersonal white-collar world. The loss of autonomy was real. As large corporations grew, swallowing smaller enterprises, the numbers of self-employed men in small businesses shrank dramatically. David Riesman recognized that the corporate structure forced middle-class men into deadening, highly structured peer interactions; he argued that only in the intimate aspects of life could a man truly be free. Industrial laborers were even less likely to derive intrinsic satisfactions from the job itself; blue-collar and white-collar employees shared a sense of alienation and subordination in the postwar corporate work force. Both Riesman and William Whyte saw the suburbs as extensions of the corporate world, with their emphasis on conformity. Yet at the same time, suburban home ownership and consumerism offered compensations for organized work life.

For women, who held jobs in greater numbers than ever before, employment was likely to be even more menial and subordinate. Surveys of full-time homemakers indicated that they appreciated their independence from supervision and control over their work, and had no desire to give up their autonomy in the home for wage labor. Educated middle-class women whose career opportunities were severely limited hoped that the home would become not a confining place of drudgery, but a liberating arena of fulfillment through professionalized homemaking, meaningful childrearing, and satisfying sexuality.

While the home seemed to offer the best hope for freedom, it also appeared to be a fragile institution, in many ways subject to forces beyond its control. Economic hardship had torn families asunder, and war had scattered men far from home and thrust women into the public world of work. The postwar years did little to alleviate fears that similar disruptions might occur again. In spite of widespread affluence, many believed that reconversion to a peacetime economy would lead to another depression. Peace itself was also problematic, since international tension was a palpable reality. The explosion of the first atomic bombs over Hiroshima and Nagasaki marked not only the end of World War II but also the beginning of the cold war. At any moment, the cold war could turn hot. The policy of containment abroad faced its first major challenge in 1949 with the Chinese revolution. That same year, the Russians exploded their first atomic bomb. The nation was again jolted out of its sense of fragile security when the Korean War broke out in 1950, sending American men abroad to fight once again. Many shared President Truman's belief that World War III was at hand. . . .

Americans were well poised to embrace domesticity in the midst of the terrors of the atomic age. A home filled with children would provide a feeling of warmth and security against the cold forces of disruption and alienation. Children would also provide a connection to the future, and a means to replenish a world depleted by war deaths. Although baby-boom parents were not likely to express conscious desires to repopulate the country, the deaths of hundreds of thousands of GIs in World War II could not have been far below the surface of postwar consciousness. The view of childbearing as a duty was painfully true for Jewish parents, after six million of their kin were snuffed out in Europe. But they were not alone. As one Jewish woman recalled of her conscious decision to bear four children, "After the Holocaust, we felt obligated to have lots of babies. But it was easy because everyone was doing it—non-Jews, too." In secure postwar homes with plenty of children, American women and men might be able to ward off their nightmares and live out their dreams.

In the face of prevailing fears, Americans moved toward the promise of the good life with an awareness of its vulnerability. The family seemed to be one place left where people could control their own destinies, and maybe even shape the future. Of course, nobody actually argued that stable family life could prevent nuclear annihilation. But the home did represent a source of meaning and security in a world run amok. If atomic bombs threatened life, marriage and reproduction affirmed life. Young marriage and lots of babies offered one way for Americans to thumb their noses at doomsday predictions. Commenting on the trend toward young marriages, *Parents Magazine* noted in 1958, "Youngsters want to grasp what little security they can in a world gone frighteningly insecure. The youngsters feel they will cultivate the one security that's possible—their own gardens, their own . . . home and families."

Thoughts of the family rooted in time-honored traditions may have allayed fears of vulnerability. Nevertheless, the "traditional" family was quickly becoming a relic of the past. Much of what had previously provided family security became unhinged. For many Americans, the postwar years brought rootlessness. Those who moved from farms to cities lost a way of life familiar to them and rooted in the land itself. Children of immigrants moved from familiar ethnic neighborhoods with extended kin and community ties in order to form nuclear families in the homogeneous suburbs, and invested them with extremely high hopes. Suburban homes offered freedom from kinship obligations, along with material comforts that had not been available on the farm or in the ethnic urban ghetto. As William Whyte noted about the promoters of the Illinois suburb he studied, "At first they had advertised Park Forest as housing. Now they began advertising happiness." But consumer goods would not replace community, and young mobile nuclear families could easily find themselves adrift. Whyte noted the "rootlessness" of the new suburban residents. Newcomers devoted themselves to creating communities out of neighborhoods comprised largely of transients: "In suburbia, organization man is trying, quite consciously, to develop a new kind of roots to replace what he left behind." . . .

Young suburbanites were great joiners, forging new ties and creating new institutions to replace the old. Park Forest, Illinois, had sixty-six adult organizations, making it a "hotbed of Participation." Church and synagogue membership reached new heights in the postwar years, expanding its functions from prayer and charity to include recreation, youth programs, and social events. Church membership rose from 64.5 million in 1940 to 114.5 million in 1960— from 50 percent to 63 percent of the entire population (a hundred years earlier only 20 percent of all Americans belonged to churches). In 1958, 97 percent of all those polled said they believed in God. Religious affiliation became associated with the "American way of life." Although many observers have commented upon the superficiality and lack of spiritual depth in much of this religious activity, there is no question that churches and synagogues provided social arenas for suburbanites, replacing to some extent the communal life previously supplied by kin or neighborhood.

Still, these were tenuous alliances among uprooted people. As William Whyte observed, suburbs offered shallow roots rather than deep ones. With so much mobility in and out of neighborhoods, and with success associated with moving on to something better, middle-class nuclear families could not depend upon the stability of their communities. Much as they endeavored to form ties with their neighbors and conform to each other's life-styles, they were still largely on their own. So the nuclear family, ultimately, relied upon itself. As promising as the new vision of home life appeared, it depended heavily on the staunch commitment of its members to sustain it. The world could not be trusted to provide security, nor could the newly forged suburban community. What mattered was that family members remained bound to each other, and to the modern, emancipated home they intended to create.

To help them in this effort, increasing numbers of women and men turned to scientific expertise. Inherited folkways would be of little help to young people looking toward a radically new vision of family life. The wisdom of earlier generations seemed to be increasingly irrelevant for young adults trying self-consciously to avoid the paths of their parents. As they turned away from "old-fashioned" ways, they embraced the advice of experts in the rapidly expanding fields of social science, medicine, and psychology. After all, science was changing the world. Was it not reasonable to expect it to change the home as well?

Postwar America was the era of the expert. Armed with scientific techniques and presumably inhabiting a world above popular passions, the experts had brought the country into the atomic age. Physicists developed the bomb; strategists created the cold war; scientific managers built the military-industrial complex. It was now up to the experts to make the unmanageable manageable. As the readers of *Look* magazine were assured, there was no reason to worry about radioactivity, for if ever it became necessary to understand its dangers, "the experts will be ready to tell you." Science and technology seemed to have invaded virtually every aspect of life, from the most public to the most private. Americans were looking to professionals to tell them how to manage their lives. The tremendous popularity of treatises such as Dr. Benjamin Spock's *Baby and Child Care* reflects a reluctance to trust the shared wisdom of kin and community. Norman Vincent Peale's *The Power of Positive Thinking* provided readers with religiously inspired scientific formulas for success. Both of these bestselling authors stressed the centrality of the family in their prescriptions for a better future. . . .

Experts fostered an individualist approach to family life that would appeal to postwar Americans who felt cut off from the past as they forged into a world both promising and threatening. The new home had to be fortified largely from within. Couples embarking on marriage were determined to strengthen the nuclear family through "togetherness." With the guidance of experts, successful breadwinners would provide economic support for professionalized homemakers, and together they would create the home of their dreams.

Testimonies drawn from a survey of six hundred husbands and wives during the 1950s reveal the rewards as well as the disappointments resulting from these fervent efforts to create the ideal home. The respondents were among the cohort of Americans who began their families during the early 1940s, establishing the patterns and setting the trends that were to take hold of the nation for the next two decades. Their hopes for happy and stable marriages took shape during the depression, while many couples among their parents' peers struggled with disruption and hardship. They entered marriage as World War II thrust the nation into another major crisis, wreaking further havoc upon families. They raised children as the cold war took shape, with its cloud of international tension and impending doom. Yet at the same time, they were fiercely committed to the families they formed, determined to weather the storms of crises.

These women and men were hopeful that family life in the postwar era would be secure and liberated from the hardships of the past. They believed that affluence, consumer goods, satisfying sex, and children would enhance and strengthen their families, enabling them to steer clear of potential disruptions. As they pursued their quest for the good life at home, they adhered to traditional gender roles and prized marital stability highly. Very few of them divorced. They represented a segment of the predominantly Protestant white population that was relatively well-educated and generally lived a comfortable middle-class life. In other words, they were among those Americans who would be most likely to fit the normative patterns. If any Americans had the ability to achieve the dream of a secure, affluent, and happy domestic life, it would have been these prosperous young adults.

These women and men were among the first to establish families according to the domestic ideology taking shape at the time. Their children would be among the oldest of the baby-boom generation. By the time their families were well established in the 1950s, they easily could have been the models for the American way of life Nixon extolled in Moscow. Relatively affluent, more highly educated than the average, they were among those Americans who were best able to take advantage of postwar prosperity. They looked toward the home, rather than the public world, for personal fulfillment. No wonder that when they were asked what they felt they sacrificed in life as a result of their decision to marry and raise a family, a decision that required an enormous investment of time, energy, and resources, an overwhelming majority of both men and women replied "nothing." Their priorities were clear.

One of the most striking characteristics of these respondents was their apparent willingness to give up autonomy and independence for the sake of marriage and family. Although the 1950s marked the beginning of the glamorization of bachelorhood, most of the men expressed a remarkable lack of nostalgia for the unencumbered freedom of a single life. Typical were the comments of one husband who said he gave up "nothing but bad habits" when he married, or another who said he relinquished "the empty, aimless, lonely life of a bachelor. I cannot think of anything I really wanted to do or have that have been sacrificed because of marriage." Many of these men had been married for over a decade, and had seen their share of troubles. Particularly poignant was the comment of a man with an alchoholic wife whom he described as sexually "frigid." Brushing aside these obvious difficulties, he wrote, "Aside from the natural adjustment, I have given up only some of my personal independence. But I have gained so much more: children, home, etc. that I ought to answer . . . 'nothing at all.'"

Women were equally quick to dismiss any sacrifices they may have made when they married. Few expressed any regret at having devoted themselves to the homemaker role—a choice that effectively ruled out other lifelong occupational avenues. Although 13 percent mentioned a "career" as something sacrificed, most claimed that they gained rather than lost in the bargain. One wife indicated the way in which early marriage affected the development of her adult identity. Stating that she sacrificed "nothing" when she married, she continued, "Marriage has opened up far more avenues of interest than I ever would have had without it . . . I was a very young and formative age when we were married and I think I have changed greatly over the years. . . . I cannot conceive of life without him."

Many of the wives who said they abandoned a career were quick to minimize its importance. One said she gave up a "career—but much preferred marriage," suggesting that pursuing both at the same time was not a viable option. Many defined their domestic role as a career in itself. As one woman wrote of her choice to relinquish an outside profession: "I think I have probably contributed more to the world in the life I have lived." Another mentioned her sacrifices of "financial independence. Freedom to choose a career. However, these have been replaced by the experience of being a mother and a help to other parents and children. Therefore the new career is equally as good or better than the old." Both men and women stressed the responsibilities of married life as a source of personal fulfillment rather than sacrifice. One man remarked that "a few fishing trips and hunting trips are about all I have given up. These not to keep peace in the family, but because the time was better (and more profitably) spent at home."

Further evidence of the enormous commitment to family life appears in response to the question, "What has marriage brought you that you could not have gained without your marriage?" While the most common responses of both men and women included family, children, love, and companionship, other typical answers included a sense of purpose, success, and security. It is interesting to note that respondents claimed that these elements of life would not have been possible without marriage. Women indicated that marriage gave them "a sense of responsibility I wouldn't have had had I remained single," or a feeling of "usefulness I have had for others dear to me." One said marriage gave her a "happy, full, complete life; children, feeling of serving some purpose in life other than making money." Another remarked, "I'm not the 'career girl' type. I like being home and having a family. . . . Working with my husband for our home and family brings a satisfaction that working alone could not."

Men were equally emphatic about the satisfactions brought about by family responsibility. Responding in their own words to an open-ended question, nearly one-fourth of all the men in the sample claimed that their marriages gave them a sense of purpose in life and a reason for striving. Aside from love and children, no other single reward of marriage was mentioned by so many of the husbands. Numerous comments pointed to marriage as the source of "the incentive to succeed and save for the future of my family," "above all, a purpose in the scheme of life," or "a motivation for intensive effort that would otherwise have been lacking." One confessed, "Being somewhat lazy to begin with the family and my wife's ambition have made me more eager to succeed businesswise and financially." A contented husband wrote of the "million treasures" contained in his family; another said that marriage offered "freedom from the boredom and futility of bachelorhood."

Others linked family life to civic virtues by claiming that marriage strengthened their patriotism and morals, instilling in them "responsibility, community spirit, respect for children and family life, reverence for a Supreme Being, humility, love of country." Summing up the feelings of many in his generation, one husband said that marriage "increased my horizons, defined my goals and purposes in life, strengthened my convictions, raised my intellectual standards and stimulated my incentive to provide moral, spiritual, and material support; it has rewarded me with a realistic sense of family and security I never experienced during the first 24 years of my life."

The modern home would provide not only virtue and security, but also liberation and expressiveness. Most of the survey respondents agreed with the widely expressed belief that "wholesome sex relations are the cornerstone of marriage." Sexual expertise was one of several skills required of modern marital partners; as one historian has noted, by the 1940s experts had fully articulated the "cult of mutual orgasm." The respondents repeatedly noted that sexual attraction was a major reason they married their particular partners, while sexual compatibility and satisfaction were deemed essential elements in a marriage. One man wrote about his future wife, "I like particularly her size and form. . . . She attracts me strongly, physically." Others wrote about the centrality of "sex desire" in their relationships, and how important it was that they were "passionately attracted to each other." Women as well as men were likely to mention the "great appeal physically" of their partners. In essence, sexual liberation was expected to occur *within* marriage, along with shared leisure, affluence, and recreation. The modern home was a place to feel good.

These comments express a strong commitment to a new and expanded vision of family life, one focused inwardly on parents and children, and bolstered by affluence and sex. The respondents claimed to have found their personal identities and achieved their individual goals largely through their families. Yet on some level the superlatives ring a bit hollow—as if these women and men were trying to convince themselves that the families they had created fulfilled all their deepest wishes. For the extensive responses they provided to other questions in the survey reveal evidence of disappointment, dashed hopes, and lowered expectations. Many of the respondents who gave their marriages high ratings had actually resigned themselves to a great deal of misery.

As postwar Americans endeavored to live in tune with the prevailing domestic ideology, they found that there were costs involved in the effort. The dividends required a heavy investment of self. For some, the costs were well worth the benefits; for others, the costs turned out to be too high. Ida and George Butler were among those who felt the costs were worth it. After more than a decade of marriage, they both claimed that they were satisfied with the life they had built together. When they first embarked on married life, they brought high hopes to their union. Ida wrote that George "very nearly measures up to my ideal Prince Charming." George, in turn, noted Ida's attractiveness, common sense, and similar ideas on home life and sex. He was glad she was "not the 'high stepping' type," but had "experience in cooking and housekeeping." For this down-to-earth couple, the home contained their sexuality, her career ambitions, his success drive, and their desires for material and emotional comforts.

Yet like all things worth a struggle, it did not come easy. Ida's choices reflect the constraints that faced postwar women. She sacrificed her plans for "a professional career—I would [have] liked to have been a doctor—but we both agreed that I should finish college which I did." Following her marriage, "there were obstacles" to her continuing to pursue a career in medicine. It was nearly impossible to combine a professional life with a family. For one thing, the children were primarily her responsibility. "My husband works very hard in his business and has many hobbies and friends. The care and problems of children seem to overwhelm him and he admits being an 'only' child ill prepared him for the pull and tug of family life. We work closely together on discipline and policies but he is serious minded and great joy and fun with the children is lacking."

If Prince Charming's shining armor tarnished a bit with the years, Ida was not one to complain. She had reasons for feeling contented with the family she helped to build. "I think a *stability* which runs through my life is important. I cannot recall any divorce or separation in my immediate family—We are a rural—close-to-the-soil group and I was brought up 'to take the bitter with the sweet'—'marry-off not on (your family)'—'you make your own bed—now lie in it' philosophy so it would not occur to me 'to run home to mother.'" Although marriage was not her first career choice, it eventually became her central occupation: "Marriage is my career—I chose it and now it is up to me to see that I do the job successfully in spite of the stresses and strains of life." She felt that the sacrifices she made were outweighed by the gains: "children—a nice home—companionship—sex—many friends." Her husband George also claimed to be "completely satisfied" with the marriage. He wrote that it brought him an "understanding of other people's problems, 'give and take,' love and devotion." He felt that he sacrificed "nothing but so-called personal freedom." Her medical career and his "so-called personal freedom" seemed to be small prices to pay for the stable family life they created together.

For men and women like George and Ida Butler, the gains were worth the sacrifices. But their claims of satisfaction carried a note of resignation. Combining a profession with a family seemed an unrealistic goal for Ida; combining personal freedom with the role of provider seemed equally out of reach for George. They both felt they faced an either/or situation, and they opted for their family roles. At first glance, this case appears rather unremarkable: two people who made a commitment to marriage and made the best of it. But the Butlers' choices and priorities take on larger significance when we keep in mind that they were part of a generation that was unique in its commitment to family life. The costs and benefits articulated by the Butlers, and their willingness to settle for somewhat less than they bargained for, were conditions they shared with their middle-class peers. . . .

The cold war consensus, politically as well as domestically, did not sustain itself beyond this single generation. The politics of the 1930s, 1940s, and 1950s had helped to shape the postwar home. In turn, the postwar home had a direct bearing on the politics of the 1960s. Much of what sparked the social and political movements forged by the baby-boom children as they came of age stemmed from a rejection of the values of postwar domesticity and the cold war itself. The children were keenly aware of the disappointments of their parents—that the domestic ideal had not fully lived up to its promise. Unlike their depression- and war-bred parents, they were less security-minded and less willing to tolerate the restraints and dissatisfactions experienced by their elders. Yet they did not wholly give up on the dream of a more liberated and expressive life; they simply looked for the fulfillment of that promise elsewhere. This new quest took more overtly political forms, since much of their energy poured out of the family into public life. In many ways, then, the children's effort to gain what their parents had failed to achieve in the way of true liberation gave rise to the new left, the antiwar movement, the counterculture, and the new feminism. As a result, by the late 1960s they had shattered the political and familial consensus that had prevailed since the 1940s.

In the years since the 1960s, politics and personal life have remained intertwined. The lines remain drawn around the same sets of values. Militant cold warriors still call for the virtues of "traditional domesticity"; critics on the left challenge the assumptions of the cold war and champion gender equality inside and outside the home. Issues of personal life, such as abortion and day care, have landed squarely in the center of hot political debates. Although it is unclear which side will ultimately prevail, there can be no doubt that public and private life continue to exert a powerful influence on each other.

ALAN BRINKLEY

The Illusion of Unity in Cold War Culture

Critics of American culture in the 1950s and many scholars since have given much of the credit to the Cold War itself: to the political repression that accompanied the rivalry with the Soviet Union, to the pressures that rivalry created to celebrate American society and affirm its right to leadership of the "Free World." That was what Lary May meant in 1987 when he spoke of a "paradigm shift"—a new sense of the national self, driven in large part by the imperatives of the Cold War. Such observers are surely correct that the Cold War played a significant role in shaping the culture of its time. The official and unofficial repression of political belief, the pervasive fear among intellectuals and others of being accused of radical sympathies, the ideological fervor that the rivalry with the Soviet Union produced: all had a powerful effect on the way Americans thought about themselves and their culture and on what they dared do, say, and even think. . . .

And yet, hard as it is, many contemporaries and many scholars have overstated the role of the Cold War in shaping postwar American culture, indeed have suggested that it was virtually the only significant factor in shaping that culture. The Cold War provides a partial explanation of the character of postwar culture, but it is only one—and perhaps not the most important one—of several causes. Other social and cultural transformations had at least as much to do with the shaping of what we now call "Cold War culture" as did the Cold War itself.

The most obvious of these changes was the remarkable expansion of the American economy in the postwar years. It was, quite simply, the greatest and most dramatic capitalist expansion in American history, perhaps even in world history. It was often described at the time, not without reason, as the American "economic miracle." One economic historian, writing in the early 1960s, said of it: "The remarkable capacity of the United States economy represents the crossing of a great divide in the history of humanity." Through much of the twentieth century, particularly during the economic crises of the 1930s, substantial numbers of Americans had retained some skepticism about industrial capitalism. But during and after the war—as the prosperity rolled on and on and the new depression that so many had predicted in 1945 never came—it became possible for many Americans to believe that there were no limits, or at least no restrictive limits, to economic growth, that capitalism was capable of much greater feats than most Americans had once believed possible.

The economist John Kenneth Galbraith, hardly an uncritical defender of capitalism through his long career, published a small book in 1952 entitled simply *American Capitalism*. In it he expressed some of the wonder and enthusiasm with which intellectuals and others faced this new discovery. About capitalism he had one succinct, almost breathless comment: "It works!" More than that, it obviated many of the principal dilemmas that had frustrated the reformers of earlier eras:

> In the United States alone there need not lurk behind modern programs of social betterment that fundamental dilemma that everywhere paralyzes the will of every responsible man, the dilemma between economic progress and immediate increase of the real income of the masses.

Increasing the income of the masses, in other words, did not have to come at the expense of investment; the two things would reinforce one another. Poverty could be eliminated and social problems could be solved—not through the ideologically unattractive and politically difficult task of redistributing limited wealth, as many Americans had once believed would be necessary, but simply through growth. Or, as a member of the Council of Economic Advisers wrote in the late 1950s, somewhat more prosaically: "Far greater gains were to be made by fighting to enlarge the size of the economic pie than by pressing proposals to increase equity and efficiency in sharing the pie."

A generation earlier economists, policymakers, and much of the public had despaired of ever seeing dynamic growth again. Many had talked of the arrival of a "mature economy" that had reached something close to the end of its capacity to grow, an economy whose fruits would have to be distributed more equally and perhaps more coercively given that those fruits seemed unlikely to expand. Now the same men and women were celebrating their discovery of the secret of virtually permanent economic growth. They were trumpeting the ability of economic expansion to solve social problems without requiring serious sacrifices, without the need for redistribution of wealth and power. When compared with what had come before, this was a paradigm shift of major proportions.

The belief that economic growth was the best route to a just society was part of a larger set of ideas, often called the "consensus" and associated most prominently with scholars and intellectuals. Consensus theorists promoted a set of ideas that, together, described America as a nation not only liberated from economic scarcity but also—and partly as a result—liberated from social conflict. That argument is associated most prominently with the sociologist Daniel Bell, the title of whose 1960 book *The End of Ideology* has become something of a label for American intellectual life in the 1950s. More revealing is the book's subtitle: *On the Exhaustion of Political Ideas in the Fifties.* In the absence of heated battles over scarce economic resources, Bell argued, Americans had run out of grand ideas:

> Ideology, which once was a road to action, has come to be a dead end. . . . Few serious minds believe any longer that one can set down "blueprints" and through "social engineering" bring about a new utopia of social harmony. . . . In the Western world, therefore, there is today a rough consensus among intellectuals on political issues: the acceptance of a Welfare State; the desirability of decentralized power; a system of mixed economy and of political pluralism. . . . The ideological age has ended.

And that, Bell concluded, was a good thing because, he wrote, "the tendency to convert concrete issues into ideological problems, to color them with moral fervor and high emotional charge, is to invite conflicts which can only damage a society." It was much better, in short, to live in a culture in which most people rejected great moral visions and broad social crusades and concentrated instead on the more prosaic, less exalted but also less dangerous business of competing for material advancement.

The "end of ideology" idea helps explain why in the early and mid-1950s there was something of a decline in liberal activism, why many people had difficulty sensing great urgency in addressing social problems or launching new initiatives. For a time, at least, consensus ideology helped make American liberalism cautious, passive, even conservative. It was a worldview that sometimes seemed to rest on fear of what might happen if society embarked on any great crusades: a fear of class conflict, a fear of "mass irrationality, a fear of the dark passions that fanaticism could and had unleashed in the world." A distinguishing characteristic of the "consensus" liberalism was its fundamentally unradical, even antiradical quality.

Complacency would be too strong a word to describe the social outlook of consensus intellectuals. Many of them were harshly critical of American society and culture, even highly critical of the consensus itself. "A repudiation of ideology, to be meaningful," Daniel Bell wrote, "must mean not only a criticism of the utopian order but of existing society as well." The historian Richard Hofstadter, one of the first and most prominent spokesmen for the consensus idea, wrote scornfully in his classic 1948 study of a series of political leaders, *The American Political Tradition:*

> The sanctity of private property, the right of the individual to dispose of and invest it, the value of opportunity, and the natural evolution of self-interest and self-assertion . . . have been staple tenets of the central faith in American political ideologies. . . . American traditions also show a strong bias in favor of equalitarian democracy, but it has been a democracy in cupidity rather than a democracy of fraternity.

Yet the concerns that Bell, Hofstadter, and other intellectuals expressed about the moral quality of the consensus did not alter their belief in the strength of the economic successes that supported it. Nor did it alter their essential (if slightly jaundiced) faith in the ability of the system to thrive. As they viewed their world, they concluded—to overstate things slightly—that there was no need to worry any longer about corporate power. Capitalism, after all, had proved that it worked. There was no need to worry about inequality; economic growth and social mobility would take care of that. Hofstadter, for example, wrote of the unemployed of the Great Depression: "The jobless, distracted, and bewildered men of 1933 have in the course of the years found substantial places in society for themselves, have become home owners, suburbanites, and solid citizens." Bell argued that "in a politico-technological world, property has increasingly lost its force as a determinant of power, and sometimes even of wealth. In almost all modern societies, technical skill becomes more important than inheritance as a determinant of occupation, and political power takes precedence over economic. What then is the meaning of class?" The problems of American life, consensus theorists believed, were less those of inequality and injustice than of shallowness, banality, and alienation that modern culture produced.

And yet, for all the criticism that consensus intellectuals often directed at their culture, there was also an unmistakably smug tone in some of the intellectual discourse of the 1950s: a tendency for writers to refer to their audience as "we," confident that the reading public was a homogeneous entity that shared their own values and assumptions. The great critic Lionel Trilling, for example, wrote with somewhat uncharacteristic ebullience that there comes a moment "when the tone, the manner and manners of one's own people become just what one needs, and the whole look and style of one's culture seems appropriate." Prosperity, abundance, consumerism, and the loosening of cultural prejudices that once would have barred Trilling, Bell, and other Jews from a place at the center of American life shaped this new view of the nation's culture. The Cold War simply reinforced it.

These ideas—the assumption of increasing and virtually universal abundance, the assumption of shared values and goals, the belief in the end of conflict—reflected the experiences of members of the white middle class and of educated white middle-class men in particular. That suggests another set of changes of considerable importance to the shaping of postwar culture: changes in the size and character of the American bourgeoisie.

Definitions of the middle class are subject to dispute. Yet by almost any reasonable definition, the American middle class was expanding dramatically in the postwar years. It was expanding occupationally. In 1956 for the first time in American history, government statistics showed that white-collar workers outnumbered blue-collar workers in the United States. It was expanding economically through a rapid growth in the number of people able to afford what the government defined as a "middle-class" standard of living. In 1929, 31 percent had achieved that standard. In 1955, 60 percent had achieved it. It was expanding educationally. The percentage of young people graduating from high school rose from just under 47 percent in 1946 to over 63 percent in 1960, and the percentage of young people attending college rose from 12.5 to 22 over the same period. In terms of consumption patterns, things traditionally considered middle-class attributes were becoming more common. Home ownership rose from 40 percent in 1945 to 60 percent in 1960. By 1960, 75 percent of all families owned cars; 87 percent owned televisions; 75 percent owned washing machines. Owning such things did not by itself make someone middle class, any more than attending college or holding a white-collar job did. But such changes in the material conditions of life tended to transform the self-image of many people, helping them to consider themselves part of the great middle class, beneficiaries of what has now come to be called the "American Dream" of education, home ownership, material comfort, and economic security. They were the products of what the sociologist William Whyte called the "second great melting pot," a process of socialization that helped men and women transcend not ethnicity but class, that created a new and more pervasive American bourgeoisie. The newcomers to the middle class, Whyte wrote, "must discard old values" and adopt new ones.

The middle class was not simply becoming more numerous in these years. It was also becoming more homogeneous and more self-conscious. One reason for this was the growing pervasiveness of middle-class images, ideas, and values in American popular culture, a result in part of changes in the media in the 1950s. The most important of those changes was the emergence of television, which within a decade moved from being a curiosity to being a central fact of life for virtually everyone in America—the most powerful force in American culture. Far more than newspapers or magazines or even radio or movies, television linked society together and provided a common cultural experience.

What, then, was that cultural experience? What message did television convey? There were many messages, then as now. But after a brief period in the early 1950s of diverse and innovative programming, television began to succumb to its own economic imperatives and for many years studiously avoided controversy and conflict. It offered instead a relatively homogeneous image of American life, dominated by middle-class lifestyles and middle-class values. This was, to use the Marxist phrase, "no accident."

Television programming in the 1950s was dominated by a very few people—the executives of the three major networks and the commercial sponsors they were attempting to attract. It was a very different programming world from the one Americans came to know in later decades. The power of sponsors over television programming today is relatively limited. Most shows are produced long before sponsors are even approached; advertisers simply buy time slots and only rarely have anything to say about program content. But in the 1950s the network had to court advertisers. Each program was generally supported by a single sponsor who exercised considerable and often direct and prior control over program content.

Many televsion programs in the 1950s actually bore the names of their sponsors: the Pepsi Cola Playhouse, the General Electric Theater (whose host, Ronald Reagan, helped launch his political career through his identification with the company and its programming), the Dinah Shore Chevy Hour, Alcoa Presents, the Camel News Caravan, and others. Corporations whose identities were tied up so directly with particular programs were reluctant to permit them to become controversial, divisive, or even unusual. That was a reflection in part of the advertising assumptions of the 1950s: effective advertising tried to appeal to everyone and to alienate no one. Network executives believed, probably correctly, that to attract sponsors they needed to provide programs that were consistently uncontroversial. One executive, responding to a proposal for a television series dealing with problems of urban life, wrote: "We know of no advertiser or advertising agency in this country who would knowingly allow the products which he is trying to advertise to the public to become associated with the squalor and general down character of this program."

From such assumptions emerged the characteristic programming of the late 1950s and early 1960s: westerns, variety shows, quiz shows, and above all situation comedies, the quintessential expression of the middle-class view of American life. Popular situation comedies—The Adventures of Ozzie and Harriet, Father Knows Best, Leave It to Beaver, Dennis the Menace—were set in virtually interchangeable suburban houses, with virtually interchangeable families, in virtually interchangeable situations. Almost everyone was upper middle class. Almost everyone was white. Almost everyone lived in a stable nuclear family. Most situation comedies reinforced prevailing notions of gender roles: women did not work outside the home, or if they did they were unmarried and were working principally as secretaries and teachers. Men left the house in the morning to go to nameless white-collar jobs in the city.

The world of television entertainment programming was, with only a very few exceptions, a placid, middle-class world. Even the exceptions—shows such as The Honeymooners or I Love Lucy or The Life of Reilly—which revealed elements of working-class or ethnic life or presented women as something more than contented housewives, took images of difference and domesticated them, so that in the end they too reinforced rather than challenged assumptions about the universality of middle-class ideas and experiences. Middle-class Americans, seeing such constant confirmation of their own world on television, could easily conclude that this was the world in which virtually all Americans lived.

Another development that played an important role in shaping the distinctive outlook of the American middle class was the rise of the new, or at least newly expansive, suburban culture in the 1950s. Suburbanization isolated many Americans from the diversity and abrasiveness of urban life. It also provided them with what were at first stable and relatively homogeneous communities. All suburbs were not alike; but within most suburbs, particularly within many of those that grew up in the 1950s, there was a striking level of uniformity and conformity. The most obvious effect of suburbanization, therefore, was a standardizing of the outward lives of those who lived in the suburbs.

This was visible even in the architecture of suburbia. Most suburban developments tended to be built all at once, by a single developer, often designed by a single architect or no architect at all, many characterized by similar and often identical houses. The most famous examples of this are the Levittowns, which became models for other, relatively inexpensive suburban developments. Relatively few suburbs were built by the same kind of mass production that the Levitt family pioneered for their developments. But many were built in ways that produced a similar homogeneity. Even the more expensive suburbs used elaborate zoning and building codes to ensure that homes would not diverge too radically from the community norm. In almost all suburbs, homes were designed to thrust the focus of the family inward on itself, not outward into the community. Suburbanites used their back yards, not their front yards, for recreation. They built back, not front, porches. They valued privacy more than interaction with the neighborhood.

There was a cultural uniformity as well within many suburbs. Sociologists and others who studied suburban communities in the 1950s were often highly critical of the overpowering conformity they found there. David Riesman wrote, "The suburb is like a fraternity house at a small college in which likemindedness reverberates upon itself." William Whyte, who studied a suburb outside Chicago, found there what he called "a belief in 'belongingness' as the ultimate need of the individual." Riesman and Whyte were only half right. Suburbs did not create a pressure to conform as much as they were products of a desire to conform—a desire of men and women to gather in communities of likeminded people, of common class and often common ethnic and religious characteristics. But whatever the reasons, suburbs insulated their residents from social and cultural diversity.

The suburban population as a whole was highly diverse—economically, ethnically, even racially. There were working-class suburbs, ethnic suburbs, black suburbs. Yet few individual suburban communities were diverse; few were places where white Anglo Americans lived alongside African Americans or Hispanic Americans or other minorities. One of the reasons for the massive movement of middle-class whites into suburbs—although not the only reason—was the desire to escape the racial and class heterogeneity of the cities. "Suburbia . . . is classless," William Whyte wrote in 1956, "or at least its people want it to be." There was in most suburbs, another social critic observed, "no elite, no wealthy, prestigious upper class. There were no shanty families, no clusters of the ethnically 'undesirable.'"

But in the larger world, of course, there were wealthy elites, there were poor people, and there were racial and ethnic minorities. The growth of suburbs did not reduce their numbers. Instead it protected the middle class from contact with them, even from active awareness of them. It was not so much a force for homogenizing American society at large as it was a force for dividing it. But in the process it helped make possible an increasingly uniform middle-class culture and an increasingly common middle-class view of the world.

Another of the large social forces that were forging a distinctive middle-class culture in the postwar era was the increasing bureaucratization of white-collar work, the growing proportion of middle-class men and a slowly increasing number of middle-class women whose lives were embedded within large-scale corporate and government organizations that created pressures of their own for conformity and homogeneity. Some of the same social critics who attacked the suburbs as stifling and alienating launched similar attacks on the "organization." Employees of large corporate organizations, according to their critics, were becoming something close to automatons. They were pressured to dress alike, to adopt similar values and goals and habits, to place a high value on "getting along" within the hierarchical structure of the corporation. The organization, its critics argued, posed a challenge to the capacity of individuals to retain their psychological autonomy. It was creating alienated conformists afraid to challenge prevailing norms; people who would take no risks; people who feared to be different.

In his 1956 book *The Organization Man,* William Whyte criticized the bureaucracy in much the same way he criticized the suburb. Corporate workers, he argued, faced constant pressures to get along by going along; they were victims of a social ethic "which makes morally legitimate the pressures of society against the individual." David Riesman's 1950 book *The Lonely Crowd,* one of the most influential works of postwar sociology, argued that the modern organizational culture was giving birth to a new kind of individual. In earlier eras, most men and women had been "inner-directed" people, defining themselves largely in terms of their own values and goals, their own sense of their worth. Now the dominant personality was coming to be the "other-directed man," defining himself in terms of the opinions and goals of others, or in terms of the bureaucratically established goals of the organization. This new form of character was blind to distinctions of class, Riesman argued. "Both rich and poor avoid any goals, personal or social, that seem out of step with peer-group aspirations." And it was debilitating to true freedom. "Men are created different," he lamented; "they lose their social freedom and their individual autonomy in seeking to become like each other." . . .

The stifling uniformity of modern suburban and organizational life was a common theme in the work of literary figures of the 1950s. Writers such as John Cheever, Norman Mailer, John Updike, Saul Bellow, J. D. Salinger, and Walker Percy wrote novels that centered around lonely, frustrated, white, middle-class, male protagonists struggling to find some way to bring meaning and fulfillment to empty, rootless, unsatisfying lives. The Beat poets whose critique of modern society was far more sweeping and more radical in its implications than those of mainstream middle-class writers nevertheless shared their fear of the stifling quality of bureaucratic life. "Robot apartments. Invincible suburbs. Skeleton treasuries. . . . Spectral nations," Allen Ginsberg wrote in his searing poem *Howl,* which became an anthem of the Beat generation. These were not new themes in the 1950s, certainly. But they were newly directed toward suburban life, toward the corporate work place, toward the facelessness and homogeneity of bourgeois society.

Such critiques are striking in retrospect because they almost entirely overlooked what later history has made clear was the most frustrated group within the middle class: not the men but the women. They are striking, too, because they say very little about the vast numbers of Americans outside the middle class altogether, barred from its successes either by economic circumstance or by active barriers of discrimination. And they are striking because almost nowhere in these diagnoses of the character of middle-class society, or of the angst it created among some of its members, was there any significant discussion of the Cold War. What shaped the world of the American bourgeoisie, both its critics and its celebrants were suggesting, were the cultural, economic, and demographic forces of a rapidly evolving industrial society and only incidentally the pressure of the struggle against communism.

The smooth surface of postwar middle-class culture—and the discontents festering below its surface, which would in the 1960s challenge and even shatter it—parallel the smooth surface of postwar American foreign policy and the critiques that would shake it, too, in the 1960s. American culture and American foreign policy reinforced one another in countless ways in the age of the Cold War. Yet they did not cause one another. American society and culture would likely have looked much the same in the 1940s and 1950s with or without a Cold War.

Margaret Rose

Gender and Civic Activism
in Mexican American
Barrios in California

"We want food, we want beds, we want bathrooms." Esperanza Quintero, the wife of striking miner Ramón, was one of the many women denouncing jail conditions in this powerful scene from the now-classic film *Salt of the Earth*. The labor struggle depicted in this motion picture, the 1950 zinc strike in Bayard, New Mexico, became one of the landmarks of Mexican American history in the immediate postwar years, although other confrontations took place before and after the war. Produced and released in the Cold War era, the movie about the fifteen-month walkout by members of Local 890 of the International Union of Mine, Mill and Smelter Workers, the great majority of whom were Mexican Americans or Mexican nationals, generated extraordinary controversy. A focus on the struggles of workers, of an ethnic minority, and of women filmed by blacklisted Hollywood activists (director, screenwriter, actors, and technicians) guaranteed a strong reaction and criticism during this politically charged period.

The film not only chronicled the successful outcome of the bitter strike but also conveyed a strong message about women's equality, rights, and concerns as it vividly portrayed the transformation of the heroine, Esperanza, from a passive to an active participant in the clash between workers and the company. She and other miners' wives insisted that better housing, hot water, and indoor plumbing be added to traditional demands of wages and safety. Moreover, the film illustrated the changes in the balance of power in her marriage. The startling personal and domestic issues raised in the movie offer tantalizing clues about gender, women's issues, family relations, and activism in the Mexican American community during the years after the war. . . .

[T]he publicity accorded to the film eclipsed other instances of collective action on the part of the Mexican American community. Of equal importance, and perhaps more lasting, were the many organizations that sprang up after World War II. Groups such as the American G.I. Forum, founded in Texas by returning Mexican American veterans, or the Unity Leagues, organized by Mexican Americans in California, indicate heightened awareness of discrimination and the desire to combat it in expanding urban areas. The Community Service Organization (CSO) is still another example of postwar social activism. Mexican heritage women participated in all these groups.

. . . Yet the postwar history of Mexican American women has received almost no attention. Traditional accounts of Mexican American history mask Latinas' postwar activism through narratives that recognize the leadership of men and only assume the support and cooperation of women. And by focusing on domestic and apolitical women living in the suburbs, recent interpretations of U.S. women's history neglect the experiences of a great many women of color living in the barrios, black ghettos, and rural communities of the postwar era. . . .

An analysis of the CSO suggests that the postwar cultural emphasis on home, family, and community had a less conservative meaning among Mexican American activist women and men. Women used their roles in the home, family, and community to organize for social change. In mixed-sex organizations they brought traditional female skills (cooking, neighborliness, clerical work, and teaching) and conventional women's issues (neighborhood improvements, education, and health) into the mainstream of the CSO reform agenda. Women and men did not establish a rigid division of labor but tended to participate in different ways in the CSO. Whatever the form of their participation, women's and men's civic activities in the late 1940s and 1950s laid the foundation for the better-known social activism of the 1960s.

The heightened awareness of inequality raised by World War II and its aftermath stimulated civic and political activism in Mexican American communities across the Southwest. In southern California's Pomona Valley, Ignacio López, a local newspaper editor, formed the Civic Unity League, considered a precursor to the CSO, to mobilize for political representation for the barrio. Assisted by Anglo activist Fred Ross, the group succeeded in electing Andrew Morales to the City Council of Chino. Obtaining funding from the Industrial Areas Foundation, a Chicago group established by Saul Alinksy, who had organized such midwestern immigrant groups as Polish and Italian stockyard workers, Ross hoped to duplicate this success in the Southwest. At the same time, in East Los Angeles, a small coterie of civic-minded individuals, angered by postwar discrimination, inferior city services, and the narrow defeat in 1947 of Edward R. Roybal, who had run for a seat on the Los Angeles City Council, began to meet to discuss their grievances. Out of the keen disappointment over Roybal's loss, former campaign workers, other community activists, and Fred Ross cooperated to form the CSO.

Despite the catalyst of the Roybal campaign and his installation as the first chair, the CSO defined itself as a nonpartisan group. In its literature it publicized itself as a "self-help, civic action agency, endeavoring to improve living conditions; to promote inter-community harmony; to work for more adequate education and youth-welfare programs; to protect group and individual interests; to protect, remedy and prevent violations of human and civil rights, and to provide a medium for social expression and 'on the spot' leadership development." This broad conception of its role placed the CSO in the tradition of mutual benefit cooperatives established in the late nineteenth century in the Southwest. *Mutualistas,* as they were called, had begun locally and then had expanded regionally; they became important resources for recently arrived immigrants, as well as first- and second-generation families.

CSO organizational accounts from the early 1950s provide insight into the participants' ethnicity, citizenship, occupation, age, and gender. A 1953 report calculated the CSO's membership at thirty-five hundred. Mexicans and Mexican Americans, three-fourths of whom were U.S. citizens, accounted for more than 85 percent of supporters. In its early years, meetings were conducted in both Spanish and English. Those not of Mexican origin were Jewish, black, or Anglos, like Fred Ross. A few supporters were professionals or small business people, but the majority of the membership was "white collar, factory and field workers in the low income bracket." The CSO was a youthful organization with the largest cohort ranging in age from twenty-five to thirty-five. Women were hardly token members. According to one report, "the branches are composed of men and women in about equal proportion." Although no breakdown was given on marital status, the CSO, like other Mexican American organizations of the time, was interested in involving the entire family. It would seem likely that the majority of female and male participants were married.

Women's and men's participation in mixed-sex organizations is not easily separated, as clear division exists in some areas, but overlap and cooperation mark others. . . .

From time to time, women emerged in leadership positions in the CSO. Sara López served as president of the Madera CSO in central California in the mid-1950s. After the CSO matured as a national organization, women served on its Executive Board. Carmen García, from the Oakland CSO, was elected second vice-president in 1956, and Rosita Moreno, of the Harbor area CSO, won office as third national vice-president in 1956 and 1957. Probably the best-known woman to emerge from the CSO was Dolores Huerta, who later became a prominent labor leader. Huerta, a third-generation New Mexican on her mother's side of the family and second-generation on her father's, benefited from her mother's relocation to Stockton, California, where she operated a hotel with her second husband. Huerta's comfortable lifestyle and family resources enabled her to graduate from high school and the local community college, a rare accomplishment for Mexican-heritage women in the years after World War II. Her association with the CSO began in 1955, when a chapter was established in Stockton. Reflecting Cold War anxieties, Huerta requested an FBI check on Fred Ross through local authorities to certify that he was not connected with radical elements before she joined the group. At first, she performed a variety of traditionally "female" tasks, such as making arrangements for CSO meetings, but soon she moved into the more demanding and responsible position of paid legislative advocate for the CSO in Sacramento. An unusual undertaking for a woman in the 1950s, particularly so for an ethnic woman, this position broadened her exposure to political and labor issues as her involvement with the AFL-CIO–sponsored Agricultural Workers Organizing Committee (AWOC) demonstrates. A divorced mother of two when the CSO was established, she moved up in the CSO while bearing and rearing five more children in an increasingly troubled second marriage. Family responsibilities were eased with the help of a supportive mother.

Dolores Huerta, however, was not typical of women in the CSO. In terms of class and educational background, Hope Schechter (formerly Mendoza) was more representative. Her personal history was not unlike many Mexican-heritage women at midcentury. "My parents came from Mexico. So I'm first generation," she noted in an interview. Further describing her mother's history, she added, "Her papers read 'walked'; they [her mother and her mother's brothers] walked across the border into Texas and then came into Arizona." Hope Mendoza was born in Arizona in 1921. When she was a year old, the family moved to Belvedere, part of the East Los Angeles barrio, and when she was a toddler her parents separated. Her mother worked as a domestic before remarrying and bearing six more children with her second husband.

Mendoza's upbringing was fairly typical of the Mexican immigrant working-class family. But her stepfather's steady employment with Swift Packing Company and union membership provided unusual security during the 1930s when many unemployed families were thrust on public assistance and vulnerable to the repatriations and deportations of the era. "All through the Depression he [her stepfather] was one of the few who had a job, and while it was on the poverty level we never had to go on welfare. He was able to support us." Nevertheless, a large family, a paycheck stretched thin, and discouragement from school-teachers placed limitations on education: "I went to the eleventh grade. It was rough going to school without proper clothes. I remember one winter I didn't have a coat. It was one of the coldest winters. . . . So that's when I decided that I would go to work." Although she would return to school as an adult, her choice to seek employment expanded her world beyond the barrio.

In 1938 the teenager went to work in the garment industry. Enjoying a new independence, she worked there several years before finding a union position on the wartime assembly line at Lockheed. As the female defense job market contracted after the war, she returned to lesser-paid employment. Disturbed by conditions at her new post, she soon became attracted to the International Ladies' Garment Workers Union: "I became interested in the union because I was working a non-union job. So I brought the girls to the union to talk about joining. The union, as usual, had a very difficult time finding women, who are on the militant side, who are articulate." Afterward, Mendoza volunteered her time organizing her shop as well as other plants. She coaxed other young women to join, made signs, walked picket lines, and was arrested. Eventually ILGWU official Sigmund Arywitz "insisted" that the eager garment worker enroll in union-sponsored leadership-training classes. Identified as a determined and bright leader, she was hired as an organizer and business agent in the sportswear division.

These activities gave Hope Mendoza valuable experience, confidence, and prominence in local labor circles and in the Mexican American community. . . . Because of her union activism, Mendoza had a solid base from which to work for political and social change in the barrio. Although Mexican-heritage women were rank-and-file union members, it was unusual for them to emerge as leaders in the white, male-dominated world of union organizing. In this regard, Hope Mendoza occupied a unique position. For many women in the CSO, however, exposure to unions, at whatever level, emerged as a significant factor in predisposing them to community activism—much as military service had done for men. . . .

The antilabor, anticommunist, and antialien climate of the late 1940s and 1950s placed further demands on Hope Mendoza as she confronted the challenges of the Cold War era, "playing a dual role—as an activist in the Mexican-American community, and as part of the labor movement." In the eyes of a rapidly expanding number of conservative politicians and the general public, unionism and subversion became increasingly linked. This combination put the Mexican American community at risk in a rising tide of nativism. The consequences were especially stressful on Mexican parents and their American-born children, who were intimidated by fears of deportation. The immediate causes of this new vulnerability were congressional laws and presidential programs that reflected the growing anticommunism. In particular, the McCarran-Walter Immigration Act of 1952, although not specifically directed at Mexican-heritage people, imposed stringent controls on all immigrants, aliens, and naturalized citizens and subjected them to harassment and deportations by the FBI and the Immigration and Naturalization Service (INS) for any "suspect" political views or activities. "Operation Wetback," initiated by the Eisenhower administration in 1953, did target Mexican immigrants and deported massive numbers of undocumented workers. Under the cumulative impact of these measures, one historian estimated that 3 million Mexicans were expelled from the United States between 1951 and 1954. Although the vast majority of Mexican American activists were members of mainstream organizations, their protests and demands for collective bargaining and social justice were interpreted as "un-American" and exposed them to jeopardy.

The impact of these developments cannot be underestimated in the Southwest, California, and the Los Angeles barrio. A headline of an article appearing in the *Belvedere Citizen* noted: *More than 196,000 L.A. Aliens Begin Annual Registration.* Civic organizations and political officials were besieged by requests for aid. The CSO announced meetings to discuss the "controversial [McCarran-Walter] act." It also responded by setting up an Immigration Committee in addition to its Civil Rights Committee. Sensitive to these concerns, Hope Mendoza served on the Immigration Committee. Congressman Chet Holifield, who represented much of the barrio, cooperated with local organizations to resolve problems. To coordinate and service his constituency better, in 1953 Holifield appointed Mendoza, who was well connected with the Democratic party, as his immigration liaison with the community. Most of her cases were routine; nevertheless, they inflicted great hardship and anxiety on individuals and families. . . . She recalled the difficulties of one particular case: "There was one woman who was being deported, and she had five children and a husband who was going blind. She was a garment worker. Her remaining in this country with five children *born* in this country was crucial, and she was being deported. . . . Through Chet Holifield's office, we worked it out so we got all the paperwork done here." The extent of the disruption of personal lives remains relatively undocumented. But the CSO, through Mendoza and others, exerted a critical impact on Mexicans and Mexican Americans throughout the turbulent 1950s not only in Los Angeles but elsewhere in the state. . . .

Hope Mendoza's almost total immersion in the causes of the late 1940s and 1950s was in part a response to an unhappy first marriage to a husband who did not share her intense convictions: "I married a man who was very provincial, extremely so. . . . He wouldn't give me a divorce. So it took me a good two years before I could get a divorce. The way I finally did it was I'd stay out late; he never saw me. I just wore him down. Never, never saw me and I never got home before—at the earliest—ten o'clock. Sometimes two o'clock in the morning." Mendoza remained single until she met and married Harvey Schechter, a community activist and eventually regional director for the Anti-Defamation League of B'nai B'rith. This marriage, based on shared interests and commitments, proved an enduring success: "We're both so active in the community. We both understand the problems of two people who are activists. . . . It works out beautifully, because we both understand each other very well in that sense."

Although Hope Mendoza achieved recognition in Mexican American labor, political, and CSO circles, the contribution of many more CSO women has gone largely unnoted. Women in the CSO functioned in a wide range of positions from paid to unpaid office work, fund raising, voter registration, and community activism. Mostly we know these women through glimpses of the activities they engaged in. María Durán (later Lang) was "active in trade union work on the Eastside," a CSO founding member, and the first treasurer of the CSO; Bertha Villescas was a CSO assistant executive director and utilized her skills in behalf of the group's education and neighborhood projects; Pauline Holguin, formerly a secretary for the International Ladies' Garment Workers Union, became the executive secretary for the CSO; María Marichilar translated her interest in health issues into programs; and untold others exemplified Mexican American women's commitment and dedication to change during the 1950s.

Mexican American women became the backbone of the CSO. They used traditional female skills—clerical work, hostessing, cooking, neighborliness, and teaching—in behalf of the groups. They contributed to the structural survival of the organization by assuming responsibility for the routine operation of the office. While men became chapter presidents, women occupied the positions of recording and corresponding secretaries. In the late 1940s and early 1950s Bertha Villescas, Carmen Medina, and Margarita Durán (daughter of María) staffed CSO headquarters, managing internal affairs, handling correspondence, running the mimeograph machine, and interacting with the public on a regular basis. Pauline Holguin shouldered this responsibility in mid-decade. Women were also essential in organizing CSO state and national conventions. . . .

Women were also vital in providing operating funds for the CSO. In the first years of its existence the group survived with grants from Alinsky's Industrial Areas Foundation, a temporary arrangement until the group became firmly established. Nevertheless, the donated moneys never covered all the costs. CSO social committees were responsible for organizing the annual and semiannual meetings, banquets, and dances that not only brought the members together to celebrate accomplishments but were also an important source of funds. *Across the River,* a Los Angeles CSO brochure, recognized the committee's role: "Far from being what its name might imply, the group is one of the hardest working, most regular committees in the organization. The committee is a jack-of-all-trades, from its activities from cooking to cleaning at every social affair. In the last analysis the committee is the financial crutch on which the organization leans heavily for support." Women often chaired such committees. Carmen Pujo, for instance, headed the Social Affairs Committee for the Imperial County CSO, as did Viola Cadena for the Santa Clara County branch. . . .

Women also played a major role in perhaps the main program of the CSO in its early years—voter registration. Motivated by the defeat of Edward R. Roybal in his run for the City Council in 1947, the CSO launched its first voter registration drive. According to its literature the following year, "the group made its first large scale attempt to induce members to become Deputy Registrars and a contest was undertaken among them to see who could register the most people." The drive began in Boyle Heights and spread to other areas in the barrio, first Belvedere, then Lincoln Heights, and finally the *colonias,* outlying areas such as San Fernando and San Gabriel. Concurrently, the effort stimulated the development of independent CSO chapters in these communities. In the 1950 campaign, "twenty men and women divided themselves into four teams of five each." The CSO volunteers and deputy registrars "painstakingly covered 2,242 blocks in 373 precincts, devoting 16,000 man-hours" to their effort. Although available records do not reveal the breakdown by gender, a photo in the *Los Angeles Daily News* in 1950, which published a series of stories on the CSO, demonstrates that nearly half the deputy registrars were women. Another photo and story in the series lauded Eliza Baker, "champ CSO registrar," for signing up a thousand new voters. Deputy registrar Hope Mendoza commented, "We just went out, door to door, literally door to door. . . . I think CSO is one that really had the greatest impact in terms of grass roots." Housewives, students, and other unemployed CSO members added 32,000 new voters to the rolls. The result of those early efforts was the election of Edward Roybal to the City Council representing the Ninth District and the selection of Ernesto Padilla to the San Fernando Council. CSO efforts were repeated throughout the 1950s, a particularly daunting task because failure to vote in a general election caused voters to be removed from the rolls.

As CSO deputy registrars scoured their neighborhoods for potential voters, they were confronted with the fact that many long-time residents could not participate in the political system because they were not citizens. To overcome this obstacle, the CSO formed citizenship committees. Announcements of citizenship programs began appearing in the local press. In 1953 the *Eastside Sun* noted: "75 Spanish Speaking Aliens to Be Given Citizenship Classes by CSO in Three Eastside Locations," and praised the "untiring efforts" of Bertha Villescas. Five months later, the *Belvedere Citizen* announced: "200 Students Graduate from CSO Citizenship Classes Tonight." The female membership was prominent in these campaigns. In the late 1950s more intensive activities were reported: "Los Angeles CSO's Citizenship Committee is going strong under the direction of Executive Secretary PAULINE HOLGUIN and

Chairman PRISCILLA ENCINITAS. There are 14 classes now in progress and more could be started if additional teachers were available." As CSO chapters spread to other parts of California, more women became involved. The Visalia branch described its program: "Eighteen persons are ready for their citizenship examinations and many thanks are due to the two fine teachers, MRS. RUBY DE LA CRUZ and MRS. RAY LAUFFENBERGER. forty-five persons are ready to start in Basic and Advanced English classes." Women predominated in this area, but men were also involved. Forty-four students were enrolled, for example, in a citizenship course taught by Leo Rojas of the Madera County CSO.

Women also concentrated on municipal concerns, such as neighborhood improvements. Growing political awareness and power mobilized the Mexican American community to press local government to respond to barrio needs. As one CSO summary noted: "As lists of registered voters with Spanish surnames increased, authorities began to move." *The C.S.O. Story*, a brief pamphlet history of the organization, recorded that "a neighborhood improvement committee was one of the very first in CSO's organization. What can we do, they asked, about the problems of East Los Angeles' blighted areas, poor houses, unpaved streets and muddy walks?" Bertha Villescas, chair of the CSO Neighborhood Improvement Committee, helped define the problems, publicize the issues, and focus community action. These concerns touched women directly as they moved throughout the barrio. Through petition drives, women organized to fight for their children's safety after injuries and deaths of youngsters occurred at dangerous intersections with no traffic lights. Women demanded improved street lighting. The lack of mobility and security were revealed by a concerned husband, who illustrated the dilemma plainly: "Suppose your neighborhood had so few street lights that your wife could not step out to the store after dark." Numerous announcements, such as "CSO to Launch Sidewalk, Curb Campaign Tonight," appeared in the barrio press. Participation in such campaigns to provide services "like those on the Westside" furnished women with important knowledge and insight into local economic relations and political obstacles to change. CSO activist Hope Mendoza underwent such an awakening: "We were fighting to get sidewalks and that's when we found out about the tremendous number of absentee ownerships—the kind of situation that exists in these poor areas. . . . I found out about the word absentee landlord, and I never had heard about it before. You can't be effective if you don't know about the community, where the pressure points are." Awareness of complex power relationships aided in confronting equally intransigent political forces arrayed against the interests of the Mexican American community. Bertha Villescas spearheaded the drive in opposition to county supervisors' plans to locate dumps in East Los Angeles. She arranged visits to proposed dump sites with other CSO officers and organized protests to the proposal.

These and other efforts resulted in measurable renovations in the area. A 1950 article in the *Los Angeles Daily News* described the changes initiated by the CSO since its inception.

Three years ago, dirt roads and walkways stretched the length and breadth of Belvedere. In Boyle Heights were trash-strewn vacant lots, junk-jammed alleyways, cracked and rutted roads, broken curbings.

Today pavements cover most of Belvedere's streets, and more than half of them are bordered by neat curbs and shining sidewalks.

In Boyle Heights, street lights glow from 50 new installations, crosswalks protect youngsters in 35 places; stoplights at 20 corners and traffic signals at 25 other intersections safeguard lives; miles of roads have been repaved.

Although these achievements seemed substantial, they were only the beginning of a sustained struggle judging from the repeated calls for meetings to press for more action throughout the 1950s. These improvements represented the persistent efforts of CSOers—and the female membership in particular. While the accomplishments may not have drawn headlines, they embodied tangible advances in the immediate surroundings as well as increased empowerment for barrio women and their families.

There were important victories, but the CSO also experienced crushing defeats in urban affairs. This was particularly evident in the painful destruction of parts of the barrio at the hands of highly organized and well-financed real estate interests and their political allies in the urban renewal and freeway projects in the late Eisenhower years. The battle over Chavez Ravine was one example of the disruption and displacement of barrio residents relocated from their homes in order to make way for Dodger Stadium despite the vigorous protests of the CSO and other local organizations. María Durán Lang, Henrietta Villaescusa, and Ralph Guzmán circulated petitions as part of an unsuccessful campaign to maintain the integrity and identity of the neighborhood.

Voter registration and education and neighborhood concerns provide a general indicator of women's activism in the Mexican American community in the 1950s; however, these were not their only interests. They also turned their attentions to family health issues, a traditional preoccupation of women. Early in the decade, the CSO scheduled a "Health Hints Talk" and conducted first-aid classes for a largely female audience. Programs for children figured prominently in the group's calendar of events. In one project the organization sponsored hearing tests for children. María Marichilar, chair of the Los Angeles CSO's Health and Welfare Committee, addressed an important concern for mothers in her 1957 plans: "On March 30th of this year, 100 free shots of Salk polio vaccine were administered at the CSO office by the Health Department and other shots will be given later." The Visalia CSO undertook a similar project to vaccinate children before the start of the polio season. Women in the Oakland CSO cooperated in an effort to offer free tuberculosis examinations in 1959. These and other endeavors, such as recreational programs and scholarships for adolescents and aid to the elderly, further demonstrate the range of women's community activism in the postwar years.

Far from being a stagnant period for Mexican-heritage women, the late 1940s and 1950s were years of involvement and commitment. Despite the pall cast by the Cold War on political, social, and community activism, the CSO provided an important vehicle for women and men to attain a Mexican American version of the American dream—first-class citizenship, community services, and a decent standard of living.

To achieve their ideal of the Mexican American family, women in Mexican American communities in the Southwest joined organizations to protect themselves against deportation; through voter registration and education drives, they became active in campaigns to secure political rights taken for granted by others; and they engaged in efforts to correct substandard living and health conditions in their neighborhoods.

The CSO maintained this mainstream vision in the 1960s and after, continuing to work for local issues and to address neighborhood concerns not only in the Los Angeles barrio but also in Mexican American communities throughout the Southwest. One of its major Los Angeles programs during the decade was to establish credit unions and promote consumer education for its membership. The passage of state old-age assistance for elderly noncitizens in 1961 was a result of an eight-year struggle generated by CSO chapters across California. In the 1970s, 1980s, and

1990s the CSO continued to sponsor dances and banquets, raise money for scholarships, hold queen and king contests, and deal with such pressing local concerns as drug use.

While the CSO was an organization on the leading edge of change in the Mexican American community, particularly in California in the 1950s, its preeminent role would come under challenge from new groups, more diverse constituencies, and different strategies for change in the 1960s. Instead of representing a clean break between the tactics and aspirations of the 1950s, however, the CSO can best be interpreted as an important bridge to the expanding options of the 1960s, whether exercised through new political associations, government programs, union organizing, or women's organizations. . . .

While it lost its preeminence as a leader for social change, the CSO retained a historic legacy as an important foundation for the emergence of the more militant activism of the Chicano generation. Its voter registration drives of the 1950s foreshadowed the emergence of the Southwest Voter Registration Education Project (SWVRP), founded by Willie Velásquez in 1974. It thrived because of female participation in voter, citizenship, and other civic crusades and transformed a generation of Mexican American women.

Like the fictional heroine Esperanza Quintero in *Salt of the Earth,* CSO women combined family life with community activism. Like her, they brought living conditions and health concerns to their organization's agenda and applied their traditional female skills on behalf of their community. Like Esperanza, they learned organizing and leadership skills that they used effectively behind the scenes and sometimes in front. Both the film *Salt of the Earth,* with its powerful messages of organizing, solidarity, and women's rights, and the CSO laid the groundwork for activists of the 1960s and 1970s. As the once banned film reemerged to inspire the next stage of twentieth-century reform movements, the CSO provided practical training and experience to a generation of women who continued to push for social change.

Further Reading

Largely favorable overviews of American society and culture in the 1950s include William O'Neill, *American High: The Years of Confidence, 1945–1960* (New York: The Free Press, 1989) and John Patrick Diggins, *The Proud Decades: America in War and Peace, 1941–1960* (New York: Norton, 1989). Douglas T. Miller and Marion Novak, *The Fifties: The Way We Really Were* (Garden City, NY: Doubleday, 1977) recovers the uneven realities beneath the cliché of the "affluent society," and Marty Jezer, *The Dark Ages: Life in the U.S., 1945–1960* (Boston: South End Press, 1981) is sharply critical. David Halberstam's *The Fifties* (New York: Random House, 1993), though a massive 700-plus pages, is a breezy account that takes a topical approach.

Critical explorations of family, women's lives, and gender issues in the 1950s include *Homeward Bound: American Families in the Cold War Era* (New York: Basic Books, 1988), by Elaine Tyler May; *The Way We Never Were: American Families and the Nostalgia Trap* (New York: Basic Books, 1992), by Stephanie Coontz, which looks at the family in the larger context of changes since the late nineteenth century; and *Not June Cleaver: Women and Gender in Postwar America, 1945–1960* (Philadelphia: Temple University Press, 1994), edited by Joanne Meyerowitz.

The popular culture of the 1950s has attracted considerable attention from historians in recent years. Few developments are seen as more emblematic of the era's popular culture than the television sitcom. For an authoritative history of early television, see *Tube of Plenty: The*

Evolution of American Television (New York: Oxford University Press, 1990), by Erik Barnouw, who worked in the industry. Lynn Siegel explores popular culture and gender in her important study, *Make Room for TV: Television and the Family Ideal in Postwar America* (Chicago: University of Chicago Press, 1992). For studies of the movies of the 1950s, see *All That Hollywood Allows: Re-Reading Gender in 1950s Melodrama* (Chapel Hill: University of North Carolina Press, 1991), by historian Jackie Byars; and *Seeing is Believing: How Hollywood Taught Us to Stop Worrying and Love the Fifties* (New York: Owl Books, 2000), by Peter Biskind, a film critic who uncovers the political messages of popular films of the era. For a probing look at the preceding period, see Dana Polan, *Power and Paranoia: History, Narrative, and the American Cinema, 1940–1950* (New York: Columbia University Press, 1986). George Lipsitz, *Time Passages: Collective Memory and American Popular Culture* (Minneapolis: University of Minnesota Press, 1980) is an influential work that looks at the ways in which class and race shaped popular culture. *A Cycle of Outrage: America's Reaction to the Juvenile Delinquent in the 1950s* (New York: Oxford University Press, 1986), by James B. Gilbert, examines the wide concern over youth and culture in the years when the "baby-boomers" were growing up. The interest in studying culture through the exploration of material artifacts is revealed by several recent books on the history of plastic, a material that came into widespread use in the 1950s. See *American Plastic: A Cultural History* (New Brunswick, NJ: Rutgers University Press, 1997), by art historian and American studies professor Jeffrey Meikle; Stephen Fenichell's accessible and celebratory *Plastic: The Making of a Synthetic Century* (New York: HarperCollins, 1996); and Alison J. Clarke, *Tupperware: The Promise of Plastic in 1950s America* (Washington, DC: Smithsonian Institution Press, 1999), an interesting and readable history of Tupperware that focuses on gender issues.

The social and cultural realities of suburbanization and the consumer culture of the 1950s are scrutinized in great detail in Lizabeth Cohen, *A Consumer's Republic: The Politics of Mass Consumption in Postwar America* (New York: Knopf, 2003), and in Rosalyn Baxandall and Elizabeth Ewen, *Picture Windows: How the Suburbs Happened* (New York: Basic Books, 2000). For a history of suburbanization that takes a long perspective, beginning with the late nineteenth century, see Kenneth T. Jackson's classic *Crabgrass Frontier: The Suburbanization of America* (New York: Oxford University Press, 1987). See Adam Rome, *The Bulldozer in the Countryside: Suburban Sprawl and the Rise of American Environmentalism* (Cambridge: Cambridge University Press, 2001) for an interesting study that locates the roots of American postwar environmental concerns in Americans' response to suburban developments.

Primary Sources

For the text of a 1995 address to Smith College students by Democratic presidential candidate Adlai Stevenson in which he praised motherhood as a proper and socially meaningful role for women, go to www.americancivilrightsreview.com/docs-stevensonwomensplace(1955).htm. For typically disparaging descriptions of unmarried women and unmarried men in the Fifties, see the two articles—"Women without Men," and "Men without Women"—published in *Look* magazine in 1960, which may be found at historymatters.gmu.edu/d/6271 and historymatters.gmu.edu/d/6564. For a copy of a 1950 brochure, "Atomic Bombing: How to Protect Yourself," go to foody.org/atomic/atomic00.html. The Web site www.tnema.org/Archives/EMHistory/TNCDHistory9.htm provides images of 1950s-era advertisements run by Tennessee's Civil Defense and Emergency Management office as well as pictures of fallout shelter supplies.

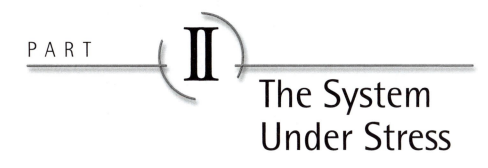

PART II

The System Under Stress

CHAPTER 5

The Black Freedom Struggle

INTRODUCTION

The struggle of African Americans for rights, equality, and freedom stands at the center of the period of U.S. history stretching between 1945 and the present. Often called "the civil rights movement," this struggle marked a crucial turning point separating the conservative 1950s from the new world of the 1960s, an era of widespread citizen mobilization and political protest. The freedom movement burst into the national consciousness as a new and potent force in 1955 with the boycott of segregated bus lines in Montgomery, Alabama. The boycott was sparked by the refusal of activist Rosa Parks to give up her seat on a bus, and its leading public voice was a 27-year-old minister named Martin Luther King, Jr. In 1954, the U.S. Supreme Court had ruled in its historic *Brown v. Board of Education* decision that public school segregation was unconstitutional. These events traditionally have been seen as marking the beginning of a new movement to abolish "Jim Crow" segregation—a system of rules that, since the late nineteenth century, had enforced a regime of white supremacy in the American South. Within a decade, the freedom movement had achieved historic victories. The Civil Rights Act of 1964 struck Jim Crow regulations from the law of the land, and the Voting Rights Act of 1965 provided powerful tools with which the federal government could enforce the Constitutional right of African Americans to vote, a right that white-run local governments had routinely denied.

The Southern system of racial apartheid entailed more than the physical separation of black and white and the disenfranchisement of African Americans; it also involved the economic domination of blacks by whites. And political subordination and economic exclusion marked the black experience on a national basis, not just in the South. The black movement of the post-World War II decades aimed to overturn all of these conditions, not just Southern segregation. During the 1930s and 1940s, African American activists, working through labor unions, the National Association for the Advancement of Colored People (NAACP), and other groups, laid the groundwork for the freedom struggle of the 1950s and 1960s, when black churches in the South became the leading sites of protest against Jim Crow. After legal segregation was outlawed, the black movement did not disappear. The idea of "black power," which expressed an intensified racial pride and anger at white America and which asserted that African Americans needed to accrue political and economic resources among themselves, became powerful among black activists. After 1965 the freedom movement sought to press forward on a wide front of personal, political, and economic issues in a quest for social equality and recognition. Many historians today conclude that the label of "the civil rights movement" is too narrow to encompass the African American movement's wide-ranging agenda.

Until recently, most historians of the freedom movement focused their attention on the campaign against Southern segregation, often asking how the black movement achieved its signal successes of the 1960s. For all the different emphases that historians have put on various factors, there is wide agreement that the movement itself created the legislative victories of 1964 and 1965. The white-dominated power structures of America were not moving toward major changes on their own in the area of race relations during the movement's heyday, with the exception of the federal courts. Movement activists displayed shrewd political insight and organizational prowess, using boycotts, marches, and other tactics to generate so much disruption in the South that white leaders felt compelled to support major concessions to restore order. The movement in this period embraced the tactics of nonviolent protest, borrowing ideas from India's struggle for independence from Great Britain and refusing to respond in kind to violent actions by white authorities. The methods of nonviolence proved effective in mobilizing citizens in large enough numbers to overwhelm the machinery of Southern law enforcement. The embrace of nonviolence, and repeated appeals to the traditional American value of civic equality, also enabled the black movement to seize the moral high ground in national and international contexts, gaining many white supporters outside the South and putting additional pressure on white authorities to abandon the Jim Crow system.

The historical literature on the black freedom struggle is not shaped by contentious disputes between conflicting interpretations. Scholars working in this area have distinguished themselves from one another by seeking to explore the history of this movement from different vantage points. Some have produced detailed studies of individual leaders and elite groups, such as King and his colleagues or the NAACP's lawyers. Others have conducted detailed studies of protest in particular cities and states to capture the "grassroots," or "bottom-up" perspective of less famous activists. It was the willingness of these "ordinary" women and men to confront the violent regime of Southern race domination that distinguished the movement and inspired so many who came into close contact with it. The internal workings of the movement, including the complex gender dynamics of the struggle and the tensions between charismatic leaders and rank-and-file activists, have received much attention.

In recent years, scholars have challenged some traditional ideas about the history of the black freedom movement and have expanded its definition in a variety of ways. They have widened the geographic and chronological boundaries of the movement's history, documenting protest against various aspects of white supremacy, particularly against economic inequality, in the North and the West as well as in the South, and during the decades of the 1930s and 1940s as well as in the 1950s and 1960s. Some scholars have demonstrated the consistent appeal of calls for "race pride" and "self-help" among African Americans throughout the post-World War II era, showing, for example, that some black Americans had reservations about pursuing racial integration with whites during the years from 1955 to 1965. They have pointed out that a strategy focusing on economic development by and for African Americans has always attracted a substantial following among black citizens who have seen this as the best route to ultimate equality. During the late 1960s and 1970s, such ideas—often criticized as "separatist"—became associated with the idea of black power. According to the traditional narrative of the African American movement, the black power tendency appeared in the mid-1960s after the strategy of nonviolent protest seemed to have run its course and when some activists had become disillusioned with King's vision of reconciliation with whites through redemptive suffering and love. Black power was embodied in organizations like the Black Panther party (BPP), in leaders such as Huey Newton and Eldridge Cleaver, and in the black arts movement that flourished around the country in the 1960s and 1970s.

The readings in this chapter, in different ways, challenge some of the received or traditional ideas about the black freedom movement, rendering it more complex, more fraught with internal conflict, and more ambiguous in both its spirit and its outcomes than customarily thought. The first reading is a 1987 consideration of Martin Luther King, Jr., and his relationship to the broader freedom struggle by the theologian and historian Vincent Gordon Harding. Harding protests the "official" King honored with a holiday and argues that the real King was more radical and, from the viewpoint of the U.S. power structure, more threatening than the figure whose birthday we now celebrate. For King, "nonviolent" did not mean "nondisruptive" or "nonthreatening." Instead, the philosophy of nonviolence moved King, as Harding explains, to challenge the spiritual and economic basis of American life and to protest the actions of the United States in the world; all of these things King ultimately condemned as essentially unjust and violent. Harding also sees King himself being challenged by the anger rising within the black movement starting in 1965, when rioting broke out in the Watts neighborhood in Los Angeles among young African Americans outraged over police brutality and a lack of economic opportunities. The cry of "black power" was first heard in 1966 during a march in Mississippi sparked by James Meredith (the central figure in an earlier desegregation battle); King was on that march and was confronted with this new rhetoric. Harding presents King as working to keep up with increasingly militant young voices in the freedom movement, but not as standing in outright opposition to black power. Harding emphasizes King's radicalism, finally, in his deepening identification with the poor and dispossessed of the United States and the world.

The second reading in this chapter, by historian Timothy B. Tyson, comes from a 1998 article surveying the career of Robert F. Williams, a largely forgotten figure who gained notoriety in the 1960s for advocating armed self-defense by black Americans against whites who would do them harm. Tyson seeks to erode the customary distinction between, on the one hand, a Southern civil rights movement shaped by nonviolence, committed to gaining legal rights "within the system," and dominant among African American activists in the period from 1955 to 1965, and, on the other hand, a Northern black power movement arising in the late 1960s, focused on racial identity, hostile to American society, and willing to consider the option of violent militancy. Tyson seeks to bring aspects of African American history sometimes associated with black power—such as armed self-defense and the influence of leftist ideology—back into the story of the freedom struggle during the heyday of civil rights, arguing that these elements were always present.

Williams, an army veteran of World War II, led an armed NAACP chapter in Monroe, North Carolina, debated the wisdom of nonviolence with King, and later was hosted by various Communist governments as a fugitive from U.S. law. As Tyson shows, the advocates of nonviolence within the black freedom struggle saw Williams as a serious challenge to their thinking, so much so that the Student Nonviolent Coordinating Committee (SNCC), the youth activist organization that spread the gospel of grassroots nonviolent agitation at that time, dispatched activists to Monroe in the early 1960s to show that their methods could succeed in making change in Williams's own backyard. The sensational aspects of Williams's story risk blowing the significance of his career out of proportion, and historians have not always made such a sharp distinction between civil rights and black power as Tyson claims they have. Nonetheless, Tyson succeeds in showing that the story of the freedom movement in the 1960s is a complex one of competing tendencies and philosophies, not one of a perfectly united nonviolent army marching toward inevitable victory.

The third reading, taken from a 2004 article by Charles M. Payne, a leading historian of grassroots activism, raises probing questions about the significance of formal desegregation—specifically, about school desegregation beginning with the *Brown* decision—in the context of the broad disadvantages that African Americans continue to experience up to the present. Payne does not go so far as to question whether African Americans were right to focus on attacking Jim Crow segregation. But he does lament the narrow understanding of racism that, in his view, was reflected in the whole long debate over segregation, stretching from the Supreme Court's 1896 *Plessy v. Ferguson* decision, which endorsed the Jim Crow system, to the *Brown* ruling, which overturned *Plessy* and ruled that segregated facilities were inherently unequal. Payne criticizes the American tradition of discussing race relations in terms of individual feelings of discomfort, rather than in terms of objective and "structural" inequality and disadvantage. He also contends that the dividends ultimately paid by the antisegregation strategy were decidedly mixed. Political and economic exclusion were not ended by formal desegregation of schools. Public schools themselves, throughout the United States, have in fact remained highly segregated by race, as is widely known, due to "white flight" from cities and the gerrymandering of school district boundaries by local authorities. Moreover, Payne argues, a political backlash by angry white Americans against the African American movement, starting in the 1960s, has pushed the entire U.S. political system sharply to the right, making it less hospitable to demands for further government redress of black grievances. So, to him, the freedom movement's history is filled with ironies, even if all historians of the movement continue to view it as inspiring and as a part of American history worth celebrating.

VINCENT GORDON HARDING

The Radicalism of Martin Luther King, Jr.

In the 1970s, as a fascinating variety of voices began to press the nation to decide where it stood concerning the memory and meaning of Martin Luther King, Jr., and as we instinctively sought an easy way to deal with the unrelenting power of this disturber of all unjust peace, a black poet perhaps best reflected our ambivalence. Carl Wendell Hines wrote:

> Now that he is safely dead
> let us praise him
>   build monuments to his glory
>   sing hosannas to his name.
>   Dead men make

such convenient heroes; They
cannot rise
To challenge the images
we would fashion from their lives.
And besides,
it is easier to build monuments
than to make a better world.

Then as the voices of artists and family and millions of black people (and their votes, and their nonblack allies) began to build, the sad wisdom of Hines's words seemed to sharpen and to cut deeper at every moment. For it became increasingly clear that most of those who were leading the campaign for the national holiday had chosen, consciously or unconsciously, to allow King to become a convenient hero, to try to tailor him to the shape and mood of mainstream, liberal/moderate America.

Symbolic of the direction given the campaign has been the unremitting focus on the 1963 March on Washington, the never-ending repetition of the great speech and its dream metaphor, the sometimes innocent and sometimes manipulative boxing of King into the relatively safe categories of "civil rights leader," "great orator," harmless dreamer of black and white children on the hillside. . . .

It appears as if the price for the first national holiday honoring a black man is the development of a massive case of national amnesia concerning who that black man really was. At both personal and collective levels, of course, it is often the case that amnesia is not ultimately harmful to the patient. However, in this case it is very dangerous, for the things we have chosen to forget about King (and about ourselves) constitute some of the most hopeful possibilities and resources for our magnificent and very needy nation. Indeed, I would suggest that we Americans have chosen amnesia rather than continue King's painful, uncharted, and often disruptive struggle toward a more perfect union. I would also suggest that those of us who are historians and citizens have a special responsibility to challenge the loss of memory, in ourselves and others, to allow our skills in probing the past to become resources for healing and for hope, not simply sources of pages in books or of steps in careers. In other words, if as Hines wrote, Martin King "cannot rise to challenge" those who would make him a harmless black icon, then *we* surely can—assuming that we are still alive.

Although there are many points at which our challenge to the comfortable images might be raised, I believe that the central encounters with King that begin to take us beyond the static March-on-Washington, "integrationist," "civil rights leader" image are located in Chicago and Mississippi in 1966. During the winter of that year King moved North. He was driven by the fires of Watts and the early hot summers of 1964 and 1965. Challenged and nurtured by the powerful commitment of Malcolm X to the black street forces, he was also compelled by his own deep compassion for the urban black community—whose peculiar problems were not fundamentally addressed by the civil rights laws so dearly won in the South. Under such urgent compulsion, King left his familiar southern base and stepped out on very unfamiliar turf. For Hamlin Avenue on Chicago's blighted West Side was a long way from the marvelous, costly victories of Selma, St. Augustine, and Birmingham, and Mayor Richard Daley was a consummate professional compared to the sheriffs, mayors, and police commissioners of the South. But King had made his choice, and it is one that we dare not forget.

By 1966 King had made an essentially religious commitment to the poor, and he was prepared to say:

I choose to identify with the underprivileged. I choose to identify with the poor. I choose to give my life for the hungry. I choose to give my life for those who have been left out of the sunlight of opportunity.

> I choose to live for and with those who find themselves seeing life as a long and desolate corridor with no exit sign. This is the way I'm going. If it means suffering a little bit, I'm going that way. If it means sacrificing, I'm going that way. If it means dying for them, I'm going that way, because I heard a voice saying, "Do something for others."

We understand nothing about the King whose life ended in the midst of a struggle for garbage workers if we miss that earlier offering of himself to the struggle against poverty in America, to the continuing battle for the empowerment of the powerless — in this nation, in Vietnam, in South Africa, in Central America, and beyond.

In a sense, it was that commitment that took him from Chicago to Mississippi in the late spring of 1966, as he responded to the attempted assassination of James Meredith, taking up with others that enigmatic hero's "march against fear." There on the highways of the Magnolia State we have a second crucial encounter with the forgotten King. He was an embattled leader, the King who was challenged, chastened, and inspired by the courageous, foolhardy Young Turks of the Student Nonviolent Coordinating Committee. He was attentive to those veterans of the struggle who raised the cry for "Black Power," who made public the long simmering challenge to King's leadership, who increasingly voiced their doubts about the primacy of nonviolence as a way of struggle, and who seemed prepared to read whites out of the movement. Perhaps the most important aspect of the Meredith March for King's development was the question the young people raised in many forms: "Dr. King, why do you want us to love white folks before we even love ourselves?" From then on the issues of black self-love, of black and white power, and of the need to develop a more militant form of nonviolence that could challenge and enlist the rising rage of urban black youth were never far from King's consciousness. Along with his deepening commitment to the poor, those were the subjects and questions that did much to shape the hero we have forgotten.

One of the reasons for our amnesia, of course, is the fact that the forgotten King is not easy to handle now. Indeed, he never was. In 1967, after spending two hectic weeks traveling with the impassioned black prophet, David Halberstam, a perceptive journalist, reported that

> King has decided to represent the ghettos; he will work in them and speak for them. But their voice is harsh and alienated. If King is to speak for them truly, then his voice must reflect theirs; it too must be alienated, and it is likely to be increasingly at odds with the rest of American society.

Halberstam was right, but only partly so. After the Selma matches of 1965, King's voice did sound harsher in its criticism of the mainstream American way of life and its dominant values—including the assumption that the United States had the right to police the world for "free enterprise." Not only did the white mainstream object to such uncompromising criticism from a "civil rights leader" who was supposed to know his place, but respectable black people were increasingly uncomfortable as well. For some of them were making use of the fragile doorways that the freedom movement had helped open. Others, after years of frustration, were finally being promoted into the positions of responsibility and higher earnings that their skills and experience should have earlier made available. Too often, King was considered a threat to them as well, especially as his commitment to the poor drove him to increasingly radical assessments of the systemic flaws in the American economic order, an order they had finally begun to enjoy.

But Halberstam, a man of words, saw only part of the picture. King did more than *speak* for the ghettos. He was committed to mobilizing and organizing them for self-liberating action. That was his deeper threat to the status quo, beyond words, beyond alienation. That was what King's friend Rabbi Abraham Heschel surely understood when he introduced King to an assembly of rabbis in these words: "Martin Luther King is a voice, a vision and a way. I call upon every Jew to harken to his voice, to share his vision, to follow in his way. The whole future of America will depend on the impact and influence of Dr. King."

Part of what we have forgotten, then, is King's vision, beyond the appealing dream of black and white children holding hands, beyond the necessary goal of "civil rights." From the outset, he held a vision for all America, often calling the black movement more than a quest for rights—a struggle "to redeem the soul of America." By the end of his life, no one who paid attention could mistake the depth and meaning of that vision. At the convention of the Southern Christian Leadership Conference (SCLC) in 1967, King announced, "We must go from this convention and say, 'America, you must be born again . . . your whole structure must be changed.'" He insisted that "the problem of racism, the problem of economic exploitation, and the problem of war are all tied together." These, King said, were "the triple evils" that the freedom movement must address as it set itself to the challenge of "restructuring the whole of American society." This was the vision behind the call he issued in his final public speech in Memphis on April 3, 1968: "Let us move on in these powerful days, these days of challenge to make America what it ought to be. We have an opportunity to make America a better nation."

That final speech was delivered to a crowd of some two thousand persons, mostly black residents of Memphis who had come out in a soaking rain to hear King and to support the garbage workers' union in its struggle for justice. King's challenge to his last movement audience reminds us that he also carried a large and powerful vision concerning the role of black people and others of the "disinherited" in American society. His vision always included more than "rights" or "equal opportunity." On December 5, 1955, at the public meeting that launched the Montgomery bus boycott and Martin Luther King, Jr., into the heart of twentieth century history, King had announced,

> We, the disinherited of this land, we who have been oppressed so long, are tired of going through the long night of captivity. And now we are reaching out for the daybreak of freedom and justice and equality.

As a result of that decision and that movement, King said,

> when the history books are written in the future somebody will have to say "There lived a race of people, of black people, fleecy locks and black complexion, a people who had the moral courage to stand up for their rights, and thereby they injected a new meaning into the veins of history and of civilization." And we're gonna do that. God grant that we will do it before it's too late.

From beginning to end, the grand vision, the magnificent obsession never left him, the audacious hope for America and its disinherited. Only in the light of that dual vision can we understand his voice, especially in its increasing alienation from the mainstream, in its urgent movement beyond the black and white civil rights establishment. In his last years, the vision led him to call repeatedly for "a reconstruction of the entire society, a revolution of values." Only as we recapture the wholeness of King's vision can we understand his conclusion in 1967 that "something is wrong with capitalism as it now stands in the United States." Only then can we grasp his word to his co-workers in SCLC: "We are not interested in being integrated into *this* value structure. Power must be relocated." The vision leads directly to the voice, calling for "a radical redistribution of economic and political power" as the only way to meet the real needs of the poor in America.

When our memories allow us to absorb King's vision of a transformed America and a transforming force of black people and their allies, then we understand his powerful critique of the American war in Vietnam. After he struggled with his conscience about how open to make his opposition, after he endured intense pressure to be quiet from Washington and from the civil rights establishment, King's social vision and his religious faith stood him in good stead. He spoke out in a stirring series of statements and actions and declared:

> Never again will I be silent on an issue that is destroying the soul of our nation and destroying thousands and thousands of little children in Vietnam. . . . the time has come for a real prophecy, and I'm willing to go that road.

Of course, King knew the costly way of prophets—as did the rabbi who called us "to follow in his way." We must assume that neither the black prophet nor his Jewish brother was speaking idle words, opening up frivolous ways. Rather those were visions, voices, and ways not meant to be forgotten.

Indeed, in a nation where the gap between rich and poor continues to expand with cruel regularity, where the numbers of black and Hispanic poor vie with each other for supremacy, where farmers and industrial workers are in profound crisis, where racism continues to proclaim its ruthless American presence, who can afford to forget King's compassionate and courageous movement toward justice? When the leaders of the country spew reams of lies to Congress and the people alike, in public and private statements, when the official keepers of the nation's best hopes seem locked in what King called "paranoid anti-communism," when we make cynical mercenaries out of jobless young people, sacrificing them to a rigid militarism that threatens the future of the world, do we dare repress the memory of a man who called us to struggle bravely toward "the daybreak of freedom and justice and equality"? Dare we forget a man who told us that "a nation that continues year after year to spend more money on military defense than on programs of social uplift is approaching spiritual death"?

Clearly, we serve our scholarship and our citizenship most faithfully when we move ourselves and others beyond amnesia toward encounters with the jagged leading edges of King's prophetic vision. When we do that we recognize that Martin King himself was unclear about many aspects of the "way" he had chosen. In his commitment to the poor, in his search for the redistribution of wealth and power in America, in his relentless stand against war, in his determination to help America "repent of her modern economic imperialism," he set out on a largely uncharted way. Still, several polestars pointed the way for him, and they may suggest creative directions for our personal and collective lives.

As King searched for a way for Americans to press the nation toward its best possibilities, toward its next birth of freedom and justice, he held fast to several basic assumptions. Perhaps it will help to remember them:

1. He seemed convinced that in the last part of the twentieth century, anyone who still held a vision of "a more perfect union" and worked toward that goal had to be prepared to move toward fundamental, structural changes in the mainstream values, economic and political structures, and traditional leadership of American society.

2. King believed that those who are committed to a real, renewed war against poverty in America must recognize the connections between our domestic economic and political problems and the unhealthy position that we occupy in the military, economic, and political wards of the

global community. In other words, what King called "the triple evils of racism, extreme materialism and militarism" could be effectively fought only by addressing their reality and relationships in our life at home and abroad.

3. Unlike many participants in current discussions of poverty and "the underclass" in American society, King assumed that his ultimate commitment was to help find the ways by which the full energies and angers of the poor could be challenged, organized, and engaged in a revolutionary process that confronted the status quo and opened creative new possibilities for them and for the nation. Surely this was what he meant when he said,

> the dispossessed of this nation—the poor, both white and Negro—live in a cruelly unjust society. They must organize a revolution against that injustice, not against the lives of . . . their fellow citizens, but against the structures through which the society is refusing to lift . . . the load of poverty.

4. By the last months of his life, as King reflected on the developments in the freedom movement since its energies had turned northward and since some of its participants had begun to offer more radical challenges to the policies of the federal government at home and abroad, he reached an inescapable conclusion. The next stages of the struggle for a just American order could no longer expect even the reluctant support from the national government that the movement had received since Montgomery. Now, he said, "We must formulate a program and we must fashion the new tactics which do not count on government good will, but instead serve to compel unwilling authorities to yield to the mandates of justice."

5. Defying most of the conventional wisdom of black and white America, King determined to hold fast to both of his fundamental, religiously based commitments: to the humanizing empowerment and transformation of the poor and of the nation and to the way of nonviolence and creative peace making. His attempt to create a Poor People's Campaign to challenge—and, if necessary, to disrupt—the federal government on its home ground was an expression of this wild and beautiful experiment in creating nonviolent revolution. Planning for a massive campaign of civil disobedience carried on by poor people of all races, aided by their un-poor allies, King announced, "We've got to make it known that until our problem is solved, America may have many, many days, but they will be full of trouble. There will be no rest, there will be no tranquility in this country until the nation comes to terms with [that problem]."

For those who seek a gentle, non-abrasive hero whose recorded speeches can be used as inspirational resources for rocking our memories to sleep, Martin Luther King, Jr., is surely the wrong man. However, if there is even a chance that Rabbi Heschel was correct, that the untranquil King and his peace-disturbing vision, words, and deeds hold the key to the future of America, then another story unfolds, another search begins. We who are scholars and citizens then owe ourselves, our children, and our nation a far more serious exploration and comprehension of the man and the widespread movement with which he was identified.

Recently, the Afro-American liberation theologian Cornel West said of King, "As a proponent of nonviolent resistance, he holds out the only slim hope for social sanity in a violence-prone world." What if both the black theologian and the Jewish scholar-mystic are correct? What if the way that King was exploring is indeed vital to the future of our nation and our world? For scholars, citizens, or celebrants to forget the real man and his deepest implications would be not only faithless, but also suicidal. For in the light of the news that inundates us every day, where else do we go from here to make a better world?

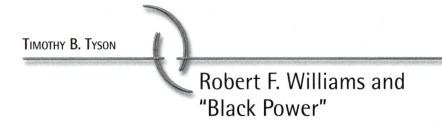

Timothy B. Tyson

Robert F. Williams and "Black Power"

The life of Robert F. Williams illustrates that "the civil rights movement" and "the Black Power movement," often portrayed in very different terms, grew out of the same soil, confronted the same predicaments, and reflected the same quest for African American freedom. In fact, virtually all of the elements that we associate with "Black Power" were already present in the small towns and rural communities of the South where "the civil rights movement" was born. The story of Robert F. Williams reveals that independent black political action, black cultural pride, and what Williams called "armed self-reliance" operated in the South in tension and in tandem with legal efforts and nonviolent protest. . . .

The still-new historiography of Black Power touches on such issues, though its chronology tends to begin after 1965 and its geography remains largely urban and northern or western. Ephemeral early works echoed the vacuous mainstream journalism of the period, portraying Black Power as a "new black mood" or a "radical response to white America"—a black backlash to the betrayals of white liberals and the assaults of white reactionaries. The first major breakthrough in the literature, Clayborne Carson's *In Struggle,* recognized that Black Power "affirmed the legitimacy of a long-standing tradition of armed self-defense in the rural deep South" and that it reflected "dormant traditions of black radicalism" in Dixie. Carson recognizes that Black Power represented "a logical outgrowth" of the freedom movement's efforts "to instill in the minds of black people the notion that they could create a better world for themselves." In these frameworks, however, Black Power still represents a tragic departure from the civil rights dream—whether pointless, necessary, unfortunate, or inevitable. . . .

The life of Robert F. Williams suggests that both Black Power and the civil rights movement have their roots in what Patricia Sullivan's important history of race and democracy in the New Deal–era South calls the "traditions of freedom and citizenship" that, "born in the crucible of Reconstruction, sustained communities of resistance." World War II afforded the black southerners who carried those traditions forward unprecedented political opportunities; many who seized them came from families with long traditions of resistance to white supremacy. And those traditions are only remotely related to nonviolence as it is conventionally depicted. In fact, it might be argued that nonviolent interracialism, rather than Black Power, is the anomaly. A careful sifting of historical evidence from across the South reveals the widely held distinction between the civil rights movement and Black Power as largely an intellectual architecture of political convenience.

. . . In 1946 twenty-one-year-old Robert Williams stepped down from a segregated Greyhound in Monroe wearing the uniform of his country. Williams had moved to Detroit four years earlier to work at Ford Motor Company. Coming home from Belle Isle Amusement Park on the evening of June 11, 1943, he and his brother battled white mobs in one of the worst race riots in United States history. Williams was drafted in 1944 and endured the ironies of marching for freedom in a segregated army. . . . Military training had given black veterans "some feeling of security and self-assurance," he recalled. "The Army indoctrination instilled in us what a virtue it was to fight for democracy and that we were fighting for democracy and upholding the Constitution. But most of all they taught us to use arms." Like thousands of other black veterans whom John Dittmer has characterized as "the shock troops of the modern civil rights movement," Robert Williams did not come home to pick cotton.

Another returning black veteran, a friend of Williams's named Bennie Montgomery, did come home to raise cotton on the farm that his father operated as a sharecropper for W. W. Mangum, a white landowner near Monroe. Saturday, June 1, 1946, was a regular workday on the Mangum place, but Montgomery asked Mangum for his wages at noon, explaining that he needed to go to Monroe to have his father's car repaired. Mangum apparently kicked and slapped the young veteran, and Montgomery pulled out a pocketknife and cut his employer's throat. The Ku Klux Klan wanted to lynch the black sharecropper, but instead state authorities whisked Montgomery out of town, tried and convicted him of murder, and ten months later executed him in the gas chamber at Central Prison in Raleigh.

State authorities shipped the sharecropper's remains back to Monroe. Robbed of their lynching, however, members of the local klavern of "the invisible empire" let it be known that Bennie Montgomery's body belonged, not to his family, but to the Ku Klux Klan. "They was gonna come and take Bennie's body out and drag it up and down the streets," J. W. McDow, another African American veteran, recalled. "I rather die and go to hell before I see that happen." A group of former soldiers met at Booker T. Perry's barbershop and devised a battle plan. When the Klan motorcade pulled up in front of the Harris Funeral Home, forty black men leveled their rifles, taking aim at the line of cars. Not a shot was fired; the Klansmen simply weighed their chances and drove away. Former United States Army Pfc. Robert F. Williams cradled a carbine that night. So did three men who would become key lieutenants in the "black militia" that Williams organized ten years later. "That was one of the first incidents," Williams recalled, "that really started us to understanding that we had to resist, and that resistance could be effective if we resisted in groups, and if we resisted with guns."

Williams soon left the South for almost a decade, working briefly at Cadillac Motor Company in Detroit before using his G.I. Bill benefits to write poetry and study psychology at three different black colleges: West Virginia State College, Johnson C. Smith College, and North Carolina Central College for Negroes. "Someday," he vowed in a 1949 article for the Detroit edition of the *Daily Worker,* "I would return seasoned from the fight in the north and more efficient in the fight for the liberation of my people." In 1952, Williams wrote an essay for Paul Robeson's newspaper, *Freedom,* in which he predicted that African American college students would soon become "the most militant agitators for democracy in America today. They have nothing to lose and all to gain." At Johnson C. Smith, Williams met one of his literary heroes, Langston Hughes, who considered Williams a promising poet and sent him handwritten poems as an encouragement. In 1953, however, Williams ran out of money for college and reenlisted in the armed forces, this time in the United States Marine Corps.

"Wherever he has gone," an FBI observer noted during this period, "Williams has constantly complained, both in the Army and at previous places of employment, that he has been discriminated against." The Marine Corps was no different. Objecting bitterly to racial discrimination, Williams clashed with his officers, spent much of his sixteen months in the Marine Corps in the brig, and received an undesirable discharge in 1955. "Subject in a letter to the President of the United States expressed his desire to renounce his citizenship and live in a country 'which would not let his family starve,'" United States Naval Intelligence reported. His one bright moment as a Marine came on May 17, 1954, when he heard that the United States Supreme Court had struck down school segregation. "At last I felt that I was a part of America and that I belonged," he wrote. "I was sure that this was the beginning of a new era of American democracy."

Upon his return to Monroe in 1955, Williams joined both the local branch of the NAACP and a mostly white Unitarian fellowship. In a Sunday sermon delivered to his fellow Unitarians in 1956, Williams hailed the Montgomery, Alabama, bus boycott and celebrated what he called "the patriots of passive revolution." His bitter collision with the Marine Corps had not dampened his commitment to equal rights for all under the United States Constitution and to those elements in the American political tradition that he believed undergirded black liberation. Invoking "the spirit of Concord, Lexington and Valley Forge," Williams declared from the pulpit that, as he put it, "the liberty bell peals once more and the Stars and Stripes shall wave forever."

The atmosphere at the Monroe NAACP was less exuberant. In the wake of the *Brown v. Board of Education* decision and the triumph at Montgomery, Ku Klux Klan rallies near Monroe began to draw crowds as big as fifteen thousand. Dynamite attacks on black activists in the area were common and lesser acts of terror routine. "The echo of shots and dynamite blasts," the editors of the freedom movement journal the *Southern Patriot* wrote in 1957, "has been almost continuous throughout the South." The Monroe NAACP dwindled to six members, who then contemplated disbanding. When the newest member objected to dissolution, the departing membership chose him to lead the chapter. "They elected me president," Robert Williams recalled, "and then they all left."

Finding himself virtually a one-man NAACP chapter, Williams turned first to the black veterans with whom he had stood against the Klan that night back in 1946. Another veteran, the physician Dr. Albert E. Perry Jr., became vice president. Finding it "necessary to visit homes and appeal directly to individuals," Williams informed the national office, he painstakingly recruited from the beauty parlors, pool halls, and street corners, building a cadre of some two hundred members by 1959. The largest group of new recruits were African American women who worked as domestics. The Monroe branch of the NAACP became "the only one of its kind in existence," the novelist Julian Mayfield, a key supporter of Williams in Harlem's black left, wrote in *Commentary* in 1961. "Its members and supporters, who are mostly workers and displaced farmers, constitute a well-armed and disciplined fighting unit." The branch became "unique in the whole NAACP because of a working class composition and a leadership that was not middle class," Williams later wrote. "Most important, we had a strong representation of black veterans who didn't scare easily."

In response to the drownings of several local African American children whom segregation had forced to swim in isolated farm ponds, the Monroe NAACP launched a campaign to desegregate the local tax-supported swimming pool in 1957. Harry Golden, a prominent Jewish liberal from nearby Charlotte, observed that the specter of interracial sexuality "haunts every mention of the race question" and thought it "naive" of Williams to "experiment with the crude emotions of a small Southern agricultural community." Not surprisingly, the Ku Klux Klan blamed the affluent Dr. Perry for the resurgent black activism and a large, heavily armed Klan motorcade attacked Dr. Perry's house one night that summer. Black veterans greeted the night riders with

sandbag fortifications and a hail of disciplined gunfire. The Monroe Board of Aldermen immediately passed an ordinance banning Ku Klux Klan motorcades, a measure they had refused to
consider before the gun battle. . . .

An even more vivid local drama dragged Monroe onto the stage of international politics on
October 28, 1958. Two African American boys, David E. "Fuzzy" Simpson and James Hanover
Thompson, ages eight and ten, met some white children in a vacant lot. A kissing game ensued
in which the ten-year-old Thompson and an eight-year-old white girl named Sissy Sutton kissed
one another. Rarely in history has an incident so small opened a window so large into the life of
a place and a people. The worldwide controversy that stemmed from the "kissing case" under-
lined the power of sexual questions in racial politics and demonstrated both the promise and the
problems of Cold War politics for the African American freedom struggle.

After the kissing incident, Sissy Sutton's mother reported, "I was furious. I would have killed
Hanover myself if I had the chance." Sissy's father took a shotgun and went looking for the two
boys. Neighbors reported that a white mob had roared up to the Thompson home and threatened not only to kill the boys but to lynch their mothers. Later that afternoon, police officers
spotted Hanover Thompson and Fuzzy Simpson pulling a red wagon loaded with soft drink bottles. "Both cops jumped out with their guns drawn," Thompson recalled. "They snatched us up
and handcuffed us and threw us in the car. When we got to the jail, they drug us out of the car
and started beating us." The local juvenile court judge reported to Gov. Luther H. Hodges that
the police had detained the boys "for their own good, due to local feeling in the case." . . .

Robert Williams saw the "kissing case" as more than a local expression of the irrational sexual lynchpin of white supremacy; the bizarre clarity of the case and the strange politics of the
Cold War suggested a larger strategy. As Martin Luther King Jr. and the Southern Christian
Leadership Conference (SCLC) would do in Birmingham four years later, Williams and his
friends in Monroe set out to use the international politics of the Cold War as a fulcrum to move
the United States government to intervene. Determined to make the "kissing case" a global
metaphor for the American racial dilemma, they fired off press releases, pestered reporters,
hounded the wire services, and put in motion what *Time* magazine called "a rolling snowball"
of worldwide publicity. . . .

"The kissing case," the activist lawyer Conrad Lynn observed years later, "was the case that
got [Williams] in national and international attention." The case not only furnished Williams
with a network of seasoned activists in the American left but with a growing number of supporters among black nationalists in Harlem. Audley "Queen Mother" Moore, an important figure in
both Communist and black nationalist circles in Harlem from the 1920s to the 1970s, organized
support for Williams. He became a regular visitor to Louis Michaux's National Memorial African
Bookstore on Seventh Avenue off 125th Street, where Michaux welcomed Williams to the
podium the store provided for the legendary Harlem street speakers of the day. The most important of Williams's contacts among the Harlem nationalists was Malcolm X, minister at the Nation
of Islam's Temple no. 7. "Every time I used to go to New York he would invite me to speak,"
Williams recalled. Malcolm would tell his congregation "that 'our brother is here from North
Carolina, and he is the only fighting man that we have got, and we have got to help him so he
can stay down there,'" Williams recounted. Williams found ready support among Harlem intellectuals, including Julian Mayfield, John Henrik Clarke, John Oliver Killens, and other literary and political figures. "They all saw something in Monroe that did not actually exist—an
immediately revolutionary situation," Harold Cruse observed. Later, in an unpublished autobi-
ography, Julian Mayfield disclosed that "a famous black writer made contact with gangsters in

New Jersey and bought me two sub-machine guns which I took to Monroe." Williams was not the best-known black leader in the United States, but he may have been the best armed. . . .

On February 1, 1960, four students from North Carolina Agricultural and Technical College walked into Woolworth's in Greensboro, sat down at a segregated lunch counter, and asked to be served. Within two months, the sit-ins had spread to fifty-four communities across nine states of the old Confederacy, infusing the freedom movement with fresh troops and new tactics. "Only in 1960, when black students entered the fray in large numbers, did a broad assault on segregation become possible," Adam Fairclough points out. "Young people made up the initial phalanx, the entering wedge." King flew to Durham, North Carolina, on February 16 to encourage the students with a speech, telling them that their protest was "destined to be one of the glowing epics of our time." He returned to Atlanta the following day. "While others were pioneering innovative methods of nonviolent direct action," Fairclough observes, "King seemed strangely ambivalent about embracing the new tactics by personal example. Although fulsome in his praise of the lunch counter protests, for example, he showed little interest to lead a sit-in himself."

On March 1, by contrast, Robert Williams followed a dozen black youths into Gamble's Drug Store in downtown Monroe and was the only person arrested. Marched down the street in handcuffs, a shotgun-toting guard on either side of him, Williams spoofed himself as "the dangerous stool-sitter bandit" and vowed that he had "never felt prouder in my life." Young insurgents in Monroe mounted an aggressive campaign of sit-ins that displayed its own unique style. "The Negroes remained in each store only a short time," the *Charlotte Observer* reported, "usually until management closed the counters." Under court orders to abide by the law or face imprisonment, Williams defied the judge and marched with his young troops. "We're using hit-and-run tactics," Williams told reporters. "They never know when we're coming or when we're going to leave. That way we hope to wear them down," he said, managing to sound like a platoon leader even while participating in a passive resistance campaign. "They were always doing something," the manager of Jones Drug Store recalled. "It's a wonder somebody didn't kill him." It was no mystery to Williams; the main difference between sit-ins in Monroe and elsewhere was that "not a single demonstrator was even spat upon during our sit-ins," Williams claimed.

The uneasy peace in Monroe would soon be broken, in large measure by followers of Dr. King. In 1961, Rev. Paul Brooks, an activist in the Nashville student movement investigating for SCLC, and James Forman, soon to become president of SNCC, came to Monroe in the company of seventeen Freedom Riders fresh out of jail in Jackson, Mississippi. The young insurgents arrived in Monroe to launch a rather incoherent nonviolent campaign in Robert Williams's backyard; some participants, including Forman, sought to support Williams, who was under enormous pressure from the Ku Klux Klan; others wanted to prove Williams wrong. One of the Freedom Riders announced that he had come to Monroe because he considered "Mr. Robert F. Williams to be the most dangerous person in America." Another proclaimed: "If the fight for civil rights is to remain nonviolent, we must be successful in Monroe. What happens here will determine the course taken in many other communities throughout the South."

Williams welcomed the Freedom Riders warmly but had a similar understanding of the stakes. "I saw it first as a challenge," he recalled, "but I also saw it as an opportunity to show that what King and them were preaching was bullshit." Two weeks of picketing at the Union County Courthouse grew progressively more perilous for the Freedom Riders. Crowds of hostile white onlookers grew larger and larger. Finally, on Sunday afternoon, August 28, a mob of several thousand furious white people attacked the approximately thirty demonstrators, badly injuring many of them; local police arrested the bleeding protesters. In his classic memoir, *The Making of Black*

Revolutionaries, James Forman later called this riot his "moment of death," "a nightmare I shall never forget." To the consternation of SCLC, the nonviolent crusade swiftly deteriorated into mob violence; throughout the community, white vigilantes attacked black citizens and even fired fifteen shots into the home of the former mayor J. Ray Shute, a white moderate who had befriended Williams.

At the height of this violent chaos, a white married couple, for reasons that are unclear, entered the black community and drove straight into an angry black mob milling near Robert Williams's house. "There was hundreds of niggers there," the white woman stated, "and they were armed, they were ready for war." Black residents, under the impression that the demonstrators downtown were being beaten and perhaps slaughtered, threatened to kill the white couple. Williams, though busy preparing to defend his home, rescued the two whites from the mob and led them into his house, where they remained for about two hours. White authorities later charged Williams and several other people with kidnapping, although the white couple met two police officers on their way home and did not report their alleged abduction. The woman later conceded that "at the time, I wasn't even thinking about being kidnapped . . . the papers, the publicity and all that stuff was what brought in that kidnapping mess." During a long night of racial terror, Williams slung a machine gun over his shoulder and walked several miles with his wife and two small sons to where Julian Mayfield waited with a car. "I didn't want those racist dogs to have the satisfaction of legally lynching me," he explained to Dr. Perry.

The Williams family fled first to New York City, then Canada, then on to Cuba to escape the hordes of FBI agents who combed the countryside in search of them. Supporters of Williams gloried in the escape. Some black residents of Monroe still maintain that Fidel Castro sent helicopters for Williams. Others tell of how he got away in a hearse owned by a black funeral director from Charlotte. An agent assigned to search for Williams locally reported his frustrations to FBI director Hoover: "Subject has become something of a 'John Brown' to Negroes around Monroe and they will do anything for him."

The FBI dragnet never snared Williams, but it did not take Hoover long to hear from him. Every Friday night from eleven to midnight on Radio Havana, Williams hosted *Radio Free Dixie,* a program that from 1961 to 1964 could be heard as far away as New York and Los Angeles. KPFA Radio in Berkeley and WBAI in New York City occasionally rebroadcast the show, and bootleg tapes of the program circulated in Watts and Harlem. An activist in Watts wrote to Williams in 1962, "I am letting my other nationalist friends make copies [of the tapes] and telling each of them to let someone make a copy of theirs." During the early 1960s folk revival, Pete Seeger performed the "Ballad of Monroe" all over the country—"Robert Williams was a leader, a giant of a man," the leftist troubadour sang. From Cuba, Williams continued to edit the *Crusader,* which was distributed via Canada and sometimes Mexico, for a circulation that eventually grew to forty thousand. In 1962, his book *Negroes with Guns,* published from Cuba, became the single most important intellectual influence on Huey P. Newton, soon to found the Black Panther Party in Oakland, California. A play based on *Negroes with Guns,* Frank Greenwood's *If We Must Live,* ran in Watts from July to December of 1965 to eager crowds and enthusiastic reviews. Copies of the *Crusader* traveled down the Mississippi back roads with Student Nonviolent Coordinating Committee organizers: "this leaflet is being distributed by SNCC and COFO workers among U.S. Negroes," the Mississippi State Sovereignty Commission complained in the spring of 1964. Later that year, when SNCC began to veer away from nonviolence, members cited Williams approvingly in the fierce internal debates.

As black activists began to reject even the tactical pretense of nonviolence, the influence of Robert Williams continued to spread. By spring 1962 "the example of the North Carolina militant," August Meier and Elliott Rudwick observe, had "had a profound effect" within the Congress of Racial Equality (CORE). "Armed self-defense is a fact of life in black communities— north and south—despite the pronouncements of the 'leadership,'" a North Carolina activist wrote to Williams. Long before Stokely Carmichael and Willie Ricks led the chants of "Black Power" that riveted national media attention in the summer of 1966, most elements invoked by that ambiguous slogan were already in place. "Your doctrine of self-defense set the stage for the acceptance of the Deacons For Defense and Justice," Lawrence Henry told Williams in the spring of 1966. "As quiet as it is being kept, the Black man is swinging away from King and adopting your tit-for-tat philosophy."

Williams's influence was not limited to the South. "As I am certain you realize," Richard Gibson, editor of *Now!* magazine in New York, wrote to Williams in 1965, "Malcolm's removal from the scene makes you the senior spokesman for Afro-American militants." *Life* magazine reported in 1966 that Williams's "picture is prominently displayed in extremist haunts in the big city ghettos." Clayborne Carson names Williams as one of two central influences—the other being Malcolm X—on the 1966 formation of the Black Panther Party for Self-Defense in Oakland, "the most widely known black militant political organization of the late 1960s." The Central Intelligence Agency (CIA) exaggerated considerably in 1969 by reporting that Williams "has long been the ideological leader of the Black Panther Party." It is closer to say that the Panthers were "a logical development" from the philosophy of Williams, as Reginald Major asserted in his 1971 book, *A Panther Is a Black Cat.* According to Williams, he "talked to Bobby Seale and Mrs. [Kathleen] Cleaver by telephone when [he] was in Africa" in 1968, and the leadership "asked me to become Foreign Minister of the Panthers." At that moment, Williams had already been named president-in-exile of two of the most influential revolutionary nationalist groups: the Revolutionary Action Movement, which the CIA believed to be "the most dangerous of all the Black Power organizations," and the Detroit-based Republic of New Africa, an influential group with hundreds of members that sought to establish an independent black republic in Mississippi, Louisiana, Alabama, Georgia, and South Carolina. "Despite his overseas activities," the CIA reported in 1969, "Williams has managed to becom[e] an outstanding figure, possibly *the* outstanding figure, in the black extremist movement in the United States.". . .

A week after his death [in 1996], Rosa Parks climbed slowly into a church pulpit in Monroe, North Carolina. Beneath her lay the body of Robert F. Williams, clad in a gray suit given to him by Mao Zedong and draped with a black, red, and green Pan-African flag. Parks told the congregation that she and those who marched with Martin Luther King Jr. in Alabama had always admired Robert Williams "for his courage and his commitment to freedom. The work that he did should go down in history and never be forgotten." Her presence in that pulpit, nearly inexplicable when placed in the traditional narrative of "the civil rights movement," demonstrates in almost poetic fashion that historians should reexamine the relationship between "civil rights" and "Black Power." Our vision of the African American freedom movement between 1945 and 1965 as characterized solely and inevitably by nonviolent civil rights protest obscures the full complexity of racial politics. It idealizes black history, downplays the oppression of Jim Crow society, and even understates the achievements of African American resistance. Worse still, our cinematic civil rights movement blurs the racial dilemmas that follow us into the twenty-first century.

The life of Robert Williams underlines many aspects of the ongoing black freedom struggle. . . . But foremost it testifies to the extent to which, throughout World War II and the postwar years, there existed among African Americans a current of militancy—a current that included the willingness to defend home and community by force. This facet of African American life lived in tension and in tandem with the compelling moral example of nonviolent direct action. No doubt those who began to chant "Black Power" in the mid-1960s felt that slogan with an urgency specific to their immediate circumstances. But then, as now, many aspects of its meaning endure as legacies from earlier African American struggles. Above the desk where Williams completed his memoirs just before his death, there still hangs an ancient rifle—a gift, he said, from his grandmother.

CHARLES M. PAYNE

Brown v. Board and the Mystification of Race

*B*rown v. Board of Education* (1954) is becoming a milestone in search of something to signify. It would be going too far to think of the case as an early example of a media event, as more hype than substance, but even with a half century of perspective, it is difficult to say with confidence just why *Brown* has seemed to matter so much. School desegregation on a broad scale does not seem to be feasible public policy. In 1962, after eight years of experience with *Brown*, one writer observed that at the then-current pace, Deep South schools could be completely desegregated in just a bit over seven thousand years. Some of the progress made toward desegregation in the 1960s and 1970s has eroded. When desegregation does occur, the social and academic outcomes are not so uniformly positive as was once hoped. The oft-repeated idea that *Brown* inspired more civil rights activism is plausible, but no one has made more than an anecdotal case for it. Indeed, a better case can be made for *Smith v. Allwright*, the 1944 Supreme Court decision outlawing the white primary. In 1940, the percentage of all southern blacks who were registered to vote was estimated at below 5 percent. In 1947 the percent registered jumped to 12 percent, by 1952 to 20 percent. The increase seems directly attributable to the black voter registration drives that occurred across the South following *Smith*. The decision energized the modern civil rights movement and ended black political exclusion. As for *Brown*, in perhaps the most important revisionist critique of the decision, the legal scholar Michael J. Klarman argued that strong links exist between the decision and the mobilization of white southern resistance to racial change.

If the legacy of *Brown* seems clouded now, its significance seemed perfectly clear to many audiences in 1954. *Time* magazine called it the most important Supreme Court decision of all time, excepting only the *Dred Scott* decision; the *Chicago Defender* saw in the decision the beginning of the end of a dual society, while the more extreme defenders of segregation saw virtually the end of Western society. What does it mean that so many commentators, coming at it from so many different directions, got it so wrong? What does it mean that supporters and opponents of segregation alike overestimated the impact of *Brown?* What does that imply about the level of understanding of the racial system? Clearly, part of the miscalculation involved a widespread tendency to overestimate the power of the law to make change and to underestimate the degree of racial intransigence outside the South. Those miscalculations, though, may reflect a larger pattern. What the initial misreadings of *Brown* tell us is that by midcentury, national discourse about race had become thoroughly confused; the nature of racial oppression had been effectively mystified. A part of that mystification process was the reduction of the systemic character of white supremacy to something called "segregation." The historian John W. Cell points out that the term is "profoundly ambiguous and self-contradictory" and contends "that this state of ambiguity and contradiction was skillfully and very deliberately created. Confusion has been one of segregation's greatest strengths and achievements."

A discussion of the nature of that confusion could start with the 1896 *Plessy v. Ferguson* decision, white supremacy's legal fig leaf. Even as white supremacy was being institutionalized, it was developing a rhetoric that hid its nature:

> We consider the underlying fallacy of the plaintiff's argument to consist in the assumption that the enforced separation of the two races stamps the colored race with a badge of inferiority. If this be so, it is not by reason of anything founded in the act, but solely because the colored race chooses to put that construction upon it.

So, in the familiar theme, the problem is that there is something wrong with black people; they are just overly sensitive. Still, the Court was also willing to grant that part of the problem was the social prejudices of white people:

> The argument also assumes that social prejudices may be overcome by legislation, and that equal rights cannot be secured to the negro except by an enforced commingling of the two races. We cannot accept this proposition. If the two races are to meet upon terms of social equality, it must be the result of natural affinities, a mutual appreciation of each other's merits and a voluntary consent of individuals. . . . Legislation is powerless to eradicate racial instincts or to abolish distinctions based upon physical differences, and the attempt to do so can only result in accentuating the difficulties of the present situation.

The race problem, then, has nothing to do with power or privilege or exploitation—all of which the law might do something about—it is all a question of how white and black people feel about each other. In his famous dissent from *Plessy,* Justice John Marshall Harlan—as irony would have it, a former slaveholder—rejected the idea that the separation of the races was merely an expression of individual social preferences, seeing it instead as a "brand of servitude and degradation," one element in a system of racial oppression:

> In my opinion, the judgment this day rendered will, in time, prove to be quite as pernicious as the decision made by this tribunal in the Dred Scott case. . . . The present decision, it may well be apprehended, will not only stimulate aggressions, more or less brutal and irritating, upon the admitted rights of colored citizens, but will encourage the belief that it is possible, by means of state enactments, to defeat the beneficent purposes which the people of the United States had in view when they adopted the recent amendments of the Constitution.

Harlan was only stating the obvious truth; segregation was the result of systematic racial domination and would only facilitate more brutal aggressions, more transgressive state laws. He lost on the decision, of course, but he also lost the larger battle to determine how the racial system in the South was to be framed. It became increasingly common for white southern spokespersons to do what the Court did: to separate the act of segregation from the systematic oppression of which it was but a part by framing the racial system in a language of "separation," "customs," "our way of life," and "social equality." That language constructed race in interpersonal, not structural, terms and put the most acceptable public face on political disenfranchisement, economic exploitation, racial terrorism, and personal degradation. The language also implied a system that worked to everyone's benefit, "enabling each group to develop to its highest potential, at its own pace, in its own way, maintaining its distinctive cultural values." . . .

The historian David Brion Davis has argued that the Confederacy won the Civil War ideologically. That is, southern interests disproportionately shaped the way the nation came to think about the issues embedded in the war. Race came to be understood through what Davis calls a Confederate-dominated paradigm: Confederate interests and northern apologists were able to shape a national memory that minimized the role of slavery in shaping the nation. In addition, "the reconciliation of North and South required a national repudiation of Reconstruction as 'a disastrous mistake'; a wide-ranging white acceptance of 'Negro inferiority' and of white supremacy in the South; and a distorted view of slavery as an unfortunate but benign institution that was damaging for whites morally but helped civilize and Christianize 'African savages.'"

To this, we might add some corollaries and slight changes of emphasis. First, what Davis calls the Confederate paradigm has always been most comfortable attributing racial inequality to the characteristics of black people—if not their outright inferiority, something at least problematic about their attributes. Thus discussions about poverty, which is usually a racialized topic, become attacks on or defenses of the character of the poor. Or, echoing *Plessy*, for many majority-group college students the key problem of race on their campus is the oversensitivity of minority students. Second, southern elites have always preferred discussions about race in which they are presented as the aggrieved party, whether that means bearing the burden of having to civilize and support blacks in the nineteenth century or having to put up with reverse discrimination in the twentieth. The states' rights argument is another version of this. When he stood in the schoolhouse door at the University of Alabama in 1963, temporarily blocking two black students from entering, Alabama governor George Wallace was trying to frame desegregation as the trampling of his rights by federal authority, not as his doing anything to black people. Last, apologists for the southern way of life have always preferred to frame race relations in interpersonal, not structural, terms. Endless anecdotes have been told about how close blacks and whites were under the old system, how much they looked out for one another. When southerners spoke of "good" race relations under Jim Crow, they almost invariably meant an absence of conflict between the races, conveniently overlooking the fact that power relations were so skewed that conflict was extremely unlikely. When contemporary college students reduce race to who eats lunch with whom instead of, say, who gets access to higher education, they are proceeding from the same paradigm that privileges the interpersonal over the structural. That few of them could even conceive of a structural way to pose the problem is further proof of Confederate victory.

It is, of course, not difficult to find national leaders interpreting black struggle through a rigidly nonstructural paradigm. Dwight D. Eisenhower, no fan of *Brown*, framed his opposition in terms that could have come directly from *Plessy*, in terms of the delicacy of human relationships. "I do not believe that prejudices . . . will succumb to compulsion. Consequently, I believe that Federal law imposed upon our States . . . would set back the cause of race relations a long, long time." For that statement not to be preposterous, one has to conceive of race relations without including violence, exploitation, or the deprivation of effective citizenship for millions of people. If we upset white people, we are going backward. Later, Eisenhower carefully pointed out to Chief Justice Earl Warren that white southerners "are not bad people."

To take an example from the sixties, it is now largely forgotten that George H. W. Bush began his political career "emphatically" in opposition to what became the 1964 Civil Rights Act and was particularly critical of the public accommodations component in the legislation. Echoing Eisenhower, he maintained that legal coercion was ineffective. What counted in the quest for civil rights, he explained, was what is in a person's heart.

Brown, then, was being interpreted in an ideological context in which many Americans almost reflexively understood race in nonstructural terms. *Brown* was seen as an obvious watershed in part because it seemed to address the presumably all-important issue of how blacks and whites were going to interact as individuals. From a mid-1950s viewpoint, it was reasonable to believe that having children go to school together would change the role of race in people's lives (although experience has proven the matter more complicated). As they first looked at *Brown,* conservative southern white elites were trapped in fifty years of their own self-serving construction of race. Over time, they began to understand, in the historian Joseph Hardin Crespino's useful phrase, that black aspiration could be strategically accommodated. Accumulated social privilege—class-segregated residential patterns, for example—afforded middle- and upper-class whites significant protection from desegregation. When that did not work, district lines could be gerrymandered, classes could be tracked, and segregationist academies could be established. Perhaps most important, southern leadership could learn to use the fear of school desegregation in the rest of the country to blunt pressures for desegregation in the South. The ugliest aspects of white supremacy had to be relinquished—unrestrained racist violence, the constant degradation of blacks, their complete exclusion from formal citizenship—but that did not necessarily call for fundamental shifts in power and privilege, certainly not at the elite levels. The Byrds of Virginia, the Lotts of Mississippi, Strom Thurmond in South Carolina, even George Wallace in Alabama—were able to reinvent themselves. In the process, they were able to pull the nation in their direction, to pull the ideological center of gravity to the right, in part through their skillful exploitation of the racial anxieties and racism of the rest of the nation. One suspects that if someone had told southern elites in the late 1950s that in exchange for concessions of civil liberties to blacks, they would be able to eliminate the idea of liberalism as a legitimate term of political discourse, at least some of them would have considered the bargain well worth it.

African American attitudes toward racial separation have always been complex. The southern racial system, in fact, allowed for a great deal of personal contact across racial lines, perhaps more so than in other parts of the country; it just had to be contact on terms defined by white people. Southern cities, for example, traditionally had lower indices of housing segregation than their northern counterparts. Jokesters were quick to point out that the numerous light-skinned blacks were living proof that plenty of integration was happening after dark. Part of the social scientist Gunnar Myrdal's optimism about American race relations was based on his finding that while southern whites were most concerned with preventing social equality—which in this context can be taken to mean unregulated cross-racial contact—blacks were primarily concerned with access to jobs, housing, and schooling and least concerned with anything like social inequality. The first black students to desegregate schools were frequently chided for their disloyalty to black schools. One 1955 poll found only 53 percent of southern blacks in agreement with *Brown.* In his study of black working-class protests over segregated public transportation in World War II Birmingham, Alabama, the historian Robin D. G. Kelley concluded that segregation itself was not the key issue:

Sitting with whites, for most black riders, was never a critical issue: rather, African Americans wanted more space for themselves, they wanted to receive equitable treatment, they wanted to be personally treated with respect and dignity, they wanted to be heard and possibly understood, they wanted to get to work on time, and above all, they wanted to exercise power over institutions that controlled them or on which they were dependent.

In short, after World War II blacks were virtually all opposed to the stigma that was involved in segregation and to segregation insofar as it was used as a tool—often a very important tool—to prevent access to a decent life. But that did not always translate into any deep commitment to integration as an end in itself.

Within the leadership of the National Association for the Advancement of Colored People (NAACP), however, one could find a very strict focus on ending segregation, so much so that W. E. B. Du Bois accused the leaders of myopia. The essays he wrote during the 1930s calling on blacks to continue to build strong race-based institutions even as they continued to assail segregation might have been regarded as unexceptional in the sense that they described how most blacks were living their lives anyway. Yet Du Bois's essays led to his being drummed out of the organization he had helped create. Like Du Bois, the NAACP's membership often saw a more problematic side to a strict focus on defeating segregation. In the years leading up to *Brown,* the historian Adam Fairclough contends, "NAACP officials had a hard time convincing their members that integration would be more effective than equalization in obtaining a better education for their children." When some expressed fear for the future of black colleges, Walter White, the organization's executive secretary, replied that blacks needed to "give up the little kingdoms" that had developed under segregation. When others pointed out that integration often led black children to feel isolated and alienated, one NAACP lawyer responded that if integration led some black children to drop out, that would have to be borne since there were casualties in all social change. When it was suggested that black teachers and principals might find themselves unemployed in desegregated systems, the leadership responded that that, too, was the price of change. Robert Carter, one of the NAACP lawyers who argued *Brown,* noted that the legal team "really had the feeling that segregation itself was the evil—and not a symptom of the deeper evil of racism. . . . The box we were in was segregation itself, and most of the nation saw it that way, too."

If that was true of most of the nation, it is not clear that it was true of most of the nation's black people, either before or after the *Brown* decision. Initial reactions to *Brown* among blacks ranged widely. While the NAACP lawyer Thurgood Marshall claimed that segregated schools could be stamped out in five years—although he expected it to take a lot more lawsuits—and the writer Ralph Ellison saw the decision as opening a "wonderful world of possibilities" for children, a *New York Times* reporter was clearly surprised at the lack of enthusiasm in the black neighborhoods of Washington, D.C., the day after the Court delivered the opinion. He entitled his story "Capital's Negroes Slow in Reacting." According to the writer Richard Kluger, that was not unusual; the mood in many black communities was muted and wary. One black columnist said of Memphis that "there was no general 'hallelujah 'tis done' hullabaloo on Beale Street over the Supreme Court's admission that segregation in the public schools is wrong. Beale Streeters are sorta skeptical about giving out with cheers yet."

One way in which *Brown* really was a milestone is that it marked the hegemony of a certain way of thinking about race. Later, that way of thinking would lead many Americans to believe that the Civil Rights Acts of 1964 and 1965 had essentially solved America's racial problems, or at least the black-white component of them. The declaration that *Brown* was a major turning point bespeaks a similar triumphalism. To the scuffling folks on America's Beale Streets, who had to meet the Man the day after *Brown,* just as they had the day before, it may not have been so clear just what *Brown* was going to do for them. It may have been a blow against segregation, but it did not speak to the range of political, economic, and extralegal constraints on their lives.

The historian Dan T. Carter tells a wonderful George Wallace story. After his 1963 stand in the schoolhouse door, Wallace got more than one hundred thousand telegrams. Over half came from outside the South, and 95 percent of those were supportive of what Wallace had done. It was a moment of revelation: "They all hate black people, all of them. They're all afraid, all of them. Great God! That's it! They're all Southern! The whole United States is Southern!" One of the most important ways Wallace was right is that the nation had learned to understand race in southern—that is, nonsystemic, nonstructural—terms. Had more people understood the implications of that way of thinking, expectations for *Brown* might have been more restrained.

Further Reading

The sprawling scholarship on the black freedom movement is larger by far than that of any other social movement of post-1945 America. Adam Fairclough, "State of the Art: Historians and the Civil Rights Movement," *Journal of American Studies* (vol. 24/3 [December 1990], 387–90) is a fine discussion of the literature. Strong overviews include Robert Weisbrot, *Freedom Bound: A History of America's Civil Rights Movement* (New York: Norton, 1990), a narrative written from a centrist-liberal perspective, and Manning Marable, *Race, Reform, and Rebellion: The Second Reconstruction in Black America, 1945–1990* (Jackson: University Press of Mississippi, 1991), which views matters from the left. Taylor Branch, *Parting the Waters: America in the King Years, 1954–63* (New York: Simon & Schuster, 1988) is an enthralling but very detailed account of the early years. Recent avenues of inquiry can be sampled in *New Direction in Civil Rights Studies* (Charlottesville: University Press of Virginia, 1991), edited by Armstead Robinson and Patricia Sullivan.

Historians taking a top-down approach to studying the movement have focused on a variety of areas. The foremost study of government policy in this area is Hugh Davis Graham, *The Civil Rights Era: Origins and Development of National Policy, 1960–1972* (New York: Oxford University Press, 1990). Mary L. Dudziak, *Cold War Civil Rights: Race and the Image of American Democracy* (Princeton, NJ: Princeton University Press, 2000) is also significant. Those interested specifically in Martin Luther King, Jr., may wish to compare Michael Eric Dyson, *I May Not Get There with You: The True Martin Luther King, Jr.* (New York: The Free Press, 2000) with the earlier work by David Levering Lewis, *King: A Biography* (Urbana: University of Illinois Press, 1978). *Making Civil Rights Law: Thurgood Marshall and the Supreme Court, 1936–1961* (New York: Oxford University Press, 1994), by Mark V. Tushnet, analyzes the NAACP's strategy of fighting for change in the federal courts. Steven F. Lawson, *Running for Freedom: Civil Rights and Black Politics Since 1946* (New York: McGraw-Hill, 1991) provides a concise accounting of the freedom movement's ramifications for the formal political system of the United States. Richard H. King, *Civil Rights and the Idea of Freedom* (New York: Oxford University Press, 1992) is an excellent history of the movement's central concept.

Clayborne Carson, *In Struggle: SNCC and the Black Awakening of the 1960s* (Cambridge, MA: Harvard University Press, 1981) is a leading early study done from the viewpoint of grassroots organizers. *The Origins of the Civil Rights Movement: Black Communities Organizing for Change* (New York: The Free Press, 1984), by Aldon D. Morris, is a crucial examination of the links between leaders like King and local activists around the South. Important local studies include William H. Chafe, *Civilities and Civil Rights: Greensboro, North Carolina, and the Black Struggle for Freedom* (New York: Oxford University Press, 1980); John Dittmer, *Local People: The Struggle for Civil Rights in Mississippi* (Urbana: University of Illinois Press, 1995); and Charles M. Payne, *I've Got the Light of Freedom: The Organizing Tradition and the Mississippi Freedom Struggle* (Berkeley: University of California Press, 1995). Recent scholarship on the central role of women in the African American movement has focused on important grassroots organizers. Leading examples are Barbara Ransby, *Ella Baker and the Black Freedom Movement: A Radical Democratic Vision* (Chapel Hill: University of North Carolina Press, 2003) and Chana Kai Lee, *For Freedom's Sake: The Life of Fannie Lou Hamer* (Urbana: University of Illinois Press, 1999).

The black power phase of the movement has until recently remained largely the province of memoir. *New Day in Babylon: The Black Power Movement and American Culture* (Chicago: University of Chicago Press, 1992), by William L. Van DeBurg, views black power through the prism of cultural history. Scholarship on the freedom struggle and reactions against it in the American North during this period has recently begun to expand quickly. See the studies collected in *Freedom North: Black Freedom Struggles outside the South, 1940–1980* (New York: Palgrave, 2003), edited by Jeanne Theoharis and Komozi Woodard. *Liberation, Imagination and the Black Panther Party* (New York: Routledge, 2001), edited by Kathleen Cleaver and George Katsiaficas, although hagiographic, presents many new writings on the Black Panther Party.

On white opposition to the black movement, the classic by Numan V. Bartley, *The Rise of Massive Resistance: Race and Politics in the South during the 1950s* (Baton Rouge: Louisiana State University Press, 1969) is now supplemented by Dan T. Carter, *From George Wallace to Newt Gingrich: Race in the Conservative Counterrevolution, 1963–1994* (Baton Rouge: Louisiana State University, 1996); Arnold Hirsch, "Massive Resistance in the Urban North: Chicago's Trumball Park, 1953–1966," *Journal of American History* (vol. 82, no. 2 [September 1995], 522–50); and the influential work by Thomas J. Sugrue, *The Origins of the Urban Crisis: Race and Inequality in Postwar Detroit* (Princeton, NJ: Princeton University Press, 1996).

Primary Sources

The majority opinion in *Brown v. Board of Education* is available at www.nationalcenter.org/brown.html. A number of Martin Luther King, Jr.'s speeches, including "I Have a Dream," "I See the Promised Land," and "Loving Your Enemies," as well as the letter he dispatched from jail in Birmingham in 1963, may be found at www.mlkonline.net. A number of oral histories of participants in the civil rights movement in Mississippi, some of which include audio clips, are available at www.usm.edu/crdp/html/transcripts.shtml. Several key documents in the history of the Student Nonviolent Coordinating Committee (SNCC), including SNCC's Founding Statement and "The Basis of Black Power," are available at lists.village.virginia.edu/sixties/HTML_docs/Resources/Primary/Manifestos under the heading "SNCC." The Black Panther Party Platform and Program, as well as the Rules of the Black Panther Party, may be found at this same Web site, under the heading "Black Panther Party." For scanned copies of pamphlets, many of which include photographs put out by the Blank Panthers, go to digital.lib.msu.edu/collections/index.cfm?CollectionID=20. Two speeches by Malcolm X, "The Ballot or the Bullet" and "Message to the Grassroots," may be found, respectively, at www.americanrhetoric.com/speeches/malcolmxballot.htm and www.americanrhetoric.com/speeches/malcolmxgrassroots.htm. Both of these speeches are also available in audio format at these sites.

CHAPTER 6

The New Radicals

INTRODUCTION

In the 1960s, Americans began to hear and read about "the young radicals." Usually this term referred to the white college students who had revived the political left after the conservative era of the Fifties and who were becoming known collectively as the "new neft." These radicals offered ringing indictments of American society during the Kennedy years. Calling America a land of inequality, they pointed to the huge numbers mired in poverty and to the racial minorities experiencing oppression and discrimination on a daily basis. They also criticized the life of the comfortable, white middle class, characterizing it as soulless, materialistic, and superficial. And they lamented a society in which the vast majority lacked real power and where unaccountable elites and massive bureaucracies lorded over citizens who were unable to control their own destinies. These charges were made forcefully in the "Port Huron Statement," the 1962 manifesto of Students for a Democratic Society (SDS), the national new left organization, and young radicals repeated them ceaselessly throughout the Sixties.

The new radicals initially hoped that if people rose up in social movements like the black freedom struggle, "the system" would respond with meaningful reforms. But as the 1960s wore on and the new left grew, its members became far less optimistic about the possibilities of reform. Radicals began to castigate the United States as a morally bankrupt society based in racism and predatory capitalism, and some began to spell "America" as "Amerika," as if to suggest a similarity to Nazi Germany. By the end of the 1960s, many of them declared themselves in favor of a socialist revolution of some kind. This change in outlook and tone reflected in large measure the bitter frustration that had developed in response to the escalation and duration of the Vietnam War. The war disillusioned many idealistic young people and led the young radicals to condemn the United States as an empire and to sympathize with third-world revolutionaries. But this alienation from American life also stemmed from the influence of the African American freedom movement, undergoing its own process of radicalization in the second half of the 1960s. The white radicals, despairing of making America the country they wanted it to be, had disappeared from public view by the mid-1970s. However, the new left's anti-imperialist perspective had a lasting impact on American intellectual life.

Beginning in the late 1960s, the new left also seemed to converge with the "hippie" counterculture that had arisen among the same middle-class, white youth that had produced the new radicals. The hippies condemned mainstream America as hopelessly materialistic and emotionally repressed. They sought an alternative way of life that was more expressive, simple, and communal, and they often experimented with drugs and unconventional living arrangements. Young white people in these years spoke of "the movement," suggesting that there was a single phenomenon, albeit with different branches, that was seeking a new America to replace the old one, which new left revolutionaries and hippies alike found decrepit and intolerable.

Contemporary observers of this movement differed over whether the new radicals brought a welcome idealism or a destructive immaturity to American life. Early on, liberal academics, viewing campus leftists up close, charged that the radicals lacked tolerance for those with opposing views, and displayed a rude, offensive style. Such elders, whether liberals or conservatives, often were anticommunists and leery of any political left, even if the new left was, in their view, merely naïve about communism and authoritarian in temper, rather than Communist-controlled.

Until recently, most scholars of the new left were one-time members of this movement who sought to justify and celebrate it, even if they acknowledged the mistakes of their youth. Early work focused on chronicling the rise and fall of SDS, which existed from 1960 until 1969, when it broke up amid fighting among sectarian political groups. These early historians fondly recalled "the movement" and upheld it as a model of fearlessness and principle to be emulated. However, even among those who admired the new left, a serious difference of opinion arose in the late 1980s and 1990s. This disagreement revolved around the question of whether the early, hopeful Sixties radicals were the "good" characters in the story, and whether late-Sixties radicalism had been "bad." Some historians viewed the harsh criticism of American society and the romanticism concerning Cuban, Vietnamese, and other foreign revolutionaries that marked the post-1968 left as a disaster, and placed part of the blame for the new left's demise on its own late-stage foolishness and anti-Americanism. Others rejected sharply that narrative of decline, asserting that the radicalism of the late 1960s was laudable and well-founded, a reasonable and constructive response to a destructive social order. Radical feminism and black nationalism, both of which came on the scene forcefully starting in the late 1960s, were viewed as welcome presences in American life by those who admired the post-1968 left.

In recent years, historians of 1960s radicalism have sought to expand our understanding of the influences on the new left and, indeed, to expand the very definition of that movement. Some scholarship has scrutinized the origins of the new left to reveal previously unappreciated sources of this renewed radicalism, whereas other work has emphasized the need to bring heightened attention to the later years of "the movement." In this chapter, we present one example of recent work that has revised our understanding of the new left's early years, and a second reading that challenges prevailing views of the later period of Sixties youth radicalism.

The first reading, an excerpt from a 1994 article by Doug Rossinow, offers a new version of the new left's origins. Earlier works focused on SDS, on the relations between the new left and the remnants of left-wing groups of the 1930s and 1940s, on the impact of 1950s popular culture on the "baby-boom" generation, and on the effect of the civil rights movement on young white Americans. Rossinow also emphasizes the formative influence of civil rights protest, but he does so in a more specific way than did earlier works, focusing on one local setting in the South—Austin, Texas, home to the University of Texas (UT). He also brings to light the influence of Christianity on the emergence of youth dissidence between 1956 and 1964. Early works on Sixties radicalism eschewed local events in favor of a national narrative, and drew largely on northern and West Coast locales as the basis for national generalizations. These early works also presented the new left as a strongly secular political movement. Although Rossinow does not present it as a religious movement, he shows how the idea of sharp political dissent became legitimate to some young people in the idiom of Christianity. He demonstrates the presence of two different forms of Christian social criticism in this setting: Christian liberalism, which was embodied in the campus YMCA/YWCA in Austin, the hotbed of political liberalism in that environment; and Christian existentialism, which promoted individual rebellion and placed a high value on "authenticity," or personal and spiritual integrity and wholeness. In the late 1950s and early 1960s, a time when the African American movement was taking off, some young white southerners, influenced by these particular religious forces, came to identify with the black freedom movement. That identification, in turn, placed a positive value on the idea of personal and social transformation, opening the door to visions of change that had seemed frightening and illegitimate during the McCarthy era.

The general applicability of Rossinow's local study can be questioned, and some of the factors he identifies in this setting seem distinctive to the South, or at least to conservative areas of the United States. But the specific links he establishes between the conservative environment of the 1950s and the movements of the 1960s help to explain how the new radicalism could have emerged following an intensely right-wing period in American history. Moreover, in describing how Christian liberalism and existentialism were communicated to young people at this time, Rossinow highlights the spiritual yearnings that underlay the development of radicalism among relatively privileged young white people in that era.

The second reading, an excerpt from a 2002 article by Max Elbaum, explores the new left in the years between 1968 and the mid-1970s, providing a fresh account of the later years of "the movement." Much of the early scholarship on the new left portrayed 1968 as the year when all hell broke loose in American society, and when the radical movement began to decline intellectually and to disintegrate as a political force. Elbaum is among those who disagree with that assessment of the later new left. Here, he offers the most detailed and extended alternative history to date of the world of radicalism starting in 1968. Indeed, Elbaum sees 1968 as a new beginning rather than as the beginning of the end, as the start of an exciting new era of a multiracial left-wing coalition in America determined to resist what it perceived as the malign power of U.S. imperialism. In some respects, Elbaum sees the left of the 1968 to 1975 years as the forgotten forerunner to the "antiglobalization" protests of recent years, such as the protests against the World Trade Organization that erupted in Seattle in 1999 (see Chapter 14). He describes the founding and activism of numerous radical youth organizations among a stunning variety of social groups, including Mexican Americans, Puerto Ricans, Native Americans, Asian Americans, African Americans, and whites (or Anglos). He also shows how they were united by their common antipathy to U.S. capitalism and racism and by their support for revolutionary and nationalist trends in the third world (or "global South," as Elbaum refers to it at one point.) These trends included the Non-Aligned Movement, a coalition of countries that declared neutrality in the U.S.–USSR conflict; the Cultural Revolution, which Mao initiated in the mid-1960s, purportedly to restore Communist China's supposedly lost revolutionary zeal; and a host of guerilla movements in countries around the world. Elbaum radically revises and expands the definition of the new left beyond the SDS-centered and exclusively white movement that has been the subject of most historical scholarship. He sees anti-imperialism and what he calls "third world Marxism" as the broad categories uniting these diverse social forces in the late 1960s and long afterward.

One can question whether all these forces really formed a single movement, especially because the term "new left" was claimed almost exclusively during the 1960s and 1970s by young white people. Furthermore, Elbaum's explanations for the gradual fading from American politics of third world Marxism, which emphasize the resiliency of U.S. capitalism and the unfortunate sectarianism of radical activists, may seem cursory. Some readers no doubt will find Elbaum's clear sympathy for anti-imperialism to be very radical indeed. But Elbaum offers something new in the written history of 1960s radicalism, vigorously telling the later part of the story in fresh detail and as a positive narrative of citizen efforts to make a better world, not as a sorry tale of indecent anti-Americanism.

As both these works indicate, the emphasis on SDS that marked early scholarship in this area has shifted to a broader understanding of 1960s radicalism. Much of the activism of that era was locally based and organized on an ad hoc basis. Frequently, little attention was paid to formal membership and organizational records. Therefore, the retrieval of the true complexity of the activism of that era by historians has proved a somewhat difficult process, one that likely will continue in the future.

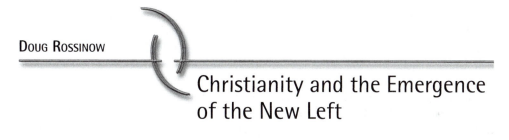

DOUG ROSSINOW

Christianity and the Emergence of the New Left

In works on the "new left"—the white youth movement against racism and imperialism and for radical democracy that flourished on American campuses in the 1960s—religion is absent from the historical picture. . . . Yet, throughout the depths of the cold war and into the 1960s, connections persisted between the realms of religion and political activism. Religion and spirituality remained rich repositories of oppositional values in these years, and political historians of the period might do well to follow the example of historians of earlier American reform and radicalism by putting religion back into "the sixties."

. . . Almost all the scholarly work on the new left has been based on the experiences and memories of northern activists. The founding elite of this movement was largely from northern, metropolitan areas where the influence of the strongly materialist old left of the 1930s and 1940s was relatively strong. Many of the most widely read studies of the new left either were written by members of this "old guard" or focused on their experiences. Even those accounts that do not center entirely on the old guard still focus on the national leadership of students for a democratic society (SDS), the largest new left organization, whose elite was always tilted strongly toward the North. The old guard included many young Jews for whom religious identity had become a secular ethnic identity, and the relative religious-ethnic diversity of the old guard discouraged any emphasis on religion in their politics. This disinclination has passed into most accounts of the new left's origins. Examination of a southern environment, as well as of a less elite group within

From " 'The Break-through to New Life': Christianity and the Emergence of the New Left in Austin, Texas, 1956–1964," by Doug Rossinow, from *American Quarterly,* Vol. 46 (Sept. 1994). Reprinted by permission of the Johns Hopkins University Press.

the emerging student movement of the 1960s, clarifies the role of religion, specifically Christianity, in the new left's emergence.

Looking to the South during the 1950s and 1960s reveals that the obvious connection between religion and democratic political activism lies in the civil rights movement. The centrality of Christian religion in the civil rights movement is well established institutionally and intellectually, but, for the most part, historians have associated religion specifically with *black* civil rights activism. Virtually no one has considered seriously that religion may have motivated and shaped *white* participation in the civil rights movement. Some scholars have documented the roots of the new left in this white civil rights activism. (Interestingly, however, those narratives of the new left that focus on the old guard of SDS underplay the role of the civil rights movement.) I suggest that the important role religion played in mobilizing white civil rights activism in the South indicates a religious element in the formation of the new left. In the South, both an old tradition of Christian liberalism and a newer force, Christian existentialism, played important roles in the emergence of white youth radicalism in the 1960s.

The role of Christian existentialism is noteworthy to historians of the cold war for existentialism of various kinds was evident in radical thought throughout the country during this period. Unfortunately, historians of the new left have mentioned existentialism merely to disparage it. Whatever one thinks of it, existentialism was a crucial element in the creation of the new left. Indeed, the presence of existentialism may have been so pervasive among American youth in the late 1950s and 1960s that, ultimately, historians will ask not why the new left became so influenced by existentialism but why so much youth existentialist sentiment in the 1960s took the form of *leftist* existentialism. In the South, the existentialist element often appeared in a specifically Christian form.

A close examination of a local environment, Austin, Texas, reveals the way in which all these factors—Christian existentialism, Christian liberalism, and civil rights activism—interacted with one another. My study of Austin, home of the University of Texas (UT) and the largest center of white youth radicalism in the South during the 1960s, demonstrates the convergence of all these forces in the years around 1960. The watershed of white student participation in civil rights protests in Austin occurred in the year between the fall of 1960 and the fall of 1961. Christian liberalism and Christian existentialism, in various ways, motivated, organized, and influenced the white participation in this activity. In turn, these traditions combined with the experience of political activism to result in the radicalization of many participants and to point the way toward a new left in the South.

The political environment in Texas during the first decade of the cold war, from the late 1940s to the late 1950s, was characterized by an exaggerated version of the conservative trend apparent nationwide, an exaggeration rooted in regional and local history. Here, liberals found themselves on the defensive and were easily accused of communist sympathies or race treason when they advanced programs that enjoyed greater legitimacy in other parts of the country. Liberalism was a far more politically oppositional force in Texas than in less right-leaning areas. In a sea of conservatism, the main island of liberalism was the University of Texas in Austin; it was also the state capital. . . .

Within the university environment, the least vulnerable center of liberalism was the local church network. Through the 1940s and 1950s, a group of ministers from churches surrounding the university was "right up there on the front edge" of political liberalism, as one protegé said. The most politically active of the group was Blake Smith at University Baptist Church, who was known for his view that "racial segregation is a betrayal of democracy, an affront to human dignity, and an insult to God." These ministers occasionally testified at legislative hearings at the capitol in support of liberal positions on free speech and other issues; they took a firm position favoring the rigid separation of church and state. In a politically and culturally conservative environment, political liberalism enjoyed its widest legitimacy when it was lent the authority of Christian religion.

Most students came to the university from churchgoing backgrounds; they were usually from congregations that were both theologically and politically conservative. Once at UT, however, they encountered a different combination: theological and political liberalism. Jim Neyland, who became prominent among liberal Christian activists at UT in the early sixties, recalled that he and his friends were "concerned about" both "religious hypocrisy" and "political and social hypocrisy." For young people who chafed at a fundamentalist heritage that increasingly seemed to belong to another era, Christian liberalism offered a way to remain in the Christian fold. Austin ministers presented this accommodating religion to them, in the tradition of the social gospel, as inextricably bound to political liberalism, particularly on the issue of race.

For UT students, the center of both theological liberalism and political activity was the university YMCA/YWCA (Y), which had its own building located directly across the street from the campus, on Guadalupe, the retail strip known as "the Drag." Y activities involved hundreds of students each school year, and the Y formed undergraduates into study and discussion committees on subjects ranging from "Psychology and Religion" and "Contemporary Literature" to "Race Relations" and "Pacifism and Disarmament." Each committee was cochaired by a woman and a man. This institutionalization of gender equality afforded women opportunities to rise to leadership positions that they did not enjoy in other settings. Women who became leaders in the Y at UT because of its binary structure, and who subsequently became leaders in the civil rights activity off-campus, included Dorothy Dawson and Sandra "Casey" Cason in the late 1950s and Vivien Franklin in the early 1960s. The Y structure and atmosphere seemed inviting to women generally; as of December 1961, the overall student membership of the Y at UT was nearly two-thirds women.

. . . The conception of Christianity that the Y promoted was highly practical and not very theistic. It was pragmatic, in a philosophical sense, and to Jim Neyland, who was president of the YMCA in the 1960–61 school year, this pragmatism required an atmosphere of free discussion. "To be liberal in the way the 'Y' is liberal," he said, "is to be willing to hear all sides of an issue and to refuse to accept at face value the 'standard' interpretation of what is happening in the world. It means to refuse to accept any value without . . . testing and applying it to life." For students who felt they came from provincial backgrounds, the Y was an oasis of open-mindedness.

The Y played this role at UT largely because of the efforts of its staff. "We've tried to show that Christianity isn't just something for Sunday exercise, that Christianity is something that has to do with living seven days a week if it's worth a hoot, that it has something to do with your treatment of people," said Block Smith, who ran the Y from 1921 until his retirement in 1954. One student in the mid-1950s called him "a primitive Christian" for the simplicity of his egalitarian outlook. . . .

Two issues that epitomized the university Y's political and intellectual role on campus were internationalism and civil rights. The Y, as a world-wide organization, had an international perspective built into it. For liberal students in Texas, a concern about international issues was a variation on the larger theme of cosmopolitanism versus provincialism. Through its frequent speakers and discussions on world affairs, the Y broadened political discussion on the Austin campus. In

1961, for example, UT professors and black South African students spoke at the Y about politics in South Africa, and representatives from student Christian groups in the United States and Cuba discussed relations between their countries.

Equally important, students active in the Y had opportunities to travel abroad with Christian student groups, and these experiences often became formative political moments. They visited third world countries and, most unusually, Eastern Europe. Consequently, they were able to put a human face on socialism, the greatest cold war bogey. In 1961, Susan Reed went to Poland and returned still anticommunist but convinced that socialism had helped the Polish people. Another student visited Russia and reported on his return that the Russians "want peace more than any [*sic*] people in the world." Vivien Franklin went to the Soviet Union and several Eastern Bloc countries. She came back and began telling people that she now thought "business interests" in the United States were "blocking disarmament for political reasons." Travels such as these drew some liberal student activists to the left flank of American liberalism and led to expressions of dissent from cold war orthodoxy, which many Texans found alarming indeed.

The 1958–59 National Student Assembly of the Ys (NSAY—a quadrennial gathering), held at the University of Illinois at Urbana, passed resolutions that clearly expressed such dissent from the "'standard' interpretation" of social and political issues. Casey Cason of the UT contingent chaired the section titled "In Search of World Community." These students saw a "shocking" ignorance of world affairs, of foreign cultures, and of the activities of the U.S. government abroad among the American public. They suggested the American government and press could not be trusted when it came to reporting foreign affairs. They urged a nonbelligerent approach to international relations, which in itself was a form of dissent from the cold war.

Expressions of sympathy for civil rights were equally controversial. Students who became involved in the Y in Austin came into contact with people who told them, by both word and example, that they thought racism contradicted simple Christian belief. The few black students at the school—UT started to admit a trickle of black undergraduates starting in 1956, but, by the early 1960s, there were still fewer than two hundred African-American students in a university of over twenty thousand—were more welcome at the Y than in any official UT building. A few black students became quite involved in Y activities. Action in behalf of an integrationist viewpoint by Y activists in Austin quickened after the 1958–59 NSAY, which Jim Neyland also attended. The assembly turned into a civil rights rally, with three thousand attendees, white and black, joining hands and singing "Kumbaya" and "We Shall Overcome" at the closing session. Back in Austin, the UT delegation was inspired to try their hands at sitting-in. Neyland's first sit-in was at a downtown bus station cafe with Jennie Franklin and Gwen Jordan, two black women. The manager closed the shop rather than serve them. The students were left with a feeling of "liberation and exhileration [*sic*]," Neyland remembered. "It was a victory for us, because we now knew that 'Christian non-violence' could work; we did not know how long it would take, but we were certain our rectitude would eventually wear down the opposition." . . .

Y activists thought they had to take action in the world to affirm their values, and they thought they needed to affirm their values in order to live meaningful lives. "Only in the enactment of [a student's] values in concrete life experience," the UT-Y leaders wrote in spring 1962, "does he divulge his faith to himself and others." This was crucial, for the "major task" of the University of Texas Y, a student reporter wrote after interviewing its staff, was "that of confronting all persons in the University with the necessity of choosing what they will value." Neyland wrote, "Real personal commitment is the goal of the 'Y,' as it encourages a free and open search for meaning." Values, commitment, meaning—these were the things that students should search for, said the Y activists. In the years around 1960, for many of these activists, the search ended in the civil rights movement.

The concern to find meaning in life underlay all the discussion and activity of Y activists. Student Y activists constantly invoked the student "search for meaning" in both their internal literature and their publicity materials. They felt this was a real longing among their contemporaries; it was not just a search that they, as activists, recommended. Another liberal student at UT in the late fifties, *Daily Texan* editor Robb Burlage, thought he heard among his generation "a new call for a meaningful life, as if it sprang from the heart of meaninglessness." Actually, the search for meaning implied a commitment neither to political activism nor to political liberalism. But student Y activists strove mightily to hitch that search to their political vision. Liberal activists of all kinds were making this connection at this time, but, in Austin, Y activists, who developed the connection in the context of Christian liberalism, made it most consistently. . . .

Despite this fusion of the personal and the political, the university Y was best known on the UT campus for its concern with political issues. The Christian Faith-and-Life Community (CFLC)—or "the community," as its members tended to call it—was the place on campus most closely associated during those same years with expressly theological discussion, and the discussion that occurred there placed personal concerns front and center. This residential and religious education center was part of the campus's liberal political culture. Between 1958 and 1963, many university Y leaders who became involved in civil rights activism and other liberal or radical politics lived for some time at the community. Dick Simpson, who lived at the CFLC for a year and who was president of the YMCA in 1962–63, wrote that there was "no place else in conservative Texas quite like [the community]." These student activists came in contact with new ideas at the CFLC that spoke powerfully to their cultural situation, ideas that imparted a radical experimentalism to their thought and action. This was Christian existentialism.

Like the more diffuse "search for meaning" that pervaded youth discussion around this time, existentialism implied a sympathetic response to neither political liberalism in general, the civil rights movement in particular, nor certainly to leftist radicalism. However, in this time and place, it is clear that these themes *did* contribute to the development of white youth liberalism and radicalism, which was crystalized in the crucible of civil rights protest. In a conservative environment such as that in Texas, people of both conservative and critical inclinations were likely to associate all forms of dissidence with one another. This imparted a political tenor to theological and intellectual dissent that it might not have acquired in different circumstances.

The community did not seem likely to nurture any type of radicalism at its inception in 1952. Because the CFLC's "mission," as the staff put it, was framed in terms of theological study, it received the blessings of many local establishment figures, including the UT administration, from the start. It was the task of W. Jack Lewis, the Presbyterian campus minister who founded the CFLC and a man firmly rooted in mainstream Texas culture—as an undergraduate at UT in the 1930s he had been chief "yeller," or cheerleader, for pep rallies—to round up and maintain this kind of establishment approval for his experiment. . . .

By forming an explicit and intentional "covenant" that expressed their collective purpose in living and studying together, he believed, students could ease the sense of social and spiritual alienation that, many social observers in the 1950s claimed, plagued American youth. As the

"Moral Covenant" averred, "Authentic, self-consciously disciplined community does not swallow the individual; it rather creates the very possibility of personhood by pushing the individual against the necessity to decide for himself."

Men and women lived in separate residences, but they had a more coeducational experience than any other students at UT. They took community classes together, ate Friday dinners together, and attended lectures and prayer services together. Judy Schleyer Blanton, who lived at the community in 1960, remembered students there sneaking in and out of bedroom windows, but, in general, there is little reason to believe that more sex went on in the CFLC than elsewhere around campus at the time. Female students there remembered functioning as equals with men in the classroom. Numerous participants in the civil rights protest of 1960–61 remembered Cason, who lived in the women's residence starting in 1958, as the driving force in their group, the initial "mover." . . .

Cason's mentor at the community was Joseph Wesley Mathews, whose arrival as head of curriculum in 1956 decisively changed the course of the "Austin experiment." Until he departed for Chicago in 1962, Mathews's teaching and personality were an omnipresent influence on the character of life and study at the CFLC. Jack Lewis conducted rather conventional Bible-study classes for the residents during the first four years of the experiment but felt that this curriculum lacked an "existential 'bite.'" He hired Mathews to develop a curriculum with sharper teeth. Mathews instituted a rigorous course of study that used not only biblical texts but also contemporary plays and stories and, most heavily, avant-garde Protestant theology— much of it written since the 1920s, much of it imported from Germany, much of it existentialist. The most important theologians to whom he introduced students in Austin were Rudolf Bultmann; Paul Tillich; and, perhaps the greatest influence politically, Dietrich Bonhoeffer.

Mathews had started his career as an evangelical preacher with fundamentalist leanings, but he had undergone a spiritual and intellectual crisis as a chaplain during World War II, when he found his simple religious precepts could not help him cope with the death all around him. After the war he went to Yale Divinity School to study with H. Richard Niebuhr, and he became immersed in existentialism. After this, Mathews combined the evangelistic zeal of his American Protestant tradition with the European theology he had adopted at Yale, and it proved a combustible mix. He became a local celebrity at Perkins Theological Seminary in Dallas and was well known for his iconoclastic sermons, during which he was known to rip pages out of a church's Bible to illustrate his belief that the book was not sacred. Mathews also became renowned at UT for his public performances. In the mid-1950s, he and the liberal philosophy professor John Silber engaged in a series of debates, which drew hundreds of students, over the question, "What is the most important thing in life?" The two later debated the meaningfulness (or meaninglessness) of Beckett's *Waiting for Godot*. Cason, like others, found in Mathews someone sympathetic to her questioning spirit. She lived in a women's dorm when she first came to UT and hated it. She did not feel she could reveal this reaction to most authority figures on campus, but she felt she could talk about it with Mathews. There was "a lot of façade everywhere" in the 1950s, she remembered, and Mathews was one of the few people who seemed to be trying to strip the façade away from things and people. He wanted to ask, "What's eating at the core of people?" It was a question she was also ready to ask.

It was as if Mathews wanted his young charges at the community to experience some of what he had experienced: a crisis of belief, a crisis of identity. What he hoped to accomplish by boring toward a person's "core" was a "breakthrough"—perhaps the pivotal idea of the community. This concept was rooted in both Protestant theology and modern psychological theory. It meant a rebirth into a new life, just as Mathews had started a new life—a personal breakthrough, which, if duplicated enough times, could produce a social breakthrough. . . .

The idea of breakthrough came most directly from the writings of Tillich and Bonhoeffer. Tillich combined psychoanalytic theory with Christian theology to develop a life-affirming ontology of love. In a discussion of Tillich's ideas, James Moeser, an undergraduate in the community who shared an apartment with Jim Neyland in the 1960–61 school year in which many of the planning meetings for political activities took place, emphasized that the experience of grace only arrived in moments of profound crisis. "It comes to us in our darkest moments of deepest despair. It strikes our consciousness just at the moment that we realize our own inadequacy to deal with our existence." This was what Tillich called "the human boundary-situation," which followed the archetype of Jesus's experience on the cross.

The grace received during this kind of crisis meant "reunion," said Moeser. It meant the end of the human experience of "estrangement," of "separation—separation from all other men, separation from the self, and separation from the Ground of Being." This "estrangement" was the basic existentialist concept of alienation, which Tillich thought was the great problem of twentieth-century culture. He identified alienation from God with a sense of alienation from one's true or potential self and recast God as "the Ground of our Being." Furthermore, he identified alienation with sin and preached that grace would bring the opposite of alienation—it would bring self-acceptance and community.

In Tillich's hands, the political implications of the idea of breakthrough as basically an end to alienation were ambiguous. But for students at the CFLC, the concept of breakthrough received a clear political emphasis from the life and work of Dietrich Bonhoeffer. Bonhoeffer is best known not for his life but for his death, in a German prison camp in 1945. He was executed for his involvement in the indigenous German anti-Nazi resistance. For some students in Austin around 1960, Bonhoeffer's influence helped tether the promise of a personal breakthrough to the prospect of political breakthrough. His account of his experience overseeing a renegade Lutheran seminary in Germany in the 1930s, *Life Together,* became a model for the CFLC's "common life together." In *Life Together,* he spoke of a "break-through to new life." Bonhoeffer asserted that the new life in Christ would be a communal life and that the "break-through to new life" would also be a "break-through to community." This breakthrough to community, he said, would occur most clearly in the process of confession. "Confession in the presence of a brother is the profoundest kind of humiliation," he wrote, and this was exactly its usefulness. As it had for Jesus, abasement had to precede breakthrough. Like Tillich, Bonhoeffer drew on the drama of the crucifixion for his discussion of the contemporary human prospect.

Bonhoeffer's vision of community seemed to harbor considerable appeal for the young people gathered at the CFLC. One student there called on her contemporaries, in 1962, to "face the breakdown of authentic human relations in [our] marriages and homes." Perceiving this kind of social alienation, the CFLC stated that its goal was the development of "new and creative modes of corporate existence." Where "the struggle" to create such "creative modes" occurs, they said, "there is the breakthrough. There is the future alive in the present." In a way both personal and social, out of "breakdown," a "breakthrough" could arrive. . . .

The new life into which the students and staff at the CFLC hoped to be reborn would not be merely a sensorium of personal discovery, however. They, like Bonhoeffer, made it clear that the "worldliness" of the new life was to be a political participation in the world. In their prayer services, they prayed for strength "to be responsible" in "politics . . . the social order . . . education . . . vocation." Students at the community expressed disdain for those so caught up in their own selves that they refused to take action in the world around them. Although they read a great deal of psychoanalytic theory, some of them—Carol Darrell, for example—derided the type of student whom she thought was *too* fond of psychology or who was so analytic that he "assumed the posture of a mere spectator." Like students active in the Y, she thought action, in addition to thought, was necessary. In some cases, only a decision to take action would clarify thought. Although the two Christian groups offered different paths to this conclusion, the familiar tradition of Christian liberalism and the newer tradition of Christian existentialism did indeed converge on this point—the need for action.

At the community as at the Y, this call to action had a politically oppositional orientation. Casey Hayden recalled the importance of the image of the "tragic hero or heroine," which she and her friends took from both Christian existentialists, such as Bonhoeffer, and atheist existentialists on the near left, such as Albert Camus. She thought it was important to take action in behalf of one's beliefs, in spite of the risks—perhaps because of the risks. Like Bonhoeffer at his life's end, the community members vowed solidarity with the downtrodden. In a prayer service in early 1961, the students said, "let us take upon ourselves the urgencies of this world." They pleaded,

> may we have compassion for
>> the starving
>> the sick
>> the estranged
>> the oppressed
>> the imprisoned.

The title of this section of the service was "The Life," and it followed some morbid comments on "death" and "fragmentation." The new life that overcame fragmentation, finally, was a life of commitment to the oppressed.

If the students wanted to make a commitment to the oppressed, in the South, the challenge of combating racial oppression presented itself to them, especially after the beginning of the civil rights movement in the mid-1950s. In fact, community members on several occasions expressed solidarity with African Americans. Allen Lingo remembered preaching at local, small-town, white churches in favor of civil rights for blacks as part of his training as a member of the CFLC's staff. As a student resident at the community, another student there had challenged Lingo to protest the annual blackface minstrel show at UT, and he had done so. He did not think a student anywhere else on campus would have challenged him in this manner. The CFLC as a whole took a stand for racial equality when, in 1954, they admitted a black woman and became the only racially integrated student housing at UT. Students remembered this move as a conscious political decision by the group, and it cost the community some sorely needed financial support. Other black students, like Robert Bell, lived there in subsequent years; he remembered it as "a real enjoyable place to live . . . people were real friendly." Solidarity with black students continued at the community, most dramatically when, in 1960, a large group of students went "en masse" to join the civil rights protests occurring just off campus. More than anything else, race was the focus of the political efforts that emerged from the CFLC in the 1956–62 period.

. . . As discussed earlier, an interracial group of Y activists began sitting in at whites-only restaurants in the spring semester of 1959. In early 1960, the wave of sit-ins that swept through the historically black colleges of the South inspired student activists in Austin to continue their efforts. Black students at Bishop College and historically black Wiley College in Marshall, Texas, conducted a series of militant sit-ins, which were animated by the philosophy of Gandhian nonviolence. A coalition of mostly black students from UT, Huston-Tillotson—a historically black college in Austin—and a couple of local seminaries staged demonstrations soon afterward against segregation in Austin. By May 1960, over thirty lunch counters and cafes in Austin had desegregated in response to these and other pressures.

Activists at the Y then decided to step up their activity. The student activists at Bishop had contacts with the Y in Austin; in April, a woman representing the Bishop students came to the Y to recount the events in Marshall. The Y activists at UT felt that they, too, should be part of the student movement for civil rights, and, in the summer of 1960, they started to plan more concerted action. Cason spent part of that summer in New York City working as a tutor in a parish in East Harlem. In August, she attended an NSA seminar on civil rights and stayed for the NSA Congress in Minneapolis, where she first came to national attention among young activists by delivering a dramatic speech challenging the gathered students to risk their own security by committing civil disobedience in behalf of racial equality. Here she, like Dorothy Dawson and Robb Burlage, came in contact with the Liberal Study Group within the NSA, which included Al Haber and Tom Hayden of the University of Michigan and which formed the nucleus of SDS. By September 1960, a circle of activists that included Cason, Houston Wade—"one of the evangels of the new left" and the only member of the group from an old left family—Jim Neyland, Jennie Franklin, and others settled on a strategy of protests directed at the two movie theaters on the Drag that did not admit blacks. Holding all their planning meetings at the Y, they insulated the Y politically and gave themselves complete autonomy by organizing as a non-Y, nonuniversity group—even though most of them were UT students and Y activists. They called themselves Students for Direct Action (SDA).

Starting in early November, SDA organized "stand-ins" at the two theaters in the evenings, often several times a week. White students would line up at the ticket windows to buy tickets if the theaters would also admit their black friends; when they were refused, they would go to the back of the line and wait to do the same thing again. The black students simply asked to buy tickets for themselves and, of course, were likewise refused. This strategy succeeded in clogging up the ticket line and, thus, slowing ticket sales; it also drew a great deal of attention both from passersby and from the local media. Eleanor Roosevelt wrote one of her daily "My Day" columns about the stand-ins. The protestors, 70 percent to 80 percent of them white, received a fair amount of petty harassment and verbal threats, but no one suffered violence during the stand-ins; an early planning meeting in the Y basement was interrupted by a lame bombing incident in which no one was hurt. In November 1960, Glenn Smiley, who worked for the pacifist organization the Fellowship of Reconciliation, visited the UT-Y and delivered a talk on the methods of nonviolent resistance. The students in SDA practiced nonviolence but not nonviolent resistance to authority; there were no planned arrests. For six months, SDA regularly put between forty and two hundred people on the streets for this evening activity; the turnout reached five hundred at the high point of protest in February 1961. This perhaps attested to the organizational skills acquired by the leaders in the varied activities of the student Y. As noted earlier, a large number of participants, as well as leaders, came from the CFLC. Couples sometimes went to the stand-ins for a cheap date. Students avoided complete boredom by singing made-up songs, such as "When the Saints Go Standing In." After each evening's actions, they returned to the Y for a follow-up group meeting; sometimes they sang as they went. Their humor and good spirits reflected their belief that they were part of a vibrant movement for change and that ultimately they would win.

Indeed, by September 1961, they won their demand; the theaters promised to integrate. The protests had put into practice the idea that action was required to affirm one's values, to make life meaningful, and to exercise the human potential for freedom. This activity satisfied the imperatives of both Christian liberalism and existentialism. Furthermore, it left an influential legacy of direct action to subsequent waves of student activists. Real freedom, real community, new life—young activists in the 1960s came to believe that these things could not be achieved if one's politics remained just talk. These convictions were established firmly, and the path to radicalization was opened, by the civil rights activism that erupted on campuses all over the country in the early 1960s. . . .

Christianity did not *cause* the involvement of these young people in civil rights protest or in the new left. A compound of political and cultural forces moved them in those directions, a compound that was forged in the heat of activism. However, the important role of Christian religion and Christian institutions in the emergence of white youth activism in Austin during this time is unmistakable. It is possible that the stand-in activity of 1960–61 would not have occurred had it not been for the safe haven that the university Y provided. There, students, white and black, who were supportive of civil rights could come together without fear of disapproval or harassment to plan their actions and to reinforce one another's commitments. . . .

The intellectual role Christianity played in this story is more complex. Christian liberalism taught students to practice, as well as preach, religious beliefs. It taught that an affirmation of one's values could bring meaning and coherence to one's life. Existentialism gave a name to the feelings of meaninglessness and incoherence that some young white people sought to assuage, and that name was alienation. Christian existentialism searched for ways of replacing alienation with feelings of wholeness, authenticity, and community. One can see these longings in a Christian liberal context like the student Y, but, at a place like the CFLC, these longings received more elaborate expression and deeper exploration. At this historical moment, these two intellectual and political frameworks worked well together; existentialism gave liberalism intellectual grounding, and liberalism helped to keep existentialism politically engaged. In other places, this configuration may have appeared in thoroughly secular settings and terms, but, in Austin, the discussion took place in a Christian idiom. . . .

The personal and the political were fused from the start of "the sixties." . . .

Resonating with North American Protestant traditions of evangelism and individual regeneration, Christian existentialism was a body of ideas from foreign soil that spoke to the situation of these youths in the American South. In the future, we will have to inquire searchingly into the cultural history of the twentieth-century United States if we wish to understand why it spoke to them so. Only by seriously considering the hollowness that white middle-class youth perceived at the center of their good fortune will we comprehend their desire to embark on radical campaigns for change in the society and culture they inherited and to which they looked "uncomfortably." By recognizing the religious component in the new left's beginnings, we can see that this emptiness they saw was, to them, spiritual as well as psychological. Their search for meaning, authenticity, and social justice stands as a reflection on the culture of advanced industrial capitalism in the United States, and it is here that their movement's abiding historical significance may lie.

MAX ELBAUM

What Legacy from the Radical Internationalism of 1968?

Seattle used to be just a city. Since December 1999, it has become shorthand for grassroots protest against the injustices of global capitalism.

This is hardly the first time a place-name has come to symbolize a watershed in opposition movements. There were a host of such markers in the huge wave of U.S. protests against racism and the Vietnam War during and after 1968: "Chicago" (referring to the 1968 Democratic Convention where police beat demonstrators as they chanted "the whole world is watching"); "San Francisco State" (where a 1968–69 strike led by students of color made the first major breakthrough in the fight for Ethnic Studies); and "Cambodia" and "Kent State" (referring to Richard Nixon's ill-fated 1970 invasion of Cambodia and the shooting of four white students by the Ohio National Guard).

For the rebellious youth of the late 1960s, those locations-turned-emblems did not just register as external events. They spurred personal transformations that led thousands to adopt a revolutionary anticapitalist outlook. Radicalization ran both broad and deep. In 1968 more college students (20 percent) identified with Latin American revolutionary Che Guevara than with any of the candidates for the U.S. presidency. A 1971 *New York Times* survey indicated that four out of ten students—nearly 3 million people—thought that a revolution was needed in the United States. Radical sentiment ran even stronger in the African American community and by the early 1970s had penetrated deeply into the Puerto Rican, Chicano, Asian American, and Native American populations. A 1970 survey showed that 30.6 percent of black enlisted men in the armed forces planned "to join a militant Black group like the Panthers" when they returned home. The radical battalions of 1968 and after were not unified around one program or doctrine. Still, their perspective was characterized by a few predominant themes, reflecting the fifteen years of civil rights, Black Power, and antiwar protests that had shaped their political evolution.

Antiracism and anti-imperialism were in the forefront of the new radical outlook. Its main international inspiration came from the national liberation movements that seemed to be daily shattering the notion of U.S. invincibility. It was a time when the Vietnamese and Cuban Revolutions, People's China, and Marxist-led armed movements in Latin America, Asia, Africa, and the Middle East appeared to mesh into one unstoppable torrent. The activists of 1968 regarded solidarity with the Third World (the period's most common term for what today is usually called the global South) as their prime internationalist responsibility. Well into the 1970s, the militants galvanized by this outlook, which most regarded as a Third World–oriented variant of

Marxism, constituted a dynamic political trend and were considered by capitalism's guardians as a force to be reckoned with. Even after this trend passed its peak, its most tenacious partisans played important roles in the antiapartheid movement, the Central America solidarity movement, the Rainbow Coalition electoral upsurge, and other battles of the 1980s.

Yet today the nature—indeed the existence—of this current has been largely erased from even the left's historical memory. The civil rights movement and the broad anti–Vietnam War movement have been extensively chronicled and receive much deserved scholarly and activist attention. But the dominant view even in progressive circles is that the young people who embraced revolutionary ideas after 1968 had essentially "gone crazy," and that the early "good sixties" were replaced by a later "bad sixties" characterized by political madness. The post-1968 work of organizations rooted in communities of color—the Black Panther Party, and to a lesser extent the Young Lords Party, La Raza Unida Party, the American Indian Movement, and a few others—is sometimes given a certain due. But for the most part intellectually ghettoized, these experiences are not seen as central to a United States left that remained vital into the 1970s.

Now is a good moment to set the record straight, to appreciate the influence Third World Marxism once enjoyed, and to analyze why the broad revolutionary trend inspired by this outlook failed to make an effective transition to the changed terrain of later years. The special timeliness of this task is due to "Seattle"—to the stirrings of a new generation against global capitalism, to the emergence of a new internationalist current manifesting impulses toward solidarity with the global South. Such a current especially has much to learn from an earlier generation that exhibited the same impulses, albeit under very different conditions, thirty years ago.

The explosive radicalism of the late 1960s evolved out of the sustained, large-scale protests that had gathered steam ever since the mid-1950s. The prime force initiating the evolution from 1950s conformism to 1968 revolutionism was the civil rights movement. . . .

Beginning in the mid-1960s, the antiracist upsurge was joined by an outpouring of protest against the Vietnam War. The first major nationwide antiwar demonstration, called by Students for a Democratic Society (SDS) for April 17, 1965, beat back a harsh red-baiting campaign and mobilized a then unexpected turnout of 15,000 plus. Just two years later, more than six times that number would march on the Pentagon, militant antiwar actions would sweep the country, and Martin Luther King would denounce the war and link it to the maintenance of racism and poverty.

These movements, moreover, were growing at a time when fights against Western colonialism and neocolonialism gripped the entire Third World. Vietnam stood at the pivot, but new armed organizations such as Uruguay's Tupamaros and Chile's Movement of the Revolutionary Left (MIR) sprouted throughout Latin America. Marxist-led guerrilla movements were gaining ground in every country of Portugal's African empire—Angola, Mozambique, and Guinea-Bissau. The Palestine Liberation Organization (PLO) was picking up the banner of popular struggle against Israeli settler colonialism, and armed left-wing movements were spreading in Asia from India to the Philippines. Che Guevara's 1967 call to "create two, three, many Vietnams" did not appear to be just an expression of sentiment, but resounded as an eminently practical program.

Meanwhile, the Non-Aligned Movement, which numbered twenty-five countries at its first summit in 1961, grew to fifty-plus member states by 1970 and consistently expressed its solidarity with armed liberation efforts. Plans to build a new society in China (the Cultural Revolution) and Cuba seemed to offer fresh, grassroots-based models of socialism.

This Third World rebellion against U.S. and West European domination also and inevitably constituted a head-on challenge to white supremacy. It resonated with young people across the globe, particularly in U.S. communities of color, where a new generation of activists termed their constituencies "Third World peoples" within this country's borders.

Through the 1960s, world and national politics became ever more volatile, and then came the jolts of that turning-point year: 1968. The nationwide Tet offensive in Vietnam, which came as a near complete surprise to the U.S. command, revealed the complete failure of Washington's counterinsurgency efforts and raised the prospect of the first outright U.S. defeat in its long war-making history. Tet, and the antiwar surge it intensified at home, also led directly to the ouster of the first of two presidents to be driven from office by the upheavals of the 1960s and early 1970s. On March 31, 1968, a besieged Lyndon Johnson announced that he was abandoning his reelection bid and that peace talks with the Vietnamese liberation forces would soon begin.

Four days later Martin Luther King was assassinated, setting off black rebellions in more than a hundred cities. In Washington, D.C., flames reached within six blocks of the White House, and machine guns were mounted on the Capitol balcony and White House lawn. King's murder convinced tens of thousands of activists that "the system" was incorrigibly corrupt and could not be reformed. This sentiment was reinforced by the assassination of Robert Kennedy two months later, by the bloody police riot at the Chicago Democratic Convention, and by both major parties fielding pro–Vietnam War candidates (Nixon vs. Hubert Humphrey) for the White House.

On the eve of the Democratic Party's gathering in Chicago, the Soviet Union invaded Czechoslovakia, a watershed not only in international politics but also for the new radical generation. Just as a new wave of young people were becoming revolutionaries, the Soviet Union was acting like anything but a force for freedom and liberation. The Soviet response to the Prague Spring and "socialism with a human face," along with the suspicion and even hostility with which the Communist Party USA (CPUSA) viewed most of the 1960s left, led the vast bulk of new radicals to look elsewhere for strategies and models.

For tens of thousands, that elsewhere turned out to be the communist parties of China, Vietnam, Cuba, and other Third World countries. Inspired by these parties and the ideology they espoused, layer upon layer of U.S. activists decided that a Third World–oriented version of Marxism was the key to building a powerful left within the "belly of the beast."

Third World Marxism saw national liberation in the global South as the cutting edge of the worldwide progressive movement, and it put opposition to racism and military interventionism at the very center of activists' vision. It riveted attention on the intersection of economic exploitation and racial oppression, pointing young organizers toward the most disadvantaged sectors of the working class. It embraced the revolutionary nationalist impulses that then held tremendous initiative in communities of color, where Marxism, socialism, and nationalism intermingled and overlapped. . . .

In terms of building a popular base, Third World Marxism struck its deepest roots in communities of color. The Black Panther Party (BPP) was pivotal in this regard. The Panthers were not a Marxist organization in any strict sense, but combined shifting strands of nationalism and Marxism into an eclectic mix. Still, they were the most prominent revolutionary organization in the country in 1968 (and in the immediate years after), and they proved the single most important group in the transition of thousands of activists from new left radicals, Black Power advocates, or militants of color to partisans of Third World Marxism. In September 1968, FBI chief J. Edgar Hoover publicly termed the Panthers "the greatest [single] threat to the internal security of the country" and ordered the intensification of efforts to disrupt and destroy the BPP via the FBI's infamous Counterintelligence Program, COINTELPRO.

The year 1968 also proved a watershed for the Asian American and Chicano movements. Until 1968, organizations of Chinese, Japanese, Filipinos, Koreans, or other U.S. residents of Asian descent had formed on a nationality-specific basis. But the formation of the Asian American Political Alliance at the University of California-Berkeley that spring set in motion a new dynamic. A few months later, a similar group was formed at San Francisco State University. That summer saw the first nationwide Asian American student conference, and by the end of the year a radical Asian American movement was spreading nationwide.

Almost simultaneously, a pivotal event revived the Chicano community's militant political tradition. On March 3, 1968, over one thousand Mexican American students walked out of Lincoln High School in Los Angeles in the first of a series of high school "blow-outs." That same year saw the formation of the militant Brown Berets and of *CASA-Hermandad General de Trabajadores* (Center for Autonomous Social Action-General Brotherhood of Workers), a socialist-led group based among Mexicano workers.

Fueled by the intersection of class exploitation and racial oppression, a vibrant radical current took root among black workers in Detroit. On May 2, 1968, a group of black activists calling themselves the Dodge Revolutionary Union Movement (DRUM) spearheaded the first wildcat strike in fourteen years to close Detroit's Dodge main plant. Within weeks, hundreds of workers were attending DRUM-sponsored rallies, challenging the United Auto Workers' leadership, and flocking to newly formed Revolutionary Union Movements (RUM's) at other facilities. The resulting shock waves extended into the inner sanctums of corporate America: "No less an authority than the *Wall Street Journal* took them [DRUM] very seriously from the day of the first wildcat, for the *Wall Street Journal* understood . . . that the Black revolution of the sixties had finally arrived at one of the most vulnerable links of the American economic system—the point of mass production, the assembly line."

Simultaneously, a new generation was revitalizing the long struggle for Native American sovereignty, and 1968 saw the founding of the American Indian Movement (AIM). While Marxism would not gain as strong a following in the Indian movement as it did in several other constituencies, this movement's stress on self-determination, its links with indigenous peoples across the globe, and its belief in the legitimacy of armed resistance (punctuated a few years later by the seventy-one-day standoff with federal troops at Wounded Knee in 1973) reinforced key themes struck by Third World Marxism.

On campuses, the cataclysms of 1968 accelerated a radicalization process that had already begun spreading nationwide. Students of color were frequently in the forefront. The first ever building takeover on a college campus took place in March 1968 at Howard University, and after 102 hours, the black student militants won most of their demands. The Third World Liberation Front launched one of the hardest fought student strikes of the decade at San Francisco State in November, and, after four-and-half months and hundreds of arrests, forced the administration to set up an Ethnic Studies program.

Reflecting the racially separate workings of most of the 1960s left, the thousands of white students moving toward Third World Marxism were organized in different, overwhelmingly white groups. The most important of these was SDS, expanding frenetically amid the upheavals of 1968. During that single year, SDS went from roughly 30,000 members and 250 chapters to 80,000–100,000 members and 350–400 chapters. Its internal politics were becoming both more influenced by Marxism and more factional, due in part to the presence of cadres from the then Maoist Progressive Labor Party (PL) since 1966. SDS leaders opposing PL, unwilling to be out-flanked on the left, increasingly came to embrace a form of Third World Marxism. Contact was established between influential members of SDS and Cuban and Vietnamese communists. An alliance was also forged between key SDS leaders and the Black Panther Party; Panther support work became an integral part of many chapters' activity and the Panther influence on SDS became not just generally ideological but direct and personal. PL was beginning to issue bitter critiques of the Panthers ("all nationalism is reactionary") and the Vietnamese ("negotiating with the United States is selling out the revolution") just as thousands of non-PL SDSers were starting to give their allegiance to these forces as the standard-bearers of worldwide revolution.

Most SDSers did not participate directly in the internal debate over doctrine or support any of the main sides. But several thousand—including a large percentage of those who were by now devoting nearly all their waking hours to politics—were invested in the outcome. And tens of thousands more, while repelled by the messiness of factional battle, shared the broad Third World Marxist view that seemed to inform all sides. . . .

The years immediately following 1968 constituted the heyday of Third World Marxism's influence. It was a volatile, no-business-as-usual time. Richard Nixon's inauguration in January 1969 did not bring his campaign-promised end to the war in Vietnam, but rather it brought with it further escalation and killing. Nixon's policy of "Vietnamization"—gradually withdrawing U.S. ground troops to lower U.S. casualties while conducting a ferocious bombing campaign that encompassed Cambodia and Laos as well as Vietnam—failed to assuage antiwar sentiment. Protests surged and, linked to the advance of revolutionary movements throughout the Third World, more and more antiwar activists embraced a broader anti-imperialist perspective. Meanwhile the economic costs of the war began to come home with a vengeance. The polarization between communities of color, where expectations and aspirations had been significantly raised during the 1960s, and the myriad institutional forms of white supremacy stayed razor-sharp.

The spread of large-scale protest movements to whole new constituencies added fuel to the fire. Between 1969 and 1973 women's liberation became a mass social force, the modern gay liberation movement was born, and a broad-based prisoner and prisoners' rights movement took shape. Also, in an unprecedented development, resistance to authority bordering on continuous open mutiny began to characterize the U.S. armed forces on the ground in Vietnam. A top pro-war army officer concluding a tour of military installations bluntly told it like it was: "By every conceivable indication, the U.S. army in South Vietnam is approaching a state of total collapse, with individuals and units avoiding or having refused combat, murdering their officers, drug-ridden, and dispirited, where not near mutinous . . . the morale, discipline, and battle-worthiness of the U.S. armed forces are, with a few salient exceptions, lower and worse than at any time in this century and possibly the history of the U.S."

In this context, the institutions and informal circles based on Third World Marxism expanded manyfold. The *Guardian* went all out to popularize Third World Marxist ideas, and the paper became a key site of communication and debate for the emerging revolutionary trend. By the end of 1969, the paper had doubled its number of pages and increased paid weekly readership to 24,000, the highest total since its initial years. Favorable coverage of Third World revolutions, along with iconic imagery of Mao, Che, and dozens of anonymous (and often female) guerrillas, began to permeate what was then termed the "underground press." As of 1970, the Underground Press Syndicate included 200 papers with 6 million readers, and another 500 underground papers existed in high schools. Hundreds of new black community newspapers were also launched between 1968 and 1973. The *Black Scholar* was launched in 1969 and quickly achieved a circulation of 10,000. The magazine featured consistently positive coverage of Marxist-led African, Cuban, and Chinese movements. Dozens of new Chicano publications appeared, linked together by the radical Chicano Press Association.

Such rapid expansion of the radical press both reflected and spurred extended outreach campaigns and base-building projects. Following longstanding Marxist tradition, Third World Marxists targeted the working class as the key agent of revolutionary change. Yet this trend distinguished itself by making a priority of reaching workers of color and all strata suffering from racial and nationality-based oppression and of integrating antiracism and Third World solidarity into its day-to-day work with workers of all backgrounds.

The BPP continued to set the pace. Despite being the government's central target for infiltration and repression, the group kept expanding in numbers and influence from 1969 through 1971. At its peak, the BPP attained a membership of roughly 4,000 in several dozen cities and circulation of its newspaper reached 100,000 per week. Panther leaders visited and gave glowing reports about China. They praised Cuba, a country that gave sanctuary to many party members fleeing the United States to escape frame-ups and arrests. The most Marxist and internationalist aspects of the Panthers' efforts receded after a bitter split between Huey Newton– and Eldridge Cleaver–led factions in 1971. But for four of the most crucial years in the ideological formation of a new radical generation (1968–71), those features of the Panthers' program had a tremendous impact. The group's emphasis on reaching the poorer strata of urban blacks, who had demonstrated their capacity to rebel during the previous years' urban uprisings, combined with their stress on multiracial alliances, influenced most other groups that identified with Third World Marxism.

Indeed, for many the Panthers served as a direct organizational model. This was especially true within the Puerto Rican movement, which experienced a *"Nuevo Despertar"* (new awakening) in the late 1960s. A pioneer group in that awakening, the Young Lords Party (YLP), aimed to be a Puerto Rican counterpart to the BPP, and some activists briefly held dual membership in both organizations.

The first Young Lords were former Chicago gang members who became politicized and worked closely with the Panthers. But the center of gravity quickly shifted to New York City, whose Young Lords chapter plunged into an ambitious grassroots campaign in Spanish Harlem. Drawing support from Puerto Ricans of all generations, the Young Lords expanded geographically to build chapters in Newark, Philadelphia, Bridgeport, Boston, and Detroit as well as in New York neighborhoods beyond Spanish Harlem. The YLP launched a bilingual newspaper, *Pa'lante,* which in 1970–71 sold almost 10,000 copies every other week.

Puerto Ricans and other Latinos fighting urban renewal on New York's Upper West Side launched El Comité, another revolutionary group, in 1970. It soon turned explicitly to Marxism and developed a student sector and a workers' organization. El Comité members also began the process that in 1975 would result in launching the Latin Women's Collective, a key institution in the decade's efforts to organize working-class Latinas.

The Puerto Rican Socialist Party (PSP), which became the largest group on the Puerto Rican left, grew out of the island-based Movement for Independence (MPI). Radicalized by the student protests, labor militancy, and antiwar demonstrations that swept Puerto Rico in the 1960s, MPI transformed itself into a Marxist-Leninist party. The PSP regarded Puerto Ricans in the United States as an integral part of a single Puerto Rican nation, and its program stated that PSP's "primary role in the U.S. is to unleash the national liberation struggle, in all its fury, in the very hearts of North American cities to which a significant portion of our colonized population was forced, and to link that struggle to the struggle for revolutionary transformation of North American society." More than 2,000 people attended the founding meeting of the PSP's U.S. branch in 1973.

The years 1969 to 1973 saw an explosion of Asian American activism, with young militants spotlighting the racist character of Washington's war in Vietnam, turning to community organizing in Chinatowns, Japantowns, and Manilatowns, and linking up with Asian farmworker militants and left-wing veterans of earlier generations. Third World Marxist ideas held virtually undisputed hegemony within Asian American radicalism, not least because of the prestige of the Communist Parties in Vietnam, China, Korea, and the Philippines and of the Zengakuren student movement in Japan. Militants formed a host of new Asian American revolutionary organizations, including the Red Guard Party and Wei Min She in the San Francisco Bay Area, the East Wind Collective in Los Angeles, and I Wor Kuen (IWK) and the Asian Study Group in New York. In 1973, a year after Ferdinand Marcos declared martial law in the Philippines, revolutionary Filipino activists formed the Union of Democratic Filipinos *(Katipunan ng mga Demokratikong Pilipino/KDP)*, which for the next fifteen years anchored solidarity work with the Communist-led armed struggle against Marcos and advocated socialist revolution in the United States.

The Chicano movement grew substantially, with watersheds in spring 1969 when the first ever National Chicano Youth Liberation Conference was held and, a month later, when Mexican American student leaders founded *El Movimiento Estudiantil de Aztlán* (MEChA). CASA, whose Marxist leadership had ties to Mexico's sophisticated communist movement, expanded its base among workers of Mexican descent. Likewise, an important section of the La Raza Unida Party (LRUP), which took shape as probably the most broadly based center of Chicano militancy between 1970 and 1972, located itself in the Third World Marxist milieu. A strong Marxist current also existed within the early 1970s movement for Chicano Studies and among the radical artists who linked the new generation to the tradition of Mexican revolutionary artists such as David Alfaro Sequieros and Diego Rivera.

In June 1969, the various RUMs that had formed in Detroit combined to found the League of Revolutionary Black Workers. Expanding its work within the auto plants and via community and student organizing, the League argued that black workers would play the pivotal role in a working-class revolution. The League recruited some of the period's most talented organizers, including James Forman, known nationwide for his contributions as executive director of SNCC. The group established ties with caucuses of militant black workers throughout the country, and League offshoots remained a significant force in Detroit even after it broke apart in 1971.

One of the most innovative organizing efforts of the period was the Third World Women's Alliance (TWWA), which grew out of the SNCC Black Women's Liberation Committee and was formally founded in 1970. The Alliance pioneered the concept of "triple jeopardy": that women of color faced the combined and intersecting burdens of capitalism, racism, and sexism. It declared in 1971: "Whether we are Puerto Rican, Black, Chicana, Native American, or Asian, our struggle is one. There is one enemy to be smashed: imperialism and capitalism. The Vietnamese people, and in particular the Vietnamese women, have taught us these lessons."

Discussion of strategies for bringing revolutionary politics to the working class meanwhile moved center stage within white student radicalism. Debate over contending approaches became ever more heated within the SDS, and the group could not survive its escalating factional warfare, splitting into PL and anti-PL camps at its June 1969 national convention. The PL-aligned section quickly faded and was altogether gone within a year or two; the opposing Revolutionary Youth Movement (RYM) group split into RYM I, the Weatherman faction, whose few hundred core members abandoned mass organizing and went underground less than a year later, and RYM II, whose cadre sought to build revolutionary collectives among working-class youth and within a year was immersed in trying to build a new communist party.

This organizational disaster disoriented and disillusioned many SDS members and constituted a serious setback for post-1969 efforts to organize on campuses. But for several more years at least, most of the thousands of SDSers who had embraced Third World Marxism carried on in other forms. A large contingent relocated from college towns to large cities, moved into working-class neighborhoods, and took jobs in auto plants, other industrial sectors, post offices, hospitals, or public schools. Flush with optimism, they believed prospects were good for building a solid base in what seemed an increasingly restive and angry working class. There were more and harder fought strikes in 1969 and 1970 than there had been in any year since 1946. The early 1970s also saw the outbreak of rank-and-file insurgent movements in a number of major unions, with black workers, young workers, and often Vietnam vets in the forefront.

Other ex-SDSers plunged into prisoner support efforts anchored by organizations of color. Protests "behind the walls," spearheaded by black and Latino inmates, frequently turned into open revolt, and there were at least sixteen prison rebellions during 1970 alone. The bloodiest confrontation took place in September 1971 at Attica: 1,200 inmates, many advocating revolutionary politics, seized control of half the prison and took hostages. Negotiations were stonewalled by Governor Nelson Rockefeller; the ensuing military assault left twenty-nine inmates and ten hostages dead, every single one shot by the attacking police.

Still other battle-hardened student radicals persevered as anchors of the continuing antiwar movement. After Nixon invaded Cambodia, these cadre were stalwarts of the largest campus protests in U.S. history: close to 4 million students took part in strikes at upwards of one thousand colleges and universities. A year later many of these same people organized for the half-million strong antiwar protest in Washington, D.C., on April 24, while others took part in the "Mayday" effort to literally shut down the capital. The latter effort resulted in the largest number of arrests in U.S. history (12,614; most of them were later ruled illegal).

Though militancy on U.S. campuses began to ebb after 1970, activists who had turned to Third World Marxism continued to see student organizing as an important supplement to reaching workers and communities of color. These cadre set up Radical Student Unions and "Attica Brigades" on numerous campuses. Supporters of the Panthers, the League of Revolutionary Black Workers, and nationalist groups such as the All African People's Revolutionary Party, launched in 1969 by former SNCC leader Stokely Carmichael (Kwame Ture), gained influence within Black Student Unions. Revolutionary politics predominated in numerous chapters of MEChA and leftists led the Puerto Rican Student Union. Third World Liberation Fronts modeled on those at San Francisco State and Berkeley formed on dozens of other campuses. Finally, ex-student revolutionaries helped start new radical caucuses in the academic and professional worlds (Union for Radical Political Economics, Health Policy Advisory Center, etc.), while partisans of Third World Marxism for a time led the National Lawyers Guild.

Given their internationalist focus, Third World Marxists prioritized solidarity efforts with national liberation revolutions and sought especially to reach workers and the racially oppressed with their anti-imperialist message. They played central roles in local affiliates of one of two major national anti–Vietnam War coalitions—the People's Coalition for Peace and Justice—and anchored anti-imperialist contingents at continuing antiwar actions between 1969 and the final end of the war. Coalitions like New York's Third World Front Against Imperialism, formed, among other groups, by the Black Panther Party, El Comité, and the Third World Women's Alliance, took shape in numerous cities.

The Union of Vietnamese in the United States, which supported the peace program of the National Liberation Front (NLF), was a vital component of early 1970s antiwar efforts. So, too, was Vietnam Veterans Against the War (VVAW), whose 1971 Operation Dewey Canyon III in Washington provided some of the most dramatic moments of the entire antiwar movement. The Operation began with a 1,500 vets, wives of dead GI's and Gold Star Mothers marching to Arlington Cemetary; it culminated at the steps of the Capitol with hundreds of veterans tossing their silver stars, Navy crosses, battle ribbons, and purple hearts over the fence. By this time VVAW, which had started in spring 1967 with a half-dozen members, numbered 11,000 and included a left wing that called for an outright NLF victory. In 1973, VVAW adopted an explicitly anti-imperialist program. . . .

The Venceremos Brigade (VB) was another project that drew strength from direct contact between North Americans and Third World revolutionaries. The idea of organizing U.S. activists to work and travel in Cuba originated after a SDS delegation visited Havana. The first Brigade, with 216 participants, left for Cuba in November 1969. A much larger second Brigade went in March 1970, more contingents followed, and the Brigade became an annual activity that has lasted to the present day. The Brigade gave priority to recruiting young people of color and became a key site of ideological development as well as networking among black, Puerto Rican, Chicano, Native American, and Asian American activists.

Solidarity with Chile was also a focal point of early 1970s internationalist work, both before and after the bloody 1973 United States–backed coup that toppled the elected government of Socialist Salvador Allende. Work promoting sympathy with China and the normalization of United States–China relations, spearheaded by United States–China Friendship Committees formed beginning in 1971, also played a significant role. In 1973, coalitions involving these Friendship Committees and revolutionary groups sponsored celebrations of the anniversary of the Chinese Revolution (October 1) in over two dozen localities, with 5,000 attending the events in New York and the Bay Area. These years also saw the launch of many publications, still extant, focusing on Third World solidarity, for example the *Bulletin of Concerned Asian Scholars* (begun in 1969) and the *Middle East Report* (launched as *MERIP Reports* in 1970). . . .

With such an impressive array of organizational initiatives encompassing thousands of the most hardworking and skilled cadre from the tumultuous 1960s, Third World Marxism seemed poised to transform spectacular short-term growth into institutional durability and broad influence. But after 1973 its progress stalled, by the end of the 1970s its prestige had sharply declined, and by the late 1980s it had nearly disappeared altogether. The reasons lay in a combination of economic and political changes beyond its control and its own shortcomings and misjudgments.

Third World Marxists had based their strategy on a few cornerstone premises: Following an anticipated Vietnamese victory, national liberation movements would win power in many other countries and break free of the capitalist world economy; Third World nations would develop ever greater unity against imperialism; U.S. capital would face steadily mounting economic troubles as it lost control of its far-flung empire; and the resulting domestic squeeze would push the population, especially the working class, toward anticapitalism. Further, it was believed that the traditional ways of "doing politics" had become so discredited that it was possible to consolidate a large left-wing base while essentially ignoring the electoral arena.

This perspective seemed plausible in the very early 1970s. Indeed, anxieties along those exact lines gripped important sections of the policy-making elite. And some elements of these views did turn out to be at least partially correct: Third World struggles continued to register advances in several regions through the 1970s, and the U.S. economy did experience some very rough going as the long postwar boom came to an end.

But overall, the strength of Third World movements was exaggerated and the resilience of U.S. capitalism qualitatively underestimated. Moreover, anticipation that the 1970s would see a steady, if uneven, shift of popular sentiment leftward proved completely off the mark. The overriding reality of the 1970s was an across-the-board capitalist counteroffensive and a tectonic shift to the right in mass politics.

Third World movements for self-determination did not actually have the economic base to achieve the results revolutionaries hoped for and imperialists feared. Rather than beginning a new wave of innovative socialist projects, the 1970s national liberation victories proved to be the final phase of the post–World War II anticolonial tide. While the Vietnamese and other communist-led struggles were able to achieve national independence—no small accomplishment—they were not able to escape the capitalist-dominated world economy and in fact were terribly bled by Washington's economic retaliation and sophisticated use of "low-intensity warfare."

This limitation was closely connected to the structural weaknesses of the largest countries that had embarked on the socialist path. During the 1970s, deep-seated flaws in the models employed by both the USSR and China began to eat away at those societies' apparent stability. Further, the Sino-Soviet split that had erupted in the early 1960s widened into an unbridgeable chasm by the end of that decade. The two strongest anticapitalist powers were unwilling to make common cause against imperialism, qualitatively weakening the international progressive front.

In the United States, meanwhile, the guardians of capitalism successfully maneuvered to regain the initiative. Some retrenchments (cutting U.S. losses by withdrawing from Southeast Asia) were required. But the technological, financial, political, and ideological reserves at capital's disposal meant that, after considerable scrambling, such adjustments could be made without the level of shock and crisis the left (and many nonleftists) had anticipated. Plus, a host of factors were at play that made translating popular discontent into durable radical allegiance a formidable task. These have deep roots: The weakness of the socialist tradition within the U.S. working class and, in contrast, the widespread consensus behind an essentially pro-imperialist version of patriotism; the pervasive racial fault lines that, among other things, lead so many white workers to believe they have more in common with their white exploiters than their nonwhite coworkers; an entrenched two-party, winner-take-all electoral arrangement that erects tremendous structural obstacles to radicalism's ability to gain a stable footing in the political system. . . .

Of course, all of these events involved powerful social forces far beyond the control of the entire U.S. left. No matter what policies they had pursued, Third World Marxists in the United States could not have reversed the rightward motion of U.S. politics or stopped Washington's military muscle-flexing around the globe. To the contrary, it was all but inevitable that these shifts would take a toll on the Third World Marxist ranks and that the damage would be exacerbated by the bitter conflict among the Third World countries (China vs. Cuba and Vietnam) that had once seemed a unified vanguard of world revolution. But things were made worse by Third World Marxism's own shortcomings.

Having come of age in the turbulent late 1960s, most Third World Marxists made undue generalizations from their youthful experience and embraced a "voluntarist" perspective on the pace and ease of social change. They came to believe that virtually anything could be accomplished if revolutionaries only had sufficient determination and correct ideas. When combined with Third World Marxism's overoptimistic assessment of the balance of class forces (in the Third World and within the United States), this led to serious misassessments of the actual realities of the late 1970s. The right's influence tended to be regarded as far more fragile than it was, and prospects for a 1960s- (or 1930s-) style mass radicalization were still considered strong (as long as the revolutionaries remained faithful and pure). Such misjudgments led directly to ultra-left tactics in mass movements and sectarian policies toward progressive groups and reform leaders who did not share all the movement's goals. It fostered inflated rhetoric and encouraged building organizational structures and an overall style of work that was out of touch with the sentiments of the social base the revolutionaries were trying to reach. . . .

In addition, most Third World Marxist formations were unable to match their resolute antiracism, anti-imperialism, and commitment to working-class organizing with similar strengths on other battlefronts. They offered some of the most penetrating criticisms of the racial, class, and national-chauvinist blindspots of the dominant tendencies in the women's, lesbian/gay, environmental, and antinuclear movements. But, with a handful of exceptions, these groups were unable to incorporate the insights of those movements into an inclusive vision that dealt adequately with the complex interweaving of class, race, gender, and sexuality, or with the urgency of environmental protection. And since these newer movements were among the most vital of the late 1970s, especially among youth, Third World Marxism's shortcomings in these areas cut it off from potential sources of renewal.

Further Reading

James Miller, "Democracy Is in the Streets": From Port Huron to the Siege of Chicago (New York: Simon & Schuster, 1987) and Todd Gitlin, The Sixties: Years of Hope, Days of Rage (New York: Bantam, 1987) are the standard "declensionist" accounts of the new left. Winifred Breines, "Whose New Left?" Journal of American History (vol. 75, no. 2 [September 1988], 528–45), and Alice Echols, "'We Gotta Get Out of This Place': Notes toward a Remapping of the Sixties," in Echols, Shaky Ground: The '60s and Its Aftershocks (New York: Columbia University Press, 2002), 61–74, reject that narrative. A collection of essays, The New Left Revisited (Philadelphia: Temple University Press, 2003), edited by John McMillian and Paul Buhle, displays recent directions in research.

On the conflict between young radicals and older liberals during the 1960s, consult the opening chapter of E. J. Dionne, Why Americans Hate Politics (New York: Simon & Schuster, 1991). If I Had a Hammer. . . : The Death of the Old Left and the Birth of the New Left (New York: Basic Books, 1987), by Maurice Isserman, addresses the difficult relations between the brash young leftists and their radical elders. Sociologists led the way in early scholarly treatments of the white radicals. The Formation of the New Left: The Early Years (Lexington, MA: Lexington Books, 1975), by George R. Vickers, stands out as a probing discussion.

Various works have addressed the links between white political radicalism in the 1960s and other contemporary movements. Personal Politics: The Roots of Women's Liberation in the Civil Rights Movement and the New Left (New York: Knopf, 1979), by Sara Evans, is an influential analysis of relations between women and men among the young radicals. Van Gosse, Where the Boys Are: Cuba, Cold War America, and the Making of a New Left (London: Verso Books, 1993) also explores the gender dynamics within political radicalism in the context of 1960s anti-imperialism. Kenneth J. Heineman, Campus Wars: The Peace Movement and American State Universities in the Vietnam Era (New York: New York University Press, 1993), although not asking deep interpretive questions, sheds light on student leftists and antiwar activists on university campuses that typically get little attention. William J. Rorabaugh, Berkeley at War: The 1960s (New York: Oxford University Press, 1989) juxtaposes all the major dissident movements of the era in one famous locale, although it offers little in the way of new ideas.

For work on other movements discussed in Elbaum's article, see Youth, Identity, Power: The Chicano Movement (London: Verso, 1989), by Carlos Muñoz; The Asian American

Movement (Philadelphia: Temple University Press, 1993), by William Wei; *Legacy to Liberation: Politics & Culture of Revolutionary Asian/Pacific America* (Edinburgh: AK Press, 2000), edited by Fred Ho; and *Agents of Repression: The FBI's Secret War against the Black Panther Party and the American Indian Movement* (Boston: South End Press, 2002), by Ward Churchill and Jim Vander Wall.

Scholarship focusing specifically on the hippie counterculture is considerably more scarce than that on the new left. Peter Braunstein and Michael William Doyle, *Imagine Nation: The American Counterculture of the 1960s and '70s* (New York: Routledge, 2002) collects the best of the emerging research. Thomas Frank, *The Conquest of Cool: Business Culture, Counterculture, and the Rise of Hip Consumerism* (Chicago: University of Chicago Press, 1997), although somewhat repetitive, presents a pungent, revisionist interpretation, contending that the "hip" rebellion of the young was hardly the revolution often described back in the 1960s.

Primary Sources

The text of the Port Huron Statement is available at lists.village.virginia.edu/sixties/HTML_docs/ Resources/Primary/Manifestos/SDS_Port_Huron.html. Additional SDS documents, including the 1968 pamphlet "Don't Mourn, Organize," are available at digital.lib.msu.edu/collections/ index.cfm?CollectionID=19. The text of a pamphlet explaining the May 2nd movement, a radical antiwar group that evolved into one of the major SDS factions of the late 1960s, is available at lists.village.virginia.edu/sixties/HTML_docs/Resources/Primary/Manifestos/PL_M2d_ manifesto.html. One well-known episode in the development of the new left was the Free Speech Movement (FSM), a student protest movement that erupted on the University of California campus in Berkeley in the fall of 1964. "Do Not Fold, Bend, Mutilate or Spindle," an important document from the FSM, is available at lists.village.virginia.edu/sixties/HTML_docs/Resources/ Primary/Manifestos/FSM_bend.html. A collection of documents related to the FSM is available at the Free Speech Movement Archives (findaid.oac.cdlib.org/texts/fsm.html). For the text of documents on the May 4, 1970, campus protests and the killings at Kent State University, go to may4archive.org/appendices.shtml. These documents include Nixon's April 30, 1970, speech announcing the invasion of Cambodia, the Justice department's summary of FBI investigations of the Kent State killings, the Report of the Special Grand Jury, and excerpts of the President's Commission on campus unrest. Eyewitness accounts and recollections may be found at may4archive.org/index.shtml. Go to www.berkeleymecha.org/documents/epeda. html for a copy of "El Plan Espiritual de Aztlan," a founding document of the organization MEChA. A set of scanned documents from the American Indian Movement (AIM) is available at www.aics.org/ WK/index.html, which includes copies of the Indigenous Voice of Resistance and the Red Power newsletters. The Stonewall Riots in New York in 1969 are generally considered to be the opening act of the gay rights movement, which is not discussed in this chapter but which was an impotant movement with numerous links to the youth radicalism of the 1960s. For a contemporary news account of the riots that displays the homophobia of the era, go to www.trikkx.com/ history2.html. Go to www.diggers.org/digger_papers.htm for documents on the leading countercultural group, The Diggers, which was based in the Haight-Ashbury neighborhood of San Francisco. The Web site luminist.org/archives/session.htm features a 1967 article, "Session Games People Play: A Manual for the Use of LSD." For the program and platform of the Black Student Union, go to lists.village.virginia.edu/sixties/HTML_docs/Resources/Primary/ Manifestos/BSU_platform.html.

CHAPTER 7

Second-Wave Feminism

INTRODUCTION

If one change in American life after 1945 affected more individuals than any other, many would say it was the altered place of women in American society. This change was multifaceted. It was economic, rooted in the enormous increase in the proportion of women—particularly married women—working for pay. It was cultural, reflected in new attitudes of both women and men about the proper roles and true character of women. It was also political, represented in the appearance, starting in the 1960s, of an organized feminist movement pursuing equal treatment and opportunities for women in society. The economic and cultural changes proved impossible to stop, although each encountered various degrees of resistance. The political side of feminism met stiffer opposition but still achieved remarkable success. Although the Equal Rights Amendment (ERA) was narrowly defeated, women, through their own activism, have gained a host of rights and opportunities that they did not previously enjoy. One ambiguous note in this story of achievement is the fact that many young women today are reluctant to identify themselves as feminists, even as many of them pursue careers premised on the idea of women's equality with men.

Although a vigorous feminist movement had existed in the United States in the nineteenth and early twentieth centuries, the ideas and goals of the earlier movement had seemingly disappeared by 1960 and feminism was to most Americans a strange, unfamiliar word. In the early 1960s, Betty Friedan sought to explain what had happened to feminism. The result was *The Feminine Mystique*, which became a bestseller after its publication in 1963 and is considered by many to represent the reemergence of feminism in America. Other significant events marking the first stirrings of a new feminism in the 1960s include the establishment by President John Kennedy in 1961 of a Commission on the Status of Women; the passage of the 1964 Civil Rights Act, which outlawed "sex discrimination," along with racial discrimination, in employment; and the formation in 1966 by Friedan and others of the National Organization for Women (NOW), the most prominent feminist group in America.

If in *The Feminine Mystique* Friedan tried to explain why feminism seemed to disappear at midcentury, historians of the new, or "second-wave," feminism, have largely sought to explain why and how it reappeared when it did, given the inhospitable climate for feminism as of 1960. Early explorations of second-wave feminism hewed closely to Friedan's work, which focused on middle- and upper-class women (Friedan drew heavily on a survey she had done of her fellow graduates of Smith, an elite women's college) and offered cultural and psychological analyses.

These women, according to Friedan, had embraced, consciously or otherwise, the "feminine mystique," a notion of proper femininity that was promoted by institutions throughout American society in the 1940s and 1950s. This "mystique" made college-educated women feel that they were not true women if they yearned for any source of satisfaction beyond a husband, children, and a home to care for. In Friedan's telling, second-wave feminism fed on the discontent created by the gap between the conventional view of what was natural and appropriate for women and the broader ambitions that young college-educated women harbored. This explanation of the new feminism—as a protest by a subordinate group within a privileged class—reigned almost unchallenged among scholars for the next two decades.

This orthodoxy, which cast second-wave feminism as a white, middle-class movement, was both reinforced and amended by historians focusing on young radical activists. The most influential work in this vein was the 1979 study *Personal Politics: The Roots of Women's Liberation in the Civil Rights Movement and the New Left,* by historian Sara M. Evans. Like Friedan, Evans focused on college-educated women. But Evans's protagonists were of a younger generation; they were the firebrands who protested the Miss America pageant in 1968, who turned to militant action in their campaign to legalize abortion, and who gained as much attention, perhaps, for wearing blue-jeans and eschewing makeup as for anything else. These pioneers of "women's liberation," as they called it, also developed a political organizing method they dubbed "consciousness-raising." This involved bringing women together in small groups to talk about their personal experiences; through these conversations, women came to realize that their experiences were not peculiar to them as individuals but were part of a pattern, even a social system, experienced by women as a group. This model of group discussion became widely influential in American culture, sometimes in settings shorn of the political context in which consciousness-raising first appeared. As illustrated by consciousness-raising, these feminists, unlike many of their older counterparts, embraced the idea that "the personal is political." Unlike NOW, they made central to their variety of feminism a direct and public campaign to change matters traditionally deemed private, even intimate. To them, the institutions of marriage and the family embodied sharply unequal relations of power. Women's liberationists, unlike Friedan and her associates, did not hesitate to denounce these gender relations as a system of inequality and exploitation in which one group (men) oppressed another group (women). The radicals demanded that both private and public institutions be restructured to create equality between women and men.

These young feminists, sometimes called "radical feminists," had been shaped by the black and white youth movements of the 1960s. Gaining self-confidence and acquiring radical perspectives on American society through their engagement in civil rights activism and community organizing, they also experienced anger and frustration at the sexism of the men in these supposedly radical movements. These women then moved on to advocate for the interests of women as a group as well as to seek liberation in their own lives. Although she presented women's liberationists as radicals, Evans, like Friedan, drew attention to the gap between the hopes of the white, middle-class women she wrote about and their experience of sexist limitations and attitudes: this was still seen as the engine driving the emergence of second-wave feminism.

In the 1980s, politics as traditionally understood received significant attention from historians of the new feminism. In this decade as in the preceding one, women ran for office in growing numbers, and elected officials of both sexes increasingly responded to lobbying by women's advocacy groups concerning a wide range of public policy issues. Pressure to encode equality for women in the law culminated in the dramatic, last-minute defeat of efforts to incorporate an ERA in the U.S. Constitution. Traditionally, small, upper-class women's organizations had championed an ERA, whereas advocates of wage-earning women had opposed it as a threat to "protective legislation," which limited working hours and conditions for women. But in the 1960s and 1970s, the idea of plain-and-simple equality of women and men as embodied in the ERA took the new feminism by storm. Opposition was left solely to conservatives, who, led by Phyllis Schlafly, a longtime Republican activist, succeeded in defeating the ERA. In the wake of this surprising outcome, scholars began to study antifeminist sentiment. In general, neither this work nor the new scholarship on the political system offered a substantially new interpretation of second-wave feminism. But the work that examined elections and policies at least suggested that feminism was relevant to a much broader spectrum of American women than just the college-educated protagonists of the standard interpretation.

The demographic focus of feminist scholarship continued to broaden and diversify as historians in the 1990s turned their attention to wage-earning women, insisting that the experiences of these women and the promotion of their bread-and-butter interests were part of the story of second-wave feminism. At the same time, historians began articulating an economic explanation of the new feminism's origins, which had first been suggested by William Chafe in the early 1970s but had then gone largely unexplored. A history of feminism that focused solely on the radicals failed to explain why millions of women who were not in this vanguard nonetheless endorsed feminist demands. To fill this gap, historians began exploring economic pressures and workplace frustrations as the source of popular support for both the new feminist movement and, more broadly, the feminist agenda.

The agitation of women for equality in pay, hiring, and promotions has received greatly increased attention from historians in recent years. Scholars have traced such activities within labor unions such as the United Auto Workers and in service occupations such as clerical work and waitressing, which employ far more women than the manufacturing sector and the highly skilled "craft" trades combined. Career lobbyists for working women's economic interests, whether employed by government bureaucracies, trade unions, or other nongovernmental organizations, have also been incorporated into the story of second-wave feminism; they have been recognized as tireless workers for the cause, even in cases when they did not call their work "feminism." Even Betty Friedan, the original source for the "frustrated homemaker" narrative of the new feminism, was revealed in recent work to have been a veteran of the labor movement, someone who worked as a left-liberal union journalist in the 1940s before "settling down." She subsequently concealed her past as a labor activist for her own reasons, but contemporary scholarship has brought the story of feminism full circle symbolically in her case.

The first reading in this chapter is an excerpt from an article by Sara Evans, which summarizes the thesis of her book, *Personal Politics,* that young white women active in the movements of the 1960s formed the vanguard of women's liberation. She emphasizes experiences within the Student Nonviolent Coordinating Committee (SNCC), the main youth group in the black freedom movement, and in the new left, the white student-based radical movement of the 1960s. These young middle-class women were inspired by these movements to believe in both personal and social transformations, but the sexism that marred these movements drove radical women to conclude that they could pursue the transformation of gender relations only within a new, separate movement. Always controversial, "the personal is political" became a powerful theme in some precincts of the new feminism, and Evans seeks to explain why.

The second reading, an excerpt from a 1999 article by historian Nancy MacLean, represents the recent interest in economic issues and the role of working-class women in second-wave feminism. Examining the experiences of women firefighters, secretaries, and newspaper employees, MacLean emphasizes the legal and political aspects of women workers' fight for equal employment opportunities and against sexual harassment. The wage-earners' equivalent to the consciousness-raising groups about which Evans writes was the women's "caucus" that MacLean pinpoints as central to workplace women's organizing. In caucuses, women in different occupational niches within a single workplace met to share stories and develop strategies for challenging the limits placed on them as well as the humiliations sometimes inflicted on them by their male colleagues and bosses. Thus these caucuses often cut across divisions of occupation, and even of social class, leading many women to view gender as the salient feature of their work experiences and their problems. MacLean also underlines the political coalitions that working women formed with men of color on the job. Her discussion of how both of these groups pressed for change, despite resistance from employers and from labor unions traditionally dominated by white men determined to maintain their seniority and status as members of a privileged caste, reveals the complexity of the internal politics of the American working class in the 1970s.

Although the women she studied bear little resemblance to those portrayed in Evans's work, MacLean, like Evans, recognizes the significance of the civil rights movement as a catalyst and model for second-wave feminism. In MacLean's study, it is not the involvement of women in earlier civil rights struggles that provides the crucial link between these two movements, as it does in Evans's work. Rather, it is the legislation that the black movement pushed the federal government to enact that proved critical, specifically Title VII of the 1964 Civil Rights Act, which prohibited sex discrimination as well as race discrimination in employment. By 1965, one year after enactment of the law, more than one-fourth of the total number of complaints that came to the Equal Employment Opportunity Commission (EEOC), which was created by the 1964 law, had come from women. MacLean also maintains that affirmative action policies were crucial in opening up economic opportunities for women of all races, and for both male and female nonwhite workers. Thus her discussion offers a rejoinder of sorts to the commonly stated view that affirmative action policies primarily have benefited middle-class people of color. In MacLean's view, the legal struggles to achieve redress of women's workplace grievances contributed significantly to the development of a widespread consciousness of gender and its meaning in the lives of American women (and men), and to a feminism whose full scope historians are now recognizing.

SARA M. EVANS

The Origins of the Women's Liberation Movement

It is a new and striking characteristic of the contemporary women's movement that at the center of its existence is the assertion that "the personal is political." Such an assumption came first from the young women in the new left and has since penetrated the more conservative "women's

From "The Origins of the Women's Liberation Movement," by Sara Evans, from *Radical America*, Vol. 9 (Mar.–Apr. 1975). Copyright © Sara M. Evans, 1975. Reprinted by permission of the author.

rights" portions of the movement. As a result, contemporary feminism has focused not simply on legal or public inequities but on the broader questions of sex roles, socialization, and the economic function of women's work in the home.

. . . Throughout the 1950's and 1960's the group entering the labor force at the greatest rate was married women from middle income families.

These same women, however, were thoroughly caught up in the resurgence of domestic ideology, the "feminine mystique." They constituted the sector of the female population who married early, had more children, and moved to suburbia. Yet the home as workplace was becoming increasingly alienating. The fantasy of total emotional and intellectual fulfillment in marriage and family frequently led to "colossal disappointment, guilt, and self-castigation" when it failed to be realized. Growing suburbs isolated women and children farther and farther from the centers of public and community life. The intensification of the family's function as a private enclave to which members escape from the outside world for warmth, nurture and support resulted in an inexhaustible stream of emotional demands placed on women. And finally, as the household technology developed, new standards of housework maintained the amount of work required at a high level. Consumption oriented, psychologically manipulative advertising reinforced and multiplied these new demands. For example, it used to be that soap would clean everything. By the 1950's the housewife was expected to choose and use a different cleanser for every surface in her home and on her body. And "clean" meant sootless, odorless, and antiseptic.

The women who found themselves simultaneously pushed out of the home and pulled back into it suffered an alienation at least as deep as the women who chose to stay at home. They may well have wanted to work, to escape loneliness and boredom. Yet a woman's work was likely to be threatening to her husband. It implied that he was not being a "good provider." Her guilt required that she avoid training, long-range planning, or high aspirations. As a result she could not resist discrimination when the only jobs open to her were repetitious and boring. This structural inability to take oneself seriously induced deep insecurity and a negative self-image. In addition these women were shouldering two jobs. They continued to be the ones responsible for household work and they defined themselves as wives and mothers. Their bodies were at work but their psyches remained at home.

The oppression of those women revolved around their primary self-definition as "housewives" whether they worked inside the home or outside. Any revolt which drew on their discontent could neither accept a traditional stereotypic view of "female nature" as particularly suited to home and motherhood nor could it restrict itself simply to a critique of inequities in the public realm.

For this reason the emergence of NOW in 1966 did not initiate a massive feminist movement. NOW was the product of contradictions experienced by professional women. Professional women throughout the 1950's were the most unmistakably "deviant," and often harbored among themselves the few remnants of feminism left. Precisely because they perceived their work as important, they felt even more acutely the discrimination against them. Having openly admitted a certain level of drive and ambition, they were far more likely to see discriminatory hiring, training, promotion, and payrates as unfair. Other women could justify their unwillingness to fight against such barriers by saying "I wouldn't be here if I didn't have to" or "I am only doing this for my family, not for myself." Professional women could not do this. In addition, Jo Freeman has demonstrated that throughout the 1950's and 1960's the relative deprivation of professional women increased at a greater rate than for any other group.

These women, in general, accepted the division between the public and the private. Betty Friedan's devastating critique of housewifery ends up with a prescription that women, like men, should be allowed to participate in both realms. In effect she urges women to do it all—to be super women—by assuming the dual roles of housewife and professional. She makes no serious assault on the division of labor within the home. For Friedan it was easier to imagine a professional woman hiring a professional "housewife" to take her place in the home than to challenge the whole range of sex roles or the division of social life into home/work, private/public, female/male domains.

The catalyst for a more thoroughgoing critique and a mass mobilization of American women developed among young female participants in the social movements of the 1960's. These daughters of the middle class had received mixed, paradoxical messages about what it meant to grow up female. On the one hand the cultural ideal—held up by media, parents, and schools—informed them that their only true happiness lay in the twin roles of wife and mother. At the same time they could observe the reality that housewifery was distinctly unsatisfactory for millions of suburban women, and furthermore that despite the best efforts of the Ladies Home Journal, most American women could expect to work outside the home a substantial portion of their lives. Such contradictions left young, educated women in the 1960's dry tinder for the spark of revolt. The preconditions for that spark developed within the southern civil rights movement and portions of the new left.

Many former activists in the civil rights movement and the new left have attributed the rise of women's liberation to the discrepancy within the movement between the goal of equality and the actual subordination of women within it. I have found, however, that the preconditions for female revolt developed in those parts of the movement which offered women the greatest space in which to develop their own potential and discover their own strength. In the process they also accumulated many of the tools for movement building: a language to describe oppression and justify revolt, experience in the strategy and tactics of organizing, and a beginning sense of themselves collectively as objects of discrimination.

The two most important incubators of feminism within the new left were the Student Nonviolent Coordinating Committee (SNCC) and the community organizing projects of Students for a Democratic Society (the Economic and Research Action Projects: ERAP) which were modeled on SNCC. By late 1965 an interconnected group of experienced female organizers had articulated an analysis of women's oppression which focused squarely on the issues of sex roles.

The most important source for new self-images within the movement lay in the nature of women's work. In contrast to the later mass mobilizations which placed a premium on public speaking and self-assertion in large groups, the vision of SNCC and of ERAP translated into daily realities of hard work and responsibility which admitted few sexual limitations. Young women's sense of purpose was reinforced by the knowledge that the work they did and the responsibilities they assumed were central to the movement.

In direct action demonstrations many women discovered untapped reservoirs of courage. Rarely did women expect or receive any special protection in demonstrations or jails. Frequently direct action teams were equally divided between women and men on the theory that the presence of women might lessen the violent reaction.

Working in local communities, organizing around voter registration, teaching in freedom schools, running libraries, creating block organizations or groups of welfare mothers, many women reached well beyond their previously assumed limits. One participant in the Mississippi "freedom summer" of 1964 wrote:

> I was overwhelmed at the idea of setting up a library all by myself. . . . Then can you imagine how I felt when at Oxford, while I was learning how to drop on the ground to protect my face, my ears, and my breasts, I was asked to coordinate the libraries in the entire project's community centers. I wanted to cry "HELP !" in a number of ways. . . .

In SDS projects a few men were good organizers but most good organizers were women. The skills required by community organizing meshed with the social training of females: warmth, empathy, compassion, interpersonal radiation. Furthermore, community organizing tends to draw upon a largely female constituency. In northern communities, while male leaders futilely attempted to organize streetcorner youth, winos, and unemployed men, women successfully created welfare rights organizations, though their efforts received much less attention.

Female community leadership in both the south and the north provided new role models as well. In 1962 SNCC staff member Charles Sherrod wrote the office that in every southwest Georgia county "there is always a 'mama.' She is usually a militant woman in the community, out-spoken, understanding, and willing to catch hell, having already caught her share." The newsletters of ERAP were likewise filled with stories of courage in the face of hardship, of women who stood up for themselves against any and all authority. For many middle-class white women in the new left these women were also "mamas" in the sense of being substitute mother-figures, new models of the meaning of womanhood.

The opportunities to develop new strengths and a heightened sense of self were strengthened by the personal nature of new left politics. The new left consistently emphasized the importance of building new kinds of human relationships, and the political import of personal choice. Jane Stembridge, daughter of a Southern Baptist minister who left her studies at Union Seminary in New York to become the first paid staff member of SNCC, put it:

> . . . finally it all boils down to human relationship. . . . It is the question of . . . whether I shall go on living in isolation or whether there shall be a we. The student movement is not a cause . . . it is a collision between this one person and that one person. It is a I am going to sit beside you. . . . Love alone is radical.

Three years later the SDS University Committee reported:

> The free university is not defined by a particular structural arrangement, but by the questions the participants ask. . . . The central question of the free university seems to be "what kind of interpersonal relations allow people to treat each other as human beings?"

Within the student movement the intensely personal nature of social action and the commitment to equality resulted in a kind of anarchic democracy and a general questioning of all the socially accepted rules. "Let the people decide" and "participatory democracy" were the ideological passwords of SNCC and SDS. A spirit of moral idealism permeated the new left.

The ideas and ideals of students in the new left reflected the fact that they were in many ways engaged in a cultural revolt. The counter culture of the late 1960's grew from the perceptions of thousands of young people that suburban material "success" constituted a hollow promise and from their determination to build their lives around more meaningful goals. It was a natural extension for women to apply the same critique to sexual relationships: Casey Hayden and Mary King wrote in 1965:

> Having learned from the movement to think radically about the personal worth and abilities of people whose role in society had gone unchallenged before, a lot of women in the movement have begun trying to apply those lessons to their own relations with men. Each of us probably has her own story of the various results. . . .

According to Casey and Mary, however, such ideas could be discussed seriously only among women. Despite their own cultural rebellions, men in the movement clung to traditional notions of sexual relationships. The effort to create a haven, a "beloved community" of equality either racially or sexually, foundered in a movement so deeply enmeshed in the very culture it set out to challenge. Feminism was born out of this contradiction: that the same movement which permitted women to grow and to develop self-esteem, new strength and skills, generally kept them out of public leadership roles and reinforced expectations based on woman's role as housewife: houseworker, nurturer, sex object, unintellectual.

In the years after 1965 the movement became increasingly alienating for women. Women were increasingly relegated to running the mimeograph machines, preparing and serving coffee, washing dishes, and being available for sex. Draft card burning, mass demonstrations, strident oratory left women more and more alienated and secondary.

But women had developed along the way too much self-respect and too much organizing skills to acquiesce quietly. They rounded out the new left focus on the personal nature of political work by asserting that personal life was in itself political. They drew on the analogy with black oppression in defining a complex of discriminatory attitudes (sexism) comparable to racism which were backed by an infrastructure of discriminatory institutions and laws. They also understood quickly by analogy that women had internalized many of the negative things attributed to them and that mutual solidarity and support were necessary to wage a struggle that was at once internal and external.

When young women from middle-income families revolted against the replication of the housewife role within the new life, they did so with a sense of strength that allowed them to name and to politicize a dilemma experienced by millions of women. Where the public ideology of NOW had focused on legal inequities, the newer radical women's liberation movement made a critique of family and personal life the cornerstone of its existence. It created a medium, the consciousness-raising group, through which individual women could develop a sense of the social nature and political import of deeply ingrained attitudes, habits, and assumptions.

Without their critique, there could have been no mass movement, only a strong feminist lobby. For millions of American women only a movement which addressed their oppression as housewives—both in the home and in the outside workplace—could have generated the massive shift in consciousness which we can observe in the past six to eight years.

Nancy MacLean

The Hidden History
of Affirmative Action

In 1993, the New York City Fire Department issued a curious order: no pictures could be taken of Brenda Berkman, on or off duty, inside or outside of a firehouse. Berkman was a firefighter, a fifteen-year veteran of the force. The order was the latest shot in a protracted battle against

Nancy MacLean, "The Hidden History of Affirmative Action: Working Women's Struggles in the 1970s and the Gender of Class," was originally published in *Feminist Studies,* Volume 25, Number 1 (Spring 1999): 43–78. Reprinted by permission of the publisher, *Feminist Studies,* Inc.

Berkman and others like her: women claiming the ability to do a job that had been a men's pre-serve for all the New York City Fire Department's 117-year, tradition-conscious history. The struggle began in 1977, when the city first allowed women to take the Firefighter Exam—and then promptly changed the rules on the physical agility section when 400 women passed the written portion of the test. Five years and a victorious class-action suit for sex discrimination later, forty-two women passed the new, court-supervised tests and training and went on to become the first female firefighters in New York's history. Among them was Berkman, founding president of the United Women Firefighters, and the most visible and outspoken of the group.

Their struggle dramatizes many elements in the larger story of women and affirmative action, which involved remaking "women's jobs" as well as braving male bastions. What Berkman and her colleagues encountered when they crossed those once-undisputed gender boundaries was not simply reasoned, judicious skepticism from people who doubted the capac-ity of newcomers to do the job. Repeatedly, what they met was elemental anger that they would even dare to try. Hostile male coworkers used many tactics to try to drive the women out, includ-ing hate mail, telephoned death threats, sexual harassment, refusing to speak to them for months on end, scrawling obscene antifemale graffiti in firehouses, and organizing public demonstra-tions against them. Male firefighters also slashed the tires of women's cars, urinated in their boots, and, in one instance, tried to lock a woman in a kitchen that they had filled with tear gas. Sometimes, the men resorted to violence: one woman was raped, and a few others endured less grave sexual assaults. Some men even carried out potentially deadly sabotage—as when one newcomer found herself deserted by her company in a burning building and left to put out a four-room fire on her own.

Frozen out by white male coworkers and betrayed by the firefighters union, the women found their only dependable internal allies in the Vulcan Society, the organization of Black male firefighters, who had themselves fought a long battle against discrimination in the department. They now stood by the women, even to the point of testifying in support of their class-action suit, despite "enormous pressure to remain silent." The tensions surrounding the entrance of women into the fire department were explosive although women constituted a mere 0.3 percent of the city's 13,000-member uniformed fire force. The no-photographs order from the top, the uncoordinated acts of hostility from would-be peers, as well as the support of the Vulcan Society, signal us that a great deal was at stake. Even in cases less egregious than the New York firefighters, boundary crossing backed by affirmative action affected something that mattered deeply to many men, especially many white men, in a way that often transcended logic.

Yet, historians of the modern United States have only begun to examine workplace-based sex discrimination and affirmative action struggles such as those of the United Women Firefighters. More attention is in order. On the one hand, disgust with discrimination and low-paying, dead-end jobs moved large numbers of working women to collective action in the last quarter-century. On the other hand, these struggles produced an unprecedented assault not just on previously unyielding patterns of occupational sex and race segregation and the economic inequality stem-ming from them but also on the gender system that sustained men's power and women's disad-vantage and marked some women as more appropriate for certain types of work than others. . . .

Interestingly . . . the first big challenges to sex discrimination in the 1960s . . . came from wage-earning women in factory jobs, who discovered a new resource in legislation won by the civil rights movement in 1964. . . . When the Equal Employment Opportunities Commission (EEOC) opened for business in the summer of 1965, all observers were stunned at the number of women's complaints, which made up more than one-fourth of the total. Some 2,500 women in the initial year alone, overwhelmingly working-class and often trade union members, challenged unequal wages, sex-segregated seniority lists, unequal health and pension coverage, and male-biased job recruitment and promotion policies—among other things. Alice Peurala, for example, who had been stymied each time she tried for promotion since she was first hired at U.S. Steel Corporation in 1953, said that when the Civil Rights Act came along "I thought, here's my chance." The protests of women such as Peurala, we can see now, prompted the development of an organized feminist movement. It was, after all, the EEOC's negligence in handling these charges of sex discrimination that led to the formation of NOW, whose founders included labor organizers and women of color as well as their better-known, affluent, white counterparts. In other words, noted the labor historian Dennis A. Deslippe, "women unionists did not merely complement the efforts of middle-class feminists; they helped construct second-wave feminism."

Such efforts were brought to the attention of a broad audience by the mass media. By the early 1970s, television news, magazines, and newspapers all carried stories about sex discrimination in employment and women's struggles against it, as well as reports of the wider women's movement. Whether the reporters were sympathetic, hostile, or patronizing, their coverage helped widen the ranks of the struggles they described. For example, the *Chicago Tribune* in 1972 published a questionnaire to discover women's views about the issues the movement raised. To the question "have you ever felt discriminated against because you are a woman?" the answer from over 3,200 women who wrote in response "was an overwhelming, often angry, YES." With responses ranging from one paragraph to eight pages, women readers divulged their experiences. The resulting list was long and varied, but job discrimination loomed large.

The gender consciousness promoted by such stories stimulated women to look at their jobs afresh and to imagine class itself in new ways. By 1970, large numbers of American women began to act on this new thinking at work. Borrowing a tactic from mostly male, blue-collar African Americans, and taking strength from the general ferment among rank-and-file workers in the early 1970s symbolized by the famed Lordstown wildcat strike, these women joined together with like-minded coworkers to organize women's caucuses as their characteristic vehicle of struggle. The caucuses embodied, in effect, a new social theory: Blacks of both sexes and women of all races who joined together implicitly announced that traditional class tools—such as unions—were ill suited to the issues that concerned them. In form, the caucuses crossed divisions of occupation in order to overcome the isolation and competition that allowed their members to be pitted against one another. Using separate structures, they fought not simply to achieve racial and gender integration at work but also to redefine it.

Having first appeared about 1970, the caucuses spread rapidly within a few years, one sparking the next like firecrackers on a string. An article on the phenomenon that appeared in 1972 reported that caucuses were "known to exist in more than a hundred companies," the list of which read like a Who's Who of American business and culture. Having set out to write about "The Ten Best Companies for Women Who Work," a *Redbook* author ended up writing in 1977 about women's caucuses instead, because all eighty of the responses to her inquiry agreed that "no corporation was doing anything it hadn't been forced into, and that grudgingly." Women were organizing in steel plants and auto factories, in banks and large corporations, in federal and university employment, in trade unions and professional associations, and in newspaper offices and television networks. Few sites remained undisturbed. Although women's historians have shown how consciousness-raising groups (mainly white and middle-class) broadened and deepened the women's movement, the importance of these caucuses (working-class and sometimes mixed-race) has been overlooked. Caucuses not only developed a critical consciousness among working women but they also won tangible improvements. Without their efforts, Title VII would have been a dead letter for women.

These early women's caucuses nearly always came about because a few women suddenly rejected some expectation arising from contemporary constructions of gender and class. "*Without exception,*" a contemporary news story reported (using italics to drive home the point), "*a principal demand of the women's caucuses is for respect.*" Although the demand for respect and dignity had recurred with regularity in the struggles of working people, now it assumed a clearly feminist form as a way to challenge the denigration of women workers in particular. Time after time, the fresh recognition of some longstanding practice as sexist—a practice usually first identified as such in the course of casual lunchtime conversation among female coworkers—impelled women to organize. Often a small slight triggered a sense that a broader pattern of discrimination had just been revealed. For example, when *Newsweek* editors assigned a cover story on women's liberation to a nonstaff writer (the wife of a senior editor), women at the magazine suddenly looked around. They saw that management confined virtually all women on staff to what they called "the 'research' ghetto" and hired only one woman to fifty-one men as writers. Armed with Title VII, they organized, complained to the EEOC, and forced change at the magazine. In another variation of the process around the same time, the refusal of editors at the *New York Times* to allow the title "Ms." in the paper led several women on staff to wonder whether "this style rigidity was symptomatic of more basic problems."

As it happens, one of the best documented examples of such workplace-based efforts is the resulting *New York Times* Women's Caucus. Its members challenged the newspaper to practice the fairness it preached to its readers. Prompted by the editors' curious resistance to nonsexist language, nine female employees in the news department began to compare experiences in 1972. Ironically, the *New York Times* had once boasted in an advertisement that one of the leaders, then a copy editor, had a "passion for facts." Now, however, the facts so carefully assembled by Betsy Wade, the self-proclaimed "Mother Bloor" of this particular struggle, brought less pride to management. The investigation and organizing continued until eighty women drew up a petition that complained of sex-based salary inequities; the confinement of women to poorer-paying jobs; the failure to promote female employees even after years of exemplary service; and their total exclusion from nonclassified advertising sales, management, and policy-making positions. The more women came to understand and label discrimination, the more of it they discovered. When "nothing happened" to address their complaints, the women secured a lawyer and filed charges with the EEOC. In turning to the state, they found they had to broaden their ranks beyond the original group to include secretarial staff and classified ad workers. That this was a stretch for some was evident in the private comment of one organizer about the latter: "We really gotta have one." Ultimately, in 1974, the enlarged group filed a class-action suit for sex discrimination on behalf of more than 550 women in all job categories at the *New York Times,* including reporters, clerks, researchers, classified salespeople, and data processors. For the next four years, as the suit wound its way through the courts, the caucus held meetings, put out newsletters, and continued to agitate. By 1978, management was willing to concede. Settling out of court, the *New York Times* compensated female employees for past discrimination and agreed to a precedent-setting affirmative action plan. "Considering where we were in 1972," said one of the original plaintiffs, the settlement was "the sun and the moon and the stars."

That settlement highlights a more common pattern: in virtually every case where women's caucuses came together, demands for affirmative action emerged logically out of the struggle against discrimination. So striking is this pattern that I have yet to come across a case in which participants did *not* see affirmative action as critical to the solution. Examples are legion: they range from the *New York Times* group, to steel workers, telephone operators, and NBC female employees, of whom two-thirds (600 of 900) were secretaries when they began organizing in 1971. Even the Coalition of Labor Union Women (CLUW), loyal to a trade union officialdom skeptical about affirmative action, came out strongly in its favor. Prioritizing seniority over diversity where the two came in conflict, CLUW nonetheless fought to establish affirmative action for women—and to keep it in place. The logic appeared inescapable: if male managers had for so many years proven oblivious to women's abilities and accomplishments and unwilling to stop preferring men when they hired and promoted, and if women themselves could have been unaware of or resigned to the discrimination taking place, then something was needed to counterbalance that inertia. Successful efforts by African American men to wield affirmative action as a battering ram against discrimination only reinforced women's resolve.

Time and again, it was affirmative action that women embraced to open advertising of jobs, broaden outreach for recruitment, introduce job analysis and training, set specific numerical goals for recruiting and promoting women, and mandate timetables for achieving these changes, all commitments for which management would be held accountable. The centerpiece of the *New York Times* settlement, goals and timetables, could also be found in other settlements from *Reader's Digest* and NBC, on the one hand, to the steel industry and the New York City Fire Department on the other. Many other employers, such as Polaroid and Levi Strauss, voluntarily adopted such programs in response to pressure from female employees. As early as 1971, NOW literature was thus proclaiming affirmative action as "the key to ending job discrimination," and numerical goals and timetables as "the heart of affirmative action." Typically, and contrary to the notion that affirmative action benefitted only privileged women, these plans covered the gamut of female employees. No longer restricted to clerical and cleaning work, women in lower-paying positions—Black and white—could now get more lucrative jobs as, for example, security guards, machine operators, mail carriers, and commissioned salespeople.

Yet, the largest single number of wage-earning women—one in three—remained in clerical jobs, and they became the target of the second kind of organizing initiative. These jobs were among the most sex segregated: in 1976, for example, women made up 91.1 percent of bank tellers and 98.5 percent of secretaries and typists. The income of clerical workers fell below that of male wage earners in every category except farming. Seeking to make the women's movement more relevant to working-class women, some feminists set out in 1973 to develop an organizing strategy geared to women office workers and to build a network that could spread the new consciousness. "The women's movement was not speaking to large numbers of working women," remembered Karen Nussbaum, one of the national leaders of the effort, "we narrowed the focus of our concerns, in order to broaden our base." Among the groups thus created were 9 to 5 (Boston), Women Employed (Chicago), Women Office Workers (New York), Cleveland Women Working, Women Organized for Employment (San Francisco), and Baltimore Working Women. By the end of the 1970s, a dozen such groups existed and had affiliated with an umbrella network called Working Women; together, they claimed a membership of eight thousand. The racial composition of the groups varied by locality, but Black women appeared to participate in larger numbers in these than in the women's caucuses, sometimes making up as much as one-third of the membership.

What linked all the members together was a categorical rejection of the peculiar gender burdens of their work: above all, the low pay and demands for personal service. Of these expectations, making and fetching coffee for men quickly emerged as the most resented emblem of women's status. Of the low pay, one contemporary said: "As long as women accepted the division of work into men's and women's jobs—as long as they *expected* to earn less because women *deserved* less—the employers of clerical workers had it easy." Now, however, the women active in these groups insisted on their standing as full-fledged workers who deserved, in what came to be the mantra of the movement, both "rights and respect." Appropriating National Secretaries' Day for their own purposes, the groups demonstrated for "Raises, Not Roses!" and a "Bill of Rights" for office workers. "What we're saying," as one 9 to 5 speaker explained in 1974, "is that an office worker is not a personal servant, and she deserves to be treated with respect and to be compensated adequately for her work." . . .

I do not want to overstate the changes that occurred. If women tried to rewrite the script, so could men. Resistance was common, and sometimes fierce, as the example of the New York City firefighters illustrates. To take one obvious case: as if to certify their own now-uncertain masculinity and remind women of their place, some men turned to sexual harassment. Although hardly new, this tactic seemed to be used more aggressively and self-consciously where men found treasured gender privileges and practices in question—as in the case of the New York firefighters. It was almost as though the men involved were marking the workplace as their territory, as indeed they were when they posted up pornography—a common practice in these situations. As one observer grasped: "By forcing sexual identities into high relief, men submerge the equality inherent in the work and superimpose traditional dominant and subordinate definitions of the sexes." The support of Black firemen complicated but did not forestall this development.

Putting face-to-face resistance to the side for the moment—which may in any case distract us from the variety and complexity of male responses—it is plain to see that the struggles described here have left much undone. By and large, working women still face serious obstacles in trying to support themselves and their families. As much as occupational sex and race segregation have diminished, they have hardly disappeared, as any glance at a busy office or construction site will show. For women and men to be equally represented throughout all occupations in the economy today, 53 out of every 100 workers would have to change jobs. The absolute number of women in the skilled trades has grown, but they hold only 2 percent of the well-paying skilled jobs. In any case, these good jobs for people without higher education, as each day's newspaper seems to announce, are themselves an endangered species. In fact, although the wage gap between the sexes has narrowed, only about 40 percent of the change is due to improvement in women's earnings; 60 percent results from the decline in men's real wages. The persistent disadvantage in jobs and incomes contributes to another problem that has grown more apparent over the last two decades: the impoverishment of large numbers of women and their children, particularly women of color. Many of these poor women, moreover, are already employed. In 1988, more than two in five women in the work force held jobs that paid wages below the federal poverty level. So I am not arguing that some kind of linear progress has occurred and all is well.

Still, affirmative action was never intended as a stand-alone measure or panacea. From the outset, advocates were nearly unanimous in their insistence that it would work best in conjunction with full employment above all but also with such measures as pay equity, unionization, and improvements in education and training. Affirmative action's mission was not to end poverty, in any case, but to fight occupational segregation. And there it has enjoyed unprecedented, if modest, success. The best indicator is the index of occupational segregation by sex: it declined more in the decade from 1970 to 1980, the peak years of affirmative action enforcement, than in any other comparable period in U.S. history. As of 1994, women made up over 47 percent of bus drivers, 34 percent of mail carriers, and 16 percent of police—all jobs with better pay and benefits than most "women's work." This lags slightly behind nontraditional jobs requiring postsecondary training: women now account for nearly 40 percent of medical school students (20 percent of practicing physicians), nearly 50 percent of law school students (24 percent of practicing lawyers), and almost one-half of all professionals and managers. The ways that white women and women of color fit into these patterns complicate analyses based on sex alone. Yet whether in blue-collar, pink-collar, or professional jobs, white and Black women have gained benefits from breaking down sex barriers.

It would be absurd, of course, to give affirmative action exclusive credit for these changes. The policies described here came to life as the result of a broader history involving women's own determination to close the gap between the sexes in education and labor force participation, institutional fears of lawsuits for discrimination, new developments in technology and labor demand, and changes that feminism and civil rights brought about in U.S. culture. The mass entry of women into hitherto "men's work" in particular is deeply rooted in the breakdown of the family wage-based gender system. It is both result and reinforcement of a host of other changes: new expectations of lifelong labor force participation among a majority of women, the spread of birth control, the growing unreliability of marriage, the convergence in women's and men's patterns of education, the demise of associational patterns and sensibilities based on stark divisions between the sexes—even the growing participation of women in sports. But if it would be foolish to exaggerate the causative role of affirmative action, it would also be sophistry to deny or underrate that role. It has furthered as well as been fostered by these other developments. Women simply could not have effected the changes described here without its tools and the legal framework that sustained them. There are sound reasons why by 1975 virtually every national women's organization from the Girl Scouts to the Gray Panthers supported affirmative action, and why today that support persists from the African American Women's Clergy Association at one end of the alphabet to the YWCA at the other.

Yet there is a curious disjuncture between these organizations and the female constituency they claim to represent: repeated polls have found that white women in particular oppose affirmative action by margins nearly matching those among white men (which vary depending on how the questions are worded). No doubt several factors help to explain this paradox, not least of them the racial framing of the issue, which encourages white women to identify with white men against a supposed threat from nonwhites. The preference for personal politics over political economy at the grassroots has also led many women to interpret feminism in terms of lifestyle choices rather than active engagement in public life. Struggles for the ERA and reproductive rights ultimately eclipsed employment issues on the agenda of the women's movement in the 1970s. And most major women's organizations have come to emphasize service or electoral politics over grassroots organizing, and staff work over participation of active members. All these developments help to explain why today there is so little in the way of a well-informed, mobilized, grassroots female constituency for affirmative action—a vacuum that, in turn, has made the whole policy more vulnerable to attack.

Surely another reason, however, for the paradoxical gulf between national feminist organizations and grassroots sentiment on this issue is the historical amnesia that has obliterated the workplace-based struggles of the modern era from the collective memory of modern feminism—whether women's caucuses, clerical worker organizing, the fight for access to nontraditional jobs, or union-based struggles. If not entirely forgotten, these efforts on the part of working women are so taken for granted that they rarely figure prominently in narratives—much less interpretations—of the resurgence of women's activism.

Further Reading

Blanch Linden-Ward and Carol Hurd Green, *American Women in the 1960s: Changing the Future* (New York: Twayne Publishers, 1993), and Winifred D. Wandersee, *On the Move: American Women in the 1970s* (Boston: Twayne Publishers, 1988) are comprehensive accounts of American women's experiences. Ruth Rosen, *The World Split Open: How the Modern Women's Movement Changed America* (New York: Viking, 2000) and Sara M. Evans, *Tidal Wave: How Women Changed America at Century's End* (New York: The Free Press, 2003) are fine recent overviews. *No Turning Back: The History of Feminism and the Future of Women* (New York: Ballantine Books, 2002), by Estelle B. Freedman, places American feminism in a global context. *Daring to Be Bad: Radical Feminism in America, 1967–1975* (Minneapolis: University of Minnesota Press, 1989), by Alice Echols, is a detailed work that picks up where Evans left off, pursuing the byways of women's liberation in its heyday.

Many historians have sought to expand and diversify the Friedan-derived picture of second-wave feminism, with varying degrees of success. Paula Giddings, *When and Where I Enter: The Impact of Black Women and Race and Sex in America* (New York: William Morrow, 1984), part 3, and Jacqueline Jones, *Labor of Love, Labor of Sorrow: Black Women, Work, and the Family from Slavery to the Present* (New York: Basic Books, 1985), chaps. 7 and 8, offer perspectives on the experiences of African American women after 1945. Lillian Faderman, *Odd Girls and Twilight Lovers* (New York: Columbia University Press, 1991), chaps. 8 and 9, documents American lesbians' lives.

Cynthia Harrison, *On Account of Sex: The Politics of Women's Issues, 1945–1968* (Berkeley: University of California Press, 1988) and Susan M. Hartmann, *From Margin to Mainstream: American Women and Politics Since 1960* (Philadelphia: Temple University Press, 1989) are basic sources on feminist politics. Much scholarship on feminist campaigns and the opposition to them deals with the ERA and the issue of abortion. On abortion rights, see Kristin Luker, *Abortion and the Politics of Motherhood* (Berkeley: University of California Press, 1984); Leslie J. Reagan, *When Abortion Was a Crime: Women, Medicine, and the Law in the United States, 1867–1973* (Berkeley: University of California Press, 1997); Laura Kaplan, *The Story of Jane: The Legendary Underground Feminist Abortion Service* (Chicago: University of Chicago Press, 1997); and Faye Ginsburg, *Contested Lives: The Abortion Controversy in an American Community* (2nd ed. [Berkeley: University of California Press, 1998]). On the ERA, see Rebecca E. Klatch, *Women of the New Right* (Philadelphia: Temple University Press, 1987), and Jane Sherron DeHart and Donald G. Mathews, *Sex, Gender, and the Politics of ERA: A State and the Nation* (New York: Oxford University Press, 1990).

The American Woman: Her Changing Social, Economic, and Political Roles, 1920–1970 (New York: Oxford University Press, 1972), by William H. Chafe, deserves recognition as an early work documenting economic changes in the lives of American women in general. Its lead was not followed up for many years. Important recent works on women's bread-and-butter concerns are Nancy F. Gabin, *Feminism in the Labor Movement: Women and the United Auto Workers, 1935–1975* (Ithaca, NY: Cornell University Press, 1990), Dorothy Sue Cobble, *The Other Women's Movement: Workplace Justice and Social Rights in Modern America* (Princeton, NJ: Princeton University Press, 2004), and Susan M. Hartmann, *The Other Feminists: Activists in the Liberal Establishment* (New Haven, CT: Yale University Press, 1998). Daniel Horowitz revisits Friedan's past in his absorbing work, *Betty Friedan and the Making of the Feminine Mystique: The American Left, the Cold War, and Modern Feminism* (Amherst: University of Massachusetts Press, 1998).

Primary Sources

For an excerpt from the congressional hearings on the Equal Pay Act of 1963, go to historymatters.gmu.edu/d/6196. The text of the Equal Rights Amendment may be found at www.now.org/issues/economic/eratext.html; Shirley Chisholm's speech, "For the E.R.A.," is available at www.americanrhetoric.com/speeches/shirleychisholmequalrights. htm. NOW's "Statement of Purpose" is available at www.now.org/history/purpos66. html. The majority opinion in *Roe v. Wade,* the historic Supreme Court opinion legalizing abortion, may be found at www.ku.edu/carrie/docs/texts/roevwade.html. The text of the November 1964 memo written by women in SNCC critical of the treatment of women in that organization is available at lists.village.virginia.edu/sixties/HTML_docs/Resources/Primary/ Manifestos/SNCC_women.html. Go to scriptorium.lib.duke.edu/wlm/ for a rich repository of documents from the women's liberation movement, organized by topic. These include Kathie Sarachild, "Consciousness-Raising as a Radical Weapon" (scriptorium.lib.duke.edu/wlm/fem/ sarachild.html); Shulamith Firestone, "Women and the Radical Movement" (scriptorium.lib.duke.edu/wlm/notes/#radical); Mirta Vidal, "Women: New Voice of La Raza" (scriptorium.lib.duke.edu/wlm/chicana/#women); Mary Ann Weathers, "An Argument for Black Women's Liberation as a Revolutionary Force" (scriptorium.lib.duke.edu/wlm/fun-games2/ argument.html); an abortion rally speech by Anne Koedt (scriptorium.lib.duke.edu/ wlm/notes/ #abortion); and "Socialist Feminism: A Strategy for the Women's Movement," issued by the Chicago Women's Liberation Union, Hyde Park Chapter (scriptorium.lib.duke.edu/ wlm/socialist).

CHAPTER 8

The War on Poverty

INTRODUCTION

The 1960s was a period of great prosperity in the United States. And yet, in 1960, one in five Americans—20 percent of the U.S. population—lived below the official poverty line, earning less than $3,000 per year. This vexing phenomenon of want amid plenty was first brought to wide public attention in 1962 with the publication of Michael Harrington's *The Other America*, an exposé of poverty in America. It was easier for Harrington and others concerned about poverty to describe the deprivation they observed than to pinpoint its cause. Common explanations in the early 1960s focused either on the cultural nature of poverty or on its roots in economic or structural factors. The culture of poverty was a familiar idea: prolonged deprivation made the poor hopeless and apathetic, incapable of envisioning a better life, and thus unable to take action to improve their lot. The poor were said to exhibit behaviors such as a lack of discipline and an inability to defer gratification, which they transmitted from one generation to the next, creating an unbroken cycle. Structural poverty, on the other hand, had nothing to do with the behavior of the poor themselves; it represented various failures of the economic system to provide adequate employment and income to all. Regardless of which explanation one believed—and many embraced aspects of both—the implication was clear: to address the problem, government action was needed.

Aware of the stir caused by Harrington's book, President John F. Kennedy authorized a federal antipoverty initiative shortly before his death; his focus was Appalachia, one of the most destitute regions of the country. His successor, Lyndon Johnson, soon expanded Kennedy's plan to include the entire nation; in 1964, in rhetoric that reflected the optimism and idealism of the times, he declared "unconditional war on poverty."

Johnson's War on Poverty included the establishment of the Office of Economic Opportunity (OEO), headed by Kennedy's brother-in-law, and the former head of the Peace Corps, Sargent Shriver. The slogan of OEO was "a hand up, not a handout." The OEO did not dispense welfare. It sought to address the problems created by the culture of poverty, to help the poor gain the skills necessary to become gainfully employed and fully participating members of American society. Among the programs OEO established were Headstart, which offered early childhood education to the disadvantaged; the Job Corps, which provided skills training to poor high school students; and legal services for the poor. It also initiated a Community Action Program (CAP), which aimed to break the cycle of poverty by engaging the poor in finding solutions to their own problems.

In addition to OEO's service programs, a significant number of other federal programs were created to address the needs of the poor in the 1960s. Among them were health care for the poor and indigent (Medicaid) as well as for the elderly, poor and rich alike (Medicare); aid to elementary and secondary schools, some of which was targeted at improving the performance of children from low-income families; food stamps; and a number of initiatives to improve housing for the poor, including the creation of the cabinet-level office of Housing and Urban Development (HUD). These initiatives, along with the historic civil rights legislation of 1964 and 1965, were part of a far broader program to improve American society that Johnson dubbed "the Great Society."

The Johnson presidency marked the high point of the antipoverty rhetoric that later became associated with liberalism and big government. But concerted efforts by the federal government to address the issue of poverty in America continued after Johnson left office. Although Republican Richard Nixon dismantled OEO when he became president, he greatly increased Social Security benefits, expanded food stamps, and proposed a Family Assistance Plan to provide government subsidies to all those considered poor, including those who worked as well as those without jobs. Further, the number of Americans on welfare soared during Nixon's presidency. However, the War on Poverty remains closely associated in the public's mind with Johnson, as well as with the 1960s; it is also often conflated by its critics with the Great Society, although that rubric encompasses much more, including such programs as the beautification of America's highways, the creation of public television, and aid to higher education.

How successful was the War on Poverty? Statistics reveal that, by 1970, the national poverty rate had fallen to less than 13 percent from its high of 20 percent a decade earlier. Is this evidence of success? Or, given that so many Americans still remained poor in 1970, a sign of failure? Were some antipoverty programs more effective than others?

Although the War on Poverty initially enjoyed widespread support, it did draw criticism from the left and the right. Those on the left viewed it as a halfway measure at best. They argued that OEO's budget—which amounted to less than 1 percent of the gross national product in those years—was too small to address the problems of one-fifth of the nation. Many were also disappointed with Johnson's refusal to consider large-scale job creation (through New Deal-style public works programs) or the redistribution of income (by taxing the well-off and giving cash payments to the poor). To these critics, Johnson's commitment to creating jobs through tax cuts, and his insistence on "a hand up, not a handout," ignored the structural basis of poverty and was thus unlikely to succeed. Most historians of the War on Poverty have voiced a similar opinion, noting the gap between the rhetoric of ending poverty and the small amount of money devoted to the project.

Those to Johnson's right were also scornful of his War on Poverty. Their criticism gained influence over time with the rise of the conservative political movement (see Chapter 10) and with the tendency, since the mid-1970s, of many voters to favor lower taxes in preference to social welfare programs that benefit the poor. Conservatives charged that the War on Poverty promoted rather than undercut the culture of poverty; as Ronald Reagan liked to quip, America waged a war on poverty and poverty won. These critics on the right claimed that Johnson's antipoverty programs undermined the incentives that traditionally forced the poor to work and, in the case of women, to marry in order to support their children. The War on Poverty was a handout to people who lacked a work ethic, in their view. They linked welfare to "family breakdown"—decreased marriage rates and increased rates of out-of-wedlock births among the poor. Some in the 1980s, including President Reagan, even claimed that government assistance encouraged unmarried women to have as many children as possible as a way to increase the size of their welfare checks. Many white Americans associated welfare with African Americans, even though a majority of welfare recipients were white; Reagan and others pandered to such preconceptions by using racially loaded terms such as "welfare queen" in making their criticisms. Conservative criticisms reached their apogee with the publication of *Losing Ground* by Charles Murray in 1984; the book was sometimes referred to as the "bible" of the social policymakers in Reagan's administration.

Among the shortcomings of this perspective is that it confuses the Johnson-era War on Poverty with Aid to Families with Dependent Children (AFDC)—what Americans commonly refer to as "welfare," a program created in the 1930s, not in the 1960s, and whose beneficiaries grew in number most dramatically during the Nixon, not the Johnson, presidency. And although federal spending for social programs did rise significantly between 1965 and 1970, the increase in expenditures was almost entirely for programs that are universal, rather than means-tested, and overwhelmingly popular with the American public, such as Medicare and the expansion of Social Security.

Despite these serious flaws, the conservative argument maintained traction and, by the mid-1990s, captured the political center. Perhaps the best evidence of this is that a Democratic president, Bill Clinton, spearheaded welfare "reform," ending in 1996 the legal guarantee of assistance that the AFDC program had made. Ironically, Clinton's stated preference for helping the poor and unemployed through job training rather than through welfare payments had been Lyndon Johnson's and OEO's preference as well. Forty years after the War on Poverty, "a hand up, not a handout" remains the politically acceptable formula for poor relief in the United States.

The first reading in this chapter is an excerpt from historian Allen J. Matusow's *The Unraveling of America: Liberalism in the 1960s*, which was published in the early 1980s, a period when the Great Society, "the Sixties," and more broadly, liberalism and the welfare state came under sharp attack from Reagan and other conservatives. Matusow's view of the Johnson-era effort to address poverty is unremittingly negative; in his words, it was "one of the great failures of twentieth-century liberalism." Although his critique bears some similarity to that of conservatives, Matusow analyzes the limitations of the welfare state from a radical perspective. A central problem of the War on Poverty, in his opinion, was conceptual; administration officials presumed that, in a growing economy, the poor would be lifted up along with everyone else. But in Matusow's view, poverty is a relative condition resulting from inequality of income, and economic growth does nothing to alleviate inequality.

The basis of Matusow's judgment of the Johnson-era antipoverty initiatives, then, is whether they contributed to reducing inequality. Again, Matusow renders a harsh verdict. Johnson's War on Poverty included two approaches: programs that provided government services to ease the difficult lot of impoverished Americans, such as health care, affordable housing, and food stamps; and programs to expand economic opportunity. In the excerpt here, Matusow analyzes Medicare and Medicaid, the health care programs created in 1965 that, of all the Great Society initiatives, drew most heavily on the federal budget. Poor substitutes for universal health care, these programs helped line the pockets of health-care professionals; they did not increase the income of the poor, in Matusow's view. Matusow is even skeptical of claims that these programs, if they did not reduce poverty, at least contributed to improved health, arguing that the reduction in both infant mortality and death rates overall are attributable to other factors. He also argues, as have conservatives, that the government-run Medicare program actually increased the cost of health care to society, and that the poor and indigent, prior to the creation of Medicare and Medicaid, received good medical attention on a charity basis.

Matusow is equally grim in his assessment of the antipoverty programs that had as their slogan "a hand up, not a handout," and that sought to give the poor the same opportunity as the more privileged to find employment. Although he recognizes the benefits that were provided by Headstart and Legal Services, he deems the Job Corps—the program to teach job skills to the unemployed, which he discusses in this excerpt—to have been misguided and ineffectual.

Although Matusow does concede that the incidence of poverty dropped significantly in the handful of years that President Johnson held office, he attributes this to the booming war economy and not to any of the service or assistance programs initiated by Johnson. A more radical approach to eliminating poverty was needed—one that involved redistributing income from the haves to the have nots—but Johnson, concerned with not alienating middle-class and affluent voters, was not about to take this step and never seriously considered it. Although certain in his diagnosis of failure, Matusow also seems pessimistic about his own prescription for change. Although believing that redistributing wealth is necessary to eliminate poverty, he shares the concern of conservatives that higher taxes on the wealthy could lead to an unacceptable slowdown in economic growth that would ultimately hurt the poor.

The second selection is an excerpt from Michael Katz's *The Undeserving Poor: From the War on Poverty to the War on Welfare.* Written in 1989, after almost a decade of policies and rhetoric unsympathetic to the poor, Katz's book offers a more tempered judgment of the War on Poverty, recognizing how much it actually achieved in light of how harshly society and government can treat the poor. Katz shares Matusow's view that the War on Poverty initiated by Johnson was fundamentally flawed. His criticism, however, focuses not so much on the administration's failure to redistribute wealth as on Johnson's refusal to use government funds to create jobs, despite the view within his administration that a lack of jobs lay at the root of the poverty problem. Thus, like Matusow, Katz sees Johnson's programs as moderate, and in tune, rather than at odds, with the values and aspirations of middle America.

Although Matusow focuses on the Johnson era, Katz includes under the rubric of the War on Poverty all the initiatives that sought to address poverty, including those of the Nixon administration. Katz provides the useful reminder that government spending on welfare actually reached its height in the Nixon, not the Johnson, years. He also notes that the most radical antipoverty initiative of all—the plan to offer direct cash payments rather than services or training to the poor—originated in the Nixon, not the Johnson, administration.

Katz shares Matusow's judgment that the spate of initiatives and programs aimed at the poor not only failed to eliminate poverty but also left many millions mired in economic deprivation. But Katz still finds much to admire. He credits Medicare, Medicaid, and the Nixon-era increases in Social Security payments with lifting millions of older Americans out of poverty. Using quality of life rather than increased income as a yardstick, Katz also lauds Medicare and Medicaid, along with the food stamp and housing programs for improving health, and reducing hunger and overcrowding among millions of America's poor. He concludes that the government programs of the Great Society era were humane and helpful, not only in intention but also in their impact.

ALLEN J. MATUSOW

The Failure of the Welfare State

President Johnson's 1964 declaration of war on poverty precipitated instant controversy. On the right Barry Goldwater attacked the "Santa Claus of the free lunch" and implied that the "attitude or actions" of the poor themselves might be the cause of their problem. On the left socialist Michael Harrington predicted that the likely result of the war would be not to abolish poverty but to enrich the politicians. Skepticism permeated even the great amorphous public, 83 percent of whom, according to Gallup, doubted that the war could ever be won. Nonetheless, Johnson's declaration seemed at the time a master stroke. As policy, it perfectly suited the nation's post-assassination mood of idealism. And, as politics, it embarrassed the Republicans in the midst of the presidential campaign, since to oppose the war seemed tantamount to approving poverty. . . .

Johnson knew, of course, that he was running grave political risk by attacking poverty. There were far more affluent than impoverished voters, which meant that whatever he did for the poor must not impinge on the perceived interests of the middle classes—or else they would destroy him. Accordingly, he went to extraordinary lengths to convince well-heeled voters that his poverty programs conformed to traditional American values, would turn tax eaters into taxpayers, and were designed to forestall radicalism. "What you have and what you own . . ." the president told the Chamber of Commerce, "is not secure when there are men that are idle in their homes and there are young people that are adrift in the streets."

Johnson's commitment to class harmony decisively influenced the administration's answer to the crucial question—what is poverty? In its 1964 annual report the Council of Economic Advisers defined poverty, sensibly enough, as lack of income. If a family of four received $3,000 or less annually it could not maintain "a decent standard of living," hence it was poor. The arresting feature of the Council's definition was its treatment of poverty as a fixed condition with a permanent boundary. Any family able to purchase more than $3,000 worth of goods and service (in constant dollars) was then and thereafter to be considered nonpoor. One corollary of this definition was that, even if the government took no special measures to help the poor, the percentage of people living below the poverty line could be expected to decrease—since economic growth by itself would raise the real income of all classes. This conception of poverty had two political benefits from Lyndon Johnson's point of view: It virtually guaranteed that so long as the economy remained strong his promise to reduce poverty would be kept—regardless of the efficacy of his poverty programs. And, even more important, it meant that fighting poverty did not necessarily require the rich to be cast down, only that the poor be raised up.

From *The Unraveling of America: A History of Liberalism in the 1960s* (1984), by Allen J. Matusow. Reprinted by permission of the author.

Though politically serviceable, the Council's definition of poverty was intellectually indefensible. The concept of poverty as a fixed or absolute condition made sense only for past ages or for developing continents, in which to be poor meant command of resources—food, clothing, shelter—so meager that life itself was threatened. But poverty of this character hardly existed anymore in advanced industrial countries. Though undernourished children did exist in the United States, even among the poor they were the exception. Compared to poor people in Bangladesh or the poor in Western countries only a century ago, most of the American poor enjoyed a living standard that far removed them from the margin of existence. Indeed, poverty in advanced societies differed so radically from other forms that it required a definition quite different from the one advanced by Johnson and his advisers.

The clue to the meaning of modern poverty was embedded in a paradox: real income for all classes of Americans in this century kept growing; yet estimates of the size of the poor population have rarely varied. In 1904 Robert Hunter's classic study estimated that "in all probability, no less than 20 percent" of the population in industrial states was poor "in ordinarily prosperous years." In 1925 economist (later U.S. senator) Paul Douglas established a poverty standard for larger cities that translated into about 20 percent of their population. And in 1964 the Council of Economic Advisers estimated that 20 percent of American families were poor. The poverty line in each of these periods approximated half of median family income. In the mid-1920s when median income was roughly $2,000, the 20 percent of families considered poor by Douglas received $1,000 or less. And in 1963, when median income was $6,000, the poverty line set by the Council of Economic Advisers was $3,000. The bottom 20 percent of American families kept getting richer, thanks to economic growth, but they lagged just as far behind everybody else as before. They were, in short, chasing a moving poverty line—and not gaining.

Contrary to the Council, then, modern poverty was a relative, not a fixed, condition, for the concept of a "decent standard of living" expanded along with the Gross National Product. "Solely as a result of growing affluence," a presidential commission said in 1969, "a society will elevate its notions of what constitutes poverty." Expectations about consumption rose, and so too did the quantity of goods actually required to become a participating member of society. Yesterday's luxuries became today's necessities. At the beginning of the century only wealthy Americans had cars, central heating, or refrigeration. In 1970, 41 percent of *poor* families had cars, 62 percent had central heating, and 99 percent had refrigerators. But by the standards of the 1960s it did not matter that children fighting off rats in the Bronx or coal miners living in shacks in Appalachia or Mrs. Johnson's tenants in Alabama were better off than people living in other times and places or even that some of them drove old cars and had TV sets. What mattered was that they enjoyed so much less of a good life than other contemporary Americans that their condition was generally regarded as pitiable.

If poverty was not a matter of absolute want but of relative deprivation, then its cause was simple enough to grasp. It could only be income inequality. It followed that, to attack poverty, the government would have to reduce inequality, to redistribute income, in short, to raise up the poor by casting down the rich. By American standards, this was radicalism, and nobody in the Johnson White House ever considered it. As Ralph Lampham, staff member of the Council of Economic Advisers, wrote Walter Heller during the earliest phase of planning for the poverty program, "Most people see no political dynamite in the fact that our income distribution at the low end is about the same as it has always been"—the bottom fifth receiving about 5 percent of national income. "Probably a politically acceptable program must avoid completely the use of the term 'inequality' or of the term '*redistribution*' of income or wealth." It was not only the terms that were spurned, but the policies they implied. So Johnson went off to fight his war declaring that there would be no casualties. As in other wars, of course, so in this one—no casualties, no victories.

In fact, the War on Poverty was destined to be one of the great failures of twentieth-century liberalism. Most of its programs could be grouped under two strategies. One of these emphasized opening new opportunities for poor people either by investing in their education or by investing in areas, like Appalachia, where they were heavily concentrated. The other strategy, recognizing that mere opportunity would not be enough for many of the poor, provided subsidies to increase their consumption of food, shelter, and medical care. The administration hastened to assure that the cost of the new subsidies would be paid painlessly from expanding federal revenues generated by existing tax rates. Taken together, the programs spawned by these two strategies did little to diminish inequality and therefore, by definition, failed measurably to reduce poverty. . . .

The most ambitious effort ever made by the government to furnish in-kind income to some of its citizens was popularly known as Medicare. Climaxing nearly a decade of debate, President Johnson asked Congress in January 1965 to enact compulsory hospital insurance for nearly all persons over sixty-five, financed by contributions to the social security system. After all, advocates argued, old people used hospitals three times as frequently as the non-aged, had average incomes only half as large, and possessed inadequate health insurance. Given the overwhelming liberal majority in the 89th Congress, there was no doubt that this case would prevail. What no one foresaw was that Congress would take Johnson's bill, rewrite it, and legislate a program dramatically more generous.

It was Wilbur Mills, chairman of the House Ways and Means Committee and a Medicare opponent, who took note of the nation's liberal mood and presided over the bill's expansion. Many old persons incorrectly believed that Johnson was proposing to pay all their medical costs, not just hospitalization, and few Congressmen cared to risk the consequence of their disappointment. At a committee session in March, Mills suddenly suggested that some elements of a Republican substitute be reworked and added to the administration's measure. Medicare now would provide not only compulsory hospital insurance for the aged under social security; it would offer voluntary insurance covering doctors and surgical fees, the premiums to be split between the government and the beneficiary. . . .

Almost casually, Mills tacked on a new program that would benefit not the old primarily, but the poor, regardless of age. This was Medicaid, a real antipoverty program that could potentially affect as many people and cost as much money as Medicare, but which received only cursory attention from the Congress enacting it. Medicaid was an appendage of the welfare, not the social security, system. States electing to participate would receive matching grants from the federal government to pay medical bills for two classes of citizens—welfare recipients and the medically indigent. Medically indigent persons were those in certain categories (the blind, the disabled, the aged, or children in single-parent families), who were ineligible for welfare but could not afford to pay for medical care. Conspicuously absent from Medicaid coverage were the working poor. . . .

Like so many other welfare programs, Medicare-Medicaid represented a ruinous accommodation between reformers and vested interests, in this case the organized doctors. So desperate was the American Medical Association to exorcise the specter of socialized medicine that in the climactic final days of congressional debate it paid twenty-three lobbyists a total of $5,000 a day to prevent passage. Though the doctors were no longer strong enough to defeat Medicare, they nevertheless extracted their pound of flesh. HEW's Wilbur Cohen recalled that he had had to pledge to the Ways and Means Committee "that there would be no real controls over hospitals or physicians. . . . I promised very conscientiously that I would see to it there was no change in the basic health delivery system because so far as the AMA and Congress were concerned, this was sacred." The law, therefore, provided that hospitals would be reimbursed for their reasonable costs and physicians for customary fees. As it turned out, this formula not only guaranteed that the medical profession could continue as before; it guaranteed galloping medical price inflation as well.

The major cause of medical price inflation was health insurance, of which Medicare was only one example. Private health insurance had begun to spread after 1950, and as it did, medical prices spurted upward, especially hospital prices, which account for 40 percent of the nation's health bill. Most hospitals were nonprofit organizations. Before the widespread availability of insurance, hospital administrators had every incentive to keep costs down, because customers (i.e., patients) had to bear most of them. But insurance reduced the net price of hospital services for the patient at the time he consumed them and thereby removed the chief motive for cost restraint. Patients and doctors typically responded to lower net prices by demanding the best or, more accurately, the most expensive care that other people's money could buy. In other words, patients demanded more expensive care than they would elect if they paid all of the bill directly. Administrators could now please doctors by buying the latest equipment, patients by adding amenities, workers by raising wages, trustees with grandiose visions by adding beds—and pass on the added costs in the form of higher prices, increasingly paid through the painless mechanism of insurance. The process fed on itself. "People spend more on health because they are insured and buy more insurance because of the high cost of health care," one economist explained. Insurance was the main reason why, between 1950 and 1965, hospital prices rose 7 percent annually, while the general price level went up less than 2 percent a year.

Doctor's fees, accounting for 20 percent of medical expenditures, also rose in response to the spread of private health insurance. Unlike most hospitals, most doctors were in business for a profit. Insurance reduced the net price of physician services for covered patients, causing demand to increase. Doctors exploited the favorable market by raising fees. Insurance caught on more quickly for hospital than for doctor care; so inflation in doctors' fees was less acute, rising at 3 percent annually from 1950 to 1965. Insurance was not the only reason for medical price inflation, but it was the most important.

With passage of Medicare-Medicaid in 1965, the quantity of insurable services stood on the verge of significant increase. By the logic of medical economics, inflationary pressure on medical prices was bound to mount. The new programs, after all, imposed no cost controls and did not alter the way hospitals and doctors ordinarily conducted their business. Hospital prices, which had risen 7 percent in the year before Medicare, jumped by 14 percent in the year after and continued to rise, on the average, 14 percent annually over the next decade. Physicians' fees rose 7 percent a year.

Medicare not only increased the cost of medicine for society as a whole; it provided far fewer financial benefits for most recipients than was commonly believed. For that small minority of old people who had both long periods of hospitalization and small savings, Medicare was everything it was cracked up to be. But the average aged person was little better off. True, he paid only 29 percent of his medical bills directly out of pocket in 1975, compared to 53 percent before Medicare; but his total bill was also much higher. The average beneficiary spent $237 out of pocket in the year before Medicare and $390 ten years later—in constant dollars almost exactly the same. Aged persons not only had to buy drugs, eye glasses, and dental care, which Medicare did not cover; they expended increasing out-of-pocket sums for physicians' and hospital bills, part of which Medicare did cover. For example, in 1975 beneficiaries paid a deductible for each stay in a hospital, reaching $104 (up from $40 when the program began); and they paid, on the average, $156 for physician services (up from $66). Some additional expenditure could be explained by increased consumption of medical services and by better services. But, ironically, medical price inflation fueled by Medicare itself helped erode much of Medicare's benefits. So many gaps existed in Medicare's coverage that 24 percent of health care expenditures for the aged in 1970 had to be covered by state and local government, mainly in the form of Medicaid payments.

Medicaid helped states pay for a wide assortment of medical expenses for welfare recipients and the medically indigent. What prompted this generosity on the part of the government is not entirely clear. Most likely, Congress theorized that lack of income was a barrier to treatment. Actually, the poor had not fared all that badly prior to Medicaid, thanks to the willingness of doctors and hospitals to dispense charity medicine. In the last year before Medicaid the hospital admission rate for families with incomes below $3,000 was 107 per 1,000 families; for families with incomes $10,000 and above, it was only 89 per 1,000 families. Before Medicaid, the average low-income person visited a doctor 4.3 times a year—not dramatically less than the 5.1 visits made by high-income persons. Granted that the poor are more frequently ill, these figures do not sustain a thesis of gross inequality. Still, if its purpose was to increase access to medical services, Medicaid succeeded. By 1968 the hospital admission rate for poor families had climbed from 107 to 123 per 1,000, while the admission rate for the affluent fell slightly. And low-income persons now actually saw doctors more frequently than high-income persons (5.6 visits compared to 4.9 visits). The question is, were the benefits worth the cost?

For one thing, Medicaid did not buy a better brand of service than charity medicine had dispensed. The typical doctor shunned Medicaid patients not only from considerations of status and paperwork, but also from income—state governments usually setting fees far below customary charges. In New York City only an estimated 8 percent of the city's 12,000 doctors, often the least capable, accepted Medicaid patients. . . .

Medicaid had other problems as well. While it reduced some inequalities, it created others: annual benefits in 1974 varied from $214 per recipient in Missouri to $911 in Minnesota; 40 percent of the poor were not on welfare and so received no benefits; 30 percent of Medicaid recipients were not poor at all. Fraud haunted the program. Medical entrepreneurs, often in so-called Medicare mills, bilked the government by dispensing unnecessary services or charging for nonexistent services, abuses that cost the state of New York an estimated $250 million annually. And finally, it was absurd on the face of it that nearly $6 of every $10 spent on public assistance in 1975 took the form of Medicaid payments. Undoubtedly, most poor people would have preferred the cash.

In the end Medicare-Medicaid relied on a simple equation: more medicine equals better health. After 1965 death rates resulting from the major diseases dropped sharply, and so did infant mortality rates. Friends of these programs hailed these trends as evidence that increased utilization of medical services by the poor and the aged had paid off. Skeptics had their doubts. After Medicare, old people saw doctors more frequently and stayed in hospitals more days per admission (though their admission rate did not rise). Still, according to one prominent medical economist, "there is no evidence that Medicare has had a significant effect on the mortality rate of the aged." As for the rapidly declining infant mortality rate, it may be linked to the increasing proportion of poor pregnant women who visit doctors in the first trimester, or just as plausibly, to improved birth control techniques that have reduced the number of unwanted births.

Equalitarians had their own standards for judging Medicare and Medicaid. Since some Medicare benefits and all Medicaid benefits aided poor and near-poor persons, these programs appeared to reduce income inequality. Taxpayers lost money income, and the needy gained income in kind. But, as so often happens in the world of welfare, appearances can be deceiving. Most of the government's medical payments on behalf of the poor compensated doctors and hospitals for services once rendered free of charge or at reduced prices. Only that small fraction of Medicare-Medicaid payments purchasing additional services for the poor constituted real additions to their income. Aside from middle-class old persons protected from the financial ravages of long illness, the clearest beneficiaries of Medicare and Medicaid were doctors, who, according to one estimate, enjoyed an average income gain of $3,900 in 1968 as a result of these programs. Medicare-Medicaid, then, primarily transferred income from middle-class taxpayers to middle-class health-care professionals. In this way, once again, the politics of consensus prevailed over the policy of redistribution. . . .

No aspect of poverty worried liberals more than the one million young men, ages sixteen through twenty-one, who were unemployed or out of the work force in 1963. As superfluous labor, this population stood as a threat to the social peace and an indictment of the social system. Years of agitation by reformers to offer these young people special vocational education finally paid off in 1964 when Congress created the Job Corps as part of the Economic Opportunity Act. The Job Corps intended annually to recruit 100,000 unemployed young men and women, remove them far from slum environments, and provide them skills to exploit the abundant opportunities of the American economy. Training would take place either in "urban centers" (most of which were actually abandoned military bases) or, at the insistence of the conservation lobby, in rural conservation camps where the least literate would receive basic education and work experience. Sargent Shriver, director of the Office of Economic Opportunity, waged fierce warfare with the Labor Department to win control of the Job Corps, hoping that it would yield instant results and cover him with quick glory. He never made a greater mistake.

Shriver launched the Job Corps with a major promotional drive to attract recruits, a drive so successful that by mid-1965 the Corps had received 300,000 applications for the available 10,000 slots. Most of the thousands turned away never returned. Shriver tapped some of the most prestigious corporations in America, including General Electric, IBM, Litton Industries, RCA, and Westinghouse to run the urban centers, convinced they would provide the most efficient but innovative training programs possible. The corporations pioneered no pedagogical breakthroughs, and the cost-plus contracts under which they operated offered no incentives for efficiency. Shriver launched the Job Corps, excited by the therapeutic possibilities of residential training centers far from the slum neighborhoods of the recruits. But this experiment never paid off, creating so many problems and generating so much bad publicity at the beginning that the Job Corps never really recovered.

The first recruits typically found themselves 1,200 miles away from home, isolated from members of the opposite sex, subjected to unaccustomed discipline, and disappointed in the Corps's facilities and programs. The first year—1965—troubles abounded. Several corpsmen were arrested at the Atterbury center in Indiana for forcing a fellow trainee to commit sodomy. In Austin, Texas, a trainee on leave from Camp Gary got stabbed in a fight. At Camp Breckinridge in western Kentucky a food riot had to be quelled by federal marshals. Corpsmen were charged with burglaries in Laredo, promiscuity in St. Petersburg, and window smashing in Kalamazoo. Meanwhile congressmen expressed shock on learning that the average cost per enrollee at a residential center in 1966 exceeded $8,000 and debated whether a Harvard education cost as much. In 1966 Shriver was disappointed when Congress limited Job Corps slots to 45,000, though applicants to fill even this number would soon prove exceedingly difficult to find.

During the second year, the Job Corps solved its worst problems and settled down to dispense vocational education. To its everlasting credit, it recruited from a clientele that nearly every other institution in America had abandoned. One of every four corpsmen had an eighth-grade education or less; more than half were black; all came from poor families. But, while many no doubt benefited from the experience, only a minority emerged notably more employable than before they began. Throughout the first decade, two-thirds of enrollees quit before completing the typical six-to-nine-month course, and nearly half were gone in three months or less. Those who did graduate received better wages and had lower unemployment rates than Corps dropouts but, according to surveys made in 1966 and 1967, did no better in the labor market than "no-shows" (applicants who had been accepted by the Job Corps but had not shown up). Six months after leaving the Corps, 28 percent of *graduates* were unemployed and only one-third had jobs related to their training.

At root, the problem of the Job Corps, as with other government manpower programs, was the nature of the training. It was simply unrealistic to expect any educational institution to take young men and women as culturally handicapped as Job Corps recruits and train them for really good jobs. Corps courses prepared trainees only for entry-level proficiency in occupations such as cook, baker, janitor, welder, construction worker, meat cutter, and auto-body repairer. These were jobs for which employers could easily hire workers from the existing labor pool and provide simple on-the-job training. The probable effect of the Job Corps, therefore, was to give its graduates a slight advantage over other similarly disadvantaged youths competing for the same openings. Because jobs obtained by corpsmen would have gone to someone else, the program had little or no effect on the overall unemployment rate, nor did it achieve much income redistribution, except perhaps from one group of the disadvantaged to another. . . .

In October 1968, during the gloomy twilight of his presidency, Lyndon Johnson entertained a group of regional OEO directors at the White House. "Here are the campaign ribbons that you and I have earned during the past 5 years," he said, whereupon he rattled off figures showing that his administration had moved people out of poverty at "the fastest rate in all of our history." Updated, these figures were his consolation and his vindication. Federal spending on the poor had risen from nearly $12 billion to more than $27 billion in six years. The incidence of poverty had gone down from 20 percent of the population to 12 percent. And 12 million people had moved across the official poverty line. He had had failures along with successes, Johnson admitted, but he could say at the end, as he had at the beginning, "we must continue."

That the war on poverty had much to do with reducing poverty is doubtful. Its programs were too recent to make much difference and too misconceived ever to do so. Indeed, those who most directly benefited were the middle-class doctors, teachers, social workers, builders, and bankers who provided federally subsidized goods and services of sometimes suspect value. The principal cause of the mass migration across the administration's fixed poverty boundary was not the war on poverty but the war in Vietnam. That war helped overheat the economy, generated rapid increases in GNP, and moved the poor up with everybody else, temporarily even a little faster.

Johnson's boast that poverty had diminished was, in any case, only as good as the official definition of the problem. Those who regarded poverty not as a fixed but a relative condition could argue that no progress at all had occurred. As confirmed by recent opinion surveys, the public continued to regard half of median family income as a realistic poverty line. In 1963, when median income was $6,000 and the poverty line $3,000, 20 percent lived beneath it. In 1976, more than a decade after Johnson launched his poverty war, the median had risen to $15,000, and 20 percent still received less than half. By this view of the matter, income inequality had not been reduced and therefore the extent of poverty had remained constant.

Agreeing that the reduction of inequality was the test of success, some defenders of Johnson's war eventually argued that merely looking at the distribution of money income was not enough. Great Society programs to provide in-kind income to the poor—food stamps, Medicare-Medicaid, housing subsidies—were just as good as money, they said. If the dollar value of in-kind income was added to the money income, the poor received a larger share of national income than if money income alone was considered. Inequality, hence poverty, had diminished after all. The argument was as ingenious as it was spurious. Approximately 85 percent of in-kind income took the form of medical services provided by Medicare-Medicaid. But, since most payments under these programs compensated doctors and hospitals for services previously rendered free of charge or for reduced charges, Medicare-Medicaid added little to the real income of poor people. Of the government's in-kind expenditures, only food stamps were income as good as cash for the poor.

While Great Society programs accomplished little redistribution, older government measures did. Cash transfer programs originating in the New Deal—public assistance, social security, unemployment insurance—provided disproportionate benefits to poor people. In 1972 the bottom 20 percent had only 1.7 percent of national income before transfers but 5.4 percent afterward—not enough to raise them above half the median but a significant addition to income nonetheless. Many reformers came increasingly to advocate more generous cash transfer programs as the way to move families at the bottom of the income scale above the poverty line, no matter how defined.

But, even from the point of view of equalitarians, these schemes posed problems. A reasonable program to lift most American families above even the official, fixed poverty line in 1972 would have required additional tax transfers of $30 to $40 billion. Since there were not all that many rich people, and tax rates at the top were already steep, much of the burden of redistribution would have fallen on families with incomes between $15,000 and $25,000, families not so very affluent. Moreover, redistribution of that magnitude might seriously inhibit the incentive to work. High taxes had not yet encouraged a taste for leisure among earners in the top brackets, but at some undetermined higher level they almost certainly would. The effects of generous cash transfers on the work incentives of low-wage workers were easier to measure. A painstaking experiment in 1971–1972 tested a variety of income-maintenance schemes to aid poor families in Denver and Seattle. Testifying before a dismayed congressional committee in 1978, the director of the study reported a significant work disincentive. "On the average," he said, "we found that the experiments caused a reduction in annual hours of work of about 5 percent for the male heads of families, about 22 percent for wives and 11 percent for female heads of families."

Finally there remained the perennial puzzle of what effect higher taxes would have on the willingness to save and invest. Progressive tax rates had not so far affected the rate of investment, but if high enough would undoubtedly do so. By inducing less work and less investment, more drastic income redistribution would result in less economic growth. Less growth would mean fewer jobs and a slower rise in living standards, important to poor people above all. It was indeed a hard world when redistribution, which alone could reduce the extent of poverty, might in the long run hurt the poor.

Michael B. Katz

From the War on Poverty to the War on Welfare

Between 1964 and 1972, the federal government unleashed a barrage of new antipoverty programs. Those most directly associated with the Office of Economic Opportunity fought poverty by trying to expand opportunity and empower local communities. Others radically altered procedures for redistributing income. Even though the former never had resources sufficient to realize their goals, spending on distributive social programs—Social Security, Medicare and Medicaid, food stamps, Aid to Families with Dependent Children—escalated until the end of Richard Nixon's first administration.

Public memory, and much subsequent history, treats the War on Poverty harshly. The nation fought a war on poverty and poverty won, has become a summary judgment assented to without reservation even by many liberals. These years deserve a more discriminating verdict. Although social policy did not seriously dent the forces that generate want, although many new programs failed spectacularly and others disappointed their sponsors, the federal government did alleviate the consequences of poverty. Millions of Americans, most of them elderly, who would have remained poor escaped poverty; others whose incomes remained below the poverty line found medical care, food, housing assistance, and income security at a level unprecedented in America's past.

The idea of a comprehensive assault on poverty had been formulated by President John F. Kennedy. On November 23, 1963, the day after Kennedy's assassination, President Lyndon Johnson met with Walter Heller, chairman of the Council of Economic Advisors, and instructed him to continue planning the antipoverty program. Johnson used the phrase "unconditional war on poverty" for the first time on January 8, 1964, in his State of the Union message. On February 1, he appointed Sargent Shriver to direct the new antipoverty program. Shriver, along with a planning committee that drew members from various branches of the federal government, developed a strategy for the program and drafted the Economic Opportunity Act (creating OEO), passed by the Senate on July 23, 1964, and by the House on August 8. President Johnson signed it into law on August 20. . . .

From the start, internal contradictions plagued the War on Poverty. Among the most debilitating was the translation of a structural analysis of poverty into a service-based strategy. As David Austin reflected in 1973: "The issue is really why a service strategy when you had a structural diagnosis." Although the most influential analyses of poverty stressed its roots in unemployment, federal antipoverty planners deliberately avoided programs that created jobs. In his economic report for 1964, Lyndon Johnson summarized the problem of poverty in America in structural terms. His presentation drew on the detailed second chapter of a report by the Council of Economic Advisors (CEA), written primarily by Robert Lampman, an economist from the University of Wisconsin and an expert in poverty statistics. Using the most detailed data yet published, the CEA's report argued that economic growth by itself would not eliminate poverty in America. Despite echoes of the culture of poverty thesis, it anchored poverty in income distribution, employment, discrimination, and inadequate transfer payments by government, and it proposed a comprehensive program for its reduction. "By the poor," asserted the report, "we mean those who are not now maintaining a decent standard of living—those whose basic needs exceed their means to satisfy them." It also firmly rejected explanations based on character or heredity: "The idea that the bulk of the poor are condemned to that condition because of innate deficiencies of character or intelligence has not withstood intensive analysis." Those in poverty lacked "the earned income, property income and savings, and transfer payments to meet their minimum needs." Many employed people earned inadequate wages, while other poor people could not work on account of "age, disability, premature death of the principal earner, need to care for children or disabled family members, lack of any saleable skill, lack of motivation, or simply heavy unemployment in the area." For others, low pay reflected racial discrimination or "low productivity" that resulted from inadequate education and skills.

Property and savings income were most important for the elderly, but many had earned too little to save, and about half of them had no hospital insurance. Without such transfer payments as existed, many more families would have been poor. Nonetheless, only half the poor received any transfer payments at all, and the most generous payments (private pensions and Social Security) offered the least help to those employed irregularly or in the worst-paying jobs. Aside from earnings, poverty's roots, according to the report, lay in a "vicious circle." Poverty bred poverty because of "high risks of illness; limitations on mobility; limited access to education, information, and training." As a consequence, parents passed on their poverty to their children. With discrimination often an insurmountable barrier, escaping poverty proved nearly impossible for "American children raised in families accustomed to living on relief."

Despite its structural diagnosis, the Council of Economic Advisors laid the foundation for a War on Poverty based on economic growth, civil rights, and new social and educational services designed to equalize opportunity. The council stressed removing the handicaps that denied the poor "fair access to the expanding incomes of a growing economy" and introducing new federal programs "with special emphasis on prevention and rehabilitation." As for jobs, the council urged their indirect creation through a tax cut that would stimulate the economy.

The CEA report revealed the hallmarks of American liberalism in the early 1960s: an uneasy mix of environmental and cultural explanations of poverty; a continuation of the historic American reliance on education as a solution for social problems; trust in the capacity of government; and faith in the power of experts to design effective public policies. Notably absent were community action and the creation of new jobs by government.

An early poverty warrior, Adam Yarmolinsky, remembered: "You ask yourself do you concentrate on finding jobs for people or preparing people for jobs. There our tactical decision was let's concentrate first on preparing people for jobs." The strategists thought the 1964 tax cut would create jobs; they believed poor people needed a long process of job preparation; and they knew that "it was less expensive to prepare people for jobs than to create jobs for people."

Like other domestic and international policies of the era, this strategy assumed the continuation of growth and abundance, for an antipoverty plan that stressed increased educational opportunity and work preparation depended on the continued expansion and easy availability of jobs. Because growth would stimulate demand and enlarge the available rewards, the eradication of poverty required no painful reallocation of money and power. In the buoyant economy of the early 1960s this analysis still remained plausible, and an analysis of poverty as primarily a problem of employment reasonably could result in a relatively cheap public policy directed toward equalizing opportunity through education and job preparation.

Not all members of the administration agreed, however. The Department of Labor, led by Secretary Willard Wirtz, proposed a poverty program which stressed employment. Wirtz's objections drew on the Labor Department's commitment to macroeconomic policies based on reducing unemployment, where necessary, through public employment. In 1961, Arthur Goldberg, then secretary of labor, advocated a Full Employment Act of 1961, and Wirtz continued to press this Labor Department position. He "violently attacked" the CEA report, which was "published over his strenuous objection." In a memo to Theodore Sorenson, who had circulated a proposal for a poverty program, Wirtz emphasized: *The Poverty Program must start out with immediate, priority emphasis on employment* [italics in original]." Because poverty "is a description of income," he argued, the major "single immediate change which the poverty program could bring about in the lives of most of the poor would be to provide the family head with a regular, decently paid job." Job creation did not depend solely on direct action by the federal government. The attack, Wirtz believed, should be launched principally at the *local* level, because *"the private forces are stronger than the public* [italics in original]." The tax bill was "an anti-poverty bill, probably the principal weapon we have." Nonetheless, the problem of unemployment demanded "special programs designed to create useful jobs." Wirtz, in common with other advocates of a poverty program, also stressed health and education, but his emphasis on job creation set the Department of Labor apart from the Council of Economic Advisors.

Wirtz apparently persuaded the staff designing the poverty program, because at the last minute it added a job component. Armed with a proposal for a supplementary tax on cigarettes to finance it, Sargent Shriver presented the plan at a cabinet meeting, where Wirtz also argued vigorously on its behalf. President Johnson, however, wanted neither expanded economic transfers nor direct job creation, and he finessed the question of income transfers by appointing a commission. As for the job creation plan, "I have never seen a colder reception from the president," recalled Adam Yarmolinsky. "He just—absolute blank stare—implied without even opening his mouth that Shriver should move on to the next proposal."

Direct attacks on unemployment never had a serious chance of passage in either the Kennedy or the Johnson administrations. Kennedy did not appoint the most influential advocate of Keynesian policies, John Kenneth Galbraith, to the Council of Economic Advisors. His three appointees, led by Walter Heller, did not share Galbraith's interventionist approach. Instead, they stressed aggregate economic objectives, particularly economic growth. Because they believed tax cuts would achieve their goals most efficiently, the focus of the War on Poverty and the Great Society, as Margaret Weir concludes, "shifted from the structure of the economy to the characteristics of the individual, characteristics that training was supposed to modify." By default, the War on Poverty adopted the culture of poverty.

As finally approved by the president, the poverty program linked two major strategies: equal opportunity and community action. As an antipoverty strategy, equal opportunity stressed improved and expanded services, especially those related to education and job preparation—for example, Operation Headstart for preschool children and the Job Corps for adolescents. (It also led to the massive infusion of funds into the schools attended by poor children, which resulted not from the poverty program itself but from the Elementary and

Secondary Education Act of 1965.) Community action refers to an emphasis on the active participation of community residents in the formulation and administration of programs. Community action required the establishment of local agencies to receive and spend federal funds. As a strategy, it deliberately bypassed existing local political structures, empowered new groups, and challenged existing institutions. . . .

Neither community action nor the War on Poverty's new service programs increased the amount of money spent on social welfare. Nonetheless, between the late 1960s and the early 1970s, the federal government expanded public social spending in five major ways. First, the number of persons receiving Aid to Families with Dependent Children (AFDC) exploded. Second, food stamps became more widely available and free to the poor. Third, through Supplemental Social Security, the aged, blind, and disabled received a guaranteed minimum income. Fourth, Social Security benefits increased dramatically and were linked to inflation. Fifth, Medicaid and Medicare created a system of national health insurance for welfare recipients and the elderly. Still, Congress defeated the most dramatic proposal for expanding public [social] provisions: Richard Nixon's guaranteed minimum income for families. In many ways, Nixon's abortive Family Assistance Plan remains the most interesting part of the story because it was the first major attempt to overhaul the social welfare structure erected in the 1930s. As such, it rested on ideas about antipoverty strategy that differed sharply from the service-based programs of the War on Poverty.

On August 8, 1969, President Richard Nixon proposed a Family Assistance Plan that would guarantee all families with dependent children a minimum yearly income ($1,600 for a family of four). He also proposed that states pay a prescribed federal minimum to disabled, blind, and elderly people eligible for welfare. . . .

Conservatives objected to Nixon's plan because it would expand the number of families eligible for aid and because it violated their beliefs about the limited role of government and the harmful effects of welfare. On the left, opinion divided between those who supported the bill as an important precedent and those who believed its benefits to be woefully inadequate and its workfare provisions punitive.

No such coalition formed to defeat the other expansions of public social provision in the same years. Because everyone grows old, Social Security cuts across class lines and draws on the massive political power of the elderly. As for food stamps, hunger historically has moved Americans more than any form of deprivation. In 1968, after a powerful television documentary on hunger, Senator George McGovern, chair of a new Senate Committee on Nutrition and Human Needs, began public hearings on the issue. By proposing the expansion of the food stamp program, Nixon preempted what otherwise surely would have become a major political issue for the Democrats. Poll after poll has demonstrated that for decades public opinion has favored national health insurance. Without the active opposition of the powerful American medical profession, America would not be the only Western democracy without it. The 1965 passage of Medicare for the elderly and Medicaid for welfare recipients therefore reflected a political compromise, not a major ideological shift.

Unlike the other expansions of public social provision, the explosion of the welfare rolls required only modest legislative changes. In 1960, 745,000 families received AFDC at a cost of less than $1 billion; by 1972, the number of families had become 3 million and the cost had multiplied to $6 billion. The reasons were several. The migration of southern blacks to northern cities increased the number of poor people dependent on cash incomes and reduced the number of subsistence farmers. Starting in 1961, Congress permitted states to extend aid to families headed by unemployed male parents. (As of 1988, only 28 states had taken advantage of this opportunity, which was a minor factor in the increase.) Some states loosened the standards for eligibility. More important, mobilized by the welfare rights movement, the proportion of poor families applying for welfare increased dramatically, as did the proportion of applicants accepted, which skyrocketed from about 33 percent in the early 1960s to 90 percent in 1971. The latter event reflected the efforts of the nascent welfare rights movement to recast welfare as an entitlement, reduce its stigma, and mobilize poor people to claim assistance as a right. Indeed, welfare rights became a social movement acted out in demonstrations that pressured reluctant welfare officials and in courtrooms where lawyers successfully challenged state laws restricting eligibility.

Welfare rights was a new idea in American social policy. "Prior to the 1960s," writes Rand Rosenblatt in his review of its legislative history, "recipients of benefits under programs such as AFDC were not seen as having 'rights' to benefits or even to a fair process for deciding individual cases." The achievement of welfare rights required both the mobilization of poor people and new legal doctrines. Funded by the poverty program, the Legal Services Corporation for the first time in American history provided poor people with lawyers to act on their behalf. With the example of civil rights victories in the courts, a new generation of welfare and poverty lawyers successfully challenged state laws in the Supreme Court. . . .

Neither the War on Poverty, the Great Society, nor the extension of public social benefits challenged the structure of the American welfare state. Instead, they reinforced the historic distinction between social insurance and public assistance that has defined welfare in America since the 1930s. Social welfare expanded along well-worn tracks. Social Security benefits increased and were indexed. Supplemental Social Insurance, on the other hand, folded programs into a new form of means-tested relief. Congress added a broadened and liberalized food stamp program to public assistance, whose benefits were lower than Social Security. Health insurance also divided into two programs, one part of the social insurance apparatus and the other part of the structure of public assistance. The benefits they provided, and the reimbursement they offered providers, differed sharply.

Social insurance received by far the greatest share of public funds and provided the highest benefits. In 1970, Social Security payments to the elderly, $30.3 billion, already exceeded AFDC payments by about ten times. By 1984, Social Security payments, which were indexed to inflation, had mushroomed to $180.9 billion. AFDC, which was not indexed, had risen to only $8.3 billion.

Although the Great Society did not alter the structure of social welfare, its accomplishments belie contemporary conventional wisdom that either ignores or belittles the great achievements of the era. Between 1965 and 1972, the government transfer programs lifted about half the poor over the poverty line. Between 1959 and 1980, the proportion of elderly poor people dropped, almost entirely as a result of government transfer programs, from 35 percent to 16 percent. Medicare and Medicaid improved health care dramatically. In 1963, one of every five Americans who lived below the poverty line never had been examined by a physician, and poor people used medical facilities far less than others. By 1970, the proportion never examined had dipped to 8 percent, and the proportion visiting a physician annually was about the same as for everyone else. Between 1965 and 1972, poor women began to consult physicians far more often during pregnancy, and infant mortality dropped 33 percent. Food stamps successfully reduced hunger, and housing programs lessened overcrowding and the number of people living in substandard housing.

Of course, there are less sanguine ways to read the evidence: poverty remained unacceptably high; millions of Americans still lacked medical insurance; in the 1980s, housing became a major problem for virtually anyone with a low income; and hunger reappeared as a national disgrace. Indeed, as the rate of poverty before income transfer programs shows, neither public policy nor private enterprise had moderated the great forces that generate poverty in America. At best, they alleviate its effects. Nonetheless, the expansion of public social benefits from 1964 to 1972 transformed the lives of millions of Americans and demonstrated the capacity of government as an agent of social change.

Further Reading

James T. Patterson, *America's War on Poverty, 1900–1994* (Cambridge, MA: Harvard University Press, 1994) and Edward D. Berkowitz, *America's Welfare State: From Roosevelt to Reagan* (Baltimore: The Johns Hopkins University Press, 1991) are highly informative overviews. *Poverty Knowledge: Social Science, Social Policy, and the Poor in Twentieth-Century U.S. History* (Princeton, NJ: Princeton University Press, 2001), by Alice O'Connor, is a challenging intellectual history critical of U.S. practices.

The Moynihan Report and the Politics of Controversy (Cambridge, MA: MIT Press, 1967), by William L. Yancey and Lee Rainwater, is an early account of the debate over "family breakdown." Daniel P. Moynihan expresses many now-familiar criticisms of the OEO in *Maximum Feasible Misunderstanding* (New York: The Free Press, 1969). Charles Murray, *Losing Ground: American Social Policy, 1950–1980* (New York: Basic Books, 1984) takes these criticisms much further and makes them pointedly political; its infelicitous style makes it more likely to have been cited than read.

From the left, Frances Fox Piven and Richard A. Cloward, *Regulating the Poor: The Functions of Public Welfare* (New York: Random House, 1971) offers a provocative, if not easily proven, argument that welfare is intended as a safety valve through which a capitalist society keeps the poor at bay. *Women, the State and Welfare* (Madison: University of Wisconsin Press, 1990), edited by Linda Gordon, is an important collection of essays representing the recent emphasis on gender issues in analysis of the U.S. welfare state. However, most of this new literature deals with the period before 1945. Martha F. Davis, *Brutal Need: Lawyers and the Welfare Rights Movement, 1960–1973* (New Haven, CT: Yale University Press, 1993) focuses on the human actors who pressed "from below" for expanded aid in the 1960s.

As the 1980s ended, works appeared representing a gloomy view on "the underclass "(a new term for the urban poor) and the kind of help they needed. William Julius Wilson, *The Truly Disadvantaged: The Inner City, the Underclass, and Public Policy* (Chicago: University of Chicago Press, 1987) is the work of a celebrated sociologist. Adolph L. Reed, Jr., furiously refuted the widespread emphasis on family breakdown and included Wilson in his indictment in "The 'Underclass' as Myth and Symbol: The Poverty of Discourse about Poverty," in Reed, *Stirrings in the Jug: Black Politics in the Post-Segregation Era* (Minneapolis: University of Minnesota Press, 1999), 179–96. *Chain Reaction: The Impact of Race, Rights, and Taxes on American Politics* (New York: Norton, 1991), by Thomas Byrne Edsall and Mary B. Edsall, is a detailed account of relevant political developments that shows sympathy for conservative complaints about the welfare state.

Primary Sources

For Lyndon Johnson's message to Congress upon submitting to it the Economic Opportunity Act of 1964, go to www.fordham.edu/halsall/mod/1964johnson-warpoverty.html. Go to www. americanrhetoric.com/speeches/lbjthegreatsociety.htm to read Johnson's 1964 speech at the University of Michigan in which he introduced his vision of the Great Society. (This site also offers an audio version of the speech.) The text of Johnson's remarks on signing the bill creating Medicare is available at www.lbjlib.utexas.edu/johnson/archives.hom/speeches.hom/ 650730.asp. For a chart showing the number of families below the poverty level and the poverty rate between 1959 and 2003, go to www.census.gov/hhes/poverty/histpov/hstpov13.html. Go to www.census.gov/hhes/poverty/histpov/hstpov16.html for a chart showing the distribution of the poor, by age and race, 1959–2003.

CHAPTER 9

The Vietnam War

INTRODUCTION

Few events after World War II brought the United States more grief than the Vietnam War. The war between the U.S. military and the Vietnamese revolutionary forces lasted two decades and cost between two million and five million lives, some 59,000 of them American. By the time the United States was driven from Vietnam in 1975, strong majorities of Americans regretted the entire enterprise, considering it both a failure and a mistake. But the American political elite were far more reluctant than the public to acknowledge the failures of U.S. policy, for which that elite bore responsibility. In addition, the grim public consensus on the war masked continuing popular disagreements about the morality of America's original intentions in fighting the war, and about whether the humbling of U.S. power by a seemingly much weaker foe ought to alter U.S. relations with the wider world. Some Americans responded to the U.S. defeat in Vietnam with anger; others, with self-criticism.

Scholarship on the Vietnam War has proceeded along many different fronts and has been undertaken by specialists in the history of diplomacy, domestic politics, warfare, and American culture. Yet historians have expended the most energy seeking answers to two essential questions about the war: Why did the United States become engaged in a war in a small, impoverished country thousands of miles from its shores? Why did the United States, the greatest military power in the world, lose? The U.S. government's official explanations for its involvement in Vietnam pointed to the need to protect the sovereignty of its ally, South Vietnam, against externally directed aggression, and to stem the global tide of communism and thus forestall a threat to U.S. national security. These explanations proved increasingly unconvincing to the American public as the war dragged on, as the U.S. body count continued to rise, and as the revelation of government lies about particular facets of the war created a "credibility gap." The title of a 1967 novel—*Why Are We in Vietnam?*—echoed the question that many Americans had begun to ask by the late 1960s. The first phase of scholarship on the war, which extended from the 1970s into the 1980s, searched for the answer. Most historians working on this question focused on diplomacy and international relations, stressing either the power politics among nations or the competing ideologies of the cold war. Many scholars narrated the decisions of individual presidents, from Franklin Roosevelt to Richard Nixon, often simply trying to get straight the details of a complicated story. Frequently, they presented these leaders as beset by forces over which they had little control, such as the post-1945 drive for nationalist revolution within the countries of the third world, or the need to preserve U.S. "prestige" by continuing a war effort even when it was going badly.

Historians have also explored the history of the war by following the story of the Vietnamese. Some of the early U.S. chroniclers of the Vietnamese revolutionary forces had links to the U.S. war effort; others were neutral or sympathetic to the revolutionaries. Although sympathies differed, historians agree that impressive organization and ideological coherence among the revolutionaries help explain why the United States ultimately failed to subdue them. This body of work points to what became the major question for historians of the Vietnam War in the 1980s and 1990s: why did the United States lose?

Many scholars interested in this question have sought answers on the battlefields rather than in Washington, DC. In the 1980s, a right-wing perspective on the war, exemplified by the book *On Strategy,* by retired military officer Harry G. Summers, Jr., drew considerable attention. Ironically, this view was dubbed "revisionist," a term generally associated with left-wing interpretations. Summers argued that, had U.S forces been deployed differently, U.S. leaders could have brought military victory in Vietnam. Very few historians of the Vietnam War endorsed Summers's argument (although it was shared by many Americans), and it did not spawn a substantial body of scholarship. However, the questions that Summers pointedly raised about U.S. military strategy did help spur other historians to search for more precise explanations of U.S. defeat, whether through focusing on military or political matters or through exploring American failings or the revolutionaries' strengths.

In the first of the two readings presented here, historian Robert Buzzanco explores the questions of how and why U.S. leaders took their country to war in Vietnam, its third major war in Asia in twenty years. The United States had been openly committed to resisting the spread of communism and socialism anywhere in the world since President Harry S Truman enunciated the 1947 doctrine that bears his name (see Chapter 2). The French had controlled Vietnam as part of their Indochina colony, but lost it to the Japanese during World War II. After the Japanese defeat in 1945, Ho Chi Minh, a nationalist in favor of independence for Vietnam, and also a leading Vietnamese Communist, declared the establishment of the Democratic Republic of Vietnam (the DRV or DRVN) in Hanoi. Rejecting Ho's appeal for American recognition and aid for the fledgling country, the United States chose instead to support and fund the French effort to retake Vietnam. When the French sued for peace in 1954 after suffering a devastating battlefield defeat, the United States stepped in to prevent the revolutionaries led by Ho from coming to power. A 1954 peace conference in Geneva negotiated a temporary division of Vietnam, with democratic elections to be held within two years to determine Vietnam's form of government. But fearful that the Communists would win the elections, the United States acted to prevent the referendum, to make partition permanent, and to maintain an anticommunist ally—critics said a "puppet"—in the south, in Saigon, at the head of what U.S. leaders called the "Republic of Vietnam" (RVN). But the question remains, why did the United States care so deeply about preventing remote Vietnam from becoming an independent, even if communist, country?

The large contours of U.S. relations with the world after 1945 provide Buzzanco's frame of reference, and he finds the basic imperatives of U.S. cold war policy adequate to explain America's commitment to Vietnam. He simply sees no great mystery here. He also conveys the monumental scale of force employed on the American side, offering a pointed response to those who, especially during the conservative period of the 1980s and 1990s, charged that the United States lost because American leaders would not permit the U.S. military to fight the war effectively. Germane in this regard is the striking evidence Buzzanco produces that high officers in the U.S. armed forces knew and said, throughout the war, that the war could not be won with any amount of U.S. firepower because of the political weaknesses of U.S. allies in South Vietnam. This is exactly what critics of the war have said for decades. Buzzanco sees Vietnam as a civilian's war, with the military cast as truth tellers and reluctant war makers.

Actually, the military command played a double game in the war's complex politics. Privately they expressed sharp doubts about the enterprise, but in public, beginning in the late 1960s, they maintained to their allies in Congress that President Lyndon Johnson and his subordinates were preventing success in the field by restricting U.S. bombing targets. To deflect blame for a looming defeat, the military planted the seeds for the subsequent, widespread belief among Americans that the United States lost because it "fought with one hand tied behind its back," a belief that Buzzanco criticizes as false.

Several popular beliefs have taken hold among Americans since the Vietnam War ended as to why the United States lost. In addition to blaming a supposedly too-limited military strategy on Lyndon Johnson, they identify a failure of "will" among the public, spreading to the political leadership, to see a difficult war through to the finish; in this connection the antiwar movement is often blamed as the source of this contagion of self-doubt. In his 1981 essay, "The 'Vietnam Syndrome' and American Foreign Policy," George Herring, long a leading historian of the Vietnam War, tackles the vexing question of how the United States, perhaps the most awesome military power in human history, could possibly have suffered defeat at the hands of revolutionaries in an impoverished peasant society. The "Vietnam syndrome" was the name given to the skittishness of the American public, in the years following the Vietnam experience, about waging further wars, particularly in the third world. A syndrome, of course, is a sickness or an otherwise undesirable condition; the implication is that it is in need of healing or being overcome. Those who spoke of a Vietnam syndrome clearly regretted its existence and hoped it would disappear. Herring, writing at the beginning of President Ronald Reagan's administration, views Reagan's efforts to present the lost war in Vietnam as, in Reagan's words, a "noble cause" in light of his administration's desire to gain public support for military involvements in Central America, interventions justified with the same anticommunist rhetoric that had framed the U.S. war in Vietnam. To achieve this hawkish goal, it was just as important for the cold warriors of the 1980s to explain away U.S. military frustration in Vietnam as it was for them to assert the goodness of American intentions there. After all, the fear of another defeat was, many would say, more responsible for the Vietnam syndrome than was American self-doubt about the morality of the United States in the world.

Herring reviews the popular explanations for the U.S. defeat, mentioned previously, and finds them wanting. He argues that we should look to events in Vietnam, not in America, for an explanation of the war's outcome. The military resiliency and political strength of America's adversaries in Vietnam and the corresponding weakness of America's Vietnamese allies, Herring contends, may well have doomed the U.S. effort from the start. The "balance of forces" was not favorable to the United States, which fought a ground war inside South Vietnam with no clear front and enemies all around, and an air war that was unprecedented in its scale but that failed to achieve its goals. It appears that simply inflicting the maximum possible damage on one's enemy—whether through "attrition" on the ground or through detonation and defoliation from the air—is not necessarily a plausible strategy for victory. Herring is careful not to identify any one reason as the cause of the U.S. defeat; he sees a number of important factors at work. But he fairly summarizes the dominant view among historians of the Vietnam War when he argues that it is misleading, and perhaps dangerous, for Americans to think they can win any war if only they desire victory badly enough.

ROBERT BUZZANCO

Why (Not) Vietnam?

"Most of the men I commanded were like Rambo," Captain J. B. Wilcox explained in an interview with Mark Slackmeyer in the comic strip *Doonesbury;* "they wanted to win. But I had my orders: 'Don't win. We're not here to win. Take it easy on the enemy.'" Garry Trudeau's satire of the *Rambo* movies of the 1980s still draws laughs, but also offers a realistic depiction of a popular view about Vietnam. Many supporters of the war—politicians, military officials, media representatives—have an explanation for the US defeat there: Americans actually won the war on the battlefield but were sold out at home. The United States, many of them argued, lost because weak politicians did not authorize American forces to take the measures necessary to win, anti-war protestors undermined the war effort, and the media was too critical. Had the Americans invaded North Vietnam, dropped more bombs, or activated the Reserves, the war might well have been won. Indeed, as he began the [1991] Gulf War, George Bush told a national television audience that "our troops . . . will not be asked to fight with one hand tied behind their back."

Such views, while attractive to large numbers of Americans, do not make good history. In fact, the United States, in its efforts to contain nationalism and Communism in Vietnam, employed a full array of the military assets at its disposal. From the 1960s—when John F. Kennedy began to send in military personnel and helicopters, and approve the use of napalm and chemicals against the enemy, to the American withdrawal in January 1973, following the so-called Christmas Bombings just weeks earlier—the United States inflicted massive damage against Vietnam, both north and south of the seventeenth parallel. Indeed, American forces destroyed the land of their ally, the RVN in the south, as much as that of their foe, the DRVN in the north. Using its vastly superior technology, the American military pulled few punches in Indochina. In the decade prior to the end of the war, the United States dropped 4.6 million tons of bombs on Vietnam and another 2 million tons on Cambodia and Laos. American forces sprayed over 11 million gallons of Agent Orange, an herbicide containing dioxin, a cancer-causing agent, and dropped over 400,000 tons of napalm. The impact of such warfare was immense: over 9,000, or about 60 percent, of southern hamlets were destroyed, as were 25 million acres of farmland and 12 million acres of forest. American bombs created about 25 million craters, many still containing active ordnance today. Most tragically, the Vietnamese suffered about 2 million deaths in the war, the Cambodians and Laotians had about 300,000 killed, and a greater number was wounded. And by 1975, there were 15 million refugees in Indochina and nearby countries. All in a nation roughly the size of New Mexico.

Ironically, many of the men who were responsible for that warfare, senior military officers, had hoped to avoid such destruction. Vietnam was very much a civilian's war. Liberals in the

From *Vietnam and the Transformation of American Life* (1999), by Robert Buzzanco. Reprinted by permission of Blackwell Publishing Ltd.

John F. Kennedy and Lyndon B. Johnson administrations made the crucial decisions to fight there and to constantly escalate the conflict. But from the 1950s on, a significant number of ranking military leaders had argued against war in Vietnam. They believed that it was not an area of vital importance to US security, that the enemy had the capability to fight a long-term guerrilla war on its own terrain, that the allied government and military of the RVN was corrupt and weak, and that America's heavy firepower would be ineffective or counterproductive. At the same time, huge numbers of American soldiers—in Vietnam and on bases in the United States, Europe, and elsewhere—were suffering from low morale, discipline problems, drug abuse, racial conflict, or were actively involved in the anti-war movement.

The United States, then, dropped more bombs on Vietnam than were used by all countries in World War II *combined*. At the peak of the war, it had over 500,000 soldiers in the country and overall spent perhaps $200–300 billion to wage war there. America's military leaders were divided and often pessimistic about their chances for victory, while maybe a majority of soldiers were stoned, angry at their officers or each other, or opposed to the war. To somehow conclude from these conditions that the United States "won" all the battles, or was not allowed to "win" by politicians and protestors at home, or fought with hands tied behind their backs, is a convenient and often popular alibi. An examination of America's motives, its role, and its actions in Vietnam indicates otherwise.

. . . [T]he Vietnamese Revolution, throughout the 1940s and early 1950s, was closely linked to various international developments. While the United States had little knowledge of or interest in Vietnam at the end of World War II, it quickly became an important national interest due to factors that lay far beyond Indochina, including the Cold War, European politics, and western economic expansion.

Ho had sought American support throughout his struggle against the French. In 1943, he initiated contacts with US intelligence agents in southern China, and the Viet Minh, it was reported, helped rescue American pilots downed behind Japanese lines, and may have even received light armaments from the Office of Strategic Services (OSS). . . . Ho wrote letters to President Harry S. Truman in 1945 seeking friendship and assistance, but Washington, DC never even acknowledged his overtures. In 1945 and 1946, various American military officials had close contact with the Viet Minh and came away impressed. One OSS agent called Ho "an awfully sweet guy." Other American operatives in Hanoi had helped him write and translate his declaration of independence speech in September 1945. Major Allison Thomas, head of an intelligence mission to Indochina, wrote quite positive reports about the Viet Minh to his superiors. And General Philip Gallagher, a US adviser in northern Vietnam, called Ho "an old Bolshevik," but nonetheless hoped that the Vietnamese "could be given their independence." Even General George Marshall, who served as both Secretary of State and of Defense, understood early on that the French "have no prospect" of victory in Vietnam, and he warned that their war against the Viet Minh "will remain a grievously costly enterprise, weakening France economically and all the West generally in its relations with Oriental peoples." And the Joint Chiefs of Staff (JCS) recognized in 1949 that it was the "widening political consciousness and the rise of militant nationalism" among the Vietnamese that was motivating the war against France; any attempt to stop the Viet Minh would thus be "an anti-historical act likely in the long run to create more problems than it solves and cause more damage than benefit."

Despite these prophetic military warnings regarding the danger of intervention in Vietnam, the United States became progressively more involved there. Although US military officials saw

Ho's popularity, the rise of nationalism, and French weakness as huge barriers to success, American civilian officials took an opposite view. To them, it was crucial to support France and stop Asian Communism. Over the military's objections, then, the United States began to send hundreds of millions of dollars to French Indochina, even though Air Force Chief of Staff Hoyt Vandenberg compared it to "pouring money down a rathole." To American officials in the White House and Department of State, such policy was necessary for three interrelated reasons: to maintain French support in the European Cold War, to contain Communism in Asia, and to encourage economic development. Whereas military officers looked at conditions *inside* Vietnam and saw great risks, civilian officials had a *global* outlook and they saw Vietnam as part of a much larger contest—the Cold War.

. . . Ho, though he wrote to Truman for support, nonetheless complained that the Americans were "only interested in replacing the French . . . They want to reorganize our country and control it. They are capitalists to the core." US behavior bore him out. Although not thrilled with the French re-entry into Vietnam, the United States believed that events in Europe were much more important than those in Indochina and did not want to alienate its allies in Paris. After 1945, the United States was pursuing containment, and to do this cooperation from the western Europeans—the British, Germans in the western zones, and of course the French— was essential. Complicating matters, French President Charles De Gaulle was trying to re-establish his country's prestige and influence . . . while the political left—the Communist and Socialist Parties and the trade unions—was quite popular and netting impressive numbers of votes in free elections. If the United States tried to push France out of Vietnam, American officials feared, it might endanger De Gaulle politically and encourage the left, which in turn could lead to the loss of a valuable ally in the fight against Euro-Communism.

Although containment . . . was to be applied politically in Europe, the focus of the Cold War shifted eastward and led to hot wars in Asia. At the end of World War II, the United States had two principal economic-strategic objectives in Asia: to rebuild Japan along western, capitalist lines and to maintain the pro-American government of Jiang Jieshi in China. While America met its goals in Japan, China appeared to be a disaster. When, in 1949, Mao won the Civil War and established a Communist government in the world's most populated country (about a half billion), American leaders found it imperative to halt any other such advances in Asia. As a result, the United States intervened in the Korean War in 1950 to prevent victory by the nationalist-Communist forces of Kim Il Sung. In Vietnam, the spectre of Mao loomed just as large. Despite US military recognition of Ho's nationalist credentials, American civilian officials saw him simply as a Communist, a puppet of Mao and Stalin. From 1949 on, then, US policy toward Vietnam would be determined according to the greater need to keep the People's Republic of China (PRC) isolated and to make sure that unfriendly governments did not emerge in proximity to Japan. "The East is Red," Chinese Communists boasted, but "the West is Ready," Americans responded.

The escalating Cold War and the extension of containment had a powerful economic component, which was a fundamental and vital factor in the US intervention into Vietnam. In 1945, at war's end, the United States hoped to construct a "new world order" based on free trade and global investment. The major barrier to that, however, was a shortage of American dollars in Europe. Because of this "dollar gap," other nations, especially the British and French, could not buy American goods, thus hurting both the European and US economies and hampering Japanese reconstruction in Asia, which depended in large measure on trade with Southeast Asia, including Indochina. To address those problems, American leaders believed that it was necessary to purchase goods from Europe's colonies in Southeast Asia, and thus put dollars into their hands that would in turn be used to buy products made in the United States. But in the two most important areas—British Malaya and French Indochina—Communist insurgencies were already strong and growing. Thus, to help the domestic economy and rebuild their allies, American officials had to support the British and French wars against the Malayan Communists and the Viet Minh. . . .

The combination of these factors—maintaining French support in the Cold War, containing Asian Communism, expanding markets—created a new sense of urgency with regard to Vietnam. Thus in 1950 the United States supported the return of the deposed Emperor Bao Dai from the brothels and casinos of the Riviera to the Vietnamese throne. Bao Dai did not have a deep interest in governance and would rather be playing baccarat or escorting beautiful blondes, but his presence gave the appearance of legitimacy. So the United States recognized his government and sent $25 million, mostly in military aid, to Indochina in the spring, and another $130 million later that year. . . . American military officials remained staunchly opposed to US involvement in Vietnam. "France will be driven out of Indochina," the Army's Chief of Staff J. Lawton Collins predicted, and was "wasting time and equipment trying to remain there." If the French requested air or naval support, the JCS insisted, "they will have to be told point blank that none will be committed." Indeed, military officials—despite the intensity of the Cold War—continued to recognize that the Viet Minh's appeal was widespread. Ho enjoyed the support of 80 percent of the population, Army planners reported, yet 80 percent of his followers were *not* Communists.

The Truman and Eisenhower administrations, however, essentially disregarded military warnings regarding Vietnam. While armed forces officers might have recognized the political and military peril of war against the Viet Minh, civilian officials had more global concerns. Vietnam was thus a pawn in a geopolitical Cold War game. Though not strategically or even economically critical in its own right, Vietnam became the centerpiece in the effort to contain Communism when viewed within the context of French needs, Chinese Communism, and economic development. So Charles Cabell, an Air Force General and JCS official, might conclude that "terrain difficulties and the guerrilla nature of Vietminh operations" would make it impossible to dislodge the enemy, but President Eisenhower and Secretary of State John Foster Dulles, with the "big picture" in mind, would send another $785 million to Vietnam in 1953 alone. . . .

Ho . . . emerged from Geneva with [his] glass only half full. The United States, represented by Dulles, remained hostile to the very idea of negotiating with Communists such as the DRVN or PRC and so refused to recognize Ho as the leader of a unified Vietnam. Vietnam's allies did not serve it much better. Zhou Enlai, the Chinese representative, did not back Ho either. To the Chinese, Vietnam was not a principal concern . . . and traditional mistrust between the two countries was still strong. Thus, Ho, with dedicated enemies and no effective allies, had to accept compromise at Geneva: rather than unifying Vietnam under his rule, he acquiesced in the temporary partition of his country at the seventeenth parallel, in Annam, with the DRVN recognized north of the demarcation line and some type of anti-Communist entity to be established south of it. In 1956, according to the Geneva settlement, elections would be held to unify Vietnam and elect a president. The Viet Minh, feeling betrayed and isolated, was furious, but Ho counselled patience once more. Declaring that Geneva was a "great victory," he urged the Vietnamese to be "capable of enduring the present. Doing so will bring them great honor." With little outside support, but great confidence in victory in 1956, Ho could do little else.

Indeed, American officials recognized the Viet Minh's strength too. Military leaders, the Department of State, and the White House all conceded that Ho would win 80 to 90 percent of the vote in any free election. . . . Rather than accept the Viet Minh as elected representatives of an internationally recognized DRVN, the United States assumed the French role in Vietnam and created the conditions for the Second Indochina War. . . . [T]he United States would, most importantly, essentially invent a nation, the Republic of Vietnam (RVN), below the seventeenth parallel. It would, moreover, establish a military training mission to Vietnam and a regional anti-Communist force, the Southeast Asia Treaty Organization (SEATO). With these decisions, the United States created a rival government to the DRVN and backed it with American arms and dollars. In 1956, the RVN, with US encouragement, canceled the Geneva-scheduled elections and thus left Ho and his supporters in the south with little choice but to again wage a war for liberation, unification, and Vietnamese socialism.

Decades later, as we study Vietnam, the events of 1954–5 are still decisive. Because of the Viet Minh's popularity and nationalist credentials, there was no real opposition to Ho inside Vietnam. Thus the United States had to establish and nurture the RVN with little indigenous support. Like the French, the Americans had to find and put in power Vietnamese officials, who would remain tainted as US puppets throughout the next generation. As a result, the RVN could never be seen as a legitimate alternative to Ho. The Vietnamese people, with their legacy of conquering the Chinese, Mongols, Japanese, and French, were not about to accept the rule of Americans and their clients. But the United States would try. In June 1954, Americans persuaded Bao Dai to appoint a Vietnamese elite named Ngo Dinh Diem to be Prime Minister. In so far as he hated the French, Diem was a nationalist, but he had little knowledge of Vietnamese society and no concern for the Vietnamese people. He had spent the previous decade in a monastery in the United States where, quite unlike Bao Dai, he practiced sobriety and celibacy. He did, however, have influential friends, including Cold War icons such as Francis Cardinal Spellman and Senators Mike Mansfield and John F. Kennedy. So when it came time for the Americans to find a leader for the RVN, they looked no further than Diem. . . .

Air Force General and psychological warfare expert Edward Lansdale, a strong supporter of Diem, . . . admitted that the Viet Minh had "exemplary relations" with Vietnamese villagers, while the southern soldiers were only "adept at cowing a population into feeding them [and] providing them with girls." Army officers reported that Ho . . . had about 340,000 troops . . . with nearly 100,000 *below* the seventeenth parallel. And General J. Lawton Collins, whom Eisenhower sent to Saigon as his personal representative, consistently advised the White House to consider abandoning the unpopular and repressive Diem regime. Likewise, . . . others warned that it was "hopeless" to expect the training mission to succeed in the absence of popular government and political stability in the south, . . . that American troops would get stuck in the middle of a "civil war" in Vietnam. The JCS meanwhile pointed out that a training program for the RVN would cost almost a half billion dollars, a steep price for an area of "low priority" such as Vietnam. Eisenhower . . . dismissed such critiques, though, and, after Diem survived an overthrow attempt in early 1955, [was] set to put American money, soldiers, and credibility on the line to preserve the RVN. . . .

The American defeat in Vietnam was a natural outcome of the way the war was developed and fought. The enemy . . . was popular, dedicated, and effective—while the ally, the government and army of the RVN, was corrupt, repressive, and not terribly competent, and American soldiers were often as interested in getting high or fighting among themselves as with engaging the enemy. America's military leaders were never enthused about intervening in Vietnam and, once there, were internally divided over the nature of the war and US strategy; they never achieved the unity of purpose so essential to warmaking. Significant segments of the public at home resisted the war as well, adding to the sense of crisis that Vietnam was causing. . . . In retrospect, all these factors put the United States at a great political and military disadvantage in Vietnam. The Americans were simply on the wrong side of history, fighting an implacable enemy which had a national tradition of ousting foreign interlopers. While the United States was not even 200 years old when the Vietnam War occurred, the Vietnamese had 2,000 years of experience fighting for independence under their belts.

America's defeat, even if it was unavoidable, caused anguish at home. The air of invincibility that had developed throughout the Cold War was punctured and Americans, for the first time in many of their lives, had to think about the limits of US power. For a few years after Vietnam, this debate continued, but by the 1980s, influential Americans were trying to rewrite the memory of the war. In the immediate aftermath of Vietnam, the United States conducted itself in a somewhat more circumspect manner internationally, but remained clearly engaged in world affairs. Because of the economic effects of the war, Nixon had significantly reduced defense spending after 1970, and, perhaps because of the bad taste left by Vietnam, did not intervene in a civil war in Angola ultimately won by a Socialist group. At the same time, Nixon escalated the amount of American weapons sold abroad, had the CIA sabotage the Cuban economy by introducing a swine flu virus, supported the apartheid regime in South Africa, and helped facilitate the overthrow of President Salvador Allende in Chile in 1973. Despite the impression that Vietnam was causing America to retreat from its global "responsibilities," it was, in many fundamental ways, "business-as-usual" in the Nixon years. Indeed, any funk or malaise associated with the Vietnam War did not last terribly long.

In 1980, Republican presidential candidate Ronald Reagan called the Vietnam War a "noble cause" and many national leaders, military officials, and scholars began to re-evaluate the war in a more positive light, often claiming that the United States had gone to war for all the right reasons—anti-Communism, democracy, national security—in Vietnam, had conducted itself with skill and admiration during the war, but had been "stabbed in the back" by the media and anti-war movement at home. Hollywood added to this revival with pro-war or pro-military movies such as *Uncommon Valor, Red Dawn,* and especially Sylvester Stallone's *First Blood* and *Rambo II,* while the militarist novels of Tom Clancy helped lift Americans out of their post-Vietnam self-doubt as well. To some degree, then, this rehabilitation of the war emboldened the Reagan administration to conduct large-scale and initially "secret" wars against insurgent groups in Latin America and the leftist Sandinista government in Nicaragua, using much the same rationale in that part of the world in the 1980s as its predecessors had in Indochina in the 1960s. In fact, Secretary of Defense Caspar Weinberger invoked the revisionist interpretation of Vietnam explicitly when he claimed that, unlike in Vietnam, "we must never send Americans into battle unless we plan to win." In 1991, that school of thought reached its apex as George Bush linked the US war against Saddam Hussein with Vietnam, and at its conclusion boasted that "by God, we've kicked the Vietnam Syndrome once and for all."

. . . [C]omparisons to Vietnam would pop up whenever the United States was debating involvement in foreign lands. During the 1980s, following the example of the Vietnam anti-war movement, a strong anti-intervention movement emerged to protest Reagan's aggression in Central America, and a popular slogan was "El Salvador is Spanish for Vietnam." Likewise, references to the war in Indochina were omnipresent whenever US policy toward Haiti, Somalia, Bosnia, and other lands was discussed. It seems as if virtually every interview concerning US foreign policy today ultimately comes to the question of whether this could turn into "another Vietnam." And the American people continue to believe that the war was "fundamentally wrong and immoral"—70 percent in a 1991 poll.

On a more personal level, the war hurt millions of Americans too. In addition to the over 58,000 soldiers killed in the war, untold numbers of veterans have had a difficult adjustment back to "normal" lives after Vietnam. Although Hollywood often has unfairly stereotyped veterans as being deranged and troubled, in fact hundreds of thousands suffer from "Post-Traumatic Stress Disorder," a psychological and emotional condition involving a wide array of problems such as recurring nightmares, jumpiness, flashbacks, paranoia, and others. Many other veterans are addicted to drugs and alcohol, and have violent or abusive personalities, while, amazingly, almost twice as many veterans have committed suicide since the war ended than died in Vietnam. Thousands of other Vietnam-era soldiers have also suffered health problems such as cancer and immune system disorders, as well as high rates of birth defects in their children, due to their exposure to Agent Orange and other herbicides.

In 1982, one of the more powerful moments in the Vietnam era occurred when "The Wall," the Vietnam Memorial, was dedicated on the Mall in Washington, DC. Two long narrow blocks of black concrete which contain the names of every American killed in Vietnam, the monument emotionally details the human costs of the war to the United States. But the country of Vietnam would need perhaps 40 or 50 such "walls" to commemorate their own losses during the American War. Instead, still-destroyed buildings, burned-out villages, land mines, disabled young men, and bitterness and recrimination mark their war. It will certainly be some time, if ever, before the Vietnamese, as Ho Chi Minh wished, will build a country "ten times more beautiful."

GEORGE C. HERRING

The "Vietnam Syndrome" and American Foreign Policy

[A] new phrase has entered the American political vocabulary. It is called the "Vietnam syndrome." It was apparently coined by Richard Nixon. As employed by the Reagan administration, it presumably means that America's failure in Vietnam and the backlash from it have been primarily responsible for the malaise that has allegedly reduced the United States to a state of impotence in a menacing world. Doctor Reagan and his associates seem determined to cure the disease. Some of the administration's defenders have even justified intervention in

From "The 'Vietnam Syndrome' and American Foreign Policy," by George C. Herring, from *Virginia Quarterly Review*, Volume 661 (Winter 1990). Reprinted by permission of *Virginia Quarterly Review*.

El Salvador as essential to that end; and although the White House and State Department may not go that far, their public statements leave no doubt of their determination to exorcise the Vietnam syndrome.

The notion of a Vietnam syndrome presupposes a view of the war which, although rarely articulated in full, nevertheless clearly influences the administration's foreign policy. Reagan himself has stated—contrary to a long-prevailing view—that Vietnam was "in truth a noble war," an altruistic attempt on the part of the United States to help a "small country newly free from colonial rule" defend itself against a "totalitarian neighbor bent on conquest." He and Secretary of State Alexander M. Haig, Jr. have also insisted that it was a necessary war, necessary to check the expansionist designs of the Soviet Union and its client states and to uphold the global position of the United States. They have left no doubt that they regard it as a war that we should have won. America failed, Reagan recently stated, not because it was defeated but because the military was "denied permission to win." Haig has argued that the war could have been won at any of several junctures if American leaders had been willing to "apply the full range of American power to bring about a successful outcome." The defeat was thus self-inflicted, and the consequences have been enormous. "America is no longer the America it was," Haig has stated, and "that is largely attributable to the mistakes of Vietnam."

These views are not, of course, new, nor is it suprising that they have gained credence in recent years. The aggressiveness of the Soviets and the Hanoi regime have made it easier for us to justify our own actions morally and in terms of national security. An explanation of failure which places blame on ourselves rather than elsewhere is probably easier for us to live with. Scholars had begun to revise conventional dovish views of the war well before Reagan took office, and films such as the *Deerhunter,* whatever their artistic merit, promoted a form of redemption. What *is* significant is that this now seems to be the official view and is also a partial basis for major policy decisions. Equally important, it is getting little challenge from Congress and the media, the centers of respectable dissent in the late 1960's and early 1970's. . . .

It seems particularly urgent, therefore, that we examine this view critically in terms of the following very difficult questions: was Vietnam a just and necessary war as is now being proclaimed? Was it a winnable war, our failure primarily the result of our own mistakes? Has the so-called Vietnam syndrome been responsible for our recent inability to control world events and meet foreign challenges?

. . . [W]as Vietnam a winnable war, our failure there primarily the result of our mistakes, our lack of will, the disunity within our society? Because it has such profound implications for future policy decisions, this is the most important of our questions and deserves the most extended commentary. Those who argue that our defeat was self-inflicted focus on the misuse of our admittedly vast military power. Instead of using air power to strike a knockout blow against the enemy, they contend, Lyndon Johnson foolishly hedged it about with restrictions, applied it gradually, and held back from the sort of massive, decisive bombing attacks that could have assured victory. Similarly, they argue, had Johnson permitted U.S. ground forces to invade North Vietnamese sanctuaries in Laos, Cambodia, and across the 17th parallel, General Westmoreland's strategy of attrition could have worked and the war could have been won.

These criticisms are not without merit. Johnson's gradual expansion of the bombing did give North Vietnam time to disperse its resources and develop a highly effective air defense system, and the bombing may have encouraged the will to resist rather than crippled it as Johnson had intended. A strategy of attrition could not work as long as the enemy enjoyed sanctuary. If losses reached unacceptable proportions, the enemy could simply retreat to safety, regroup and renew the battle at times and places of his own choosing. He retained the strategic initiative.

To jump from here to the conclusion that the unrestricted use of American power could have produced victory at acceptable costs raises some troubling questions, however. Could an unrestricted bombing campaign have forced North Vietnam to accept a settlement on our terms? Obviously, there is no way we can ever know, but there is reason to doubt that it would have. The surveys conducted after World War II raised some serious doubts about the effect of bombing on the morale of the civilian population of Germany and Japan, and the capacity of air power to cripple a pre-industrial society such as North Vietnam may have been even more limited. There is evidence to suggest that the North Vietnamese were prepared to resist no matter what the level of the bombing, even if they had to go underground. The United States could probably have destroyed the cities and industries of North Vietnam, but what then? Invasion of the sanctuaries and ground operations in North Vietnam might have made the strategy of attrition more workable, but they would also have enlarged the war at a time when the United States was already stretched thin. Each of these approaches would have greatly increased the costs of the war without resolving the central problem—the political viability of South Vietnam.

We must also consider the reasons why Johnson refused to expand the war. He feared that if the United States pushed North Vietnam to the brink of defeat, the Soviet Union and/or China would intervene, broadening the war to dangerous proportions, perhaps to a nuclear confrontation. Johnson may, of course, have overestimated the risks of outside intervention, but the pressures would certainly have been large and he would have been irresponsible to ignore the dangers. And even if the United States had been able militarily to subdue North Vietnam without provoking outside intervention, it would still have faced the onerous, expensive, and dangerous prospect of occupying a hostile nation along China's southern border.

Those who argue that the war was winnable also emphasize the importance of American public opinion in sealing our defeat. They shift blame from those who waged the war to those who opposed it, contending that an irresponsible media and a treacherous antiwar movement turned the nation against the war, forcing Johnson and later Nixon to curtail U.S. involvement just when victory was in grasp. As much mythology has deveoped around this issue as any other raised by the war, and we probably know as little about it as any. Studies of public opinion do indicate that despite an increasingly skeptical media and noisy protest in the streets, the war enjoyed broad, if unenthusiastic support until that point early in 1968 when it became apparent that the costs might exceed any possible gains—and, even then, Nixon was able to prolong it for four more years. Until the early 1970's, moreover, the antiwar movement was probably counterproductive in terms of its own goals, the majority of Americans finding the protestors more obnoxious than the war. Indeed, it seems likely that the antiwar protest in a perverse way may have strengthened support for the government. After 1969, public opinion and Congress did impose some constraints on the government, and the media probably contributed to this. But to pin the defeat on the media or the antiwar movement strikes me as a gross oversimplification.

The problem with all these explanations is that they are too enthnocentric. They reflect the persistence of what a British scholar has called the illusion of American omnipotence, the traditional American belief that the difficult we do tomorrow, the impossible may take awhile. When failure occurs, it must be *our* fault, and we find scapegoats in our own midst: the poor judgment of our leaders, the media, or the antiwar movement. The flaw in this approach is that it ignores the other side of the equation, in this case, the Vietnamese dimension. I would contend that the sources of our frustration and ultimate failure rest primarily, although certainly not exclusively, in the local circumstances of the war: the nature of the conflict itself, the weakness of our ally, the relative strength of our adversary.

The Vietnam War posed extremely difficult challenges for Americans. It was fought in a climate and on a terrain that were singularly inhospitable. Thick jungles, foreboding swamps and paddies, rugged mountains. Heat that could "kill a man, bake his brains, or wring the sweat from him until he died of exhaustion," Philip Caputo tells us in *Rumor of War*. "It was as if the sun and the land itself were in league with the Vietcong," Caputo adds, "wearing us down, driving us mad, killing us." Needless to say, those who had endured the land for centuries had a distinct advantage over outsiders, particularly when the latter came from a highly industrialized and urbanized environment.

It was a people's war, where the people rather than territory were the primary objective. But Americans as individuals and as a nation could never really bridge the vast cultural gap that separated them from all Vietnamese. Not knowing the language or the culture, they did not know what the people felt or even how to tell friend from foe. "Maybe the dinks got things mixed up," one of novelist Tim O'Brien's bewildered G.I.s comments in *Going After Cacciato* after a seemingly friendly farmer bowed and smiled and pointed the Americans into a minefield. "Maybe the gooks cry when they're happy and smile when they're sad." Recalling the emotionless response of a group of peasants when their homes were destroyed by an American company, Caputo notes that they did nothing "and I hated them for it. Their apparent indifference made me feel indifferent." The cultural gap produced cynicism and even hatred toward the people Americans were trying to help. It led to questioning of our goals and produced a great deal of moral confusion among those fighting the war and those at home.

Most important, perhaps, was the formless, yet lethal, nature of guerrilla warfare in Vietnam. It was a war without distinct battlelines or fixed objectives, where traditional concepts of victory and defeat were blurred. It was, Caputo writes, "a formless war against a formless enemy who evaporated into the morning jungle mists only to materialize in some unexpected place." This type of war was particularly difficult for Americans schooled in the conventional warfare of World War II and Korea to fight. And there was always the gnawing question, first raised by John Kennedy himself—how can we tell if we're winning? The only answer that could be devised was the notorious body count, as grim and corrupting as it was unreliable as an index of success. In time, the strategy of attrition and the body count came to represent for sensitive G.I.s and for those at home killing for the sake of killing. And the light at the end of the tunnel never glimmered. "Aimless, that's what it is," one of O'Brien's G.I.s laments, "a bunch of kids trying to pin the tail on the Asian donkey. But no . . . tail. No . . . donkey."

Far more important in explaining our failure is the uneven balance of forces we aligned ourselves with in Vietnam. With the passage of time, it becomes more and more apparent that in South Vietnam we attempted a truly formidable undertaking on the basis of a very weak foundation. The "country" to which we committed ourselves in 1954 lacked most of the essential ingredients for nationhood. Had we looked all over the world, in fact, we could hardly have found a less promising place for an experiment in nation-building. Southern Vietnam lacked a viable economy. The French had destroyed the traditional political order, and their departure left a gaping vacuum, no firmly established political institutions, no native elite capable of exercising effective political leadership. Southern Vietnam was rent by a multitude of conflicting ethnic and religious forces. It was, in the words of one scholar, a "political jungle of war lords, bandits, partisan troops, and secret societies." When viewed from this perspective, there were probably built-in limits to what the United States or any outside nation could have accomplished there.

For nearly 20 years, we struggled to establish a viable nation in the face of internal insurgency and external invasion, but the rapid collapse of South Vietnam after our withdrawal in 1973 suggests how little was really accomplished. We could never find leaders capable of mobilizing the disparate population of southern Vietnam. We launched a vast array of ambitious and expensive programs to promote sound and effective government, win the support of the people, and wage war against the Vietcong. When our client state was on the verge of collapse in 1965, we filled the vacuum by putting in our own military forces. But the more we did, the more we induced a state of dependency among those we were trying to help. Tragically, right up to the fall of Saigon in 1975, the South Vietnamese elite expected us to return and save them from defeat. This is not to denigrate the leaders or people who sided with us or to make them the scapegoats for our failure. The point rather is that given the history of southern Vietnam and the conditions that prevailed there in 1954, the creation of a viable nation by an outside power may have been an impossible task.

The second point central to understanding our failure is that we drastically underestimated the strength and determination of our adversary. I do not wish to imply here that the North Vietnamese and Vietcong were supermen. They made blunders. They paid an enormous price for their success. They have shown a far greater capacity for making war than for building a nation. In terms of the balance of forces in Vietnam, however, they had distinct advantages. They were tightly mobilized and regimented and fanatically committed to their goals. They were fighting on familiar soil, and they employed methods already perfected in the ten years' war against France. The Vietcong were close to the rural population of South Vietnam, adapted its ideology and tactics to traditional Vietnamese political culture, and used the American presence to exploit popular distrust of outsiders. North Vietnam skillfully employed the strategy of protracted war, perceiving that the Americans, like the French, could become impatient, and if they bled long enough they might tire of the war. "You will kill ten of our men, but we will kill one of yours," Ho once remarked, "and in the end it is you who will tire." The comment was made to a French general in 1946, but it could as easily have been said of the Second Indochina War.

Our fatal error, therefore, was to underestimate our adversary. We rather casually assumed that the Vietnamese, rational beings like ourselves, would know better than to stand up against the most powerful nation in the world. It would be like a filibuster in Congress, Lyndon Johnson speculated, enormous resistance at first, then a steady whittling away, then Ho Chi Minh hurrying to get it over with. Years later, Henry Kissinger confessed great surprise with the discovery that his North Vietnamese counterparts were "fanatics." Since our own goals were limited and from our standpoint more than reasonable, we found it hard to understand the total, unyielding commitment of the enemy, his willingness to risk everything to achieve his objective.

The circumstances of the war in Vietnam thus posed a dilemma that we never resolved. To have achieved our goal of an independent non-Communist South Vietnam required means that were either morally repugnant to us, posed unacceptable risks, or were unlikely to work. Success would have required the physical annihilation of North Vietnam, but given our limited goals, this would have been distasteful and excessively costly, and it held out a serious threat of Soviet or Chinese intervention. The only other way was to establish a viable South Vietnam, but given the weak foundation we worked from and the cultural gap, not to mention the strength of the internal revolution, this was probably beyond our capability. To put it charitably, we may very well have placed ourselves in a classic, no-win situation.

Further Reading

Fine overviews of the subject include George D. Herring, *America's Longest War* (4th ed. [New York: Random House, 2002]), a standard, oft-revised account; Marilyn B. Young, *The Vietnam Wars, 1945–1990* (New York: HarperCollins, 1991), a bitingly critical treatment; and William S. Turley, *The Second Indochina War: A Short Political and Military History, 1954–1975* (Boulder, CO: Westview Press, 1986), which is out of print, but worth consulting for its concision and its coverage of strategy on all sides of the conflict. Almost all important scholarly articles dealing with any aspect of the war are gathered in *The Vietnam War: Significant Scholarly Articles* (New York: Garland Publishing, 2000), edited by Walter L. Hixson, a superlative six-volume set. *Major Problems in the History of the Vietnam War* (3rd ed. [Boston: Houghton Mifflin, 2003]), edited by Robert J. McMahon, presents an excellent selection of writings by historians.

The best books on the U.S. path to war are George McT. Kahin's satisfyingly detailed work, *Intervention* (New York: Knopf, 1986) and Andrew J. Rotter, *The Path to Vietnam: Origins of the American Commitment to Southeast Asia* (Ithaca, NY: Cornell University Press, 1987). The most absorbing treatments of the much-debated topic of John F. Kennedy's inclinations in Vietnam remain those written by amateur historians. David Halberstam, *The Best and the Brightest* (New York: Random House, 1972) paints an unforgettable picture of U.S. policymakers in the 1960s, although portraiture takes pride of place over analysis. *Rethinking Camelot* (Boston: South End Press, 1993), by Noam Chomsky, although marred by the author's sarcasm, is a well-documented, damaging attack on Kennedy's policy that places it in a broader context. Richard Nixon's prosecution of the war has been a topic relatively neglected by serious scholars. Larry Berman, *No Peace, No Honor: Nixon, Kissinger and Betrayal in Vietnam* (New York: The Free Press, 2001) begins to right that wrong.

Those interested in the development of Vietnamese revolutionary nationalism might start by reading William Duiker, *Ho Chi Minh: A Life* (New York: Hyperion, 2000), the latest work of a scholar who has spent a career plumbing the depths of this general subject. Mark David Bradley, *Imagining Vietnam and America: The Making of Postcolonial Vietnam, 1919–1950* (Chapel Hill: University of North Carolina Press, 2000) is an intriguing work of cultural history tracing connections between two countries fated to go to war. Qiang Zhai, *China and the Vietnam Wars* (Chapel Hill: University of North Carolina Press, 2000) is an enlightening study based on previously unavailable Chinese and Vietnamese sources.

The most compelling explanations for the U.S. defeat can be found "on the ground." *The Dynamics of Defeat: The Vietnam War in Hau Nghia Province* (Boulder, CO: Westview Press, 1991), by Eric M. Bergerud, a dense and challenging book, is not to be missed by those interested in military strategy and tactics and their relationship to political conflict. Jeffrey P. Kimball, "The Stab-in-the-Back Legend and the Vietnam War," *Armed Forces and Society* (vol. 14/3 [1988], 433–58) is the best survey of the "revisionist" arguments that the U.S. military could have won the war if the civilians had let them. Ronald H. Spector, *After Tet: The Bloodiest Year in Vietnam* (New York: The Free Press, 1993) is very good on military affairs later in the war. Christian Appy, *Working-Class War: American Combat Soldiers and Vietnam* (Chapel Hill: University of North Carolina Press, 1993) is an outstanding social history of the U.S. troops.

Diverse antiwar constituencies receive able treatment in *Because of Their Faith: CALCAV and Religious Opposition to the Vietnam War* (New York: Columbia University, 1990), by

Mitchell K. Hall; *The Turning: A History of Vietnam Veterans Against the War* (New York: New York University Press, 1999), by Andrew Hunt; *Apocalypse Then: American Intellectuals and the Vietnam War, 1954–1975* (New York: New York University Press, 1998), by Robert R. Tomes; and *Give Peace a Chance: Exploring the Vietnam Antiwar Movement* (Syracuse, NY: Syracuse University Press, 1992), edited by Melvin Small and William D. Hoover. Howard Schuman, "Two Sources of Antiwar Sentiment in America," *American Journal of Sociology* (vol. 78, no. 3 [1972], 513–36) dispels much confusion about public opinion on the war and the impact of antiwar protest.

Primary Sources

A good starting point is vietnam.vassar.edu/abstracts.html, which offers twenty key documents on the conflict between the U.S. and North Vietnam, beginning with the Final Declaration of the Geneva Conference in 1954 and ending with the Paris Peace Accords of 1973 and including a few documents from Hanoi, such as the 1971 DRV peace proposal. A good site which focuses on the diplomatic history of the war from 1950 through 1964 is www.yale.edu/lawweb.avalon/intdip/indoch/indoch.html. The most compendious collection of documents may be found at www.mtholyoke.edu/acad/intrel/vietnam.htm. Organized chronologically, the site includes the Pentagon Papers, relevant correspondence and speeches by Presidents Truman through Ford, letters and cables of the U.S. State Department, CIA and National Security Council documents, as well as documents from North and South Vietnam. In addition to the documents that cover the period from World War II to 1975, there are retrospectives and maps as well as links to other Web sites with information about the Vietnam War. For those interested specifically in the overthrow of South Vietnamese President Ngo Dinh Diem, go to www.gwu.edu/~nsarchiv/NSAEBB/NSAEBB101 for a narrative of events, as well as 29 key documents. Go to www.hpol.org/lbj/vietnam/ to hear audio excerpts of Lyndon Johnson's telephone conversations in which he expresses doubts about the course of the war. For oral histories of over 250 U.S. veterans of the war, as well as a few veterans who fought either in the South Vietnamese Army or with the Viet Cong, go to www.vietnam.ttu.edu/oralhistory/interviews/index.htm and click on "Interviews available online." A collection of documents related to the My Lai Massacre, which resulted in the court martial of Lt. William Calley, can be found at www.law.umkc.edu/faculty/projects/ftrials/mylai/mylai.htm, along with a brief history of the events. Documents include excerpts of the court martial transcripts, the general conventions on the law of war, public opinion polls, and the Peers report. For documents related to Vietnam Veterans Against the War, including John Kerry's statement to the Senate Foreign Relations Committee in 1971, go to lists.village.virginia.edu/sixties/HTML_docs/Resources/Primary.html.

10

The Crisis of
the State

INTRODUCTION

In August 1974, less than two years after his landslide reelection, President Richard Nixon resigned from office in the face of certain impeachment by the U.S. House of Representatives and a likely conviction in a Senate trial. The crisis that brought about Nixon's downfall is often referred to as "Watergate," named for the Washington, DC, apartment and office complex, where in 1972, burglars working for Nixon's reelection campaign (known by the acronym CREEP) were arrested while planting electronic surveillance equipment in the national headquarters of the Democratic party. Although evidence has never been produced to show that Nixon himself ordered the burglary, tapes of his Oval Office conversations did reveal that Nixon directed a cover-up of the crime, including the payment of hush money to the burglars and the use of the CIA to thwart the FBI investigation of the felony.

But Nixon's misdeeds extended well beyond an attempt to block the investigation of an election-year crime. Watergate was not an isolated incident but was representative of a mindset and mode of operation in the Nixon White House. Critics of the administration, especially opponents of the war in Vietnam, were viewed as enemies to be punished, and the president and his aides felt they were entitled to ignore the law and the Constitution to achieve their aims. Although the full range of Nixon's misdeeds and crimes are not known, they included the illegal wiretapping of the phones of those on Nixon's "enemies" list; the use of the IRS to audit the tax returns of enemies (Nixon personally scrutinized the returns of his leading enemies, having obtained them illegally from the IRS); the ordering of government officials to fabricate documents to implicate President John F. Kennedy in the assassination of South Vietnamese president Ngo Dinh Diem; and the burglary of the office of the psychiatrist of Daniel Ellsberg (the Defense Department consultant who leaked the in-house history of the Vietnam War, known as the "Pentagon Papers," to the press) in search of damaging information to discredit Ellsberg.

Richard Nixon always maintained, despite evidence to the contrary, that he had violated no laws, stating his position most clearly in an interview in 1977 with talk-show host David Frost when he explained, "When the President does it, that means it is not illegal." But in 1974, when Nixon resigned, most Americans did not agree with this odd doctrine. In another era, perhaps Nixon would not have been held accountable for his illegal activities. President Ronald Reagan also violated the law, but the congressional inquiry into the Iran-Contra scandal of the 1980s dealt gently with him, and there was no wide public outcry for his impeachment. But Nixon's crimes were exposed at the end of the era known as "the Sixties," a period of extraordinary public activism, civic mobilization, and criticism of authority. The leaking of the Pentagon Papers had fed the wider public's realization that their government had misled them—even lied to them—about the progress of the Vietnam War; in this context, revelations about Nixon's illegal activities confirmed growing perceptions about the untrustworthiness of government. Others in positions of authority and power took their responsibilities to the public seriously as well. Although the news of the break-in at the Watergate complex was initially relegated to a small story in the "Metro" section of the Washington *Post*, a handful of journalists pursued the story doggedly. Key officials in the Justice Department, disturbed by the government's abuse of power, acted in accordance with the law rather than with political loyalties. The Democrats in Congress launched serious rather than superficial investigations into Watergate. As inquiries began to pry the lid off of Nixon's illegalities, the president's impulse was to commit further crimes to block the investigations, giving rise to the truism that "the cover-up is worse than the crime."

The House Judiciary Committee, which drew up the articles of impeachment, charged Nixon with obstructing justice (for seeking to cover up Watergate), with abusing presidential power (for using executive branch agencies and employees to persecute his "enemies"), and with refusing to comply with Congress's legally proper demands for evidence (when Nixon would not hand over the secret Oval Office tapes). Nixon intended to face impeachment and a Senate trial, until leading Republican senators informed him that he could count on few in their ranks to vote in his favor.

Once the crisis had played out and Nixon had left office, the dominant interpretation of Watergate was that the "system worked": Nixon's violations of the Constitution had been uncovered, and through processes outlined in that same Constitution, Nixon had been held accountable. But the fallout from the crisis was great: large sectors of the public lost faith in the integrity of their leaders and developed a deep skepticism about government. Revelations in the mid-1970s that the United States had been involved in overthrowing or attempting to assassinate world leaders, which were brought to light by congressional investigations into the cold war activities of U.S. intelligence agencies, confirmed the suspicions of some that Nixon was not unique and that other cold war presidents had similarly misused their powers.

And yet, from the start, certain misconceptions plagued public understanding of Watergate. First, many Americans believed that Nixon's secret Oval Office tapes themselves constituted an offense for which he was punished, and concluded that, since other presidents, beginning with Franklin Roosevelt, had taped Oval Office conversations, Nixon was just the one who "got caught." In fact, the taping was not a crime; the tapes simply provided irrefutable evidence of Nixon's crimes. Second, the cover-up has gotten the most attention, overshadowing the extent of the earlier crimes committed by CREEP and White House officials and the deep roots of these activities in the politics of the era. Third, the connection between Watergate and conflicts over foreign policy has remained shadowy to the public, although historians have sought to make the connection clear. Perhaps this element would have garnered more public attention had the House Judiciary Committee not put aside a fourth article of impeachment, which they considered, and indicted Nixon for ordering the invasion of Cambodia in 1970. (A fifth potential article of impeachment concerning Nixon's tax evasion was dropped in committee as well.)

Scholarly inquiry into Watergate initially focused on the odd personality of Richard Nixon, his towering resentments and his determination to "fix" his adversaries. Indeed, Nixon's compelling weirdness fed the craze among scholars in the 1970s for what was called "psychohistory," in which historians made elaborate use of psychological and psychiatric models of individual personality to shed light on past leaders. This biographical framework of interpretation has persisted among historians. Only rarely have they sought to place Nixon's presidential crimes in a broader sweep of history. Notable in this regard is Arthur M. Schlesinger, Jr.'s *The Imperial Presidency,* published in 1973, as the Watergate scandal was unfolding. Schlesinger argued that over the course of the cold war, the executive branch had shockingly aggrandized its power in ways that were inconsistent with Constitutional precepts and dangerous to American liberty. During an age when Americans perceived their country to be engaged in a constant battle against a global enemy, the increasing latitude enjoyed by presidents in the conduct of foreign policy had made possible the consolidation of power and authority at the top, in a steady drift toward authoritarianism. Placed in this context, Nixon's crimes looked like a continuation of alarming trends that his predecessors in the White House had done much to advance.

In recent years, some commentators have compared Watergate to two subsequent scandals—the Iran-Contra imbroglio of Reagan's presidency and Whitewater (also referred to as "Monica-gate"), the scandal involving President Bill Clinton. Iran-Contra involved criminal and secret government policies. Reagan, despite avowals to the contrary, covertly and illegally furnished arms to the anti-American government of Iran in an effort to free U.S. hostages held by terrorist groups. Also in defiance of U.S. law, he ordered his staff to find and provide covert financial support for the Contras, a rebel army seeking to overthrow the internationally recognized Sandinista government of Nicaragua. (Oliver North, a White House national-security aide, diverted funds from the Iran arms sales to the Contras, thus establishing the "Iran-Contra" link.) In 1986, Congress initiated an investigation into Iran-Contra. Numerous administration officials were eventually convicted of crimes, but in 1992 President George H. W. Bush, who had served as Reagan's vice president, pardoned several of the most senior figures involved, thus preventing high-profile trials from occurring and keeping the trail of investigation from approaching Bush himself. Although Reagan's involvement in Iran-Contra injured his popularity, the Constitutional peril posed by his activities never seemed palpable to a majority of voters, as it had in Nixon's case. Democrats, although holding the upper hand in Congress in the late 1980s, chose not to pursue impeachment.

President Bill Clinton received harsher treatment from the Republicans who controlled Congress in the late 1990s. The House impeached him in 1998, after finding that he had obstructed justice and given false testimony in relation to a civil lawsuit brought against him by Paula Jones for sexual harassment allegedly committed by Clinton when he was governor of Arkansas. Fueling the disgust for Clinton in many quarters were the revelations of his sexual escapades in the White House with the young intern Monica Lewinsky. "Monica-gate" had its beginnings in the extensive investigation, led by Kenneth Starr, of Clinton's pre-presidential life, beginning with a real estate transaction known as Whitewater. Despite the enormous media attention given to the sexually explicit details disclosed by Starr, Clinton's job-approval ratings actually rose during the impeachment proceedings. Although voters decried Clinton's personal behavior, they did not see it, or his dishonesty about it, as grounds for removal from office, and the Senate declined to convict him.

Efforts to render Whitewater, Iran-Contra, and Watergate equivalent fall short of persuasion. All three featured abysmal judgment by presidents, investigations by Congress and by special prosecutors, and efforts by the White House to conceal or deny the full truth. But the similarities end there. Iran-Contra was arguably the most serious of the three scandals, involving many high executive-branch officials in a secret foreign policy designed to violate U.S. law and to subvert the Constitutional balance of powers. Watergate also involved the criminal manipulation of government powers, with the intent mainly to punish the president's opponents. Whitewater revealed pathetic behavior and stunted moral judgment on the part of the president, but it did not reach the same alarming level of White House criminality as did Watergate and Iran-Contra. Both Nixon and Reagan, unlike Clinton, got into trouble because of their official behavior while serving as president. Yet Nixon's fate was unique. Nixon, and the era in which he served, created together the perfect conditions for a presidential downfall: a vigilant citizenry, a hostile Congress, and presidential behavior not only threatening to the Constitutional system but also so crude and thuggish that the public was able to believe that the occupant of the White House was in fact a criminal.

The first reading in this chapter is by Lewis L. Gould who, as have most historians, focuses on Richard Nixon's career and personality in explaining Watergate. But Gould also connects Nixon's misbehavior in office to longer trends in America's political history. He highlights the thorough politicization of Nixon's White House operations, viewing his presidency as a "permanent campaign" from which there was no respite during which reflective policymaking might occur. The preoccupation of Nixon and his closest aides with manufacturing positive appearances for the president, and with targeting and smearing their political opponents, built on earlier tendencies in American politics, Gould argues. But he emphasizes that Nixon took these tendencies to new extremes. In the "us-versus-them" atmosphere that Nixon cultivated in the White House, the skullduggery that became associated with the term "Watergate" did not seem out of the ordinary. The Oval Office tapes reveal that Nixon and his aides did not see their actions as wrong, although their comments that they were just playing "hardball," as previous administrations had, may suggest an unspoken awareness of the illegality of their acts. Gould sees such rationalizations as self-serving and inaccurate. He also suggests that, even though no subsequent administration matched Nixon's for criminal scheming and paranoia, presidents and their top appointees since 1974 have increasingly followed Nixon's example in keeping politics and the next election uppermost in mind throughout the four years after inauguration day. It is a telling comment on the evolution of American public life that, for the duration of the twentieth century, the presidents whose White House operations were commonly accused of practicing politics incessantly (Reagan and Clinton) were elected to second terms, whereas those who were unsuccessful in gaining reelection (Carter and George H. W. Bush) were criticized for their lack of political acumen as much as for policy failures.

The second reading is taken from *Watergate in American Memory*, a 1993 book by Michael Schudson, a scholar of mass communications. Schudson tackles head-on the question of whether we should interpret Watergate as a story about Richard Nixon or as a story of the "imperial presidency." Although he does not come down on one side or the other of this question, Schudson clearly thinks that the Watergate scandal was part of a deeper crisis of political authority in America, and that this bigger story is too seldom remembered. Neither the phrase "Nixon was a terrible man" nor the cynical refrain of "Nixon just got caught" is an adequate summary of what happened in the 1970s, in his view. Schudson argues that the cover-up among the Watergate conspirators, although it got them into trouble, also succeeded in obscuring the roots of Watergate, especially its roots in foreign policy and intelligence gathering.

Public anger at revelations of Nixon's surveillance of law-abiding U.S. citizens, combined with the lingering strength of the antiwar movement, led to an atmosphere of reform and a renewed zeal for scrutiny of spy agencies. Investigations followed, most famously committee hearings led by Representative Otis Pike of New York in the U.S. House and by Senator Frank Church of Idaho in the Senate. These inquiries cast aside, for the first and last time, the normal congressional agreement to keep CIA and FBI operations largely secret, parting the curtains of secrecy to reveal a cold war history of overthrowing foreign governments, trying to kill foreign leaders, spying on American citizens, and incompetence and wastefulness to boot. Church called the CIA a "rogue elephant"; in calling this characterization unfounded, Schudson implies that presidents really had more culpability in the Agency's doings than even the populist-spirited Church was willing to admit. In any case, the U.S. government had never before conceded that it did such things, and the revelations of the Church Committee further stoked both public outrage and a growing cynicism about the American state. But instead of leading to more aggressive grassroots actions against the state, as some feared, this cynicism led to greater disengagement from politics.

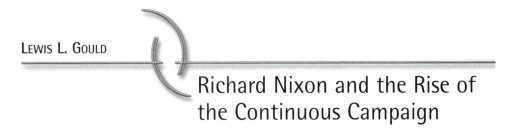

LEWIS L. GOULD

Richard Nixon and the Rise of the Continuous Campaign

More than any other chief executive before him, Nixon embraced the concept of the permanent political campaign as president. He geared up institutions within the White House to sustain such an effort. "The staff doesn't understand that we are in a continuous campaign," Nixon told his chief of staff, H. R. Haldeman, on 25 March 1971. His example was followed by his immediate Republican successors as well as by Bill Clinton.

Previous presidents, including Lyndon Johnson and Franklin D. Roosevelt, certainly had interwoven governance with politics in their administrations. But there had not been, even in the most partisan cases, such a direct nexus between the style of a presidential campaign—fund-raising, jockeying for partisan advantage, and efforts to frustrate the opposition—and the way the White House functioned, as proved true during Nixon's five and a half years in office. Even if the principle was often violated, the notion existed that a president should govern in a style that subordinated partisan considerations to the national interest. Between inauguration and the start of a reelection campaign, for example, stretched several years in which the president should not always be thinking of how a second term could be won.

Under Nixon, this concept, timeworn and obsolete as it had become, vanished. The campaign never stopped, and the presidency itself emerged as an extension of that effort. Added to the mix was Nixon's conviction that such an approach was necessary in a political universe that was hostile to him and all his goals. Facing enemies who he believed would stop at nothing,

Nixon was convinced that all measures were justified to retain political supremacy. In his view, Kennedy and Johnson had used illegal methods against him in the 1960 and 1968 campaigns, and their friends would use them again to oppose his presidency if they had the opportunity. He therefore resolved to use the same weapons, once he held power. The result was a presidency that moved inexorably toward illegality from its earliest days.

Thus, Richard Nixon had a dual impact on the evolution of the modern presidency. His involvement in the Watergate scandal cover-up and the other crimes of his presidency brought about his resignation in August 1974 and produced serious restrictions on the power and autonomy of future chief executives. The measures that he had instituted in the way of implementing the permanent campaign that did not involve illegal activity remained an important if troubling legacy of his years in office.

Richard Nixon was one of the most puzzling and enigmatic personalities ever to occupy the presidency. He could be brilliant in his analysis of foreign policy questions, and he had an encyclopedic grasp of American politics. Whether he meant to or not (and that is still a subject of much dispute), his administration pushed through environmental legislation and expanded spending on social programs. Nixon has in fact been dubbed "the last liberal president." His defenders credit him with opening a new relationship with the People's Republic of China and with pursuing policies toward the Soviet Union that eased tensions between the two superpowers. Despite the disgrace of Watergate, Nixon, in this view, was a president of substantial achievements brought down by political enemies and personal excesses.

To his detractors, Nixon's crime-ridden presidency was the fulfillment of a career driven by paranoia and a dark view of his political adversaries, along with hefty doses of racism and anti-Semitism. From his first entry into politics, Nixon had practiced political hardball and a win-at-any-cost mentality. The presidency simply gave him greater scope to pursue his divisive policies and to deal with his personal demons. Watergate was thus the logical culmination of his personality defects.

There is no doubt that Nixon was a strange and tormented individual. His family background in California was one of insecurity and a lack of genuine affection. One of his aides, Bryce Harlow, believed that Nixon "as a young person was hurt very deeply by somebody . . . a sweetheart, a parent, a dear friend, someone he deeply trusted. Hurt so badly he never got over it and never trusted anybody again." Nixon grew up introverted and shy but wanted very much to be accepted and included in male activities. He played football at Whittier College despite a lack of physical coordination that relegated him to the scrub team.

Following law school at Duke and a stint in the navy during World War II, Nixon returned to Southern California, ran as a Republican for Congress in the 1946 election, and won. From the start of his public career, he proved adept at debating his opponents and using the issue of anticommunism to advance his fortunes. He had little regard for the voters he represented. "You've got to be a little evil to understand those people out there," he once remarked. Nixon won a Senate race in 1950 and two years later went on the Republican ticket as Dwight D. Eisenhower's running mate. Eight years as vice president enriched his knowledge of American politics but did not bring him close to real power. He lost a close presidential contest in 1960 to John F. Kennedy and a gubernatorial race in California two years later, but people who predicted his political demise were premature. He won the Republican nomination in 1968 and defeated Hubert Humphrey and George C. Wallace in the fall election.

Nixon wanted to be a great president in foreign affairs to outdo Eisenhower and Kennedy, two men whom he very much envied. He told a reporter in 1967 that the nation "could run itself domestically without a President. All you need is a competent Cabinet to run the country at home. You need a President for foreign policy." That may explain his detachment from economic and domestic policy issues except as they related to his reelection chances or how history might view his presidency. As he said about matters relating to the international economy and the value of the dollar, "I don't give a shit about the lira."

. . . [S]ince Nixon was intent on presenting an image to the world of a confident, self-assured executive in the model of a Harry Truman or a Jack Kennedy, it was necessary that the public at large not know of the president's insecurities or emotional needs. The result was the dedication of much staff time to presidential image making on a scale that even Nixon's predecessors had not attained. Once institutionalized, this process became self-perpetuating in subsequent administrations.

It was not enough that President Nixon be judged by his deeds in office in the fashion of William Howard Taft or Harry Truman. From the earliest days of his presidency, the press and public received a barrage of information about how hard Nixon was working, how cool he was in moments of crisis, and how nonpolitical and objective his decisions were. Frequently, Nixon compared himself in private with other presidents, always to his advantage, and then sought to have his subordinates get the word out to the press about his superiority. Though the presidency had always had a self-referential quality for its occupants, most of those who preceded Nixon had been largely content to let their deeds shape their public image. In Nixon's case the need to depict himself as a strong, confident chief executive was a major element in his reliance on White House institutions to promote his positive self-image and to build domestic support for his policies.

To accomplish these results, the traditional role of the White House press secretary as a link with the reporters who covered the president was clearly inadequate. Nixon neither liked nor trusted the press, and their needs had a low claim on his time and energy. "I was bored by the charade of trying to romance the media," Nixon later wrote. He installed Ron Ziegler as his press secretary because Ziegler's modest abilities and lack of public stature meshed with Nixon's desire to diminish the direct impact of the print and electronic media. "Nixon was able to program Ziegler. He was absolutely programmable," concluded the White House aide Charles Colson. It did not take long for the press corps to determine that the youthful and uninformed Ziegler had no real access to serious White House information. Once a figurehead was in place, the president then took further steps to render the White House reporters an inconsequential element in covering his presidency.

At first the new administration wanted to relocate the White House press corps to the Old Executive Office Building across the street. When that idea aroused a tepid response from journalists, who saw themselves being moved away from the center of power, the Nixon people covered over the swimming pool that had been in the White House since Franklin D. Roosevelt's day and created a new press headquarters that has remained in use ever since. With a podium for the press secretary and other officials, and the reporters placed as an audience, the press briefings became mini press conferences of their own each day.

The upgrading of press facilities was cosmetic. The effort of the Nixon years was to downgrade independent press coverage and to relegate the Washington reporters and the electronic media to the margins. Nixon's infrequent nighttime press conferences were changed from the afternoons, as under Kennedy, so that these events occurred in prime time on the East Coast. That made it harder for morning newspapers with tight deadlines in the East to have much coverage and analysis of what the president had said. The number of actual presidential news conferences fell to 39 during Nixon's time in office, down from Lyndon Johnson's 132 during a similar period in the White House. The multitude of such conferences held during the Coolidge, Roosevelt, and Truman presidencies came to seem utopian. Nixon accelerated the descent of the press conference as a presidential institution from the heights it had attained during the period from Roosevelt through Eisenhower.

Nixon delighted in making statements about what he had done first as president, even if some of these comments were based on faulty historical arguments. In 1970, using third-person, as he often did, he wrote that "RN is the first president who came into the Presidency with the opposition of all these major communication powers." This statement would have puzzled Franklin D. Roosevelt, who faced more press hostility from the owners of the large Republican newspapers than Nixon ever did, but it clearly exemplified Nixon's near paranoia about his relations with the mainstream media. "Do you think, for Christ sakes, that the *New York Times* is worried about all the legal niceties?" he asked in June 1971 as the controversy over the Pentagon Papers developed. "Those sons of bitches are killing me."

The solution in the new president's mind was to install White House institutions that would allow his administration to circumvent the press. To that end, an Office of Communications was established with the longtime Nixon friend Herbert Klein as its first director. Its public purpose was, as Klein told the press, "to eliminate any possibility of a credibility gap for this administration." Nixon himself promised an emphasis on "the need for free access to information in all departments of the government, to the extent that it does not endanger national security." These reassuring statements proved to be largely window dressing for an administration intent on reducing the flow of information to the media.

The actual purpose of the Communications Office was to create a kind of quasi-journalistic operation that would put out favorable information on the Nixon administration in the guise of news. Klein and his staff prepared news releases, facilitated access for reporters outside of Washington, and provided speakers to defend Nixon's policies. It functioned, as Nixon intended it to do, very much like a continuing political campaign. Even Klein later remarked that in the Nixon White House "an amazingly excessive amount of time was spent worrying about plans to conjure up better and more favorable coverage."

Although the Office of Communications represented in theory an effort to broaden ties between the White House and its various constituencies, it soon became a means of generating popular opinion itself. Nixon believed that the Democrats and especially John Kennedy had benefited from "a constant representation in letters to the editor columns and a very proper influence on the television commentators." Though the direct evidence for such influence may have existed only in Nixon's mind, he concluded that it would be wise to create such sentiment from the White House on a sustained basis. He constantly urged his aides to devise ways to plant stories and favorable letters in newspapers that the administration deemed unfriendly. He told Haldeman in November 1969 before a major address on Vietnam, "if only do one thing get 100 vicious dirty calls to the *New York Times* and *Washington Post* about their editorials (even though no idea what they'll be)."

The techniques employed included a letter-writing operation directed by the Republican National Committee that produced up to sixty letters weekly to major media outlets. An aide estimated that each letter cost about one hundred dollars to produce, a bargain when one of the missives appeared in the *Washington Post* or the *New York Times*. The White House also used phone banks to stimulate calls to newspapers and radio stations, asking for fairer coverage of Nixon and his policies. Aides set up shadow committees that endorsed Nixon's initiatives in foreign and domestic policy. These panels then sent out mass mailings asking for support of the president. For Nixon, who believed that his goals were supported by a great "silent majority," it made sense for the presidency to evoke and even to produce the sentiments he wished that majority to adopt.

These activities imparted a sense of accomplishment to the men and women who worked for Nixon. They believed that they were creating favorable attitudes toward the president. They also demonstrated that the modern presidency had become less about dealing with real national problems and more about presenting favorable impressions of the presidency and its occupant. Engaging issues, however, lacked the emotional wallop that went with defeating a political enemy or re-creating the ethos of a campaign. Many times the practitioners of presidential make-believe under Nixon and his successors convinced themselves that they had been engaged in the public's business when all they had done was to take part in executive ballyhoo.

The campaign-style thinking that these activities reflected blended with the melodramatic point of view of the president and his men to move the Nixon White House in less legal directions. If the president was opposed by unscrupulous "bad guys" and "evil" enemies, as Haldeman noted in his diary, then it was important to preempt any assaults that these adversaries might launch. Properly outraged at the excesses of the Kennedy and Johnson administrations when they were directed against him, Nixon did not conclude that such tactics were beneath the dignity of a president and wisely to be avoided. Instead, he decided that it was both appropriate and prudent for his administration to strike first through the use of government agencies such as the Internal Revenue Service and by taking other, even less savory measures. Believing that the "IRS is full of Jews," Nixon urged his men to launch probes of "the big Jewish contributors of the Democrats," or, as he put it, "Could we please investigate some of the cocksuckers?"

Another element moving Nixon's presidency toward illegality was the obsession with secrecy that permeated the White House. To carry out his diplomatic initiatives toward Vietnam and later China, Nixon believed, as did Henry Kissinger, that absolute confidentiality was essential. Their valid point, however, lost some of its persuasive power when it became evident that their lust for secrecy was directed not so much at keeping enemies such as North Vietnam and China in the dark as it was at preventing the American people from being informed about what was being done in their name. The impulse for widespread wiretapping, for example, derived from press disclosures about bombing in Cambodia in 1969, which was no news to its targets, but it was not common knowledge in the United States. Embarrassment to the administration rather than a concern for national security launched a campaign to root out leakers that became a recurring obsession of the Nixon White House.

Like most of his twentieth-century presidential counterparts who faced the problem of leaks to the press, Nixon displayed outrage when they occurred. Although Nixon had said that "LBJ and other presidents have overreacted, and he won't" when confronted with leaking, precisely the opposite response occurred. The concern with leaks affected how the administration responded to the disclosures of the Pentagon Papers in the *New York Times* and the *Washington Post* during summer 1971. To placate the outrage of Nixon and Kissinger over the disclosure of these secrets of the Johnson administration and Vietnam, the president approved the formation of what evolved into the White House Plumbers unit. The task of this cadre of inept counterespionage types was to punish those people in and out of government who had the temerity to leak classified documents. The Justice Department was seen as too legalistic and constrained by the rule of law to handle such matters. Since no administration has been immune from leaks of one sort or another, the determination that Nixon and his men evidenced to cut down on all such unauthorized disclosures was bound to prove self-defeating.

Several forces came together to facilitate decisions in the Nixon White House to engage in what Haldeman called "hardball politics." Like most politicians, Nixon and his associates expected to be throwing the hardballs, not standing at home plate receiving them. So by mid-July 1969, Nixon was telling aides of his desire to "set up and activate 'dirty tricks'" operations from the White House. The money for such endeavors came from leftover campaign funds from the 1968 presidential race. With ready access to then unregulated and unreported cash, it seemed easy and effective to set seasoned operatives in motion against likely political opponents. Convinced that the presidency was above legal restraints, Nixon did not expect that these illicit endeavors would ever see the light of day. At the same time, he did not take any discernible steps to ensure that trained and experienced people were used for a risky venture. He accepted the assurances of his advisers that the White House could rely on men such as sometime spy and spy novelist E. Howard Hunt.

From his own experience, Nixon proved creative at finding things for his men to do in the dark shadows of American politics. Using the Internal Revenue Service to harass partisan enemies, which his predecessors had also done, was too tempting a tactic to resist. Compiling a list of enemies for future reprisals came naturally as well. With a future presidential election in mind, identifying possible opponents and undermining their chances were logical steps for the Nixon White House to pursue. The president should not just be the leader of his own political party; he should employ the weapons of the presidency to determine the choice of the Democrats in 1972.

That these steps had to be taken in secret attested to their novelty as direct actions of the presidency. Even more staff time had to be allocated to these White House activities. In turn, the need for secrecy bred the desire for ever more political intelligence and inside dope about potential opponents. Most such information about the fractious Democrats and their chronic arguments could easily be gleaned from a careful reading of daily newspapers, but that was either too mundane an approach for presidential aides or not enough to satisfy Nixon's conspiratorial lust for reassurance that he was always one step ahead of his unscrupulous enemies.

The late 1960s and early 1970s were a time of social turmoil as the passions that the Vietnam War had stirred produced repeated protests and sporadic acts of violence. Like the Johnson administration before it, the Nixon White House was convinced that the antiwar left had ties to the Communist world. In January 1969, Nixon told Kissinger: "I want to hear a CIA analysis in depth of worldwide common factors of youth disturbances." When the CIA and the FBI could not identify such ties, these conclusions did not comfort Nixon and his associates. In their minds, the absence of evidence attested to the inefficiency and incompetence of these investigative agencies. The president's men would simply have to find the facts on their own.

The next step in the chain of logic then was to create within the executive branch more coordination in the gathering and processing of "internal domestic intelligence." Though there were legitimate issues about how well the FBI and even the CIA operated in this field, the underlying problem was that they were not telling Nixon what he wanted to know. Therefore, Nixon set in motion efforts to establish his own sources for intelligence gathering through a White House aide, Tom Huston. The zealous Huston embarked on a plan that would have had a serious impact on the civil liberties of American citizens while simultaneously diminishing the role of the FBI. Naturally, such an initiative encountered opposition from the aging J. Edgar Hoover, which in turn generated more time and effort in the Nixon White House to resolve the bureaucratic impasse.

Previous presidents had often criticized the performance of the chief executives who had come before them, but Nixon proved innovative in his use of government records to blacken the reputations of his predecessors. And if the records did not show what Nixon's operatives wanted them to demonstrate, then some plausible fabrications were in order. With the assistance of such unscrupulous operatives as Charles Colson and E. Howard Hunt, Nixon proposed to concoct phony historical documents to implicate John F. Kennedy in such mistakes or misdeeds as the Bay of Pigs in 1961 or the murder of South Vietnamese leader Ngo Dinh Diem in 1963. To have the agents of the president engage in fakery on such a potentially grand scale was another of Nixon's unique contributions to the evolution of presidential power.

These wacky schemes did not produce the results that Nixon desired, and his efforts to stem leaks through the FBI and CIA also proved futile. When the White House Plumbers broke into the office of Daniel Ellsberg's psychiatrist, the caper yielded no usable information and was carried off in a notably inept manner. The key point in the history of the presidency was the establishment of a covert operation in the White House itself. In essence, Nixon believed that the presidency was not a part of the government required to interact with other agencies. It should function instead as a government in itself, in which illegal activities were acceptable because they were being carried out in the name of and with the knowledge of the president.

With the barrier against illegal activity broken and the 1972 presidential election approaching, the development of surreptitious means to disrupt the political opposition was no great stretch for the men in the Nixon White House. Convinced that the president was indispensable to world peace because of his initiative with Communist China and the apparent winding down of the Vietnam War, Nixon and his colleagues were persuaded that electing a Democrat would be a national calamity. No one asked if Nixon's achievements would be enhanced if he simply stood on the historical legacy of his term and retired. For Nixon himself, with his addiction to power, another elected term would move him past Kennedy, Johnson, and Truman and into a league with his mentor Eisenhower.

Since the national interest demanded a Nixon triumph, any chance of a Democratic success must be extinguished. Confronting the opposition only with the tough weapons of American politics left open the slim possibility of an upset in the fall. The electorate could not be allowed even the chance of a fatal error in judgment when the presidency was at stake. The incumbent must see to it that democracy produced the correct result, even if extralegal measures were employed. So by early 1972, the White House and the attorney general, John Mitchell, opened discussions about how to disrupt the Democratic National Convention and undermine the leading anti-Nixon candidates. Only questions of practicality and the risk of possible disclosure figured in the discussion of these schemes. Otherwise, using the presidency as a means of covert action seemed entirely appropriate.

By the time these clandestine ventures were in progress, Richard Nixon had long since put aside his initial opposition to Lyndon Johnson's practice of taping conversations in the White House. In 1971 an even more elaborate voice-activated system of recording conversations in the Oval Office was in place. Nixon's purpose in authorizing these tapes was to provide an accurate record for himself that he could use in writing his memoirs after the presidency. Voice activation had to be employed because he was so inept in dealing with even the simplest machinery that he could not be relied on to press a button to start the tape rolling. Sometimes he remembered that the system was in operation and guided the conversations accordingly. In other instances, he forgot the recorders' presence and indulged in the profane, often anti-Semitic, language that characterized the private Nixon.

So convinced was Nixon that he would never be caught and that presidents could move beyond legality with impunity that he did not consider the tapes any kind of threat to his continuation in office, even while he initiated the cover-up of the Watergate scandal that led to his potential downfall. The possibility that the tapes might ever be the focus of legal action such as a subpoena from an independent counsel seemed outside the scope of political reality. Nixon had internalized the assumptions of the modern presidency to such an extent that he never contemplated the diminution of executive authority in the future.

Yet by 1971 and 1972, a reaction against the imperial aspects of presidential power had begun to appear, and it intensified during the two years that followed. The scholarly literature produced such works as Arthur Schlesinger Jr.'s *The Imperial Presidency* (1973), in which a defender of the use of executive authority under Franklin D. Roosevelt, Harry S Truman, and John F. Kennedy had second thoughts after the performance of Lyndon Johnson and Richard Nixon. Congress sought to restrict what Nixon and other presidents could do in foreign policy through the War Powers Act (1973), which was passed over Nixon's veto. For the moment, the temper of the nation was turning against the excesses of the modern presidency as the dimensions of Nixon's assertion of executive primacy became clear.

Although the Watergate scandal broke open with the arrest of the burglars in the Democratic headquarters located in that building in June 1972, the White House was able to contain it throughout Nixon's successful race for reelection against the divided Democrats and their candidate, George S. McGovern. The power of incumbency and the ineptitude of the Democrats produced a landslide victory for Nixon and Spiro Agnew. In the aftermath of the result, Nixon hoped to consolidate his power over the executive branch and exert enhanced influence with the press. As Haldeman recorded in his diary, Nixon had said, "Most second terms have been disastrous and . . . someone should write this, because [Nixon's] determined that his won't be." With the end of direct American involvement in Vietnam in early 1973, Nixon could believe that, except for Watergate, a period of presidential accomplishment lay ahead and there was no reason for him not to push on with his agenda as forcefully as he had done in the first term.

But the Watergate scandal did break during the first half of 1973, and Nixon's presidency never recovered.

MICHAEL SCHUDSON

Watergate in American Memory

In the terms proposed by Leonard Garment, Nixon's law partner and counselor, there are two kinds of perspectives on Watergate: "Nixon theories" and "imperial presidency theories." Nixon theories typically argue that what Nixon did was unique; "imperial presidency" theories generally argue that what he did was part of a long-term pattern of the aggrandizement of constitutional and extraconstitutional authority by the presidency. These latter

From *Watergate in American Memory: How We Remember, Forget and Reconstruct the Past,* by Michael Schudson. Copyright © 1992 by Michael Schudson. Reprinted by permission of Basic Books, a member of Perseus Books, L.L.C.

theories emphasize that American foreign policy since World War I has been conducted on a wartime footing, that "national security" is a rationale to cover a multitude of sins and crimes, and that Watergate's lesson was that a nation's misconduct abroad "can come home to haunt it."

Was Richard Nixon's offense an aberration or, instead, the logical consequence of a system in which he was no more guilty than other presidents? The House Judiciary Committee was very interested to know if Nixon's offenses could be distinguished from those of his predecessors. Counsel John Doar even asked eminent Yale historian C. Vann Woodward in May 1974 to do a historical study of presidential misconduct. Woodward and fourteen other historians dropped everything else to do the work and determine if Nixon's transgressions were unlike those of his predecessors. Their conclusion: Nixon was unique. Typically American presidents were the victims rather than perpetrators of malfeasance, betrayed by friends or associates. Presidential offense "usually lay in negligence or in indecision about correcting the offensive practices or discharging the accused." Nixon, in contrast, was "the chief coordinator of the crime and misdemeanor charged against his own administration" and "the chief personal beneficiary of misconduct in his administration." For all the many variations of misconduct in the White House from 1789 to 1969, Woodward concluded, "they do little to prepare us for the innovations of the ensuing period of five and a half years."

But Woodward's study looked only at publicly acknowledged presidential scandals, not presidential misdeeds that might have come to light after a president's term of office ended. In 1974 and 1975, a mountain of information poured out from the news media, a presidential commission, and two congressional committees to reveal massive abuses of power by presidents back to Franklin Roosevelt. Woodward's hurried study was irrelevant by 1976. By 1977, when the conservative political writer Victor Lasky published what might be viewed as a rebuttal to Woodward, *It Didn't Start with Watergate,* he had a powerful case. Lasky did not refute a "Richard Nixon" theory with an "imperial presidency" theory. His position was simply that politicians, at least Democrats, are sleazy human beings beneath contempt, particularly if their names are John Kennedy or Lyndon Johnson. Crude as Lasky's book is, it is packed with information gleaned largely from public documents and respectable newspapers. By the time it was published, it was believable in a way it could not have been a few years earlier. In 1973 the kinds of arguments Lasky would later make were stock dodges for Nixon defenders. Humorist Art Buchwald made a list of them, which included "Everybody does it," "What about Chappaquiddick?" "What about Harry Truman and the deep freeze scandal?" "Franklin D. Roosevelt did a lot of worse things," and "LBJ used to read FBI reports every night." By 1977 such rationalizations for Nixon's conduct were not so easily dismissed.

The impeachment inquiry promoted "Nixon" theories, but the meaning of Watergate by 1977 had shifted, "Nixon" theories losing ground to "imperial presidency" theories, and views of Watergate as symptom of systemic faults coming to compete with views of Watergate as aberration. Three factors made this possible. First, the legal and cultural need to attribute blame for criminal activity to specific, morally responsible individuals had been at least partially satisfied. President Nixon left office in disgrace, and many of his aides had served or were still serving prison terms. With the matter of criminal responsibility resolved, there was more room to consider broader interpretations of Watergate without necessarily suggesting Nixon's exoneration. Second, the meaning of Watergate was to some extent fuzzy to begin with, because Watergate was in no small measure a crime against memory itself. The Watergate cover-up was an effort to misdirect attention, to destroy evidence, to make accurate historical reconstruction impossible. Though the cover-up fell apart it was successful enough to leave ambiguity about just what went on. Bolstered by the pardoning of Nixon, it left wiggle room for varying interpretations.

Third, as I have indicated, investigations in the years after Watergate brought out new and damning information about the abuses of power in presidents before Nixon. C. Vann Woodward worked only with public historical records. The question he examined was: What kinds of malfeasance in office or abuse of power have presidents or their chief aides been responsibly charged with through the years? The question that became of greater interest in 1975 was quite different: What abuses of power have presidents been guilty of even if the public never knew about them? How was Watergate routine rather than aberration? While this question was asked during 1972 to 1974, it never became a matter for intense public attention. It slid, or was pushed, to the side. But once asked seriously, it reconfigured the meaning of Watergate. It propelled to new prominence the question, "Did Richard Nixon just have the bad luck to get caught?" It forced people connected with earlier administrations and campaigns who had themselves engaged in dirty tricks painfully to rethink their own deeds. It reestablished what would pass as plausible interpretations of Watergate. . . .

The Ford administration was barely in place when the nation was stunned by a series of revelations about American covert military and intelligence operations. In mid-September, while responses to the pardon were still electrifying the media, Seymour Hersh wrote in the *New York Times* that CIA covert operations had been designed and enacted, with some success, to bring down the government of the democratically elected Marxist leader of Chile, Salvador Allende. On 22 December 1974, Hersh broke an even more explosive story: that the CIA had spied on domestic antiwar protesters and other left-wing organizations during the 1960s. Daniel Schorr, the CBS News correspondent covering the story, recounts that this disclosure "caused a public stir in a way that a covert operation against a distant South American regime had not. It twinged the Watergate-raw 'invasion of liberties' nerve that the Ford administration had been trying to assuage."

"Watergate-raw" is a term that certainly fit the CIA. In May 1973, the public learned that Howard Hunt, a White House "plumber" acting with authorization from John Ehrlichman and using CIA equipment to collect materials for a CIA "psychiatric profile" of Daniel Ellsberg, broke into Ellsberg's psychiatrist's office. The administration was looking for information to discredit Ellsberg in retaliation for his release of the Pentagon Papers. CIA director James Schlesinger was outraged. He directed all CIA employees, past and present, to disclose any improper agency activity they knew of. The Inspector General's office came up with a 693-page report of possible violations of the CIA's legislative charter, known inside the agency as the "family jewels" or, by Deputy Director of Plans William Colby, as "our skeletons in the closet."

So when Ford asked William Colby, Schlesinger's successor as CIA director, to respond to the *New York Times* charges, Colby delivered "the family jewels" to the president. On 4 January 1975, Ford appointed a commission of inquiry headed by Vice President Nelson Rockefeller to examine CIA domestic operations that violated its charter. While this was intended to cool things off, Ford unintentionally provoked another bombshell. In an off-the-record luncheon with *New York Times* editors, he defended the generally conservative cast of the Rockefeller commission by saying he wanted people who would stick to the mission at hand (illegal and unauthorized domestic surveillance) and not get into matters that could blacken the reputation of presidents back to Truman. "Like what?" asked managing editor A. M. Rosenthal. "Like assassinations!" said Ford, adding, "That's off the record!"

The *Times* did not print the remarks or investigate the story, but word began to get around. After Daniel Schorr obtained an unintentional confirmation from Colby that the CIA may have assassinated foreign leaders, he broke the story for CBS News, and assassinations were added to the topics within the Rockefeller commission's mandate.

By then the Rockefeller commission was not operating alone. Senator Frank Church, Democrat from Idaho, was running a Senate investigation of the CIA, too, as chair of the Senate Select Committee to Study Government Operations with Respect to Intelligence Activities, established 27 January. The House set up a comparable committee in February, although internal bickering left it floundering for months. The Rockefeller commission ran out of time, or will, even with a two-month extension, to complete a study of assassination attempts; it turned over its assassination materials to the Senate Intelligence Committee. Even so, the Rockefeller report, made public 10 June, was anything but the whitewash many had expected. It documented the domestic surveillance charges, including "Operation Chaos," in which the Johnson administration and later the Nixon administration had collected files on foreign contacts of left-wing American activists. Although the CIA had no statutory authority in domestic intelligence, it developed files on Americans and infiltrated new left organizations. The CIA during the Nixon administration helped draw up a plan "at the President's personal request" for a major assault on the peace movement, under the direction of a White House aide, Tom Huston. The infamous Huston plan was squelched by FBI director J. Edgar Hoover's opposition.

As for assassination plots, the Church committee revealed that there had been assassination plots or coup attempts under Presidents Eisenhower, Kennedy, Johnson, and Nixon directed against a number of foreign leaders. Efforts had been made, but failed, to assassinate Patrice Lumumba in 1960 in the Congo (internal opponents assassinated him). Efforts were made to assassinate Rafael Trujillo, the dictator of the Dominican Republic, in 1961. Trujillo was killed by dissidents who apparently had received American arms. The CIA aided a coup against South Vietnamese president Ngo Dinh Diem in 1963 that led to his death. The CIA sought to kidnap General René Schneider, chief of staff of the Chilean army, who had foiled a CIA-backed military coup against President Allende; when he resisted, Schneider was killed by CIA-supported Chileans. A number of imaginative CIA plots had been launched to assassinate Fidel Castro. Poison cigars were delivered to Havana, but it appears no one got them to Castro. Mafia gangsters were retained to help poison Castro's drink. A diving suit with disease-bearing fungus was to be delivered to Castro as a gift for his recreational diving.

No foreign leader, as Daniel Schorr reported for CBS, "was directly killed by the CIA. But it wasn't for want of trying." On 18 July Senator Church suggested that the CIA may have been acting like "a rogue elephant on a rampage," but that was a conclusion Church did not have evidence to support. It was not clear whether the CIA acted on its own or with the knowledge of presidents. The Church committee could not demonstrate either that the CIA acted under presidential directive or that it did not. It is still not clear. Robert McNamara, testifying before the Church committee, avowed that all senior officials in the Kennedy administration opposed assassinations but claimed at the same time that the CIA took no major actions without proper authorization from senior officials. "I understand the contradiction that this carries with respect to the facts." Richard Helms, defending the CIA, felt the Church committee hypocritically conducted an assault on U.S. intelligence. Surely the senators knew that the CIA was the agency of the president precisely to provide a policy option midway between persuasion and military conduct; the point of covert activity is that it be covert. When the committee asked how the CIA could engage in horrible acts like assassination without presidential authorization, Helms felt they surely knew there *was* such authorization but that no president would be so stupid as to put it in writing.

Assassination plots were not the Church committee's only bombshell. The committee revealed that CIA scientists developed and retained deadly poisons, violating President Nixon's directives to comply with international treaties. The public learned also of twenty years of CIA opening of mail, including that of Martin Luther King, Jr., Arthur Burns, Senator Edward Kennedy, and Senator Frank Church. Mail opening stopped only in 1973 because of fears inspired by the Watergate investigations. The FBI, too, had been engaged in unauthorized interception of mail.

The investigations of the abuses of the intelligence agencies led to new patterns of congressional oversight of the CIA and, at least in the short term, major demoralization within the agency. In the long term, it may have led to a more conscientious effort to reconcile the irreconcilable forces of secrecy and democracy than had existed since government secrecy rapidly expanded during and after World War II.

The CIA revelations reshaped the public's image of Watergate. They achieved what President Ford had feared they might: They depressed the reputations of presidents before Nixon, especially Kennedy and Johnson. They lent credence to Nixon's own fumbled defense of himself: that in many of the abuses of power detailed in Article II of the Watergate bill of impeachment, he was pursuing politics as usual. While Article I obstruction of justice charges were untouched by "the year of intelligence" events, Article II abuse of power charges were shown to be ones that might well have been leveled with equal merit at John Kennedy and Lyndon Johnson—and perhaps other presidents, too. Then was there any legitimate basis for distinguishing Richard Nixon's offense? In terms of scope? Perhaps. In terms of central direction? Perhaps. In terms of how Nixon's use of intelligence agencies for political purposes dominated White House activities and provided a central thrust in the administration's outlook? Perhaps. In the Nixon administration's obliviousness to legal and constitutional issues, in its mode of operation less embarrassed and, indeed, less covert than that of earlier presidents? Perhaps. In the warlike footing in which opponents were transformed into enemies and dissension perceived as civil war? Perhaps this, too. All of these are plausible bases for distinguishing the character or scope of Richard Nixon's abuses of power from those of his predecessors. But there is no definitive or consensual judgment among lawyers, judges, or scholars on these matters. The blurring of the line remains between what offenses Richard Nixon alone committed and which offenses were a habitual part of an arrogant, imperial presidency by the time he assumed office. . . .

For radicals of the left, Watergate was a scandal, not a crisis, managed by establishment forces to preserve the general system of the national security state. As Marcus Raskin put it, "to forestall a politically revolutionary consciousness, it was necessary to develop a theory that Nixon and his activities were distinguishable from the System's usual operations." Watergate posed danger to the system by revealing a fundamental corruption of democracy incompatible with national aspirations and popular expectations. To keep these obvious contradictions from threatening the system as a whole, Congress, the media, and other leading forces helped make Richard Nixon the scapegoat for systemic dysfunctions. A political issue of overriding importance was turned into a criminal matter that the nation would after a time be able to put behind it.

For ultraconservatives, Watergate was likewise a scandal but one in which Richard Nixon (and the political forces he represented) was genuinely the object, not a scapegoat. Powerful institutions were not united to save their power as a whole; instead, power was sharply divided between liberals and conservatives. The liberals used their hegemony in the media and in the Congress to drive conservatives from office. The proof that Article II-type presidential abuses of power were rife among Nixon's immediate predecessors strongly reinforced the legitimacy of conservative and ultraconservative charges that liberal forces had been out to get Nixon and not out to locate truths about the presidency.

For liberals Watergate was a constitutional crisis of a troubled system, one that should force the nation to legislative reform to prevent future Watergates, educational reform to prevent the socialization of the kinds of people who made Watergate possible, and general soul-searching to uproot the failings in all of us that enabled Watergate to happen. But central to the liberal position is that Watergate was a constitutional crisis in which the separate branches of government stared each other down. The executive and the legislature—the president and the Congress—went eyeball to eyeball in Watergate, and the president blinked first, honoring the Supreme Court decision on the tapes and choosing to resign for lack of political support in the legislative branch. For liberals Article I obstruction of justice was a kind of subset of Article II abuses of power; both revealed an overreaching presidency and a dangerously reckless president who believed himself above the law.

The liberal position waffles, moving first to Article I to indict Nixon, then to Article II to reform the system. Take, for instance, Theodore Sorensen's lectures at MIT on presidential accountability in the fall of 1974. Sorensen, chief speech writer for President Kennedy, took issue with *both* those who saw Watergate as "a culmination of past trends" and those who asserted that Nixon was "a total aberration." Nixon, he said, was not the first president to receive and dispense unreported campaign contributions, to engage in political espionage, to sanction dirty tricks, to deal ruthlessly with opponents. But, Sorensen argued, turning exclusively to Article I transgressions, "I know of no other President who was personally and directly involved in the cover-up of crimes, the obstruction of justice, and the defiance of those congressional committees, courts, and prosecutors who then investigated these misdeeds." This is unarguable. But see how Sorensen first recognizes but then dodges the more complicated and fateful issues of Article II transgressions to rest on the more plainly established uniqueness of those detailed in Article I.

It is not illogical to claim both that the growth of executive power made possible someone like Nixon and that Nixon was distinctive, unlikely, unprecedented. It may be a virtue of the liberal position that it alone maintains a focus on *both* Article I and Article II abuses, but it opens liberals to charges of confusion. Liberals emphasize systemic explanation while still insisting on the moral and legal accountability of individuals.

For conservatives, as for liberals, Watergate was a constitutional crisis, but it was caused by the follies of one man and his administration, not by systemic distress and disproportion between the powers of the executive and the legislative branches. What Watergate demonstrated is that the political system was strong enough and flexible enough to handle even so serious a threat to political liberty as Watergate turned out to be. For conservatives, Watergate should be viewed ultimately as an opportunity for national self-congratulation rather than for soul-searching and reform.

The question of whether Watergate abuses were aberrational and Nixonian or common and systemic was raised before the Church committee, the Pike committee, and the Rockefeller commission. The "year of intelligence" simply added powerful corroboration for the "system" theories. No one doubted the validity of the CIA inquiry revelations. No one questioned the veracity of Seymour Hersh's reporting. Now no one denied that the CIA under Kennedy and Johnson had been involved in trying to assassinate foreign leaders. And no one could easily define a bright line separating Richard Nixon's Article II abuses of power in office from the abuses of other presidents.

After the cover-up, the pardon, and the "year of intelligence," the shape of Watergate discourse was set. This is a somewhat arbitrary conclusion, of course; the meaning of Watergate has changed in some measure since 1975 and may one day change again. But I think the framework for debate about Watergate today was well articulated by the end of 1975. Was Watergate a personal aberration or a systemic fault? Were Nixon's abuses of power the same as or different from those of other presidents? Was Watergate a constitutional crisis of mammoth dimensions or a scandal of malfeasance blown out of proportion? Was it a turning point in American history or no more than a systemic spasm at the end of the Vietnam era?

These questions figure in the Watergate story in most of its renditions. While this leaves plenty of room for significant debate, the framework of Watergate discussion also precludes consideration of some topics. What is left out of Watergate memory may be more important than what is contained in it. If the Nixon administration did its own frantic editing of Watergate, the Congress did editorial work, too, but more deliberately. Of real importance, a fourth article of impeachment concerning Nixon's prosecution of a secret war in the territory of neutral Cambodia rarely receives more than passing mention in accounts of Watergate. This article (as well as another one concerning Nixon's tax returns and his use of federal money for personal home improvements) was voted down in the Judiciary Committee 26 to 12. The Judiciary Committee was reluctant to challenge the president's authority in foreign policy, especially when the administration had in fact notified a few members of Congress of the military action in Cambodia. The Congress was thus compromised; what was secret from the American public was not entirely unknown to the Congress. The Cambodia issue was thus removed from the story of Watergate, shearing off the largest source and original center of conflict between President Nixon and the Congress: the Vietnam War. Watergate has come to mean, in some interpretations, the matters of the cover-up detailed in Article I; and, in other interpretations, the abuses of power in the domestic sphere discussed in Article II. But the issue of presidential prerogatives in foreign policy raised by the Cambodia article is left aside, too painful a topic to pursue and too divisive a topic on which to reach consensus. Both liberal and conservative versions of Watergate may have provided a signal to presidents that foreign policy is safe territory for unilateral action.

Further Reading

Stanley I. Kutler, *The Wars of Watergate: The Last Crisis of Richard M. Nixon* (New York: Alfred A. Knopf, 1990) should be the definitive comprehensive account of these matters for many years. It is, however, very long, and narrative displaces analysis within its pages. Keith W. Olson, *Watergate: The Presidential Scandal that Shook America* (Lawrence: University Press of Kansas, 2003) is a concise, readable treatment. Among the many journalistic accounts, two of the best are *Nightmare: The Underside of the Nixon Years* (3rd ed. [Athens: Ohio University Press, 1999]), edited by J. Anthony Lukas, an enormous work; and *The Time of Illusion* (New York: Vintage Books, 1976), by Jonathan Schell, which offers serious reflection.

For a good, thorough overview of Nixon's presidency, see Melvin J. Small, *The Presidency of Richard M. Nixon* (Lawrence: University Press of Kansas, 1999). *Nixon Reconsidered* (New York: Basic Books, 1995), by Joan Hoff, is an interesting effort to challenge the conventional wisdom, but at times Hoff's interest in rebutting the standard view becomes an end in itself, at the expense of coherence.

There have been many biographies of Nixon. Stephen Ambrose *Nixon: The Triumph of a Politician, 1962–1972* (New York: Simon & Schuster, 1989) and *Nixon: Ruin and Recovery, 1973–1990* (New York: Simon & Schuster, 1991) are considered fine academic treatments of Nixon's mature years. *The Arrogance of Power: The Secret World of Richard Nixon* (New York: Viking, 2000), by Anthony Summers, an amateur historian and a professional muckraker, is sensationalistic but ventures into areas that academics have found too delicate for their attentions. Fawn M. Brodie, *Richard Nixon: The Shaping of His Character* (New York: Norton, 1981) is a classic example of psychohistory.

The few works that have followed the lead of Arthur M. Schlesinger, Jr., *The Imperial Presidency* (Boston: Houghton Mifflin, 1973) include Godfrey Hodgson, *All Things to All Men: The False Promise of the American Presidency* (New York: Simon & Schuster, 1980) and Barton J. Bernstein, "The Road to Watergate and Beyond: The Growth and Abuse of Executive Authority since 1940," *Law and Contemporary Problems* (vol. 40 [Spring 1976], 58–86).

The body of scholarship that connects Watergate to foreign policy and intelligence skullduggery is slightly larger. Kathryn Olmsted, *Challenging the Secret Government: The Post-Watergate Investigations of the CIA and FBI* (Chapel Hill: University of North Carolina Press, 1996) offers a sobering account of the CIA and FBI scandals, showing that press coverage overall was timorous. Seymour M. Hersh, *The Price of Power: Kissinger in the Nixon White House* (New York: Simon & Schuster) is an essential but exceedingly detailed work by one of the few journalists to dig deeply. *Spying on Americans: Political Surveillance from Hoover to the Huston Plan* (Philadelphia: Temple University Press, 1978), by Athan J. Theoharis, looks at domestic surveillance.

For a scholarly effort by a political scientist to compare Watergate, Iran-Contra and Whitewater, see James P. Pfiffner, "Three Crises of Character in the Modern Presidency," in *Understanding the Presidency* (3rd ed. [New York: Pearson Longman, 2005]), edited by James P. Pfiffner and Roger H. Davidson, 424–441. For a reliable account of the scandal that rocked the Clinton presidency, see Jeffrey Toobin, *A Vast Conspiracy: The Real Story of the Sex Scandal that Nearly Brought Down a President* (New York: Random House, 2000). *Firewall: The Iran-Contra Conspiracy and Cover-Up* (New York: Norton, 1997), by Lawrence E. Walsh, the special prosecutor who investigated Iran-Contra, is an authoritative discussion of that presidential scandal.

Primary Sources

For a number of significant primary sources regarding the Watergate affair, including Nixon's resignation and farewell speeches, the articles of impeachment, and transcripts of several key Watergate tapes, including Nixon's June 23, 1972, conversation with chief aide H. R. Haldeman, known as the "smoking gun" tape, go to www.ku.edu/carrie/docs/amdocs_index.html#1970 and click on the documents listed under "Watergate Affair, 1972–1976." Those wishing to listen to portions of the Watergate tapes should go to www.hpol.org/master.php?t=browse&s=speaker&id=19. Click on a tape excerpt; then click on the option "Listen". Transcripts are also accessible by clicking on the option "View Transcript/Log." A collection of well-known Herblock cartoons about Nixon and Watergate, which gives a good sense of the liberal dismay over Nixon's illegal actions and more generally of the political climate of the Nixon era, may be found at www.loc.gov/rr/print/swann/herblock/crook.html. The reports of the Church Committee (the Senate Select Committee to Study Governmental Operations with Respect to Intelligence Activities), including "Alleged Assassination Plots Involving Foreign Leaders," may be found at historymatters.com/archive/church/contents.htm. An overview of the Reagan-era Iran-Contra scandal, in the form of the Final Report of the Independent Counsel for Iran/Contra Matters, may be found at www.fas.org/irp/offdocs/walsh/. For documents on the impeachment of President William Jefferson Clinton, including grand jury testimony, articles of impeachment and the Independent Counsel Report, go to www.lib.umich.edu/govdocs/ impeach.html.

PART **III**

A New Domestic and World Order

11

The Conservative Ascendancy

INTRODUCTION

The election of Ronald W. Reagan to the presidency in 1980 proved to be a political watershed for America. Reagan represented the right wing of the Republican party, a movement whose radicalism had been rejected decisively in 1964 when voters overwhelmingly chose Democrat Lyndon Johnson over Republican Barry Goldwater for president. Sixteen years after that debacle for the political right, Reagan gained the highest office in the land, articulating an antitax, antiwelfare, antiregulation agenda that challenged the views that had dominated political and economic discourse in the United States since the New Deal of the 1930s, and on some issues, since the turn-of-the-century presidency of Theodore Roosevelt. Reagan also campaigned against many of the developments associated with the Sixties, criticizing environmental protections, civil rights laws, and abortion rights. The conventional wisdom in 1980, as recalled by one journalist, was that Reagan was "too old, too unserious and most of all, too conservative" to win the election. But he did win—decisively—and that victory transformed politics in America, putting liberalism on the defensive and making mainstream views that, a short time earlier, had routinely been described as marginal and reactionary.

Such significant and rapid change requires explanation. In the years since Reagan's election, scholars have sought to explain the history of conservatism (the term long used to denote the American right) and to explore how the right propelled itself out of the doldrums of the 1960s to a position of commanding influence. Some have focused on the major conservative figures who preceded Reagan, such as Goldwater and Alabama Governor George Wallace, whose insurgent presidential campaigns in 1964, 1968, and 1972 helped establish themes for right-wing political appeals in later years. Other historians have turned much-needed attention to conservatism's base, scrutinizing grassroots organizing in particular locales and documenting the development of the "Christian right" as a political force. Also receiving attention have been the so-called Reagan Democrats—the blue-collar and lower-middle-class white voters who, beginning in the late 1960s, began shifting their support from the Democratic party to right-wing politicians. These inquiries into the ranks of "downscale" conservative voters are of particular interest because the right, traditionally, had difficulty attracting such support because of its association with wealth and privilege and its often explicit elitism.

Collectively, this work has shown that the American right drew on a succession of issues to rally support in the three-and-a-half decades between 1945 and Reagan's election in 1980. First, in the 1940s and 1950s, anticommunism galvanized the right (see Chapter 3). Then, in the 1950s and 1960s, conservatives drew on white opposition, first and foremost in the South, to the civil rights movement and its agenda of social equality. Starting in earnest in the late 1970s and up to now, the right has championed "family values" as a challenge to the sexual revolution, the gay rights movement, the legalization of abortion, and the expansion of women's social roles, all of which "movement" conservatives have viewed as symptoms of a spreading moral decadence in American society, a decay that purportedly began or at least advanced greatly in the Sixties. The burdens of government taxation also became an important conservative theme in the 1970s. The antitax movement achieved its signal success in the passage by California voters in 1978 of Proposition 13, a ballot initiative that radically limited property tax increases for both businesses and homeowners, and popularized the notion of a citizen-based tax revolt. Reagan's adoption of antitax rhetoric in the campaign of 1980 contributed to his defeat of Jimmy Carter.

The right worked effectively to link each of these perceived evils—communism, government-mandated racial equality, changes in the family and morality, and onerous taxation—to political liberalism in the public mind. Starting with Wallace, political leaders and thinkers on the right used the figure of the "government bureaucrat" bent on social engineering to embody the liberalism they opposed. Such bureaucrats were included in the broader category of the "cultural" or "liberal" elite, which, in the view of the right, advanced all four evils, wittingly or not. Richard Nixon and Ronald Reagan followed Wallace's lead and used the twin bogies of liberal bureaucrats and the cultural elite to fashion a right-wing populism, much in the way that liberals had earlier played on the enmity toward an economic elite to create a winning coalition of blue-collar, "ethnic," and African American voters. That earlier "New Deal coalition," dating from the 1930s and rooted in a desire for economic opportunity and security, had joined black and white voters and working-class and middle-class Americans in a successful formula for the Democratic party. That coalition had been the bane of the Republicans for decades by the 1960s, and the new right-wing populism proved effective in driving a wedge between different elements of the New Deal coalition.

Because the scholarly work on the post-1945 right has developed so recently and rapidly, the major interpretive differences are still becoming clear. Here we reproduce three readings that offer different perspectives on the rise of the right. The first reading is an excerpt from the influential 1991 book *Chain Reaction: The Impact of Race, Rights, and Taxes on American Politics,* by the journalists Thomas B. Edsall and Mary Edsall. As the book's title indicates, the Edsalls believe that a wide array of issues came together in the 1970s and 1980s to make the appeal of conservatism newly powerful. But they state emphatically that the issue of race was the catalyst that provoked the "chain reaction" leading to the formation of a conservative political majority in America. The success of the right, in their view, depended on the reaction against the liberalism that began to take shape in the Sixties—a "new liberalism" that was epitomized in Democrat George McGovern's 1972 presidential campaign. The new liberalism endorsed new rights for criminal defendants, for women, and for racial minorities, and advocated new methods of achieving racial equality, including affirmative action and busing of school children to achieve integration. According to the Edsalls, these ideas and the accompanying government policies caused many working-class and middle-class white Americans to switch their loyalties from the Democratic party to the Republican party and to vote for Nixon, who gave voice to this "white backlash" with his appeals to the "silent majority" and the "nonshouters, the nondemonstrators."

If Nixon, with his staunch opposition to busing, began the process of winning these former Democrats over to the Republican party, it was Reagan who completed the conversion process. Campaigning in the South in 1980, he championed the doctrine of "states' rights," a widely understood code for opposition to racial integration, and one that had been taboo in presidential politics ever since Goldwater (with Reagan's support) had embraced it in 1964. In the Edsalls' view, Republicans gained their hold on national power through a racially charged ensemble of issues that secured the allegiance of enough swing voters to ensure electoral victory. Although one may question whether the new liberalism was really as prominent within the Democratic party and as pro–African American as the Edsalls assert, *Chain Reaction* makes a powerful case that many white Americans shared these perceptions, and that this image of the Democratic party as too focused on helping African Americans was a key factor in the conservative ascendancy within American politics.

The second reading is an excerpt from the 2001 book, *Suburban Warriors: The Origins of the New American Right,* by Lisa McGirr. In her view, the essential story in the rise of the right is not that of the swing voters whom the Edsalls highlight; rather, it is that of the grassroots movement conservatives—the activists who brought the right from the political margins in the early 1960s to center stage in later decades. McGirr argues that, in geographic terms, we should direct our attention to the "Sunbelt" of the Southwest, particularly to the "southland" of California, the highly conservative region that was friendly to Barry Goldwater and home to Ronald Reagan. She tells the stories of individuals who were the foot soldiers of the right in Orange County, a suburban area south of Los Angeles that was developed largely after World War II. McGirr documents the transition of the right from the older preoccupation with communism (Orange County was the birthplace of the John Birch Society, the embodiment of anticommunist extremism) to a new set of issues after Reagan's 1966 election as governor of California on a platform opposing various aspects of Sixties-era social liberalism and radicalism. McGirr shows how the "social issues" of obscenity, sex education, abortion, and feminism brought longtime rightists together with new recruits from Catholic Democratic families and Protestant evangelicals in the late 1960s and 1970s. To her, these were the issues that brought coherence to a new generation of the American right. She closes her discussion, however, by arguing that these social issues tended to be divisive, not only in society as a whole but also within the ranks of the right. Thus McGirr suggests that the very issues that fueled the grassroots right after domestic communism and formal desegregation faded as political concerns in the United States also imposed limits on the right's political appeal.

By the time Reagan left the White House in 1989, many movement conservatives expressed disappointment with his leadership on the "social issues" that motivated the Republican political base. Reagan had pledged to support a Human Life Amendment to the Constitution, which would have outlawed abortion, but it never came close to passage. His Justice Department took positions on a number of issues that enraged the civil rights lobby, but Reagan generally lost these battles in the end. The conservative movement moved on to new efforts to influence American society through the force of government action, mainly in connection with the Republican party.

The third reading for this chapter, taken from the 2004 book *What's the Matter with Kansas?* by historian and journalist Thomas Frank, focuses not on the Sunbelt but on a midwestern state that he sees as epitomizing the political turn to the right in the nation as a whole. He also explores a later period than do McGirr and the Edsalls, looking at developments after 1994, a year when the Republican party gained control of both houses of Congress and numerous representatives of the new-wave right gained power and prominence. In Frank's view, the essence of this form of right-wing politics is an obsessive focus on America's alleged moral decline—as reflected in the increasing acceptance of homosexuality, the supposedly liberal stranglehold on the nation's education system, and a general coarsening of popular culture—largely as a way to distract voters from economic concerns and significant inequalities of wealth among social classes. Like McGirr, Frank pays attention to the shock troops of the right; in this case, these are the working-class people who, through hard work and good organization, have done so much to advance their moral agenda. Frank respects the dedication of the conservative movement's cadres, and he is sympathetic to some of their concerns, agreeing in particular that popular culture has become crude and morally offensive in recent years. But he also sees them as having been gulled by the political leaders of the right, who have succeeded in stirring their moral outrage and at the same time gotten them to advance a plutocratic agenda that favors the wealthy and hurts those with modest incomes. In other words, these citizens, many of them middle class or working class, have been misled by representatives of the rich into voting and working against their own objective economic interests. Frank's contention that the moral issues that have motivated these voters are not as important or fundamental as economic concerns has led some to accuse him of condescension. But in his passionate denunciation of the right's agenda and logic, Frank unapologetically asserts that people do have objective economic interests, and that no one understands this better than the wealthy interests who have allied themselves with and helped steer the conservative movement.

THOMAS BYRNE EDSALL
AND MARY D. EDSALL

Race, Rights, and American Politics

For Richard Nixon, the commitment of the Democratic party in 1972 to an expanding rights revolution provided the ideal opportunity to enlarge upon the strategies he—and George Wallace—had pioneered in 1968. Focusing public attention on the costs of the new liberalism, Nixon sought to provide positive moral and ideological legitimacy to those who did not want to pay those costs. Of the worker concerned about high taxes, Nixon said: "I don't think it is right to charge him with selfishness, with not caring about the poor and the dependent." To the mother concerned about court-ordered busing, he declared: "When a mother sees her child taken away from a neighborhood school and transported miles away, and she objects to that, I don't think it's right to charge her with bigotry."

In a critically important expansion of these arguments Nixon set out to establish positive grounds for the rejection of the kinds of social responsibilities that were raised by the civil rights movement—presaging the conservative ideological framework articulated far more consistently by Ronald Reagan. Nixon concluded an October 21, 1972, radio address with a direct assault on the demand for middle-class sacrifice in behalf of the most disadvantaged that had become an integral aspect of the liberal position:

> There is no reason to feel guilty about wanting to enjoy what you get and what you earn, about wanting your children in good schools close to home or about wanting to be judged fairly on your ability. Those are not values to be ashamed of; those are values to be proud of. Those are values that I shall always stand up for when they come under attack.

Nixon in 1972, seeking to secure the shifting loyalties of the white working class, turned presidential rhetoric against the major civil rights initiative of his own first administration—[the affirmative action initiative known as] the Philadelphia Plan. Although Nixon had fought for the plan in 1969, by 1972 he sought to reap political reward from stockpiled blue-collar resentments: "When young people apply for jobs . . . and find the door closed because they don't fit into some numerical quota, despite their ability, and they object, I do not think it is right to condemn those young people as insensitive or even racist."

In retrospect, two elements of Nixon's 1972 campaign strategy are striking: 1) the degree to which the underlying theme of race is repeatedly stressed, in the references to busing and to affirmative action; and, 2) the extraordinary degree to which Nixon anticipated the social-issue agenda of the conservative Republican revolution that swept Ronald Reagan into office in 1980. Nixon, expanding on themes introduced into national politics by Wallace, effectively established the groundwork for the anti-tax ideology of the 1980s, repeatedly rejecting a "liberal" paradigm centered around "social responsibility," in favor of a conservative paradigm centered around "legitimate self-interest."

Nixon saw the polarizing power of racial issues such as busing and affirmative action—issues that came to dominate the civil rights agenda in the wake of the demolition of legal barriers to equal opportunity. In the process of both provoking and responding to voter concerns about race, Nixon, and a handful of strategists within the Republican party, recognized the catalytic power of race to transform the content of the political debate. Race facilitated the beginning of an ideologically conservative conversion of the electorate, as the social costs of programs such as housing integration, busing, and affirmative action became indissolubly fused in the minds of crucial numbers of voters with steeply rising taxes, cultural metamorphosis, increases in violent crime, expanding welfare rolls, greater numbers of illegitimate children, and evidence of the deterioration of both black and white family structures.

Race gave new strength to themes that in the past had been secondary—themes always present in American politics, but which had previously lacked, in themselves, mobilizing power. Race was central, Nixon and key Republican strategists began to recognize, to the fundamental conservative strategy of establishing a new, non-economic polarization of the electorate, a polarization isolating a liberal, activist, culturally-permissive, rights-oriented, and pro-black Democratic party against those unwilling to pay the financial and social costs of this reconfigured social order.

Nixon in 1972 advanced an emerging conservative strategy, using new techniques and tactics to insure his own landslide re-election; but the circumstances were not yet ripe to bring these techniques and tactics to bear on the task of deliberately building a broadened Republican party.

In 1972, the post–World War II economic boom had not quite come to a halt, and the Democratic party still dominated the legislative agenda. . . .

By 1980, the opportunity to merge the interests of the white working man with those of traditional Republican pro-business, free-marketeers had arrived in full force. The issues of taxes, of an ailing economy, and of the collective set of grievances closely linked to race and rights— including crime, affirmative action, welfare spending, busing, IRS regulation of the Christian school movement, women's liberation, homosexual rights, abortion, etc.—had reached an unprecedented level of intensity among key segments of the white electorate. This intensity provided Reagan and the Republican party with the opportunity to activate a new set of polarizing issues to rupture the frayed class base of a traditional, economically-oriented Democratic liberalism.

Inflation, spiraling interest rates, and rising taxes during the last two years of the Carter administration effectively ensured a Republican presidential victory in 1980—and insured as well substantial GOP House and Senate gains. But the scope of the conservative victory depended heavily on an underlying ideological shift: the Republican party and an emerging populist-conservative ideology, for the first time in fifty years, captured from the Democratic party and from liberalism a piece of the moral high ground, staking out a new conservative claim by key segments of the white electorate to the long-standing tradition of an idealized American egalitarianism.

The political equation was relatively straightforward. Democratic liberalism by the end of the 1970s was judged by many voters to have failed to live up to a basic political obligation: that of rewarding and protecting its own constituents. At the height of Democratic liberal ascendancy—between 1974 and 1980—core Democratic voting blocs suffered from the consequences of economic stagnation and, in many sectors, from outright economic decline.

At the same time, the national Democratic party became more closely associated with a rights agenda that had moved past equal opportunity to support for overtly remedial and redistributive measures—particularly for busing and racial preferences. These preferential measures, seeking to rectify the effects of past discrimination against one group, now inevitably imposed substantial costs on another.

Racially preferential remedies, particularly those created by the federal judiciary, were largely instituted without being subjected to the political or legislative process. Court-established remedies, in consequence, regardless of their moral justifiability or of their merits in creating an enlarged black middle class, not only lacked firm public support, but were, in fact, opposed by decisive majorities of white voters.

The positions adopted by the national Democratic party in favor of racial preferences and busing were critical in allowing the national Republican party to take over the political and philosophical center. Sixteen years earlier, in the 1964 election, Goldwater's conservative stands on privacy, property, and states' rights had served as an umbrella sheltering and protecting from the taint of an explicit ideology of white supremacy Southern voters seeking to avoid integration.

In the context of the civil rights issues of 1964—at a time when a majority of the northern public, moved by the nonviolent, church-based struggle of blacks, was in favor of the relatively modest goals of the early civil rights movement—Goldwater was widely perceived as being *against* "equality of opportunity." By 1980, the content of the civil rights agenda had shifted so that Ronald Reagan—who in 1964 had shared Goldwater's views—was able to become the *advocate* of "equal opportunity," and to remain at the same time firmly in the conservative camp.

As racial battles were fought less over legally prohibited *access* to opportunity—prohibitions institutionalized under legal segregation—and fought more, as the sixties and seventies unrolled, over such affirmative remedies as minority preferences in hiring and busing, "equal opportunity" became a Republican standard, and included among its supporters racial conservatives, including those who were in fact anti-black, as well as much of the moderate center, and the ideological right.

In terms of public opinion among whites, the Republican stand, focused on "opportunity"—however illusory—was backed by the overwhelming majority of voters. As early as 1972, 97 percent of whites polled said blacks should have "as good a chance" to get any job as whites, and by 1980, 88 percent of whites said black and white students should go to the same schools. Whites, however, sharply opposed out-and-out racial preferences. The number of whites in a 1980 poll opposed to the government providing "special help" to minorities outnumbered those favoring such help by a margin of 65–35. By 1985, when tougher questions asked respondents specifically about racial preference in hiring, whites were opposed by a margin of 87–13; in the case of college and university admissions, whites were opposed to racial preferences by a margin of 74–26.

The changing politics of civil rights permitted the Republican party to achieve its central goal—the establishment of a putatively egalitarian, ideologically respectable, conservatism. In 1980, Reagan and the GOP portrayed *opposition* to central elements of civil rights enforcement—opposition to the use of race and sex preferences in hiring and in college admittance, to court-ordered busing, and to the introduction of means-tested programs for the poor—as deriving from a principled concern for fairness: as a form of populist opposition to the granting of special privilege.

"The truths we hold and the values we share affirm that no individual should be victimized by unfair discrimination because of race, sex, advanced age, physical handicap, difference of national origin or religion, or economic circumstance," the 1980 Republican Platform declared. "However, equal opportunity should not be jeopardized by bureaucratic regulation and decisions which rely on quotas, ratios and numerical requirements to exclude some individuals in favor of others, thereby rendering such regulations and decisions inherently discriminatory."

Together with opposition to rising taxes on the working and middle classes, conservatism—with its new "anti-discriminatory," meritocratic, and egalitarian rhetoric—became a powerful political weapon.

The racial basis of conservative egalitarianism served as a key factor in the diversion of populist resentment away from the rich and toward the poor, toward minorities, and toward the federal government. Unlike liberal egalitarianism, which focused public attention on the regressive distribution of income, on the need for a progressive tax system, and on the exploitation of working men and women by a political and social system controlled by and for an economic elite, conservative egalitarianism focused on the inequities imposed by liberalism.

The fundamental strategy developed by George Wallace, of creating the specter of a coercive Democratic liberal establishment—a powerful centralized, bureaucratic, and unresponsive government imposing its regulatory will and its tax collectors on a hard-pressed electorate—reached its full dimensions in the Reagan campaign of 1980.

"If you look at American politics, what you've always had is an antiestablishment thing out there. For about 150–160 years, the establishment was always business. You go back to the agrarian revolt, the establishment was always business. [Franklin] Roosevelt comes in and established another establishment and it was government. And so you have for the first time two establishments," explained Lee Atwater, who served as deputy campaign manager for Reagan, as campaign manager for George Bush, and as chairman of the Republican National Committee.

"In the 1980 campaign, we were able to make the establishment, in so far as it is bad, the government. In other words, big government was the enemy, not big business. . . . If the people are thinking that the problem is that taxes are too high and government interferes too much, then we [Republicans] are doing our job. But, if they get to the point where they say the real problem is that rich people aren't paying taxes, that Republicans are protecting the Realtors and so forth, then I think the Democrats are going to be in pretty good shape. The National Enquirer readership is the exact voter I'm talking about. . . . There are always some stories in there about some multimillionaire that has five Cadillacs and hasn't paid taxes since 1974, or so-and-so Republican Congressman hasn't paid taxes since he got into Congress. And they'll have another set of stories of a guy sitting around in a big den with liquor saying so and so fills his den with liquor using food stamps. So it's which one of those establishments the public sees as a bad guy [that determines whether conservative or liberal egalitarianism is ascendant]. . . .

In the debate over the rights and responsibilities of both government and of its citizenry that emerged out of the intensified conflict between liberalism and conservatism in the late 1970s and early 1980s, the role of race in helping to build a working conservative political majority should not be underestimated. Race was embedded in conflicts surrounding tax, spending, education, welfare, regulatory, and industrial policy. The racial consequences of policy alternatives—inescapable because of racial differences in income, in reliance on government benefits, in job and family patterns, in rates of criminality, in demographics, in suburban versus urban residential trends, as well as in a host of other measures—became integral to the structuring of the political debate, sometimes explicitly, sometimes implicitly. In the construction of a conservative ideological edifice, race served, in effect, to increase the bonding power of brick to mortar.

In making the case in 1980 for his own presidential candidacy and for a major retrenchment in domestic spending, Ronald Reagan made explicitly clear that the target of his planned assault on government would be the means-tested programs serving poor constituencies, heavily black and Hispanic, that had become the focus of much public hostility to government. One of Reagan's favorite and most often-repeated anecdotes was the story of a Chicago "welfare queen" with "80 names, 30 addresses, 12 Social Security cards" whose "tax-free income alone is over $150,000." The food stamp program, in turn, was a vehicle to let "some fellow ahead of you buy T-bone steak" while "you were standing in a checkout line with your package of hamburger."

These campaign appeals and strategies on the part of Reagan and the Republican party revived the sharply polarized racial images of the two parties—a polarization that had characterized the Johnson-Goldwater contest. By 1980, the racial polarization of the two parties was to prove highly profitable to Republicans, with racial conservatism contributing decisively to the GOP advantage.

This shift in the marketability of racial conservatism to the majority electorate reflected the degree to which public attitudes toward civil rights had changed in a matter of sixteen years. If, in 1964, Goldwater's racial conservatism had been catastrophic for his party, by 1980, the white public had become far more ambivalent—torn between support for the principle of racial justice, but opposed to aggressive mechanisms to remedy discrimination. In 1980, the majority public saw Reagan and the Republican party as conservative on matters pertaining to minority America, but this was no longer a liability; it had, in fact, become an advantage.

In 1964, . . . 60 percent of respondents said that the Democratic party was more likely to provide fair employment treatment of blacks, while only 7 percent said the GOP was more likely. This gap between the parties narrowed somewhat after 1964, when the GOP presidential banner was carried by Richard Nixon and Gerald Ford, each more moderate on civil rights than

Goldwater. In 1972 and in 1976 (in response to a slightly different question), the number of voters who saw the GOP as unlikely to help minorities outnumbered, by a very small 4–3 margin, those who saw the Republican party as supportive of minority interests. In 1976, for example, with Carter and Ford as the presidential nominees, 33 percent of poll respondents described the GOP as likely to help minorities, and 40 percent described the party as unlikely to do so, for a net 7 percent point balance on the conservative side of the ledger (with the remainder placing the party in the center or holding no opinion). The Democratic party throughout this period remained the party of racial liberalism: 64.8 percent of those surveyed in 1976 said the Democratic party was likely to adopt policies favoring minorities, while only 14 percent said the Democratic party was unlikely to help minorities, for a liberal tilt of 50.8 percentage points.

In 1980, with Reagan at the top of the ticket (Reagan's record included opposition to the Civil Rights Acts of 1964 and 1965, opposition to fair-housing legislation, and opposition to a holiday honoring Martin Luther King, Jr.), the public image of the Republican party became again sharply more conservative on racial issues. That year, by a margin of better than 6 to 1, the electorate saw the GOP as unlikely to help minorities.

With Reagan heading the ticket, the racial conservatism of the GOP matched the racial liberalism of the Democratic party. The racial polarization of the parties coincided with the larger fusion of race, partisanship, and ideology that had been building throughout the 1970s, a process that culminated in the sharp turn to the right in domestic politics in 1980. Liberalism, which before the civil rights revolution had been seen by a majority of voters as largely race-neutral—as primarily an economic philosophy of government intervention in behalf of the nation's "have-nots"—became, in the wake of the civil rights movement, closely associated with issues linked to race.

Analysis of 1972 and 1976 National Election Studies (NES) data by political scientists Edward G. Carmines and James A. Stimson shows that some of the strongest divisions between voters identifying themselves as liberals and conservatives were over attitudes toward black protests and urban unrest, attitudes toward segregation and integration, and attitudes toward protecting the rights of criminal defendants, and that these divisions paralleled the more traditional liberal-conservative conflict over the responsibility of government to provide employment and fair wages. In both 1972 and 1976, racial issues were more important in defining differences between liberals and conservatives than stands on the question of the progressivity of tax rates—a traditional centerpiece of economic liberalism.

The growing salience of racial issues in determining liberal-conservative differences applied even more strongly to the parties themselves. John Petrocik of UCLA, found that through the 1970s, "Republican identifiers became less sympathetic toward blacks, Democratic identifiers adopted a distinctly pro-black posture compared with the 1950s, and the size of the interparty difference [on race] began to rival Democratic-Republican disagreement" on such traditionally partisan economic issues as domestic government spending.

Carmines and Stimson, in turn, have tracked this growing divergence on racial policy between self-identified Democratic and Republican voters. On the basis of responses to a range of questions (including, "Are civil rights leaders pushing too fast, too slow or about right?" "Should the federal government prevent discrimination in housing, schools and public accommodations?" and "Do you support segregation, desegregation or something in between?") Carmines and Stimson found that the racial attitudes of Republicans and Democrats began to diverge sharply in 1964, with Republicans becoming decisively conservative and Democrats decisively liberal.

In other words, in the years following the civil rights legislation of the 1960s, racial attitudes became a central characteristic of both ideology and party identification, integral to voters' choices between Democrats and Republicans, and integral to choices between policy positions on a range of non-racial issues traditionally identified with liberalism and conservatism. At the same time, a wide range of social developments, including the emergence of a growing urban underclass and the associated problems of crime, joblessness, and urban school failure, were becoming, in the public mind, indelibly associated with race through the growing body of statistical information demonstrating disproportionate black involvement; through media coverage of crime, of declining labor-force participation among black males, and of a long-term (sometimes multi-generational) welfare clientele; and through increased public policy and academic interest in the intractable persistence of black and Hispanic poverty.

The intensified racial polarization of the two parties coincided with a shift to the right in public opinion—a shift with strong racial overtones and one that made the electorate more receptive to the Reagan administration's 1981 budget-cutting and tax-cutting proposals. The intensified conservatism of the majority public by 1980 on policy issues relating to race should not be misread as an across-the-board movement to the right or towards economic conservatism in general: within overall trends showing increased opposition to government spending and to federal tax levels, the focus of the electorate's ire was measurably on programs serving the poor and blacks.

One of the strongest signals of a rising anti-government form of conservatism lay in the response to questions asking whether government was getting too powerful. In 1980, 49 percent of the polled electorate viewed government as too powerful, more than triple the 15 percent who thought government was not too strong. This was the highest anti-government ratio since the question was first asked in 1964. Similarly, support for government action to reduce income inequality fell to a low point in 1980, while the percentage of voters who thought their federal income taxes were too high reached 68 percent that year.

On close examination, the anti-tax, anti-government view of the electorate in 1980 was very specifically directed. It did not, for example, reflect diminished support for higher government spending on education, health, Social Security, crime control, drug addiction control, and environmental protection—all of which retained unstinting, and in some cases growing, majority support. In the case of the military, public support for increased spending grew decisively after the Soviet invasion of Afghanistan and after the seizure of hostages in Iran. While the percentage of the electorate saying that "too little" was being spent on defense had remained in the range of 23 to 31 percent through most of the 1970s, in 1980, it shot up to 56 percent.

Public anger at government in 1980, in fact, was directed at programs serving heavily minority and poor populations. This closely paralleled the findings of surveys of California voters during the tax revolt debate of the late 1970s, when the only programs that a majority of voters sought to cut were welfare and public housing. In 1978 and 1980, national support for increased spending to improve the condition of blacks fell to a record low, 24 percent. Opposition to welfare spending reached its highest level in 1976, and remained there through 1980. The percentage of respondents in 1980 saying that blacks and other minorities should help themselves, 41 percent, versus those saying that government should improve the social and economic position of blacks, 19 percent, was at an all-time high, compared to 37–29 in 1976, and 38–31 in 1972.

A significant segment, a "swing" sector, of the white public had come to make a distinction between what Republican pollsters called "good welfare"—Social Security, education, health, police—and "bad welfare"—food stamps, Aid to Families with Dependent Children, and other means-tested programs favoring poor or near-poor heavily black and Hispanic constituencies. This distinction provided the ideal wedge for the Republican party to use to further divide the Democratic coalition, a wedge that Reagan was ideally situated to exploit to maximum advantage.

LISA McGIRR

Suburban Warriors

By the late 1960s, the right had made important political gains in both California and the nation. Ronald Reagan, an unabashed conservative ideologue, had won a resounding victory in his run for governor. Richard Nixon, a centrist Republican who courted the Republican right, had become his party's presidential nominee and won the election through an embrace of a new middle-class conservatism, even while George Wallace, a law-and-order populist, had garnered 13.5 percent of the national vote on a third-party ticket. Building on new opportunities, the right had refashioned itself, gaining new political respectability. As the late 1960s witnessed antiwar protests, a flourishing counterculture, and riots in the nation's inner cities, the conservative critique of liberalism resonated with an increasing number of Americans.

Increased political opportunities and the rise of new social issues had an uneven impact on the decade-old conservative movement in Orange County. Older organizations that had been so critical to the mobilizations earlier in the decade declined, and new conservative initiatives sprang up—often led by activists who had gotten their start in politics in the Goldwater movement. The center of grassroots activity moved away from the anticommunist study groups and home meetings of the early 1960s and toward new single-issue campaigns, as well as to a conservative religious awakening. Moreover, while some older recruits and activists dropped out, new participants joined the fray. . . .

As conservative elites moved closer to the halls of power, the grassroots activists invigorated their movement by increasingly focusing on single-issue campaigns. These new issues expressed some of the same general concerns over moral corruption and traditional values that previously had been subsumed under the rubric of anticommunism. But these concerns now took on new dimensions, in large part in reaction to changes in family life, sexual liberation, a growing youth culture, and liberal Supreme Court decisions that expanded the scope of personal freedoms. As a result, various forms of "domestic corruption"—obscenity, sex education, abortion, and, by the late 1970s, an ever more assertive gay liberation movement—became the new targets of attack. And the enemy responsible for such ills was no longer an international, public, and political opponent, but the secular humanists in one's own community. These new issues drew in activists from among discontented Democrats who had previously been part of the liberal coalition.

Obscenity was one arena in which conservatives expressed growing dismay over the expansion of personal freedoms. Concerns over "filth" and "immorality" had preoccupied conservatives since early in the decade, after a Supreme Court decision of 1962 made prosecution of "obscenity" increasingly difficult. The Catholic newspaper the *Tidings,* among others, had warned southland Catholics of the dangers posed by pornography to the values and morals of the nation. When, in 1964, the Supreme Court, in *Jacobellis v. Ohio,* required that questionable material must be without "redeeming social importance" to be censored, making prosecution of obscenity even more difficult, conservatives feared that "decadence" and "moral decay" would destroy the moral fiber of the nation.

These concerns led southland right-wing forces to sponsor Proposition 16 for the November ballot in 1966. The measure was promoted by a group calling itself California League for Enlisting Action Now (CLEAN), whose advisory board included such future national Christian right leaders as Timothy LaHaye (then pastor of Scott's Memorial Baptist Church in San Diego) and William Dannemeyer (then state assemblyman from Orange County). The initiative gained the support of prominent businesspeople, such as Patrick Frawley of the Eversharp and Schick Razor Company, Joe Crail of the Coast Federal Savings and Loan Association, and Orange County's Walter Knott. They and others were attracted to the measure because it promised to redefine pornography, disregarding the Supreme Court's exemption of works tinged with "redeeming social importance"—and it sought to put regulatory control in the hands of local communities. Reagan strongly endorsed the ballot initiative, gaining the accolades and gratitude of social conservatives. It had sufficient backing in Orange County to win a majority at the polls. While the measure did not convince the state's voters, conservative Orange Countians continued to mobilize around the issue within their local communities. In 1969, spurred on by a campaign led by the *Anaheim Bulletin* (part of libertarian R. C. Hoiles's "Freedom" newspaper chain), they shut down the Anaheim Chamber of Commerce for a day to display the "lewd and lascivious materials" that were available at local newsstands. Local business boosters were central to the anti-obscenity crusade. The educational arm of the local Anaheim Chamber of Commerce, for example, eagerly worked to root out "smut."

Following these campaigns, in the early 1970s, the county itself undertook the prosecution of obscenity when a Newport Beach restaurant owner complained to the police after receiving mail advertising illustrated books and films for adults. The incident eventually led to the influential 1973 Supreme Court decision in *Miller v. California,* which cheered anti-obscenity advocates while raising the hackles of civil libertarians. In it, the Court favored respecting local sentiments in making decisions about what constituted obscenity and held that prurient, offensive depictions must have "serious literary, artistic, political, or scientific value" to merit First Amendment coverage. The decision, which historian Margaret Blanchard described as "another aspect of the conservative revolution being engineered by Richard Nixon," was, in her words, a "giant step backward" for the cause of free speech.

The fight over sex education in the school systems was another arena where grassroots conservatives voiced concerns over "domestic corruption." In 1969, a band of dedicated Orange County conservatives made national headlines with their vigorous, and eventually successful, campaign to uproot a prominent and innovative sex education program. The issue clearly marked the reorientation of the movement not only in its focus on explicit moral issues but also in its language and the cast of enemies it targeted. While earlier in the decade such a struggle would certainly have been blamed on a communist drive to undermine the morals of youth, now "secular humanists" were targeted as the force lurking behind the threat to morals, values, and the family. In a similar vein, however, the accusations were tinged with conspiratorial utterances, demonstrating the linkages to an earlier discourse.

The conflict was rooted in the development of a curriculum by Paul Cook, superintendent of the Anaheim Union School District. Under Cook's guidance, the district became one of the first large school districts in the country to establish a broad sex education program, with the help of the Sex Information and Education Council of the United States (SIECUS). The district encompassed more than 30,000 pupils in twenty-five schools. In 1968, a year after the course had gone into full operation, it came under attack. Eleanor Howe, an Anaheim mother of four and a receptionist at Kwik-Set Lock Company, whose husband was a retired Marine Corps pilot, sparked the initiative when she wrote a letter to the *Anaheim Bulletin* condemning the program and calling for action against it. Howe, a devout Catholic and a conservative who had cast her first Republican vote for Goldwater in 1964, gathered information about the program and sought to mobilize opposition. She and Jim Townsend, who had been active in local conservative circles since the Conservative Coordinating Council was born in 1961, spearheaded opposition under the rubric of the California Citizens' Committee, a grassroots organization he helped found that had strongly backed Goldwater. Later, they were joined by Jan Pippinger, a born-again Christian whose husband was the manager of a meat storage center for the Lucky Food Stores chain, along with other concerned parents, mostly women, many of them devoutly religious. In the summer of 1968, they came before the school board to launch a formal complaint, demanding an end to the program. While the program had faced opposition before, in 1968 it came under full-scale attack as "godless, pornographic, and an affront to family privacy."

The viciousness of the opposition to the sex education program was in some ways surprising because the curriculum itself was hardly radical. Developed with the support of local clergy and community organizations in response to changing sexual mores, it emphasized the negative consequences of premarital sex and was, according to its proponents, "designed to produce good family members." Still, it represented a departure: Its broad and inclusive nature was an entirely new arena of "social engineering," usurping an area of authority that had previously been left to parents. Moreover, the Anaheim school administrators asserted that FLSE [Family Life and Sex Education] program discussion groups were intended to encourage students to make their own moral judgments about sexual and social behavior within the context of community norms. Many religious conservatives resented this relativizing of moral absolutes, seeing in it a threat to Christian beliefs and values.

Clearly, fears about the social changes of the decade underpinned support for the sex education struggle and for the right-wing conspiratorial utterances with which it was tinged. Conspiracy theories, embraced by the most zealous opponents, provided middle-class conservatives a safe explanation for young people's challenge to an older set of values. . . .

The sex education programs did promote more liberal values than those of staunch religious conservatives. This, opponents believed, undermined parental authority. As one pamphlet argued, "What the sex educators have in mind is simply this: Sex should be as easily discussed as any other subject in the curriculum, and any inhibitions, or moral and religious taboos should be eliminated. This obviously drives a wedge between the family, church and school, bolstering the authority of the school while casting doubts on the traditional moral teachings of the home or church."

The battle occupied the Anaheim Union School Board for two years between 1968 and 1970. By the fall of 1970, the program was, for all intents and purposes, dismantled. When the Citizens' Committee of California had launched the anti-sex education campaign, almost

99 percent of the district's more than 30,000 students in grades seven through twelve were enrolled in the course; by 1970, about 24 percent of students were enrolled at only three grade levels, and the film and text lists were drastically limited. By that fall, Superintendent Paul Cook had resigned, and Sally Hansen, a SIECUS member and a program consultant, had been fired.

The struggle, moreover, had ramifications beyond the local level. John Schmitz, state senator from Orange County, successfully led the passage of a law requiring parents' permission for their children to enter a sex education class and mandating that the curriculum material be open for inspection in advance. . . .

As with many other issues, this conflict caused some Democrats and former liberals to rethink their political allegiances. A Mrs. Burns of Cypress, a prominent sex education opponent and recent migrant to Orange County, remarked, "I was a Democrat. And I'm still a registered Democrat and I thought I was a liberal, but I really don't understand the meaning of the word." Jan Pippinger, a born-again Christian, demonstrated that religious conservatism did not always go hand in hand with a clear overall embrace of conservative economic ideology when she remarked to the school board: "Over a million dollars has been spent on this program and for what? More kids on dope than ever before, more young girls pregnant. . . . Kids walking out and leaving home. . . . Gentlemen, I am not satisfied with the answer that I received as to why our children cannot have a hot meal at noon in our schools because there is no money for that purpose. . . . I suggest you satisfy their stomachs, not their curiosity about sex." Obviously, social conservatives' allegiance and votes were up for grabs, and conservative Republicans, rather than the liberal California Democratic party, had something to offer them, responding to their concerns over "sexual liberation," the youth culture, and changes in family life.

As liberalized pornography laws and sex education in schools provoked the ire of social conservatives, a third issue that demonstrated the shifting nature of conservative mobilization was the rising storm over abortion. By 1969, the women's liberation movement and abortion rights supporters had made important gains in liberalizing abortion laws. In California, Governor Reagan had signed the Therapeutic Abortion Act in 1967, a reform bill proposed after a group of physicians were indicted for performing abortions on women who had rubella. While the bill was intended to serve as a clarification of existing law, in practice, its stipulation that doctors could perform abortions if the birth of a child would "gravely impair the physical or mental health of the mother," or when the pregnancy was the result of rape or incest, led to a rapid sea change. The number of legal abortions in the state rose dramatically, from 5,018 in 1968, the first year under the new law, to more than 100,000 by 1972. At the same time, the debate that had been a reform argument among professionals was recast as a call by women's organizations for the repeal of all abortion laws. In 1969, the California Supreme Court became the first in the nation to strike down an abortion law. In *People v. Belous,* the court recognized that a woman possessed the constitutional right "to life and to choose whether to bear children." The court's decision struck down important provisions of the Therapeutic Abortion Act, passed only two years earlier. By 1972, the court had invalidated nearly all provisions of the 1967 law, providing for abortion on demand.

Conservatives were profoundly dismayed by the growing sentiment in favor of abortion reform, which they saw as an attack by the state on their religious and family values. Concerns over abortion were driven, in part, by a belief in the sanctity of life. As one religious conservative from Orange wrote in 1971, "All lives have a right to live. . . . The Bible, God's word, says 'Thou shalt not kill.' And what are those doctors doing, they are breaking God's law, also killing a life." Mrs. Thomas Tiernan, a Catholic from Santa Ana, put it just as starkly: "Who among us is so all-knowing as to say with certainty the exact moment that the life-giving principle joins the mass and becomes a human person?. . . Abortion is murder, period."

But if concerns over abortion were driven by conservative religious beliefs, these beliefs encompassed a broader worldview in which God ordained natural roles for men and women. Abortion posed a threat to women's traditional identities as wives and mothers by upsetting "natural roles" and enabling women to control their fertility. In religious conservatives' eyes, it was part of a broader mentality that flouted the law of God by seeking to deny biological realities. Not surprisingly, then, the women's rights movement was seen as responsible for promoting this "abortion mentality" and came under heavy attack. The interplay of antifeminism and pro-life issues was evident in the trajectories of activists who organized against both abortion and equal rights causes, and in joint "pro-family" and "pro-life" initiatives.

As women's organizations won support for their call for legalized abortion, a small number of grassroots conservatives organized in response. Cathy Sullivan, who had been a Goldwater supporter . . . received a request in 1969 from two local priests asking her if she would head up the founding of the county's first antiabortion organization, the Citizens Action Committee. It was, in Sullivan's words, "an antipornography, pro-education, antiabortion grassroots organization comprised of both Democrats and Republicans." The group symbolized the new alliance struck between Catholics and Protestant evangelicals at the grassroots level around abortion, as well as the early politicization of some churches around the issue.

Not only was a new alliance struck between Protestants and Catholics, but the abortion issue also helped forge an alliance between registered Democrats and registered Republicans. In Orange County, according to Sullivan, "You had all these brand-new, former Democrats that were upset about this issue, some of them becoming Republican." One of them was Beverly Cielnicky, who explained that for herself and her husband, their identities as conservative Republicans gradually emerged from their pro-life position. They had been Democrats in college, but "when we first got into pro-life, we said, well let's be one of each so we'll get all the information from both parties. Then we gradually learned that the Democratic party had been taken over by the pro-abortionists." The Cielnickys' strong pro-life stance and activities as part of the Protestant Church–based Crusade for Life eventually drew them into a broader conservative mobilization. Cielnicky, for example, opposed the Equal Rights Amendment. She attended a rally at the University of Southern California where Phyllis Schlafly was a guest speaker, supported Schlafly's anti-ERA crusade, and joined "miniconventions" and rallies in San Diego led by Beverly LaHaye that eventually led to the founding of Concerned Women for America, the largest women's organization of the Christian right during the 1980s and 1990s. Further demonstrating Cielnicky's deepening conservative commitment, she left the mainline American Lutheran Church after years of unsuccessfully lobbying for it to take a pro-life stand. Eventually, she and her husband joined the Central Baptist church in Huntington Beach, which she described as "very, very pro-life." Her pro-life stand remained at the core of her self-definition as a conservative for more than twenty-five years. While this might not be typical, the synthesis of social conservatism with the libertarian discourse on freedom and antistatism bespoke a common impulse among grassroots conservatives. According to Cielnicky:

> Pro-life is number one. That's respect for all human life from the moment of conception until natural death. So that the human being in the image of God is the primary focus. . . . Secondly, to keep government from dictating, taking away freedoms. Some of it is pro-life and some of it is just basic, such as in the schools. The conservative position is that . . . parents, the family be the center.

Although the pro-life movement remained small in the early 1970s, it created the institutional base and networks that would provide the foundation for its rapid growth after the Supreme Court, in *Roe v. Wade,* legalized abortion in 1973. Sullivan, for example, helped to found the Pro-Life Political Action Committee of Orange County, using as a model the bylaws of the California Republican Assembly: "We started it, then Californians for Life, the California Pro-Life Council, other organizations started to come about, bigger organizations." But Sullivan, true to her conservative leanings, sought to keep everything under local control: "I felt very strongly that we should never get any bigger than our little county, and we never have."

Another early Orange County pro-life activist was Don Smith of La Habra, who had heard about Sullivan's Citizens Action Committee through a protest held in Anaheim on the occasion of the American Medical Association's annual convention. Smith contacted some of the organizers, who put him in touch with Sullivan, and he soon became active in pro-life circles. He established Crusade for Life in 1971, a Protestant evangelical pro-life group that went on to become one of the largest pro-life organizations in the state. Smith also influenced the national abortion debate. The Anaheim-based American Portrait Films he established in 1983 produced the controversial *Silent Scream,* depicting a suction abortion performed on a twelve-week fetus. The film was described by pro-life supporters as "a weapon of battle for the right to life troops" and by opponents as a distorted propaganda piece.

The continuities and discontinuities between the new social issues mobilizations of the late 1960s and early 1970s and the conservative initiatives ten years earlier are highlighted by the front ranks of the early pro-life movement in Orange County. In contrast to Sullivan, Smith, though a convert to rock-ribbed conservatism already by the mid-1960s, did not become an activist until the early 1970s. The antiabortion struggle increasingly drew in new activists like Smith and Cielnicky. Yet these recruits often depended on the networks and initiatives established by earlier pioneers. More important, established activists such as Sullivan or, in the sex education struggle, Jim Townsend, played important roles in propelling the new issues to the forefront of the conservative movement's concerns.

Buffeted by the feminist movement, a vibrant youth culture, and broader social change, religious conservatives lamented the decline of "traditional values" and changes in family life. These concerns had emerged earlier in the 1960s, but issues such as sex education and abortion pushed them to new heights in the late 1960s and the 1970s. Yet while new social issues galvanized the grassroots conservative movement and resonated with growing numbers of Americans, they would not prove to be the issues that could sway the broader middle class to the conservative agenda. Indeed, even those within conservative ranks did not always agree on the centrality of social issues like abortion to their cause. As Cathy Sullivan expressed it, "The conservatives even at that time weren't looking at that as a big political issue. . . . Finally . . . they saw it. I would say the biggest influence in getting them to see it would have been the evangelicals." But even once conservatives adopted the issue, not all agreed on the role the state should play in regulating abortion. Edna Slocum, for example . . . asserted years later, "I think that it's too bad that it ever became a national issue that's in the political arena. I could never have an abortion because, to me, it is a religious belief. But my feeling is, if somebody else differs, if there is such a thing as a final judgment, they'll have to answer for it there, and I'm not going to concern myself with that issue. It's become so divisive." Similarly, staunch libertarians believed that "the better way to deal with it and perhaps succeed in reducing the number of abortions are nongovernmental ways." By no means, however, were all libertarians pro-choice; abortion had been a contentious issue with the Libertarian party since its founding in 1972. In Orange County, one activist noted, "There was a big movement of libertarians for life . . . they weren't an enemy . . . they were split." The issue was a divisive one for the movement that has continued to haunt it into the twenty-first century.

Aside from abortion, other social issues wrought divisions within the movement. Government regulation of pornography was one of them. While important to religious conservatives, it was not a priority to others. Libertarians such as David Bergland remembered being annoyed by conservative attempts to limit personal freedoms. Referring to efforts by United Republicans of California to get rid of pornography in the late 1960s, he remarked, "They did some things that I thought were just stupid, which were not tolerant. They wanted to shut down adult bookstores or something." Social conservative issues divided the movement between those who prioritized libertarian issues and those who sought to build a godly world.

These divisions made themselves felt in conservative Orange County in 1972 when another anti-obscenity measure was placed on the ballot in California. In contrast to Proposition 16, which had won a majority in Orange County in 1966, Proposition 18 lost by a large margin. The different outcomes can be attributed, in part, to the far-reaching scope of Proposition 18, which went beyond the earlier measure in seeking to define obscenity, providing extremely detailed descriptions of "obscene acts." The broad scope of Proposition 18 generated national opposition and must have appeared, even to many conservative voters, to be a threat to privacy. Just as important, Orange County had, in the intervening years, continued its upward spiral of growth, bringing many new voters into the county. The difference in outcomes hints that while Orange Countians continued to embrace a staunch law-and-order, limited-government, and pro-defense ethos, new residents were shifting the package of Orange County conservatism. Libertarian sentiments were taking hold among a broader group. Such changes, however, did not discourage social conservatives; in contrast, they encouraged them to become more vocal. Now they sought not only to limit but also to roll back cultural change.

THOMAS FRANK

What's the Matter with Kansas?

The poorest county in America isn't in Appalachia or the Deep South. It is on the Great Plains, a region of struggling ranchers and dying farm towns, and in the election of 2000 the Republican candidate for president, George W. Bush, carried it by a majority of greater than 80 percent.

This puzzled me when I first read about it, as it puzzles many of the people I know. For us it is the Democrats that are the party of workers, of the poor, of the weak and the victimized. Understanding this, we think, is basic; it is part of the ABCs of adulthood. When I told a friend of mine about that impoverished High Plains county so enamored of President Bush, she was perplexed. "How can anyone who has ever worked for someone else vote Republican?" she asked. How could so many people get it so wrong?

Her question is apt; it is, in many ways, the preeminent question of our times. People getting their fundamental interests wrong is what American political life is all about. This species of derangement is the bedrock of our civic order; it is the foundation on which all else rests. This derangement has put the Republicans in charge of all three branches of government; it has elected presidents, senators, governors; it shifts the Democrats to the right and then impeaches Bill Clinton just for fun.

If you earn over $300,000 a year, you owe a great deal to this derangement. Raise a glass sometime to those indigent High Plains Republicans as you contemplate your good fortune: It is thanks to their self-denying votes that you are no longer burdened by the estate tax, or troublesome labor unions, or meddling banking regulators. Thanks to the allegiance of these sons and daughters of toil, you have escaped what your affluent forebears used to call "confiscatory" income tax levels. It is thanks to them that you were able to buy two Rolexes this year instead of one and get that Segway with the special gold trim.

Or perhaps you are one of those many, many millions of average-income Americans who see nothing deranged about this at all. For you this picture of hard-times conservatism makes perfect sense, and it is the opposite phenomenon—working-class people who insist on voting for liberals—that strikes you as an indecipherable puzzlement. Maybe you see it the way the bumper sticker I spotted at a Kansas City gun show puts it: "A working person that *supports* Democrats is like a chicken that *supports* Col. Sanders!"

Maybe you were one of those who stood up for America way back in 1968, sick of hearing those rich kids in beads bad-mouth the country every night on TV. Maybe you knew exactly what Richard Nixon meant when he talked about the "silent majority," the people whose hard work was rewarded with constant insults from the network news, the Hollywood movies, and the know-it-all college professors, none of them interested in anything you had to say. Or maybe it was the liberal judges who got you mad as hell, casually rewriting the laws of your state according to some daft idea they had picked up at a cocktail party, or ordering your town to shoulder some billion-dollar desegregation scheme that they had dreamed up on their own, or turning criminals loose to prey on the hardworking and the industrious. Or perhaps it was the drive for gun control, which was obviously directed toward the same end of disarming and ultimately disempowering people like you.

Maybe Ronald Reagan pulled you into the conservative swirl, the way he talked about that sunshiny, Glenn Miller America you remembered from the time before the world went to hell. Or maybe Rush Limbaugh won you over, with his daily beat-down of the arrogant and the self-important. Or maybe you were pushed; maybe Bill Clinton made a Republican out of you with his patently phony "compassion" and his obvious contempt for average, non-Ivy Americans, the ones he had the nerve to order into combat even though he himself took the coward's way out when his turn came.

Nearly everyone has a conversion story they can tell: how their dad had been a union steelworker and a stalwart Democrat, but how all their brothers and sisters started voting Republican; or how their cousin gave up on Methodism and started going to the Pentecostal church out on the edge of town; or how they themselves just got so sick of being scolded for eating meat or for wearing clothes emblazoned with the State U's Indian mascot that one day Fox News started to seem "fair and balanced" to them after all.

Take the family of a friend of mine, a guy who came from one of those midwestern cities that sociologists used to descend upon periodically because it was supposed to be so "typical." It was a middling-sized industrial burg where they made machine tools, auto parts, and so forth. When Reagan took office in 1981, more than half the working population of the city was employed in factories, and most of them were union members. The ethos of the place was working-class, and the city was prosperous, tidy, and liberal, in the old sense of the word.

My friend's dad was a teacher in the local public schools, a loyal member of the teachers' union, and a more dedicated liberal than most: not only had he been a staunch supporter of George McGovern, but in the 1980 Democratic primary he had voted for Barbara Jordan, the black U.S. Representative from Texas. My friend, meanwhile, was in those days a high school Republican, a Reagan youth who fancied Adam Smith ties and savored the writing of William F. Buckley. The dad would listen to the son spout off about Milton Friedman and the godliness of free-market capitalism, and he would just shake his head. *Someday, kid, you'll know what a jerk you are.*

It was the dad, though, who was eventually converted. These days he votes for the farthest-right Republicans he can find on the ballot. The particular issue that brought him over was abortion. A devout Catholic, my friend's dad was persuaded in the early nineties that the sanctity of the fetus outweighed all of his other concerns, and from there he gradually accepted the whole pantheon of conservative devil-figures: the elite media and the American Civil Liberties Union, contemptuous of our values; the la-di-da feminists; the idea that Christians are vilely persecuted—right here in the U.S. of A. It doesn't even bother him, really, when his new hero Bill O'Reilly blasts the teachers' union as a group that "does not love America."

His superaverage midwestern town, meanwhile, has followed the same trajectory. Even as Republican economic policy laid waste to the city's industries, unions, and neighborhoods, the townsfolk responded by lashing out on cultural issues, eventually winding up with a hard-right Republican congressman, a born-again Christian who campaigned largely on an antiabortion platform. Today the city looks like a miniature Detroit. And with every bit of economic bad news it seems to get more bitter, more cynical, and more conservative still.

This derangement is the signature expression of the Great Backlash, a style of conservatism that first came snarling onto the national stage in response to the partying and protests of the late sixties. While earlier forms of conservatism emphasized fiscal sobriety, the backlash mobilizes voters with explosive social issues—summoning public outrage over everything from busing to un-Christian art—which it then marries to pro-business economic policies. Cultural anger is marshaled to achieve economic ends. And it is these economic achievements—not the forgettable skirmishes of the never-ending culture wars—that are the movement's greatest monuments. The backlash is what has made possible the international free-market consensus of recent years, with all the privatization, deregulation, and deunionization that are its components. Backlash ensures that Republicans will continue to be returned to office even when their free-market miracles fail and their libertarian schemes don't deliver and their "New Economy" collapses. It makes possible the policy pushers' fantasies of "globalization" and a free-trade empire that are foisted upon the rest of the world with such self-assurance. Because some artist decides to shock the hicks by dunking Jesus in urine, the entire planet must remake itself along the lines preferred by the Republican party, U.S.A.

The Great Backlash has made the laissez-faire revival possible, but this does not mean that it speaks to us in the manner of the capitalists of old, invoking the divine right of money or demanding that the lowly learn their place in the great chain of being. On the contrary; the backlash imagines itself as a foe of the elite, as the voice of the unfairly persecuted, as a righteous protest of the people on history's receiving end. That its champions today control all three branches of government matters not a whit. That its greatest beneficiaries are the wealthiest people on the planet does not give it pause.

In fact, backlash leaders systematically downplay the politics of economics. The movement's basic premise is that culture outweighs economics as a matter of public concern—that *Values Matter Most,* as one backlash title has it. On those grounds it rallies citizens who would once have been reliable partisans of the New Deal to the standard of conservatism. Old-fashioned values may count when conservatives appear on the stump, but once conservatives are in office the only old-fashioned situation they care to revive is an economic regimen of low wages and lax regulations. Over the last three decades they have smashed the welfare state, reduced the tax burden on corporations and the wealthy, and generally facilitated the country's return to a nineteenth-century pattern of wealth distribution. Thus the primary contradiction of the backlash: it is a working-class movement that has done incalculable, historic harm to working-class people.

The leaders of the backlash may talk Christ, but they walk corporate. Values may "matter most" to voters, but they always take a backseat to the needs of money once the elections are won. This is a basic earmark of the phenomenon, absolutely consistent across its decades-long history. Abortion is never halted. Affirmative action is never abolished. The culture industry is never forced to clean up its act. Even the greatest culture warrior of them all was a notorious cop-out once it came time to deliver. "Reagan made himself the champion of 'traditional values,' but there is no evidence he regarded their restoration as a high priority," wrote Christopher Lasch, one of the most astute analysts of the backlash sensibility. "What he really cared about was the revival of the unregulated capitalism of the twenties: the repeal of the New Deal."

This is vexing for observers, and one might expect it to vex the movement's true believers even more. Their grandstanding leaders never deliver, their fury mounts and mounts, and nevertheless they turn out every two years to return their right-wing heroes to office for a second, a third, a twentieth try. The trick never ages; the illusion never wears off. *Vote* to stop abortion; *receive* a rollback in capital gains taxes. *Vote* to make our country strong again; *receive* deindustrialization. *Vote* to screw those politically correct college professors; *receive* electricity deregulation. *Vote* to get government off our backs; *receive* conglomeration and monopoly everywhere from media to meatpacking. *Vote* to stand tall against terrorists; *receive* Social Security privatization. *Vote* to strike a blow against elitism; *receive* a social order in which wealth is more concentrated than ever before in our lifetimes, in which workers have been stripped of power and CEOs are rewarded in a manner beyond imagining.

Backlash theorists . . . imagine countless conspiracies in which the wealthy, powerful, and well connected—the liberal media, the atheistic scientists, the obnoxious eastern elite—pull the strings and make the puppets dance. And yet the backlash itself has been a political trap so devastating to the interests of Middle America that even the most diabolical of string-pullers would have had trouble dreaming it up. Here, after all, is a rebellion against "the establishment" that has wound up abolishing the tax on inherited estates. Here is a movement whose response to the power structure is to make the rich even richer; whose answer to the inexorable degradation of working-class life is to lash out angrily at labor unions and liberal workplace-safety programs; whose solution to the rise of ignorance in America is to pull the rug out from under public education.

Like a French Revolution in reverse—one in which the sans-culottes pour down the streets demanding more power for the aristocracy—the backlash pushes the spectrum of the acceptable to the right, to the right, farther to the right. It may never bring prayer back to the schools, but it has rescued all manner of right-wing economic nostrums from history's dustbin. Having rolled back the landmark economic reforms of the sixties (the war on poverty) and those of the thirties (labor law, agricultural price supports, banking regulation), its leaders now turn their guns on the accomplishments of the earliest years of progressivism (Woodrow Wilson's estate tax; Theodore Roosevelt's antitrust measures). With a little more effort, the backlash may well repeal the entire twentieth century.

As a formula for holding together a dominant political coalition, the backlash seems so improbable and so self-contradictory that liberal observers often have trouble believing it is actually happening. By all rights, they figure, these two groups—business and blue-collar—should be at each other's throats. For the Republican party to present itself as the champion of working-class America strikes liberals as such an egregious denial of political reality that they dismiss the whole phenomenon, refusing to take it seriously. The Great Backlash, they believe, is nothing but crypto-racism, or a disease of the elderly, or the random gripings of religious rednecks, or the protests of "angry white men" feeling left behind by history.

But to understand the backlash in this way is to miss its power as an idea and its broad popular vitality. It keeps coming despite everything, a plague of bitterness capable of spreading from the old to the young, from Protestant fundamentalists to Catholics and Jews, and from the angry white man to every demographic shading imaginable.

It matters not at all that the forces that triggered the original "silent majority" back in Nixon's day have long since disappeared; the backlash roars on undiminished, its rage carrying easily across the decades. The confident liberals who led America in those days are a dying species. The new left, with its gleeful obscenities and contempt for the flag, is extinct altogether. The whole "affluent society," with its paternalistic corporations and powerful labor unions, fades farther into the ether with each passing year. But the backlash endures. It continues to dream its terrifying dreams of national decline, epic lawlessness, and betrayal at the top regardless of what is actually going on in the world.

. . . The high priests of conservatism like to comfort themselves by insisting that it is the free market, that wise and benevolent god, that has ordained all the economic measures they have pressed on America and the world over the last few decades. But in truth it is the carefully cultivated derangement of places like Kansas that has propelled their movement along. It is culture war that gets the goods.

From the air-conditioned heights of a suburban office complex this may look like a new age of reason, with the Web sites singing each to each, with a mall down the way that every week has miraculously anticipated our subtly shifting tastes, with a global economy whose rich rewards just keep flowing, and with a long parade of rust-free Infinitis purring down the streets of beautifully manicured planned communities. But on closer inspection the country seems more like a panorama of madness and delusion worthy of Hieronymous Bosch: of sturdy blue-collar patriots reciting the Pledge while they strangle their own life chances; of small farmers proudly voting themselves off the land; of devoted family men carefully seeing to it that their children will never be able to afford college or proper health care; of working-class guys in midwestern cities cheering as they deliver up a landslide for a candidate whose policies will end their way of life, will transform their region into a "rust belt," will strike people like them blows from which they will never recover.

Further Reading

The Odyssey of the American Right (New York: Oxford University Press, 1980), by Michael W. Miles, is an early work that touches on most of the key points. Up-to-date surveys include *Roads to Dominion: Right-Wing Movements and Political Power in the United States* (New York: The Guilford Press, 1995), by Sara Diamond, which emphasizes grassroots movements and extremists, and *America's Right Turn: From Nixon to Bush* (Baltimore: The Johns Hopkins University Press, 1998), by William C. Berman, which stresses the political mainstream. Recent trends in historical scholarship are reflected in the essays collected in *The Conservative Sixties* (New York: Peter Lang Publishing, 2003), edited by David Farber and Jeff Roche. On the development of antiliberal populism, see Michael Kazin's long-term account, *The Populist Persuasion* (New York: Basic Books, 1995) and Terri Bimes's richly documented analysis, "Reagan: The Soft-Sell Populist," in *The Reagan Presidency: Pragmatic Conservatism and its Legacies,* edited by W. Elliot Brownlee and Hugh Davis Graham (Lawrence: University Press of Kansas, 2003), 61–81.

Besides McGirr's book, other local histories, which emphasize the "white backlash" are Jonathan Rieder, *Canarsie: The Jews and Italians of Brooklyn against Liberalism* (Cambridge, MA: Harvard University Press, 1985) and Ronald P. Formisano, *Boston against Busing: Race, Class, and Ethnicity in the 1960s and 1970s* (Chapel Hill: University of North Carolina Press, 1991).

Documenting the conservative triumph within the Republican party are Robert Alan Goldberg, *Barry Goldwater* (New Haven, CT: Yale University Press, 1995), Mary C. Brennan, *Turning Right in the Sixties: The Conservative Capture of the GOP* (Chapel Hill: University of North Carolina Press, 1995), and Rick Perlstein, *Before the Storm: Barry Goldwater and the Unmaking of the American Consensus* (New York: Hill and Wang, 2001). *The Politics of Rage: George Wallace, the Origins of the New Conservatism, and the Transformation of American Politics* (New York: Simon & Schuster, 1995), a definitive biography by Dan T. Carter, examines a different conservative insurgency within the Democratic party.

On the concerns and activities of the Christian right during this period, see the well-informed discussions in Margaret Lamberts Bendroth, "Fundamentalism and the Family: Gender, Culture, and the American Pro-Family Movement," *Journal of Women's History* (vol. 19, no. 4 [Winter 1999], 35–54); Michael Lienisch, *Redeeming America: Piety and Politics in the New Christian Right* (Chapel Hill: University of North Carolina Press, 1993); and David H. Watt, *A Transforming Faith: Explorations of Twentieth-Century American Evangelicalism* (New Brunswick, NJ: Temple University Press, 1991). Focused analyses of gender issues relating to the Christian right include Rebecca E. Klatch, *Women of the New Right* (Philadelphia: Temple University Press, 1987), and Donald G. Mathews and Jane S. DeHart, *Sex, Gender, and the Politics of ERA: A State and the Nation* (New York: Oxford University Press, 1990).

Primary Sources

For examples of the early rhetoric of politicians of the right, see Barry Goldwater's acceptance speech at the 1964 Republican Convention (www.ku.edu/carrie/docs/texts/goldwater1964. html), Ronald Reagan's address on behalf of Barry Goldwater at that same convention (www.ku.edu/carrie/docs/texts/reagan101964.html), and Reagan's widely noted 1964 speech, "A Time for Choosing" (www.fordham.edu/halsall/mod/1964reagan1.html). The text of a brochure from George Wallace's 1968 presidential campaign can be found at www.4president.

org/brochures/wallace68.pdf. For examples of speeches by Nixon's vice president, Spiro Agnew, who specialized in attacking the liberal elite, go to www.geocities.com/ Pacific_Future/ speech_agnew220570.html ("An Effete Corps of Impudent Snobs") and www.americanrhetoric. com/speeches/spiroagnew.htm ("Television News Coverage"). Both text and audio versions of Nixon's well-known "The Great Silent Majority" speech may be found at www.americanrhetoric. com/speeches/richardnixongreatsilentmajority.html. For excerpts from 1978 issues of *Tax Revolt Digest* that describe and analyze California's Proposition 13 as well as similar measures proposed in other states, go to www.lib.niu.edu/ipo/1978/ii781213.html. To read or listen to Ronald Reagan's first inaugural address, go to www.americanrhetoric.com/speeches/ rreagandfirstinaugural.html. A copy of Newt Gingrich's 1994 "Contract with America" may be found at www.house.gov/house/Contract/CONTRACT.html.

12

Reaganomics and Beyond

INTRODUCTION

For roughly the first three decades after World War II, the American economy performed remarkably well. Between 1945 and 1973, the average yearly growth in productivity was an impressive 2.8 percent, enough to double living standards over the course of these years. And then, as economist Paul Krugman has written, "the magic went away." Shortages of oil, brought about by the actions of the oil-exporting members of the OPEC cartel, combined with high unemployment and high inflation—the notorious "stagflation" of the 1970s—to create widespread and urgent concern about the prospects for the American economy to continue to expand indefinitely and to support, much less to expand, the large middle class that had formed after World War II. The drop in productivity, the key to economic growth, to 1 percent annually confirmed a developing unease about America's economic future. In 1980, for the first time in years, the state of the economy was a major factor when American voters went to the polls to select a president, and economic difficulties would become a perennial political issue throughout the remaining decades of the twentieth century.

President Jimmy Carter spoke to the nation about the state of the American economy, as well as about what he called the nation's "crisis of confidence" in July 1979. In what commentators labeled his "malaise speech," he exhorted Americans to remember that material possessions were not the only way to the good life. A few months later, Ronald Reagan, in announcing his candidacy for president, rejected the notion that Americans needed to alter their economic expectations or consumption patterns, offering a simple explanation for why the American economy had faltered: the problem was the government itself. He also offered neat solutions, tax cuts and large reductions in federal spending, to free up capital for investment in the profit-making private sector. Reagan handily defeated Carter and proceeded to implement his economic plan, which the press and pundits referred to as "Reaganomics."

Reaganomics was hotly debated at the time and initially scoffed at by most economists and journalists. They considered Reagan's economic plan to be financially unsound and a thinly disguised version of 1920s "trickle-down economics," according to which wealth, if placed in the hands of "haves," eventually finds its way, at least in some small part, to the "have-nots"—which had been discredited by the Great Depression of the 1930s. Reagan's advocacy of tax cuts and criticism of big government were rooted in his personal experiences, and they were championed by a handful of journalists associated with the *Wall Street Journal.* They were also supported by a minority of professional economists, who were known as "supply-siders" because they believed that focusing on generating supply (the creation of products and services) rather than on increasing demand (the purchase of goods and services) was the key to economic recovery. Attention to demand had been orthodoxy since the 1940s; supporters of this approach were referred to as Keynesians, after the economist John Maynard Keynes, who had championed it. Keynesians believed in the use of temporary government spending or tax cuts to provide consumers of modest means with income to buy goods and services; this increased demand, they argued, would in turn lead businesses to hire more workers, thus ending an economic slump. But supply-siders argued that government spending was the wrong solution, as were tax cuts aimed at putting more cash in consumers' pockets. The way to stimulate the economy, they argued, was to give massive tax cuts specifically to the wealthy and to businesses. This would unleash investment capital, which would in turn create the jobs that would provide workers with the wages needed to purchase things. This approach would not only pull the economy out of the doldrums, according to supply-siders, but also improve the economy's long-range prospects for growth.

George H. W. Bush, one of Reagan's political rivals in 1980, referred to supply-side theories as "voodoo economics," because he doubted, as did many others, that the numbers would add up. Reagan had campaigned on the promise of balancing the government's books, but he also proposed large tax cuts, securing a 25 percent across-the-board tax cut over three years and a drop in the highest marginal rate from 70 percent to 50 percent in one fell swoop. (Top marginal rates—paid only on annual income over $215,400—would fall to 28 percent by the end of Reagan's presidency, the lowest rate in over fifty years.) The result was a dramatic worsening of government budget deficits. The predictions of Reagan and the supply-siders that the tax cuts would stimulate so much economic growth that government revenues would actually increase were not borne out. By the end of Reagan's eight years, the federal debt was three times what it had been when he entered office in 1981. This was not only the result of cutting tax rates. As president, Reagan proved loath to cut spending on programs other than those for the poor. He also oversaw massive increases in military spending. Despite Reagan's verbal attacks on "big government," the actual size of the government grew on Reagan's watch.

Although historians' evaluations of Reagan as president have softened over time, partly because he is now often credited with having brought down the Soviet Union (see Chapter 12), and perhaps also because there is sympathy for him as a victim of Alzheimer's disease, their views of Reaganomics have remained almost uniformly unfavorable. The tax cuts failed in their stated aim of increasing investment levels, instead spurring lavish spending by the rich. They also brought no relief to middle- and working-class Americans. Their tax burden actually got heavier, due to higher state and local taxes (to make up for the federal spending cuts that had been made) and increased Social Security taxes (raised by Reagan); the combination of these tax hikes was greater than the value of their federal income-tax cut under Reagan. Historians have regarded Reagan's economic policies as responsible, at least in part, for the stunning growth in inequality over the 1980s and for the creation of a federal debt of crushing proportions. Where disagreements have emerged, they have been modest, ranging from how great a drag on the economy the Reagan deficits and accumulating debt were, to how much Reagan's tax cuts contributed to the growth in inequality. Although a hard core of Reagan loyalists (none of whom are professional historians) continue to claim that Reaganomics realized what it set out to achieve, few of the countless fond recollections of Reagan's presidency after his death in June 2004 even mentioned the supply-side economics with which Reagan was so closely associated, so overwhelming is the evidence for this doctrine's failure to achieve the goals its advocates proclaimed.

Historians and commentators have also noted the extent to which the economic developments and policies associated with Reagan and the 1980s cannot be bound by that decade or the years of his presidency. In terms of economic trends, historians recognize that the disparity in wealth between the upper and lower strata of American society, as well as the pinch experienced by the middle class, has, if anything, grown in the decades since Reagan's presidency, under Republican and Democratic administrations. Additionally, some of the ideas associated with Reaganomics, such as deregulation and tax cuts for businesses, and the tightening of the money supply to curb inflation, were actually first implemented in the waning years of Carter's presidency. Reagan's successor, George H. W. Bush, overcame his objections to Reaganomics and worked during his term in office to lower taxes on capital gains, a long-held goal of supply-siders. And the "end of welfare as we know it," a long-standing aim of Reagan, was the work of President Bill Clinton, a Democrat.

The fact that a Democrat would enact a policy arguably detrimental to the poor is simply evidence, some would say, of Reagan's impact. Further evidence might be the enormous attention paid by Clinton to reducing the deficit that was created by Reaganomics. (George H. W. Bush was also concerned with the huge imbalance in the budget; his agreement to reduce the deficit by raising taxes contributed to his defeat at the polls in 1992, when some Reagan loyalists stayed home rather than support a supposed betrayer of Reaganomics.) In the view of many, Clinton acted responsibly by focusing on deficit reduction. To some, however, attending to the deficit instead of trying to stimulate economic growth was simply another twist on Reaganomics, reflecting the same class loyalties, because deficit reduction was in the interest of wealthy bondholders and entailed tight money policies that hurt middle- and lower-class Americans, whose personal debt levels skyrocketed in the 1980s and 1990s. The conservative nature of his economic policies was recognized by Clinton himself when, in talking to his advisors about the budget, he commented "I hope you're all aware we're the Eisenhower Republicans here." Although Republicans had historically called for balanced budgets—achieved for the first time since Lyndon Johnson's 1969 budget by Democrat Clinton in 1998—Reagan had easily abandoned this goal early in his presidency, discovering that voters, as opposed to the bond market, did not object to a deficit, even an enormous one, especially if reducing it meant raising taxes.

The first selection in this chapter is from journalist and author Barbara Ehrenreich's 1989 book, *Fear of Falling,* which discusses the increasingly precarious condition of the American middle class over the course of the 1980s, as well as the cultural change leading to a celebration of wealth and an orgy of ostentatious consumption. Although not focused on Reagan himself, Ehrenreich makes clear that Reagan was partially responsible for the inequalities in wealth that cracked open in the 1980s, through tax policies that favored the wealthy and through his crushing of the 1981 strike by PATCO, the air traffic controllers' union, which in her view gave industry the go-ahead to engage in union busting and other actions hostile to workers, including plant closings. The trends that Ehrenreich describes continued largely unabated into the 1990s and beyond, raising the question of whether they may have developed regardless of whether Reagan had been elected president.

The second selection is from historian Robert Collins's 2000 history of economic policy and politics, *More.* Although Collins recognizes that economic difficulties, as well as well-developed criticisms of Keynesian economics, antedated Reagan's presidency, he sees Reagan's innate optimism and skills as a communicator as central to promoting and implementing supply-side economics. In this selection, Collins discusses Reaganomics and its impact, paying particular attention to the contradiction between Reagan's campaign pledges to balance the budget and the unprecedented budgetary deficits during his presidency. Taking a gentler, more measured tone than do some historians who discuss Reagan, Collins sees Reagan as an engaging and gifted salesman, and in this sense, as an effective leader. However, in keeping with the developing historical consensus, he also sees Reagan as ill-informed about policy, inclined toward a figurehead presidency, and personally passive and lazy; for example, Reagan declined to read essential briefing material the evening before an international economic summit because he preferred to watch *The Sound of Music* on television. All of these traits contributed to his inability or unwillingness to follow through in the implementation of certain ideas, notably to make the tough decisions on spending cuts to bring the budget into balance.

But, it may be argued, the unbalanced budget helped Reagan meet his pledge to slow the growth of (if not in fact to cut back) government spending, as it became impossible for liberals to propose new government programs in the face of such astoundingly large deficits. At the time, some Democrats suspected that this was the real purpose of the deficit; Collins argues that this was not Reagan's initial motive, but that it was a side benefit well understood by him and others in his administration. Finally, Collins argues that the deficits themselves were not terribly harmful in economic terms, although they did dampen the prospects for long-term growth, the achievement of which had been the stated aim of Reaganomics.

The final selection is from the economist Michael Meeropol's 2000 book, *Surrender,* which argues that Democratic President Clinton, far from being the liberal that Republicans claimed he was, actually completed the "Reagan Revolution." Citing the welfare reform bill of 1996 along with Clinton's commitment to and achievement of a balanced budget, Meeropol sees Clinton as accepting the vast inequalities in wealth that began developing during the Reagan years and rejecting the traditional kinds of liberal economic policies that involve government spending to help the less fortunate during economically difficult times. One problem with this argument is that Meeropol sees achieving a balanced budget as part of the Reagan Revolution, whereas Reagan himself never showed more than a rhetorical interest in balanced budgets, as Collins describes. But Meeropol does raise the interesting question of whether the old labels of "conservative" and "liberal" are still valid in a political arena where supposedly liberal Democrats champion the traditional Republican aim of budget balancing and restrained government spending, and supposedly conservative Republicans—most recently President George W. Bush—engage in deficit spending of such magnitude that the deficits associated with the liberal administrations of Franklin Roosevelt and Lyndon Johnson appear small in comparison.

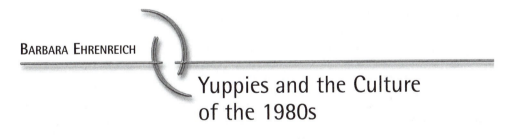

BARBARA EHRENREICH

Yuppies and the Culture of the 1980s

Sometime in the late sixties American society had begun to lurch off the track leading to the American dream of affluence and equality. No one could have known it at the time, but those were the last years in which economic inequality among Americans declined. Since then, in a sharp reversal of the equalizing trend that had been under way since shortly after World War II, the extremes of wealth have grown farther apart and the middle has lost ground. Some economists even began to predict that the middle class—defined simply as those with middling amounts of money—would disappear altogether, leaving America torn, like many third-world societies, between an affluent minority and an army of the desperately poor. . . .

The change is evident no matter how you slice up the population—whether you compare the top fifth to the bottom fifth, or the top 40 percent to the poorest 40 percent—and whether you look at individual earnings, household earnings, or employ occult-sounding measures of inequality like the economists' "Gini coefficient." In 1985, for example, the top fifth of American families—those earning more than $48,000 a year—took in 43 percent of all family income, a postwar high. The bottom fifth—families earning less than $13,200 a year—got only 4.7 percent, their lowest share in twenty-five years. Families in a somewhat arbitrarily defined middle range ($15,000 to $35,000 a year) saw their share fall to 39 percent of total family income from 46 percent in 1970. According to the Census Bureau, the income gap between the richest and the poorest families was wider in the mid-eighties than at any time since the bureau began keeping statistics in 1946.

The widening gap between the extremes was in no small part the result of the conscious efforts of the Reagan administration. At the same time that the administration sliced viciously away at social programs designed to help the down-and-out, it rewarded Reagan's constituency of wealth with a series of generous tax reductions. The combination of spending cuts for the poor and tax cuts for the rich produced a massive, government-induced upward redistribution of wealth. Between 1980 and 1984 alone, the richest one-fifth of American families gained $25 billion in income and the poorest one-fifth lost $6 billion.

Meanwhile, income at the extremes was also diverging. The poor faced wages held down by that miserly standard, the minimum wage, which remained, throughout most of the eighties, at $3.35 an hour, or $6,900 a year—more than $4,000 less than what the federal government defined as the poverty level for a family of four. In early 1988, *U.S. News and World Report,* which had once questioned the very existence of "poverty" in the United States, acknowledged that there were now 9 million working American adults whose wages were not sufficient to lift them and their families above the poverty level:

> They are people like Glen Whitbeck, a short-order cook whose $8000 annual salary doesn't stretch to cover his two little girls' medical bills. Or like Charlie Scott, a construction worker whose money woes forced him and his wife into a shelter and then, most recently, provoked a separation. Or Pamela Kelley, a onetime airline-passenger screener who shifted to canned food at home because pot roast was too expensive for her and her two-year-old daughter.

As if rubbing its eyes in disbelief, *U.S. News* noted that the poor of the eighties did not fit the stereotype defined by the culture of poverty and the ideologues of the new right. The concept of the poor as "shiftless, black urban males unable to hold jobs, or as inner-city mothers on welfare whose sole work experience is the repeated bearing and raising of illegitimate children," the magazine admitted, was "woefully overblown."

At the other extreme, where wages are known more elegantly as "compensation," there is of course no parallel to the minimum wage—no "maximum wage" to contain the greed of the already rich. In the eighties, while the median income of American families actually declined, the compensation of top executives rose dizzily. In 1986, top executives earned an average of $679,000 a year, up 9 percent from the year before. Executive incomes over $1 million (from salary and bonuses) became routine; only incomes over $10 million raised eyebrows. Reporting on then-chairman of NCR Inc. William S. Anderson's annual compensation of $13,229,000, the *New York Times* noted dryly:

> The kind of salary reported for Mr. Anderson brings out strong feelings in those who believe that the men at the top of the corporate pinnacle are wildly overpaid, members of an elite that pretty much sets its own pay. . . .

No one could any longer imagine that America was the land of one vast, undifferentiated middle class. In cities like Los Angeles and New York, the contrasts in wealth and poverty scandalized European visitors: high-rise buildings where two-bedroom apartments cost more to rent than most Americans earn in a month, while at street level, makeshift cardboard structures sheltered the homeless. The streets carried fleets of stretch limos, their windows discreetly shaded to frustrate the curious, while on the sidewalk, beggars of all ages searched trash cans for edible crusts; breakdancers performed for quarters; hawkers sold ballpoint pens, watches, used clothing, old magazines, drugs.

While these lurid, distinctly un-American images came to characterize the extremes of wealth and poverty, no less dramatic changes were taking place in the middle range of income. For one thing, a middle-level income no longer guaranteed such perquisites of middle-class status as home ownership. According to the National Association of Homebuilders, in 1984 a family needed an income of approximately $37,000 to afford a median-priced home, but in the same year the median family income was only $26,167—almost $11,000 short. That gap marked a sharp deterioration in the prospects of middle-income, mostly working-class people. According to economists Frank S. Levy and Richard Michel, a typical wage-earner in the 1950s faced housing costs equivalent to about 14 percent of his gross monthly pay. In 1984, however, a thirty-year-old man who purchased a median-priced home had to set aside a staggering 44 percent of his income for carrying charges. For the first time in postwar America, a middle-level income no longer guaranteed what we have come to think of as a middle-class lifestyle.

But the big news was that the "middle class," or more precisely, the middle range of income, was becoming ever more sparsely inhabited. If the middle range was defined as lying between family incomes of $20,000 and $50,000, the fraction of families with middle-range incomes declined from 53 percent in 1973 to less than 48 percent in 1984. Some people were climbing out and up, but others were sinking down toward the bottom. . . .

The phrase *the disappearing middle class,* which I, among others, used to describe the enormous changes of the eighties, in some ways missed the point. It was the blue-collar working class that was "disappearing," at least from the middle range of comfort. In the new right's imagination the working class was a precious avatar of "traditional values," a human bulwark against permissiveness. But to the business interests that commanded the new right's deepest loyalties, the American blue-collar working class—with its once-strong unions and real tradition of workplace defiance—had become a burden.

Beginning in the seventies, the corporate elite did everything possible to shake this burden loose. They "out-sourced" their manufacturing jobs to the lower-paid and more intimidated work force of the third world. They shifted their capital from manufacturing to the quick-profit realm of financial speculation—corporate mergers, leveraged buyouts—leaving American plants and technology to decay. And they led a brutal assault on the wages and living standards of those who still had jobs to cling to. For it is well to remember that what we call the working class, and picture as people striving to make a living, exists in the business literature only as *labor costs.*

The corporate abandonment of manufacturing—or what economists Barry Bluestone and Bennett Harrison have called "the deindustrialization of America"—violently disrupted the life of the blue-collar working class. Between 1979 and 1984, 11.5 million American workers lost their jobs because of plant shutdowns or relocations. Only 60 percent were able to find new jobs, and nearly half of the new jobs were at lower pay than the lost jobs. One study found that laid-off steelworkers in Chicago saw their incomes fall, on the average, by one-half, from $22,000 a year to $12,500 a year, just slightly above the official poverty level.

Throughout America's industrial "rust belt," whole towns and neighborhoods fell into decline as factories shut their doors. There were plenty of alternative jobs in the service sector— as bank tellers, hotel clerks, fast-food workers—but these tended to be low-paid, nonunion, and otherwise foreign to men whose skills lay in working with things, not people. A laid-off copper miner in Butte, Montana, a huge man wearing cowboy boots, overalls, and a scruffy beard, told me indignantly that he had been offered retraining—as a nurses' aide. Usually it was women or young, often black or Hispanic, men who took the proliferating service jobs; and one of the paradigmatic images of the eighties was that of the laid-off steelworker whose homemaker-wife has gone out to support the family on her wages at Burger King.

According to Harrison and Bluestone, though, the biggest reason for the declining fortunes of the working class was not job loss but wage loss. In every industry, employers launched a fierce initiative against labor costs: demanding wage concessions as the price of continued employment; instituting two-tier wage structures whereby the recently hired are paid on a vastly lower scale than those with seniority; replacing full-time workers with part-time employees who do not have to be offered benefits such as health insurance; and, of course, old-fashioned union-busting. In the eighties, law firms did a brisk business in union-busting services to employers, including public-relations drives to discredit the union and psychological methods of dividing and demoralizing the work force. More brutal, brass-knuckle approaches also flourished. Between 1986 and 1988, three New York–area union organizers of my acquaintance were beaten by company thugs, and two Queens factory workers who had participated in an organizing drive were pistol-whipped, in front of their coworkers, by the factory owners.

The Reagan administration set the tone of labor relations in the 1980s by busting PATCO, the air traffic controllers' union, in 1981. The administration then proceeded to all but eviscerate the Occupational Safety and Health Administration and the National Labor Relations Board, which guarantee minimal legal protections to labor. While the ideologues of the new right extolled the virtues of the working class, the government of the new right abetted the worst capitalist assault on America's working people since the 1920s.

Middle-class people, professionals and managers, also suffered in the economic dislocations of the eighties. They too lost jobs when plants closed or when government-financed social-welfare agencies shut down their services. They too experienced the stresses of a polarizing society, in which the poor were becoming ever more desperate and the rich were becoming more numerous and brash. While the poor were increasingly to be avoided for safety's sake, the rich presented a different kind of threat to people in the middle: bidding up the cost of real estate to astronomical values and uncomplainingly accepting college tuitions in the range of $20,000 a year. If staying in the economic and social middle ground had become impossible for much of the working class, it had also become a challenge for those whose education and occupation entitled them to believe they *were* the middle class.

But the professional middle class is more resilient than those below it. A laid-off manager is more likely to find a decent-paying job than a laid-off assembly-line worker. Public-sector professionals, like doctors, social workers, and administrators, can switch over to the private sector when the funds for public services are cut. And compared to blue- or pink-collar workers, white-collar professionals are in a better position to negotiate higher pay to meet the rising costs of housing and education. Above all, the young of the professional middle class are flexible. Starting in the seventies, they began to abandon the long, penurious path leading to professional status, and to go for the money. . . .

The first element of what might be called the "yuppie strategy" was to choose a college major that corporate recruiters would look favorably upon. In one short decade, American campuses went from being hotbeds of dissent to hothouses for the production of corporate cadres. Between the early seventies and the early eighties, the number of students receiving bachelor's degrees in English fell by almost 50 percent, while the number graduating with degrees in business nearly doubled. The social sciences also took an almost 50 percent cut, and mathematics and the natural sciences—which presumably are essential for the future technological competitiveness of the United States—could together claim fewer than 4 percent of the college seniors graduating in 1983. . . .

With nineteen-year-olds redirecting their energies from sociology to spreadsheets, a negative, self-centered mood settled over the campuses. UCLA's annual survey of undergraduate attitudes found a steady rise in avarice and a decline in "altruism and social concern." In 1987, for example, a record 73 percent of students reported "being very well off financially" as their top goal, compared to 39 percent in 1970. Only 16 percent were interested in doing something to preserve the environment, compared to 45 percent in 1972. In other areas, students were now at least as conservative as the general public: Only 21 percent favored legalizing marijuana in 1987, compared to 53 percent in 1977. In 1984, only 49 percent believed abortion should be available to married women, down from 68 percent in the seventies. Peter Carlson, a former sixties radical, returned to his old dorm room at Boston University in 1986 to find

> posters of Miss Piggy, Sesame Street's Bert and Ernie, Kermit the Frog . . . a mural-sized photo of a bottle of Cordon Rouge champagne popping its cork, a poster of elegant sushi arrangements . . . and a cartoon captioned, "Shop till you drop." Almost lost amid this collage of cuteness, I spied a postcard of Ron and Nancy atop a desk. I wondered: Is that a genuine *hommage* or some sort of ironic protest?
>
> It was a genuine *hommage.*

A lucky, highly publicized minority of the new generation of pragmatists leaped directly from the academy to instant wealth. Beginning in the late seventies, graduates of Harvard Law School and a few other elite, business-oriented institutions could expect to be courted with starting salaries above $40,000 a year. In Wall Street's bustling money factories, the goal of amassing a million by age thirty was neither uncommon nor entirely unrealistic. Baby high-rollers were proliferating, and New York's $50-a-lunch restaurants were jammed, by the late eighties, with fresh-faced young people barely above drinking age. These financial prodigies were, in at least one sense, the true descendants of the sixties radicals: They had scorned the arduous apprenticeship traditionally required for middle-class membership—scorned, in fact, the middle class itself. . . .

The hallmark of the yuppie—male or female, married or single—was consumption. The yuppie of stereotype drove a $40,000 foreign car, vacationed vigorously in all seasons, and aspired to a condominium with an intimidating address. Even those who could not afford the big-ticket items—condos and Porsches—infused their daily lives with extravagant details: salad dressings made of raspberry vinegar and walnut oil, imported mineral water, $100 sneakers, $50 meals at the restaurant of the moment. Yuppie spending patterns represented a new, undreamed-of level of capitulation to the consumer culture: a compulsive acquisitiveness bordering on addiction, a mental state resembling the supposed "present-orientation" and "radical improvidence" of the despised underclass.

Yuppie consumerism was not simply a distortion built into the stereotype. America was on a consumer binge, or as some economists put it, in a new stage of "hyperconsumption." Someone was spending, and it was not the laid-off industrial worker or unemployed woman on a dwindling welfare allowance. In fact, even during the recession of 1982–83, even after the stock-market crash of 1987, sales of luxury goods boomed. The truly rich—roughly the 5 percent of Americans who hold over 50 percent of the nation's wealth—accounted for a disproportionate share of the boom, particularly in the markets for yachts, gems, jets, real estate, and such collectibles as classic cars. But at the low end of luxury—which includes vacation trips, restaurant meals, and sports cars—America's newly rich, double-income business professionals were holding up their share of the binge.

In defense of yuppie spending habits—and it is a tribute to the enduring anxiety of the middle class that they still needed *any* defense at the height of Reagan-era profligacy—*New Republic* editor Michael Kinsley described the yuppies as engaged in a kind of compensatory spending. The $40,000 or so that a young business person might earn did not, after all, measure up so well when compared to the purchasing power enjoyed by his or her parents a few decades ago. It would hardly be enough to cover the house, station wagon, stay-at-home spouse, and three children that the white-collar man of the fifties expected as a matter of right. So, in Kinsley's argument, the raspberry vinegar, *crème fraîche,* and so forth had to be seen as "affordable luxuries":

> They serve as consolation for the lack of unaffordable luxuries like a large house. You may not have a dining room, but you have a dining room table, and everything on it can have a complicated explanation involving many foreign words.

But the compensatory-spending argument misses the profound change in middle-class attitudes toward consumption. In a previous generation, a young couple who lacked the money for a house and other family-oriented purchases would simply have skipped the raspberry vinegar (or its fifties equivalent) and saved their pennies. Spending was the reward for saving; and "leisure products," which include all the yuppie favorites, took second place to the moral solidity represented by a house and heavy appliances. The profligacy of the yuppies, which set a standard for all the middle class as a whole, was the surrender to hedonism that middle-class intellectuals had been warning against for over thirty years.

The consumer binge of the eighties is all the more startling when contrasted to the trend that immediately preceded it—the fashionable austerity of the seventies, symbolized by Jimmy Carter's low-budget 1976 inauguration and the popularity of E. F. Schumacher's *Small Is Beautiful.* "Voluntary simplicity," as this brief interlude of abstemiousness has since been termed, gave concrete expression to the middle-class fears of affluence that had been voiced since the fifties. The counterculture and student movement of the sixties were its immediate inspiration; the oil shortage of the early seventies and the new environmentalism imbued it with a high sense of moral purpose. A 1977 Harris poll found Americans increasingly concerned with "learning to get our pleasure out of nonmaterial experiences," rather than "satisfying our needs for more goods and services." According to a study by the Stanford Research Institute, this attitude was particularly strong among young, educated, middle-class people, who were no longer likely to be political activists but at least tended "to prefer products that are functional, healthy, nonpolluting, durable, repairable, recyclable or made from renewable raw materials, energy-cheap, authentic, aesthetically pleasing, and made through simple technology." These preferences easily accommodated the new marketing emphasis on "leisure products," such as sports equipment, cameras, and stereos. The requirements of being functional and healthy did not, however, extend to such eighties favorites as *crème fraîche* and Beluga caviar. . . .

Whatever the reasons, the yuppie spending pattern, (whether indulged in by demographically official yuppies or not) represented a frantic positioning—an almost desperate commitment to the latest upscale fad. In the fashionable intellectual discourse of the time, possessions were important only as "signifiers," elements of an ever-shifting language that spoke of wealth and promise. The trick was to understand the language as it changed from month to month, leaving behind the ignorant and the less than affluent. As soon as an affordable fad—the example is often given of pita-bread sandwiches—sedimented down to the general public, it would be rendered useless as a mark of status and abandoned by the cognoscenti.

Hence that favorite magazine and newspaper filler in the mid-eighties, the list of what's in and what's out, calculated to both mock and alarm the status-conscious reader. For example, in 1985 the *Miami Herald* published a largely predictable list of what's "hot" and "not hot": Conservatives, dinner parties, and gilt were hot; liberals, cookouts, and minimalism were not. The joke was at the end of the long lists, where, under *hot,* one found *what's not hot,* and under *not hot,* of course, *what's hot.*

But there was a certain consistency to the dominant upscale tastes. Conservatism had triumphed over liberalism, gilt over minimalism, expensive over modestly priced. The obvious impetus was the sudden visibility of the truly rich, who reentered public consciousness with the triumphal display of the 1981 Reagan inauguration. The rich, of course, are always with us. But throughout most of the postwar period they had not been too eager to announce their presence, as a class, to the potentially resentful public. All this changed with the ascent to power of the new right, whose populist language conflicted openly with its aristocratic allegiances. According to historian Deborah Silverman, the Reagan era introduced a "new cultural style" consistent with right-wing politics:

> A style aggressively dedicated to the cult of visible wealth and distinction, and to the illusion that they were well earned; a style that adopted the artifacts of Chinese emperors, French aristocrats, and English noblemen as signs of exclusivity and renunciation; a style of unabashed opulence, whose mixture of hedonism, spitefulness, and social repudiation was captured in the slogan "Living well is the best revenge."

Not to mention the even nastier and more popular slogan "He who dies with the most toys wins."

What was pathetic and ultimately embarrassing about the stereotypical yuppie was that he or she was such a poor copy of the truly rich. People who have yachts and private jets do not have to agonize over "what's hot" and "what's not." People who employ their own chefs do not have to engage in yuppie-style "competitive eating" to establish their place in the world. In moving from minimalism to gilt, from voluntary simplicity to a parodic profligacy, the upwardly mobile middle class began to lose its own fragile sense of dignity. The rich can surrender to hedonism because they have no reason to remain tense and alert. But the middle class cannot afford to let down its guard; it maintains its position only through continual exertion—through allegiance to the "traditional values" of hard work and self-denial. In the eighties, the middle class came dangerously close to adopting the presumed wantonness of the poor—that is, the actual wantonness of the very rich.

ROBERT COLLINS

The Reagan Revolution

Reagan proved to be one of the most deceptive of America's presidents. The fact that he also appeared to be the most obvious and transparent of politicians merely deepened the enigma. Few national leaders in U.S. history have been at once so limited and so gifted. Reagan, who turned seventy just a few weeks after his first presidential inauguration, struck the longtime Washington insider Clark Clifford as "an amiable dunce," and, in truth, he was strikingly ill-informed and unanalytical. Blessed with a memory that was near-photographic when it worked but notoriously spotty in its overall performance, he compiled a record of embarrassing gaffes that included a much-talked-about failure even to recognize his secretary of housing and urban development, Sam Pierce, whom he mistakenly addressed as "Mr. Mayor" while greeting a delegation of visiting mayors to the White House half a year into his first term. (That Pierce was the only African American in the cabinet magnified the significance of Reagan's faux pas in the minds of liberal critics.)

Over time, Reagan's ignorance and intellectual laziness became the stuff of legend among both insiders and observers. An economic adviser has recalled rather delicately that the Californian had "a low tolerance for analysis"; Richard Darman, a White House adviser who spent several hours each day with Reagan during his first term, noted that the president was hardworking when pressed—he had "a compulsive insistence upon completing whatever work was given to him"—and was blessed with "a natural analytic facility," but observed that Reagan's capacity for hard work and talent for analysis had, over time, atrophied "because his charm, good looks, and memory served to get him a long way without additional effort." In a similar vein, well-informed journalistic observers have concluded that Reagan's "biggest problem was that he didn't know enough about public policy to participate fully in his presidency—and often didn't realize how much he didn't know" and that the Reagan presidency would have been far more successful "had Reagan not been so lazy."

Notwithstanding such weaknesses, Reagan's opponents learned quickly enough the cost of underestimating his leadership gifts. Speaker of the House Thomas P. "Tip" O'Neill greeted the incoming president during the transition with the derisive comment "Welcome to the big leagues!" When, within months, Reagan managed to defeat the Democratic majority in the House on a number of crucial votes, a constituent at home asked O'Neill what was happening.

"I'm getting the shit whaled out of me," he replied. Jim Wright, the Democratic House majority leader, expressed a similar shocked disbelief in a June 1981 diary entry: "Appalled by what seems to me a lack of depth, I stand in awe nevertheless of . . . [Reagan's] political skill. I am not sure that I have seen its equal." The big leagues, indeed!

O'Neill, Wright, and others often learned the hard way that Reagan's intellectual weaknesses were counterbalanced by a number of leadership strengths. The most basic of these was what the conservative columnist George Will described as Reagan's "talent for happiness," an unshakable optimism as infectious as it was deeply grounded. A classic example was one of Reagan's favorite stories during his early days in the White House (until reporters began to make it the butt of their own gibes). There were, it went, two youngsters, one an incurable malcontent and the other an incorrigible optimist. The boys' parents decided to temper their sons' inclinations by means of very different Christmas gifts. Given a roomful of toys, the malcontent just cried in the corner, certain that all his wonderful presents would soon break on him. Meanwhile, his brother, given a pile of horse manure, dove in with great relish, exclaiming with a huge grin as he dug into the manure, "I just know there's a pony in here somewhere!"

Reagan projected his personal penchant for positive thinking onto the broader canvas of American life as well. The nation's problems, he told the onlookers at his inauguration in 1981, required "our best effort and our willingness to believe in ourselves and to believe in our capacity to perform great deeds, to believe . . . we can and will resolve the problems which now confront us." "And after all," he added, in what was the most telling line of his entire speech, "why shouldn't we believe that? We are Americans." On this foundation of sunniness rested a personality seemingly so at ease with itself, so engaging and winning, that even confirmed political adversaries felt its warm influence.

Reagan also had an unusual ability to cobble together his few core beliefs and ideas into something grander—a vision, which was itself made all the more coherent and powerful by its simplicity. There might be much that Reagan did not know, but he knew well the few big things that he hoped to achieve as president. Isaiah Berlin has reminded us of the observation by the Greek poet Archilochus that "the fox knows many things, but the hedgehog knows one big thing." Nothing so set Reagan apart from Jimmy Carter as that difference between the fox and the hedgehog. Carter knew an astounding array of facts about how government worked; Reagan knew what he wanted. In the 1980 election, and likely in the larger judgment of history as well, this particular hedgehog bested that particular fox. Moreover, Reagan managed not only to focus on those central goals but also to sustain that focus over time. As Edwin Meese III, a close adviser throughout Reagan's government career in both California and Washington, has written, "He kept his eye on the main objective at all times—astonishingly so, considering the number and complexity of the issues involved."

Finally, Reagan had the ability to communicate his agenda clearly and compellingly, not simply through the smoothness of his speaking delivery or by means of his impressive physical presence, but most important through his uncanny ability to manipulate the symbols and imagery of presidential leadership. Behind what sometimes appeared to be a shallow fondness for the pomp of office lay the fact that Reagan, as White House communications aide David Gergen noted, "understood, better than anyone since de Gaulle, the dramatic and theatrical demands of national leadership." The former actor and his aides made the previously innocuous "photo op" into a potent instrument of governance. Reagan's carefully scripted projections of presidential imagery came to be seen, one political analyst has written, "as synonymous with the act of governing itself, as distinct from merely being adjuncts or backdrop."

In his run for the presidency, Reagan put his various strengths in the service of a handful of simply stated but impressively large goals. The big things Reagan hoped to achieve—what he conceived as his heroic missions—are best remembered as the three "r's." First, he sought to revitalize the U.S. economy by defeating stagflation and moving back to the fast growth track of the earlier postwar decades. "The Republican program for solving economic problems is based on growth and productivity," he proclaimed to a rapt audience in accepting the presidential nomination at the GOP national convention in July 1980. Second, he was determined to restore U.S. military strength and international prestige. "No American should vote," he told the assembled Republicans, "until he or she has asked: Is the United States stronger and more respected now than it was three and a half years ago? Is the world a safer place in which to live?" Finally, Reagan meant to reverse what he perceived as the nation's drift in the direction of a European welfare state by halting the growth of the federal government. "Our federal government is overgrown and overweight," he declared to the convention. Once elected, the new president added famously in his inaugural address that government was not the solution to the nation's problems so much as it was their cause. The tasks of revitalization, restoration, and reversal remained the lodestars by which Reagan steered his presidency, consistently, albeit with uneven success, through two terms.

The economic program Reagan adopted to help achieve these large ends—the three "r's"—further demonstrated the incoming administration's ability to focus at the outset on a few essentials and to sustain that focus over time. In August 1979, Martin Anderson, Reagan's chief domestic policy adviser, drafted the Reagan for President Campaign's "Policy Memorandum No. 1," which sketched out the economic strategy the Californian would take to the voters. "It is time the United States began moving forward again," Anderson told the candidate, "with new inventions, new products, greater productivity, more jobs, and a rapidly rising standard of living that means more goods and services for all of us." To regain the economy's former momentum, Anderson suggested across-the-board tax cuts of at least three years' duration in conjunction with the indexation of federal income tax brackets; reduction in the rate of increase in federal spending; the balancing of the federal budget; vigorous deregulation; and a consistent monetary policy to deal with inflation.

Despite George Bush's stinging criticism during the primary campaign that, when combined with the massive military buildup Reagan promised, such a program constituted "voodoo economics," Reagan stuck to the blueprint laid out in Policy Memorandum No. 1. With only minor adjustments and some change in emphasis—a slight downplaying of the balanced budget goal, attainment of which was pushed farther into the future, and an underscoring of the immediate need to fight inflation—that early strategy was the program President Ronald Reagan presented to the American people in February 1981. As Anderson later wrote, "Again and again, in the campaign, during the transition, and all during his tenure as president . . . [Reagan] adjusted his economic plan to accommodate changes in the economy and political opposition in the Congress, but he did not adjust the blueprint." Both its champions and its critics labeled the blueprint Reaganomics.

The rationale behind Reaganomics was varied. Several members of Reagan's Council of Economic Advisers have noted that there was much more agreement on what the administration should do than on why it should do those things. The president's commitment to the regimen of tax cuts and spending constraints, tight money, and deregulation reflected, in large part, his own emotional and experiential view of economics. He abhorred big government and had a primordial dislike of high taxes rooted in his own experiences in the film industry. During his peak earning years as an actor at Warner Brothers, Reagan found himself in the 94 percent marginal tax bracket: "The IRS took such a big chunk of my earnings," he remembered, "that after a while I began asking myself whether it was worth it to keep on taking work. Something was wrong with a system like that." Moreover, the problem was not simply the confiscatory level of taxation but also the ultimate economic impact of such disincentives to work: "If I decided to do one less picture," Reagan later wrote, "that meant other people at the studio in lower tax brackets wouldn't work as much either; the effect filtered down, and there were fewer total jobs available."

When the Californian left acting to become an increasingly visible spokesman for American conservatism in the early 1960s, he told his audiences that the progressive income tax had come "directly from Karl Marx who designed it as the prime essential of a socialist state." Reagan's disdain for the progressive income tax, together with his alarm at the growth of the federal government, predisposed him to favor the supply-side approach championed by Jack Kemp and his politico-intellectual allies. The practical preferences were marrow-deep, the theoretical rationale skin-deep, but both counted. Reagan's sunny nature reinforced his inclinations, pushing him farther toward a doctrine suffused with an optimism as boundless as his own. "Jack [Kemp] was basically pushing on an open door," recalled Ed Meese, because Ronald Reagan "was a supply-sider long before the term was invented." For Reagan, such ideas were less economic doctrine than simple "common sense."

It nevertheless helped immensely that Reagan's version of common sense coincided with an economic dogma that legitimated and bolstered his predilections. Supply-side economics provided a coherent, if controversial, rationale for Reagan's policies and exercised a decisive influence on a number of his key advisers. Martin Anderson, the author of the "Reagan for President Campaign's Policy Memorandum No. 1," was an early convert to the supply-side approach and in 1976, while reviewing grant applications for the Richardson Foundation, helped Jude Wanniski get the funding that allowed him to leave the *Wall Street Journal* in order to write his supply-side tract *The Way the World Works.* During the race to the presidency, Anderson took what he called "the simple idea that was supply-side economics" and helped make it into "an important part of President Reagan's economic program."

Supply-side ideas also influenced Reagan's "economic professionals" on the Council of Economic Advisers. In announcing the administration's Program for Economic Recovery in February 1981, Murray Weidenbaum, the first of Reagan's several CEA chairmen, noted that "in contrast to the inflationary demand-led booms of the 1970s, the most significant growth of economic activity will occur in the supply side of the economy." When the CEA later set forth the philosophical and intellectual underpinnings of the administration's economic program in the 1982 *Economic Report,* it embraced a supply-side perspective. While never persuaded that tax cuts would so stimulate economic activity as to automatically and immediately make up for lost revenue . . . Weidenbaum and his CEA colleagues subsequently recalled that they nevertheless "really believed in supply-side economics."

Shaped by both personal experience and economic doctrine, Reaganomics also had a larger inspiration and rationale. The Reagan program was, at bottom, yet another expression of postwar growthmanship. William Brock, the Republican party chairman, later recalled the "very clear sense that . . . the basic aim of the policy we were trying to implement was to restore growth." Reaganomics, Kemp observed, was "really the classical prescription for economic growth." Thus, it was no coincidence that Reagan entitled his major 1980 campaign speech on economic policy "A Strategy for Growth: The American Economy in the 1980s." In his first presidential address on the economy, he reminded his live national television audience, "Our aim is to increase our national wealth so all will have more, not just redistribute what we already have [*sic*] which is just a sharing of scarcity."

In this way, the Gipper finally achieved unambiguously what Richard Nixon had earlier attempted with characteristic indirection—he stole the Democrats' most potent politico-economic appeal and placed it at the center of his conservative Republicanism. Running for reelection in 1984, Reagan joyfully offered voters a choice "between two different visions of the future, two fundamentally different ways of governing—their government of pessimism, fear, and limits, or ours of hope, confidence, and growth." Moreover, like both Nixon and the growth liberals before him, Reagan harnessed growth to a larger ideological crusade. The growth liberals had used growth to underwrite a new level and style of governmental activism at home and abroad; Nixon had sought to use it to reestablish a republic of Whiggish virtue; Reagan now turned to growth to help him dismantle the modern welfare state.

The apparent brilliance of Reagan's approach and much of its consequent appeal to conservatives lay in the fact that the same mechanisms that would spur economic growth—tax cuts, spending controls, and deregulation—would also serve to restrain the growth of the federal government. Reagan's disdain for government was real and ran deep. In January 1982, he complained in his diary that "the press is trying to paint me as trying to undo the New Deal. I remind them I voted for FDR four times." As Reagan saw it, the charge was off the mark, if only by a little: "I'm trying to undo the Great Society. It was LBJ's war on poverty that led us to our present mess." Believing that the federal government would "grow forever unless you do something to starve it," Reagan perceived his growth program to be both good economics and good ideology. "By cutting taxes," he later wrote, "I wanted not only to stimulate the economy but to curb the growth of government and reduce its intrusion into the economic life of the country." As both candidate and president, Reagan gave top priority to an economic program designed to stimulate economic growth and to achieve these larger, heroic objectives as well. The relationship between the goals was reciprocal: the tax and spending cuts designed to generate growth would shrink government, and the shrinkage of government would in turn contribute to still more growth. Once again, economic growth became both vehicle and camouflage for a larger ideological agenda.

The administration took full advantage of Reagan's single-mindedness in pursuing its economic agenda. It also benefited mightily from the surge of public affection for the president generated by his brave and graceful performance after an assassination attempt only weeks into his first term in the spring of 1981. The combination of purposefulness and luck enabled the administration to implement large parts of its economic program with a speed that stunned its Democratic opponents. In August, Congress passed the Economic Recovery Tax Act of 1981 (ERTA), which phased in a 23 percent cumulative reduction in personal income tax rates over three years, lowered immediately the top marginal personal income tax rate from 70 to 50 percent, committed the federal government to begin indexing the personal income tax for inflation in 1985, and liberalized depreciation guidelines and increased the business investment tax credit. It was the largest tax cut in U.S. history, and it was permanent.

Reagan achieved similar success on the monetary front, although there he necessarily acted mainly by indirection while the notionally independent Federal Reserve took the lead. Encouraged by Reagan's campaign commitment to fight inflation unmercifully, the Fed, which had already adopted a more strictly monetarist policy approach in October 1979, tightened monetary policy soon after the 1980 election and again in May 1981. Most important, when critics both inside and outside the administration clamored for relief from the economic pain caused by the Fed's attempt to wring inflation out of the economy once and for all, Reagan protected the central bank politically. . . .

To the extent that the battle against inflation was psychological, and it was partly so, Reagan's firmness in firing the 11,400 air traffic controllers who went out on strike over a pay dispute in August 1981 made an important symbolic contribution. As Volcker later recalled, "The significance was that someone finally took on an aggressive, well-organized union and said no." Equally important for the campaign against inflation, Reagan's strong action against the air traffic controllers dramatically established his determination and willingness to court short-term risks and to absorb short-term costs in the pursuit of larger goals or principles. The decision to fight the 1982 midterm elections under the slogan "Stay the Course" and the subsequent reappointment of Volcker to a new term as Fed chairman in 1983 drove home the anti-inflation message. Although the Fed's tight money campaign came at an exceedingly high price in both joblessness and lost production—the policy played a major role in bringing about the sharpest recession of the postwar era in 1981–82—the payoff was considerable: in 1982, the consumer price index increased only 3.8 percent, and it remained in that vicinity for the remainder of the decade. As the economist Michael Mussa has observed, "the demon of inflation . . . had finally been tamed."

The administration also made some initial progress in the attempt to reduce the growth of federal spending and to further the efforts, already under way and often far advanced during the Carter years, to reduce the extent of federal regulation. Reagan's first budget proposal, presented in February 1981 for fiscal year 1982, called for spending cuts of slightly more than $45 billion; in the end, the legislative package passed in August was estimated to trim spending by $35 billion. The latter figure was sufficient to cause the Democratic chairman of the House Budget Committee to claim that the reduction in spending constituted "the most monumental and historic turnaround in fiscal policy that has ever occurred." In its drive to deregulate the economy, the new administration immediately created a task force on regulatory reform under the leadership of Vice President George Bush, terminated the price controls on oil remaining from the 1970s, put a blanket hold on the imposition of new regulations, and filled important posts with champions of regulatory relief.

However, the administration's substantial initial progress in all these areas was quickly overtaken and overshadowed by a budgetary crisis that developed even as the basic building blocks of Reaganomics were being put into place in the summer of 1981. Weeks before the president signed the Economic Recovery Tax Act of 1981 into law, OMB director David Stockman warned of a brewing fiscal disaster. From the outset Stockman, a former Michigan congressman, had been a driving force in the framing and implementation of Reaganomics. He possessed, his compatriot Martin Anderson has written, "the zeal of a newly born-again Christian, the body of a thirty-four-year-old, and the drive to work fourteen-hour days, including Saturdays and some Sundays." His personality wore better with some people than with others—Treasury Secretary Donald Regan thought him "arrogant and antidemocrat"—but his intellectual grasp of budgetary matters impressed both friend and foe and made him a powerful figure in White House circles and beyond. Nobody in the administration, perhaps the whole government, knew as much about the budget, and in early August 1981 Stockman told Reagan and his top aides, "The scent of victory is still in the air, but I'm not going to mince words. We're heading for a crash landing on the budget. We're facing potential deficit numbers so big that they could wreck the president's entire economic program."

The problem that Stockman presented to the seemingly barely comprehending president and his aides was real, and it quickly got worse. The administration's predicament could be stated all too simply: Revenue growth lagged more than originally anticipated but spending continued to rise. The widening gap between intake and outgo threatened to eventuate in a round of the biggest deficits in peacetime U.S. history. The reasons for the fiscal debacle were some-what more complicated than the distressingly simple arithmetic that underlay them. On the rev-enue side of the fiscal equation, several factors were at work. First, the administration won not simply the largest tax cut in the nation's history, but a tax cut far larger overall than even it had originally envisioned. Tax-cutting was obviously a political exercise—there were benefits to be gained and disadvantages to be avoided—and, once under way, the process touched off a con-gressional frenzy, a bidding war in which both political parties courted support by offering special tax relief for favored constituencies. Consequently, the Economic Recovery Tax Act of 1981 came to include not merely the massive reductions in the personal income tax a la Kemp-Roth but also a host of lesser "ornamental" tax breaks, income tax indexation (a big revenue loser when it corrected the individual income tax structure for inflation from 1985 onward), and large cuts in business, estate, and gift taxes.

In addition, the administration had based its initial budget projection of a balanced budget by fiscal year 1984 on a very optimistic forecast, which came to be known as the "Rosy Scenario." As it turned out, economic growth—and hence revenue growth—was much slower than pro-jected, in part because the much-heralded incentive effects of supply-side policies proved both less potent and less immediate in their impact than some had predicted, and in part because when the Fed constricted the money supply to battle inflation, it helped trigger a recession in 1981–82 that further weakened the flow of revenue. Ironically, even the Fed's success in bring-ing down inflation worked against the administration's hope for a balanced budget, since the slackening of inflation meant less bracket creep in the tax system and consequently less revenue, even before indexation took effect.

Developments on the spending side of the ledger proved similarly disastrous to the administra-tion's initial projections of a balanced budget by 1984. As revenues lagged, expenditures con-tinued to grow. Here, too, the reasons were several. First, even the most dedicated budget slashers within the administration found that gutting the modern welfare state was easier said than done. Stockman was a true radical, an ideologue who wanted a revolutionary reduction in the size and scope of the federal government, what he later termed "a frontal assault on the American welfare state." But, as he himself admitted, his "blueprint for sweeping, wrenching change in national economic governance would have hurt millions of people in the short run." To his disappoint-ment, Stockman discovered that although Reagan genuinely wanted to slow the growth of the federal apparatus, the president was temperamentally "too kind, gentle, and sentimental" for the kind of draconian expenditure reductions his budget director thought necessary to balance the budget and dismantle the existing welfare state. Liberals took a rather different view, complaining that Reagan's cuts in domestic spending signaled "the return of social Darwinism," this time presided over by a former movie actor playing "Herbert Hoover with a smile." The truth actually lay somewhere in between these contrasting assessments. Real spending for nondefense programs other than interest on the national debt did grow in the Reagan years, but at an average annual rate—less than 1 percent—far below that of previous postwar decades.

Reagan was committed to slowing the growth of established federal programs, but he carefully avoided pledges to abolish outright any specific existing ones. Here, as elsewhere, he preferred the protective cover of his unique combination of rhetorical generalities about gov-ernment being the problem, not the solution, and anecdotal specificity about Cadillac-driving welfare queens and feckless bureaucrats. Although he lacked his budget director's command of fiscal detail, he was savvy enough to recognize Stockman's call for "the ruthless dispensation of short-run pain in the name of long-run gain" as political dynamite. After all, Stockman had been appointed OMB director; Reagan had been elected president. He and his political advisers entertained hopes for a second term, and their aversion to bloated government, although genuine, was not so great as to incline them to political suicide attacks. When on one occasion Stockman did manage to engineer Reagan's acquiescence in a plan to cut Social Security benefits to early retirees (those who left the workforce at age 62 instead of 65), the resulting political firestorm persuaded the president and his advisers that Social Security was, in Niskanen's phrase, "a minefield for the administration." Consequently, the White House placed such middle-class entitlements as Social Security and Medicare off-limits to budget cutters, preferring to believe, erroneously, that large budget reductions could be made just by cutting out waste and fraud.

Moreover, when the administration did move to trim discretionary spending, it encountered resistance from both within and without that in the long run often proved overpowering. When Stockman sought to trim what he called the "vast local transportation pork barrel"—federal funding for the local building and upkeep of streets, roads, and mass transit—he found himself in a losing battle with Transportation Secretary Drew Lewis, most of Congress, and a huge constituency of state and local officials, contractors, and unions. "In the end," the budget director ruefully recounted later, "the transportation sector of the pork barrel never even knew the Reagan Revolution had tilted at it." "It was a dramatic case of everything staying the same," he added, "but it would be only one of many."

Finally, the administration compounded its budget-cutting woes by implementing a massively expensive military buildup even more energetically than the candidate had promised in the 1980 campaign. . . . The pace of military spending slowed in his second term, but overall Reagan presided over an unparalleled peacetime defense buildup that totaled nearly $2 trillion.

In this fashion, a combination of ineluctable arithmetic and the vagaries of politics immersed the Reagan presidency in a tide of red ink. By the end of the administration's second year, the fiscal picture was, Stockman later admitted, "an utter, mind-numbing catastrophe." It worsened with time. The final Reagan record on deficits was unprecedentedly bad: all eight of the administration's budgets ran deficits, the smallest $127.9 billion (current dollars) in fiscal year 1982 and the largest $221.2 billion in fiscal year 1986; in fiscal year 1983 the deficit reached a peacetime record of 6.3 percent of GNP; and, overall, the national debt tripled on Reagan's watch, from $914 billion in fiscal year 1980 to $2.7 trillion in fiscal year 1989. James M. Poterba, an MIT economist, has estimated that one-third of the deficit growth under Reagan resulted from tax reduction, two-thirds from expenditure growth in the form chiefly of increased transfer payments to individuals, increased interest payments on federal borrowing, and increased defense spending.

The reaction to this budgetary distress was a series of grudging tactical retreats that came to dominate federal budget policy for the remainder of the 1980s and beyond. For the most part, the impetus for these efforts to recapture a measure of fiscal probity came from fiscal moderates and old-style budget-balancers in Congress, abetted by those of Reagan's advisers, the budget wizards Stockman and his OMB deputy Richard Darman foremost among them, who too late recognized that their original economic design contained, in the so-called out years of their own projections, the seeds of fiscal havoc. Reagan himself was most often a passive spectator or, at best, a hesitant participant in the subsequent attempts at correction, while the unrepentant "punk supply-siders" among his advisers and elsewhere vigorously opposed them. The salvaging effort took the form chiefly of corrective tax increases (the Tax Equity and Fiscal Responsibility Act of 1982 [TEFRA], the 1983 Social Security Amendments, the Deficit Reduction Act of 1984 [DEFRA], and the Omnibus Budget Reconciliation Act of 1987 [OBRA]) and spending control measures (Gramm-Rudman-Hollings, passed in 1985, and Gramm-Rudman of 1987) that set precise deficit targets and specified the mechanisms to achieve them. In the end, these efforts, rather than eliminating the deficit as a problem, merely underscored the fact that record budget deficits and the tripled national debt had become the central economic and political realities of the Reagan era.

As a result of the unprecedented red ink, the decade from the mid-1980s through the mid-1990s may well be remembered as the era of the budget. Between 1982 and 1995, the federal government was forced twelve times technically to halt operations, however briefly, for lack of funds. Former presidents Gerald Ford and Jimmy Carter warned Reagan's Republican successor, George Bush, before his inauguration that the federal deficit had come to dominate decision making "in Congress, in the White House, throughout the Federal government." By the end of the 1980s, wrote the political scientists Joseph White and Aaron Wildavsky, the budget had become "to our era what civil rights, communism, the depression, industrialization, and slavery were at other times." Extravagant perhaps, but New York's Democratic senator Daniel Patrick Moynihan agreed that the deficit had become "the first fact of national government."

The overriding political consequence of this defining fact of governance was its shattering impact on the sort of federal activism strongly identified with Democratic liberalism. The Reagan administration's persistent efforts to dismantle social programs by restricting eligibility, slashing benefits, and privatizing activities met with only uneven success, but where direct assault failed, fiscal policy succeeded by indirection: Reagan's budget deficits effectively defunded the welfare state. The recurring deficits and growing national debt forced liberals to scurry to protect existing social programs from budget cuts and made it almost impossible for them to mount new efforts at the federal level. The fiscal crisis was "Reagan's revenge," complained the liberal historian Alan Brinkley, "a back door for doing what many on the right had been unable to achieve with their frontal assaults in the 1950s and 1960s." As Reagan White House aide Tom Griscom observed with palpable satisfaction, "You can no longer just say, 'Well, let's do this and not worry about either where the money is going to come from or whether we are going to have to take away from another program or shift priorities.'" Reduced support for existing programs and the forestalling of new ones further hurt liberalism by contributing to a general loss of faith by voters in the capacity of government to address national concerns. To the horror of liberals, Reagan's economic ineptitude seemed to weaken their programmatic potency and political appeal!

Daniel Patrick Moynihan believed this outcome deliberate. The senator from New York favored a supply-side tax cut of some sort in 1981 in order to improve incentives and boost investment, but he distrusted the promises of the enthusiastic supply-siders around Reagan, observing that they bore the same relationship to genuine conservatives that anarchists did to liberals. Moynihan realized almost immediately that the ERTA of 1981 was too large, and he predicted presciently that it would result in crushing deficits. Within weeks of the ERTA's passage, he asked a New York business audience, "Do we really want a decade in which the issue of public discourse, over and over and over, will be how big must the budget cuts be in order to prevent the deficit from being even bigger. Surely, larger, more noble purposes ought to engage us."

By the end of 1983 the senator became convinced, partly on the basis of conversations with Stockman, who had been a Moynihan protégé (and that family's live-in babysitter) while studying at Harvard Divinity School, that "the early Reagan deficits had been deliberate, that there had been a hidden agenda." . . .

Was Moynihan's charge accurate? Had there been a conspiracy purposely to generate huge deficits in order to bring the welfare state to its knees by "starving the beast"? Stockman denied the charge, asserting that both the administration's "rosy scenario" forecast and the Congressional Budget Office projections used by Congress in developing the ERTA of 1981 had predicted falling deficits under the administration's budget proposals; he also denied that anyone within the administration really believed they were creating huge deficits that could be used effectively to discipline congressional spending. In other words, the deficits were too much of a surprise to have been put to the conspiratorial uses suggested by Moynihan. Stockman's deputy at OMB, Richard Darman, called Moynihan's charge "way overdrawn," but granted that both Reagan and Stockman had believed that the threat or reality of reduced revenue could be used to rein in the spending habits of the profligate Congress. . . .

It is one of the great ironies of the 1980s that Reagan's stumbling success in his ideological endeavor to limit the perceived leftward drift of government came at the expense of his economic goal of accelerated long-term growth. The deficits that effectively prevented any substantive extension of the welfare state (beyond the inertial advance of middle-class entitlements) at the same time compromised the drive to make the economy more productive. The administration's record on growth was lackluster. It is a further irony that when the deficits generated by the administration's supply-side approach helped the economy recover from the 1981–82 recession, they succeeded because they boosted demand in the short run; the impact of the deficits on the supply side of the economy—investment and productivity—operated in the long run to undercut economic growth.

The economic impact of the large Reagan deficits was substantial, but just how substantial and to what degree harmful have proven to be controversial questions. It will not do to oversimplify a complex matter. Even among professional economists, there was much empirical and analytical uncertainty regarding the effect of the Reagan budget "disasters." William Niskanen, a veteran of Reagan's CEA, wrote in 1988 that although economists had been studying the economic effects of government borrowing for years, "the economics community has probably never been more confused about this issue." Another economist noted that the confusion was compounded by the fact that virtually everyone who approached the topic of Reagan's deficit spending had "some kind of ax to grind." Consequently, professional opinion ranged widely: some said large deficits mattered little, if at all; others saw in them the road to ruin.

If the Reagan deficits were indeed harmful, the damage they did was not immediately obvious to the casual eye. In truth, Reagan's economic record was not nearly so catastrophic as liberal critics insisted. The administration's initial tax cuts helped fuel the recovery from the 1981–82 recession by substantially increasing consumer spending, and the economy subsequently enjoyed what was to become the longest peacetime expansion in U.S. history (to that point). Most important, the Reagan expansion was sustained alongside a significant decline in inflation. Even Charles L. Schultze, Carter's CEA chairman, admitted that "the reduction in inflation was worth the pain" of the 1981–82 recession. The conventional wisdom that large deficits fueled inflation proved in this case to be wrong. A massive inflow of foreign capital appeared to mitigate the immediate impact of the deficits on investment in the United States. This was surely not the immediate meltdown some critics predicted.

Nevertheless, the massive deficits constituted a real problem in several regards. First, they required drastically increased interest payments, which themselves came to constitute a significant source of increased federal spending (no small irony!), further distending subsequent budgets in a compounding fashion. Second, as the Harvard economist Benjamin Friedman has written, "Deficits absorb saving. When more of what we save goes to finance the deficit, less is available for other activities that also depend on borrowed funds. . . . The more of our saving the deficit absorbs, the harder everyone else must compete for the rest and the higher interest rates go." Thus, the sustained large deficits kept real interest rates (that is, interest rates corrected for inflation) high even after the Federal Reserve eased monetary policy to deal with the 1981–82 recession, and those high real interest rates, both short-term and long-term, in turn caused both business and individual net investment (relative to income) to lag significantly in the Reagan years. The end result was, in Friedman's words, an "extraordinary shrinkage of America's capital formation in the 1980s." Third, the string of deficits meant that government subsequently skimped on the sorts of long-term investment in infrastructure and human capital (education and training) required for future economic growth. Finally, the deficits left policymakers with little fiscal purchase for fine-tuning the economy for either growth or stability. Without very much discretionary fiscal income to manipulate through spending and taxing decisions, "all that is left is monetary policy," wrote the economic journalist Thomas Friedman, "[which] is like trying to play a piano with only the black keys."

Thus, in the name of growth, the Reagan administration ended up damping one of the chief postwar engines of growth. Paul Krugman of MIT concluded that, all told, the Reagan deficits constituted "a moderate drag on U.S. economic growth." The administration's policies were, he wrote, "if anything biased against long-term growth." Ironically, the administration's vaunted supply-side approach ended up working more to boost demand in the short run than to effect long-term growth by increasing investment and productivity on the supply side. If this was less than the calamity claimed by Democratic partisans, it was nevertheless a rather incongruous and disappointing outcome for an administration embarked on a supply-side growth crusade.

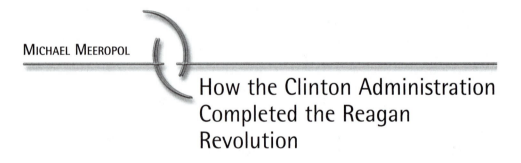

MICHAEL MEEROPOL

How the Clinton Administration Completed the Reagan Revolution

On November 5, 1996, Bill Clinton was elected to a second term as president of the United States. That same night, in congressional races, Republican majorities were returned to both the House of Representatives and the Senate. Lost in the sound and fury of the election campaign was a striking fact. When President Clinton had submitted his budget proposal the previous February, he had effectively surrendered to the policies demanded by the Republican majority in Congress. Though there had been two shutdowns of the federal government and a

From *Surrender: How the Clinton Administration Completed the Reagan Revolution,* by Michael Meeropol. Published 1998 by the University of Michigan Press. Copyright © 1998 by the University of Michigan. Reprinted by permission of the University of Michigan Press.

raucous debate between the president and the majority of Congress, they were merely arguing over the method of achieving a policy on which they had already agreed. The agreement was that by 2002 the federal budget deficit would be reduced to zero without raising taxes—in fact, there would be some tax cuts. This was not the president's only surrender. He later "compromised" with the Republican majority in Congress by signing a welfare reform bill that ended a sixty-year federal guarantee of income to poor children in single-parent homes.

Eight months after the election, on July 30, lopsided majorities in both houses passed a budget and tax agreement that had been crafted by the Clinton administration and the Republican majority in Congress. Due to the strong economic growth that had occurred in 1996 and 1997, the amount of spending reductions necessary to achieve budget balance by 2002 was significantly lower than when Congress had passed a bill with the same goal in 1995. The tax cuts were much less than the Republicans had proposed in 1995. Nevertheless, the overall result of this agreement was to complete a revolution in economic policy making.

To understand the significance of that agreement, compare the policies adopted by the United States government between 1975 and 1979 to the policies followed from 1991 to the present. The years have been chosen because these are the years following recessions, which, by law, the government of the United States must take action to counter. After the recession of 1974, economic policy was designed to increase the rate of growth, reduce the level of unemployment, and soften the blow of unemployment and poverty for those unable to find work or earn a decent level of income. After 1990 the policymakers focused on cutting the budget deficit and slowing the economy in order to keep inflation from rearing its ugly head. Making sure the unemployed were receiving unemployment compensation and that the poor could take advantage of governmental assistance were not merely less important than achieving budget balance, they were considered counterproductive.

The policies followed in response to the 1974 recession were consistent with a general expansion of the role of government in the economy from the Great Depression through 1979. The election of Ronald Reagan to the presidency in 1980 signaled the beginning of a serious effort to alter that trend. Though the so-called Reagan Revolution was only partially successful in changing policy and though the effects it had on the economy have been the subject of hot dispute, with the hindsight of history it is clear that those initial efforts finally met success in the bipartisanship before and after the presidential election of 1996.

. . . Government tax and spending policy will no longer be used to reduce unemployment. Instead, the Federal Reserve System, the U.S. Central Bank, has been conceded total authority to battle either inflation or unemployment. In practice, the Central Bank has focused more on preventing inflation, so that anytime the unemployment rate gets "too low" they feel it necessary to raise it in order to slow down the economy. The Congress and the president are silent in the face of such action. Thirty—and even twenty—years ago, such actions would routinely produce howls of protest from Congress and even the president.

Redistribution of income to the nonelderly poor is no longer a federal responsibility. Even redistribution of income to the elderly is to be constrained so as to permit the federal budget to achieve balance. After an expansion of the role of the federal government in redistributing income between 1960 and 1980, the new priority for government, both at the federal and at the state and local levels, is to finance the Defense Department and a growing police and prison industry.

Between 1960 and 1979, the Social Security system went from representing 12.6 percent of the federal budget to 20.7 percent. In 1960, Medicare did not exist; by 1979 it covered 5.2 percent of the budget. Redistributing income to the poor (identified as income security) went from 8 percent of the federal budget to 13 percent. The "Reagan Revolution" made a strenuous effort to cut this redistribution but mostly succeeded in cutting taxes. In terms of overall spending it was unsuccessful. In 1989, the proportion of the budget covered by Social Security and Income Security had fallen slightly to 32.2 percent (from just over one-third), but Medicare had risen to cover 7.4 percent of the federal budget.

The 1997 law puts controls on the growth of Medicare spending. Looking to the long term, there are proposals in the air to privatize some aspects of Social Security, to automatically reduce cost-of-living increases because the government's measuring rod for the cost of living has been judged faulty, and otherwise control what the pundits and policymakers have called "runaway entitlement spending."

Meanwhile, income distribution, which had trended toward more equality between 1945 and 1979, had become more unequal in the period between 1979 and 1993, and it was unclear whether the period after 1993 had merely interrupted a trend or actually reversed it. Income distribution is a very important economic-policy issue from a political point of view. During the 1994 congressional election, Democrats had criticized the Republicans' campaign document, called the *Contract with America,* on the basis of "fairness." The policies advocated by the Republicans would, in the words of Representative Carrie Meek (D.-FL), "produce another tax windfall for the wealthy while leaving the middle class and poor behind."

The effect of proposed policy changes on income distribution is one of the major arguments between those who approved of and wanted to extend the Reagan economic legacy and those who wanted to reverse it. Both sides appealed to the principle of fairness. From Representative Meek's perspective, fairness involved less inequality in the distribution of income. For supporters of the Reagan Revolution, fairness involved avoiding undue burdens on individuals who work, produce, and invest, thereby creating more income for everyone. The Republican majority in Congress and not a few Democrats claim that policies that might increase income inequality are acceptable if they have such a positive influence on the rate of growth of income that even the poorest individuals would benefit greatly. In other words, economic growth raising the absolute level of income for the poor would more than make up for increased inequality. This is the key idea behind the statement attributed to President Kennedy, "A rising tide lifts all boats." Those who agree with Representative Meek argue that the middle class and the poor were hurt by the Reagan economic program, that the economy's growth did not benefit them.

The linchpin of the revolution was the drive to balance the federal budget and cut taxes as a means toward shrinking the role of the federal government in the economy. The desire to do this was based on a general view of how the (economic) world functions: a belief that, left to their own devices, individuals pursuing their self-interest and constrained only by competition will interact in such a way as to produce the best of all possible (economic) results. On the theoretical level, this is an argument that government should stay out of the way as much as possible, though it has some clearly important roles, such as enforcing the law and providing for the defense of the nation against foreign enemies.

On a more practical, political level, the requirement of a balanced budget provides significant support for policymakers who do not wish to expand government spending on programs that might be popular, such as guaranteeing all children equal educational opportunity, repairing every bridge and road that needs it, fixing every leaky roof in a public school, and wiring every public library for the Internet. It also makes it difficult to introduce new spending initiatives such as providing complete cradle-to-grave health coverage for all citizens. In response to felt needs, leaders can exclaim, as President George [H. W.] Bush did in his inaugural address, "We have more will than wallet," and that ends the argument in favor of such expensive items as guaranteed health care for all Americans.

President Reagan created the first installment of the revolution by pushing through a significant tax cut in 1981. However, he never was able to follow through with the spending cuts necessary to avoid big increases in government borrowing. In 1990, George Bush compromised with Congress on a combination of tax increases and spending cuts that some saw as a betrayal of the Reagan policies, but that in the long run reduced borrowing and constrained spending increases. In 1992, Bill Clinton was elected in part on a promise to reverse Reagan's policies. His package of tax increases and spending cuts in 1993 supposedly repudiated Reagan's policies, but except in very minor ways they were consistent with them. More importantly, over the years after 1993, the federal budget deficit declined significantly, and federal spending fell a bit in relation to total income. The one effort made by the Clinton administration to move economic policy in a different direction, the full reform of the health care system, was soundly defeated by a coalition of Republicans and conservative Democrats.

In 1994, the Republicans gained control of the House and Senate after a campaign where they featured a series of promises in the Contract with America. The economic policies promised in that document included a balanced-budget amendment to the Constitution, a series of tax cuts, and a sweeping reform of the welfare system. From the beginning of that congressional campaign, Democrats such as Representative Meek attacked the proposals as trickle-down economics, enriching a few and claiming that the rest of society would benefit from the crumbs. When the Republicans won the election and introduced their proposals as legislation, Democrats blasted them as "extremist." In 1995 and 1996 the battle was joined between the president and the Republican Congress over budget proposals that were vetoed by the president. As mentioned above, the government actually was shut down twice over these budget battles before Congress and the president reached a compromise in April 1996.

Hidden in the noise from the "battlefield," the Clinton administration's surrender was barely noticed by the public, which was focusing instead on the lead-up to the presidential election campaign and then the campaign itself. But as the compromise emerged during the discussions over the 1998 fiscal year budget, the success of the revolution was no longer in doubt. First had been Reagan's election, then a decade of change and even more revolutionary proposals thwarted by a Democratic Congress. Then there was the alleged Bush betrayal in 1990. Some saw the election of Bill Clinton as a repudiation of Reaganomics, with the Republican Contract with America as its revival. Clinton's "tough stand" against Republican "extremism" allegedly blunted that revolution, but in fact when Bill Clinton submitted his budget in February 1996 and signed the welfare reform law in August 1996 he signaled surrender: the Reagan Revolution was going to achieve its major goals.

With the signing of the budget and tax bills in August 1997, the surrender was complete. Budget balance was an iron-clad pledge from both political parties and both branches of government. As a result of the constraint of budget balance and the (albeit modest) tax cut approved for the 1998–2002 budget years, the impact of government on the economy, which had grown from the Great Depression through the 1970s, was bound to shrink.

Further Reading

See Burton I. Kaufman, *The Presidency of James Earl Carter, Jr.* (Lawrence: University Press of Kansas, 1993) on the presidential policies of Jimmy Carter, as well as Daniel Horowitz, *Jimmy Carter and the Energy Crisis of the 1970s: The "Crisis of Confidence" Speech of July 15, 1979: A Brief History with Documents* (Boston: Bedford Books, 2004).

For an overview of Reagan's presidency and American society in the 1980s, see *Sleepwalking Through History: America in the Reagan Years* (New York: Norton, 1991) by long-time Washington journalist Haynes Johnson; the best short overview by an historian is *Reckoning with Reagan: America and Its President in the 1980s* (New York: Oxford University Press, 1992), by Michael Schaller.

For the most recent research on various aspects of the policies and politics of the Reagan administration, see the essays in *The Reagan Presidency: Pragmatic Conservatism and Its Legacies* (Lawrence: University Press of Kansas, 2003), edited by W. Elliott Brownlee and Hugh Davis Graham. More accessible and considerably less mild in its judgments of Reagan's economic policies is Iwan W. Morgan, *Deficit Government: Taxing and Spending in Modern America* (Chicago: Ivan R. Dee, 1995).

Kevin P. Phillips, *Wealth and Democracy: A Political History of the American Rich* (New York: Broadway Books, 2002) and his earlier *The Politics of Rich and Poor: Wealth and the American Electorate in the Reagan Aftermath* (New York: Random House, 1990) document the growing inequality of American society since the late 1970s as well as the "middle-class squeeze." For an analysis of tax policy that details the way in which Reagan-era tax reform did not help the middle class, see Donald L. Bartlett and James B. Steele, *America: Who Really Pays the Taxes?* (New York: Simon & Schuster, 1994). *The Next American Nation: The New Nationalism and the Fourth American Revolution* (New York: The Free Press, 1995), by Michael Lind, is an arresting effort to map the changing landscape of class and race in America. *Peddling Prosperity: Economic Sense and Nonsense in an Age of Diminished Expectations* (New York: Norton, 1994), by Paul Krugman, is essential, although somewhat challenging, reading on the economic policy debates of the 1980s and early 1990s.

Serious biographers of Reagan are critical of Reagan's domestic policies, although they vary somewhat in how harshly they indict Reagan himself, with some emphasizing Reagan's intellectual emptiness and lack of engagement, and others expressing admiration for his skills as a communicator and salesman. Among those who seek to combine both viewpoints is William E. Pemberton, *Exit with Honor: The Life and Presidency of Ronald Reagan* (Armonk, NY: M. E. Sharpe, 1997). For a sympathetic account that strives to be balanced and objective, see *President Reagan: The Role of a Lifetime* (New York: Simon & Schuster, 1991), by Lou Cannon, who covered Reagan's career as a journalist both in Sacramento and in Washington, DC. One of the earlier studies of Reagan, Garry Wills's *Reagan's America: Innocents at Home* (Garden City, NY: Doubleday, 1987) is still indispensable reading for its effort to place Reagan's life and political success in a broader cultural context. For a highly critical and brief overview of Reagan's presidency, see Robert Erwin's essay, "Reagan in Retrospect," *Virginia Quarterly Review* (vol. 77/3 [Summer 2001]), 377–90. See journalist Sidney Blumenthal, *Our Long National Daydream: A Political Pageant of the Reagan Era* (New York: Harper & Row, 1988), and Joan Didion's essay on Reagan, "The West Wing of Oz," in her collection, *Political Fictions* (New York: Knopf, 2001) for examples of works that stress Reagan's intellectual vacuity and hands-off approach to governing. For the argument that Reagan was in charge and engaged by a critic of the president, see *Firewall: The Iran-Contra Conspiracy and Cover-Up* (New York: Norton, 1997), by Lawrence E. Walsh, the special prosecutor who led the official investigation of the Iran-Contra foreign-policy scandal of the 1980s. Most of the enthusiastic accounts of Reagan's presidency lack scholarly merit; the best among them is Dinesh D'Souza's *Ronald Reagan: How an Ordinary Man Became an Extraordinary Leader* (New York: The Free Press, 1997). For a recent iconoclastic view of Reagan as a liberal, see Joshua Green, "Reagan's Liberal

Legacy: What the New Literature on the Gipper Won't Tell You," *Washington Monthly* (January/February 2003, 28–33).

The shelf of good books on the post-Reagan era of national politics and policy is relatively short. For the presidency of George H. W. Bush, see Michael Duffy and Dan Goodgame, *Marching in Place: The Status Quo Presidency of George Bush* (New York: Simon & Schuster, 1992). *The Postmodern Presidency: Bill Clinton's Legacy in U.S. Politics* (Pittsburgh, PA: University of Pittsburgh Press, 2000), edited by Steven E. Schier, is an early attempt by scholars to come to grips with the Clinton era. See also Theda Skocpol, *Boomerang: Clinton's Health Security Effort and the Turn Against Government in U.S. Politics* (New York: Norton, 1996) for an account by an eminent sociologist of the failure of Clinton's effort to create national health care, and Elizabeth Drew, *Showdown: The Struggle between the Gingrich Congress and the Clinton White House* (New York: Simon & Schuster, 1996) for a veteran political reporter's insight into the political struggles during Clinton's presidency.

Primary Sources

For Jimmy Carter's Crisis of the American Spirit speech, go to www.americanrhetoric.com/speeches/jimmycartercrisisofconfidence.htm, which provides both text and audio versions. Carter had planned to deliver a speech on energy conservation but was dissuaded from doing so by his pollster, Pat Caddell; for the text of the undelivered speech, go to www.americanrhetoric.com/speeches/jimmycarterundeliveredenergyspeech.htm. The text of Ronald Reagan's first inaugural address, in which he stated that government was the source of America's economic woes, may be found at www.presidentreagan.info/speeches/in1.cfm. For information on the federal debt each year from 1950 through 2005, go to www.publicdebt.treas.gov/opd/opdhisto4.htm. For a chart based on U.S. Census data that shows how income distribution in the U.S. changed between 1947 and 2001, go to www.census.gov/hhes/income/histinc/f02.html. Go to www.truthandpolitics.org/top-rates.php?print=yes for a chart of the top marginal tax rates and how they changed between 1913 and 2003. For President Bill Clinton's 1996 State of the Union address, in which he declared "the era of big government is over" and also laid out his plan for welfare reform, go to www.law.ou.edu/hist/state96.html.

CHAPTER ⟨13⟩

The End of the Cold War

INTRODUCTION

The collapse of the Soviet Union in 1991 ended almost 50 years of cold war, leaving the United States the sole surviving superpower. Did the United States thus "win" the cold war? Republican loyalists and conservative analysts were quick to claim victory not only for the United States but also, specifically, for Republican president Ronald Reagan and his confrontational approach to the USSR during his presidency. Tough talk—most famously, Reagan's speech of March 1983 labeling the Soviet Union an "evil empire"—coupled with an aggressive military buildup and aid to insurgents challenging communist rule around the globe had pushed the Soviets into a corner, they said. Already experiencing severe economic challenges, the Soviets were forced into a renewal of an unwanted arms race with the United States that so debilitated the Soviet economy that the whole system finally imploded. Both popular and scholarly histories of the cold war have reflected this view that belligerent rhetoric and aggressive tactics paid off, and that Ronald Reagan engineered the downfall of the Soviet Union. These include the video biography of Ronald Reagan, which aired as part of the popular *American Experience* program on public television, a medium that eschews partisan identification but in the public's mind is liberal in outlook.

The challenge to this view was immediate and significant from scholars of international relations and of the Soviet Union, from some policy experts, and from journalists and others whose scrutiny of Reagan as president had uncovered little evidence of the abilities and focus implied in the view of him as the mastermind of the Soviet Union's demise. Writing in the *New York Times* in 1992, George Kennan, the longtime Soviet specialist who in the aftermath of World War II successfully advocated the policy of containment (that is, of seeking to prevent the Soviet Union from spreading communism to countries outside the East Bloc), asserted that "the suggestion that any American administration had the power to influence decisively the course of a tremendous domestic-political upheaval in another great country on another side of the globe is intrinsically silly and childish. No great country has that sort of influence on the internal developments of any other one." Others have seconded this view that events within the Soviet Union—the gross economic inefficiencies that, by the late 1970s, had become untenable, and the dynamic leadership of Mikhail Gorbachev, who was dedicated to reforming the Soviet economy and ending the arms race with the United States—were the keys to the Soviet Union's collapse.

Another line of argument focuses on the rhetoric and policies under Reagan that signaled an end to containment in favor of a more aggressive effort to "roll back" communist gains and even undermine the Soviet Union itself. Evidence of Reagan's confrontational style and policies include his support for the Contras, who were seeking to overthrow the left-wing Sandinista regime of Nicaragua, even after Congress made such assistance illegal, and the military assistance provided to the mujihadin in Afghanistan, who were fighting against the Soviet Union. Critics maintained that this kind of activity, along with Reagan's huge military buildup and his advocacy of the Strategic Defense Initiative (a space shield that purportedly could protect the United States from incoming nuclear missiles), promoted instability, posed the risk of larger war and even of nuclear disaster, and actually prolonged the cold war by provoking a hostile response from hard-liners within the Soviet Union who were opposed to reform.

A third criticism of the view that Reagan masterminded the cold war focuses on Reagan himself. According to this argument, Reagan's policies were not as coherent as his proponents recall, and he was in fact mentally disengaged and, as his presidency went on, often addled. His greatest successes vis-à-vis the Soviet Union came not in response to his saber-rattling but with his efforts at reconciliation—lifting the grain embargo on the Soviet Union that had been imposed by Jimmy Carter, for example—and at ending the arms race, to which Gorbachev responded positively.

Two of the three readings that follow represent starkly contrasting views of Reagan's role in ending the cold war. The first selection, by right-wing commentator Dinesh D'Souza, represents an extreme version of the "Reagan won the cold war" position, but it is one that has influenced significantly mainstream examinations of the end of the cold war. In it, D'Souza gives sole credit to Reagan, although he acknowledges that the Soviet Union's economy was troubled. He also admits that Gorbachev was a decent man seeking to reform his country, but insists that he acted in response to Reagan's challenges rather than to events internal to the USSR. Although D'Souza is openly scornful of those he refers to as "doves"—those who believed that the more productive approach to dealing with the Soviet Union was through negotiation and détente, or, in his term, "appeasement"—he also criticizes "hawks," who were inflexible and unable to recognize, as Reagan did, both that the Soviet Union was on its knees and that it was desirable, and not dangerous, to commit the United States to nuclear arms reductions.

The second selection, by political scientists Daniel Deudney and G. John Ikenberry, proceeds from the premise that "the ultimate cause of the cold war's outcome lies in the failures of the Soviet system itself." But why, the authors ask, did the Soviet Union collapse at the moment that it did? In their view, Ronald Reagan's actions and rhetoric vis-à-vis the USSR *did* have an impact. But it was neither his belligerent challenges to the "evil empire" nor his aggressive military buildup that brought down the Soviet Union, as D'Souza and other adherents of what they call the "Reagan victory school" assert. Deudney and Ikenberry point instead to Reagan's personal antipathy to nuclear weapons and his willingness, in the face of pressure from the grassroots peace movement, to discuss disarmament with Gorbachev despite the objections of hardliners in his administration. Initiatives toward economic cooperation and the influence of American popular culture were significant as well in the unraveling of the Soviet system, they argue, but they find no evidence that the ideological warfare waged by the Reagan administration against the Soviet Union had the desired impact. Thus a complex array of forces, of which Reagan's willingness to negotiate arms reductions was but one, brought the cold war to an end; military and ideological aggression were not among them. The authors conclude by suggesting broader policy implications: negotiation and initiatives stressing interdependence may be more effective than belligerence and confrontation in advancing U.S. foreign policy goals.

The third selection, by historian Edward Pessen, takes a longer view of the half-century-long conflict between the United States and the USSR, asking not so much why the United States "won" the cold war but at what cost. Unlike the previous authors, he attaches no particular significance to Reagan's presidency, seeing instead remarkable continuity in policy and actions from President Truman through President George H. W. Bush. All practiced containment, which included the stockpiling of nuclear weapons and military intervention in third world countries, among other things. In Pessen's view, these efforts, together, certainly achieved their aims of destroying the Soviet Union. The emphasis, in this excerpt from his book, *Losing Our Souls: The American Experience in the Cold War,* is on the price of this victory—in terms of lives lost and of threats to the environment, to the U.S. economy, and to American political life. If D'Souza believes that the end of the cold war is cause for unreserved celebration, Pessen reminds his readers that any war, even a cold one, exacts losses, and he raises issues, implicit in the selection by Deudney and Ikenberry, about means and ends and whether the latter justify the former.

DINESH D'SOUZA

How Reagan Won the Cold War

With the disintegration of the Soviet Union, the most ambitious political and social experiment of the modern era ended in failure, and the supreme political drama of the twentieth century—the conflict between the free West and the totalitarian East—came to an end. What will probably prove to be the most important historical event of our lifetimes has already occurred.

Given these remarkable developments, it is natural to wonder what caused the destruction of Soviet Communism. Yet, oddly, this is a subject that no one seems to want to discuss. The reluctance is especially acute among intellectuals. Consider what happened on June 4, 1990, when Mikhail Gorbachev addressed the students and faculty at Stanford University. The Cold War was over, he said, and people clapped with evident relief. Then Gorbachev added, "And let us not wrangle over who won it." At this point the crowd leapt to its feet and applauded thunderously.

Gorbachev's desire to avoid this topic was understandable. But why were the apparent winners of the Cold War equally resolved not to celebrate their victory or analyze how it came about? Perhaps the reason is simply this: virtually everyone was wrong about the Soviet Union. The doves or appeasers were totally and spectacularly wrong on every point. For example, when Reagan in 1983 called the Soviet Union an "evil empire," Anthony Lewis of the *New York Times* was so indignant that he searched his repertoire for the appropriate adjective: "simplistic," "sectarian," "dangerous," "outrageous." Finally Lewis settled on "primitive—the only word for it."

Adapted from *Ronald Reagan: How an Ordinary Man Became an Extraordinary Leader,* by Dinesh D'Souza. Copyright © 1998 by Dinesh D'Souza. Used by permission of Dinesh D'Souza.

In the mid 1980s, Strobe Talbott, then a journalist at *Time* and later an official in the Clinton State Department, wrote: "Reagan is counting on American technological and economic predominance to prevail in the end," whereas, if the Soviet economy was in a crisis of any kind, "it is a permanent, institutionalized crisis with which the USSR has learned to live."

Historian Barbara Tuchman argued that instead of employing a policy of confrontation, the West should ingratiate itself with the Soviet Union by pursuing "the stuffed-goose option—that is, providing them with all the grain and consumer goods they need." If Reagan had taken this advice when it was offered in 1982, the Soviet empire would probably be around today. . . .

The man who got things right from the start was, at first glance, an unlikely statesman. When he became the leader of the free world he had no experience in foreign policy. Some people thought he was a dangerous warmonger; others considered him a nice fellow, but a bit of a bungler. Nevertheless, this California lightweight turned out to have as deep an understanding of Communism as Aleksandr Solzhenitsyn. This rank amateur developed a complex, often counter-intuitive strategy for dealing with the Soviet Union which hardly anyone on his staff fully endorsed or even understood. Through a combination of vision, tenacity, patience, and improvisational skill, he produced what Henry Kissinger terms "the most stunning diplomatic feat of the modern era." Or as Margaret Thatcher put it, "Ronald Reagan won the Cold War without firing a shot."

Reagan had a much more skeptical view of the power of Soviet Communism than either the hawks or the doves. In 1981 he told an audience at the University of Notre Dame, "The West won't contain Communism. It will transcend Communism. It will dismiss it as some bizarre chapter in human history whose last pages are even now being written." The next year, speaking to the British Parliament, Reagan predicted that if the Western alliance remained strong it would produce a "march of freedom and democracy which will leave Marxism–Leninism on the ashheap of history."

These prophetic assertions—dismissed as wishful rhetoric at the time—raise the question: How did Reagan know that Soviet Communism faced impending collapse when the most perceptive minds of his time had no inkling of what was to come? To answer this question, the best approach is to begin with Reagan's jokes. Over the years he had developed an extensive collection of stories which he attributed to the Soviet people themselves. One of these involves a man who goes up to a store clerk in Moscow and asks for a kilogram of beef, half a kilogram of butter, and a quarter kilogram of coffee. "We're all out," the clerk says, and the man leaves. Another man, observing this incident, says to the clerk, "That old man must be crazy." The clerk replies, "Yeah, but what a memory!"

Another favorite anecdote concerns a man who goes to the Soviet bureau of transportation to order an automobile. He is informed that he will have to put down his money now, but there is a ten-year wait. So he fills out all the various forms, has them processed through the various agencies, and finally gets to the last agency. He pays them his money and they say, "Come back in ten years and get your car." He asks, "Morning or afternoon?" The man in the agency says, "We're talking about ten years from now. What difference does it make?" He replies, "The plumber is coming in the morning."

Reagan could go on in this vein for hours. What is striking, however, is that Reagan's jokes are not about the evil of Communism but about its incompetence. Reagan agreed with the hawks that the Soviet experiment which sought to create a "new man" was immoral. At the same time, he saw that it was also basically stupid. Reagan did not need a PhD in economics to recognize that any economy based upon centralized planners' dictating how much factories should produce, how much people should consume, and how social rewards should be distributed was doomed to disastrous failure. For Reagan the Soviet Union was a "sick bear," and the question was not whether it would collapse, but when.

Yet while the Soviet Union had a faltering economy, it had a highly advanced military. No one doubted that Soviet missiles, if fired at American targets, would cause enormous destruction. But Reagan also knew that the evil empire was spending at least 20 percent of its gross national product on defense. (The actual proportion turned out to be even higher.) Thus Reagan formulated the notion that the West could use the superior economic resources of a free society to outspend Moscow in the arms race, placing intolerable strains on the Soviet regime.

Reagan outlined his "sick bear" theory as early as May 1982 in a commencement address at his alma mater, Eureka College. He said, "The Soviet empire is faltering because rigid centralized control has destroyed incentives for innovation, efficiency, and individual achievement. But in the midst of social and economic problems, the Soviet dictatorship has forged the largest armed force in the world. It has done so by pre-empting the human needs of its people and, in the end, this course will undermine the foundations of the Soviet system."

Sick bears, however, can be very dangerous—they tend to lash out. Moreover, since in fact we are discussing not animals but people, there is the question of pride. The leaders of an internally weak empire are not likely to acquiesce in an erosion of their power. They typically turn to their primary source of strength: the military.

Appeasement, Reagan was convinced, would only increase the bear's appetite and invite further aggression. Thus he agreed with the anti-Communist strategy of dealing firmly with the Soviets. But he was more confident than most hawks that Americans were up to the challenge. "We must realize," he said in his first inaugural address, "that no weapon in the arsenals of the world is so formidable as the will and moral courage of free men and women." What was most visionary about Reagan's view was that it rejected the assumption of Soviet immutability. At a time when no one else could, Reagan dared to imagine a world in which the Communist regime in the Soviet Union did not exist.

It was one thing to envision this happy state, and quite another to bring it about. The Soviet bear was in a blustery and ravenous mood when Reagan entered the White House. Between 1974 and 1980, it had, through outright invasion or the triumph of its surrogates, brought ten countries into the Communist orbit: South Vietnam, Cambodia, Laos, South Yemen, Angola, Ethiopia, Mozambique, Grenada, Nicaragua, and Afghanistan. Moreover, it had built the most formidable nuclear arsenal in the world, with thousands of multiple-warhead missiles aimed at the United States. The Warsaw Pact had overwhelming superiority over NATO in its conventional forces. Finally, Moscow had recently deployed a new generation of intermediate-range missiles, the giant SS-20s, targeted on European cities.

Reagan did not merely react to these alarming events; he developed a broad counteroffensive strategy. He initiated a $1.5-trillion military buildup, the largest in American peacetime history, which was aimed at drawing the Soviets into an arms race he was convinced they could not win. He was also determined to lead the Western alliance in deploying 108 Pershing II and 464 Tomahawk cruise missiles in Europe to counter the SS-20s. At the same time, he did not eschew arms-control negotiations. Indeed he suggested that for the first time ever the two superpowers should drastically reduce their nuclear stockpiles. If the Soviets would withdraw their SS-20s, he said, the U.S. would not proceed with the Pershing and cruise deployments. This was called the "zero option."

Then there was the Reagan Doctrine, which involved military and material support for indigenous movements struggling to overthrow Soviet-sponsored tyrannies. The Administration supported such guerrillas in Afghanistan, Cambodia, Angola, and Nicaragua. In addition, it worked with the Vatican and the international wing of the AFL-CIO to keep the Polish trade union Solidarity going, despite a ruthless crackdown by General Jaruzelski's regime. In 1983, U.S. troops invaded and liberated Grenada, ousting the Marxist government and sponsoring free elections. Finally, in March 1983, Reagan announced the Strategic Defense Initiative (SDI), a new program to research and eventually deploy missile defenses which offered the promise, in Reagan's words, of "making nuclear weapons obsolete."

At every stage, Reagan's counteroffensive strategy was denounced by the doves, who exploited public fears that Reagan's military buildup was leading the world closer to nuclear war. Reagan's zero option was dismissed by Strobe Talbott as "highly unrealistic" and as having been offered "more to score propaganda points than to win concessions from the Soviets." . . . SDI was denounced as, in the *New York Times*'s words, "a projection of fantasy into policy."

The Soviet Union was equally hostile to the Reagan counteroffensive, but its view of Reagan's objectives was far more perceptive than that of the doves. *Izvestiya* protested, "They want to impose on us an even more ruinous arms race." General Secretary Yuri Andropov alleged that Reagan's SDI program was "a bid to disarm the Soviet Union." The seasoned diplomat Andrei Gromyko charged that "behind all this lies the clear calculation that the USSR will exhaust its material resources and therefore will be forced to surrender."

These reactions are important because they establish the context for Mikhail Gorbachev's ascent to power in early 1985. Gorbachev was indeed a new breed of Soviet general secretary, but few have asked why he was appointed by the Old Guard. The main reason was that the Politburo had come to recognize the failure of past Soviet strategies.

Reagan, in other words, seems to have been largely responsible for inducing a loss of nerve that caused Moscow to seek a new approach. Gorbachev's assignment was not merely to find a new way to deal with the country's economic problems but also to figure out how to cope with the empire's reversals abroad. For this reason, Ilya Zaslavsky, who served in the Soviet Congress of People's Deputies, said later that the true originator of *perestroika* (restructuring) and *glasnost* (openness) was not Mikhail Gorbachev but Ronald Reagan.

Gorbachev inspired wild enthusiasm on the political left and in the Western media. Mary McGrory of the *Washington Post* was convinced he had a "blueprint for saving the planet." Gail Sheehy was dazzled by his "luminous presence." In 1990 *Time* proclaimed him its "Man of the Decade" and compared him to Franklin Roosevelt. Just as Roosevelt had to transform capitalism in order to save it, so Gorbachev was credited with reinventing socialism in order to save it.

The reason for these embarrassing "Gorbasms" was that Gorbachev was precisely the kind of leader that Western intellectuals admire: a top-down reformer who portrayed himself as a progressive; a technocrat who gave three-hour speeches on how the agriculture program was coming along. Most of all, the new Soviet leader was attempting to achieve the great twentieth-century hope of the Western intelligentsia: Communism with a human face! A socialism that works!

Yet as Gorbachev discovered, and as the rest of us now know, it cannot be done. The vices that Gorbachev sought to eradicate from the system turned out to be the essential features of the system. If Reagan was the Great Communicator, then Gorbachev turned out to be, as Zbigniew Brzezinski puts it, the Grand Miscalculator. To the degree he had a Western counterpart, it was not FDR but Jimmy Carter. The hard-liners in the Kremlin who warned Gorbachev that his reforms would cause the entire system to blow up turned out to be right. Indeed, hawks in the West were also vindicated: Communism *was* immutable and irreversible, in the sense that the system could only be reformed by destroying it.

Gorbachev, like Jimmy Carter, had one redeeming quality: he was a decent and relatively open-minded fellow. Gorbachev was the first Soviet leader who came from the post-Stalin generation, the first to admit openly that the promises of Lenin were not being fulfilled.

Reagan, like Margaret Thatcher, was quick to recognize that Gorbachev was different. What changed his mind about Gorbachev was the little things. He discovered that Gorbachev was intensely curious about the West and showed a particular interest in anything Reagan could tell him about Hollywood. Also Gorbachev had a sense of humor and could laugh at himself. Moreover, he was troubled by Reagan's earlier reference to the Soviet Union as an "evil empire." To Reagan, it was significant that the concept of presiding over an evil regime bothered Gorbachev. In addition, Reagan was struck by the fact that Gorbachev routinely referred to God and Christ in his public statements and interviews. When asked how his reforms were likely to turn out, Gorbachev would say, "Only Jesus Christ knows the answer to that." This could be dismissed as merely a rhetorical device, but Reagan didn't think so.

As they sat across the table in Geneva in 1985, however, Reagan saw that Gorbachev was a tough negotiator, and he responded in a manner that may be described as "cordial toughness." While State Department communiqués warned of U.S. concerns about the "destabilizing" influence of the Soviet occupation in Afghanistan, Reagan confronted Gorbachev directly. "What you are doing in Afghanistan is burning villages and killing children," he said. "It's genocide, Mike, and you are the one who has to stop it." At this point, according to aide Kenneth Adelman, who was present, Gorbachev looked at Reagan with a stunned expression; Adelman gathered that no one had ever talked to him this way before.

Reagan also threatened Gorbachev. "We won't stand by and let you maintain weapon superiority over us," he told him. "We can agree to reduce arms, or we can continue the arms race, which I think you know you can't win." The extent to which Gorbachev took Reagan's remarks to heart became obvious at the October 1986 summit in Reykjavik. There Gorbachev astounded the arms-control establishment in the West by accepting Reagan's zero option. Gorbachev embraced the very terms that Strobe Talbott and other doves had earlier dismissed as absurdly unrealistic.

Yet Gorbachev had one condition: the U.S. must agree not to deploy missile defenses. Reagan refused. The press immediately went on the attack. "Reagan–Gorbachev Summit Talks Collapse as Deadlock on SDI Wipes Out Other Gains," read the banner headline in the *Washington Post*. "Sunk by Star Wars," *Time's* cover declared.

To Reagan, however, SDI was more than a bargaining chip; it was a moral issue. In a tele-vised statement from Reykjavik he said, "There was no way I could tell our people that their gov-ernment would not protect them against nuclear destruction." Polls showed that most Americans supported him.

Reykjavik, Margaret Thatcher says, was the turning point in the Cold War. Finally Gorbachev realized that he had a choice: continue a no-win arms race, which would utterly cripple the Soviet economy, or give up the struggle for global hegemony, establish peaceful relations with the West, and work to enable the Soviet economy to become prosperous like the Western economies. After Reykjavik, Gorbachev seems to have resolved on this latter course.

In December 1987, he abandoned his "non-negotiable" demand that Reagan give up SDI and visited Washington, D.C., to sign the Intermediate-Range Nuclear Forces (INF) treaty. For the first time ever the two superpowers agreed to eliminate an entire class of nuclear weapons. Moscow even agreed to on-site verification, a condition that it had resisted in the past.

The hawks, however, were suspicious from the outset. Gorbachev is a masterly chess player, they said; he might sacrifice a pawn, but only to gain an overall advantage. "Reagan is walking into a trap," Tom Bethell warned in *The American Spectator* as early as 1985. "The only way he can get success in negotiation is by doing what the Soviets want." Republican senators like Steven Symms and Jesse Helms planned "killer amendments" to sink the INF treaty. Howard Phillips of the Conservative Caucus even charged Reagan with "fronting as a useful idiot for Soviet propaganda."

Yet, as at least some hawks like Bethell now admit, these criticisms missed the larger current of events. Gorbachev wasn't sacrificing a pawn, he was giving up his bishops and his queen. The INF treaty was in fact the first stage of Gorbachev's surrender in the Cold War.

Reagan knew that the Cold War was over when Gorbachev came to Washington. Gorbachev was a media celebrity in the United States, and the crowds cheered when he jumped out of his limousine and shook hands with people on the street. Out of the limelight, Reagan had dinner with a group of conservative friends, including Ben Wattenberg, Georgie Anne Geyer, and R. Emmett Tyrrell Jr. As Wattenberg recounted the incident to me, the group complained that Gorbachev was getting all the media credit for reaching an agreement essentially on Reagan's terms. Reagan smiled. Wattenberg asked, "Have we won the Cold War?" Reagan hedged. Wattenberg persisted. "Well, have we?" Reagan finally said yes. Then his dinner companions understood: he wanted Gorbachev to have his day in the sun. Asked by the press if he felt over-shadowed by Gorbachev, Reagan replied, "I don't resent his popularity. Good Lord, I co-starred with Errol Flynn once."

To appreciate Reagan's diplomatic acumen, it is important to recall that he was pursuing his own distinctive course, rejecting the recommendations of both the hawks and the doves. Reagan knew that the movement for reform was fragile, and that hard-liners in the Kremlin were looking for U.S. actions that they could use to undermine Gorbachev's initiatives. Reagan recognized the importance of permitting Gorbachev a zone of comfort in which to pursue his program of reform.

At the same time, when doves in the State Department implored Reagan to "reward" Gorbachev with economic concessions and trade benefits for announcing that Soviet troops would pull out of Afghanistan, Reagan recognized that this ran the risk of restoring the health of the sick bear. Reagan's goal was—as Gorbachev himself once joked—to lead the Soviet Union to the edge of the abyss and then induce it to take "one step forward."

Thus Reagan simultaneously supported Gorbachev's reform efforts and applied constant pressure on him to move faster and further. This was the significance of Reagan's trip to the Brandenburg Gate on June 12, 1987, in which he demanded that Gorbachev prove that he was serious about openness by pulling down the Berlin Wall. The State Department kept taking that line out of Reagan's speech, and Reagan kept putting it back in. And in May 1988 Reagan stood beneath a giant white bust of Lenin at Moscow State University and gave the most ringing defense of a free society ever offered in the Soviet Union. On that trip he visited the ancient Danilov Monastery and preached about the importance of religious freedom and a spiritual revival. At the U.S. ambassador's residence, he assured a group of dissidents and "refuseniks" that the day of freedom was at hand. All of these measures were calculated to force Gorbachev's hand.

First Gorbachev agreed to deep unilateral cuts in Soviet armed forces in Europe. Starting in May 1988, Soviet troops pulled out of Afghanistan, the first time the Soviets had voluntarily withdrawn from a puppet regime. Before long, Soviet and satellite troops were pulling out of Angola, Ethiopia, and Cambodia. The race toward freedom began in Eastern Europe, and the Berlin Wall was indeed torn down.

During this period of ferment, Gorbachev's great achievement, for which he will be credited by history, was to abstain from the use of force—the response of his predecessors to popular uprisings in Hungary in 1956 and Czechoslovakia in 1968. By now not only were Gorbachev and his team permitting the empire to disintegrate, as Reagan had foreseen and intended, but they even adopted Reagan's way of talking. In October 1989 Soviet Foreign Ministry spokesman Gennadi Gerasimov announced that the Soviet Union would not intervene in the internal affairs of Eastern Bloc nations. "The Brezhnev Doctrine is dead," Gerasimov said. Reporters asked him what would take its place, and he replied, "You know the Frank Sinatra song 'My Way'? Hungary and Poland are doing it their way. We now have the Sinatra Doctrine." The Gipper could not have said it better himself.

Finally the revolution made its way into the Soviet Union. Gorbachev, who had completely lost control of events, found himself ousted from power. The Soviet Union voted to abolish itself. Serious problems of adjustment to new conditions would remain, but emancipated people know that such problems are infinitely preferable to living under slavery.

Even some who were previously skeptical of Reagan were forced to admit that his policies had been thoroughly vindicated. Reagan's old nemesis Henry Kissinger observed that while it was Bush who presided over the final disintegration of the Soviet empire, "it was Ronald Reagan's Presidency which marked the turning point." Cardinal Casaroli, the Vatican secretary of state, remarked publicly that the Reagan military buildup, which he had opposed at the time, had led to the collapse of Communism.

DANIEL DEUDNEY AND
G. JOHN IKENBERRY

Who Won the Cold War?

The collapse of the Cold War caught almost everyone, particularly hardliners, by surprise. Conservatives and most analysts in the U.S. national security establishment believed that the Soviet-U.S. struggle was a permanent feature of international relations. As former National Security Council adviser Zbigniew Brzezinski put it in 1986, "the American-Soviet contest is not some temporary aberration but a historical rivalry that will long endure." And to many hardliners, Soviet victory was far more likely than Soviet collapse. Many ringing predictions now echo as embarrassments.

The Cold War's end was a baby that arrived unexpectedly, but a long line of those claiming paternity has quickly formed. A parade of former Reagan administration officials and advocates has forthrightly asserted that Reagan's hard-line policies were the decisive trigger for reorienting Soviet foreign policy and for the demise of communism. As former Pentagon officials like Caspar Weinberger and Richard Perle, columnist George Will, neoconservative thinker Irving Kristol, and other proponents of the Reagan victory school have argued, a combination

From "Who Won the Cold War?" by Daniel Deudney and G. John Ikenberry, appearing in *Foreign Policy* 87 (Summer 1992). Reprinted with permission from *Foreign Policy* 87 (Summer 1992). *www.foreignpolicy. com* Copyright © 1992 by the Carnegie Endowment for International Peace.

of military and ideological pressures gave the Soviets little choice but to abandon expansionism abroad and repression at home. In that view, the Reagan military buildup foreclosed Soviet military options while pushing the Soviet economy to the breaking point. Reagan partisans stress that his dramatic "Star Wars" initiative put the Soviets on notice that the next phase of the arms race would be waged in areas where the West held a decisive technological edge.

Reagan and his administration's military initiatives, however, played a far different and more complicated role in inducing Soviet change than the Reagan victory school asserts. For every "hardening" there was a "softening": Reagan's rhetoric of the "Evil Empire" was matched by his vigorous anti-nuclearism; the military buildup in the West was matched by the resurgence of a large popular peace movement, and the Reagan Doctrine's toughening of containment was matched by major deviations from containment in East-West economic relations. Moreover, over the longer term, the strength marshaled in containment was matched by mutual weakness in the face of nuclear weapons, and efforts to engage the USSR were as important as efforts to contain it.

Perhaps the greatest anomaly of the Reagan victory school is the "Great Communicator" himself. The Reagan right ignores that his anti-nuclearism was as strong as his anticommunism. Reagan's personal convictions on nuclear weapons were profoundly at odds with the beliefs of most in his administration. Staffed by officials who considered nuclear weapons a useful instrument of statecraft and who were openly disdainful of the moral critique of nuclear weapons articulated by the arms control community and the peace movement, the administration pursued the hardest line on nuclear policy and the Soviet Union in the postwar era. Then vice president George Bush's observation that nuclear weapons would be fired as a warning shot and Deputy Under Secretary of Defense T. K. Jones's widely quoted view that nuclear war was survivable captured the reigning ethos within the Reagan administration.

In contrast, there is abundant evidence that Reagan himself felt a deep antipathy for nuclear weapons and viewed their abolition to be a realistic and desirable goal. Reagan's call in his famous March 1983 "Star Wars" speech for a program to make nuclear weapons impotent and obsolete was viewed as cynical by many, but actually it expressed Reagan's heartfelt views, views that he came to act upon. As *Washington Post* reporter Lou Cannon's 1991 biography points out, Reagan was deeply disturbed by nuclear deterrence and attracted to abolitionist solutions. "I know I speak for people everywhere when I say our dream is to see the day when nuclear weapons will be banished from the face of the earth," Reagan said in November 1983. Whereas the right saw antinuclearism as a threat to American military spending and the legitimacy of an important foreign policy tool, or as propaganda for domestic consumption, Reagan sincerely believed it. Reagan's anti-nuclearism was not just a personal sentiment. It surfaced at decisive junctures to affect Soviet perceptions of American policy. . . .

Contrary to the conventional wisdom, the defense buildup did not produce Soviet capitulation. The initial Soviet response to the Reagan administration's buildup and belligerent rhetoric was to accelerate production of offensive weapons, both strategic and conventional. That impasse was broken not by Soviet capitulation but by an extraordinary convergence by Reagan and Mikhail Gorbachev on a vision of mutual nuclear vulnerability and disarmament. On the Soviet side, the dominance of the hard-line response to the newly assertive America was thrown into question in early 1985 when Gorbachev became general secretary of the Communist party after the death of Konstantin Chernenko. Without a background in foreign affairs, Gorbachev was eager to assess American intentions directly and put his stamp on Soviet security policy. Reagan's strong antinuclear views expressed at the November 1985 Geneva summit were decisive in convincing Gorbachev that it was possible to work with the West in halting the nuclear arms race. . . .

Reagan's commitment to anti-nuclearism and its potential for transforming the U.S.-Soviet confrontation was more graphically demonstrated at the October 1986 Reykjavik summit when Reagan and Gorbachev came close to agreeing on a comprehensive program of global denuclearization that was far bolder than any seriously entertained by American strategists since the Baruch Plan of 1946. The sharp contrast between Reagan's and Gorbachev's shared skepticism toward nuclear weapons on the one hand, and the Washington security establishment's consensus on the other, was showcased in former secretary of defense James Schlesinger's scathing accusation that Reagan was engaged in "casual utopianism." But Reagan's anomalous anti-nuclearism provided the crucial signal to Gorbachev that bold initiatives would be reciprocated rather than exploited. Reagan's anti-nuclearism was more important than his administration's military buildup in catalyzing the end of the Cold War. . . .

The Reagan victory school also overstates the overall impact of American and Western policy on the Soviet Union during the 1980s. The Reagan administration's posture was both evolving and inconsistent. Though loudly proclaiming its intention to go beyond the previous containment policies that were deemed too soft, the reality of Reagan's policies fell short. As Sovietologists Gail Lapidus and Alexander Dallin observed in a 1989 *Bulletin of the Atomic Scientists* article, the policies were "marked to the end by numerous zigzags and reversals, bureaucratic conflicts, and incoherence." Although rollback had long been a cherished goal of the Republican party's right wing, Reagan was unwilling and unable to implement it.

The hard-line tendencies of the Reagan administration were offset in two ways. First, and most important, Reagan's tough talk fueled a large peace movement in the United States and Western Europe in the 1980s, a movement that put significant political pressure upon Western governments to pursue far-reaching arms control proposals. That mobilization of Western opinion created a political climate in which the rhetoric and posture of the early Reagan administration was a significant political liability. By the 1984 U.S. presidential election, the administration had embraced arms control goals that it had previously ridiculed. Reagan's own anti-nuclearism matched that rising public concern, and Reagan emerged as the spokesman for comprehensive denuclearization. Paradoxically, Reagan administration policies substantially triggered the popular revolt against the nuclear hardline, and then Reagan came to pursue the popular agenda more successfully than any other postwar president.

Second, the Reagan administration's hard-line policies were also undercut by powerful Western interests that favored East-West economic ties. In the early months of Reagan's administration, the grain embargo imposed by President Jimmy Carter after the 1979 Soviet invasion of Afghanistan was lifted in order to keep the Republican party's promises to Midwestern farmers. Likewise, in 1981 the Reagan administration did little to challenge Soviet control of Eastern Europe after Moscow pressured Warsaw to suppress the independent Polish trade union Solidarity, in part because Poland might have defaulted on multibillion dollar loans made by Western banks. Also, despite strenuous opposition by the Reagan administration, the NATO allies pushed ahead with a natural gas pipeline linking the Soviet Union with Western Europe. That a project creating substantial economic interdependence could proceed during the worst period of Soviet-U.S. relations in the 1980s demonstrates the failure of the Reagan administration to present an unambiguous hard line toward the Soviet Union. More generally, NATO allies and the vocal European peace movement moderated and buffered hard-line American tendencies.

In sum, the views of the Reagan victory school are flawed because they neglect powerful crosscurrents in the West during the 1980s. The conventional wisdom simplifies a complex story and ignores those aspects of Reagan administration policy inconsistent with the hard-line rationale. Moreover, the Western "face" toward the Soviet Union did not consist exclusively of Reagan administration policies, but encompassed countervailing tendencies from the Western public, other governments, and economic interest groups.

Whether Reagan is seen as the consummate hardliner or the prophet of anti-nuclearism, one should not exaggerate the influence of his administration, or of other short-term forces. Within the Washington beltway, debates about postwar military and foreign policy would suggest that Western strategy fluctuated wildly, but in fact the basic thrust of Western policy toward the USSR remained remarkably consistent. Arguments from the new right notwithstanding, Reagan's containment strategy was not that different from those of his predecessors. Indeed, the broader peace-through-strength perspective sees the Cold War's finale as the product of a long-term policy, applied over the decades.

In any case, although containment certainly played an important role in blocking Soviet expansionism, it cannot explain either the end of the Cold War or the direction of Soviet policy responses. The West's relationship with the Soviet Union was not limited to containment, but included important elements of mutual vulnerability and engagement. The Cold War's end was not simply a result of Western strength but of mutual weakness and intentional engagement as well.

Most dramatically, the mutual vulnerability created by nuclear weapons overshadowed containment. Nuclear weapons forced the United States and the Soviet Union to eschew war and the serious threat of war as tools of diplomacy and created imperatives for the cooperative regulation of nuclear capability. Both countries tried to fashion nuclear explosives into useful instruments of policy, but they came to the realization—as the joint Soviet-American statement issued from the 1985 Geneva summit put it—that "nuclear war cannot be won and must never be fought." Both countries slowly but surely came to view nuclear weapons as a common threat that must be regulated jointly. Not just containment, but also the overwhelming and common nuclear threat brought the Soviets to the negotiating table. In the shadow of nuclear destruction, common purpose defused traditional antagonisms.

A second error of the peace-through-strength perspective is the failure to recognize that the West offered an increasingly benign face to the communist world. Traditionally, the Soviets' Marxist-Leninist doctrine held that the capitalist West was inevitably hostile and aggressive, an expectation reinforced by the aggression of capitalist, fascist Germany. Since World War II, the Soviets' principal adversaries had been democratic capitalist states. Slowly but surely, Soviet doctrine acknowledged that the West's behavior did not follow Leninist expectations, but was instead increasingly pacific and cooperative. The Soviet willingness to abandon the Brezhnev Doctrine in the late 1980s in favor of the "Sinatra Doctrine"—under which any East European country could sing, "I did it my way"—suggests a radical transformation in the prevailing Soviet perception of threat from the West. In 1990, the Soviet acceptance of the de facto absorption of communist East Germany into West Germany involved the same calculation with even higher stakes. In accepting the German reunification, despite that country's past aggression, Gorbachev acted on the assumption that the Western system was fundamentally pacific. As Russian foreign minister Andrei Kozyrev noted subsequently, that Western countries are pluralistic democracies "practically rules out the pursuance of an aggressive foreign policy." Thus the Cold War ended despite the assertiveness of Western hardliners, rather than because of it.

The second front of the Cold War, according to the Reagan victory school, was ideological. Reagan spearheaded a Western ideological offensive that dealt the USSR a death blow. For the right, driving home the image of the Evil Empire was a decisive stroke rather than a rhetorical flourish. Ideological warfare was such a key front in the Cold War because the Soviet Union was, at its core, an ideological creation. According to the Reagan right, the supreme vulnerability of the Soviet Union to ideological assault was greatly underappreciated by Western leaders and publics. In that view, the Cold War was won by the West's uncompromising assertion of the superiority of its values and its complete denial of the moral legitimacy of the Soviet system during the 1980s. Western military strength could prevent defeat, but only ideological breakthrough could bring victory. . . .

Convinced that Bolshevism was quintessentially an ideological phenomenon, activists of the new right were contemptuous of Western efforts to accommodate Soviet needs, moderate Soviet aims, and integrate the USSR into the international system as a "normal" great power. In their view, the *realpolitik* strategy urged by George Kennan, Walter Lippmann, and Hans Morgenthau was based on a misunderstanding of the Soviet Union. It provided an incomplete roadmap for waging the Cold War, and guaranteed that it would never be won. A particular villain for the new right was Secretary of State Henry Kissinger, whose program of détente implied, in their view, a "moral equivalence" between the West and the Soviet Union that amounted to unilateral ideological disarmament. Even more benighted were liberal attempts to engage and co-opt the Soviet Union in hopes that the two systems could ultimately reconcile. The new right's view of politics was strikingly globalist in its assumption that the world had shrunk too much for two such different systems to survive, and that the contest was too tightly engaged for containment or Iron Curtains to work. As James Burnham, the ex-communist prophet of new right anticommunism, insisted in the early postwar years, the smallness of our "one world" demanded a strategy of "rollback" for American survival.

The end of the Cold War indeed marked an ideological triumph for the West, but not of the sort fancied by the Reagan victory school. Ideology played a far different and more complicated role in inducing Soviet change than the Reagan school allows. As with the military sphere, the Reagan school presents an incomplete picture of Western ideological influence, ignoring the emergence of ideological common ground in stimulating Soviet change.

The ideological legitimacy of the Soviet system collapsed in the eyes of its own citizens not because of an assault by Western ex-leftists, but because of the appeal of Western affluence and permissiveness. The puritanical austerity of Bolshevism's "New Soviet Man" held far less appeal than the "bourgeois decadence" of the West. For the peoples of the USSR and Eastern Europe, it was not so much abstract liberal principles but rather the Western way of life—the material and cultural manifestations of the West's freedoms—that subverted the Soviet vision. Western popular culture—exemplified in rock and roll, television, film, and blue jeans—seduced the communist world far more effectively than ideological sermons by anti-communist activists. As journalist William Echikson noted in his 1990 book *Lighting the Night: Revolution in Eastern Europe,* "instead of listening to the liturgy of Marx and Lenin, generations of would-be socialists tuned into the Rolling Stones and the Beatles."

If Western popular culture and permissiveness helped subvert communist legitimacy, it is a development of profound irony. Domestically, the new right battled precisely those cultural forms that had such global appeal. V. I. Lenin's most potent ideological foils were John Lennon and Paul McCartney, not Adam Smith and Thomas Jefferson. The right fought a two-front war against communism abroad and hedonism and consumerism at home. Had it not lost the latter struggle, the West may not have won the former.

The Reagan victory school argues that ideological assertiveness precipitated the end of the Cold War. While it is true that right-wing American intellectuals were assertive toward the Soviet Union, other Western activists and intellectuals were building links with highly placed reformist intellectuals there. The Reagan victory school narrative ignores that Gorbachev's reform program was based upon "new thinking"—a body of ideas developed by globalist thinkers cooperating across the East-West divide. The key themes of new thinking—the common threat of nuclear destruction, the need for strong international institutions, and the importance of ecological sustainability—built upon the cosmopolitanism of the Marxist tradition and officially replaced the Communist party's class-conflict doctrine during the Gorbachev period.

It is widely recognized that a major source of Gorbachev's new thinking was his close aide and speechwriter, Georgi Shakhnazarov. A former president of the Soviet political science association, Shakhnazarov worked extensively with Western globalists, particularly the New York-based group known as the World Order Models Project. Gorbachev's speeches and policy statements were replete with the language and ideas of globalism. The Cold War ended not with Soviet ideological capitulation to Reagan's anticommunism but rather with a Soviet embrace of globalist themes promoted by a network of liberal internationalists. Those intellectual influences were greatest with the state elite, who had greater access to the West and from whom the reforms originated.

Regardless of how one judges the impact of the ideological struggles during the Reagan years, it is implausible to focus solely on recent developments without accounting for longer-term shifts in underlying forces, particularly the widening gap between Western and Soviet economic performance. Over the long haul, the West's ideological appeal was based on the increasingly superior performance of the Western economic system. Although contrary to the expectation of Marx and Lenin, the robustness of capitalism in the West was increasingly acknowledged by Soviet analysts. Likewise, Soviet elites were increasingly troubled by their economy's comparative decline.

The Reagan victory school argues that the renewed emphasis on free-market principles championed by Reagan and then British prime minister Margaret Thatcher led to a global move toward market deregulation and privatization that the Soviets desired to follow. By rekindling the beacon of laissez-faire capitalism, Reagan illuminated the path of economic reform, thus vanquishing communism.

That view is misleading in two respects. First, it was West European social democracy rather than America's more free-wheeling capitalism that attracted Soviet reformers. Gorbachev wanted his reforms to emulate the Swedish model. His vision was not of laissez-faire capitalism but of a social democratic welfare state. Second, the right's triumphalism in the economic sphere is ironic. The West's robust economies owe much of their relative stability and health to two generations of Keynesian intervention and government involvement that the right opposed at every step. As with Western popular culture, the right opposed tendencies in the West that proved vital in the West's victory.

There is almost universal agreement that the root cause of the Cold War's abrupt end was the grave domestic failure of Soviet communism. However, the Soviet response to this crisis—accommodation and liberalization rather than aggression and repression—was significantly influenced by outside pressures and opportunities, many from the West. As historians and analysts attempt to explain how recent U.S. foreign policy helped end the Cold War, a view giving most of the credit to Reagan-era assertiveness and Western strength has become the new conventional wisdom. Both the Reagan victory school and the peace-through-strength perspective on Western containment assign a central role in ending the Cold War to Western resolve and power. The lesson for American foreign policy being drawn from those events is that military strength and ideological warfare were the West's decisive assets in fighting the Cold War.

The new conventional wisdom, in both its variants, is seriously misleading. Operating over the last decade, Ronald Reagan's personal anti-nuclearism, rather than his administration's hard-line, catalyzed the accommodations to end the Cold War. His administration's effort to go beyond containment and on the offensive was muddled, counter-balanced, and unsuccessful. Operating over the long term, containment helped thwart Soviet expansionism but cannot account for the Soviet domestic failure, the end of East-West struggle, or the direction of the USSR's reorientation. Contrary to the hard-line version, nuclear weapons were decisive in abandoning the conflict by creating common interests.

On the ideological front, the new conventional wisdom is also flawed. The conservatives' anticommunism was far less important in delegitimating the Soviet system than were that system's internal failures and the attraction of precisely the Western "permissive culture" abhorred by the right. In addition, Gorbachev's attempts to reform communism in the late-1980s were less an ideological capitulation than a reflection of philosophical convergence on the globalist norms championed by liberal internationalists. And the West was more appealing not because of its laissez-faire purity, but because of the success of Keynesian and social welfare innovations whose use the right resisted.

Behind the debate over who "won" the Cold War are competing images of the forces shaping recent history. Containment, strength, and confrontation—the trinity enshrined in conventional thinking on Western foreign policy's role in ending the Cold War—obscure the nature of these momentous changes. Engagement and interdependence, rather than containment, are the ruling trends of the age. Mutual vulnerability, not strength, drives security politics. Accommodation and integration, not confrontation, are the motors of change.

EDWARD PESSEN

Losing Our Souls

The swiftest glance at recent events seems to establish that the United States successfully achieved the chief objectives of its cold war policy. The Soviet empire has crumbled. The Eastern European satellites have broken the shackles that bound them, achieving independence and installing—for the most part—representative democratic governments in place of their ousted Soviet puppet regimes. The former Soviet Union has withdrawn from Afghanistan, ceased intervening in Third World affairs, and cut off its financial and military aid to radical or Marxist regimes and movements. Marxism seems almost everywhere to be in retreat. And, most dramatic of all, the Communist party has not only been removed from power in what used to be the Soviet Union but it has in some places been outlawed. The Union of Soviet Socialist

Republics has ceased to exist, replaced by what at this writing is called a commonwealth composed of those former Soviet republics that chose to join it. Amidst the debris, the United States stands alone as the sole remaining superpower, clearly the victor over its twin enemies—the Soviet Union and Marxism-Leninism.

And yet questions about American cold war policy remain. That the United States achieved its major objectives does not prove that the policy and its goals were therefore in the national interest. Questionable ends do not become worthy because they are attained. As I shall show, American policy and the means of implementing it have had negative as well as positive consequences. . . .

The most baneful effect of this anti-Soviet policy [was] the unprecedented insecurity it brought to the United States. For the first time in the nation's history it could be almost destroyed and most of its people killed in a matter of minutes by weapons against which we had no effective defense. And it was our own doing that brought us to this condition. True, a massive nuclear arsenal would enable American leaders to wipe out any nation that attacked us. But the resulting mutual destruction would be of little comfort to the few irradiated survivors. . . . President John F. Kennedy at one point doubted that the expenditure of hundreds of billions of dollars on nuclear and conventional arms had increased U.S. security at all. In fact, the nuclear weapons buildup, and the Soviet buildup it evoked, seriously undermined our security. Many thousands of misreadings of radar and frightening superpower confrontations threatened nuclear holocaust, by accident or design. American leaders neither hoped nor planned for this state of affairs, but it might have been anticipated had they given more serious thought to the likely results of their nuclear policy.

Yet another consequence of official cold war policies was the great fear and anxiety that swept over the world at the dread of a nuclear holocaust. There is no way of measuring precisely the emotional pain suffered by a generation trained to "duck and cover," but there is no reason to doubt that nuclear nightmares left psychic scars in their wake.

The manufacture and above all the testing of nuclear bombs has had a deleterious and perhaps irreversible effect on the environment, poisoning the earth, the waters, the air, the atmosphere, and causing untold injury and death to plant, animal, and human life. We have not to this point learned how to dispose of nuclear wastes.

To those who would argue that nuclear bombs, however awful their effects, were simply the latest progression in the history of weapons development and therefore not chargeable to the cold war, evidence says otherwise. President Truman's use of the atomic bomb in adopting a tougher stance toward the Soviets, and our questionable plan for control of atomic weapons, proposed to the United Nations, indicates that we aggressively seized this new weapon for policy ends.

Morally questionable presidential actions to implement their cold war policy, including an ardor for nuclear bombs, destruction of Vietnam, and the CIA's less than secret involvement in the assassination of foreign leaders, aroused strong anti-American feeling in many countries of the world. Senator Frank Church believed that the CIA's covert operations had "destroyed the moral leadership of [the United States] throughout the world. . . . Resistance, hostility, and hatred toward the United States—much of it stems from our covert operations."

Most satisfactory to the United States in international affairs was the collapse of the Soviet Union. Responding to what he felt was the excessive self-praise of President George Bush in claiming credit for bringing about the demise of the USSR, George Kennan has argued that the Soviet implosion was due to internal strains and weaknesses that had been developing over time in that vast and complex nation. Yet it seems beyond doubt that American post–World War II actions played an important role in hastening the dissolution of the Soviet order and the fall of the Communist party both in the USSR itself and in the satellite states of Eastern Europe. The amazing inefficiency and backwardness of an economy bypassed by the technological revolutions of the postwar decades were of course instrumental in undermining the Soviet Union. But the great economic strain imposed on the Soviets by an arms race that we promoted, the havoc that American-sponsored covert operations spread throughout the Soviet empire, the cold war tensions that induced the Soviet government to tighten already onerous internal controls and restraints—all contributed to the fall of the Marxist-Leninist state.

Yet these policies also accounted for at least three million Asian deaths in Southeast Asia, the wounding of millions more, the destruction of much of the Korean countryside, and the utter devastation of Vietnam, on which more bombs were dropped than on all the belligerents combined in World War II. In Korea and in Southeast Asia, American leaders made war on nations that had neither attacked nor threatened to attack the United States. Absent the cold war and absent a theory that political victories for Communist or communist-supported parties anywhere were Soviet-directed and therefore unacceptable to the United States, there would not have been wars in Korea, Vietnam, Laos, and Cambodia. Reliance on carpet bombing, napalm, Agent Orange, search-and-destroy missions, body counts, and Operation Phoenix, which killed many thousands of unarmed "communist suspects" in a war Presidents Johnson and Nixon chose to wage, were the assured results of these very tactics.

Bloodbaths in Indonesia, the Congo . . . , Angola, Iran, Guatemala, El Salvador, Chile, Brazil, and Argentina; the killing of hundreds of thousands of peasants, students, trade unionists, priests, and nuns; the wiping out of entire villages by right-wing governments, police forces, militias, secretive death squads, many of them financed and trained by and in the United States—these were other consequences of our cold war policy. A cynical Latin American noted that they had been "killing 'communists' there for centuries." American policymakers approved such executions, insisting however that they not be publicized. In Guatemala, for example, after the CIA had helped overthrow the government of Arbenz Guzman, when anti-communist Colonel Enrique Diaz balked at enforcing the American ambassador's order to kill the communist suspects on his proscription list, Diaz was quickly dumped and replaced by a more cooperative officer.

Many noncommunist Third World governments were overthrown as a result of cold war policy, and in some cases their leaders were assassinated. Among the victims were Mossadegh in Iran, Arbenz Guzman in Guatemala, Lumumba in the Congo, Diem in South Vietnam, Allende in Chile, and Sukarno in Indonesia. Castro of Cuba was not among their number, but not for want of American efforts. American leaders also promoted the civil wars that during the era plagued the Philippines, El Salvador, Nicaragua, Angola, and Peru. In Central America and elsewhere in the Third World, brutal dictatorships that came to power commanded the support of native oligarchs, large American corporations, and an American government that in many instances instructed the despots in torture and terror. The shah's notorious SAVAK which terrorized post-Mossadegh Iran, was the beneficiary of such American assistance.

In an address he gave at the University of Pennsylvania in 1962, historian Arnold Toynbee likened the United States to Rome in the days of empire, everywhere the champion of the rich against the poor and the enemy of popular revolutions. Invariably American policies supported wealthy oligarchs against the peasant masses from whose ranks, after all, came communist "suspects," thus doing the bidding of such corporations as the United Fruit Company, which profited mightily from its vast landholdings and the low wages it paid peasant labor in the Central

American banana republics it dominated. We resisted reforms that threatened the profit margins of American investors in the Third World, acquiesced in the heroic looting of the national treasury of Zaire by despot Joseph Mobutu, and poured arms and financial aid into countries ruled by our favored elites rather than assisting the beleaguered poor. In all these ways American policies helped perpetuate the poverty and inequality that reigned in the nonindustrial world. . . .

The earth's surface was pockmarked with American air bases, war planes armed with hydrogen bombs, and the military personnel called for by the treaties and alliances the United States entered into with nations on almost every continent. Since these agreements were designed to meet "indirect aggression" and internal subversion as well as to confront the Soviet Union or, as in Asia, Red China, one of their not insignificant effects was to prevent change in the status quo or, in exceptional cases like the Dominican Republic, the accession to power of democratically elected governments.

Our cold war leaders brushed aside international law and traditional restraints on the use of force against nations with which we were at peace. The United States intervened in the affairs of other countries, resorting to sabotage, demolition, assassination, and out-and-out warfare. The Founders of the nation had regarded war as a barbaric institution, to be entered into only in case of an attack or threatened attack on our country. When he became secretary of state, Daniel Webster expressed the hope that the War of 1812 would be our last war. War, he observed, should be rejected as an instrument of national policy because "the spirit of the age . . . demanded that civilized nations settle their differences by conciliation [and] moral precept rather than by narrow advantage." But during the cold war our leaders became as children of Clausewitz, willing to embrace war as a perfectly acceptable means of conducting foreign policy. . . .

Patriotism has come to be widely misdefined in the wake of the cold war. The dictionary defines it as love of country. As the generation of Washington, Jefferson, and the Adamses knew, love of country is not synonymous with love of government. When government misbehaves or pursues bad policy, "real" patriotism takes the form of open criticism of the government's actions, no matter how risky or harmful such criticism may be to one's reputation. Courage may be required of real patriots because government's power to shape public opinion is so great that it can transmute stupid into seemingly wise policy and stigmatize criticism of policy as unpatriotic if not treasonable. Cold war America . . . treated patriotism as a kind of blind, Ramboesque nationalism, according to which patriots offer uncritical, even enthusiastic approval of government actions against foreign states, no matter how illegal, cruel, and amoral the actions.

The American way of life, whose defense against communist subversion spiced so much cold war rhetoric, [took] on new meaning. In fact the concept is broad and inclusive, for it describes a complex and often discordant reality. But during the cold war it was stripped of the irreverence, the suspicion of business and ill-gotten gains, the pacifism, the sharp dissent, the sympathy for foreign revolutions that had come to be an important part of the American tradition.

The American people . . . acquiesced in the remarkably arrogant behavior of its government during the cold war. While the details of most clandestine activities were kept from public view, the broad outlines of many covert operations were known. Nor did the media and the public question whether the CIA or other government officials were involved in publicized coups or assassinations of foreign leaders. Nor were complaints heard about the tendency of presidents to resort to force on their exclusive authority in defense of what they called our vital interests. In effect, Congress's power to declare war was set in abeyance.

These interests [were] ever more elastically defined during the cold war and in its aftermath. Time was when, in accord with the principles admired by our Founding Fathers, our vital interests were peace, security against foreign invasion, and a prosperity that was most surely achievable through trade and commerce on equal terms with all willing nations. No longer. America's cold war leaders acted on the unspoken premise that the struggle against communist subversion somehow created an imposing new catalogue of interests so important as to justify illegal actions in order to safeguard and secure them. These allegedly vital interests required us to prevent a number of unacceptable circumstances: elected procommunist or insufficiently anti-communist regimes; the toppling of pro-American governments, no matter how undemocratic and repressive; the loss or unavailability to us of foreign resources which we had grown accustomed to having on our own terms; the emergence anywhere of political movements our leaders adjudged as hostile or threatening.

Almost all shades of influential American opinion in and out of government have come to regard U.S. accessibility to Middle Eastern oil, under terms to which we have become accustomed, as an American interest so vital that war would be justified in order to maintain it. We are saying in effect that we will not permit a foreign people to take control of their own resources if the United States has come to depend on getting those resources under terms of our choosing, and if we have reason to fear that the new regime may change these terms or, worse, shut off the supply. So bizarre a notion goes largely unremarked in the contemporary United States. Under international law a nation does have the right, after all, to do what it will with its own products and natural resources, no matter how much these goods are coveted by any other nation. Pursuing the cold war has evidently accustomed American leaders and the public alike to feel that whatever Uncle Sam wants anywhere on earth, Uncle Sam has the right to get, and by whatever means he thinks necessary.

Further Reading

The output of the Reagan victory school has outpaced that of those with different views. Classic examples of this viewpoint are Dinesh D'Souza, *Ronald Reagan: How an Ordinary Man Became an Extraordinary Leader* (New York: The Free Press, 1997) and Peter Schweizer, *Victory: The Reagan Administration's Secret Strategy that Hastened the Collapse of the Soviet Union* (New York: Atlantic Monthly Press, 1994); both emphasize the role of Reagan himself and his determination to follow his own (brilliant) political instincts, despite criticism from the foreign policy establishment and, at times, his own advisors. Jay Winik, *On the Brink: The Dramatic Behind-the-Scenes Saga of the Reagan Era and the Men and Women Who Won the Cold War* (New York: Simon & Schuster, 1996) focuses on four of Reagan's foreign policy advisors (Richard Perle, Elliot Abrams, Jeane Kirkpatrick, and Max Kampelman) as crucial to the formulation of Reagan's hard-line policy toward the USSR. *From the Shadows: The Ultimate Insider's Story of Five Presidents and How They Won the Cold War* (New York: Simon and Schuster), by Robert M. Gates, offers a former CIA director's perspective, which credits Presidents Harry Truman through George H. W. Bush with successfully waging cold war, but supports the view that it was Reagan's military buildup that put unbearable pressure on the Soviet Union, leading to its collapse.

Critics of the Reagan victory school include Raymond L. Garthoff, *The Great Transition: American-Soviet Relations and the End of the Cold War* (Washington, DC: Brookings Institution,

1994), which emphasizes the role of Mikhail Gorbachev in seeking to democratize and reform the Soviet Union and in initiating an end to the arms race with the United States. Stephen G. Brooks and William Wohlforth, "Power, Globalization, and the End of the Cold War: Reevaluating a Landmark Case for Ideas," *International Security* (Winter 2000/2001), 5–53 is marred by policy and international relations jargon, but is worth reading for its argument that material conditions within the Soviet Union—specifically, the economic and technological stagnation that began in the late 1970s—pushed leaders within the USSR to seek to reform their political-economic system; in their view, it was this desire for internal reform, and not fears of U.S. military strength, that led Gorbachev to seek a rapprochement with Reagan, thus initiating the end of the cold war. Easier to read is *We All Lost the Cold War* (Princeton, NJ: Princeton University Press, 1994), by Richard Ned Lebow and Janice Gross Stein, which makes a similar argument while exploring the dangers of international conflict in a nuclear age.

The End of the Cold War: Its Meaning and Implications (Cambridge: Cambridge University Press, 1992), edited by Michael J. Hogan, is an excellent volume, providing a variety of perspectives that, from the vantage point of the early 1990s, explore the reasons for, and the significance of, the end of the cold war.

Primary Sources

An archive of documents on "The End of the Cold War" (and other topics) is available at the Web site of the Cold War International History Project (www.wilsoncenter.org/index.cfm? fuseaction= topics.home&topic_id=1409). Ronald Reagan's 1983 speech to the National Association of Evangelicals, in which he used the term "evil empire" in referring to the Soviet Union, is available in text and audio formats at www.americanrhetoric.com/speeches/ronaldreaganevilempire. htm. Go to fas.org/spp/starwars/offdocs/rrspch.htm for the text of Reagan's March 1983 address to the nation in which he proposed the Strategic Defense Initiative (SDI). The transcript of a 1984 interview with Dr. Helen Caldicott, a leading antinuclear activist, is available at eee.uci.edu/97y/50070/doc/socpeace/caldicot.htm. For excerpts of the Gorbachev–Reagan arms reductions talks at Reykjavik, Iceland, in 1986, go to astro.temple.edu/~rimmerma/excerpts_of_ gorbachev_reagan.htm. For the translation of the minutes of the December 1988 meeting of the Politburo of the Central Committee of the Communist Party of the Soviet Union, in which Gorbachev mentions how his own actions have reduced tensions between the United States and the USSR, go to www.wilsoncenter.org/index.cfm?topic_id=1409&fuseaction=library.document&id= 15932. A translation of an excerpt from the diary of Anatoly Chernyaev that records his impressions of Gorbachev, go to www.wilsoncenter.org/index.cfm?topic_id=1409&fuseaction=library. document&id=15979. For a chart showing U.S. annual military expenditures from 1945 through 1996, go to www.cdi.org/issues/milspend.html. A chart showing global nuclear stockpiles from 1945 to 1996 is available at www.brook.edu/FP/PROJECTS/NUCWCOST/STOKPILE.HTM. For a table of the annual numbers and kinds of U.S. nuclear warheads from 1945 to 2002, go to www.nrdc.org/nuclear/nudb/datab9.asp; for a graph of nuclear weapons tests by all nations between 1945 and 1998, visit www.clw.org/archive/coalition/chart4598.pdf.

CHAPTER 14
Globalization

INTRODUCTION

Few economic issues in recent years have stirred as much controversy and public protest as globalization. The process of cross-border trade and investment began many years—some scholars say many centuries—ago. But the phenomenon has become closely associated with the post-cold-war years, during which free-market capitalism was proclaimed triumphant and the growing use of Internet technology seemed both to shrink the planet and to speed up global communications. Commentators on globalization often speak of it as already well underway and as inevitable, focusing on the cultural evidence. American music and movies are now within the reach of most young people anywhere on the planet, and an American hamburger can be had at any one of the 15,000 McDonald's restaurants spread across seventy-nine different countries. Americans now routinely and without a second thought purchase goods imported from a variety of other countries and dine on ethnic cuisines that would have seemed exotic to many of them several decades ago. And yet despite the talk of globalization as both inexorable and irresistible, almost 40 percent of Americans polled in 2004 by PIPA/KN stated that the United States should try to slow down, stop, or reverse the process of globalization; the same percentage, surveyed in 2000 by the polling firm of Belden, Russonello and Stewart, stated that they personally would experience more rather than fewer problems as a result of globalization.

Proponents of globalization argue that capitalism works best when unfettered by government interference in the form of regulations and tariffs, which are essentially sales taxes placed on imported goods to make them more expensive—and thus less desirable—than domestic products. In the absence of such barriers, the markets for capital and goods will expand, they argue; prosperity will then spread, and in its wake, interest in Western values and democracy will grow. Opponents insist that only some prosper from global trade and investment, chiefly large, multinational corporations. The majority lose out, including workers in America whose jobs are moved overseas where labor is cheaper and those overseas who are poorly paid and work under unsafe conditions.

This dispute reached a kind of climax in 1993 when then Vice President Al Gore and former Reform party presidential candidate Ross Perot met on the widely watched *Larry King Live* show to debate the North American Free Trade Agreement (NAFTA), then pending before Congress. The agreement removed tariffs on U.S. goods flowing into Mexico and also provided mechanisms by which a corporation operating in another country could challenge that nation's regulatory laws. Perot warned of the "giant sucking sound" that Americans would hear when, if NAFTA passed, U.S. corporations began moving their operations to Mexico to take advantage of lower labor costs and the absence of strong environmental regulations. Gore insisted that American jobs had already begun to move across the border; NAFTA, he argued, would help the United States retain and even gain jobs because U.S. companies would gain access to markets previously closed to them by excessive tariffs.

The Congress approved NAFTA and it was signed into law by President Bill Clinton, a leading champion of the treaty and the free-trade philosophy it embodied. The politics of this legislative feat reflected important changes in the power distribution within the nation's capital. The major political force opposing the trade agreement had been the organized labor movement—traditionally a key component of the Democratic party's coalition—and labor's staunch allies in the Democratically controlled Congress opposed the ratification of NAFTA. Yet Clinton lobbied hard against labor's wishes and forged a congressional majority with support from most Republicans. A dominant bipartisan coalition long in the making and based in laissez-faire, pro-business thinking seemed to have blossomed in Washington, DC. NAFTA had triggered a bitter struggle among Democrats, and Clinton pointed the way to a new social and economic orientation for his party, embracing the interests of businesspeople, professionals, and consumers interested in the low prices that globalized production and trade could bring. Organized labor was excluded from this coalition, and media observers declared the unions to be reactionaries who wished only to defend the perquisites of high-wage factory workers against the interests of all others. Likewise, Perot found himself proclaimed a political dead letter, a representative of old thinking, unable to grasp both the inevitability and the possibilities of global trade.

Yet the opposition to NAFTA and subsequent trade agreements—and, more broadly, to the globalization of the marketplace and the workplace—has persisted, particularly among supporters of labor and those concerned about the environment. This led to dramatic demonstrations in November 1999 in Seattle, Washington, that effectively broke up a meeting of the World Trade Organization (WTO), a broad consortium of governments that has pushed forward a free-trade regime; a similar protest was staged in Genoa, Italy, in 2001. This opposition to globalization united youthful environmentalists, consumer activists opposed to products made in third-world "sweatshops"—a movement that spread rapidly on college campuses in the 1990s—and the labor unions whose longtime allies in the halls of power had cast them aside. Such forces would have seemed unlikely partners in protest a mere decade before. Moreover, the international wave of protests against the WTO suggested that U.S. antiglobalization (or, to be precise, anti*corporate* globalization) activists might commence their own global phase. As the twenty-first century began, U.S. activists became newly aware of developments internationally, such as the meetings of human rights and environmental activists from around the world in Porto Allegre, Brazil, and the protests by citizens of India, including the acclaimed novelist Arundhati Roy, against World Bank sponsorship of a development project for their country. This globalization of anticorporate protest was something that the triumphant pro-NAFTA forces in the United States, Canada, and Mexico had not foreseen.

The issues today remain similar to those articulated in the 1993 Gore–Perot debate. Proponents of globalization emphasize the emergence of new markets for U.S. businesses and the creation of much-needed jobs for third-world workers. They argue that trade agreements actually help protect workers and the environment, if perhaps only in the long term, by spurring economic and social development in poorer countries and creating a global middle class that will demand the regulations, social standards, and political democracy necessary to a good "quality of life." The most enthusiastic boosters of globalization have presented it as the inevitable result of technological development, particularly the creation and widespread use of Internet-based technology, which they describe as a revolutionary innovation on par with the nineteenth-century invention of the steam engine. A few commentators have pointed out that globalization is really nothing new, that nations have been trading with each other, and businesses have been using the labor of other countries, for centuries. Given that global trade is nothing new, it is also nothing, in this view, to get exercised about.

Critics of globalization, on the other hand, argue that proponents have overlooked the "human face" of free trade, ignoring the actual lives and working conditions of those people who have been brought into the global workforce, often desperate and lacking the power to prevent their exploitation by profit-seeking transnational corporations, or TNCs, as some refer to them. Environmentalists also have argued that NAFTA and similar agreements really aren't about trade at all; rather, they are about eroding national sovereignty in a broad sense, to allow TNCs to circumvent state and national environmental regulations. (Under NAFTA, for example, a corporation located in Canada or Mexico that is barred, for environmental reasons, by the United States or one of its states from selling its product in the United States may sue that government for the loss of potential profits resulting from the environmental restriction.) Underlying the criticisms of free trade is an emphasis on power relations. Where proponents of international laissez-faire argue in favor of eliminating tariffs to create a "level playing field," critics charge that the ideology of free trade—which emphasizes equals meeting and negotiating in a free market-place—is an illusion. In reality, some people have vastly more power than others, and in this view, an unregulated economy, far from providing an escape from these inequalities, reflects them and produces unfair results. Indeed, many critics argue that global trade exacerbates, rather than reduces, these power inequalities.

In the first selection reprinted in this chapter, Evelyn Hu-DeHart, a professor of history and ethnic studies, criticizes the global economy, arguing that proponents of free trade ignore the realities of workers' lives, both in the United States and in third-world countries where U.S. corporations, like Nike, are doing business. In addition to describing vividly the terrible conditions under which these workers labor, and highlighting the gross disparity between workers' wages and the profits being reaped by global corporations from their labor, Hu-DeHart brings a gendered analysis to global trade. Globalization's "biggest losers," according to Hu-DeHart, are women, particularly poor Latinas and Asians, both outside the United States and within. Hu-DeHart thus includes immigrant labor in her discussion of the global labor force; she also looks not just at manufacturing jobs but includes domestic labor and sex work in her analysis as well.

The second selection is by Jagdish Bhagwati, an economist as well as an advisor to the WTO and the United Nations on globalization. Bhagwati rejects the criticism of Hu-DeHart and others that globalization lacks a "human face." Proponents of globalization are seeking just what Hu-DeHart and other critics are, he insists, including the reduction of poverty and child labor, an increase in real wages, gender equity, and improvement in environmental conditions. But, in his view, "anti-globalizers have it all wrong"; it is through a global economy that these things will be achieved, because trade promotes economic growth and economic growth in turn reduces poverty. And as third-world countries become more prosperous, they will become willing to embrace the values of the advanced industrialized nations, such as protection for the environment. Although he does not discuss it in this particular excerpt, Bhagwati sees trade as similarly leading to improved conditions for women, who are the main source of labor for the corporations with manufacturing facilities in the third world. The jobs the corporations offer, although poorly paid by U.S.

standards, are good jobs from the perspective of these women, who otherwise have few employment opportunities and thus no source of income independent of their husbands or fathers. This economic empowerment will lead, in Bhagwati's view, to political and personal power for women.

The third selection is by Douglas S. Massey, a sociologist specializing in the issues of immigration and race relations. In this excerpt, Massey accepts the integration of the global economy as a given and withholds judgment. Like Hu-DeHart, however, Massey is interested in the laborers in the global economy, specifically, the immigrants to the United States from Mexico. He begins by asking why, if the United States is indeed committed to the free flow of capital, goods, services, and information between the United States and Mexico, it seeks to inhibit the free flow of another component of the industrial capitalist system—labor—through the costly militarization of the border. This contradiction, in Massey's view, is rooted in a public misconception about immigration. Despite conventional wisdom, most immigrants to the United States are not fleeing destitution and social chaos and will not become, once they enter the United States, dependent on taxpayer-supported social services. Most immigrants to the United States come from the middle, not the bottom, rungs of their home countries' socioeconomic ladders. Furthermore, most immigrants come not from the poorest countries but from nations such as Mexico that are linked to the United States through commerce and information networks. This immigration is an inevitable result of global economic integration, in Massey's view.

The militarization of the U.S.–Mexican border is thus illogical and a vast waste of taxpayer dollars, from this perspective. It also is counterproductive, because it has failed to keep out undocumented immigrants and, in fact, encouraged those already in the United States illegally to stay rather than risk the hazards of crossing the border. Massey attributes the border policies and public misconceptions about immigration to politicians who purposely manipulate stereotypes about immigrants to distract voters from real issues that they do not wish to confront, such as low wages and reductions in social services. Massey's viewpoint contrasts with that of Hu-DeHart, who briefly addresses U.S. immigration policy to argue that its aim is not to prevent but rather to regulate immigration. Rather than see it as illogical, she suggests that U.S. immigration policy meshes with globalization's corporate agenda to keep wages low and inhibit the formation of labor unions.

EVELYN HU-DEHART

Globalization and Its Discontents

In recent years, we have been treated to a sense of déjà vu of the sixties. Great numbers of mostly young people, men and women, mostly white, middle-class college students, have descended on major American cities such as Seattle and Washington, D.C., as well as their own

From "Globalization and Its Discontents: Exposing the Underside," by Evelyn Hu-DeHart. Reprinted from *Frontiers: A Journal of Women's Studies,* Vol. 24, No. 2 & 3 (2003) by permission of the University of Nebraska Press. Copyright © 2004 by Frontiers Editorial Collective.

campuses to protest a new and virulent form of injustice. Only this time, instead of protesting against war or racism, they raised their voices against something called "globalization." Specifically, they named the related evils to be exposed and reformed, if not destroyed, as the World Trade Organization (WTO), which seeks to remove all barriers to world trade, such as regulations and tariffs erected by nation-states; the Multilateral Agreement on Investment (MAI), which prohibits signatory nations from impeding the flow of money and production facilities across their borders; the International Monetary Fund (IMF) and World Bank, both created by the advanced economies to help poor countries "modernize" with loans and development projects; and sweatshops, the unregulated assembly plants. All of these are linked to globalization.

The concern boiling over into outright objection to globalization has been brewing for some time. But if we have to pinpoint a specific event, we can begin with the Zapatista uprising in Mexico in January 1994. On that fateful day, the Indian peasants of Chiapas, Mexico's southernmost province, rose up in rebellion, timing the protest to coincide with the first day of implementation of the North American Free Trade Agreement (NAFTA), eagerly signed by the governments of the United States, Canada, and Mexico to consolidate neoliberal economic policies and practices in the hemisphere. Dubbed the first postmodern uprising because the rebels professed no interest in seizing state power while demonstrating uncanny sophistication in generating and maintaining international media interest in their just cause, the Zapatistas were soon joined by other Indigenous and peasant insurgents in at least six other poverty-stricken states in southern and central Mexico. What all the rural rebels of Mexico have in common is their vociferous objection to one of then-President Salinas's most controversial preparatory moves for NAFTA, the undoing of Article 27 of the constitution of the Mexican Revolution, which had created thousands of pueblos with inalienable community landholdings called *ejidos,* the centerpiece of Mexico's postrevolutionary land reform and the primary symbol of social justice for peasants. Much to the shock of observers in Mexico and abroad, Salinas violated an unspoken, sacrosanct principle that even his most corrupt and venal predecessors had upheld for decades when he allowed the communal landholdings to be broken up, sold off, and privatized. The breakup of the *ejidos* indicated just how far Salinas and Mexico's elite in the official ruling party Partido Revolucionario Institucional (PRI) were willing to go to mortgage Mexico's most vulnerable citizens to neoliberalism's New World Order, also known as globalization. For more than eighty years, peasants were assured of at least a minimum safety net; now, even this threadbare net was yanked out from under them, leaving Mexico's eighty-plus million population, half of whom were living in poverty, to sink deeper into misery. . . . Obviously, the peasants of Chiapas understood the meaning of globalization, at least as far as their well-being was concerned, sooner than many of us in the sophisticated First World, and they registered their opposition to globalization in no uncertain terms.

In fact, well before NAFTA, Mexico had been a test site and launching pad of the new globalization along its extensive northern border shared with the advanced economy of the United States, far away from the southern border zone that the Zapatistas shared with two even poorer countries, Guatemala and Belize. Indeed, for the alert observer of late-capitalist globalization, the Border Industrialization Project (BIP), which spawned the ubiquitous assembly plants called *maquiladoras,* is the prototype of export-zone production that now dominates the manufacturing landscape all over the Pacific Rim and was the forerunner of the notorious sweatshops seemingly resurrected from the ash heap of early capitalist America.

One recent report counts twenty-seven hundred *maquiladoras* in Mexico, which now, after the enactment of NAFTA, spread from the northern border zone deep into the Yucatán of southern Mexico, where labor is more stable and 25 percent cheaper. In addition to North American corporate owners, other large *maquiladora* owners came from Japan, South Korea, Taiwan, Hong Kong, and assorted European countries, such as Germany. Always in search of cheaper labor, usually embodied by women and children, similar assembly plants have penetrated Central America and parts of the Caribbean. The "giant sucking sound" that presidential candidate Ross Perot heard was that of jobs flowing southward as the United States eliminated industrial jobs. This deindustrialization process began in the 1970s in the economically powerful global core, and manufacturing jobs flowed eastward across the Pacific and south to Latin America, while the U.S. labor economy experienced the rapid rise in service employment at both the high- and low-skilled ends. In the United States, the nonmanufacturing labor force came to constitute 84.3 percent of the total hours worked by 1996, or a growth of almost thirty million jobs since 1979.

The ensuing restructured international economy set up "export-processing zones" (EPZs) or "free trade zones" (FTZs) all over the global periphery, where jerry-built factories produce consumer goods—mainly electronics, clothing, shoes, and toys—for export back to the core. In this New World Economy, finance capital from the global core flows unfettered across international borders to locate sources of cheap labor where eager local elites in control of pliant states act as "middlemen" to facilitate what is euphemistically termed global economic integration. Some Asian countries have prospered from early export-based industrialization—notably Japan, Singapore, Taiwan, and Hong Kong before reintegration with China—and have also become exporters of finance capital, setting up assembly plants in poorer Asian countries such as Indonesia, Thailand, and China, as well as in Mexico, Central America, and the Caribbean as mentioned above. Meanwhile, these more prosperous countries have continued to perform middlemen functions for large international capital in their capacity as subcontractors or outsourcers.

Nothing illustrates the relationship between the transnational U.S. corporation and Asian capital and labor better than Phil Knight's Nike, Inc. The very establishment newspaper *The Washington Post* charges that: "No other company symbolizes the mobilization of American companies overseas more than Nike, Inc. Its thirty-year history in Asia is as close as any one company's story can be to the history of globalization, to the spread of dollars—and marks, and yen—into the poor corners of the earth." Simply put, during the 1970s and 1980s Knight discovered that new computer and fax technology enabled him to export and control the production of his brand-name athletic shoes in Asian countries, where cheap, largely female, labor abounded. By the time he closed down his last U.S. sneaker plants in New Hampshire and Maine, he had discovered the virtues of out-sourcing production. He subcontracted with Asian entrepreneurs from the more affluent Asian countries, such as Taiwan, South Korea, and Hong Kong, to set up assembly plants to manufacture Nike shoes in poorer, and thus labor-cheap, Asian countries such as China, Indonesia, and Vietnam. The subcontractors did all the work of recruiting, training, and disciplining workers, monitoring production, setting wages, and paying workers—in short, handling all aspects of management-labor relations. These Asian subcontractors also took care of dealing with Asian host governments and local officials, greasing palms when necessary. One of Asia's most successful subcontractors was the Tsai family of Hong Kong, whose ninety-seven production lines employing fifty-four thousand workers in China's Pearl River Delta produced forty-five million sneakers in 1995 for Reebock and Adidas, as well as

Nike. For a long period of time, the subcontracting system allowed Nike to argue that it had no direct supervision over Asian plants, thus should be absolved from dealing with any problems arising from labor or government relations.

In this global production system, profits are good for the subcontractors, but they are really phenomenal for Nike owner Phil Knight. To expand the worldwide demand for Nike sneakers, he enlisted the alliance of National Basketball Association (NBA) Commissioner David Stern, global media mogul Rupert Murdoch, and most importantly, basketball superstar Michael Jordan. With $20 million in yearly endorsement fees from Knight, Jordan spread his impressive American game to the rest of the world while simultaneously selling the Nike shoes that seemingly propelled him to unparalleled heights. Knight became the sixth wealthiest man in the United States, and Jordan became the most successful global pitchman, but their profits and fame were founded on the labor of legions of faceless, nameless Asian girls and women.

After Jordan's retirement from basketball, Knight signed up Tiger Woods, son of a Thai mother and an African American father, to do for Nike and golf what Jordan had done for Nike and basketball. As a still more perverse turn of globalization, the next global pitchman for Nike is likely to be Yao Ming, China's seven-feet-five-inch gift to the NBA. This first pick of the 2002 NBA draft was signed by the team in Houston, home to America's fifth largest Asian American community. But his real appeal would be transnational, pitching American labels manufactured in Asian sweatshops back to consumers in his densely-packed homeland and all across Asia.

When this global production system first evolved, Knight was rather guileless in explaining his huge profits: "We were . . . good at keeping our manufacturing costs down," he said. How low? In 1992, four Indonesian plants owned by South Korean subcontractors paid young girls as little as $.15 an hour for an eleven-hour day. A pair of shoes that cost less than $5 to make in Asia sold for $150 in the United States. By the late 1990s, Indonesian factories made 70 million pairs of Nike shoes with twenty-five thousand workers, each of them receiving daily wages of $2.23, which covered only 90 percent of basic subsistence needs for one person. Their combined yearly wages did not equal Jordan's endorsement fee. Wages in Vietnam were even lower, at $1.60 for an eight-hour day in 1997.

The Nike shoe captures the essence of the new global consumer product: A particular model can be designed in Nike headquarters in Oregon, and cooperatively developed by technicians in Oregon, South Korea, and Indonesia by putting together fifty-two separate parts made in five countries. It is manufactured by young women hunched over machines and hand tools and glue, working in factories located in Vietnam, Indonesia, or China and owned by someone from Taiwan or Hong Kong. Then it is sold all over the world.

. . . [S]omewhat amazingly, global capital and production in continuous and relentless search for cheap labor, manufacturing flexibility, and spatial mobility have come full circle: The global assembly plant employing low-skilled, low-cost female labor can now be found in abundance in the global core—the United States itself—in the form of hundreds of garment sweatshops scattered throughout southern California, the San Francisco-Oakland area, and in and around New York's garment district and Chinatowns. Although clothing manufacturing has constituted a mainstay of the Mexican *maquiladoras* and fly-by-night assembly plants set up in export-processing zones by Asian subcontractors in the Caribbean, Central America, and all over Asia, the fast-changing designs and fluctuating market demands of the garment business has dictated the need to produce certain styles and quantities of garments close to the retailers, manufacturers, and consumers in the United States. New Asian and Latino immigrants (legal and undocumented) quickly meet the needs both for subcontractors and for workers, doing the same work they would in their home countries had they not migrated to the United States. Nike and other American manufacturers are reluctant to claim responsibility for labor problems in their Asian production, and they have a similar policy at home, arguing they have no control over their subcontractors who own and operate the sweatshops.

While hidden for years from the American consuming public and the media, the revived American sweatshop is no longer a secret, and its exposure is helping to fuel the antiglobalization movement. The raid on the El Monte, California, underground sweatshop in August 1995 freed sixty-seven women and five men, Thai workers smuggled into the country by the Thai-Chinese owners who contracted with several well-known U.S. brand-name manufacturers. Paid only $1.60 per hour, these workers were kept in a modern version of indentured servitude, denied their freedom to leave the barbed-wire compound, forced to pay off their passage, and threatened with retribution against family members back home and rape if they disobeyed their captors. In January 1999, the media exposed another shameful sweatshop situation that resembled El Monte. Hundreds of sweatshops owned by Asians and Asian American subcontractors were found in the U.S. Pacific territory of Saipan, where workers—predominantly young women from the Philippines, China, Thailand and Bangladesh—worked twelve hours daily, seven days weekly, living seven to a room in "dreary barracks surrounded by inward-facing barbed wire."

At the base of this system are the legions of immigrant women workers, Asian and Latina, who have seldom complained because they believe they have no other job options. In converting themselves into an available and flexible labor force almost immediately upon their arrival in the United States, they have enabled the garment industry to keep a critical part of garment production within the United States, right in the manufacturing and retail centers of New York and Los Angeles, where most of these immigrants settle. Those immigrant women absorbed into garment work likely have little formal education and little or no English-language skills, and are deemed to be low-skilled in other areas as well. Research has shown that deficiencies in education and English-language skills are also the most critical factors in determining immigrant job options in the United States. Many women are compelled to work to supplement family incomes because their equally low-skilled, English-deficient spouses also work in low-paying, often dead-end jobs. It would be wrong to dismiss their contribution to family income as merely "supplementary," for many women earn as much, if not more, than their equally trapped partners. Furthermore, with both partners stuck in these low-wage, dead-end, often seasonal jobs, poverty for many such immigrant families has become a permanent fact of life.

In addition to manufacturing, immigrant women workers from Asia and Latin America are desired in the global core for what might be termed "social reproductive labor." Whether working in domestic, cleaning, janitorial, or food service, or in nursing home or child care, or as prostitutes, sex workers, or mail- or internet-order brides, Third World immigrant women are not just making a living in low-paying, low-status, often demeaning niches that require little English or other skills. In a very crucial way, they, too, are part of the new transnational division of labor, albeit in a less visible and certainly far less acknowledged way. Their paid labor now replaces the previously unremunerated responsibilities of First World women in the social reproduction of daily and family life, both on a daily and intergenerational basis, by relieving professional First World women of much of the burden of the "second shift." Such social reproductive labor has always been associated with women's work and continues to be debased and devalued when "industrialized," that is, performed for payment by Third World women for their largely white and affluent First World "sisters" in a racial division of labor. In sum, "Most white middle class women could hire another woman—a recent immigrant, a working class woman, a woman of color, or all these—to perform much of the hard labor of household tasks," as they fulfill themselves in careers outside the home. To put it bluntly, the "private sphere" responsibilities of class-privileged women are thereby transferred to racially and socially subordinate women.

Although sex work across national boundaries is not new in the world, sex industries have greatly expanded under late capitalist globalization. Preference for Asian women as sex partners—paid or even unpaid, as in the case of military and mail- or internet-order brides—by many American men dates back to the days of America's serial military involvement in Asia, from WW II, through the Korean War, and on to the Vietnam War. "Militarized prostitution" developed around all army bases in Asia while American soldiers on furlough for "rest and relaxation" stimulated the development and growth of sex tourism to countries far beyond the battlegrounds, such as in Thailand. Just as American transnational capital has constructed Third World women as particularly adept at garment assembly work—both "over there" and after migration to the United States—so have American men fetishized these same women as particularly seductive as girlfriends and attentive and submissive as wives, uncorrupted by Western feminist ideas and values. As in Asia, sex work has greatly expanded in the Caribbean as an extension of the lucrative tourist industry, feeding off the familiar, unequal relationships between First and Third world nations.

The *maquiladoras* in Mexico, the export-processing-zone factories in Asia, the garment sweatshops in the United States, the meatpacking plants in the American heartland, the sex work and domestic work of immigrant women—these are the unattractive public faces of the New World Order. Do they represent the trickle-down dividends of globalization by creating jobs, as global cheerleaders would have us believe, or do they represent "lurid examples of random inhumanity" wrought by global capitalism, as its critics charge? What responsibilities do governments and especially the international organizations and policy-setting bodies that facilitate globalization, such as the WTO and IMF, have to ensure minimum wage and workplace standards, including environmental and health regulations? And if these organizations do not address these issues, then who will do so for them? Is globalization only about property rights, or should it also be concerned about human rights? Obviously, there are real winners, or else wealthy corporations and individuals backed up by their powerful governments would not be pushing so aggressively and relentlessly for global policies and regulatory bodies such as the WTO and MAI, but do there have to be legions of permanent losers? These are some of the compelling questions that have galvanized protesters from Chiapas to Seattle to Washington, D.C., who have forced onto the world stage the dark side of globalization. The following are some of the issues and contradictions raised by globalization and its discontents, illustrated by the scenarios described above:

1. Corporate-led globalization depends on intense exploitation of labor, *especially female labor,* exacerbated by the subcontracting system that answers to the logic of a race to the bottom of the wage scale.

To win a contract, the subcontractor must submit the lowest bid, then squeezes the workers to make his profit. Thus, Vietnamese workers in factories under contract to Nike and similar U.S. transnational corporations do not even make a living wage, defined as enough to buy three meals a day, let alone pay rent, health care, and support for a family. Subcontracting works in a particularly oppressive way in the garment industry worldwide, whether in Asia, Mexico, Central America, the Caribbean, or the United States itself. Thus, the antisweatshop movement on college campuses correctly focuses its pressure on the manufacturers and not primarily on the

Asian subcontractors, because they understand that U.S. manufacturers pocket the lion's share of profits and call the shots.

The biggest losers in this global assembly line are women—Latina and Asian women—characterized as inherently, innately, and naturally suited for the kind of low-skill labor in light manufacturing, whether in Third World export-processing factories or U.S. electronic assembly plants and sweatshops. This "myth of nimble fingers"—a purely ideological construct—is nothing less than rationalization for low wages, not to mention justification for the perpetuation of the notion of Third World women's intellectual inferiority. It is not just the gendered quality of the international division of labor that is so problematic, but that the gendered division is inferred and inscribed as a permanent hierarchy that is further reinforced by race, class, and nationality differences, as well as denial of immigration and citizenship rights in the case of the smuggled and undocumented.

We are compelled to conclude that Third World women in their home countries and after migration to the United States comprise one continuum in the same gendered, transnational workforce that lies at the base of the extremely exploitative and oppressive global subcontracting system of production. Whether she works in a Nike plant subcontracted to a Taiwanese factory owner in Indonesia or Vietnam, or as a contract worker in an Asian-owned Saipan factory, or in an unregistered, unlicensed underground sweatshop in Los Angeles operated by a Korean immigrant, or in a union shop in New York's Chinatown owned by a newly naturalized Chinese American, she may well be sewing the same style of garment for the same manufacturer, affixing the same name-brand label on the same finished product. How ironic it is that with all its "supposed modernity and wondrous technologies," the "manic logic of capitalism" has reproduced all the old barbarisms associated with early twentieth-century capitalism.

2. Increased trade spurred on by decreased regulation and removal of all barriers does not necessarily produce better jobs.

If anything, removal of regulations only serves to increase the power of the wealthier nations of the North over the poorer nations of the South, which often feel they have little choice but to go along with the dictates of the IMF, the World Bank, the WTO, and, in our hemisphere, NAFTA, and the powerful governments that stand behind these global organizations and policies. Thus, if unregulated, global free trade as we now know it will disproportionately benefit the already wealthy nations to the great disadvantage of the poor nations, enabling a few corporations and individuals to become obscenely rich while furthering the misery of the world's multitudinous poor. Many new studies have demonstrated the growing gap *between* and *within* nations, with the United States providing a notable example of both kinds of inequalities. As some critics point out, contrary to the World Bank's bald assertion that accelerated globalization has produced greater world equality, far from lifting all boats, the rising tide of globalization is "only lifting yachts"! Today, the world's richest two hundred people have more wealth than 41 percent of the world's humanity. Increasing the world's productive capacities may be a good thing for all, but it must be accompanied by a broader distribution of wealth.

3. Thus, it cannot be argued that globalization is natural and inevitable, and produces general progress for all.

Rather, it should be made clear that globalization and the global finance system is a "man-made artifact," in the inimitable words of critic William Greider, one of the most trenchant and lucid critics of corporate globalization. It is defined as, "a political regime devised over many years by interested parties to serve their ends," and if man made it, Greider concludes, then man can very well undo it, "because nothing in nature or, for that matter, in economics requires the rest of us to accept a system that is so unjust and mindlessly destructive." In short, globalization is not an inevitable force of history, "but rather the consequence of public policy choices." This is precisely what protesters in Chiapas and Seattle and on our campuses are demanding of their governments and international organizations behind globalization, and of their university administrators: Make *different* public policy choices. Societies and citizens must act to counter the "destructive social convulsions" sown by the unregulated or deregulated market forces of finance capital through so-called free trade, irresponsible investment, speculative lending, and environmental degradation.

4. Immigrants are not only *not* a drain on the U.S. economy, but an absolute necessity.

Why then, has nativism or anti-immigrant hysteria accompanied globalization in the United States and in other parts of the global core, such as Australia and Japan? Immigrant labor is indispensable for the labor-intensive, service-dependent economy of the United States, as well as the resurgent sweatshops of the light-manufacturing sector. Lately, well-educated and professionally trained immigrant labor is also in great demand in the computer programming sector of the American Silicon Valley. The primary role of the INS is not to stop the flow of immigration to the United States but to regulate the level of that flow and to control the type of immigrants who come in at any given time. In other words, rather than unregulate and deregulate immigration, as is the case with finance capital and trade in manufactured goods, the United States wants to regulate and control the free trade of labor in order to keep wages down and unions out, and thereby protect their high corporate profits, although higher wages and strong unions would ensure a broader distribution of wealth in an expanding world economy.

It is also time for the United States to acknowledge that neoliberal reforms in the Third World, such as Salinas's privatization of *ejido* land, free-trade policies, and IMF-imposed restrictions on social spending, have all created the poverty, that is, forced people from the global south to countries in the global north, including the United States, Australia, Japan, and Western Europe, only to be attacked and maligned as illegal aliens and undesirables, and a drain on society.

When demand for new workers surges in any critical sector of the economy, as periodically happens in the high-tech industries of the Silicon Valley or in the low-tech industries of agriculture in the West and meatpacking in the Midwest, the INS is perfectly capable and willing to look "the other way." In the booming U.S. economy at the end of the twentieth century, with unemployment at just 4 percent and a strong demand for people to take jobs paying $8 per hour or less—which comprise 25 percent of all jobs—documented and undocumented immigrants made up a large share of the available labor pool. Is U.S. immigration policy just an undetected glaring contradiction, or is it part and parcel of another kind of unspoken logic of global capitalism, like the manic logic of the subcontracting system? (After 9/11, national security concerns regulating movement of mostly male foreign nationals from certain countries in Asia and the Middle East have further complicated the immigration equation.) Until very recently, the U.S. labor movement actually fell for the arbitrary line invented by the government and corporate interests to differentiate between legal, thus "good" immigrants, and illegal, thus "bad" immigrants. That canard was finally laid to rest when the Service Employees International Union (SEIU) led its eighty-five hundred janitors who cleaned the high-rise office buildings in downtown Chicago and Los Angeles—many of them "illegal aliens" from Mexico, Central America, and Asia—on successful strikes in those locations. Concretely, current labor leaders such as AFL-CIO's John Sweeney has proclaimed a "new internationalism" for American unions. John Wilhelm, president of the Hotel

Employees and Restaurant Employees union (HERE), went one step further in calling for a correction of Labor's previous anti-immigrant stance. "Immigrants have the right to ask us—which side are we on," he said at the 2000 AFL-CIO convention.

Greider argues passionately that a productive world economy need not produce widespread misery that results from persistent and gross injustices. While public pressure coming from demonstrations across the nation can succeed in uncovering the veil of secrecy surrounding the instruments of corporate globalization and imposing some measure of corporate responsibility on sweatshops, these tactics can only reduce a few of the worst abuses. Ultimately, these protests and their proposed remedies illustrate the conventional liberal argument that globalization is good, just curb its excesses; moreover, it's inevitable, so mend it, don't end it. Former Clinton Labor Secretary Robert Reich expands on this liberal perspective: "The challenge for those of us who believe that free trade and global capital are essentially good things if managed correctly is to avoid the backlash by developing progressive strategies to overcome the widening inequalities and the environmental depredations."

Finally, some protesters and critics of globalization urge us to question the fundamental class relationship between this globalized working class and global capital, interrogate the supposed logic and rationality of the global assembly line, and resist accepting the inevitability of corporate-driven globalization or the permanency of the grossly unequal North-South divide. Our protests and critiques must seek answers to these more fundamental and vexing questions, not just negotiate remedies for abuses and excesses in the existing relationship between workers and capital in the global economy.

JAGDISH BHAGWATI

The Human Face of Globalization

Many politicians contend, while others simply concede, that the anti-globalizers are right in thinking that the social implications of economic globalization range from bad to worse.

The favoured phrase, used in particular by the "alternative way" politicians of social democratic persuasion, is that "globalization needs a human face"—implying, in other words, that it lacks one.

Indeed, the prevailing orthodoxy in activist groups . . . is that we need ethical globalization—since somehow economic globalization is unethical in its impact, if not its intent. But is this true?

I would argue that globalization has a human face; that, on balance, globalization advances, rather than harms, social agendas as diverse as reduction of poverty and the reduction of child labour in the poor countries, the real wages of workers in the rich countries, the pursuit of

From "The Human Face of Globalization," by Jagdish Bhagwati. From *Global Agenda,* the magazine of the World Economic Forum, Jan. 2004. Reprinted by permission of World Link Publications Ltd.

democracy worldwide, the promotion of gender equality and women's welfare, and the quality of the environment.

So, globalization is not only valuable in terms of increasing the economic pie; it is also an economic issue about which there are few existing populist critics among economists—a group rarer than, say, endangered turtles and, what's more, less worthy of preservation than such turtles.

Globalization is also beneficial to the social issues that we, as citizens, care deeply about. Its economic and social impacts are not only beneficial, they are also correlated. Increased economic prosperity contributes, generally speaking, to the achievement of social agendas such as the reduction of poverty and of child labour.

Whether or not globalization has a human face is also a question whose answer has immediate implications for the kind of governance regimes we pursue. For, if you believe that globalization lacks a human aspect, then appropriate governance will mean policy interventions that tend to inhibit, handicap and restrain globalization throwing sand into the gears to slow down its processes.

But if you believe, as I now do, that globalization has a human face, then you will want altogether different policy interventions—ones that enhance, supplement and complement the good effects that globalization can bring. Nothing is more important, therefore, than to decide which of the two conflicting views of globalization we embrace.

Consider the important issue of poverty in poor countries. Globalization has aided the reduction of poverty because, first, it promotes economic growth, and, second, growth reduces poverty.

Economists are ingenious enough to build models where trade, for instance, need not affect growth or may even reduce it. But an overwhelming amount of evidence shows that the growth of trade—both at given levels of protection and, additionally, as a result of trade liberalization—is strongly linked with the growth of income, and thus economic prosperity.

This evidence comes in a variety of ways. First, the traditional view that protectionism aided growth historically, especially in the 19th century, has now been successfully challenged. . . .

More recently, Arvind Panagariya has examined growth rates for almost 200 countries over a period of 38 [years] from 1961 to 1999. He concludes that, when you classify countries with per capita growth rates of 3% or more as miraculous and those with rates that declined in per capita terms as disastrous, it is remarkable that virtually all countries in the former group rapidly expanded their trade as well.

And the vast majority of the "debacle" countries with declining per capita incomes recorded declines in imports as well.

But growth of per capita income, in turn, is also associated with a decline in poverty. Recent work by Xavier Sala-i-Martin, and by the Indian economist Surjit Bhalla, has undermined the conviction that economic growth worldwide has been accompanied by an increase, rather than a decline, in poverty.

Sala-i-Martin has estimated poverty rates for 97 countries between 1970 and 1998, supporting a conjecture that I made in the early 1960s that economic growth has to be the principal (but not the only) force in alleviating poverty—and that growth had to be viewed as an active "pull-up" strategy for reducing poverty, rather than as a passive "trickle-down" strategy.

Contrasting the reversed role of Asia and Africa in poverty rates, Sala-i-Martin concludes that: "Poverty increased dramatically in Africa because African countries did not grow. As a result, perhaps the most important lesson to be learned . . . is how to make Africa grow."

Both he and Bhalla conclude, in absolute terms that poverty, as a proportion of the population, has diminished, not increased.

Nor should the anti-globalizers think that experience shows that income inequality among nations, as distinct from poverty, has increased in recent decades. The World Bank, a major source of the estimates that Sala-i-Martin and Bhalla debunk, has also estimated that if you were to put all households of the world next to one another and estimate the income inequality among them, world inequality has increased.

The Bank's conclusions have been undermined by Sala-i-Martin. He has calculated, in fact, nine different measures of global inequality and finds that, according to all of them, global inequality has declined in the past two decades.

So, the anti-globalizers have it all wrong: trade enhances growth and growth reduces poverty. It is good to know that, at least in this instance, economics and common sense go together.

But if poor countries profit in terms of both increased prosperity and reduced poverty, should we then worry—as labour unions do—that the labour standards of rich countries are therefore at risk, and that there is now a "race to the bottom" thanks to trade and direct foreign investment?

Admittedly, this fear is plausible. But it is misplaced. The unions believe that employers will say to them: "if, in this globally competitive economy, you do not accept lower standards, jobs will be lost to countries where these standards are lower; or we will just take our production to these other countries. So hard-won standards will be lowered."

But there is practically no evidence that standards have indeed been lowered in this way.

Consider the most competitive industry: garment manufacturing. Sweatshop conditions are common even in New York factories, where legislated standards are being flouted. But the reason why these standards are low, despite the mandated high standards, is simply because the industry employs illegal immigrants who cannot assert their rights.

Furthermore, there is virtually no enforcement. Nor is there any evidence that, because of low standards in Guatemala and similar places, the legislated standards in the United States have fallen in any way at all.

Take the furniture industry as another example. Some players in this industry crossed the Rio Grande into Mexico because the lead paint restrictions in California were too stringent, and there was almost no such regulation in Mexico. Did this lead to decline in the lead-paint standards in California? Absolutely not.

Much systematic work by political scientists today shows why this is so. There are many institutions which have evolved and worked over decades to develop the high standards; so these pressures to lower the standards are successfully fought.

It was feared that the former president Bush's Competitiveness Council, headed by vice president Dan Quayle in the early 1990s, would be a source of pressure to reduce US standards. But there was almost no instance where it succeeded, simply because any pressure was resolutely rolled back.

When competition with low-standard countries is feared, these institutions, including the unions and opposition politicians, have tried to deflect the competitiveness game into one of demanding higher standards abroad.

So, politically, there has been an attempt at creating a "race to the top" instead of succumbing to a "race to the bottom."

Indeed, as one goes down the litany of complaints and fears of the anti-globalizers—including the effects on mainstream and indigenous cultures—the conclusion is inescapable that the effects [of] economic globalization on several social dimensions are benign, on balance, rather than malign.

But then we must ask: what institutional and policy framework is necessary to improve on the benign outcomes that globalization already bears?

Three types of issues matter. First, even if the overall effect is sometimes benign, it is not always so in every instance. Therefore, we must devise institutions to deal with downsides, as and when they arise.

I have argued that developing countries often lack adjustment assistance programmes of the kind that the developed countries have evolved over time as they liberalized their trade regimes. But how can the poor countries finance such programmes?

Evidently, aid agencies such as the World Bank can be mobilized to provide funds to support trade liberalization.

Second, we need to ensure that we do not repeat the mistake made by the reformers in Russia, where shock therapy was tried and failed. Maximal speed is not necessarily optimal speed: both economics and politics require cautious adjustment.

When the economist Jeffrey Sachs insisted on shock therapy in Russia in the 1990s, he used the analogy: "You cannot cross a chasm in two leaps." The Soviet expert Padma Desai replied: "You cannot cross it in one leap either unless you are Indiana Jones; it is better to drop a bridge." Events proved her right.

Finally, we need to use supplementary policies to accelerate the pace at which social agendas are advanced. True, child labour will be reduced by the prosperity enhanced by globalization. But then what more can we do to reduce it faster?

Here, the unions in rich countries have taken the view that only trade sanctions have teeth. This is a myopic and counterproductive view. Today it is far better, as many intellectuals from the developing countries argue, to base arguments on moral suasion. After all, God gave us a tongue as well. In today's age, with democratic regimes worldwide, with CNN and with NGOs [nongovernmental organizations], a good tongue-lashing is far more powerful than sanctions imposed by governments whose own credentials are often not unblemished.

Globalization has a human face. Globalization works. But we can make it work better. That is the chief task before all of us today.

Douglas S. Massey

Closed-Door Policy

At the dawn of the 21st century, the United States offers a contradictory model of global economic openness. American policy has relentlessly promoted open commerce, leading the way by freeing its own markets to foreign investment, trade and travel. America's own borders have become increasingly open for flows of capital, goods, commodities, information and certain favored classes of people: entrepreneurs, scientists, students, tourists and corporate employees.

When it comes to the movement of ordinary labor, however, America has not sought openness. Rather, the thrust of U.S. policy since the 1950s has been to make it more difficult for workers to enter the United States in search of jobs, except via narrow programs under corporate control.

This contradiction is nowhere more apparent than in U.S. relations with Mexico, which together with Canada is our largest trading partner. Since 1986, U.S. officials have worked closely with officials in both countries to create an integrated North American economy, open to flows of goods, capital, commodities, services and information. Yet within this integrated economy we somehow, magically, do not want any labor to be moving. Against all logic, we wish to create an integrated, continent-wide economy characterized by the free movement of all factors of production except one.

This schizophrenia is manifest in the fact that, since the mid-1980s, we have moved in two diametrically opposed directions, at once promoting integration while simultaneously seeking separation. Between 1985 and 2000, total trade between Mexico and the United States increased by a factor of eight, the number of Mexican tourists quintupled, Mexican business visitors and intra-company transferees tripled, and the total number of persons crossing the border for short visits doubled. All this came about according to plan, and only intensified with enactment of the North American Free Trade Agreement.

At the same time, however, U.S. officials have sought to maintain the illusion of separation. As trade expanded between 1985 and 2000, U.S. spending on border enforcement increased by a factor of six, the number of U.S. Border Patrol officers doubled and hours spent by agents patrolling the frontier tripled. During the 1990s, two of the top 10 fastest growing job categories in the federal workforce were "Immigration Inspector" and "Border Patrol Agent." Today the Border Patrol is the largest arms-bearing branch of the U.S. government except for the military itself, with a budget well in excess of $1 billion per year. In many border communities, the Immigration and Naturalization Service is now the largest employer.

Why has the United States chosen to militarize a peaceful border with its closest trading partner, a democratic country that poses no conceivable threat to U.S. security? The answer, I fear, rests on seriously mistaken notions about the nature of immigration in today's postindustrial, globalized economy.

The most basic misconception is that, without a heavily militarized border, the United States will be invaded by an army of destitute immigrants fleeing abject poverty, or flooded by a tidal wave of poor foreigners eager to take Americans' jobs and consume public services at taxpayer expense. Politicians—liberal as well as conservative—find the imagery of invasions and floods useful during periods of economic insecurity and rising inequality, for it deflects attention from more fundamental questions about the distribution of wealth and power in the United States. Immigrants provide a convenient scapegoat to absorb voter anger about the erosion of wages, the instability of unemployment and declining access to social benefits. Politicians and the media periodically manufacture immigration and border crises as the need arises, and the restrictiveness of immigration policies is inversely correlated with the business cycle.

The truth is that most immigrants to the United States are not desperate people fleeing poverty and social chaos overseas. International migration is a well-ordered process connected to broader processes of global trade, geopolitical integration and market expansion; it is simply the labor component of a globalizing market economy. Developed nations that receive flows of capital, goods, services and commodities also receive immigrants. As a result, western Europe,

Japan, Korea, Singapore and other countries have joined traditional immigrant-receiving nations such as the United States, Canada and Australia to become net importers of labor.

The poorest and most populous nations of the world, with a large share of those who have the most to gain from international migration, generally do not send the most migrants. If emigration were caused by poverty, most immigrants would come from Africa, followed by the Caribbean, Asia and Latin America. Among immigrants to the United States during the 1990s, however, just 3 percent came from Africa whereas 11 percent came from the Caribbean, 30 percent from Asia and 36 percent from Latin America. Likewise, the rate of international migration across countries bears no relation whatsoever to the rate of demographic increase: The correlation is virtually zero.

Among sending countries, emigration does not stem from a lack of development but from development itself. International migration has always been part and parcel of broader processes of economic growth and development. In the course of its industrialization, for example, Europe exported 54 million people. Emigrants are created by social and economic transformations in societies undergoing rapid change as a result of their incorporation into the global market economy. What is remarkable about today's developing nations is not that they produce emigrants but that they produce so few. Whereas Britain ended up exporting half of its population increase in the course of its development, South Korea exported less than 5 percent of its demographic increase. At present, fewer than 3 percent of the world's people live outside their countries of birth.

Nor are those who do leave their countries of origin in search of work overseas the poorest of citizens. Indeed, labor emigrants tend to be drawn from the middle of a country's socioeconomic distribution, not the bottom. When they go, moreover, migrants typically do not go to nations that are richest or closest. Rather, they proceed along established pathways to countries that are already connected politically, socially and economically to their countries of origin. The main sources of immigrants for the United States are thus its closest trading partners (Mexico, Canada, China), former colonies (the Philippines, Puerto Rico), and regions where the United States has recently intervened militarily or politically (Central America, the Caribbean, Southeast Asia).

That Mexico is by far the largest source of U.S. immigrants is hardly surprising. In addition to sharing a land border with the United States, it was twice invaded by U.S. troops in the 20th century (in 1914 and 1917), it has been the target of two U.S.–sponsored labor recruitment efforts (during 1917–18 and 1942–64), and since 1986, at U.S. insistence, it has undertaken a radical transformation of its political economy and entered the global market. Moreover, since 1994 it has been linked to the United States by NAFTA, a comprehensive economic treaty that presently generates $250 billion per year in binational trade.

Under these circumstances, immigration between the two countries is inevitable, even though Mexico is wealthy by Third World standards. With a per capita gross domestic product of $9,000, it is one of the richest countries in Latin America. It is in the interest of the United States, therefore, to build on this economic base by accepting Mexican immigration as a reality and working to manage it in a way that minimizes the costs and maximizes the benefits for both nations.

The repressive border controls imposed by the United States since 1986 have done precisely the opposite, however. Studies have found no discernable effect of restrictive immigration policies on the inflow of Mexican immigrants, documented or undocumented. Indeed, during the 1990s, a record 2.2 million Mexican immigrants entered the country legally, constituting a quarter of all documented immigration. At the same time, the probability of apprehension for undocumented migrants fell to record-low levels, raising the odds of their ultimately gaining access. By the mid-1990s, the probability of apprehension had fallen to as low as 20 percent per attempt. The selective concentration of enforcement resources at specific locations along the border redirected migratory flows toward other sectors where fewer Border Patrol officers were stationed. Perversely, more people actually got in.

By redirecting migrants toward more remote and inhospitable sectors, the selective hardening of the border tripled the rate of border mortality, causing hundreds of needless deaths each year. Moreover, as a result of the increased risks of entering the United States, Mexican migrants rationally chose to minimize border crossings, not by remaining home but by staying longer once they got in. Paradoxically, the principal effect of border militarization has been to reduce the odds of going home, not of coming in the first place.

As the size of the return flow plummeted during the 1990s, it produced a spectacular and unprecedented increase in the Mexican population of the United States. The wall of enforcement resources erected after 1993 was especially high in San Diego, which deflected migrants away from California and toward other regions of the country. Whereas 63 percent of all Mexicans who arrived between 1985 and 1990 went to California, just 35 percent of those arriving between 1995 and 2000 did so, creating an explosion of Mexican populations in a host of new receiving states.

In addition to increasing the size of the Mexican population and spreading it throughout the United States, U.S. policies have marginalized immigrants socially and economically. The criminalization of undocumented hiring in 1986 caused employers to shift from direct employment to labor subcontracting. In the wake of this legislation, everyone who wished to work in certain sectors of the labor market—agriculture, gardening, construction, custodial services—had to go through a subcontractor. It didn't matter if they were legal residents or citizens. The subcontractor, of course, took a cut of their wages as payment, money that before 1986 would have gone to the immigrants themselves. The net effect was to reduce the wages and undermine the working conditions not of undocumented migrants but of U.S. workers.

Other laws passed in 1996 stripped legal immigrants of the right to certain social entitlements, causing a stampede toward naturalization. More naturalizations mean more immigrants at a later date, because a U.S. citizen can sponsor the entry of spouses, unmarried sons and daughters, and parents without restriction. In addition, citizens may petition for the entry of adult sons and daughters, as well as for brothers and sisters, subject to numerical limitation. Each new citizen thus creates a host of legal entitlements for additional immigration.

At the same time, a large fraction of new immigrants are undocumented and marginalized from the rest of American society; even those with legal papers find their access to social benefits constrained unless they are citizens. If U.S. authorities had set out to intentionally design a program to create a future underclass, they could not have done a better job.

The fundamental problem with U.S. immigration policy toward Mexico—and with U.S. immigration policy generally—is that it treats international migration as a pathological condition to be repressed through unilateral actions. In reality, immigration is the natural outgrowth of broader processes of market expansion and economic integration that can be managed for the mutual advantage of trading partners. By migrating in response to structural adjustments at home, migrants generally do not intend to remain abroad for the rest of their lives. Some do, of course, and others change their mind as a result of their experience in the host society. But left to their own devices, most would return home, for they are migrating not to maximize income but to overcome economic problems at home. They use international migration instrumentally as a way of overcoming the missing and failed markets that are quite common in the course of economic development. The money they earn abroad is repatriated in the form of savings and remittances, which total around $60 billion worldwide. Repressive border policies make it more difficult for migrants to achieve their ambition of returning home.

Rather than accepting immigration as a logical consequence of America's hegemonic position at the core of a global market economy, U.S. political leaders have enacted repressive unilateral policies to create the impression that immigration is not occurring, that U.S. borders are "under control" and that U.S. citizens are protected from the presumed ill effects of immigrants. In fact, such policies achieve the opposite: Immigration continues, but in a way that undermines the status and welfare of U.S. residents. . . .

The answer is not open borders, of course, but frontiers that are reasonably regulated on a binational basis. At present, all countries have the same quota of 20,000 legal immigrants per year, no matter their size or relationship to the United States. Thus, our largest and closest neighbor and most important trading partner has the same limited access to U.S. visas as Botswana, Nepal and Paraguay. A more realistic policy would recognize Mexico's unique status by increasing the annual immigrant quota, establishing a flexible temporary labor program and regularizing the status of those already here.

By bringing the flows above board, we would mitigate the downward pressures on wages and working conditions in the United States while raising tax revenues that could be used to offset the costs of immigration and to assist Mexico in overcoming the market failures that motivate so many moves north of the border. If we cannot manage migratory exchanges with Mexico as it joins with us to create an integrated North American market, how can we possibly hope to manage the migratory flows that will be coming from China as it is transformed by participating in the global market economy?

Further Reading

New York Times columnist Thomas Friedman has been a zealous advocate of globalization; for his view that globalization is both revolutionary and inevitable and that its opponents are backward-looking, see the highly readable if facile *The Lexus and the Olive Tree: Understanding Globalization* (New York: Farrar, Straus and Giroux, 2000). For a review of Friedman's book by a critic of globalization, see Thomas Frank's "It's Globalicious!" in *Harper's Magazine* (vol. 299 [October 1999]), 72–75. For a criticism of Friedman's viewpoint by a proponent of globalization, see Jagdish Bhagwati, "Globalization in Your Face," in his collection *The Wind of the Hundred Days: How Washington Mismanaged Globalization* (Cambridge, MA: MIT Press, 2000). Bhagwati's *In Defense of Globalization* (New York: Oxford University Press, 2004) is challenging reading which provides a measured but overall positive view. See Paul Krugman, *Peddling Prosperity: Economic Sense and Nonsense in the Age of Diminished Expectations* (New York: Norton, 1994) for one economist's view that globalization has not resulted in U.S. job loss or the lowering of wages. (Krugman sees technological change—particularly the use of computer technology by businesses—as leading to greater efficiency and productivity and thus the need for fewer workers.) See economist Jay R. Mandle's "Trading Up: Why Globalization Aids the Poor," *Commonweal* (vol. 127/11 [2 June 2000]), 15–18, for the argument that globalization does, in fact, result in job loss for the United States, but that these are undesirable, low-wage jobs that are better shifted to third-world countries anyway. For the view that globalization has been underway for years if not for centuries—and that is thus implicitly critical of an antiglobalization outlook—see Doug Henwood, "Beyond Globophobia," *Nation* (vol. 277/18 [1 December 2003]), 17–20.

For a thorough critique of globalization which considers environmental issues, workers' rights, sovereignty issues, and America's huge trade deficit, see journalist William Greider's *One World, Ready or Not: The Manic Logic of Global Capitalism* (New York: Simon & Schuster, 1997). *The Case Against "Free Trade": GATT, NAFTA, and the Globalization of Corporate Power* (San Francisco: Earth Island Press, 1993) is a collection of essays by leading opponents of globalization, including Ralph Nader. Concise, readable challenges to globalization from an environmentalist perspective may be found in Mark Weisbrot, "Tricks of Free Trade," *Sierra* (vol. 86/5 [Sept./Oct. 2001]), 64–72; and Jerry Mander, "Economic Globalization and the Environment," *Tikkun* (vol. 16/5 [Sept./Oct. 2001]), 33–40. For a free-trader's criticism of trade agreements as inhibiting rather than promoting free trade, see Brink Lindsey, "Free Trade from the Bottom Up," *CATO Journal* (vol. 19/3 [Winter 2000]), 359–69.

Debating American Immigration, 1882–Present, (Lanham, MD: Rowman and Littlefield, 2002), by Roger Daniels and Otis L. Graham, offers contrasting views of the history of U.S immigration policy. George J. Borjas, *Friends or Strangers: The Impact of Immigrants on the U.S. Economy* (New York: Basic Books, 1990) provides a good introduction to the much-argued topic of whether, from an economic perspective, immigration is a positive or negative phenomenon. *Between Two Worlds: Mexican Immigrants in the United States* (Wilmington, DE: Scholarly Resources, 1996), edited by David Gutierrez, is a collection of scholarly articles on Mexican immigration; see also his earlier monograph, *Walls and Mirrors* (Berkeley: University of California Press, 1997). *Across the Pacific: Asian Americans and Globalization* (Philadelphia: Temple University Press, 1999), edited by Evelyn Hu-DeHart, samples recent work in Asian American studies.

Primary Sources

For a transcript of the NAFTA debate between Vice President Al Gore and Ross Perot in 1993, go to ggallarotti.wcb.wesleyan.edu/govt155/goreperot.htm. A controversial provision of NAFTA allows multinational corporations to seek compensation from countries they deem to have limited their potential profits. Although these cases are heard, in secret, by trade tribunals, the legal briefs, witness statements, and rulings in the case of *Metalclad v. Mexico* were obtained by the PBS show *Frontline* and are available at www2.gwu.edu/-nsarchiv/NSAEBB/NSAEBB65/. Go to depts.washington.edu/wtohist/testimonies.htm for the accounts of some of those involved in the WTO protests in Seattle. For documents produced by the protesters explaining their opposition to the WTO and their criticism of the actions of Seattle police, as well as documents from the WTO explaining the benefits of globalization go to depts.washington.edu/wtohist/topten.htm. Reports and addresses of the International Labor Organization's (ILO) World Commission on the Social Dimension of Globalization may be found at www.ilo.org/public/english/wcsdg/globali/documents.htm. Articles and reports produced by the World Council of Churches, which is critical of globalization, are available at www.wcc-coe.org/wcc/what/jpc/globalization.html#1. A sampling of the vast number of articles and op-ed pieces that have been written, for and against globalization, in the past decade may be found at www.mtholyoke.edu/acad/intrel/globaliz.htm, including writings by Thomas Friedman, Nicholas Kristof, Fareed Zakaria, Amartya Sen, Arundhati Roy, and Robert Samuelson, among many others. Additional articles on the subjects of multinational corporations, trade, and the global economy may be found at www.mtholyoke.edu/acad/intrel/mnc.htm, www.mtholyoke.edu/acad/intrel/trade.htm, and www.mtholyoke.edu/acad/intrel/globecon.htm.

CHAPTER 15

The 9/11 Attacks

INTRODUCTION

On the morning of September 11, 2001, two commercial airliners, each piloted by hijackers, crashed into the Twin Towers of New York City's World Trade Center. A third hijacked plane hit the Pentagon, situated in Virginia just outside the nation's capital; a fourth, perhaps headed for the White House, crashed in a field in Pennsylvania. A radical Islamic paramilitary organization called al Qaeda (Arabic for "the base") perpetrated the assaults, which quickly became known in the United States by the shorthand "9/11." Approximately three thousand people died in the attacks, six hundred more than were killed in the 1941 bombing of Pearl Harbor by Japan, the last time that the United States had come under direct attack by a foreign power or organization.

After 9/11, the United States, assisted by some allies, chief among them Great Britain, embarked on two major foreign wars, purportedly in retaliation. In 2001, the United States invaded Afghanistan and overthrew its ruling Taliban regime, a fundamentalist Muslim government that had harbored and cooperated with Osama bin Laden, the leader of al Qaeda. In 2003, the United States invaded Iraq and overthrew the government of Saddam Hussein, a dictator who had been a sworn enemy of America since 1991, when the United States, under the leadership of President George H. W. Bush, forcibly expelled Hussein's occupying army from Kuwait during the Gulf War. The government of President George W. Bush (the son of the first President Bush) justified the 2003 invasion by suggesting that Iraq had assisted al Qaeda and by arguing that Iraq might attack the United States with "weapons of mass destruction" (WMD) in the near future. In both Afghanistan and Iraq, the United States embarked on experiments in "nation building" after deposing the old regimes, a mission not undertaken on such a scale since the United States tried it in South Vietnam in the 1950s and 1960s.

A number of books have already been published about 9/11, including accounts from those inside the U.S. government. In July 2004, the government also made available to the public the report of the National Commission on Terrorist Attacks Upon the United States (commonly known as the "9/11 Commission"). The bipartisan Commission was created reluctantly by President George W. Bush in response to insistent pressure by some of the relatives of the victims of 9/11. They were concerned that all information about the attacks be made public and that there be a full airing of what warnings the government may have had of impending strikes and of how the government responded on 9/11 itself.

The 9/11 Commission, headed by Republican Thomas Kean, former governor of New Jersey, with Democrat Lee Hamilton, former U.S. congressman from Indiana, acting as vice-chair, began its work in 2003, the year the United States embarked on the war in Iraq. Although Bush's proposal to take the United States into war had received overwhelming endorsement from the U.S. Congress (just as had his proposed war against Afghanistan's Taliban government), the conflict with Iraq generated immediate public controversy, which grew during the course of the Commission's work. Early questions were raised about the reasons for the invasion of Iraq and doubts were expressed in many quarters about the claims that Hussein had supported al Qaeda. Additionally, many Americans, along with some members of the United Nations (UN) Security Council, doubted the assertions that Hussein had amassed WMD. They preferred that the UN weapons inspections be allowed to continue. Although the 9/11 Commission did not directly tackle the question of why the United States went to war in Iraq, it did investigate the Bush administration's assertion that Iraq had ties to al Qaeda and concluded that there is no evidence to support this contention. Although this information was widely publicized at the time it was announced by the Commission in the early fall of 2004, between one-fourth and one-half of Americans, according to various measures of public opinion, continue to believe that Hussein in some way participated in the attacks on 9/11.

The war in Iraq, which is still under way, remains controversial. There is little dispute, however, over the terrorist events of 9/11. Although the U.S. government did not recognize in advance that terrorists were plotting to attack on 9/11, the participants in the attacks had not gone unnoticed. After the assault, information from the various agencies and individuals with whom the terrorists had had contact, as well as cell phone and e-mail records, were brought together to form a basic picture of the events that led up to 9/11. There remains controversy, however, about the actions of the U.S. government both prior to 9/11—specifically, about whether the U.S. government could have prevented the attacks—and on the day of 9/11—specifically, about whether the U.S. government lacked decisive direction and the ability to respond quickly and in an organized fashion. Both issues are significant if one expects, as many do, that there will at some time be another attempted terrorist attack against the United States.

The latter issue was brought directly to the attention of the public through the documentary film *Fahrenheit 9/11,* which opened in theaters in May 2004. The film presented footage of President Bush continuing to read to school children in Florida after having been informed of the attacks on the World Trade Center. The documentary also revealed that, after the grounding of all airplanes, the U.S. government allowed planes to escort members of the Saudi royal family and Osama bin Laden's relatives out of the country. The implications of incompetence and of an unusual, if not improper, relationship between the Bush family and the Saudi government were ridiculed by supporters of Bush and also by most of the media. President Bush, initially reluctant to testify before the Commission as requested, finally complied on the conditions that his vice president, Dick Cheney, also be present and that no written record be made of his testimony. To the Commission, Bush reputedly reiterated statements made earlier by members of his administration that on 9/11 he sought to project a sense of calm by not reacting in front of children to the terrible news. He also presumably addressed assorted questions of government policy.

The other issue—whether the U.S. government had failed to act on intelligence information that warned of an imminent terrorist attack by al Qaeda—also gained media attention in early summer of 2004 when the Commission took public testimony from Richard Clarke, the former head of the Counterterrorism Security Group (CSG) under Presidents Bush and

Bill Clinton and a terrorism expert who had served continuously in the U.S. government since the Reagan administration. Since an earlier bombing of the World Trade Center in 1993, Clarke had been intently focused on al Qaeda and Osama bin Laden, convinced that they would attempt another attack on American soil. According to Clarke's testimony, his deep concerns about bin Laden's organization had been appreciated by the Clinton administration's National Security Advisor, Samuel Berger, who had given Clarke direct access to the president. According to Clarke, the Bush administration's National Security Advisor, Condoleezza Rice, had lacked this appreciation and had in effect demoted Clarke, who eventually resigned. A sensational document supporting Clarke's view that the Bush administration failed to recognize—and thus failed to attempt to thwart—the likelihood of an al Qaeda-sponsored attack on the United States was written by Clarke and reprinted in the Commission's *Report*. Entitled "Bin Laden Determined to Strike the U.S.," it was handed to Bush by Rice during the President's daily national security intelligence briefing on August 6, 2001. The lack of response to this document was explained by Rice in testimony to the 9/11 Commission as unexceptional, and she raised the issue, as had several others testifying before the Commission, of the distorting quality of hindsight. Only after an event has occurred could the clues pointing to its likelihood be properly understood, she suggested.

In addition to these issues, which focus on the U.S. role in preventing terrorist attacks, some attention has been paid to the question of what could possibly motivate an organization such as al Qaeda and a person such as bin Laden to engage in such horrific acts of violence against the United States, including those that require suicide for their realization. Although the scale of the 9/11 attacks was unprecedented, neither suicide bombings nor terrorist acts are new; Palestinian insurgents, for example, have relied on both for some time now in their war against Israel. However, the basis of the dispute between the Palestinians and Israel seems to most observers to be fairly clear. But to most Americans, who before 9/11 had not even heard of al Qaeda and may have had only had a dim awareness of the politics of the Middle East, the motivations behind the 9/11 attacks may be mysterious. Soon after the attacks, President Bush offered an explanation: the terrorists attacked America out of hatred for America's freedoms. Bush did not offer an explanation for this hatred other than to suggest, at different times, that the terrorists either misunderstand how great America is or that they are simply evil. In seeking more compelling explanations, some have pointed to conditions in the Middle East, particularly the lack of economic opportunities for those with education (a group overrepresented among al Qaeda leaders), and to the repressiveness and inequality in Middle Eastern countries. Others have sought to understand the religious views of fundamentalist Muslims, and distinguish them from the views of other Muslims. Some commentators on the left have sought to explain al Qaeda's actions, at least in part, as a response to specific acts committed by the United States, such as the U.S. stationing of armed forces in Saudi Arabia and other countries in the Middle East, which some citizens of these countries view as imperialistic acts that imperil the integrity of their homelands. These explanations are not mutually exclusive.

The readings reprinted in this chapter address both the issues of the U.S. efforts to prevent and respond to terrorist attacks and the motives of the terrorists in attacking the United States. The first excerpt is from *The 9/11 Report*. Authored by the staff of the 9/11 Commission, the *Report* seeks to present a strongly factual, nonpartisan account and analysis of 9/11. Yet, despite the stance of objectivity, the Commission staff clearly made choices (as do all historians) concerning which individuals, what context, and which interpretations to emphasize in telling the history of 9/11. (Philip Zelikow, a professional historian with conservative leanings—he previously co-authored a scholarly book with Condoleezza Rice—headed the Commission's staff. He has not claimed credit for writing the *Report,* suggesting that it was a collective effort.)

In addressing what may have motivated the 9/11 attacks, the *Report* presents the generally understood facts regarding the religious and political beliefs of bin Laden and his associates. The *Report's* conclusion that the economies of many Muslim countries are stagnant and that the resulting frustration of those unable to find satisfactory employment plays a role in terrorist recruitment is not controversial. It ventures into uncertain territory, however, in its suggestion that an attitude of "entitlement" underlies this apparent frustration. Similarly, the broad assertion that the forces of "modernization" have disoriented many in the Middle East, and that these bewildered people provide bin Laden and other jihadists with a ready flock of followers, lacks substantiation. It is also doubtful whether such a vague concept as modernization, and the assertion of its purported psychological effects, offers the explanatory power assumed in the *Report.* The *Report* implicitly rejects the view of a number of critics of the government that al Qaeda was in fact an inadvertent creation of the U.S. government, which had generously funded extremist Islamic groups in the late 1970s and early 1980s, including bin Laden and his associates, to aid them in their war against the Soviet Union in Afghanistan.

In addressing the issue of whether the U.S. government might have acted to prevent the 9/11 attacks, the *Report* focuses on the administrations of President George W. Bush and of his predecessor, Bill Clinton, who was president when al Qaeda first attacked the World Trade Center in 1993 and in December 1999 when the federal government thwarted the so-called "Millenium Plot," al Qaeda's plan to attack West Coast targets. The *Report* concludes that both of these leaders were seriously concerned about al Qaeda and the threat of an attack on the United States, but that neither fully appreciated the scale of devastation that al Qaeda had in mind and thus failed to create a coordinated and successful counterterrorism effort. However, this conclusion (found at the end of the excerpt presented here), which seeks to distribute blame evenly, is not entirely supported by the details in the *Report's* presentation of the counterterrorism efforts of the Clinton and Bush administrations. As mentioned earlier, the Clinton administration, and particularly National Security Council (NSC) chair Berger, are shown to have assigned high priority to al Qaeda and to have helped prevent the Millennium attacks. Additionally, Berger worked closely with other officials such as CIA head George Tenet and Generals Hugh Shelton and Anthony Zinni to develop plans to kill bin Laden and destroy al Qaeda facilities. In contrast Rice, Bush's NSC chair, is shown to have taken little action in response to the cascade of intelligence warning of an imminent al Qaeda attack on the United States.

This excerpt also presents the Commission's understanding of the days immediately following 9/11, during which the Bush administration decided to go to war in Afghanistan. The *Report* sees this war as a direct response to the events of 9/11. Although it makes clear that the possibility of going to war with Iraq to topple Saddam Hussein was also discussed by Bush and other high-level administration officials at this time, the *Report* notes that the administration lacked any evidence of Hussein's involvement with bin Laden and al Qaeda, and thus that President Bush rejected the idea of attacking Iraq. What is left unexplained is why Bush, as the *Report* states, initially assumed, and sought evidence of, Iraq's involvement, and why, if no evidence of this involvement could be found shortly after 9/11, he led the United States into a war against Iraq a year later.

The second reading in this chapter is from the introduction to the 2004 edition of *Blowback: The Costs and Consequences of American Empire,* by Chalmers Johnson, a longtime authority on East Asian political and economic development. In recent years, Johnson has become alienated from what he believes to be a destructive and badly intentioned U.S. foreign policy. The book from which this excerpt is drawn was originally published in 2000 and helped to popularize the expression "blowback," a CIA term for the unintended consequences of a covert action. Johnson uses the term to mean the unforeseen and dangerous long-term repercussions that a great power like the United States may suffer as a result of its own arrogant intrusions into foreign lands. In his view, a classic example of blowback was the 1979 Iranian revolution, which was fueled by anger at the U.S. role in installing and propping up the hated Shah and which brought to power an anti-American, fundamentalist Muslim government in a country rich in oil and strategically important to the United States.

Provocatively, Johnson sees the 9/11 attacks as blowback. In contrast to *The 9/11 Report,* Johnson believes that the United States provided substantial aid to Osama bin Laden and associated extremist Islamist groups in the late 1970s and 1980s, encouraging them to resist the Soviet Union and their allies in Afghanistan. This U.S. assistance fueled the rise of both al Qaeda and the Taliban, he argues, and as with so many other activities it has initiated around the world, the U.S. government failed to foresee the consequences for America. In this case, once the radical Islamist forces had vanquished the Communists, they turned against what they perceived to be the other infidel power in their midst—the United States. Neither *Blowback* nor *The 9/11 Report,* which are in disagreement over the extent of U.S. involvement in supporting bin Laden and those who later formed al Qaeda, offers substantial evidence in support of its argument on this point. Both agree, however, with the broader point that the jihad in Afghanistan was the crucible in which the forces that later perpetrated the 9/11 attacks were formed.

On the subject of the U.S. response to the 9/11 attacks, Johnson believes that the wars in Afghanistan and Iraq, which have led to severe social and economic dislocation, as well as to the injury and death of thousands of civilians, have spawned further distrust and even hatred of U.S. power. In this regard, Johnson contends that U.S. leaders have given bin Laden exactly what he wanted and have exacerbated rather than lessened the terrorist threat. But Johnson also challenges the notion that these wars, particularly the conflict in Iraq, were waged in retaliation for 9/11. Instead, he suggests that 9/11 merely provided the excuse to launch a war that had long been sought by certain special interest groups to which President Bush is especially attentive. In another work—*The Sorrows of Empire* (2003)—Johnson has argued that the United States, since the end of the cold war, has embarked on a new kind of imperialism, characterized by heavy-handed interventions in foreign lands and the establishment of military bases for the sake of particular U.S. military and economic interests. The wars in Afghanistan and Iraq are but a part of this larger imperial enterprise. In his view, America's imperial goals were present during the cold war as well, but U.S. actions were constrained by concerns over the reaction of the USSR. In the "new world order" since the fall of communism, the United States as the sole superpower may act, and has acted, unilaterally.

Hard-liners within the Bush administration would agree with part of this analysis, believing that the United States may and should act unilaterally, exercising its power when and as it sees fit. Some who are close to the administration have even used the term "American empire" approvingly. But they have insisted that the post-cold-war role of the United States is shaped by the "war on terror," and have denied that special interests have advocated, and are benefiting from, the war in Iraq and other projections of power abroad. They have, however, championed the idea of "preventive war," meaning that the United States is justified in attacking a country that has not wronged the United States and poses no imminent threat, if U.S. leaders deem that country to be a potential future threat to American security or power.

THE NATIONAL COMMISSION ON TERRORIST ATTACKS UPON THE UNITED STATES

The 9/11 Report

The 9/11 attacks were a shock, but they should not have come as a surprise. Islamist extremists had given plenty of warning that they meant to kill Americans indiscriminately and in large numbers. Although Usama Bin Ladin himself would not emerge as a signal threat until the late 1990s, the threat of Islamist terrorism grew over the decade.

In February 1993, a group led by Ramzi Yousef tried to bring down the World Trade Center with a truck bomb. They killed six and wounded a thousand. Plans by Omar Abdel Rahman and others to blow up the Holland and Lincoln tunnels and other New York City landmarks were frustrated when the plotters were arrested. In October 1993, Somali tribesmen shot down U.S. helicopters, killing 18 and wounding 73 in an incident that came to be known as "Black Hawk down." Years later it would be learned that those Somali tribesmen had received help from al Qaeda.

In early 1995, police in Manila uncovered a plot by Ramzi Yousef to blow up a dozen U.S. airliners while they were flying over the Pacific. In November 1995, a car bomb exploded outside the office of the U.S. program manager for the Saudi National Guard in Riyadh, killing five Americans and two others. In June 1996, a truck bomb demolished the Khobar Towers apartment complex in Dhahran, Saudi Arabia, killing 19 U.S. servicemen and wounding hundreds. The attack was carried out primarily by Saudi Hezbollah, an organization that had received help from the government of Iran.

Until 1997, the U.S. intelligence community viewed Bin Ladin as a financier of terrorism, not as a terrorist leader. In February 1998, Usama Bin Ladin and four others issued a self-styled fatwa, publicly declaring that it was God's decree that every Muslim should try his utmost to kill any American, military or civilian, anywhere in the world, because of American "occupation" of Islam's holy places and aggression against Muslims.

In August 1998, Bin Ladin's group, al Qaeda, carried out near-simultaneous truck bomb attacks on the U.S. embassies in Nairobi, Kenya, and Dar es Salaam, Tanzania. The attacks killed 224 people, including 12 Americans, and wounded thousands more.

From *The Report of The National Commission on Terrorist Attacks Upon the United States.* Originally published 2004 by the United States Government Printing Office. In the public domain.

In December 1999, Jordanian police foiled a plot to bomb hotels and other sites frequented by American tourists, and a U.S. Customs agent arrested Ahmed Ressam at the U.S. Canadian border as he was smuggling in explosives intended for an attack on Los Angeles International Airport.

In October 2000, an al Qaeda team in Aden, Yemen, used a motorboat filled with explosives to blow a hole in the side of a destroyer, the USS *Cole,* almost sinking the vessel and killing 17 American sailors.

The 9/11 attacks on the World Trade Center and the Pentagon were far more elaborate, precise, and destructive than any of these earlier assaults. But by September 2001, the executive branch of the U.S. government, the Congress, the news media, and the American public had received clear warning that Islamist terrorists meant to kill Americans in high numbers.

Who is this enemy that created an organization capable of inflicting such horrific damage on the United States? We now know that these attacks were carried out by various groups of Islamist extremists. The 9/11 attack was driven by Usama Bin Ladin.

In the 1980s, young Muslims from around the world went to Afghanistan to join as volunteers in a jihad (or holy struggle) against the Soviet Union. A wealthy Saudi, Usama Bin Ladin, was one of them. Following the defeat of the Soviets in the late 1980s, Bin Ladin and others formed al Qaeda to mobilize jihads elsewhere.

…How did Bin Ladin—with his call for the indiscriminate killing of Americans—win thousands of followers and some degree of approval from millions more?

The history, culture, and body of beliefs from which Bin Ladin has shaped and spread his message are largely unknown to many Americans. Seizing on symbols of Islam's past greatness, he promises to restore pride to people who consider themselves the victims of successive foreign masters. He uses cultural and religious allusions to the holy Qur'an and some of its interpreters. He appeals to people disoriented by cyclonic change as they confront modernity and globalization. His rhetoric selectively draws from multiple sources—Islam, history, and the region's political and economic malaise. He also stresses grievances against the United States widely shared in the Muslim world. He inveighed against the presence of U.S. troops in Saudi Arabia, the home of Islam's holiest sites. He spoke of the suffering of the Iraqi people as a result of sanctions imposed after the Gulf War, and he protested U.S. support of Israel.

Islam (a word that literally means "surrender to the will of God") arose in Arabia with what Muslims believe are a series of revelations to the Prophet Mohammed from the one and only God, the God of Abraham and of Jesus. These revelations, conveyed by the angel Gabriel, are recorded in the Qur'an. Muslims believe that these revelations, given to the greatest and last of a chain of prophets stretching from Abraham through Jesus, complete God's message to humanity. . . .

Many Muslims look back at the century after the revelations to the Prophet Mohammed as a golden age. Its memory is strongest among the Arabs. What happened then—the spread of Islam from the Arabian Peninsula throughout the Middle East, North Africa, and even into Europe within less than a century—seemed, and seems, miraculous. Nostalgia for Islam's past glory remains a powerful force. . . .

The extreme Islamist version of history blames the decline from Islam's golden age on the rulers and people who turned away from the true path of their religion, thereby leaving Islam vulnerable to encroaching foreign powers eager to steal their land, wealth, and even their souls.

… Many Americans have wondered, "Why do 'they' hate us?" Some also ask, "What can we do to stop these attacks?"

Bin Ladin and al Qaeda have given answers to both these questions. To the first, they say that America had attacked Islam; America is responsible for all conflicts involving Muslims. Thus Americans are blamed when Israelis fight with Palestinians, when Russians fight with Chechens, when Indians fight with Kashmiri Muslims, and when the Philippine government fights ethnic Muslims in its southern islands. America is also held responsible for the governments of Muslim countries, derided by al Qaeda as "your agents." Bin Ladin has stated flatly, "Our fight against these governments is not separate from our fight against you." These charges found a ready audience among millions of Arabs and Muslims angry at the United States because of issues ranging from Iraq to Palestine to America's support for their countries' repressive rulers.

Bin Ladin's grievance with the United States may have started in reaction to specific U.S. policies but it quickly became far deeper. To the second question, what America could do, al Qaeda's answer was that America should abandon the Middle East, convert to Islam, and end the immorality and godlessness of its society and culture: "It is saddening to tell you that you are the worst civilization witnessed by the history of mankind." If the United States did not comply, it would be at war with the Islamic nation, a nation that al Qaeda's leaders said "desires death more than you desire life."...

In the 1970s and early 1980s, an unprecedented flood of wealth led the then largely unmodernized oil states to attempt to shortcut decades of development. They funded huge infrastructure projects, vastly expanded education, and created subsidized social welfare programs. These programs established a widespread feeling of entitlement without a corresponding sense of social obligations. By the late 1980s, diminishing oil revenues, the economic drain from many unprofitable development projects, and population growth made these entitlement programs unsustainable. The resulting cutbacks created enormous resentment among recipients who had come to see government largesse as their right. This resentment was further stoked by public understanding of how much oil income had gone straight into the pockets of the rulers, their friends, and their helpers.

Unlike the oil states (or Afghanistan, where real economic development has barely begun), the other Arab nations and Pakistan once had seemed headed toward balanced modernization. The established commercial, financial, and industrial sectors in these states, supported by an entrepreneurial spirit and widespread understanding of free enterprise, augured well. But unprofitable heavy industry, state monopolies, and opaque bureaucracies slowly stifled growth. More importantly, these state-centered regimes placed their highest priority on preserving the elite's grip on national wealth. Unwilling to foster dynamic economies that could create jobs attractive to educated young men, the countries became economically stagnant and reliant on the safety valve of worker emigration either to the Arab oil states or to the West. Furthermore, the repression and isolation of women in many Muslim countries have not only seriously limited individual opportunity but also crippled overall economic productivity.

By the 1990s, high birthrates and declining rates of infant mortality had produced a common problem throughout the Muslim world: a large, steadily increasing population of young men without any reasonable expectation of suitable or steady employment—a sure prescription for social turbulence. Many of these young men, such as the enormous number trained only in religious schools, lacked the skills needed by their societies. Far more acquired valuable skills but lived in stagnant economies that could not generate satisfying jobs.

Millions, pursuing secular as well as religious studies, were products of educational systems that generally devoted little if any attention to the rest of the world's thought, history, and culture. The secular education reflected a strong cultural preference for technical fields over the humanities and social sciences. Many of these young men, even if able to study abroad, lacked the perspective and skills needed to understand a different culture.

Frustrated in their search for a decent living, unable to benefit from an education often obtained at the cost of great family sacrifice, and blocked from starting families of their own, some of these young men were easy targets for radicalization. . . .

A decade of conflict in Afghanistan, from 1979 to 1989, gave Islamist extremists a rallying point and training field. A Communist government in Afghanistan gained power in 1978 but was unable to establish enduring control. At the end of 1979, the Soviet government sent in military units to ensure that the country would remain securely under Moscow's influence. The response was an Afghan national resistance movement that defeated Soviet forces.

Young Muslims from around the world flocked to Afghanistan to join as volunteers in what was seen as a "holy war"—*jihad*—against an invader. The largest numbers came from the Middle East. Some were Saudis, and among them was Usama Bin Ladin.

Twenty-three when he arrived in Afghanistan in 1980, Bin Ladin was the seventeenth of 57 children of a Saudi construction magnate. Six feet five and thin, Bin Ladin appeared to be ungainly but was in fact quite athletic, skilled as a horseman, runner, climber, and soccer player. He had attended Abdul Aziz University in Saudi Arabia. By some accounts, he had been interested there in religious studies, inspired by tape recordings of fiery sermons by Abdullah Azzam, a Palestinian and a disciple of Qutb. Bin Ladin was conspicuous among the volunteers not because he showed evidence of religious learning but because he had access to some of his family's huge fortune. Though he took part in at least one actual battle, he became known chiefly as a person who generously helped fund the anti-Soviet jihad.

Bin Ladin understood better than most of the volunteers the extent to which the continuation and eventual success of the jihad in Afghanistan depended on an increasingly complex, almost worldwide organization. This organization included a financial support network that came to be known as the "Golden Chain," put together mainly by financiers in Saudi Arabia and the Persian Gulf states. Donations flowed through charities or other nongovernmental organizations (NGOs). Bin Ladin and the "Afghan Arabs" drew largely on funds raised by this network, whose agents roamed world markets to buy arms and supplies for the mujahideen, or "holy warriors."

Mosques, schools, and boardinghouses served as recruiting stations in many parts of the world, including the United States. Some were set up by Islamic extremists or their financial backers. Bin Ladin had an important part in this activity. . . .

The international environment for Bin Ladin's efforts was ideal. Saudi Arabia and the United States supplied billions of dollars worth of secret assistance to rebel groups in Afghanistan fighting the Soviet occupation. This assistance was funneled through Pakistan: the Pakistani military intelligence service (Inter-Services Intelligence Directorate, or ISID), helped train the rebels and distribute the arms. But Bin Ladin and his comrades had their own sources of support and training, and they received little or no assistance from the United States.

April 1988 brought victory for the Afghan jihad. Moscow declared it would pull its military forces out of Afghanistan within the next nine months. As the Soviets began their withdrawal, the jihad's leaders debated what to do next. . . .

On August 7, 1998, National Security Advisor Berger woke President Clinton with a phone call at 5:35 A.M. to tell him of the almost simultaneous bombings of the U.S. embassies in Nairobi, Kenya, and Dar es Salaam, Tanzania. Suspicion quickly focused on Bin Ladin.

Unusually good intelligence, chiefly from the yearlong monitoring of al Qaeda's cell in Nairobi, soon firmly fixed responsibility on him and his associates.

Debate about what to do settled very soon on one option: Tomahawk cruise missiles. Months earlier, … Clarke had prodded the Pentagon to explore possibilities for military action. On June 2, General Hugh Shelton, the chairman of the Joint Chiefs of Staff, had directed General Zinni at Central Command to develop a plan, which he had submitted during the first week of July. Zinni's planners surely considered the two previous times the United States had used force to respond to terrorism, the 1986 strike on Libya and the 1993 strike against Iraq. They proposed firing Tomahawks against eight terrorist camps in Afghanistan, including Bin Ladin's compound at Tarnak Farms. After the embassy attacks, the Pentagon offered this plan to the White House.

The day after the embassy bombings, Tenet brought to a principals meeting intelligence that terrorist leaders were expected to gather at a camp near Khowst, Afghanistan, to plan future attacks. According to Berger, Tenet said that several hundred would attend, including Bin Ladin. The CIA described the area as effectively a military cantonment, away from civilian population centers and overwhelmingly populated by jihadists. Clarke remembered sitting next to Tenet in a White House meeting, asking Tenet "You thinking what I'm thinking?" and his nodding "yes." The principals quickly reached a consensus on attacking the gathering. The strike's purpose was to kill Bin Ladin and his chief lieutenants.

Berger put in place a tightly compartmented process designed to keep all planning secret. On August 11, General Zinni received orders to prepare detailed plans for strikes against the sites in Afghanistan. The Pentagon briefed President Clinton about these plans on August 12 and 14. Though the principals hoped that the missiles would hit Bin Ladin, NSC staff recommended the strike whether or not there was firm evidence that the commanders were at the facilities.

Considerable debate went to the question of whether to strike targets outside of Afghanistan, including two facilities in Sudan. One was a tannery believed to belong to Bin Ladin. The other was al Shifa, a Khartoum pharmaceutical plant, which intelligence reports said was manufacturing a precursor ingredient for nerve gas with Bin Ladin's financial support. The argument for hitting the tannery was that it could hurt Bin Ladin financially. The argument for hitting al Shifa was that it would lessen the chance of Bin Ladin's having nerve gas for a later attack.

Ever since March 1995, American officials had had in the backs of their minds Aum Shinrikyo's release of sarin nerve gas in the Tokyo subway. President Clinton himself had expressed great concern about chemical and biological terrorism in the United States. Bin Ladin had reportedly been heard to speak of wanting a "Hiroshima" and at least 10,000 casualties. The CIA reported that a soil sample from the vicinity of the al Shifa plant had tested positive for EMPTA, a precursor chemical for VX, a nerve gas whose lone use was for mass killing. Two days before the embassy bombings, Clarke's staff wrote that Bin Ladin "has invested in and almost certainly has access to VX produced at a plant in Sudan." Senior State Department officials believed that they had received a similar verdict independently, though they and Clarke's staff were probably relying on the same report. Mary McCarthy, the NSC senior director responsible for intelligence programs, initially cautioned Berger that the "bottom line" was that "we will need much better intelligence on this facility before we seriously consider any options." She added that the link between Bin Ladin and al Shifa was "rather uncertain at this point." Berger has told us that he thought about what might happen if the decision went against hitting al Shifa, and nerve gas was used in a New York subway two weeks later.

By the early hours of the morning of August 20, President Clinton and all his principal advisers had agreed to strike Bin Ladin camps in Afghanistan near Khowst, as well as hitting al Shifa. The President took the Sudanese tannery off the target list because he saw little point in killing uninvolved people without doing significant harm to Bin Ladin. The principal with the most qualms regarding al Shifa was Attorney General Reno. She expressed concern about attacking two Muslim countries at the same time. Looking back, she said that she felt the "premise kept shifting."

Later on August 20, Navy vessels in the Arabian Sea fired their cruise missiles. Though most of them hit their intended targets, neither Bin Ladin nor any other terrorist leader was killed. Berger told us that an after-action review by Director Tenet concluded that the strikes had killed 20–30 people in the camps but probably missed Bin Ladin by a few hours. Since the missiles headed for Afghanistan had had to cross Pakistan, the Vice Chairman of the Joint Chiefs was sent to meet with Pakistan's army chief of staff to assure him the missiles were not coming from India. Officials in Washington speculated that one or another Pakistani official might have sent a warning to the Taliban or Bin Ladin.

The air strikes marked the climax of an intense 48-hour period in which Berger notified congressional leaders, the principals called their foreign counterparts, and President Clinton flew back from his vacation on Martha's Vineyard to address the nation from the Oval Office. The President spoke to the congressional leadership from Air Force One, and he called British Prime Minister Tony Blair, Pakistani Prime Minister Nawaz Sharif, and Egyptian President Hosni Mubarak from the White House. House Speaker Newt Gingrich and Senate Majority Leader Trent Lott initially supported the President. The next month, Gingrich's office dismissed the cruise missile attacks as "pinpricks."

At the time, President Clinton was embroiled in the Lewinsky scandal, which continued to consume public attention for the rest of that year and the first months of 1999. As it happened, a popular 1997 movie, *Wag the Dog,* features a president who fakes a war to distract public attention from a domestic scandal. Some Republicans in Congress raised questions about the timing of the strikes. Berger was particularly rankled by an editorial in the *Economist* that said that only the future would tell whether the U.S. missile strikes had "created 10,000 new fanatics where there would have been none."

Much public commentary turned immediately to scalding criticism that the action was too aggressive. The Sudanese denied that al Shifa produced nerve gas, and they allowed journalists to visit what was left of a seemingly harmless facility. President Clinton, Vice President Gore, Berger, Tenet, and Clarke insisted to us that their judgment was right, pointing to the soil sample evidence. No independent evidence has emerged to corroborate the CIA's assessment.

Everyone involved in the decision had, of course, been aware of President Clinton's problems. He told them to ignore them. Berger recalled the President saying to him "that they were going to get crap either way, so they should do the right thing." All his aides testified to us that they based their advice solely on national security considerations. We have found no reason to question their statements.

The failure of the strikes, the "wag the dog" slur, the intense partisanship of the period, and the nature of the al Shifa evidence likely had a cumulative effect on future decisions about the use of force against Bin Ladin. Berger told us that he did not feel any sense of constraint. . . .

In the critical days and weeks after the August 1998 attacks, senior policymakers in the Clinton administration had to reevaluate the threat posed by Bin Ladin. Was this just a new and especially venomous version of the ordinary terrorist threat America had lived with for decades, or was it radically new, posing a danger beyond any yet experienced?

Even after the embassy attacks, Bin Ladin had been responsible for the deaths of fewer than 50 Americans, most of them overseas. An NSC staffer working for Richard Clarke told us the threat was seen as one that could cause hundreds of casualties, not thousands. Even officials who acknowledge a vital threat intellectually may not be ready to act on such beliefs at great cost or at high risk. . . .

Clarke hoped the August 1998 missile strikes would mark the beginning of a sustained campaign against Bin Ladin. Clarke was, as he later admitted, "obsessed" with Bin Ladin, and the embassy bombings gave him new scope for pursuing his obsession. Terrorism had moved high up among the President's concerns, and Clarke's position had elevated accordingly. . . . In practice, the CSG often reported not even to the full Principals Committee but instead to the so-called Small Group formed by Berger, consisting only of those principals cleared to know about the most sensitive issues connected with counterterrorism activities concerning Bin Ladin or the Khobar Towers investigation.

For this inner cabinet, Clarke drew up what he called "Political-Military Plan Delenda." The Latin *delenda*, meaning that something "must be destroyed," evoked the famous Roman vow to destroy its rival, Carthage. The overall goal of Clarke's paper was to "immediately eliminate any significant threat to Americans" from the "Bin Ladin network." The paper called for diplomacy to deny Bin Ladin sanctuary; covert action to disrupt terrorist activities, but above all to capture Bin Ladin and his deputies and bring them to trial; efforts to dry up Bin Ladin's money supply; and preparation for follow-on military action. The status of the document was and remained uncertain. It was never formally adopted by the principals. . . .

In the spring of 2001, the level of reporting on terrorist threats and planned attacks increased dramatically to its highest level since the millennium alert. At the end of March, the intelligence community disseminated a terrorist threat advisory, indicating a heightened threat of Sunni extremist terrorist attacks against U.S. facilities, personnel, and other interests. . . .

In May 2001, the drumbeat of reporting grew louder with reports to top officials that "Bin Ladin public profile may presage attack" and "Bin Ladin network's plans advancing." In early May, a walk-in to the FBI claimed there was a plan to launch attacks on London, Boston, and New York. Attorney General John Ashcroft was briefed by the CIA on May 15 regarding al Qaeda generally and the current threat reporting specifically. The next day brought a report that a phone call to a U.S. embassy had warned that Bin Ladin supporters were planning an attack in the United States using "high explosives." On May 17, based on the previous day's report, the first item on the CSG's agenda was "UBL: Operation Planned in U.S." The anonymous caller's tip could not be corroborated. . . .

Reports similar to many of these were made available to President Bush in morning intelligence briefings with DCI Tenet, usually attended by Vice President Dick Cheney and National Security Advisor Rice. While these briefings discussed general threats to attack America and American interests, the specific threats mentioned in these briefings were all overseas. . . .

A terrorist threat advisory distributed in late June indicated a high probability of near-term "spectacular" terrorist attacks resulting in numerous casualties. Other reports' titles warned, "Bin Ladin Attacks May be Imminent" and "Bin Ladin and Associates Making Near-Term Threats." The latter reported multiple attacks planned over the coming days, including a "severe blow" against U.S. and Israeli "interests" during the next two weeks.

On June 21, near the height of the threat reporting, U.S. Central Command raised the force protection condition level for U.S. troops in six countries to the highest possible level, Delta. The U.S. Fifth Fleet moved out of its port in Bahrain, and a U.S. Marine Corps exercise in Jordan was halted. U.S. embassies in the Persian Gulf conducted an emergency security review, and the embassy in Yemen was closed. The CSG had foreign emergency response teams, known as FESTs, ready to move on four hours' notice and kept up the terrorism alert posture on a "rolling 24 hour basis."

On June 25, Clarke warned Rice . . . that six separate intelligence reports showed al Qaeda personnel warning of a pending attack. An Arabic television station reported Bin Ladin's pleasure with al Qaeda leaders who were saying that the next weeks "will witness important surprises" and that U.S. and Israeli interests will be targeted. Al Qaeda also released a new recruitment and fund-raising tape. Clarke wrote that this was all too sophisticated to be merely a psychological operation to keep the United States on edge, and the CIA agreed. The intelligence reporting consistently described the upcoming attacks as occurring on a calamitous level, indicating that they would cause the world to be in turmoil and that they would consist of possible multiple—but not necessarily simultaneous—attacks.

On June 28, Clarke wrote Rice that the pattern of al Qaeda activity indicating attack planning over the past six weeks "had reached a crescendo." "A series of new reports continue to convince me and analysts at State, CIA, DIA [Defense Intelligence Agency], and NSA that a major terrorist attack or series of attacks is likely in July," he noted. One al Qaeda intelligence report warned that something "very, very, very, very" big was about to happen, and most of Bin Ladin's network was reportedly anticipating the attack. In late June, the CIA ordered all its station chiefs to share information on al Qaeda with their host governments and to push for immediate disruptions of cells.

The headline of a June 30 briefing to top officials was stark: "Bin Ladin Planning High-Profile Attacks." The report stated that Bin Ladin operatives expected near-term attacks to have dramatic consequences of catastrophic proportions. That same day, Saudi Arabia declared its highest level of terror alert. Despite evidence of delays possibly caused by heightened U.S. security, the planning for attacks was continuing. . . .

Tenet told us that in his world "the system was blinking red." By late July, Tenet said, it could not "get any worse." Not everyone was convinced. Some asked whether all these threats might just be deception. . . . Deputy Secretary of Defense Paul Wolfowitz questioned the reporting. Perhaps Bin Ladin was trying to study U.S. reactions. Tenet replied that he had already addressed the Defense Department's questions on this point; the reporting was convincing. To give a sense of his anxiety at the time, one senior official in the Counterterrorist Center told us that he and a colleague were considering resigning in order to go public with their concerns. . . .

On August 3, the intelligence community issued an advisory concluding that the threat of impending al Qaeda attacks would likely continue indefinitely. Citing threats in the Arabian Peninsula, Jordan, Israel, and Europe, the advisory suggested that al Qaeda was lying in wait and searching for gaps in security before moving forward with the planned attacks.

During the spring and summer of 2001, President Bush had on several occasions asked his briefers whether any of the threats pointed to the United States. Reflecting on these questions, the CIA decided to write a briefing article summarizing its understanding of this danger. Two CIA analysts involved in preparing this briefing article believed it represented an opportunity to communicate their view that the threat of a Bin Ladin attack in the United States remained both current and serious. The result was an article in the August 6 Presidential Daily Brief titled "Bin Ladin Determined to Strike in US." It was the 36th PDB item briefed so far that year that related to Bin Ladin or al Qaeda, and the first devoted to the possibility of an attack in the United States.

The President told us the August 6 report was historical in nature. President Bush said the article told him that al Qaeda was dangerous, which he said he had known since he had become President. The President said Bin Ladin had long been talking about his desire to attack America. He recalled some operational data on the FBI, and remembered thinking it was heartening that 70 investigations were under way. As best he could recollect, Rice had mentioned that the Yemenis' surveillance of a federal building in New York had been looked into in May and June, but there was no actionable intelligence.

He did not recall discussing the August 6 report with the Attorney General or whether Rice had done so. He said that if his advisers had told him there was a cell in the United States, they would have moved to take care of it. That never happened. . . .

We have found no indication of any further discussion before September 11 among the President and his top advisers of the possibility of a threat of an al Qaeda attack in the United States. DCI Tenet visited President Bush in Crawford, Texas, on August 17 and participated in PDB briefings of the President between August 31 (after the President had returned to Washington) and September 10. But Tenet does not recall any discussions with the President of the domestic threat during this period.

Most of the intelligence community recognized in the summer of 2001 that the number and severity of threat reports were unprecedented. Many officials told us that they knew something terrible was planned, and they were desperate to stop it. Despite their large number, the threats received contained few specifics regarding time, place, method, or target. Most suggested that attacks were planned against targets overseas; others indicated threats against unspecified "U.S. interests." We cannot say for certain whether these reports, as dramatic as they were, related to the 9/11 attacks. . . .

President Bush had wondered immediately after the attack whether Saddam Hussein's regime might have had a hand in it. Iraq had been an enemy of the United States for 11 years, and was the only place in the world where the United States was engaged in ongoing combat operations. . . .

Clarke has written that on the evening of September 12, President Bush told him and some of his staff to explore possible Iraqi links to 9/11. "See if Saddam did this," Clarke recalls the President telling them. "See if he's linked in any way." While he believed the details of Clarke's account to be incorrect, President Bush acknowledged that he might well have spoken to Clarke at some point, asking him about Iraq.

Responding to a presidential tasking, Clarke's office sent a memo to Rice on September 18, titled "Survey of Intelligence Information on Any Iraq Involvement in the September 11 Attacks." Rice's chief staffer on Afghanistan, Zalmay Khalilzad, concurred in its conclusion that only some anecdotal evidence linked Iraq to al Qaeda. The memo found no "compelling case" that Iraq had either planned or perpetrated the attacks. . . . Arguing that the case for links between Iraq and al Qaeda was weak, the memo pointed out that Bin Ladin resented the secularism of Saddam Hussein's regime. Finally, the memo said, there was no confirmed reporting on Saddam cooperating with Bin Ladin on unconventional weapons.

On the afternoon of 9/11, according to contemporaneous notes, Secretary Rumsfeld instructed General Myers to obtain quickly as much information as possible. The notes indicate that he also told Myers that he was not simply interested in striking empty training sites. He thought the U.S. response should consider a wide range of options and possibilities. The secretary said his instinct was to hit Saddam Hussein at the same time—not only Bin Ladin. Secretary Rumsfeld later explained that at the time, he had been considering either one of them, or perhaps someone else, as the responsible party.

According to Rice, the issue of what, if anything, to do about Iraq was really engaged at Camp David. Briefing papers on Iraq, along with many others, were in briefing materials for the participants. Rice told us the administration was concerned that Iraq would take advantage of the 9/11 attacks. She recalled that in the first Camp David session chaired by the President, Rumsfeld asked what the administration should do about Iraq. Deputy Secretary Wolfowitz made the case for striking Iraq during "this round" of the war on terrorism.

A Defense Department paper for the Camp David briefing book on the strategic concept for the war on terrorism specified three priority targets for initial action: al Qaeda, the Taliban, and Iraq. It argued that of the three, al Qaeda and Iraq posed a strategic threat to the United States. Iraq's long-standing involvement in terrorism was cited, along with its interest in weapons of mass destruction.

Secretary Powell recalled that Wolfowitz—not Rumsfeld—argued that Iraq was ultimately the source of the terrorist problem and should therefore be attacked. Powell said that Wolfowitz was not able to justify his belief that Iraq was behind 9/11. "Paul was always of the view that Iraq was a problem that had to be dealt with," Powell told us. "And he saw this as one way of using this event as a way to deal with the Iraq problem." Powell said that President Bush did not give Wolfowitz's argument "much weight." Though continuing to worry about Iraq in the following week, Powell said, President Bush saw Afghanistan as the priority.

President Bush told Bob Woodward that the decision not to invade Iraq was made at the morning session on September 15. Iraq was not even on the table during the September 15 afternoon session, which dealt solely with Afghanistan. Rice said that when President Bush called her on Sunday, September 16, he said the focus would be on Afghanistan, although he still wanted plans for Iraq should the country take some action or the administration eventually determine that it had been involved in the 9/11 attacks.

At the September 17 NSC meeting, there was some further discussion of "phase two" of the war on terrorism. President Bush ordered the Defense Department to be ready to deal with Iraq if Baghdad acted against U.S. interests, with plans to include possibly occupying Iraqi oil fields.

Within the Pentagon, Deputy Secretary Wolfowitz continued to press the case for dealing with Iraq. Writing to Rumsfeld on September 17 in a memo headlined "Preventing More Events," he argued that if there was even a 10 percent chance that Saddam Hussein was behind the 9/11 attack, maximum priority should be placed on eliminating that threat. Wolfowitz contended that the odds were "far more" than 1 in 10, citing Saddam's praise for the attack, his long record of involvement in terrorism, and theories that Ramzi Yousef was an Iraqi agent and Iraq was behind the 1993 attack on the World Trade Center. . . .

On September 19, Rumsfeld offered several thoughts for his commanders as they worked on their contingency plans. Though he emphasized the worldwide nature of the conflict, the references to specific enemies or regions named only the Taliban, al Qaeda, and Afghanistan. Shelton told us the administration reviewed all the Pentagon's war plans and challenged certain assumptions underlying them, as any prudent organization or leader should do.

General Tommy Franks, the commanding general of Central Command, recalled receiving Rumsfeld's guidance that each regional commander should assess what these plans meant for his area of responsibility. He knew he would soon be striking the Taliban and al Qaeda in Afghanistan. But, he told us, he now wondered how that action was connected to what might need to be done in Somalia, Yemen, or Iraq.

On September 20, President Bush met with British Prime Minister Tony Blair, and the two leaders discussed the global conflict ahead. When Blair asked about Iraq, the President replied that Iraq was not the immediate problem. Some members of his administration, he commented, had expressed a different view, but he was the one responsible for making the decisions.

Franks told us that he was pushing independently to do more robust planning on military responses in Iraq during the summer before 9/11—a request President Bush denied, arguing that the time was not right. . . .

Having issued directives to guide his administration's preparations for war, on Thursday, September 20, President Bush addressed the nation before a joint session of Congress. "Tonight," he said, "we are a country awakened to danger." The President blamed al Qaeda for 9/11 and the 1998 embassy bombings and, for the first time, declared that al Qaeda was "responsible for bombing the USS *Cole*." He reiterated the ultimatum that had already been conveyed privately. "The Taliban must act, and act immediately," he said. "They will hand over the terrorists, or they will share in their fate." The President added that America's quarrel was not with Islam: "The enemy of America is not our many Muslim friends; it is not our many Arab friends. Our enemy is a radical network of terrorists, and every government that supports them." Other regimes faced hard choices, he pointed out: "Every nation, in every region, now has a decision to make: Either you are with us, or you are with the terrorists."

President Bush argued that the new war went beyond Bin Ladin. "Our war on terror begins with al Qaeda, but it does not end there," he said. "It will not end until every terrorist group of global reach has been found, stopped, and defeated." The President had a message for the Pentagon: "The hour is coming when America will act, and you will make us proud." He also had a message for those outside the United States. "This is civilization's fight," he said. "We ask every nation to join us."

President Bush approved military plans to attack Afghanistan in meetings with Central Command's General Franks and other advisers on September 21 and October 2. Originally titled "Infinite Justice," the operation's code word was changed—to avoid the sensibilities of Muslims who associate the power of infinite justice with God alone—to the operational name still used for operations in Afghanistan: "Enduring Freedom." . . .

In December 2001, Afghan forces, with limited U.S. support, engaged al Qaeda elements in a cave complex called Tora Bora. In March 2002, the largest engagement of the war was fought, in the mountainous Shah-i-Kot area south of Gardez, against a large force of al Qaeda jihadists. The three-week battle was substantially successful, and almost all remaining al Qaeda forces took refuge in Pakistan's equally mountainous and lightly governed frontier provinces. As of July 2004, Bin Ladin and Zawahiri are still believed to be at large. . . .

Within about two months of the start of combat operations, several hundred CIA operatives and Special Forces soldiers, backed by the striking power of U.S. aircraft and a much larger infrastructure of intelligence and support efforts, had combined with Afghan militias and a small number of other coalition soldiers to destroy the Taliban regime and disrupt al Qaeda. They had killed or captured about a quarter of the enemy's known leaders. Mohammed Atef, al Qaeda's military commander and a principal figure in the 9/11 plot, had been killed by a U.S. air strike. According to a senior CIA officer who helped devise the overall strategy, the CIA provided intelligence, experience, cash, covert action capabilities, and entrée to tribal allies. In turn, the U.S. military offered combat expertise, firepower, logistics, and communications. With these initial victories won by the middle of 2002, the global conflict against Islamist terrorism became a different kind of struggle. . . .

The 9/11 attack was an event of surpassing disproportion. America had suffered surprise attacks before—Pearl Harbor is one well-known case, the 1950 Chinese attack in Korea another. But these were attacks by major powers.

While by no means as threatening as Japan's act of war, the 9/11 attack was in some ways more devastating. It was carried out by a tiny group of people, not enough to man a full platoon. Measured on a governmental scale, the resources behind it were trivial. The group itself was dispatched by an organization based in one of the poorest, most remote, and least industrialized countries on earth. This organization recruited a mixture of young fanatics and highly educated zealots who could not find suitable places in their home societies or were driven from them.

To understand these events, we attempted to reconstruct some of the context of the 1990s. Americans celebrated the end of the Cold War with a mixture of relief and satisfaction. The people of the United States hoped to enjoy a peace dividend, as U.S. spending on national security was cut following the end of the Soviet military threat.

The United States emerged into the post–Cold War world as the globe's preeminent military power. . . .

America stood out as an object for admiration, envy, and blame. This created a kind of cultural asymmetry. To us, Afghanistan seemed very far away. To members of al Qaeda, America seemed very close. In a sense, they were more globalized than we were.

If the government's leaders understood the gravity of the threat they faced and understood at the same time that their policies to eliminate it were not likely to succeed any time soon, then history's judgment will be harsh. Did they understand the gravity of the threat?

The U.S. government responded vigorously when the attack was on our soil. Both Ramzi Yousef, who organized the 1993 bombing of the World Trade Center, and Mir Amal Kansi, who in 1993 killed two CIA employees as they waited to go to work in Langley, Virginia, were the objects of relentless, uncompromising, and successful efforts to bring them back to the United States to stand trial for their crimes.

Before 9/11, al Qaeda and its affiliates had killed fewer than 50 Americans, including the East Africa embassy bombings and the *Cole* attack. The U.S. government took the threat seriously, but not in the sense of mustering anything like the kind of effort that would be gathered to confront an enemy of the first, second, or even third rank. The modest national effort exerted to contain Serbia and its depredations in the Balkans between 1995 and 1999, for example, was orders of magnitude larger than that devoted to al Qaeda.

As best we can determine, neither in 2000 nor in the first eight months of 2001 did any polling organization in the United States think the subject of terrorism sufficiently on the minds of the public to warrant asking a question about it in a major national survey. Bin Ladin, al Qaeda, or even terrorism was not an important topic in the 2000 presidential campaign. Congress and the media called little attention to it.

If a president wanted to rally the American people to a warlike effort, he would need to publicize an assessment of the growing al Qaeda danger. Our government could spark a full public discussion of who Usama Bin Ladin was, what kind of organization he led, what Bin Ladin or al Qaeda intended, what past attacks they had sponsored or encouraged, and what capabilities they were bringing together for future assaults. We believe American and international public opinion might have been different—and so might the range of options for a president—had they been informed of these details. Recent examples of such debates include calls to arms against such threats as Serbian ethnic cleansing, biological attacks, Iraqi weapons of mass destruction, global climate change, and the HIV/AIDS epidemic.

While we now know that al Qaeda was formed in 1988, at the end of the Soviet occupation of Afghanistan, the intelligence community did not describe this organization, at least in documents we have seen, until 1999. . . .

From 1998 to 2001, a number of very good analytical papers were distributed on specific topics. These included Bin Ladin's political philosophy, his command of a global network, analysis of information from terrorists captured in Jordan in December 1999, al Qaeda's operational style, and the evolving goals of the Islamist extremist movement. Many classified articles for morning briefings were prepared for the highest officials in the government with titles such as "Bin Ladin Threatening to Attack US Aircraft [with antiaircraft missiles]" (June 1998), "Strains Surface Between Taliban and Bin Ladin" (January 1999), "Terrorist Threat to US Interests in Caucasus" (June 1999), "Bin Ladin to Exploit Looser Security During Holidays" (December 1999), "Bin Ladin Evading Sanctions" (March 2000), "Bin Ladin's Interest in Biological, Radiological Weapons" (February 2001), "Taliban Holding Firm on Bin Ladin for Now" (March 2001), "Terrorist Groups Said Cooperating on US Hostage Plot" (May 2001), and "Bin Ladin Determined to Strike in the US" (August 2001).

Despite such reports and a 1999 paper on Bin Ladin's command structure for al Qaeda, there were no complete portraits of his strategy or of the extent of his organization's involvement in past terrorist attacks. Nor had the intelligence community provided an authoritative depiction of his organization's relationships with other governments, or the scale of the threat his organization posed to the United States. . . .

Whatever the weaknesses in the CIA's portraiture, both Presidents Bill Clinton and George Bush and their top advisers told us they got the picture—they understood Bin Ladin was a danger. But given the character and pace of their policy efforts, we do not believe they fully understood just how many people al Qaeda might kill, and how soon it might do it. At some level that is hard to define, we believe the threat had not yet become compelling.

It is hard now to recapture the conventional wisdom before 9/11. For example, a *New York Times* article in April 1999 sought to debunk claims that Bin Ladin was a terrorist leader, with the headline "U.S. Hard Put to Find Proof Bin Laden Directed Attacks." The head of analysis at the CTC [the CIA's Counterterrorist Center] until 1999 discounted the alarms about a catastrophic threat as relating only to the danger of chemical, biological, or nuclear attack—and he downplayed even that, writing several months before 9/11: "It would be a mistake to redefine counterterrorism as a task of dealing with 'catastrophic,' 'grand,' or 'super' terrorism, when in fact these labels do not represent most of the terrorism that the United States is likely to face or most of the costs that terrorism imposes on U.S. interests."

Beneath the acknowledgment that Bin Ladin and al Qaeda presented serious dangers, there was uncertainty among senior officials about whether this was just a new and especially venomous version of the ordinary terrorist threat America had lived with for decades, or was radically new, posing a threat beyond any yet experienced. Such differences affect calculations about whether or how to go to war. . . .

By 2001 the government still needed a decision at the highest level as to whether al Qaeda was or was not "a first order threat," Richard Clarke wrote in his first memo to Condoleezza Rice on January 25, 2001. In his blistering protest about foot-dragging in the Pentagon and at the CIA, sent to Rice just a week before 9/11, he repeated that the "real question" for the principals was "are we serious about dealing with the al Qida threat? . . . Is al Qida a big deal?"

One school of thought, Clarke wrote in this September 4 note, implicitly argued that the terrorist network was a nuisance that killed a score of Americans every 18–24 months. If that view was credited, then current policies might be proportionate. Another school saw al Qaeda as the "point of the spear of radical Islam." But no one forced the argument into the open. . . . The issue was never joined as a collective debate by the U.S. government, including the Congress, before 9/11.

We return to the issue of proportion—and imagination. Even Clarke's note challenging Rice to imagine the day after an attack posits a strike that kills "hundreds" of Americans. He did not write "thousands."

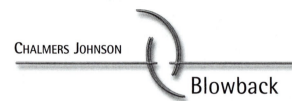

CHALMERS JOHNSON

Blowback

In a speech to Congress on September 20, 2001, shortly after the terrorist attacks of September 11, President George W. Bush posed this question: "Why do they hate us?" His answer: "They hate our freedoms—our freedom of religion, our freedom of speech, our freedom to vote." He commented later that he was amazed "that there's such misunderstanding of what our country is about that people would hate us. . . . I just can't believe it because I know how good we are."

But how "good" are we, really? If we're so good, why do we inspire such hatred abroad? What have we done to bring so much "blowback" upon ourselves? . . .

Actions that generate blowback are normally kept totally secret from the American public and from most of their representatives in Congress. This means that when innocent civilians become victims of a retaliatory strike, they are at first unable to put it in context or to understand the sequence of events that led up to it. In its most rigorous definition, blowback does not mean mere reactions to historical events but rather to clandestine operations carried out by the U.S. government that are aimed at overthrowing foreign regimes, or seeking the execution of people the United States wants eliminated by "friendly" foreign armies, or helping launch state terrorist operations against overseas target populations. The American people may not know what is done in their name, but those on the receiving end surely do—including the people of Iran (1953), Guatemala (1954), Cuba (1959 to the present), Congo (1960), Brazil (1964), Indonesia (1965), Vietnam (1961–73), Laos (1961–73), Cambodia (1961–73), Greece (1967–74), Chile (1973), Afghanistan (1979 to the present), El Salvador, Guatemala, and Nicaragua (1980s), and Iraq (1991 to the present), to name only the most obvious cases.

In a broader sense, blowback is another way of saying that a nation reaps what it sows. Although individuals usually know what they have sown, they rarely have the same knowledge on a national level, especially since so much of what the managers of the American empire have sown has been kept secret. As a concept, blowback is obviously most easily grasped in its straightforward manifestations. The unintended consequences of American policies and acts in country X lead to a bomb at an American embassy in country Y or a dead American in country Z. Certainly, any number of Americans have been killed in that fashion, from Catholic nuns in El Salvador to tourists in Uganda who just happened to wander into hidden imperial scenarios about which they knew nothing.

Adaptation of Introduction from *Blowback: The Costs and Consequences of American Empire,* by Chalmers Johnson, Copyright © 2000, 2004 by Chalmers Johnson. Reprinted by permission of Henry Holt and Company, LLC.

But blowback is hardly restricted to such reasonably straightforward examples. In its extended sense, it also includes the decline of key American industries because of the export-led economic policies of our satellites, the militarism and arrogance of power that inevitably conflict with our democratic structure of government, and the distortions to our culture and basic values as we are increasingly required to try to justify our imperialism.

The term "blowback" first appeared in a classified government document in the CIA's post-action report on the secret overthrow of the Iranian government in 1953. In 2000, James Risen of the *New York Times* explained: "When the Central Intelligence Agency helped overthrow Mohammed Mossadegh as Iran's prime minister in 1953, ensuring another 25 years of rule for Shah Mohammed Reza Pahlavi, the CIA was already figuring that its first effort to topple a foreign government would not be its last. The CIA, then just six years old and deeply committed to winning the cold war, viewed its covert action in Iran as a blueprint for coup plots elsewhere around the world, and so commissioned a secret history to detail for future generations of CIA operatives how it had been done. . . . Amid the sometimes curious argot of the spy world—'safebases' and 'assets' and the like—the CIA warns of the possibilities of 'blowback.' The word . . . has since come into use as shorthand for the unintended consequences of covert operations."

The attacks of September 11 descend in a direct line from events in 1979, the year in which the CIA, with full presidential authority, began carrying out its largest ever clandestine operation—the secret arming of Afghan freedom fighters *(mujahideen)* to wage a proxy war against the Soviet Union, which involved the recruitment and training of militants from all over the Islamic world. Various members of the current Bush cabinet were complicit in generating the blowback of 9/11. Former general Colin Powell certainly knows why "they" might hate us. He was Ronald Reagan's last national security adviser and then chairman of the Joint Chiefs of Staff during the George H. W. Bush administration. Others include former secretary of defense Dick Cheney, former National Security Council staff official Condoleezza Rice, former Reagan confidant and emissary to Saddam Hussein Donald Rumsfeld, former Pentagon official in both the Reagan and George H. W. Bush administrations Paul Wolfowitz, and many more. Throughout the 1980s, these officials designed and implemented the secret war in Afghanistan and then, after the Soviet Union's withdrawal, made the decision to abandon America's Islamic agents.

The USSR's invasion of Afghanistan was deliberately provoked. In his 1996 memoirs, former CIA director Robert Gates writes that the American intelligence services actually began to aid the *mujahideen* guerrillas in Afghanistan not after the Soviet invasion of that country, but *six months before it.* And in a 1998 interview with the French weekly magazine *Le Nouvel Observateur,* former president Carter's National Security Adviser, Zbigniew Brzezinski, unambiguously confirmed Gates's assertion.

"According to the official version of history," Brzezinski told the *Nouvel Observateur,* "CIA aid to the *mujahideen* began during 1980, that is to say, after the Soviet army invaded Afghanistan on December 24, 1979. But the reality, closely guarded until now, is completely otherwise: Indeed, it was July 3, 1979, that President Carter signed the first directive for secret aid to the opponents of the pro-Soviet regime in Kabul. And that very day, I wrote a note to the president in which I explained to him that in my opinion this aid was going to induce a Soviet military intervention."

When asked whether he regretted these actions, Brzezinski replied:

> "Regret what? That secret operation was an excellent idea. It had the effect of drawing the Russians into the Afghan trap and you want me to regret it? The day that the Soviets officially crossed the border, I wrote to President Carter, essentially: 'We now have the opportunity of giving to the USSR its Vietnam War.'"

Nouvel Observateur: "And neither do you regret having supported Islamic fundamentalism, which has given arms and advice to future terrorists?"

Brzezinski: "What is more important in world history? The Taliban or the collapse of the Soviet empire? Some agitated Moslems or the liberation of Central Europe and the end of the cold war?"

Brzezinski, Carter, and their successors in the Reagan administration, including George H. W. Bush, Gates, Cheney, Rumsfeld, Rice, Wolfowitz, Armitage, and Powell—none of whom has come forward to draw attention to this history—all bear some responsibility for the 1.8 million Afghan casualties, 2.6 million refugees, and 10 million unexploded land mines that followed from their decisions, as well as the "collateral damage" that befell New York City in September 2001 from an organization they helped create during the years of anti-Soviet Afghan resistance.

The CIA supported Osama bin Laden, like so many other extreme fundamentalists among the *mujahideen* in Afghanistan, from at least 1984 on. In 1986 it built for him the training complex and weapons storage tunnels around the Afghan city of Khost where he trained many of the 35,000 "Arab Afghans." Bin Laden's men constituted a sort of Islamic Abraham Lincoln Brigade of young volunteers from around the Muslim world who wanted to fight on the side of the Afghans against the Soviet Union. In August 1998, on President Bill Clinton's orders, the Khost complex was hit with cruise missiles, in retaliation for bin Laden's attacks that month on the American embassies in Kenya and Tanzania. For once the CIA knew exactly where the targets were, since it had built them.

Osama bin Laden, the well-connected, rich young Saudi (he was born around 1957), was well positioned to become a close ally with other friends of the CIA: Prince Turki Bin Faisal, the head of Istakhbarat, the Saudi Intelligence Service, and Lieutenant General Hameed Gul, head of Pakistan's Inter-Services Intelligence (ISI) agency, which America used to funnel money and weapons to the *mujahideen* in order to maintain a facade of deniability with the Soviet Union. Since 1982, the ISI also took the lead in recruiting radical Muslims to come to Pakistan, receive training, and fight on the Afghan side.

It was only after the Russians had bombed Afghanistan back to the stone age and suffered a Vietnam-like defeat, and the United States had walked away from the death and destruction the CIA had helped cause, that Osama bin Laden turned against his American supporters. The last straw as far as he was concerned was the way that "infidel" American troops—around 35,000 of them—remained in Saudi Arabia after the first Gulf War to prop up that decadent, fiercely authoritarian regime. Devoutly Muslim citizens of that kingdom saw the troops' presence as a humiliation to the country and an affront to their religion. Dissident Saudis began to launch attacks against Americans and against the Saudi regime itself. In June 1996, terrorists associated with Osama bin Laden bombed the Khobar Towers apartments near Dhahran airport, killing nineteen American airmen and wounding scores more.

That same year, the international relations commentator William Pfaff offered the reasonable prediction, "Within 15 years at most, if present American and Saudi Arabian policies are pursued, the Saudi monarchy will be overturned and a radical and anti-American government will take power in Riyadh." Such a course of events has occurred elsewhere many times before—in Cuba, Vietnam, Iran, Greece, the Philippines, and South Korea, where indigenous peoples fought hard to free themselves from American-backed dictatorships. Yet American foreign policy remained on autopilot, instead of withdrawing from a place where a U.S. presence was only making a dangerous situation worse. Only after the defeat of Iraq in the spring of 2003 did the United States announce that it would withdraw most of its forces from Saudi Arabia. By then, however, the gesture was meaningless. The United States has massive military forces concentrated in nearby Qatar, Kuwait, Bahrain, the United Arab Republics, and Oman, not to mention its newly acquired bases in such Muslim countries as Iraq, Afghanistan, Jordan, Kyrgyzstan, Uzbekistan, Pakistan, Djibouti, and in territories with large Muslim populations such as Kosovo, Serbia. All of this suggests future blowback against the United States.

The suicidal assassins of September 11, 2001, did not "attack America," as political leaders and news media in the United States have tried to maintain; they attacked American foreign policy. Employing the strategy of the weak, they killed innocent bystanders, whose innocence is, of course, no different from that of the civilians killed by American bombs in Iraq, Serbia, Afghanistan, and elsewhere. It was probably the most striking instance in the history of international relations of the use of political terrorism to influence events.

Political terrorism is usually defined by its strategic objectives. Its first goal is normally to turn those domestic or international conditions terrorists perceive to be unjust into unstable revolutionary situations. To a wavering population, terrorist acts are intended to demonstrate that the monopoly of force exercised by incumbent authorities can be broken. The essential idea is to disorient that population "by demonstrating through apparently indiscriminate violence that the existing regime cannot protect the people nominally under its authority. The effect on the individual is supposedly not only anxiety, but withdrawal from the relationships making up the established order of society."

Of course, such a strategy rarely works as intended: it usually has the opposite effect of encouraging people to support any strong reassertion of authority. That was indeed what happened within the United States following the attacks of September 11, but not necessarily throughout the Islamic world, where the terrorists' objective of displaying America's vulnerabilities and destabilizing the world of the advanced capitalist nations was all too effective.

A second strategic objective of revolutionary terrorism is to provoke ruling elites into a disastrous overreaction, thereby creating widespread resentment against them. This is a classic strategy, and when it works, the impact can be devastating. As explained by Carlos Marighella, the Brazilian guerrilla leader whose writings influenced political terrorists in the 1960s and 1970s, if a government can be provoked into a purely military response to terrorism, its overreaction will alienate the masses, causing them to "revolt against the army and the police and blame them for this state of things." The second Palestinian Intifada of 2000–03 illustrates the dynamic: terrorist attacks elicited powerful and disproportionate Israeli military reactions that led to an escalating cycle of more attacks and more retaliation, completely militarizing relations between the two peoples.

In our globalizing world, the masses alienated by such overreactions may be anything but domestic. The bombing of Afghanistan that the United States launched on October 7, 2001, inflicted great misery on many innocent civilians, a pattern repeated in Iraq, where the death toll of civilians as of August 2003 stood at well over 3,000, a figure that informed observers think may go as high as 10,000 as more evidence is collected. Altogether, instead of acting to resolve the post 9/11 crisis, the United States exacerbated it with massive military assaults on Afghanistan and Iraq, two ill-advised and unnecessary wars that inflamed passions throughout the Islamic world and repelled huge majorities in every democratic country on earth.

The two wars that the United States launched preemptively were the pet projects of special interest groups that used the attacks of 9/11 as a cover to hijack American foreign policy and implement their private agendas. These interest groups include the military-industrial complex and the professional armed forces, close American supporters of and advisers to the Likud party in Israel, and neoconservative enthusiasts for the creation of an American empire. This latter group, concentrated in right-wing foundations and think tanks in Washington D.C., is composed of "chicken-hawk" war lovers (that is, *soi-disant* military strategists with no experience of either the armed forces or war) who seized on the national sense of bewilderment after 9/11 to push the Bush administration into conflicts that were neither relevant to nor successful in destroying al Qaeda. Instead, the wars accelerated the recruitment of more suicidal terrorists and promoted nuclear proliferation in countries hoping to deter similar preemptive attacks by the United States. Two years after 9/11, America is unquestionably in greater danger of serious terrorist threats than it has ever been before.

The Afghan and Iraq wars resulted in easy American victories, but both soon reerupted as guerrilla struggles of attrition. Experience has shown that high-tech armed forces, such as those of the United States, are inappropriate, overly blunt instruments against terrorists and guerrillas. What was called for was international police cooperation to hunt down the terrorists and changes in foreign policy to separate militant activists from their passive supporters, whose grievances need to be addressed. The objective should have been to turn supporters into informers against the militants, thereby allowing them to be identified and captured. Serious high-level intelligence efforts against organizations like al Qaeda and intelligence sharing with other services that may have greater access or capabilities than our own are also important in this context, as are collaborative efforts to interrupt financing of terrorist activities and prevent money laundering.

Instead, in the wake of 9/11, the United States came up with a particularly cynical and destructive strategy. It sent CIA agents to Afghanistan with millions of dollars to bribe the same warlord armies that the Taliban had defeated to reopen the civil war, promising them air support in their new offensive. The warlords, with a bit of help from the United States, thus overthrew the Taliban government and soon returned to their old ways of regional exploitation. Afghanistan descended into an anarchy comparable to that which prevailed before the rise of the ruthless but religiously motivated Taliban. The propaganda apparatus of the Pentagon claimed a stupendous U.S. victory in Afghanistan, but, in fact, leaders of the Taliban and al Qaeda escaped and the country quickly became an even more virulent breeding ground for terrorists.

In the first year after Afghanistan's "liberation," the production of opium, heroin, and morphine, controlled by America's warlord allies, increased 18-fold, from 185 to 3,400 tons. Even British prime minister Tony Blair admitted in January 2003 that 90 percent of the heroin consumed in Britain came from Afghanistan. Previously vacillating supporters of terrorists have been drawn into militant organizations. Muslim governments that in the past have cooperated with the United States, especially Saudi Arabia, Egypt, Indonesia, and Pakistan, are facing growing internal dissent. In most of the world, the spectacle of the world's richest and most heavily armed country using its air power against one of the world's poorest quickly eroded the moral high ground accorded to the United States as the victim of the September 11 attacks. Our "preventive wars" insured that Afghans, Iraqis, and their supporters will have ample motives long into the future to kill any and all Americans, particularly innocent ones, just as the American military slaughtered their civilians with its "shock and awe" bombing campaigns against which there is no defense.

The war with Iraq that followed the Afghan conquest had even less justification and subverted the system of international cooperation that the United States had worked since World War II to create. Immediately following 9/11, American leaders began to fabricate pretexts for an invasion of Iraq. These were then uncritically disseminated by American print and television media, leading a majority of Americans to believe that Saddam Hussein was an immediate threat to their own safety and that he had personally supported al Qaeda in its attacks of 9/11. Since there was no evidence for any of these propositions, the American public formed its impressions based on stories planted by the president and his followers and then endlessly repeated and embellished by complicit journalists and networks.

The United States will feel the blowback from this ill-advised and poorly prepared military adventure for decades. The war has already had the unintended consequences of seriously fracturing the Western democratic alliance; eliminating any potentiality for British leadership of the European Union; grievously weakening international law, including the charter of the United Nations; and destroying the credibility of the president, vice president, secretary of state, and other officials as a result of their lying to the international community and the American people. Most important, the unsanctioned military assault on Iraq communicated to the world that the United States was unwilling to seek a modus vivendi with Islamic nations and was therefore an appropriate, even necessary, target for further terrorist attacks.

History has shown that the most important virtue in the conduct of international relations is prudence—being cautious and discreet in actions, circumspect and sensible in what one says, suspicious of ideology, and slow to jump to conclusions. During the Cold War, the superpower confrontation imposed a high degree of caution on both sides. A mistake by one party was certain to be exploited by the other, and both the United States and the USSR knew how readily the other would take advantage of impetuous and poorly thought-out policies. After 1991 and the collapse of the USSR, the United States no longer felt this pressure and seemed to lose all sense of prudence. For example, President George H. W. Bush kept a tight leash on the same ideological and inexperienced neoconservatives who, in his son's administration, have been given free rein. This loss of common sense guarantees an even more lethal era of blowback than America's policies during the Cold War have already generated. . . .

Since 9/11, the number of significant terrorist incidents has grown and increased in intensity. These include the attempt on December 22, 2001, by Richard Reid, a British citizen, to blow up a Miami-bound jet using an explosive device hidden in his shoe; the bombing on October 12, 2002, of a nightclub in Bali, Indonesia, killing 202 vacationers, most of them Australians; the May 13, 2003, explosions at three residential compounds and the offices of an American defense contractor in Riyadh, Saudi Arabia; the killings three days later, on May 16, 2003, of some 33 people at a restaurant and Jewish community center in Casablanca, Morocco; the use of a car bomb on August 5, 2003, to attack the new Marriott Hotel, a symbol of American imperialism, in Jakarta, the Indonesian capital; the deaths of at least 19 people in an explosion at the Jordanian Embassy in Baghdad, August 7, 2003; and the blowing up of the United Nations compound in Baghdad on August 19, 2003, killing Sergio Vieira de Mello, the secretary general's special representative, and many others. There have also been numerous assassinations of American officials and business people around the world and 184 American service personnel died in Iraq in the six months since May 1, 2003, when President Bush ostentatiously declared that the war was over.

Beyond terrorism, the danger I foresee is that we are embarked on a path not so dissimilar from that of the former Soviet Union a little more than a decade ago. It collapsed for three reasons—internal economic contradictions, imperial overstretch, and an inability to reform. In every sense, we were by far the wealthier of the two Cold War superpowers, so it will certainly take longer for similar afflictions to do their work. But it is nowhere written that the United States, in its guise as an empire dominating the world, must go on forever. The blowback from the second half of the twentieth century has only just begun.

Further Reading

Several books by journalists offer basic information about the Central Asian spawning ground of al Qaeda. Steve Coll, *Ghost Wars: The Secret History of the CIA, Afghanistan, and Bin Laden, from the Soviet Invasion to September 10, 2001* (New York: The Penguin Press, 2004) provides an abundance of detail on U.S. aid to the mujihadin during the 1980s. Ahmed Rashid, *Taliban: Islam, Oil and the New Great Game in Central Asia* (London: Pan Macmillan, 2002) is an updated version of the foremost account of the now-deposed Afghan regime and the far-flung political intrigue surrounding its rise and fall.

On the U.S. side, *Against All Enemies: Inside America's War on Terror* (New York: The Free Press, 2004), by Richard A. Clarke, is an absorbing insider's account of counterterrorism policy by a key government official working on those issues from the Reagan administration through the early George W. Bush administration, from which Clarke resigned in frustration. *Imperial Hubris: Why the West Is Losing the War on Terror* (Dulles, VA: Brassey's, Inc., 2004), by Michael Scheuer, is a bracing critique of U.S. policy by a top CIA analyst (originally published as the work of "Anonymous").

Several authors have tried to paint the outlines of the "new world order" that followed the cold war. For two different versions of the thesis that a global conflict of cultures marks the post-cold war world, see Samuel P. Huntington, *The Clash of Civilizations and the Remaking of World Order* (New York: Simon & Schuster, 1998) and Benjamin R. Barber, *Jihad vs. McWorld: How Globalism and Tribalism are Reshaping the World* (New York: Ballantine Books, 1996). *The Imperial Tense: Prospects and Problems of American Empire* (Chicago: Ivan R. Dee, 2003), edited by Andrew J. Bacevich, offers a diverse array of recent writings probing the extent and nature of U.S. power. Emmanuel Todd, *After the Empire: The Breakdown of the American Order,* trans. C. Jon Delogu (New York: Columbia University Press, 2003), a bestseller in the author's native France, pungently portrays recent U.S. wars as symptoms of American economic decline, and as evidence of weakness, not strength. Chalmers Johnson, *The Sorrows of Empire: Militarism, Secrecy, and the End of the Republic* (New York: Metropolitan Books, 2004) details the expansion of U.S. military bases throughout the Middle East and in the former Soviet republics since the end of the cold war.

After the second Bush administration took office in 2001 and advanced its unilateralist stance, and even more after the 9/11 attacks, scholarly debate over the place of the United States in the world became entangled with that administration's aggressive posture toward Iraq and the debate over going to war. Many of the most notable observers of the global scene settled into two camps: those who welcomed the Bush stance, and the others, many of them moderate conservatives, who deemed it unwise based on their assessment of U.S. interests. In the first camp, one can include *Power, Terror, Peace, and War: America's Grand Strategy in a World at Risk* (New York: Alfred A. Knopf, 2004), by Walter Russell Mead, an ideological moderate; and *Of Paradise and Power: America and Europe in the New World Order* (New York: Alfred A. Knopf, 2003), by Robert Kagan, a thinker on the right. Within mainstream criticism, Clyde Prestowitz, *Rogue Nation: American Unilateralism and the Failure of Good Intentions* (New York: Basic Books, 2003), the work of a longtime conservative, is striking. A more complete rejection of recent U.S. actions is found in *Hegemony or Survival: America's Quest for Global Dominance* (New York: Metropolitan Books, 2003), a recent work among many by the redoubtable Noam Chomsky, long a scathing and influential critic of U.S. foreign policy.

Primary Sources

The final report of the 9/11 Commission in its entirety is available at www.gpoaccess.gov/911/index.html. A copy of the August 6, 2001, Presidential Daily Briefing, "Bin Laden Determined to Strike in U.S.," is available at www.gwu.edu/~nsarchiv/NSAEBB/NSAEBB116/pdb8-6-2001.pdf. A copy of the July 2001 document, "U.S. Engagement with the Taliban on Usama Bin Laden," which lists the many efforts made under President Clinton and the three made under President Bush to work with the Taliban to defuse bin Laden, is available at www.gwu.edu/~nsarchiv/NSAEBB/NSAEBB97/tal40.pdf. For a comprehensive directory of links to Web sites with documents and other information related to the 9/11 attacks, al Qaeda, and the "war on terror," go to www.lib.umich.edu/govdocs/usterror.html. See also the links listed under "September 11th Sourcebooks" at www2.gwu.edu/~nsarchiv/NSAEBB/index.html. Go to www.whitehouse.gov/news/releases/2001/09/20010920-8.html for the text of President George W. Bush's speech to Congress and the American people on September 20, 2001, in which he offers his explanation for why bin Laden and his followers hate America. For a translation of the fatwa "Jihad against Jews and Crusaders" issued by bin Laden in 1988, go to www.fas.org/irp/world/para/docs/980223-fatwa.htm. To read a translation of an al Qaeda training manual, which was used as evidence in the 1993 World Trade Center bombing trial, go to www.thesmokinggun.com/archive/jihadmanual.htm. For the full text of the interview with former National Security Advisor Zbigniew Brzezinski, in which he discusses how the United States worked to provoke the Soviets to invade Afghanistan, go to www.globalresearch.ca/articles/BRZ110A.html. Regarding the history of U.S. covert activities in Afghanistan, see the 1992 *Washington Post* story, "Anatomy of a Victory: CIA's Covert Afghan War," by Steve Coll, which may be found at www.krigskronikan.com/arkiv/WP_afghanCasey92.html. (National Security Directive 166, mentioned in the article, remains classified.)